The Cambridge Handbook of Group Interaction Analysis

This handbook provides a compendium of research methods that are essential for studying interaction and communication across the behavioral sciences. Focusing on coding of verbal and nonverbal behavior and interaction, the handbook is organized into five parts.

- Part I provides an introduction and historic overview of the field.
- Part II presents areas in which interaction analysis is used, such as relationship research, group research, and nonverbal research.
- Part III focuses on development, validation, and concrete application of interaction coding schemes.
- Part IV presents relevant data analysis methods and statistics.
- Part V contains systematic descriptions of established and novel coding schemes, which allows quick comparison across instruments.

Researchers can apply this methodology to their own interaction data and learn how to evaluate and select coding schemes and conduct interaction analysis. This is an essential reference for all who study communication in teams and groups

Elisabeth Brauner is Full Professor of Psychology at Brooklyn College and The Graduate Center, City University of New York. She is former Head of the PhD Program in Cognition, Brain, and Behavior at the Graduate Center, CUNY, and Director of two MA programs in Industrial and Organizational Psychology at Brooklyn College. Her research on team processes focuses on group interaction for the purpose of developing transactive memory, as well as on the development of research methods for applied psychological research.

Margarete Boos is Full Professor of Psychology and Head of the Department of Social and Communication Psychology at the Institute for Psychology, University of Göttingen. Her research focuses on group psychology, especially coordination and leadership in teams, computer-mediated communication, and distributed teams, as well as on methods for interaction and communication analysis.

Michaela Kolbe is a member of the faculty at ETH Zurich and the Director of the Simulation Center for the University Hospital Zurich. She has been studying team processes for many years, with particular research interest in the social dynamics of "speaking up" across the authority gradient and across disciplines in health care. She publishes widely in psychological, health care, and simulation journals and books, and she is a member of the Editorial Board of *BMJ STEL* and Associate Editor of *Advances in Simulation*.

The Cambridge Handbook of Group Interaction Analysis

Edited by

Elisabeth Brauner
Brooklyn College and The Graduate Center, The City University of New York

Margarete Boos
Georg August-University of Göttingen, Faculty of Biology and Psychology, Georg Elias Müller-Institute for Psychology

Michaela Kolbe
University Hospital Zurich and ETH Zurich

CAMBRIDGE
UNIVERSITY PRESS

University Printing House, Cambridge CB2 8BS, United Kingdom

One Liberty Plaza, 20th Floor, New York, NY 10006, USA

477 Williamstown Road, Port Melbourne, VIC 3207, Australia

314–321, 3rd Floor, Plot 3, Splendor Forum, Jasola District Centre, New Delhi – 110025, India

79 Anson Road, #06–04/06, Singapore 079906

Cambridge University Press is part of the University of Cambridge.

It furthers the University's mission by disseminating knowledge in the pursuit of education, learning, and research at the highest international levels of excellence.

www.cambridge.org
Information on this title: www.cambridge.org/9781107113336
DOI:10.1017/9781316286302

© Cambridge University Press 2018

First published 2018

Printed in the United Kingdom by TJ International Ltd. Padstow Cornwall

A catalogue record for this publication is available from the British Library.

Library of Congress Cataloging-in-Publication Data
Names: Brauner, Elisabeth, editor. | Boos, Margarete, editor. | Kolbe, Michaela, editor.
Title: The Cambridge handbook of group interaction analysis / edited by Elisabeth Brauner, Brooklyn College and The Graduate Center, The City University of New York, Margarete Boos, Georg August – University of Gottingen, Faculty of Biology and Psychology, Georg Elias Muller – Institute for Psychology, Michaela Kolbe, University Hospital Zurich and ETH Zurich.
Description: New York : Cambridge University Press, 2018. | Series: Cambridge handbooks in psychology | Includes bibliographical references and index.
Identifiers: LCCN 2018012352 | ISBN 9781107113336 (hardback)
Subjects: LCSH: Social interaction. | Communication.
Classification: LCC HM1111 .C36 2018 | DDC 302–dc23
LC record available at https://lccn.loc.gov/2018012352

ISBN 978-1-107-11333-6 Hardback
ISBN 978-1-107-53387-5 Paperback

To the memory of

Renee A. Meyers

Contents

Figures

Tables

Contributors

MITJA D. BACK, University of Münster

JOSEPH A. BONITO, University of Arizona

MARGARETE BOOS, University of Göttingen

ELISABETH BRAUNER, Brooklyn College and The Graduate Center, The City University of New York

JEANNE BRETT, Kellogg School Northwestern University

JONAS BRÜNGGER, University of Applied Sciences and Arts Northwestern Switzerland

JUDEE K. BURGOON, University of Arizona

S. ALEXANDRA BURT, Michigan State University

ADAM DALGLEISH, University of Auckland

MAREE J. DAVIES, University of Auckland

JEREMY DAWSON, University of Sheffield

AARON S. DIETZ, Johns Hopkins University School of Medicine

NORAH E. DUNBAR, University of California Santa Barbara

MAAYAN DVIR, Purdue University

VALENTÍN ESCUDERO, University of A Coruña

ROSE EVISON, University of Sheffield

SAMUEL FARLEY, University of Leeds

MYRNA L. FRIEDLANDER, University at Albany, State University of New York

ERIN MARIE FURTAK, University of Colorado Boulder

KATHARINA GEUKES, University of Münster

MICHAEL GLÜER, University of Applied Sciences South-Westphalia, Germany

MARC GRÜNBERG, University of Münster

SARAH HARVEY, UCL School of Management

LAURIE HEATHERINGTON, Williams College

SIMONE KAUFFELD, Braunschweig University of Technology

SADAF KAZI, Armstrong Institute for Patient Safety and Quality, Johns Hopkins University School of Medicine

SANDRA KELLER, University of Neuchâtel

JANICE R. KELLY, Purdue University

JOANN KEYTON, North Carolina State University

KATHARINA KIEMER, Augsburg University

CORNELIA KLEINDIENST, University of Applied Sciences and Arts Northwestern Switzerland

JULIA KOCH, University of Applied Sciences and Arts Northwestern Switzerland

MICHAELA KOLBE, University Hospital Zurich; ETH Zurich

CHIA-YU KOU, School of Business, University College Dublin

ALBRECHT C. P. KÜFNER, University of Münster

MINSUN LEE, Seton Hall University

NALE LEHMANN-WILLENBROCK, University of Hamburg

ZHIKE LEI, Pepperdine University

MAGNUS S. MAGNUSSON, University of Iceland

MAGDALENA MATEESCU, University of Applied Sciences and Arts Northwestern Switzerland

JANA MATTERN, University of Münster

ANNIKA L. MEINECKE, University of Hamburg

ROCÍO MENESES, University of Barcelona

YVONNE METZGER, University of Göttingen

JOSÉ NAVARRO, University of Barcelona

ROD NICOLSON, Edge Hill University

SUSANNAH B. F. PALETZ, University of Maryland

DANIELLE M. PARSONS, Purdue University

MARSHALL SCOTT POOLE, University of Illinois Urbana-Champaign

VICENÇ QUERA, University of Barcelona

OLIVER RACK, University of Applied Sciences and Arts Northwestern Switzerland

NEIL RACKHAM, University of Sheffield

NATASHA REED, University of Göttingen

FRANK RITZ, University of Applied Sciences and Arts Northwestern Switzerland

MICHAEL A. ROSEN, Johns Hopkins University School of Medicine

CARSTEN C. SCHERMULY, SRH University of Applied Sciences

CORNELIA SCHOOR, University of Bamberg

THOMAS SCHULTZE, University of Göttingen

STEFAN SCHULZ-HARDT, University of Göttingen

CHRISTIAN D. SCHUNN, University of Pittsburgh

JULIA SEELANDT, University of Zurich

NORBERT K. SEMMER, University of Bern

JOANNA M. SETCHELL, Durham University

ALAN L. SILLARS, University of Montana

CHRISTINA SOMMER, University of Göttingen

SARAH M. STAGGS, Arizona State University

WILLIAM B. STILES, Miami University; Appalachian State University

J. LUKAS THÜRMER, University of Konstanz; University of Pittsburgh

FRANZISKA TSCHAN, University of Neuchâtel

FRANK WIEBER, University of Konstanz; Zurich University of Applied Sciences

MIKHILA N. WILDEY, Grand Valley State University

JINGJING YAO, IESEG School of Management

CARMEN ZAHN, University of Applied Sciences and Arts Northwestern Switzerland

ZHI-XUE ZHANG, Peking University

JASMIN ZIMMERMANN, University of Neuchâtel

SARAH ZOBEL, University of Tübingen

Editors' Preface

The principle which I have suggested as basic to human social organization is that
of communication involving participation in the other. This requires the appearance of the other in the self, the identification of the other with the self, the
reaching of self-consciousness through the other.

George Herbert Mead

If observing and coding interaction was a simple process, you would not be holding
this book in your hands. Much expertise, skill, and some ability are involved in
successfully applying interaction analysis methods and avoiding making rookie
mistakes. Until now, a lot of the writing on theory, methodology, statistical analysis, and practical application of observing interactive behavior was dispersed
across many books, literature reviews, and research articles in a large number of
sources and across different fields. Although no single book can ever make all those
other important publications redundant, this handbook is a complete resource for
everything related to interaction analysis but, at the same time, functions as
a gateway to those other publications.

Scholars from all areas in which interaction analysis is used and applied have
lent their expertise and written chapters that will allow newcomers, as well as
experienced researchers, to expand and deepen their knowledge, learn step by step
how to conduct interaction analysis, and find access to literature that is dispersed in
various fields.

Just as diverse as the field of our contributors is the audience to which this book
is addressed. Researchers in the fields of business, communication, education,
management studies, political science, industrial and organizational psychology,
social psychology, sociology, and linguistics will hopefully find this handbook
a useful resource for basic and applied research and for teaching graduate and some
advanced undergraduate courses. It is appropriate for researchers new to this field
as well as for expert scholars looking for a single resource or for inspiration for
further reading. It can also benefit applied researchers-practitioners who are conducting research projects based on observation in many different fields, for
instance, the health sector, human factors research, psychotherapy, consulting, or
marketing research. Practitioners in these areas can get a quick overview of the
methodology, methods, and techniques to learn to apply interaction analysis in their
respective fields.

Brief Long History of This Handbook

This book is the result of many years of using, and thinking about, interaction coding and interaction analysis and almost as many years of planning. It started with a meeting of Elisabeth Brauner, Margarete Boos, and Franziska Tschan at the conference of the Society of Experimental Social Psychology (SESP) in 2005 in San Diego, California. It was against the backdrop of the little harbor at the conference hotel, the view of the Pacific Ocean, and the scent of fish and chips that we first hashed out the plan to put this book together. Due to other projects, responsibilities, and tenure and promotion processes, it was put on the backburner for a few years before it was revived again during Elisabeth Brauner's sabbatical leave in 2010/2011 and visit with Franziska Tschan in Switzerland and Margarete Boos in Göttingen.

Due to other obligations, Franziska Tschan had to leave the project, but we (Elisabeth Brauner and Margarete Boos) were delighted that Renee A. Meyers agreed to join us. Work on the project continued until Renee's untimely passing in March 2012, which froze us and any activity on this project for over a year. It was another conference, the INTERCOM, organized by Simone Kauffeld in Braunschweig in 2013, that brought the project to the foreground again and, joined by Michaela Kolbe, motivated us to give it another try. Finally, Rebecca Taylor's (then commissioning editor at Cambridge University Press) visit to Brooklyn College led to the project getting an appropriate home and getting the ball rolling.

We gratefully acknowledge the University Syndicate Board at Cambridge University Press for believing in our project as much as we did; and we thank Rebecca Taylor, Hetty Marx, and Karen Oakes for their assistance in the first stages, as well as our editor, Janka Romero, and editorial assistant, Abigail Walkington, as well as Neil Ryan and Chloe Bradley (all at Cambridge),

Left: The first stages of the planning process of this handbook, SESP conference 2005, San Diego, California (photograph: Elisabeth Brauner); Right: Working on the handbook (from left Margarete Boos, Michaela Kolbe, Elisabeth Brauner; photograph: Margarete Boos).

Puviarassy Kalieperumal (Integra-PDY), and Matthew Bastock for taking care of us so gently and supportively in the final stages of the project.

We wish to thank all authors of this book for their confidence in this project and for the time and effort that they put into writing their chapters. This handbook would not have been possible without all of them. We also would like to recognize Anthony Caines (Academic Information Technologies, Brooklyn College) for recreating some of the figures from scratch, and we wish to express thanks to the research assistants who put the reference list in the Appendix together: Noah Ringler (Claremont Graduate University), Sascha Behrens (University of Göttingen), Lia Espe (University of Göttingen), and Roberto Alejandro Ortiz (Brooklyn College, City University of New York).

Elisabeth Brauner

Margarete Boos

Michaela Kolbe

Organization of This Handbook

Joseph E. McGrath was passionate about not making students code interaction data because it is just such torture and because it would take them too long to finish their studies (personal communication, ca. April 2001). While not in spite of, but certainly instead of McGrath's strong conviction, we decided a reference book was needed that will allow students and other researchers much easier access to theory, methodology, and methods of interaction analysis. The result is this handbook, which is divided into five parts.

Part I focuses on the theoretical and historic background of interaction analysis. It addresses what interaction analysis is and why it matters. Part II presents a variety of areas in which interaction research is applied and conducted. These chapters cover relational communication and dyadic interaction analysis, group research, nonverbal communication, and animal behavior. It also presents interaction research methods that go beyond coding interaction. Part III details what needs to be done before, during, and after coding. It presents the procedure of interaction analysis, that is, what researchers need to know to get started, to choose or develop a coding scheme, to prepare the data for coding by unitizing them, and to check whether the codings are reliable and valid. An overview of available software that can assist with interaction analysis is also part of this section. Part IV presents concrete data analysis techniques and relevant statistics that can be applied to further analyze and present coded data. The chapters focus on frequency analyses, sequential analyses, as well as special problems in interaction research, such as interdependence of data and the analysis of multiple levels. Several of the chapters also present quantitative and qualitative methods of visualizing coded data. Part V is comprised of a selection of coding schemes that can be used for different purposes in various research contexts. Each chapter in this last section is structured following a template that reflects all relevant characteristics and descriptors to enable researchers to make informed decisions. At the beginning of Part V, the template and organizational system of the coding schemes will be explained. In addition, readers will find a listing of further coding schemes with short synopses for each in the appendix.

How to Work with This Handbook

Readers can, of course, read this handbook cover to cover, although that is relatively unlikely to happen. Therefore, we would like to provide a roadmap as to how to approach this volume.

Readers unfamiliar with what interaction analysis is, and how it is done, should start with Part I, where they will learn how interaction analysis is understood here, how it is different from other forms of interaction analysis, and learn about its historic roots. Then, they should explore Part II, where the various areas are presented in accordance with which interaction analysis is being conducted: verbally and nonverbally, in dyads (close relationships and families), groups and teams, and animals. Each chapter also provides a slightly different perspective on the essentials of theory and methodology of interaction analysis.

Readers familiar with interaction analysis but interested in how it is being used and applied in other fields (e.g., a group researcher interested in learning about dyadic interaction research) should peruse Part II of the book.

Readers interested in quickly learning how to apply observational coding in their research can focus on Part III and learn how to select the appropriate coding scheme if a construct has been studied before, or how to construct a new coding scheme if previously published instruments are not suitable. Here, they can also find an appropriate software program to support the coding process and data analysis. Then, they can review Part V to explore which coding scheme would best fit their interest.

Readers who already have finished coding their data, but are not sure how to continue, should read about quality control in Part III and focus on Part IV for ideas about data analysis and further possibilities for presentation of results. If no sequential information is available in the coded data, then only certain analysis techniques will apply (e.g., frequency analyses); but if sequential information is available in the data, Part IV contains a range of possible further analysis techniques.

Finally, readers who are simply interested in getting quick access and informative descriptions of some of the available coding schemes can focus on Part V of the handbook and select the coding scheme that is most suitable for their research and their construct of interest. Additionally, the Appendix contains a reference list of published coding schemes along with short summaries of their purpose.

Throughout all chapters, cross-references enable readers to recognize connections between topics; readers can read chapters accordingly as they seem relevant to their purpose and interest. Some chapters also contain cross-references to coding schemes, thus providing examples that can be directly reviewed.

This handbook was written to be suitable for multiple audiences at different levels of expertise. Authors come from all disciplines relevant to interaction analysis: communication, education, management science, psychology, sociology, and anthropology, as well as applied fields, such as medical research and research on high reliability organizations. These various angles result in a comprehensive review of the current state of the art in interaction research and thus provide unique perspectives and new insights.

PART I

Background and Theory

1   Interaction Analysis

An Introduction

Joann Keyton

Interaction analysis has become so prominent among researchers across disciplines that a handbook is warranted as a way to review and organize what has been accomplished with this method, as well as present what we might expect as future trends or opportunities with this method. Generally, interaction analysis has been attributed to sociologist Mildred Parten, who observed preschool children in the 1930s, and social psychologist Robert Freed Bales, who developed systems for evaluating the social interaction of small groups in the 1950s.

Interaction analysis is a systematic research technique for reliably unitizing and coding sequential naturally occurring interaction behaviors and making valid interpretations and inferences from those data to the context in which the observations occurred. Even if a researcher has placed dyads or groups in experimental conditions to communicate or interact based on a prompt (usually a condition of the independent variable), researchers acknowledge that conversation naturally occurs around the premise that participants act and respond to one another spontaneously (Bavelas, Gerwing, Healing, & Tomori, 2017).

Observable behaviors in these exchanges are captured and coded. In an interaction, behaviors – verbal, nonverbal, textual – are what participants say, do, or write to one another in a dyadic or group setting and what other participants react to. That is, behaviors are artifacts that can be captured and codified. The researcher carefully and thoughtfully codes these behaviors relative to one another, within the context in which the interaction occurred, and with respect to theoretical and methodological claims. Thus, the researcher situates him/herself as an interpreter of the conversation, just as conversational partners would do in situ.

Interaction analysis is not about participants' perceptions as gathered through questionnaires. Presumably, a participant's thoughts, attitudes, and judgments guide his or her communication. However, in interaction analysis, "the details of social interactions in time and space and, particularly, in naturally occurring, everyday interactions among members of communities of practice" (Jordan & Henderson, 1995, p. 41) are the focus of study. Interaction systems vary in the type of interaction they examine. Some of the most common are task content, message function, and message structure. While most interaction analysis research designs focus on talk or text, studies of nonverbal behavior are also conducted. Let's take each term of *interaction analysis* in turn.

Interaction requires that researchers identify two or more individuals involved in some type of activity related to one another; that is, everyone participates, with conversation flowing from one to all other members, or from one member to another in front of the other members. For example, a conversation may be captured by audio or video recording (and then transcribed[1]); or the interaction may be observed and coded by researchers in real time. A public (often official) exchange of views may be captured by video or audio recording. A chat function may capture suggestions from team members recorded in an online brainstorming session. Important to all three of these examples, the interaction is natural and captured as it occurs without researcher intervention. The flow and emergent nature of conversation and other human interactivity, as well as group processes, are the key items of interest.

Analysis requires a systematic investigation in which the researcher specifies the research question (e.g., "How are team members' perceptions of strategic communication related to the way messages function?", Beck & Keyton, 2009, p. 227) or hypothesis (e.g., "Negative procedural statements will be negatively linked to team success," Kauffeld & Lehmann-Willenbrock, 2012, p. 136). Over time, several interaction analysis coding schemes have been developed and tested (see examples of interaction analysis coding schemes in Part V of this volume) that now allow researchers to generate hypotheses about which type of interaction events occur more frequently, or prior to or subsequent to one another. More typically, however, many researchers use research questions to frame their investigations as new contexts are being explored (e.g., juries, Poole & Dobosh, 2010; text and voice chat rooms, Jepson, 2005). Thus, researchers are looking to identify frequencies and patterns of interaction codes or categories, as well as detect sequential dependence among those observations (Bakeman & Gottman, 1997).

Thus, interaction analysis can answer questions such as: What do interactants do in this setting? And, how do they do it? For example, in a meeting, are interactants making decisions or managing conflict, or both? How are city council members performing their tasks of informing citizens or stalling in making a decision? Interaction analysis can also answer questions such as: How do task force members create new regulations? How is their interaction different when the most influential member is absent? Interaction analysis is a research method for helping researchers to identify and evaluate repeatable and explainable patterns in turns at talk that are beyond a level of which participants are aware at the time of its occurrence. That is, researchers using deductive or inductive theorizing can find instances and patterns in conversations that would remain hidden from the conversational partners or a casual observer.

Conducting studies with interaction analysis, however, costs researchers significant time and effort. So, why undertake such an analysis? Researchers use interaction analysis for detailed analyses of what group members say and how they say

---

[1] There is also the special case of conversation that occurs over an audio channel with push-to-talk buttons. In these cases, speakers control who hears their speaking.

it. The method allows the researcher to take on the role of a complete observer, as the unitizing, coding, and analysis of the interaction is performed out of the group setting. This allows the researcher to focus on the interaction without his or her attention being drawn back to any particular group member or to any one part of the interaction. In many ways, it's like taking a specimen back to the laboratory for refined, detailed examination. The other advantage is that the type of data produced by interaction analyses, i.e., micro-level data, can be analyzed for individuals and the group over time (within a group interaction or across many group interactions). The data can also be aggregated by interaction function, group member, or at the group level. So, while interaction analysis takes time and effort, a researcher can *see* what happened rather than rely on the perceptions of group members after the interaction is over.

Because interaction analysis is intended to be used on naturally occurring interaction, the researcher must be able to record the dyad's or group's conversation. In some cases, recordings are routinely made. Either way, persons being recorded (unless the recording is for the public record; see Beck, Gronewold, & Western, 2012) must give their consent and a high-fidelity audio or video recording is required. Most frequently, recordings are transcribed manually,[2] unitized, and then coded by at least two researchers (some software can assist in some of these steps). Reliability checks are performed for the unitizing and coding steps. Once coded, analysis begins.

Selecting interaction analysis as part of the research design carries with it several assumptions. First, the method assumes that people can make valid and reliable judgments about the text they are coding.[3] Second, interaction analysis is based on the premise that higher frequencies of coded acts are more theoretically important, as these coded acts represent the bulk of the interaction. However, recent studies have countered this assumption by suggesting that interaction types that occur less frequently may have disproportionate influence (see Keyton & Beck, 2009; Beck & Keyton, 2014). Third, interaction analysis accounts for (or codes) every utterance in the dataset. Fourth, interaction analysis is concerned with the interactive level (i.e., what acts precede or follow) over the content (i.e., topic of conversation) level of the dataset. Fifth, interaction analysis assumes the interact is a mediator, not a moderator of the interaction that follows. Sixth, interaction analysis is concerned with talk over time; a time dimension (or sequence of interactions) must be part of the study design. That is, in interaction analysis, acts only have meaning in terms of the acts that precede and follow. A researcher may only count the frequency of acts as a method of providing basic information about the conversation. However, more detail and nuance are uncovered if the interact level of analysis is also performed.

---

[2] At the date of publication, software has not yet been developed that reliably identifies a specific speaking voice from other speaking voices in a group interaction.

[3] My experience in working with many researchers, including student researchers, is that coding is a skill that not everyone has or wants to develop. Coding is very detail-oriented; some individuals can improve their skill with practice whereas others cannot. Having the time to spend on coding is another factor in addition to the skill issue.

Why Do Interaction Analysis?

Researchers use interaction analysis as a method to identify and interpret the interrelated verbal or textual features or functions from a stream of conversational elements. The next *why?* is more important. As Bonito and Sanders (2011) argue:

> Without close attention to the specifics of group members' conduct and interaction, it is easy for oversimple generalizations and unexamined assumptions to go unchecked, and to overlook that members' conduct and interaction is the basis for much that does not happen, as well as what does happen. For example, just because the conditions for conflict arise, actual conflict does not necessarily occur (p. 348).

Interaction analysis is the method by which researchers can understand the nuance of when and how, for example, conflict arises.

Acts that sequentially create conversation can be quite short (e.g., "yeah" or a spontaneous but fleeting facial gesture) or longer (a turn at talk). By coding acts (e.g., complete thought,[4] sense turn, thought turn, sentence-like units, turn at talk, utterance, 30 seconds of behavior) in their sequential order, researchers can pay close attention to the surface-level intent and function of messages, determine the effects of messages, and examine messages for their relationship to one another over time (Tucker, Weaver, & Berryman-Fink, 1981). In essence, interaction analysis provides three benefits: (a) it provides a picture of how acts are distributed across the group's conversation and across group members, (b) it showcases the interactive structure of the conversation, and (c) it makes detection of patterns and sequences of acts possible. Knowing this level of detail of human activity "helps us to understand both the development and predictability of interaction processes . . . [and] explain unexpected interaction functions or outcomes" (Meyers & Seibold, 2012, p. 341). Too often, what researchers do not capture in the sequential process of conversation is how "participants inevitably draw upon and create shared understandings, which shape their subsequent actions and meanings" (Bavelas, Gerwing, Healing, & Tomori, 2017, p. 139).

Interaction Analysis Is Quantitative

Interaction analysis is a form of textual analysis (other forms are content analysis and discourse analysis) and is quantitative as the researcher assigns acts to nominal categories. Qualitative interaction analysis research does exist.[5] As an example of quantitative interaction analysis, Keyton and Beck (2009) and Beck and

---

[4] A complete thought unit is one of the most frequently used units of analysis in interaction analysis. A complete thought unit is any statement or utterance, of any length, that has meaning on its own.
[5] An exemplar of qualitative interaction analysis is Paugh and Izquierdo's (2009) investigation of family mealtime.

Keyton (2014) captured the conversation of a breast cancer survivors group and discovered that task-related messages both preceded and followed relationally oriented messages. Moreover, task-related messages dominated the group's hour-long conversation, even though the primary task of the group was to be supportive of one another. This called the researchers' attention to the power of the less frequent relationally oriented messages, as well as how the two types of messages were interrelated within a conversation. Using descriptive statistics and chi-square analyses, the researchers drew readers' attention to how coding was distributed across the IPA categories. Then, by isolating sequences of task-relational-task interactions, the researchers provided examples of the group's conversation to support the researchers' claims. For example, use of relational talk after task talk confirmed, extended, or qualified information from another speaker; signaled the direction, continuance, or transition of the conversation; or signaled identification of other members. As a result of these analyses, the researchers could demonstrate that in a support group, advice is not simply given by one member to another. Rather, the researchers could demonstrate with examples that, in this support group setting, advice is interactive and layered.

Because of the interest in the temporality of interaction analysis, some analytical methods (e.g., ANOVA, regression) are not suitable whereas other analytic techniques are (e.g., autoregressive, integrative, moving average; cross-recurrence quantification analysis; lag-sequential analysis; Markov and semi-Markov modeling; moderated dependency analysis; multilevel modeling, phasic analysis) (Bakeman & Gottman, 1997; Bakeman & Quera, 1995; Davis, 2017; Hewes & Poole, 2012; VanLear, 2017; see also, all in this volume, Rack, Zahn, & Mateescu, Chapter 14; Quera, Chapter 15; Magnusson, Chapter 16; Bonito & Staggs, Chapter 17; and Poole, Chapter 18).

The Method of Interaction Analysis

Once verbal, nonverbal, or textual interaction is captured, the researcher creates a transcript and verifies it against the capture of the data. With transcript in hand, the next step is to isolate units of talk from within the continuous stream of talk or activity, code those units independently from at least one other coder, analyze units relative to the talk that precedes and follows it, and present a valid interpretation of the talk back to the context. Sometimes, feedback is also given to participants who generated the talk. Thus, interaction analysis is a research method that allows for the systematic capture, unitizing, coding, and interpretation of naturally occurring conversations.

Coding Schemes

The coding scheme (or set of standardized coding rules) is central to interaction analysis. Coding schemes may be developed inductively from a set of observations (see Pavitt, 2011; Sabee, Koenig, Wingard, Foster, Chivers, Olsher, & Vandergriff,

2015), be theoretically derived, or may already exist (see Part V of this volume for a list of coding schemes and Tschan, Zimmermann, & Semmer, Chapter 10, for the development of new coding schemes). This latter deductive approach allows researchers to use coding schemes of carefully defined categories based on theory (in addition to knowing the degree of reliability and validity other scholars have found). The use of decision trees is recommended by Bavelas, Gerwing, Healing, and Tomori (2017) as a way to work through the steps required to create a coding scheme. Validity and reliability studies are the next step (see Seelandt, this volume, Chapter 12).

The domain of interaction analysis coding schemes is quite varied. Some coding schemes contain only a few codes and are context dependent. In their Mother Adolescent Interaction Task coding scheme (MAIT), Pineda, Cole, and Bruce (2007) used three broad codes (e.g., critical behavior, depressive behavior, and positive behavior) to assess both the child's and mother's verbal and nonverbal behavior during their interaction. Other coding schemes are quite broadly construed and can be used in many different types of interactions. Bales' (1950) Interaction Process Analysis (IPA) coding scheme is one of these. It has 12 coding categories organized into four macro categories of socioemotional/positive reactions, socioemotional/negative reactions, task/attempted answers, and task/questions. Coding schemes can be specific to a type of conversational feature (e.g., Group Working Relationships Coding System, developed for coding conflict; Poole & Roth, 1989), or specific to a contextually specific type of conversation (e.g., Siminoff Communication Content and Affect Program, developed for health settings; Siminoff & Step, 2011). At the extreme, a coding scheme can code people simply as *talking* or as *silent* (Cappella, 1984; also see Yong, 2016).

Thus, coding schemes must define what counts as a codable *act*, making the relationship between coding scheme and codable unit of paramount importance. In early coding schemes, the most typical unit of analysis of conversation was the *act*, which Bales (1950) described as "the smallest discriminable segment of verbal or nonverbal behavior" that could be coded (p. 37). Later, Folger, Hewes, and Poole (1984) argued that units of social interaction can range from 300 milliseconds to a full exchange among speakers. Thus, the unit of analysis is not fixed, but rather is selected based on theory, the coding scheme, and the hypothesis/research question. Sometimes, the unit of analysis that becomes the pivotal aspect of a conversation is not discovered until other units of analyses have been attempted. So, while a unit of analysis is not fixed, it is also not arbitrary (see Reed, Metzger, Kolbe, Zobel, & Boos, this volume, Chapter 11 for a syntax-based method for unitizing interaction). Researchers must have good reasons for using the unit of analysis selected and describe this decision choice.

Coding schemes must also be meaningful to human interaction, but validity and reliability must be taken into account. That is, the coding scheme should not distort the meaning of the text solely to achieve acceptable levels of validity or reliability. As coding schemes are used over time, they are either validated or revised as other researchers code different types of interaction and ask different types of research questions.

Regardless of which interaction analysis coding scheme is selected, researchers are advised to consider six features before embarking on a research study (Trujillo, 1986). What philosophical perspective frames the design and study? What is the conceptual and operational focus of the coding scheme? How much and what type of observer inference will be required? Is the design suited to interaction analysis? Finally, what is the potential effect of recording the conversation on coding judgments (e.g., clarity of recording)?

Finally, it should be pointed out that training coders is a significant investment. Coders must learn the coding system, practice coding, and achieve the required level of intercoder reliability. Once the coding scheme is fully developed and verified, interaction analysis is conducted by trained individuals (scholars or their research assistants) while the interaction of interest is occurring, or afterward from an audio or video recording or transcript. Coding is aligned with a specific inter-action event and inherent to interaction analysis. When researchers code the interaction of people, they are observing naturally occurring interaction, and they are coding a behavior that just occurred. When coding is done from audio, video, or transcripts, researchers can often code for finer-grained detail than (a) research participants can rate themselves or (b) researchers can rate all research participants after the interaction has concluded (Samter & Macgeorge, 2017).

The characteristics common to all coding schemes for interaction analysis are several: (a) the focus is the interaction of two or more individuals; (b) the interaction must be naturally occurring, not scripted; (c) coding is done by trained researchers or research assistants; and (d) the data are captured sequentially allowing for more basic analyses of frequencies, and more sophisticated sequential analyses.

Distinguishing Interaction Analysis from Content Analysis and Conversation Analysis

Over a period of years, Krippendorff (2004, 2013) has set the standard for *content analysis*, which is both different from and similar to interaction analysis. Similar to both methods are the isolation and unitizing of discrete units, coding the units, and making inferences back to the context from which the text was drawn. The primary difference between the two rests on the requirement of interaction analysis for maintaining sequence of the units, which is essential to coding acts or interacts, and often not present in content analysis. Interaction analysis also has the requirement of naturally occurring interaction among multiple speakers, which content analysis does not.

For example, Humphreys, Gill, and Krishnamurthy (2014) used content analysis to code the amount and types of personally identifiable information from public Twitter messages to answer several research questions. Twitter messages are asynchronous and asymmetric. Two of the research questions were: RQ1: "How often is locational information articulated in public Twitter messages"; and RQ2: What is "the degree to which we can assess where these behaviors are occurring – work, home, or outside of work and home (or what one might call public space)" (p. 847). These questions are typical for content analysis, as the aim is to describe what is happening and how frequently a type of behavior occurs. Alternatively, analysis of text message conversations would be better suited for interaction analysis methods, as *who texts what* presents a demand on the receiver for responding in a sensible fashion. Text messages are synchronous and symmetric. Thus, units can be coupled, minimally into repeating binary exchanges, but also examined for how topics reoccur or are dropped.

Examining the relationship of conversation analysis to interaction analysis, there are few similarities. Both use naturally occurring data and rely on the sequence of talk both within and between speaking turns. However, conversation analysis is a more detailed analysis, and requires a different type of transcription – one that more finely annotates, for example, the allocation of turn taking. In conversation analysis, researchers pay attention to a particular type of discourse act within an interaction. For example, Lee, Tsang, Bogo, Wilson, Johnstone, and Herschman (2017) examine the moments in the conversation of family dyads in therapy when the therapist joins the two family members (i.e., a joining moment). Other parts of the conversation are not analyzed. For conversation analysis, transcripts are marked with the milliseconds of pauses and overlaps; all physical actions are also noted. As a result of this highly micro-level of analysis, conversation analysts typically investigate only one interaction with the goal of situating the conversation of these speakers in a location and context requiring this type of interaction (Beach, 2008). Conversation analysis studies are particularly good at determining how conversation works in different conventional settings. For example, Pontecorvo and Arcidiacono (2016) used conversation analysis to explore how children and fathers perform argument in daily talk. These authors discovered that a child can resist his father's instruction during family dinnertime conversation by using an elaborated argumentative strategy.

Coding vs. Rating

In comparison to interaction analysis, *rating* can be done by the researcher, but also by participants as self-report data, once the interaction being studied is completed. Retrospective rating is characterized by the researchers or participants assigning a number representing the degree to which the phenomenon was displayed. Ratings are more typically made on global impressions. Bales and Cohen (1979) suggest that raters making self or other retrospective ratings tend to have a positive bias in their ratings, whereas coders assign a wider distribution when coding. The positive bias phenomenon is well studied (e.g., Wilson, Meyers, & Gilbert, 2003). Thus, many researchers believe that interaction coding is closer to ground truth than self-report questionnaires or global observer ratings.

Thus, in summary, interaction analysis focuses on outward facing, contextually situated interdependent behavior among two or more individuals. These interrelated behaviors are continuously interpreted by all actors in the setting in order to proceed to the interrelated goal that brought these interactants together. *Interaction analysis* is an umbrella term for a set of systematic research techniques for reliably unitizing and coding sequential, naturally occurring interaction behaviors and making valid interpretations and inferences from those data to the context in which the observations occurred. Across these techniques, there is a great variety of (a) observable phenomena (i.e., verbal, nonverbal, textual), (b) observational modes, (c) units of analysis, (d) study designs, (e) length of interactions, (f) coding schemes, (g) types of analysis, and (h) theoretical foundations (Fairhurst & Cooren, 2004). Generally, the goal of interaction analysis research using one of these techniques is to uncover the functions of the observed phenomena, not its content (Frey, 1996). For a critique of interaction analysis, see Fairhurst (2004).

Theory and Interaction Analysis

D. J. Canary (2017) demonstrates how the theory underlying a coding scheme can result in the same act being coded differently. Some coding schemes, in this instance conflict coding schemes, do "share some similarities but differ in several behaviors and level of abstraction" (p. 5). He demonstrates this in considering how a coding scheme would treat the act of disagreement. In some coding schemes, disagreement is coded as negative; in other coding schemes, disagreement is coded as competitive or as hostility. Thus, researchers using interaction analysis need to be mindful of the theoretical foundation of their research design and develop analyses and implications within that theoretical frame.

What Can We Learn by Observing Interaction?

Using interaction analysis is ideal for learning about a number of observable human processes that can be recorded or captured for analysis. For example, consider these situated interactions. How do we engage someone to argue with us? What are the interactions that lead to a couple saying "I do"? How does a design team create a breakthrough in knowledge? All of these are human interaction processes for which sequential data are ideal to represent the manner in which these interactions occur, develop, and sustain or resolve over time. Bakeman and Gottman (1997) remind us that when descriptors such as *process* or *dynamic* are in our research goals, research questions, and hypotheses, scholars must observe over time while noting the order of events as well as the start, top, and duration of events. These are the goals of interaction analysis. As an example, Meyers and Seibold

(2012, p. 329) describe how they believe it best to analyze and explain processes in decision-making groups: The questions could not be answered adequately and/or only by predicting from inputs to outputs, or by querying group participants about what they would say (or said they did) *if* they were in a group setting, or by asking students to write communicative responses to scenarios. In order to understand the complexity and seeming ambiguity of group communicative processes, it is necessary to scrutinize the data produced during members' discussions.

These scholars make an important point. In some disciplines, researchers only code one of the interactants (see Rimal, 2001). Doing so eradicates the unique advantage of interaction analysis, which is to reveal and interpret patterns of interaction *among* interactants. Especially in the case of physician-patient interaction, knowing how the physician delivers advice is only relevant with respect to the earlier doctor-patient conversation. As this research demonstrated, a physician's interaction at the very beginning of the medical interview significantly alters the ensuing physician-patient interaction (Manning & Ray, 2002).

Interaction analysis has great strength in revealing social processes. Because the conversation remains in sequential order throughout the coding and analyses, concepts from each category of a coding scheme can be evaluated for its contribution to the conversation as a whole. A particularly compelling interactional analysis study (Holmes & Sykes, 1993) demonstrates that training for negotiators is more orderly than real hostage-negotiation sessions. The revelation of this insight provided several opportunities for increasing the validity of the training police negotiators receive.

Researchers choosing to use interaction analysis as part of their research design must be committed to the time and resources required for data collection, unitizing, coding, and interpretation. With this commitment, researchers can uncover temporal patterns in the situated context that reveal *how* a phenomenon develops (or not) and is sustained (or weakened). Its data-driven form is a foundation for developing new practices or procedures for practitioners. Likewise, interaction analysis can reveal unexpected patterns or patterns that run counter to established theory.

For example, Beck and Keyton (2009) used IPA coding and analysis as a way to understand the strategic intent and interaction of an organizational group. Their findings revealed how and why team members interpreted the same interaction in different ways. Kauffeld and Lehmann-Willenbrock (2012) identified a clear link between the interaction processes of teams and team success. Problem-focused statements, positive procedural statements, and proactive statements were associated with increased meeting satisfaction, team productivity, and organizational success. However, dysfunctional communicative behaviors such as criticizing or complaining showed numerous negative relationships with the study's outcome variables. Beck, Gronewold, and Western (2012) examined a public meeting, which was called to allow all interested parties to discuss allowing another Wal-mart™ in their city. Their interaction analyses revealed that a simple straightforward strategy for argumentation (focusing on one or two issues, placing the position in context, and avoiding confrontation) was successful. Thus, such a simple, straightforward argumentation strategy cannot necessarily be identified as unsophisticated argumentation.

The Future of Interaction Analysis

To date, most interaction analysis research has focused on verbal or physical behaviors, as those are easiest to observe in real time or capture with audio and/or video recording equipment. However, continual development of technology is expanding what interaction cues can be examined by researchers. For example, Yu et al. (2015) describe their successful capture of facial movements, facial expressions, and head movement to study the role of interactional synchrony in deception. Importantly, this research group discovered that, after controlling for false positives, automated methods for detecting synchrony between an interviewer and interviewee were better than manual coding. As technology develops, allowing researchers to capture and code both verbal and nonverbal interaction, we need to acknowledge in our research designs the fact that "both visible and audible communicative resources ... are tightly integrated with each other ... their actions must be understood as coordinated and mutually influential" (Samter, Gerwing, Healing, & Tomori, 2017, p. 133). In many instances, a gesture can serve as a conversational act (e.g., one person putting both hands up to signal *stop*).

For interaction analysis, scholars tend to think of *sequential* as a within-event phenomenon. However, between-event sequences of several task-related meetings are also important (see Bonito, Keyton, & Ervin, 2017; Ervin, Bonito, & Keyton, 2017) especially when the sequential lag is normal for participants. In studying family mealtimes, H. E. Canary (2017) notes that mealtime interaction is relatively short. However, a wide range of behaviors and interactions are likely to occur (e.g., discussion of food and family routines for eating, life and family events, joking and teasing, evaluation of behavior). The variety of interactions within-interaction and across-interaction would be important to consider within the larger ebb and flow of family dynamics.

Why This Book Now?

Scholars who design interaction analysis studies represent many disciplines. While disciplinary content may not hold us together, learning more about this methodology does create a unique community of interaction analysis scholars. Coding schemes should be theoretically based, and much time and energy is devoted to developing them. Further, researchers have used many different types of sessions or periods of interaction as data for analyses (e.g., meetings, play sessions, greetings). This handbook should expose this community of researchers (and newcomers to interaction analysis) to coding schemes (see chapters in Part V) and analytic techniques (see chapters in Part IV) of which they were unaware.

Interaction analysis requires a notable investment in time and resources. For example, Meyers and colleagues (1991) reported that two pairs of two coders were trained over a period of five weeks for more than 40 hours of training and practice coding sessions until intercoder agreement reached 80 percent. After reaching a suitable level of agreement, coders can then work individually or in pairs – still, intercoder reliability must be routinely calculated to detect if coder drift has occurred. Clearly, interaction analysis is a detailed and time-consuming process that requires a number of researchers or research assistants who can meet together to train, discuss coding discrepancies, and work further on the development of the coding scheme. Interaction analysis demands significant resources, which can be expensive. This handbook should also make this research community aware of tips and techniques that others have found helpful in this time-consuming method. Researcher collaboration has long been seen as "essential for incorporating novices because interaction analysis is difficult to describe and is best learned by doing" (Jordan & Henderson, 1995, p. 43).

Theoretically, there is still much to do. For example, more than one coding scheme can be used (e.g., starting with a more general coding scheme, such as Bales' Interaction Process Analysis [1950], and then coding for conflict management strategies with, for example, Poole and Dobosh's coding scheme [2010]). But this layering of interaction analysis is rare. One example is the study of Gottman, Markman, and Notarius (1977), who applied three coding schemes (i.e., content of the message, nonverbal delivery of the message, nonverbal reception of the message) in their investigation of marital conflict. Layering coding this way will require this research community to team up across disciplines as well as to develop innovative analysis techniques to make the best use of the data.

Technological advances have occurred that will help researchers, especially in coding a two-person conversation. But, to date, technology has not proven to be successful in coding speech from audio channels. In the area of collaborative learning (see Heisawn & Hmelo-Silver, 2014), researchers have used adjacency pairs of text chat, a unit of conversation that contains a turn at speaking by two speakers; that is, Speaker A talks followed by Speaker B. Using these units, researchers can create coding rules such that software can automatically assign these units to a coding classification scheme. While this computer-assisted coding may be helpful for a first pass through the data, only human coders can make the very fine type of distinctions required in interaction analysis. Why? Currently, computer programs can only consider the content (or the literal meaning) or the pairing of adjacent words to identify an appropriate code; the computer program also does not take into account what was said by speakers many turns before or after. Most importantly, software cannot account for *how* words were said (or the interactional meaning; i.e., the meaning created by the speakers based upon the context in which the utterance occurs; Tracy, 2002). In group interaction, turn taking is not evenly distributed among speakers. Only a human coder reading a transcript can take into account the immediate context in which the conversation occurred (including who has/has not spoken), and infer the influence of the acts of the dominant or submissive speakers. Can the interaction analysis community create interdisciplinary relationships for developing more useful software applications? For example, in this volume, Chapter 19, Bonito and Keyton report that machine learning continues to progress and is being used to code group interaction data (also see Grimmer & Stewart, 2013).

This handbook, through its contributors, has evaluated the health of interaction analysis as a research method. Learning from one another should be our first goal. Reaching out to one another can move interaction analysis forward theoretically and methodologically; that should be our second goal. I am excited to be a member of this research community and look forward to learning and developing new relationships and ways for analyzing interaction data.

References

Bakeman, R., & Gottman, J. M. (1997). *Observing interaction: An introduction to sequential analysis* (2nd edn.). Cambridge, UK: Cambridge University Press.

Bakeman, R., & Quera, V. (1995). *Analyzing interaction: Sequential analysis with SDIS and GSEQ*. New York, NY: Cambridge University Press.

Bales, R. F. (1950). *Interaction process analysis: A method for the study of small groups*. Cambridge, MA: Addison-Wesley.

Bales, R. F., & Cohen, S. P. (1979). *SYMLOG: A system for the multiple level observation of groups*. New York, NY: Free Press.

Bavelas, J., Gerwing, J., Healing, S., & Tomori, C. (2017). Microanalysis of face-to-face dialogue. In C. A. VanLear & D. J. Canary (Eds.), *Researching interactive communication behavior: A sourcebook of methods and measures* (pp. 129–157). Los Angeles, CA: Sage.

Beach, W. A. (2008). Conversation analysis. In E. W. Donsbach (Ed.), *The international encyclopedia of communication*. Malden, MA: Blackwell Publishing. doi:10.1111/b.9781405131995.2008.x

Beck, S. J., Gronewold, K. L., & Western, K. H. (2012). Intergroup argumentation in city government decision making: The Wal-mart dilemma. *Small Group Research*, *43*, 587–612. doi:10.1177/1046496412455435

Beck, S. J., & Keyton, J. (2009). Perceiving strategic meeting interaction. *Small Group Research*, *40*, 223–246. doi:10.1177/1046496408330084

Beck, S. J., & Keyton, J. (2014). Facilitating social support: Member-leader communication in a breast cancer support group. *Cancer Nursing*, *37*(1), E36–E43. doi:10.1097/NCC.0b013e3182813829

Bonito, J., Keyton, J., & Ervin, J. (2017). Role-related participation in product design teams: Individual- and group-level trends. *Communication Research*, *44*, 263–286. doi:10.1177/0093650215618759

Bonito, J. A., & Sanders, R. E. (2011). The existential center of small groups: Member's conduct and interaction. *Small Group Research*, *42*, 343–358. doi:10.1177/1046496410385472

Canary, D. J. (2017). Observing relational conflict. In C. A. VanLear & D. J. Canary (Eds.), *Researching interactive communication behavior: A sourcebook of methods and measures* (pp. 3–16). Los Angeles, CA: Sage.

Canary, H. E. (2017). Observing family communication. In C. A. VanLear & D. J. Canary (Eds.), *Researching interactive communication behavior: A sourcebook of methods and measures* (pp. 17–33). Los Angeles, CA: Sage.

Cappella, J. N. (1984). The relevance of the microstructure of interaction to relationship change. *Journal of Social and Personal Relationships*, *1*, 239–264. doi:10.1177/0265407584012006

Davis, T. J. (2017). Modeling behavioral interaction as a nonlinear dynamical system. In C. A. VanLear & D. J. Canary (Eds.), *Researching interactive communication behavior: A sourcebook of methods and measures* (pp. 261–271). Los Angeles, CA: Sage.

Ervin, J., Bonito, J., & Keyton, J. (2017). Convergence of intrapersonal and interpersonal processes across group meetings. *Communication Monographs*. doi:10.1080/03637751.2016.1185136

Fairhurst, G. T. (2004). Textuality and agency in interaction analysis. *Organization*, *11*, 335–353. doi:10.1177/1350508404041996

Fairhurst, G. T., & Cooren, F. (2004). Organizational language in use: Interaction analysis, conversation analysis and speech act schematics. In D. Grant, C. Hardy, C. Oswick, & L. Putnam (Eds.), *The Sage handbook of organizational discourse* (pp. 131–152). Thousand Oaks, CA: Sage.

Folger, J. P., Hewes, D. E., & Poole, M. S. (1984). Coding social interaction. In B. Dervin & M. J. Voigt (Eds.), *Progress in communication sciences* (p. 115–161). Norwood, NJ: Ablex.

Frey, L. R. (1996). Remembering and "re-membering": A history of theory and research on communication and group decision making. In R. Y. Hirokawa & M. S. Poole (Eds.), *Communication and group decision making* (2nd edn., pp. 19–51). Thousand Oaks, CA: Sage.

Gottman, J., Markman, J., & Notarius, C. (1977). The topography of marital conflict: A sequential analysis of verbal and nonverbal behavior. *Journal of Marriage and the Family*, *39*, 461–477. doi:10.2307/350902

Grimmer, J., & Stewart, B. M. (2013). Text as data: The promise and pitfalls of automatic content analysis methods for political text. *Political Analysis*, *21*, 267–297. doi:10.1093/pan/mps028

Heisawn, J., & Hmelo-Silver, C. E. (2014). An examination of CSC methodology practices and the influence of theoretical frameworks 2005–2009. *International Journal of Computer-Supported Collaborative Learning*, *8*, 305–334. doi:10.1007/s11412-014-9198-3

Hewes, D. E., & Poole, M. S. (2012). The analysis of group interaction processes. In A. B. Hollingshead & M. S. Poole (Eds.), *Research methods for studying groups and teams: A guide to approaches, tools, and technologies* (pp. 358–385). New York, NY: Routledge.

Holmes, M. E., & Sykes, R. E. (1993). A test of the fit of Gulliver's phase model to hostage negotiations. *Communication Studies*, *44*, 38–55. doi.10.1080/10510979309368381

Humphreys, L., Gill, G., & Krishnamurthy, B. (2014). Twitter: A content analysis of personal information. *Information, Communication & Society*, *17*, 843–857. doi:10.1080/1369118X.2013.848917

Jepson, K. (2005). Conversation—and negotiated interaction—in text and voice chat rooms. *Language, Learning, and Technology*, *9*(3), 79–98.

Jordan, B., & Henderson, A. (1995). Interaction analysis: Foundations and practice. *Journal of the Learning Sciences*, *4*, 39–103. doi:10.1207/s15327809jls0401_2

Kauffeld, S. (2006). Kompetenzen messen, bewerten, entwickeln—Ein prozessanalytischer Ansatz für Gruppen *[Measuring, evaluating, and developing competencies—A process analytical approach for groups]*. Stuttgart, Germany: Schäffer-Poeschel.

Kauffeld, S., & Lehmann-Willenbrock, N. (2012). Meetings matter: Effects of team meetings on team and organizational success. *Small Group Research*, *43*, 130–158. doi:10.1177/ 1046496411429599

Kauffeld, S., & Meyers, R. (2009). Complaint and solution-oriented cycles: Interaction patterns in work group discussions. *European Journal of Work and Organizational Psychology*, *18*, 267–294. doi:10.1080/13594320701693209

Keyton, J., & Beck, S. J. (2009). The influential role of relational messages in group interaction. *Group Dynamics*, *13*, 14–30. doi:10.1037/a0013495

Krippendorff, K. (2004). *Content analysis: An introduction to its methodology* (2nd edn.). Thousand Oaks, CA: Sage.

Krippendorff, K. (2013). *Content analysis: An introduction to its methodology* (3rd edn.). Thousand Oaks, CA: Sage.

Lee, E., Tsang, A. K. T., Bogo, M., Wilson, G., Johnstone, M., & Herschman, J. (2017). Joining revisited in family therapy: Discourse analysis of cross-cultural encounters between a therapist and an immigrant family. *Journal of Family Therapy*, *48*, 178–189. doi:10.1111/1467-6427.12148

Lehmann-Willenbrock, N., & Kauffeld, S. (2010). The downside of communication: Complaining cycles in group discussions. In S. Schuman (Ed.), *The handbook for working with difficult groups: How they are difficult, why they are difficult and what you can do about it* (pp. 33–54). San Francisco, CA: Jossey-Bass/Wiley.

Manning, P., & Ray, G. B. (2002). Setting the agenda: An analysis of negotiation strategies in clinical talk. *Health Communication*, *14*, 451–473. doi:10.1207/S15327027HC1404_3

Meyers, R. A., & Seibold, D. R. (2012). Coding group interaction. In A. B. Hollingshead & M. S. Poole (Eds.), *Research methods for studying groups and teams: A guide to approaches, tools, and technologies* (pp. 329–357). New York, NY: Routledge.

Meyers, R. A., Seibold, D. R., & Brashers, D. (1991). Argument in initial group decision-making discussions: Refinement of a coding scheme and a descriptive quantitative analysis. *Western Journal of Speech Communication*, *55*, 47–68. doi:10.1080/10570319109374370

Paugh, A., & Izquierdo, C. (2009). Why is this a battle every night? Negotiating food and eating in American dinnertime interaction. *Journal of Linguistic Anthropology*, *19*, 185–204. doi:10.1111/j.1548-1395.2009.01030.x

Pavitt, C. (2011). Communication, performance, and perceptions in experimental simulations of resource dilemmas. *Small Group Research*, *42*, 283–308. doi:10.1177/1046496411399782

Pineda, A. Q., Cole, D. A., & Bruce, A. E. (2007). Mother-adolescent interactions and adolescent depressive symptoms: A sequential analysis. *Journal of Social and Personal Relationships*, *24*, 5–19. doi:10.1177/0265407507072564

Pontecorvo, C., & Arcidiacono, F. (2016). The dialogic construction of justifications and arguments of a seven-year-old child within a 'democratic' family. *Language and Dialogue*, *6*, 306–328. doi:10.1075/ld.6.2.05pon

Poole, M. S., & Dobosh, M. A. (2010). Exploring conflict management processes in jury deliberations through interaction analysis. *Small Group Research*, *41*, 408–426. doi:10.1177/1046496410366310

Poole, M. S., & Roth, J. (1989). Decision development in small groups IV: A typology of group decision paths. *Human Communication Research*, *15*, 323–356. doi:10.1111/j.1468-2958.1989.tb00188.x

Rimal, R. N. (2001). Analyzing the physician-patient interaction: An overview of six methods and future research directions. *Health Communication*, *13*, 89–99. doi:10.1207/S15327027HC1301_08

Sabee, C. M., Koenig, C. J., Wingard, L., Foster, J., Chivers, N., Olsher, D., & Vandergriff, I. (2015). The process of interactional sensitivity coding in health care: Conceptually and operationally defining patient-centered communication. *Journal of Health Communication*, *20*, 773–782. doi:10.1080/10810730.2015.1018567

Samter, W., & Macgeorge, E. L. (2017). Coding comforting behavior for verbal person centeredness. In C. A. VanLear & D. J. Canary (Eds.), *Researching interactive communication behavior: A sourcebook of methods and measures* (pp. 107–128). Los Angeles, CA: Sage.

Siminoff, L. A., & Step, M. M. (2011). A comprehensive observational coding scheme for analyzing instrumental, affective, and relational communication in health care contexts. *Journal of Health Communication: International Perspectives*, *16*, 178–191. doi:10.1080/10810730.2010.535109

Tracy, K. (2002). *Everyday talk: Building and reflecting identities*. New York, NY: Guilford Press.

Trujillo, N. (1986). Toward a taxonomy of small group interaction-coding systems. *Small Group Research*, *17*, 371–394. doi:10.1177/104649648601700401

Tucker, R. K., Weaver, R. L., & Berryman-Fink, C. (1981). *Research in speech communication*. Englewood Cliffs, NJ: Prentice-Hall.

VanLear, C. A. (2017). Modeling and analyzing behaviors and the dynamics of behavioral interaction. In C. A. VanLear & D. J. Canary (Eds.), *Researching interactive communication behavior: A sourcebook of methods and measures* (pp. 235–260). Los Angeles, CA: Sage.

VanLear, C. A., & Canary, D. J. (Eds.). (2017). *Researching interactive communication behavior: A sourcebook of methods and measures*. Los Angeles, CA: Sage.

Wilson, T. D., Meyers, J., & Gilbert, D. T. (2003). "How happy was I, anyway?" A retrospective impact bias. *Social Cognition*, *21*, 421–446. doi:10.1521/soco.21.6.421.28688

Yong, E. (2016, January 4). The incredible thing we do during conversations. *The Atlantic.* Retrieved from www.theatlantic.com/science/archive/2016/01/the-incredible-thing-we-do-during-conversations/422439

Yu, X., Zhang, S., Yan, Z., Yang, F., Huang, J., Dunbar, N. E., Jensen, M. L., Burgoon, J. K., & Metaxas, D. N. (2015). Is interactional dissynchrony a clue to deception? Insights from automated analysis of nonverbal visual cues. *IEEE Transactions on Cybernetics*, *45*, 492–506. doi:10.1109/TCYB.2014.2329673

2 History of Group Interaction Research

Simone Kauffeld and Annika L. Meinecke

"How do groups develop over time?", "How do groups manage conflict?", "What characterizes a successful discussion?", and "How do groups solve complex problems?" These are just a few questions that started the study of group interaction research. The key to answering these questions lies in understanding group inter-action processes, that is, "the simultaneous and sequential behavior (verbal and motor) of group members as they act in relation to one another and to the task that the group is trying to accomplish, over time" (McGrath & Altermatt, 2001, p. 525). One way to get access to group interaction processes is by systematically *observing* the ongoing interaction among group members (McGrath & Altermatt, 2001). Systematically observing groups can be tedious and time consuming, which might be one reason why only a small percentage of group researchers actually devote their work to the study of group interaction processes (Moreland, Fetterman, Flagg, & Swanenburg, 2010; Wittenbaum & Moreland, 2008). Nonetheless, we can look back at a long and strong history of group interaction research.

In highlighting milestones of group interaction research, we will follow a content-driven approach by focusing on important methodological developments rather than giving a comprehensive historic account in chronological order. We will pay close attention to previous studies and literature on systematic observation and coding of group interaction processes, and not to the general history of group research such as outlined by other scholars (e.g., Forsyth & Burnette, 2005; Levine & Moreland, 2012; McGrath, 1997; Wittenbaum & Moreland, 2008).

In the following, we first trace the origins of group interaction research and explore how previous research shaped our understanding of how to study groups today. Second, we provide an overview of the manifold coding decisions that group researchers made in the past. Finally, we will touch on more recent developments in group interaction research.

Origins of Group Interaction Research

Group interaction research emerged in the early to mid-twentieth century originating from scientific disciplines such as sociology, communication studies, organizational behavior and management, as well as organizational and social psychology (McGrath, 1984; McGrath & Altermatt, 2001; Wittenbaum &

Moreland, 2008). Research endeavors stemming from these different disciplines share their focus on systematic observation of group members' actual interactive behavior. However, the ways and means of carrying out this systematic observation and analysis of group interaction varied depending on the researchers' background and training, the specific research question at hand, and the technological capabilities and opportunities at the time of research.

There is no single study that would mark the beginning of group interaction research. Instead, several notable research projects and studies were conducted between the mid-1920s and mid-1950s.

Parten's Stages of Play

One of the first systematic and quantitative approaches to group observation can be found in Parten's work (1932, 1933a, 1933b). Parten was an American sociologist and at the time a researcher at the University of Minnesota's Institute of Child Welfare. In the late 1920s, she developed her *theory of six stages of play* that encompassed the classification of social participation and play among preschool children in group settings.

Parten observed children of the age of almost two to five years. She carried out several months of preliminary observations to develop and refine her technique of observation. In her main study, three independent observers and Parten herself documented the behavior of about 40 children. The children were observed for one-minute intervals each during the morning free play hour. In doing so, all four observers simultaneously observed and documented the behavior of the same target child before turning to a new child. Parten prepared coding templates to document the children's behavior in a standardized fashion. In addition to documenting the number of children that the target child played with, the names of the children in the group, and the play activity in which they engaged, the target child's overt behavior was coded using two separate coding schemes. The first coding scheme was used to record the degree of social participation and the second to measure the degree of leadership. To illustrate, the six categories for social participation are shown in Table 2.1. Finally, Parten documented if the target child was talking or not, and she used an estimate to describe the duration of the activity (i.e., v – short time, m – most of the minute, or e – entire minute).

At least 60 of these one-minute samples were obtained for each child following the method of repeated short samples. The order in which the children were observed rotated so that each child was observed an equal number of times during the beginning, middle, and end of the one-hour free play time. Because all observers worked with the same coding template and kept records simultaneously, Parten was able to derive an early measure of inter-rater reliability (i.e., percentage of agreement). To test her hypotheses, Parten calculated percentage scores for the distribution of each category across the coded intervals and correlated these with certain characteristics of the children such as their age and IQ. Consistent with her

Table 2.1 *Parten's (1932, pp. 249–251) category system for social participation among preschool children*

Code	Definition
U – Unoccupied behavior	The child is not playing or engaged with anything specific.
O – Onlooker	The child spends most of the time watching other children play but does not join in.
S – Solidary independent play	The child plays alone and is unaffected by other children.
P – Parallel activity	The child plays independently, but the activity that is chosen naturally brings him/her among other children. The child plays beside rather than with the other children. The child does not attempt to control who is in the group.
A – Associative play	The child plays with other children. The child borrows and loans play material. There are mild attempts to control who is in the group.
C – Cooperative or organized supplementary play	The child plays in a group that is organized for some purpose (e.g., playing formal games). Control of the group is in the hands of one or two children who direct the activity of the others.

Note. Abbreviated definitions are displayed.

theory, Parten found that older children showed more associative and cooperative play than younger children.

Parten's research has had a significant impact on the understanding of play up until this day. Moreover, Parten established important standards for observation and coding of social situations. In this regard, she stressed the importance of multiple observers, a standardized and controlled environment, and a thorough coding schedule. Moreover, she introduced the use of a priori coding schemes to quantitatively categorize the behavior of individuals within groups. This allowed her to derive summary measures of coded behavior that were sound and reliable.

Early Category Systems for Coding Interactions

Early quantitative systems for coding group interactions among teenagers and adults arose shortly after Parten's work (e.g., Benne & Sheats, 1948; Miller, 1939; Newstetter, 1937; Steinzor, 1949; Wrightstone, 1934). One such category system is Wrightstone's *Code 3* coding scheme for group planning and discussion, which he described as "an instrument for measuring certain aspects and practices of democracy in the classroom" (Wrightstone, 1934, p. 643). Thus, Code 3 focused on group interactions among pupils and, specifically, on their verbal communication. In using Code 3, Wrightstone coded those pupil contributions that were heeded by the group. The coding scheme comprised seven different categories that would classify as *mutually exclusive* nowadays because each contribution could be coded into just one category: (3a) *prepared voluntary report or exhibit,* (3b) *assigned report or exhibit*, (3c) *extemporaneous contribution from real experience*, (3d) *extemporaneous contribution from vicarious experience*, (3e) *asking questions on the topic, unit, or problem*, (3f) *criticism of a contribution: praise or challenge*, and (3g) *suggesting means, methods, activities, or solutions* (Wrightstone, 1934, p. 644). In contrast to Parten's interval sampling method, Wrightstone's coding method distinguished each individual contribution. Thus, the unit of analysis was a specific event (i.e., event-coding; Bakeman & Quera, 2011; Yoder & Symons, 2010). One limitation that cannot be (entirely) disregarded is, however, that Wrightstone did not provide clear definitions for what an event actually looked like (e.g., one or several sentences long).

In addition to coding the pupils' contributions, Wrightstone also noted the number of minutes that the group was observed (i.e., total duration) and who the speaker was. Finally, Wrightstone scored each contribution of each pupil. He awarded one point for each contribution so that more active pupils received a higher score overall. This score was then averaged across all pupils within one class and divided by the amount of time that each pupil was observed. For example, if he observed 24 pupils for a total of 157 minutes, the average observation time for each pupil was 6.54 minutes. If the average pupil score was 8.62, this score would be divided by 6.54, resulting in a comparable unit of 1.31. Hence, scores were standardized to account for differences in discussion length and group size. This approach allowed Wrightstone to compare average pupil participation across different schools and grades. However, Wrightstone did not record the sequential order of the specific contributions. For example, we cannot tell whether asking a question (3e) was often followed by a suggestion (3g). This is simply because, similar to Parten, Wrightstone's research questions did not require sequential data (i.e., moment-to-moment sequences of behavior).

An early attempt to obtain sequential data can be found in Miller's (1939) study on social interaction in group discussion among students. Building on Wrightstone's Code 3 coding system, Miller (1939) developed his own set of six mutually exclusive categories: (1) *inference question*, (2) *inference statement*, (3) *supported opinion*, (4) *information question*, (5) *factual statement*, and (6) *unsupported opinion* (p. 343). The unit of analysis was a student's response (i.e., event coding). To record the student responses in a sequential fashion, Miller used a paper-pencil *flow sheet* (see also Carr, 1929). Each flow sheet listed the names of all students one below the other and provided space for coding four successive student responses. On average, a total of 35 flow sheets were needed to code a 45-minute group discussion. Based on the flow sheets, all student responses were recorded in their actual order. This observational technique allowed Miller to visualize the temporal progression of the discussion. In particular, he mapped interludes between the students and their professor, which were defined as intervals beginning with a statement by the professor and ending with the last statement of one of the students. Descriptively comparing the different maps, Miller found that less successful discussions were characterized by a simple question-answer format, with the professor asking a question and a student responding. More lively discussions with more students involved in one interlude were rated as more successful. Looking at the characteristics of the discussion process as it unfolds in time provided a new perspective for group interaction research.

Interaction Process Analysis at Harvard University

After the Second World War, interest in group interaction processes remained and flourished at Harvard University. One name that is ultimately tied to group interaction research during this time is Robert F. Bales. Bales' research mainly centered on group interaction in problem-solving groups, and the general idea behind his research was that groups are in a constant struggle of managing external pressure from the larger system in which they are embedded and from internal pressures originating from interaction among group members (Bales, 1950a; Bales & Strodtbeck, 1951). Bales was especially interested in the interplay between *task-oriented or instrumental behavior*, on the one hand, and *social-emotional behavior*, on the other hand. According to Bales (1950a), task-oriented behavior reveals how the group deals with the concern to handle the task at hand (external pressure) whereas social-emotional behavior is an expression of the group's concern to deal with internal relationships among the group members. As group members work together, only one concern or set of behaviors can be at play at one specific point in time. Thus, task-oriented behavior always constrains social-emotional behavior and vice versa (Bales, 1950a, 1953). As the group progresses, group members will give emphasis to one set of behaviors over the other, resulting in *orderly phases* of behavior. To empirically test his ideas, Bales developed what "has now become his legacy" (Frey, 1996, p. 24), the *Interaction Process Analysis* (IPA) coding scheme, a system for microanalysis of speech acts in problem-solving groups (Bales, 1950a, 1950b; see also Poole, this volume, Chapter 18; Keyton, this volume, Chapter 23). Observers using the IPA coding scheme identify the speaker of each act, the target, and the functional role of the act for the group's discussion. Overall, the IPA comprises 12 categories that either capture task-oriented behaviors or social-emotional behaviors.

Similar to Wrightstone (1934) and Miller (1939), Bales distinguished behavioral events. Each unit of analysis in the IPA coding scheme is a *thought unit*, which constitutes the smallest segment of behavior that can be coded into one of the 12 categories (i.e., microlevel of behavior; Bales, 1950a, 1950b). In tradition with previous coding schemes, the categories in the IPA coding scheme are mutually exclusive. Moreover, the categories are intended to be *exhaustive*. Thus, every single utterance made during a group discussion should be able to fit into one of the 12 categories.

The vast amount of Bales' research was based on laboratory studies with male college students. Just as the studies outlined earlier, interaction was usually not recorded for later analysis but coded at the research site. Bales' research questions were manifold but mostly focused on the nature of interpersonal interaction in small groups (for a more detailed overview see McGrath, 1984). Among other topics, Bales studied how the coded acts or events were distributed over categories (e.g., much research centered on different frequencies of coded behavior, Bales, 1950a) and over participants (e.g., functional roles of group members, Bales & Slater, 1955; Borgatta & Bales, 1953). Moreover, Bales had a high interest in his postulated process phases and studied how coded events were distributed over time within a single group discussion or throughout repeating group discussion (Bales & Strodtbeck, 1951).

The IPA was intended to be applicable in a variety of different group settings (e.g., therapy groups, Psathas, 1960; Talland, 1955). Nevertheless, it was criticized that the IPA was so tightly interwoven with Bales' underlying theoretical structure that "the IPA turn[ed] out to be theoretically barren as a system for testing any other theory" (McGrath, 1984, p. 142). By the 1960s the use of the IPA slowly decreased (for a contemporary application, see Löfstrand & Zakrisson, 2014). Nevertheless, the IPA is frequently regarded as the mother of most group interaction coding schemes that followed, and many scholars adopted the IPA coding scheme and made adjustments to it (e.g., Bales & Cohen, 1979; Borgatta, 1962; Borgatta, Couch, & Bales, 1954; Landsberger, 1955; Mann, 1961; Morris, 1966; Schermuly & Scholl, 2012).

A Multiplicity of Coding Schemes and Coding Decisions

After Bales' pioneering research, a wealth of coding schemes has emerged. There is certainly no such thing as a "perfect," one-size-fits-all coding scheme. Instead, group researchers have to choose a coding scheme that best fits the specific research questions at hand (e.g., Brauner, 1998; Weingart, 1997). Group interaction can be analyzed from many different perspectives, and over the years different coding schemes to accommodate these perspectives have been developed. Table 2.2 provides an overview of the many decisions that group researchers made in the past when developing and applying new coding schemes (for similar overviews see Hirokawa, 1988; McGrath & Altermatt, 2001; Poole, Keyton, & Frey, 1999; see Brauner, this volume, Chapter 9; Tschan, Zimmermann, & Semmer, this volume, Chapter 10). These coding decisions are interrelated. For example, ad hoc coding limits the possibility to use a very fine-grained micro coding scheme. For the sake of clarity, however, we discuss each point separately.

Focus of Interaction

Perhaps the most important consideration facing group interaction researchers concerns the selection of the particular focus of their coding scheme. Building on classifications from social psychology (McGrath & Altermatt, 2001) and communication research (Poole et al., 1999), we argue that the majority of group interaction coding systems fall into one of three categories: (1) process-focused systems, (2) activity-focused systems, and (3) content-focused systems (see also Brauner, this volume, Chapter 9).

Table 2.2 *Looking back at 100 years of group interaction research: Decisions in coding group interactions*

Decision area	Decision options
Focus of interaction	1. Process focused: behaviors are coded in terms of their function for the group process 2. Activity focused: presence or absence of (verbal) activity is coded 3. Content focused: behaviors are coded in terms of their content
Immediacy	1. Ad hoc: live coding 2. Post hoc: coding (video)-recorded behavior
Source	1. Group as a whole: no information on individual contributions 2. Individual team members: each group member is identified 3. Roles within a team: group members are identified based on their roles (e.g., leader vs. followers; male vs. female group members)
Direction	1. Directed: target is specified ("to whom"; sender and receiver) 2. Undirected: target is not specified
Exhaustiveness	1. Continuous, exhaustive coding: entire stream of behavior is coded 2. Selective coding: only behaviors or phases of interest are coded
Frequencies & sequences	1. Summary data: information on frequencies of behaviors (e.g., 2xA, 2xB, 1xC)[a] 2. Sequential data: information on succession of behaviors (e.g., A-B-B-A-C)[a]
Duration	1. Timed data: Specific onset and offset times are recorded 2. Untimed data: No temporal information
Unitizing strategy	1. Interval coding/ time sampling: e.g., 10 second intervals 2. Event coding: e.g., speaker turns, thought units, words
Granularity, ranging from	1. Micro: fine-grained behaviors are coded 2. Macro: coarse-grained behaviors are coded
Dimensionality	1. Univocal: each behavior is coded on just one dimension 2. Multifunctional: behaviors are coded on multiple dimensions
Magnitude	1. Occurrence only: information about presence/ absence of behaviors 2. Intensity: information about the intensity or quality of behaviors (e.g., +/-)
Level of observer inference, ranging from	1. High: coder judgement is vital, interpretation necessary 2. Low: coder judgement is low, interpretation negligible
Applicability, ranging from	1. Universal: coding scheme is applicable across a wide range of situations 2. Setting-specific: coding scheme is applicable in a specific situation/ context

Process-focused coding schemes, such as Bales' (1950a) IPA, classify behavior according to its function for the group process and not according to its specific content (McGrath & Altermatt, 2001). For example, the category "gives opinion" in the IPA coding schemes describes that a group member voices an opinion or gives an evaluation but it is not captured what the content of that opinion actually implies for the content of the group decision (see Keyton, this volume, Chapter 23). Many group researchers followed up on this approach and developed their own process-focused coding system. One such example is the *Time-by-Event-by-Member Pattern Observation* (TEMPO) system developed in the late 1980s by social psychologists Futoran, Kelly, and McGrath (1989; see also Kelly, Dvir, & Parsons, this volume, Chapter 24). TEMPO provides a detailed analysis of the temporal and sequential arrangement of individual member contributions and can be applied in a wide range of group task performance settings (Futoran et al., 1989). The field of communication research has also generated a wealth of process-focused group communication coding schemes, many of which center on idea generation, argumentation, and decision-making in groups (e.g., Canary, Brossman, & Seibold, 1987; Crowell & Scheidel, 1961; Fisher, 1970; Gouran & Baird, 1972; Hirokawa, 1980; Jackson & Poole, 2003; Meyers, Seibold, & Brashers, 1991; Poole, 1981; Poole & Roth, 1989; Stech, 1970). In addition, there is a growing number of process-focused coding schemes and subsequent group interaction studies coming from Europe (e.g., Becker-Beck, 1997, 2001; Boos, 1996; Brauner, 2006; Kauffeld & Lehmann-Willenbrock, 2012; Kolbe, Strack, Stein, & Boos, 2011; Schermuly & Scholl, 2012; Tschan, 2000, 2002; see Part V, this volume, for details).

Coding systems that fall into the second category (i.e., activity-focused systems) are concerned with the presence (activity) or absence (inactivity) of a specific class of overt behaviors – mainly verbal activity (McGrath & Altermatt, 2001). This approach was pioneered by Chapple (1942, 1949) who developed the *interaction chronograph method*. This method utilized a recording machine that consisted of a moving tape on which lines were drawn when the observer pressed a key. Whenever one person started to speak, the observer had to press down the key assigned to that person for as long as the speaking turn lasted (Chapple, 1942). This rather simple machine-supported way of coding allowed Chapple to analyze talk-turn structures in groups. Following the early work by Chapple, several coding techniques have been developed to analyze verbal participation in groups (e.g., Bonito, 2000, 2001; Dabbs & Ruback, 1987). Overall, this stream of research is driven by the idea that the amount of verbal participation and the distribution of speaking turns in group discussions is consequential for a variety of outcomes on both the individual and group level (for reviews on participation in groups see Bonito, 2002; Bonito & Hollingshead, 1997). Recent applications and extensions of this line of research are introduced below (see "direction").

The third group of coding systems can be described as content-focused, which means that the coding is grounded in the participants' communication specific to the purpose of the group (Poole et al., 1999). A content-focused coding approach can help to identify lines of argument, showing which ideas or topics were accepted by the group (Seibold, Lemus, & Kang, 2010; Wheelan et al., 1994). An available coding scheme that classifies content themes emerging during group discussions can be found in Mabry (1975). Alternatively, content-focused coding schemes can be deductively derived from the task used in the specific study, focusing on similar content features (Meyers & Seibold, 2012; see Tschan et al., this volume, Chapter 10).

Immediacy

Group researchers also need to decide whether group interaction is coded live or post hoc. Today, recording devices are increasingly high in portability and are gradually becoming cheaper. Thus, they are common tools in group inter-action research and can be of immense help to produce strong and reliable data (Furr, 2009). In comparison, early group researchers (e.g., Bales, 1950a; Miller, 1939) had no other choice than to engage in live coding because video recordings were just not as affordable at that time (see also Hewes & Poole, 2012). Just as video recordings became more accessible, so did software for computer-assisted coding. Today, group researchers can choose from a variety of software solutions to ease the coding process (see Glüer, this volume, Chapter 13).

Source

Moreover, there has been some variation over the years as to who is the source of the group activity (McGrath & Altermatt, 2001). Whereas most coding schemes differentiate individual group members and identify who the speaker is, subsequent findings are often reported at the group level (e.g., Miller, 1939). Dependent on the specific research question, group members have also been identified based on functional roles (e.g., leader vs. follower, Lehmann-Willenbrock, Meinecke, Rowold, & Kauffeld, 2015) or demographic characteristics (e.g., male vs. female group members, Hawkins & Power, 1999).

Direction

Another key issue that researchers treated differently in the past concerns the direction of group interaction. Some group interaction coding schemes expli-citly specify which group member is the target of each act (i.e., "to whom," e.g., Bales, 1950a; Schermuly & Scholl, 2012), which allows capturing the trajectories of interactions among group members. In recent years, the renewal of the social network perspective for understanding groups (Contractor & Su, 2012) has sparked new interest in capturing (communication) structures in groups. As a result, activity-focused coding systems have become more popular again. When applying social network analysis to coded group data, tracing the target of each act – also if the target is the entire group – is typically a necessity (e.g., Argote, Turner, & Fichman, 1989; Brown & Miller, 2000; Sauer & Kauffeld, 2013; for early applications see Bavelas, 1950; Leavitt, 1951).

Exhaustiveness

Coding can be exhaustive or selective. Over the years, most recommendations for developing new coding schemes state that coding systems should be exhaustive, thus logically complete (e.g., Meyers & Seibold, 2012; Weingart, 1997). Every unitized act should fit one category of the respective coding scheme (see Reed, Metzger, Kolbe, Zobel, & Boos, this volume, Chapter 11). This way, the entire stream of group interaction in a given situation (e.g., a group discussion among students or an organizational meeting) can be captured and classified. However, exhaustive coding can be difficult to implement in live coding settings (e.g., Schermuly & Scholl, 2012). The use of additional filler codes such as "other" can help to make a coding scheme look exhaustive, but does not necessarily lead to a logically complete coding scheme (Yoder & Symons, 2010). Selective coding schemes, on the other hand, zoom in only on those behaviors or phases that are of interest. For example, whereas Poole and colleagues have examined conflict as one of several different types of interactions in groups (e.g., Kuhn & Poole, 2000; Poole & Dobosh, 2010), Paletz and colleagues have created a coding scheme that focuses specifically on detecting microconflict in groups (Paletz, Schunn, & Kim, 2011; see Paletz & Schunn, this volume, Chapter 27). Because the focus is on specific phenomena, nonexhaustive coding schemes are easier to use on an ad hoc basis.

Frequencies and Sequences

Another choice revolves around the type of data that a specific coding scheme yields. As outlined earlier, coding group interactions in a continuous fashion (e.g., A-B-B-C with A, B, and C representing behavioral categories for units coded along a time line) leads to sequential data, which can be further analyzed to explore how group behavior unfolds in sequences (Hewes & Poole, 2012). If group researchers are mainly interested in the frequencies of certain categories, the sequentially coded behaviors can be "collapsed" to form summary scores (e.g., Kauffeld & Lehmann-Willenbrock, 2012; see Rack, Zahn, & Mateescu, this volume, Chapter 14). Alternatively, group interactions can be coded without noting their sequential order (e.g., Parten, 1932; Wrightstone, 1934). Because software solutions simplify the coding process and have mostly replaced traditional paper-pencil flow sheets, it is recommended to code group interactions in a sequential fashion because it provides more options for further analyses (Hewes & Poole, 2012; see Glüer, this volume, Chapter 13; see also Part IV).

Duration

Digital recordings and computing resources also make it easier for group researchers to collect information on the duration of behavioral events. Timed data comprise information on the specific onset and offset times of each unit of analysis (Bakeman & Quera, 2011). So far, only little group research focused on the duration of specific behaviors (e.g., van der Kleij, Schraagen, Werkhoven & De Dreu, 2009). However, researchers increasingly call for incorporating timing and duration of behaviors (Ballard, Tschan, & Waller, 2008; Cronin, Weingart, & Todorova, 2011; Herndon & Lewis, 2015). For example, new statistical methods are developed that account for the duration of individual group behavior in contingency analyses (e.g., Fairbairn, 2016).

Unitizing

Two main options can be chosen when unitizing interaction: interval coding (or time sampling) and event coding (e.g., Hatfield & Weider-Hatfield, 1987). An interval approach unitizes the group interaction process into intervals of equal length that are defined a priori. For example, Parten's (1932) research was based on repeated short intervals of one minute each. There are also a number of recent studies using interval coding (e.g., Lei, Waller, Hagen, & Kaplan, 2016; Waller, Gupta, & Giambatista, 2004; Zijlstra, Waller, & Phillips, 2012). Coding schemes that differentiate events, on the other hand, unitize the group interaction process into particular behavioral units. Many coding schemes follow the example of Bales (1950a) and differentiate thought units (e.g., Canary et al., 1987; Crowell & Scheidel, 1961; Gouran & Baird; 1972; Meyers et al., 1991). However, the respective events can also be considerably smaller (e.g., words) or larger (e.g., speaker turns). Interval coding has practical advantages because it is typically easier to implement than event coding. However, summary statistics may be estimated only approximately using interval coding (Bakeman & Quera, 2011). Thus, event coding is the preferred method of choice if researchers want to collect detailed information on the exact frequencies of specific behaviors, their duration, and possible overlaps or co-occurrences of behaviors (Bakeman & Quera, 2011; see Reed et al., this volume, Chapter 11).

Granularity

Group interaction systems that were developed over the years also differ in their level of granularity, ranging from micro to macro (see also Brauner, this volume, Chapter 9). Micro systems distinguish fine-grained behaviors such as individual statements. Bales' (1950a) IPA coding scheme is a classic example of a fine-grained group interaction coding scheme. An even more detailed analysis can be achieved using the act4teams coding scheme (Kauffeld & Lehmann-Willenbrock, 2012; see Kauffeld, Lehmann-Willenbrock, & Meinecke, this volume, Chapter 21). Similar to the IPA, act4teams can be used for a variety of group interaction settings that center on problem solving but it was specifically developed to measure naturally occurring interactions in organizational work groups. Coders using act4teams classify each statement brought up during a group's discussion into one of 43 mutually exclusive and exhaustive categories. Conversely, the macro level of interaction addresses larger segments of behavior. For example, Berg (1967) initially classified themes of group discussions into just two categories, *task* and *nontask*, which were then further divided into two subcategories (*procedural* or *substantive* for task; *disruptive* or *irrelevant* for nontask). There is no trend over time favoring either micro or macro coding schemes. Instead, the decision ultimately depends on the purpose of the study.

Dimensionality

Another consideration facing group researchers concerns the dimensionality of their coding approach. Most coding systems are univocal, meaning that each act is coded on just one dimension using mutually exclusive coding categories (e.g., Bales, 1950a; Kauffeld & Lehmann-Willenbrock, 2012). Thus, each act can be coded into just one category. Historically, this rule of mutual exclusivity, as well as the assumption of exhaustiveness described earlier, has been largely "dictated by methodological convention" (Trujillo, 1986, p. 382). Many techniques for analyzing temporal interactions (used to) assume exclusivity by default (e.g., lag sequential analysis; Sackett, 1979). However, assigning a single code to one act might be challenging if a certain behavior serves several functions at once (Poole et al., 1999). Moreover, if group researchers want to classify multiple modes of interaction – such as verbal and nonverbal behavior – multifunctional coding schemes might constitute a better choice. For example, after much research building on the IPA coding scheme, Bales and Cohen (1979) developed the multifunctional SYMLOG system, which is an acronym for **SY**stematic, **M**ultiple **L**evel, **O**bservation of **G**roups. As the name implies, SYMLOG classifies group behavior along multiple levels and acknowledges that statements have multiple meanings. In particular, statements can be coded along the following three bipolar dimensions: dominance versus submissiveness, friendliness versus unfriendliness, and acceptance of versus opposition to authority. SYMLOG's multifunctional framework aims at better representing the complexity of group interactions. At the same time, multifunctional coding schemes (see also Crowell & Scheidel, 1961) also have their shortcomings. First, they require coders to make multiple decisions simultaneously, which is not only demanding but potentially compromising for attaining high interrater reliability (Poole et al., 1999). Second, multifunctional coding draws the risk of "over-coding," which implies that coders read "more functions into an act than it serves" (Poole et al., 1999, pp. 105–106; see Poole, this volume, Chapter 18).

Magnitude

Another coding decision revolves around the question of capturing the magnitude of coded acts. Traditional coding – independent of the focus of the interaction coding system – generates nominal-scale data: Observers note the presence or absence of specific behaviors. However, observers can also rate the intensity or quality of the observed behavior. Thus, in addition to coding the occurrence of an act, observers also make judgements about the magnitude of an act, leading to ordinal or interval scale data (McGrath & Altermatt, 2001). For example, in a study on group decision making, Poole, McPhee, and Seibold (1982) used the Valence Coding System to classify each utterance according to positive, negative, or neutral valence for a particular option.

Observer Inference

The degree of observer inference required by different coding schemes has also differed significantly. Observer inference can vary from minimal, such that coder judgment is low and interpretation is negligible, to high inference (Trujillo, 1986). High observer inference encompasses that coder judgment is vital and interpretation is necessary. In other words, it would be extremely difficult to train a computer to do the coding. Coding schemes requiring high levels of coder judgment are SYMLOG (Bales & Cohen, 1979) or TEMPO (Futoran et al., 1989). Activity-focused coding schemes such as the interaction chronograph method developed by Chapple (1942) usually require few inferential judgments and are easier to learn.

Applicability

Finally, coding schemes differ in terms of their applicability, ranging from universal to setting-specific. As outlined earlier, the IPA coding scheme was intended to be a rather generic coding scheme that could be applicable across many group settings (Bales, 1950a). But coding systems can also be tailored to a specific situation. For example, there is a growing amount of group interaction research on high-risk teams such as military teams (e.g., Stout, Salas, & Carson, 1994), aviation teams (Salas, Shuffler, & DiazGranados, 2010; Zijlstra et al., 2012), nuclear power plant teams (Stachowski, Kaplan, & Waller, 2009), and medical teams (e.g., Kolbe, Burtscher, & Manser, 2013). Setting-focused coding schemes comprise behavioral categories that are specific to the context for which they have been developed. This "specificity is both the main strength and the main limitation of setting-focused systems" (McGrath & Altermatt, 2001, p. 537) as it becomes more difficult to compare findings across different studies and contexts.

Recent Developments in Group Interaction Research

In closing this chapter, we want to highlight some recent progress in group interaction research but make no claim that our overview is exhaustive. Instead, we hope to spark some enthusiasm for group interaction research so that interested readers will contribute to these new developments with their own research.

Research on groups has largely presumed that group size is fixed and members belong to just one group. However, (organizational) groups are becoming ever more fluid (Tannenbaum, Mathieu, Salas, & Cohen, 2012). Group membership can change when new employees are hired or members leave the group (maybe even just temporally such as during parental leave), groups can be split into subgroups, and individuals can be a part of different groups at once. As a result, new methods have been developed that allow for fluid group membership (e.g., in terms of participation equality, Paletz & Schunn, 2011).

Additionally, the form and means of interaction as such has drastically changed and encompasses virtuality as a key component (Gilson, Maynard, Young, Vartiainen, & Hakonen, 2015). This means that a significant part of communication is no longer represented by the standard face-to-face idea, but revolves around computer-assisted communication (e.g., emails, instant messengers). For a wholesome analysis of group interactions, the consideration of newer channels of communication provides insight into group interaction outside of face-to-face encounters (e.g., Schneider, Liskin, Paulsen, & Kauffeld, 2015). Similarly, the ease of adding an additional person to a conference call within a group discussion nowadays exemplifies the fluidity of groups and the importance of looking at groups as a dynamical rather than a static entity (see also Cronin et al., 2011; Kozlowski, 2015).

Building on the idea of groups as dynamic systems (McGrath, Arrow, & Berdahl, 2000), we can see a trend toward a stronger value of research that focuses on the dynamics of group interaction processes (Cronin et al., 2011; Mathieu, Hollenbeck, van Knippenberg, & Ilgen, 2017; Kozlowski, 2015; Waller, Okhuysen, & Saghafian, 2016). Behavioral coding provides an excellent base for exploring group dynamics (Kozlowski, 2015). However, as recently noted, "having observers watch live or videoed team interactions is both intrusive and challenging from a logistical standpoint" (Mathieu et al., 2017, p. 461). New technological advancements that put emphasis on noninvasiveness and an economic style of recording have opened new doors for group researchers and can supplement traditional video-based interaction coding. For example, the development of mobile sensors (Schmid Mast, Gatica-Perez, Frauendorfer, Nguyen, & Choudhury, 2015) and apps (Buengeler, Klonek, Lehmann-Willenbrock, Morency, & Poppe, 2017) show promise for obtaining rich and dynamic interaction data (see also Rosen, Dietz, & Kazi, this volume, Chapter 6).

In addition, and as outlined earlier, coding schemes have shortcomings in that they usually focus on one aspect of group interaction. Consequently, researchers "scratch" just one layer of group interaction. Boos (1995) summarized that communication (as one mode of group interaction) is characterized by an overlap of different aspects at the same time such as relational *and* task-focused communication. Especially by means of computer-assisted coding, the same situation can be coded with different coding schemes and in different passes. Later, these coded strings of behavior can be merged to reveal a more comprehensive picture of group interaction. Moreover, automated text analysis programs such as the *Linguistic Inquiry and Word Count* (Pennebaker, Boyd, Jordan, & Blackburn, 2015) offer potential for analyzing group interaction from yet another angle (Gonzales, Hancock, & Pennebaker, 2010; see also Bonito & Keyton, this volume, Chapter 19).

To further improve on existing and new coding schemes, increased transparency and accessibility of material for educational purposes is crucial (see also Seelandt, this volume, Chapter 12). Recent developments show promising trends in this direction. For example, the German version of the DCS (Schermuly & Scholl, 2012) includes extensive manuals and exercises to convey and solidify the understanding of the coding scheme. A different approach is the provision of supplementary material in online publishing (e.g., Klonek, Quera, & Kauffeld, 2015). Though both of these approaches require additional effort, the educational value and possible collaborative results can, over time, drastically improve the quality of coding schemes.

Finally, there are more and more promising approaches to interdisciplinary collaboration in group interaction research (e.g., Lehmann-Willenbrock, Hung, & Keyton, 2017; Beck, Meinecke, Matsuyama, & Lee, 2017). The Interdisciplinary Network for Group Research (INGRoup)[1] with its annual conference provides a platform for such interdisciplinary collaboration. For example, communication and social psychology scholars can provide the theoretical framework for hypothesizing about group processes. Scholars from fields such as organizational psychology or organizational behavior can design suitable field studies making sure that rich data are obtained and that practical implications can be drawn from the results. Finally, computer scientists working in the fields of social signal processing can develop advanced methods for, e.g., automatically detecting group cohesion (Hung & Gatica-Perez, 2010). The prospect of interdisciplinary technological innovation in the form of apps, software-assisted coding, or even automatic coding systems is promising in two ways: It eases and speeds up the process of coding and analyzing and it has the potential to simultaneously incorporate a multiplicity of streams of information to flesh out a more complete analysis of the real situation.

---

[1] See www.ingroup.net.

Conclusion

We hope that this chapter will provide the reader with an understanding of how groups have been studied in the past and to where the roots of group interaction research can be traced back. More importantly, we hope that this chapter will inspire researchers to immerse themselves into interaction research – from coding group interaction, to unraveling underlying patterns, to editing and visualizing them so that they can be used for training and development. We need to improve our toolkit and not shy away from interdisciplinary collaboration if we want to move the field of interaction research forward.

References

Argote, L., Turner, M. E., & Fichman, M. (1989). To centralize or not to centralize: The effects of uncertainty and threat on group structure and performance. *Organizational Behavior and Human Decision Processes*, *43*, 58–74. doi:10.1016/0749-5978(89)90058-7

Bakeman, R., & Quera, V. (2011). *Sequential analysis and observational methods for the behavioral sciences*. New York, NY: Cambridge University Press.

Bales, R. F. (1950a). *Interaction process analysis: A method for the study of small groups*. Cambridge, MA: Addison-Wesley.

Bales, R. F. (1950b). A set of categories for the analysis of small group interaction. *American Sociological Review*, *15*, 257–263.

Bales, R. F. (1953). The equilibrium problem in small groups. In T. C. Parsons, R. F. Bales, & E. A. Shils (Eds.), *Working papers in the theory of action* (pp. 111–161). Glencoe, IL: Free Press.

Bales, R. F., & Cohen, S. P. (1979). *SYMLOG: A system for the multiple level observation of groups*. New York, NY: Free Press.

Bales, R. F., & Slater, P. E. (1955). Role differentiation in small decision-making groups. In T. Parsons (Ed.), *Family socialization and interaction process* (pp. 259–306). Glencoe, IL: Free Press.

Bales, R. F., & Strodtbeck, F. L. (1951). Phases in group problem solving. *Journal of Abnormal and Social Psychology*, *46*, 485–495. doi:10.1037/h0059886

Ballard, D. I., Tschan, F., & Waller, M. J. (2008). All in the timing: Considering time at multiple stages of group research. *Small Group Research*, *39*, 328–351. doi:10.1177/1046496408317036

Bavelas, A. (1950). Communication patterns in task-oriented groups. *The Journal of the Acoustical Society of America*, *22*, 725–730. doi:10.1121/1.1906679

Beck, S. J., Meinecke, A. L., Matsuyama, Y., & Lee, C.-C. (2017). Initiating and maintaining collaborations and facilitating understanding in interdisciplinary group research. *Small Group Research*, 48, 532–543. doi:10.1177/1046496417721746

Becker-Beck, U. (1997). *Soziale Interaktion in Gruppen: Struktur- und Prozessanalyse* [Social interaction in groups: Structure and process analysis]. Opladen, Germany: Westdeutscher Verlag.

Becker-Beck, U. (2001). Methods for diagnosing interaction strategies: An application to group interaction in conflict situations. *Small Group Research*, *32*, 259–282. doi:10.1177/104649640103200301

Benne, K. D., & Sheats, P. (1948). Functional roles of group members. *Journal of Social Issues*, *4*, 41–49. doi:10.1111/j.1540-4560.1948.tb01783.x

Berg, D. M. (1967). A thematic approach to the analysis of the task-oriented, small group. *Central States Speech Journal*, *18*, 285–291. doi:10.1080/10510976709362891

Bonito, J. A. (2000). The effect of contributing substantively on perceptions of participation. *Small Group Research*, *31*, 528–553. doi:10.1177/104649640003100502

Bonito, J. A. (2001). An information-processing approach to participation in small groups. *Communication Research*, *28*, 275–303. doi:10.1177/009365001028003002

Bonito, J. A. (2002). The analysis of participation in small groups. Methodological and conceptual issues related to interdependence. *Small Group Research*, *33*, 412–438. doi:10.1177/104649640203300402

Bonito, J. A., & Hollingshead, A. B. (1997). Participation in small groups. In B. R. Burleson (Ed.), *Communication yearbook 20* (pp. 227–261). Thousand Oaks, CA: Sage.

Boos, M. (1995). Die sequentielle Strukturierung sozialer Interaktion [The sequential structure of social interaction]. In W. Langenthaler & G. Schiepek (Eds.), *Selbstorganisation und Dynamik in Gruppen* (pp. 209–221). Münster, Germany: LIT.

Boos, M. (1996). *Entscheidungsfindung in Gruppen. Eine Prozeßanalyse* [Decision-making in groups. A process analysis]. Bern, Switzerland: Huber.

Borgatta, E. F. (1962). A systematic study of interaction process scores, peer and self-assessments, personality and other variables. *Genetic Psychology Monographs*, *65*, 219–291.

Borgatta, E. F., & Bales, R. F. (1953). Interaction of individuals in reconstituted groups. *Sociometry*, *16*, 302–320. doi:10.2307/2785935

Borgatta, E. F., Couch, A. S., & Bales, R. F. (1954). Some findings relevant to the great man theory of leadership. *American Sociological Review*, *19*, 755–758. doi:10.2307/2087923

Brauner, E. (1998). Die Qual der Wahl am Methodenbuffet—oder: Wie der Gegenstand nach der passenden Methode sucht [Hard choice at the buffet of methods—or: How a problem is searching for the appropriate method]. In E. Ardelt, H. Lechner, & W. Schloegl (Eds.), *Neue Gruppendynamik. Theorie und Praxis, Anspruch und Wirklichkeit* (pp. 176–193). Göttingen, Germany: Verlag für Angewandte Psychologie.

Brauner, E. (2006). Kodierung transaktiver Wissensprozesse (TRAWIS): Ein Verfahren zur Erfassung von Wissenstransfer in Interaktionen [Transactive knowledge coding system: A schema for the assessment of knowledge transfer in interactions]. *Zeitschrift für Sozialpsychologie*, *37*, 99–112. doi:10.1024/0044-3514.37.2.99

Brown, T. M., & Miller, C. E. (2000). Communication networks in task-performing groups: Effects of task complexity, time pressure, and interpersonal dominance. *Small Group Research*, *31*, 131–157. doi:10.1177/104649640003100201

Buengeler, C. K., Klonek, F. E., Lehmann-Willenbrock, N., Morency, L.-P., & Poppe, R. (2017). Killer apps: Criteria and interdisciplinary opportunities for developing novel team applications. *Small Group Research 48*, 591–620. doi:10.1177/1046496417721745

Canary, D. J., Brossmann, B. G., & Seibold, D. R. (1987). Argument structures in decision-making groups. *Southern Speech Communication Journal, 53,* 18–37. doi:10.1080/10417948709372710

Carr, L. J. (1929). Experimental sociology: A preliminary note on theory and method. *Social Forces, 8,* 63–74. doi:10.2307/2570053

Chapple, E. D. (1942). The measurement of interpersonal behavior. *Transactions of the New York Academy of Science, 4,* 222–233. doi:10.1111/j.2164-0947.1942.tb00852.x

Chapple, E. D. (1949). The Interaction Chronograph: Its evolution and present application. *Personnel, 25,* 295–307.

Contractor, N. S., & Su, C. (2012). Understanding groups from a network perspective. In A. B. Hollingshead & M. S. Poole (Eds.), *Research methods for studying groups and teams: A guide to approaches, tools, and technologies* (pp. 284–310). New York, NY: Routledge.

Cronin, M. A., Weingart, L. R., & Todorova, G. (2011). Dynamics in groups: Are we there yet? *The Academy of Management Annals, 5,* 571–612. doi:10.1080/19416520.2011.590297

Crowell, L., & Scheidel, T. M. (1961). Categories for analysis of idea development in discussion groups. *The Journal of Social Psychology, 54,* 155–168. doi:10.1080/00224545.1961.9919360

Dabbs, J. M., & Ruback, R. B. (1987). Dimensions of group process: Amount and structure of verbal interaction. In L. Berkowitz (Ed.), *Advances in experimental social psychology* (pp. 123–169). San Diego, CA: Academic Press.

Fairbairn, C. E. (2016). A nested frailty survival approach for analyzing small group behavioral observation data. *Small Group Research, 47,* 303–332. doi:10.1177/1046496416648778

Fisher, B. A. (1970). Decision emergence: Phases in group decision-making. *Speech Monographs, 37,* 53–66. doi:10.1080/03637757009375649

Forsyth, D. R., & Burnette, J. L. (2005). The history of group research. In S. A. Wheelan (Ed.), *The handbook of group research and practice* (pp. 3–18). Thousand Oaks, CA: Sage.

Frey, L. R. (1996). Remembering and "re-membering": A history of theory and research on communication and group decision making. In R. Y. Hirokawa & M. S. Poole (Eds.), *Communication and decision making* (2nd edn., pp. 19–54). Thousand Oaks, CA: Sage.

Furr, R. M. (2009). Personality psychology as a truly behavioural science. *European Journal of Personality, 23,* 369–401. doi:10.1002/per.724

Futoran, G. C., Kelly, J. R., & McGrath, J. E. (1989). TEMPO: A time-based system for analysis of group interaction processes. *Basic and Applied Social Psychology, 10,* 211–232. doi:10.1207/s15324834basp1003_2

Gilson, L. L., Maynard, M. T., Young, N. C. J., Vartiainen, M., & Hakonen, M. (2015). Virtual teams research: 10 years, 10 themes, and 10 opportunities. *Journal of Management, 41,* 1313–1337. doi:10.1177/0149206314559946

Gonzales, A. L., Hancock, J. T., & Pennebaker, J. W. (2010). Language style matching as a predictor of social dynamics in small groups. *Communication Research, 37,* 3–19. doi:10.1177/0093650209351468

Gouran, D. S. & Baird, J. E. (1972). An analysis of distributional and sequential structure in problem-solving and informal group discussions. *Speech Monographs, 39,* 16–22. doi:10.1080/03637757209375734

Hatfield, J. D., & Weider-Hatfield, D. (1978). The comparative utility of three types of behavioral units for interaction analysis. *Communication Monographs*, *45*, 44–50. doi:10.1080/03637757809375950

Hawkins, K., & Power, C. B. (1999). Gender differences in questions asked during small decision-making group discussions. *Small Group Research*, *30*, 235–256. doi:10.1177/104649649903000205

Herndon, B., & Lewis, K. (2015). Applying sequence methods to the study of team temporal dynamics. *Organizational Psychology Review*, *5*, 318–332. doi:10.1177/2041386614538276

Hewes, D. E., & Poole, M. S. (2012). The analysis of group interaction processes. In A. B. Hollingshead & M. S. Poole (Eds.), *Research methods for studying groups and teams: A guide to approaches, tools, and technologies* (pp. 358–385). New York, NY: Routledge.

Hirokawa, R. Y. (1980). A comparative analysis of communication patterns within effective and ineffective decision-making groups. *Communication Monographs*, *47*, 312–321. doi:10.1080/03637758009376040

Hirokawa, R. Y. (1988). Group communication research: Considerations for the use of interaction analysis. In C. H. Tardy (Ed.), *A handbook for the study of human communication: Methods and instruments for observing, measuring, and assessing communication processes* (pp. 229–245). Westport, CT: Ablex Publishing.

Hung, H., & Gatica-Perez, D. (2010). Estimating cohesion in small groups using audio-visual nonverbal behavior. *IEEE Transactions on Multimedia*, *12*, 563–575. doi:10.1109/TMM.2010.2055233

Jackson, M. H., & Poole, M. S. (2003). Idea-generation in naturally occurring contexts. *Human Communication Research*, *29*, 560–591. doi:10.1111/j.1468-2958.2003.tb00856.x

Kauffeld, S., & Lehmann-Willenbrock, N. (2012). Meetings matter: Effects of team meetings on team and organizational success. *Small Group Research*, *43*, 130–158. doi:10.1177/1046496411429599

Klonek, F. E., Quera, V., & Kauffeld, S. (2015). Coding interactions in Motivational Interviewing with computer-software: What are the advantages for process researchers? *Computers in Human Behavior*, *44*, 284–292. doi:10.1016/j.chb.2014.10.034

Kolbe, M., Burtscher, M. J., & Manser, T. (2013). Co-ACT-a framework for observing coordination behaviour in acute care teams. *BMJ quality & safety*, *22*, 596–605. doi:10.1136/bmjqs-2012-001319

Kolbe, M., Strack, M., Stein, A., & Boos, M. (2011). Effective coordination in human group decision making: MICRO-CO: A micro-analytical taxonomy for analysing explicit coordination mechanisms in decision-making groups. In M. Boos, M. Kolbe, P. Kappeler, & T. Ellwart (Eds.), *Coordination in human and primate groups* (pp. 199–219). Berlin, Germany: Springer.

Kozlowski, S. W. J. (2015). Advancing research on team process dynamics: Theoretical, methodological, and measurement considerations. *Organizational Psychology Review*, *5*, 270–299. doi:10.1177/2041386614533586

Kuhn, T., & Poole, M. S. (2000). Do conflict management styles affect group decision making? Evidence from a longitudinal field study. *Human Communication Research*, *26*, 558–590. doi:10.1111/j.1468-2958.2000.tb00769.x

Landsberger, H. A. (1955). Interaction process analysis of the mediation of labor-management disputes. *Journal of Abnormal and Social Psychology, 51*, 552–558. doi:10.1037/h0043533

Leavitt, H. J. (1951). Some effects of certain communication patterns on group performance. *Journal of Abnormal Psychology, 46*, 38–50. doi:10.1037/h0057189

Lehmann-Willenbrock, N., Hung, H., & Keyton, J. (2017). New frontiers in analyzing dynamic group interactions: Bridging social and computer science. *Small Group Research.* Advance online publication. doi:10.1177/1046496417718941

Lehmann-Willenbrock, N., Meinecke, A. L., Rowold, J., & Kauffeld, S. (2015). How transformational leadership works during team interactions: A behavioral process analysis. *The Leadership Quarterly, 26*, 1017–1033. doi:10.1016/j.leaqua.2015.07.003

Lei, Z., Waller, M. J., Hagen, J., & Kaplan, S. (2016). Team adaptiveness in dynamic contexts: Contextualizing the roles of interaction patterns and in-process planning. *Group & Organization Management, 41*, 491–525. doi:10.1177/1059601115615246

Levine, J. M., & Moreland, R. L. (2012). A history of small group research. In A. W. Kruglanski & W. Stroebe (Eds.), *Handbook of the history of social psychology* (pp. 383–405). New York, NY: Psychology Press.

Löfstrand, P., & Zakrisson, I. (2014). Competitive versus non-competitive goals in group decision-making. *Small Group Research, 45*, 451–464. doi:10.1177/1046496414532954

Mabry, E. A. (1975). An instrument for assessing content themes in group interaction. *Speech Monographs, 42*, 291–297. doi:10.1080/03637757509375904

Mann, R. D. (1961). Dimensions of individual performance in small groups under task and social-emotional conditions. *Journal of Abnormal and Social Psychology, 62*, 674–682. doi:10.1037/h0041180

Mathieu, J. E., Hollenbeck, J. R., van Knippenberg, D., & Ilgen, D. R. (2017). A century of work teams in the Journal of Applied Psychology. *Journal of Applied Psychology, 102*, 452–467. doi:10.1037/apl0000128

McGrath, J. E. (1984). *Groups: Interaction and performance.* Englewood Cliffs, NJ: Prentice Hall.

McGrath, J. E. (1997). Small group research, that once and future field: An interpretation of the past with an eye to the future. *Group Dynamics: Theory, Research, and Practice, 1*, 7–27. doi:10.1037/1089-2699.1.1.7

McGrath, J. E., & Altermatt, T. W. (2001). Observation and interaction over time: Some methodological and strategic choices. In M. A. Hogg & S. Tindale (Eds.), *Blackwell handbook of social psychology: Group processes* (pp. 525–556). Malden, MA: Blackwell.

McGrath, J. E., Arrow, H., & Berdahl, J. L. (2000). The study of groups: Past, present, and future. *Personality and Social Psychology Review, 4*, 95–105. doi:10.1207/S15327957PSPR0401_8

Meyers, R. A., & Seibold, D. R. (2012). Coding group interaction. In A. B. Hollingshead & M. S. Poole (Eds.), *Research methods for studying groups and teams: A guide to approaches, tools, and technologies* (pp. 329–357). New York, NY: Routledge.

Meyers, R. A., Seibold, D. R., & Brashers, D. (1991). Argument in initial group decision-making discussions: Refinement of a coding scheme and a descriptive quantitative analysis. *Western Journal of Speech Communication*, *55*, 47–68. doi:10.1080/10570319109374370

Miller, D. C. (1939). An experiment in the measurement of social interaction in group discussion. *American Sociological Review*, *4*, 341–351.

Moreland, R. L., Fetterman, J. D., Flagg, J. J., & Swanenburg, K. L. (2010). Behavioral assessment practices among social psychologists who study small groups. In C. R. Agnew, D. E. Carlston, W. G. Graziano, & J. R. Kelly (Eds.), *Then a miracle occurs: Focusing on behavior in social psychological theory and research* (pp. 28–53). New York, NY: Oxford University Press.

Morris, C. G. (1966). Task effects on group interaction. *Journal of Personality and Social Psychology*, *4*, 545–554. doi:10.1037/h0023897

Newstetter, W. I. (1937). An experiment in the defining and measuring of group adjustment. *American Sociological Review*, *2*, 230–236.

Paletz, S. B. F., & Schunn, C. D. (2011). Assessing group-level participation in fluid teams: Testing a new metric. *Behavior Research Methods*, *43*, 522–536. doi:10.3758/s13428-011-0070-3

Paletz, S. B. F., Schunn, C. D., & Kim, K. H. (2011). Conflict under the microscope: Micro-conflicts in naturalistic team discussions. *Negotiation and Conflict Management Research*, *4*, 314–351. doi:10.1111/j.1750-4716.2011.00085.x

Parten, M. B. (1932). Social participation among pre-school children. *The Journal of Abnormal and Social Psychology*, *27*, 243–269. doi:10.1037/h0074524

Parten, M. B. (1933a). Leadership among preschool children. *The Journal of Abnormal and Social Psychology*, *27*, 430–440. doi:10.1037/h0073032

Parten, M. B. (1933b). Social play among preschool children. *The Journal of Abnormal and Social Psychology*, *28*, 136–147. doi:10.1037/h0073939

Pennebaker, J. W., Boyd, R. L., Jordan, K., & Blackburn, K. (2015). *The development and psychometric properties of LIWC2015*. Austin, TX: University of Texas at Austin.

Poole, M. S. (1981). Decision development in small groups I: A comparison of two models. *Communication Monographs*, *48*, 1–24. doi:10.1080/03637758109376044

Poole, M. S., & Dobosh, M. (2010). Exploring conflict management processes in jury deliberations through interaction analysis. *Small Group Research*, *41*, 408–426. doi:10.1177/1046496410366310

Poole, M. S., Keyton, J., & Frey, L. (1999). Group communication methodology: Issues and considerations. In L. Frey, D. Gouran, & M. S. Poole (Eds.), *Handbook of group communication theory and research* (pp. 92–112). Thousand Oaks, CA: Sage.

Poole, M. S., McPhee, R. D., & Seibold, D. R. (1982). A comparison of normative and interactional explanations of group decision-making: Social decision schemes versus valence distributions. *Communication Monographs*, *49*, 1–19. doi:10.1080/03637758209376067

Poole, M. S., & Roth, J. (1989). Decision development in small groups IV: A typology of group decision paths. *Human Communication Research*, *15*, 323–356. doi:10.1111/j.1468-2958.1989.tb00188.x

Psathas, G. (1960). Phase movement and equilibrium tendencies in interaction process in psychotherapy groups. *Sociometry*, *23*, 177–194. doi:10.2307/2785681

Sackett, G. P. (1979). The lag sequential analysis of contingency and cyclicity in behavioral interaction research. In J. D. Osofsky (Ed.), *Handbook of infant development* (pp. 623–649). New York, NY: Wiley.

Salas, E., Shuffler, M. L., & DiazGranados, D. (2010). Team Dynamics at 35,000 Feet. In E. Salas & D. Maurino (Eds.), *Human factors in aviation* (2nd edn., pp. 249–292). Burlington, MA: Academic Press.

Sauer, N. C., & Kauffeld, S. (2013). Meetings as networks: Applying social network analysis to team interaction. *Communication Methods and Measures*, *7*, 26–47. doi:10.1080/19312458.2012.760729

Schermuly, C. C., & Scholl, W. (2012). The Discussion Coding System (DCS)—A new instrument for analyzing communication processes. *Communication Methods and Measures*, *6*, 12–40. doi:10.1080/19312458.2011.651346

Schmid Mast, M., Gatica-Perez, D., Frauendorfer, D., Nguyen, L., & Choudhury, T. (2015). Social sensing for psychology: Automated interpersonal behavior assessment. *Current Directions in Psychological Science*, *24*, 154–160. doi:10.1177/0963721414560811

Schneider, K., Liskin, O., Paulsen, H., & Kauffeld, S. (2015). Media, mood, and meetings: Related to project success? *ACM Transactions on Computing Education*, *15*(4), 21. doi:10.1145/2771440

Seibold, D. R., Lemus, D. R., & Kang, P. (2010). Extending the conversational argument coding scheme in studies of argument quality in group deliberations. *Communication Methods and Measures*, *4*, 46–64, doi:10.1080/19312451003680525

Stachowski, A. A., Kaplan, S. A., & Waller, M. J. (2009). The benefits of flexible team interaction during crises. *Journal of Applied Psychology*, *94*, 1536–1543. doi:10.1037/a0016903

Stech, E. L. (1970). An analysis of interaction structure in the discussion of a ranking task. *Speech Monographs*, *37*, 249–256. doi:10.1080/03637757009375674

Steinzor, B. (1949). The development and evaluation of a measure of social interaction. Part 1 The development and evaluation for reliability. *Human Relations*, *2*, 103–121. doi:10.1177/001872674900200202

Stout, R. J., Salas, E., & Carson, R. (1994). Individual task proficiency and team process behavior: What's important for team functioning? *Military Psychology*, *6*, 177–192. doi:10.1207/s15327876mp0603_3

Talland, G. A. (1955). Tasks and interaction process: Some characteristics of therapeutic group discussion. *Journal of Abnormal and Social Psychology*, *50*, 105–109. doi:10.1037/h0046576

Tannenbaum, S., Mathieu, J. E., Salas, E., & Cohen, D. (2012). Teams are changing: Are research and practice evolving fast enough? *Industrial and Organizational Psychology*, *5*, 2–24. doi:10.1111/j.1754-9434.2011.01396.x

Trujillo, N. (1986). Toward a taxonomy of small group interaction-coding systems. *Small Group Research*, *17*, 371–394. doi:10.1177/104649648601700401

Tschan, F. (2000). *Produktivität in Kleingruppen: Was machen produktive Gruppen anders und besser?* [Productivity in small groups]. Bern, Switzerland: Hans Huber.

Tschan, F. (2002). Ideal cycles of communication (or cognitions) in triads, dyads, and individuals. *Small Group Research*, *33*, 615–643. doi:10.1177/1046496402238618

van der Kleij, R., Schraagen, J. M., Werkhoven, P., & De Dreu, C. K. W. (2009). How conversations change over time in face-to-face and video-mediated communication. *Small Group Research*, *40*, 355–381. doi:10.1177/1046496409333724

Waller, M. J., Gupta, N., & Giambatista, R. C. (2004). Effects of adaptive behaviors and shared mental models on control crew performance. *Management Science, 50,* 1534–1544. doi:10.1287/mnsc.1040.0210

Waller, M. J., Okhuysen, G. A., & Saghafianm, M. (2016). Conceptualizing emergent states: A strategy to advance the study of group dynamics. *The Academy of Management Annals, 10,* 561–598. doi:10.1080/19416520.2016.1120958

Weingart, L. R. (1997). How did they do that? The ways and means of studying group processes. *Research in Organizational Behavior, 19,* 189–239.

Wheelan, S. A., McKeage, R. L., Verdi, A. F., Abraham, M., Krasick, C., & Johnston, F. (1994). Communication and developmental patterns in a system of interacting groups. In L. R. Frey (Ed.), *Group communication in context: Studies of natural groups* (pp. 153–180). Hillsdale, NJ: Lawrence Erlbaum.

Wittenbaum, G. M., & Moreland, R. L. (2008). Small-group research in social psychology: Topics and trends over time. *Social and Personality Psychology Compass, 2,* 187–203. doi:10.1111/j.1751-9004.2007.00065.x

Wrightstone, J. W. (1934). An instrument for measuring group discussion and planning. *The Journal of Educational Research, 27,* 641–650. doi:10.1080/00220671.1934.10880446

Yoder, P., & Symons, F. (2010). *Observational measurement of behavior.* New York, NY: Springer.

Zijlstra, F. R. H., Waller, M. J., & Phillips, S. I. (2012). Setting the tone: Early interaction patterns in swift-starting teams as a predictor of effectiveness. *European Journal of Work and Organizational Psychology, 21,* 749–777. doi:10.1080/1359432X.2012.690399

PART II

Application Areas of Interaction Analysis

3   Dyadic Interaction Analysis

Valentín Escudero, Minsun Lee, and Myrna L. Friedlander

Double Description: The Heart of Dyadic Interaction

Listen in on this bit of dialogue, overheard between a mother and her 15-year-old daughter Chrissy:

CHRISSY [frantically searching her belongings]:	Where's my phone? Have you seen my phone?
MOTHER [POINTING TO THE PHONE]:	It's right here in front of your nose, silly!
CHRISSY [GRABBING THE PHONE]:	Whew! [laughs]
MOTHER:	You never keep track of any of your things!
CHRISSY:	Yes, I do! . . . Well, I usually do.
MOTHER:	No, you don't!
CHRISSY:	Yes, I do!
MOTHER:	You always have to have the last word in any argument, don't you?
CHRISSY:	No, I don't!
MOTHER:	Yes, you do!
CHRISSY:	No, I don't!!
MOTHER:	Yes, you do, you really do!
CHRISSY:	No, I don't, I really don't!

[Both laugh.]

Why did this interchange end in laughter? The humor is embedded not in the semantic or digital meaning of each speaking turn, but rather in the juxtaposition of speaking turns, which reveals their analogic, relational meaning. Moreover, the conversation is occurring between two people who are in a meaningful relationship with one another.

As is clear from this example, understanding dyadic interaction requires paying close attention to the relational meaning of verbal messages. In the above example, whether or not Chrissy can "keep track of her things" provides little information about her relationship with her mother. Rather, the relationship is revealed by the sustained banter that follows ("Yes, you do!", "No, I don't!"). Consider how different the relationship between mother and daughter would look if it had gone this way:

MOTHER: You always have to have the last word in any argument, don't you?
CHRISSY: I guess I do, yes. Sorry.

In other words, it's the *familiar* way that Chrissy interacts with her mother that characterizes their relationship. Despite the symmetrical competitiveness, their banter is playful, ending with laughter when they recognize that *how* they are arguing reflects *what* they are arguing about.

This brief interchange illustrates what Bateson (1979) called *double description*, or the combination of verbal actions that creates a multilayered pattern. The sequence "No, I don't!", "Yes, you do!" taken out of context is not humorous, but when this sequence is repeated several times, the pattern of sequences reveals an isomorphism between content (what is being said) and form (how it is being said) (cf. Rogers & Escudero, 2004).

The distinction of *content* versus *form* (Bateson, 1979) reflects the work of many early scholars who emphasized the "connective qualities of language" (Rogers & Escudero, 2004, p. 6). Notably, Simmel (1950) wrote that relationships "develop upon the basis of reciprocal knowledge and this knowledge upon the basis of the actual relations [interactions]" (p. 309; see also Rogers & Escudero, 2004, p. 7). Scholars have long recognized that social relationships develop over time through the repeated, cumulative interactions that create a unique and enduring culture between people. This point is reflected in the dialogue between Chrissy and her mother. Their bantering was humorous not only because of the isomorphism between form and content but also because mother and daughter recognized the familiarity in this way of interacting with one another.

When we view social relationships as reflected in enduring, reciprocal interactions, it becomes clear that any single verbal (or nonverbal, for that matter) behavior carries less meaning in isolation than when it is considered in context. In dyadic interaction, the immediate context is the comment by the other speaker. Thus, for example, Chrissy's "Yes, I do! … Well, I usually do!" means little without knowledge of her mother's preceding comment, "You never keep track of any of your things."

Moreover, some verbal messages tend to structure the listener's response more so than others. Closed questions like "Did you find your phone?" pull for a *yes* or *no* answer, whereas less structuring messages ("You never keep track of any of your things") offer the listener more leeway to respond as she sees fit. Even less structure is provided by minimal encouragers ("Mhmm … I see") since they allow the listener to continue the dialogue in any direction by, for example, providing more detail, shifting the topic, asking a question, offering advice, and so on (Friedlander, 1982).

Not only does one behavior structure the subsequent behavior, but also each behavior is structured by the behavior that preceded it. The comment "Mhmm . . . I see" carries no relational meaning in the absence of the preceding message. "Mhmm . . . I see" would not be a meaningful response to a question, for example.

In this way, understanding any verbal exchange between two people requires at least three contiguous messages. Even three messages do not tell the full story, however. Consider if we were to "punctuate" (Watzlawick, Bavelas, & Jackson, 1967) Chrissy's and her mother's dialogue like this:

CHRISSY: No, I don't!
MOTHER: Yes, you do!
CHRISSY: No, I don't!!

Although these three messages in isolation connote an argument, they carry less relational meaning than if we were to punctuate the exchange like this:

MOTHER: You always have to have the last word in any argument, don't you?
CHRISSY: No, I don't!
MOTHER: Yes, you do!

Thus we see that dyadic communication is self-regulating, in that messages by one speaker both affect and are affected by messages conveyed by the other speaker. This *coupling* prioritizes the connections *between* the behaviors of actors in a relationship (Tomm, 2014, p. 17). Some coupled messages, also called *sequences* or *transactions*, are highly probable regardless of the type of social relationship – an answer tends to follow a question, compliance tends to follow an order – but it is the likelihood of certain kinds of transactions that characterizes a particular social relationship between any two individuals (Rogers & Escudero, 2004). The symmetrical pattern of argument-counter-argument in the example with Chrissy and her mother is characteristic of the mother-daughter relationship.

Moreover, depending on the kind of social relationship, certain types of sequences are more probable than other. For example, order-command sequences are more probable when the person giving the order has some authority over the other, such as a physician or an employer. Chrissy feels free to disagree (i.e., "have the last word in an argument") with her mother, but she is unlikely to respond to a challenge in the same way from a teacher, for example.

The probability of one kind of verbal act following another kind of verbal act is what makes a social relationship predictable (Rogers & Escudero, 2004). When predictability becomes invariability, however, the transactional rigidity can be problematic (Raymond, Friedlander, Heatherington, Ellis, & Sargent, 1993; Tomm, 2014). The laughter between Chrissy and her mother suggests that not every interaction between them is characterized by a competitive struggle. If it were, they would be unlikely to see the humor in yet another argument about who has the last word.

Taking the foregoing explanation of double description in dyadic interaction as a point of departure, this chapter continues with a discussion of guidelines for analyzing dyadic interactions and techniques for identifying and examining the emergent structure and pattern of dyadic relationships. Since statistical analysis is the focus of a series of chapters in this handbook, we describe strategies for analyzing dyadic interaction rather than specific statistical procedures. The chapter continues with a synthesis of representative literature on dyadic communication in the study of several kinds of social relationships, concluding with some final thoughts about the future study of dyadic communication.

Analyzing Dyadic Sequences of Interaction

Relational Information Is Based on Probability Estimates

The starting point for exploring patterns in dyadic relationships is the identification of mutually produced sequences of interaction. This precondition is what we call the *relational information axiom*: Any behavior emitted by interactor X in an interpersonal context can potentially affect the subsequent behavior of interactor Y and is at the same time affected by Y's preceding behavior. That is, in situations where a given behavior limits Y's response options, it is easier to predict the nature of that response.

Take the example of a mother and a daughter. If a mother were to give an order to her daughter, the expected likely response would be for the daughter to comply with that order. If, in observing conversations between Chrissy and her mother, we find that the sequence Mother Order/Chrissy Comply is highly probable, we could then assert that the juxtaposition of these two behaviors (an Order-Comply interchange) provides specific information about how these two individuals relate to one another.

Thus the relationship between any two actors is characterized by the sequential association of behaviors observed in their interchange. The pattern of exchanges does not imply a causal relationship between the observed behaviors, however, but rather a probabilistic one. Thus the key to dyadic interaction analysis is simple: In a given interpersonal setting, some kinds of behaviors are more likely to follow other kinds of behaviors.

On the other hand, some kinds of behavior tend not to be sequentially associated with any other kinds of behavior. In other words, the occurrence of a given behavior does not vary as a function of prior, antecedent behaviors. For instance, in observing Chrissy and her mother interact, we might find that the high probability of Chrissy complying with an order given by her mother does not deviate from the probability of her responding with compliance to any other kind of behavior on her mother's part (an instruction, a request, a suggestion, etc.). For example, we might find that although Order-Comply seems characteristic of the relational pattern between Chrissy and her mother, a more extensive analysis might show that the probability of this specific sequence occurring does not differ from the probability of Chrissy replying to her mother with compliance regardless of the mother's preceding behavior.

Based on these simple and intuitive considerations, Gottman (1979) defined *relational information* in terms of probability estimates, such that a specific behavior of an interactor in a social context provides relational information if it reduces the uncertainty of the subsequent behavior by the other person. Specifically, the probability of behavior B following behavior A in a previous speaking turn (called a *lag*) is its *transitional* or *conditional probability*. In the interaction example of Chrissy and her mother, if a competitive (resisting or noncomplying) behavior on Chrissy's part has a greater probability of occurrence when it is preceded by an order from her mother than when it is not preceded by this kind of regulative behavior, we would conclude that a type of constriction in the interactional sequence was observed. This constriction might define, for example, a pattern of competition (Order-Noncomply) or some other kind of interaction.

Although event-based transitional probabilities operationally define an interaction pattern based on the detection of sequential associations between behaviors, the totality of the observations needs to be taken into account in order to draw reliable conclusions about a particular dyadic relationship. Two conditions are essential for making inferences: (1) the total frequency of the observed behaviors and (2) the sequential dependence of these behaviors. Moreover, it is essential to define the *context of the interaction* in order to interpret the observed relational information. For example, Chrissy's and her mother's competitiveness might characterize their lighthearted banter about who has the last word, but competitiveness might not characterize their interactions in other, more important contexts.

Structuring the Process of Dyadic Interaction Analysis

Based on this notion of *relational information*, the next methodological consideration is how to approach the analysis of interactions. Described below is a six-step analytical procedure proposed by Escudero and Rogers (2004a) for organizing and integrating all of the essential aspects of the analysis, beginning with the recording of the coded behaviors to determining the type of analysis that best characterizes the complexity of the observed dyadic patterns.

First Step: Represent the Interaction Sequence. Dyadic interaction sequences are typically represented as chains of communication codes recorded in the sequential order in which they are observed, e.g., Mother orders, Chrissy complies. There are, however, different ways to represent interactional events that depend on the specific coding system being used and the hypotheses or research questions under consideration.

It is first necessary to select a system for delineating the recording and organizing the sequential data. One such system is the Sequential Data Interchange Standard (SDIS), developed by Bakeman and Quera (1992) for formatting different forms of sequential data. Essentially the SDIS is a language for representing different types of code sequences, and is complemented with a software program, the Generalized Sequential Querier (GSEQ) (Bakeman & Quera, 1995, see also Quera, this volume, Chapter 15), that allows for the analysis of sequential data as expressed in the SDIS.

In this framework, interaction sequences can be expressed in one of five ways: (1) *Event sequences* are series of codes that are recorded in the order of occurrence. The behavioral codes are mutually exclusive and exhaustive, but the duration of the events is not taken into account. A common example is the coding of speaking turns in a conversation. (2) *Multievent sequences* are those in which various events occur simultaneously and the coding system records this multiplicity; for example, two simultaneous coding schemes for verbal and nonverbal behaviors applied to each of the speech turns of a conversation. (3) *State sequences* refer to one category or a series of categories that represent behavioral states. The transition from one state to another is recorded according to the onset and offset of the coded behavioral states. An example would be recording the change from speaking to silence. (4) *Timed-event sequences* are represented by the duration or the time of momentary occurrence using either the onset or the onset-offset timing of each event, for example, recording the duration of each coded speaking turn using an electronic time recording system. (5) *Interval sequences* are based on a series of successive timed intervals to which one or more codes are assigned; the intervals are fixed as defined a priori by the researcher.

Second Step: Identify Dyadic Information Based on Frequencies of Behaviors.

Although relational information requires the analysis of sequential interactions, it is often informative to begin by observing the frequencies of individual or dyadic behaviors. (See Rack, Zahn, and Mateescu, this volume, Chapter 14, for a description of various kinds of analyses based on frequencies.)

In many studies of dyadic interaction, it is common for researchers to compare the frequencies of coded behaviors between groups, for example, between clinical and nonclinical couples who are engaged in similar kinds of discussions, or between psychotherapist and client in successful and unsuccessful cases.

As an illustrative example, consider the usefulness of simply estimating the frequencies of three types of communication control sequences defined by the Relational Communication Control Coding System (RCCCS; Escudero & Rogers, 2004b; see details in Chapter 43 in this handbook). Two RCCCS indices are (1) *domineeringness*, which is based on the relative frequency of speech turns coded as one-up (↑), that is, attempts by an interactor to assert control in a social relationship with regard to his/her total observed interventions, and (2) *submissiveness*, or the relative frequency of speech turns coded as one-down (↓), or moves that give up control in the relationship.

The simple frequencies of RCCCS codes behaviors are also used to estimate dyadic patterns. For example, with respect to domineeringness and submissiveness, we might ask, "What is the relationship between the domineeringness of interactor X (e.g., Chrissy's mother) receiving a submissive response from interactor Y (Chrissy)?" Answering this question involves comparing the frequency with which Mother displays ↑ behaviors with the frequency with which Chrissy follows these behaviors by ↓ behaviors, thereby allowing for the observation of a dyadic pattern referred to as *dominance* or *complementarity* (↑↓).

If Chrissy's interaction with her mother went like the following, here is how the dialogue would be coded:

MOTHER: You never keep track of any of your things, do you? (↑)
CHRISSY: I guess I don't. (↓)
MOTHER: Do you know where your cell phone is, for example? (↑)
CHRISSY: No, I have no idea where it is. (↓)

This interaction depicts two domineering speaking turns ("nonsupport-questions," defined in the RCCCS as ↑ or domineering) by the mother and two submissive turns (support/acceptance assertion, defined as ↓ or submissive) by Chrissy, or 100 percent complementarity, with Mother ↑/Chrissy ↓.

Using "time event" or "interval" coding procedures, a researcher can take into account the duration of an exchange in order to describe or compare the communicative behaviors of two interactors. Interesting relational information can be provided by simple measures of time, such as the relative frequency and rate (frequency in relation to unit of time), relative duration (with respect to total time of recorded interaction), and the average duration of specific coded behaviors.

Third Step: Examine the Relational Structure of Antecedent and Consequent Behaviors. While indexes based on individual codes offer basic and often relevant information, in the third step we move toward the analysis of interactional sequences, beginning with transactional interchanges. To do so, the researcher composes transition tables, also called *contingency tables*. In these tables the entries are organized by the antecedent (prior) and consequent (subsequent) position of each interactor. For example, Table 3.1 might have Chrissy's behavior as antecedent (rows in the table) and her mother's behavior as consequent (columns in the table). Essentially, the table is a matrix, in which each row and each column represent the various codes in the observational system used in the research.

The first empirical question is whether or not sequential association exists in the table, that is, whether the relational structure of the conversation (across all codes) is significant. For example, analysis of this table will determine whether the

Table 3.1 *Contingency table with Chrissy's behavior as antecedent*

			Consequent		
			Mother's behavior		
			One-up ↑	One-across→	One-down ↓
		One-up ↑	12	18	5
Antecedent	Chrissy's behavior	One-across→	7	14	12
		One-down ↓	14	15	4

Table 3.2 *Contingency table with Mother's behavior as antecedent*

			Consequent		
			Chrissy's behavior		
			One-up ↑	One-across→	One-down ↓
		One-up ↑	22	7	4
Antecedent	Mother's behavior	One-across→	10	20	7
		One-down ↓	3	6	12

mother's messages (the consequents) are contingent on Chrissy's prior behavior (the antecedents), whereas analysis of Table 3.2 can determine the significance of the opposite pattern, i.e., whether Chrissy's messages are contingent on her mother's prior behavior. Typically Pearson's chi-square or the Likelihood-Ratio chi-square, G^2, is used to test for a significant association between the behaviors represented in the rows and the behaviors represented in the columns (Bakeman & Quera, 1995b).

Following this analysis, it is necessary to analyze contingent patterns in specific cells of each table, such as (1) the pattern of Mother's ↓ messages followed by Chrissy's antecedent ↑ messages in Table 3.1 and (2) the pattern of Chrissy's ↑ messages followed by Mother's antecedent ↓ messages in Table 3.2.

Fourth Step: Analyze the Specific Dyadic Patterns. Studies of dyadic interaction usually involve identifying specific patterns of interaction as observed in different social contexts. Observational systems with different categories of coded behavior produce a number of specific dyadic patterns. For example, the three RCCCS codes are ↑ (domineeringness), ↓ (submissiveness), and → (one-across or neutralizing). Thus the RCCCS configures nine possible dyadic patterns based on how these three control behaviors are sequenced. Two of these dyadic patterns are called *complementarity* (↑ behavior responded to by ↓ behavior, and vice versa) and *competitive symmetry* (↑ followed by a ↑ response).

In the transition table, these two types of exchanges, as well as the other seven types, are represented in a 3 x 3 matrix ($\uparrow\downarrow\rightarrow$ entries of antecedent and consequent behaviors). If, for example, we were to design a study to test the hypothesis that a pattern of competitive symmetrical interaction characterizes the discussions of stressed romantic couples, the particular cell in the transition table corresponding to the $\uparrow\uparrow$ interchange (competitive symmetry) would be of most interest. To test if the frequency of this cell, or other cells of interest, is significant, indices like adjusted residuals (Bakeman & Quera, 1995a; Haberman, 1978) can be used. The adjusted residual is a (statistically) normalized version of the difference between the observed frequency in that cell ($\uparrow\uparrow$) and the expected frequency, as a test of the hypothesis of no association between the interaction pattern represented in the cell. That is, this index indicates whether the consequent $\uparrow$ behavior is significantly influenced by antecedent $\uparrow$ behavior. Adjusted residuals can also be combined with other statistical procedures designed to control the fact that the relational patterns (represented in the different cells of a transition table) are interrelated (for example, the "winnowing technique" described by Quera & Bakeman, 2000).

Fifth Step: Test for Group Differences. Research questions often involve comparing the communication patterns of different groups (e.g., clinical versus nonclinical couples or successful versus unsuccessful psychotherapy sessions). An important methodological issue for group comparisons is that the indices mentioned earlier, i.e., the transition probability or the adjusted residuals, are not appropriate for carrying out parametric analyses. Valid alternatives for this kind of comparisons include the methods described by Bakeman, McArthur, and Quera (1996) and Yoder and Feurer (2000), who examined and compared results using different indices of sequential association, specifically the Odds Ratio, Yule's Q, transformed Kappa, and Phi. With the exception of a few disadvantages for the transformed kappa (Wampold, 1989), the other indices provide only subtle differences (see Quera, this volume, Chapter 15 for more details).

Sixth Step: Identify Complex Relational Patterns. As shown in the review of representative research in the following section of this chapter, there has been much diversity in the research questions addressed through the study of dyadic interaction. Consequently, the particular objectives of specific studies guide the type of analysis required. In general, however, one of the limitations mentioned by most investigators in this field has to do with the difficulty of analyzing complex dyadic interaction patterns, such as the conflict pattern represented in the repeated sequence of $\uparrow$ followed by $\uparrow$ in Chrissy's dialogue with her mother. Capturing interactional complexities involves the challenging task of describing patterns of patterns. Escudero and Rogers (2004a) recommended procedures for studying four levels of dyadic relational analysis: directionality, reciprocity, preponderance, and episodes, as explained below.

Directionality Consider the hypothetical dyadic pattern of interaction "Mother's domineeringness activates Chrissy's domineeringness" (which would be categorized in the RCCCS as *competitive symmetry*). What about this relationship depends on directionality? That is, does Chrissy's domineeringness "activate" or "influence" her mother's ↑ responses? A *unidirectional relational structure* would occur if Mother's relational control behaviors influence Chrissy's relational control responses but Chrissy's relational control behaviors do not influence Mother's control responses, whereas a *bidirectional relational structure* represents the association in both directions.

Specific *bidirectional dyadic circuits* are possible for unidirectional and bidirectional structure. That is, in a particular relationship we might discover significant patterns of activation and/or inhibition, such that certain behaviors on the part of one or both interactors significantly increase the probability (activate) or decrease (inhibit) certain subsequent behaviors by the other interactor. As an example, Chrissy's ↑ behavior might activate her mother's ↑ behavior and also inhibit her mother's ↓ behavior.

Reciprocity. Simply put, reciprocity occurs when the same type of bidirectional relationship is found between both interactors. This would be the case if Chrissy's ↑ behavior activates her mother's ↑ behavior and vice versa. Reciprocity is obviously salient in studying couples' relationships (Gottman, 1996; Rogers & Escudero, 2004) as well for studying psychotherapeutic relationships (Tracey & Ray, 1984).

Preponderance. When there emerges a bidirectional pattern of dyadic interaction, it is possible to determine whether the magnitude of the sequential association is greater in one direction than in the other. A significant difference in one direction would represent a preponderance of that particular dyadic pattern. This would be the case if, for example, the reciprocal activation of domineeringness between Chrissy and her mother were stronger (in terms of statistic difference of magnitude) when the direction is "Mother's domineeringness activates Chrissy's competitive response." In other words, the mother's behavior would define the preponderance of this pattern of interaction.

Some authors (e.g., Wampold, 1992) proposed specific statistical tests to analyze bidirectional dependency, reciprocity, and preponderance. Similarly, Gottman and Roy (1990) formulated the idea of measuring *asymmetry in predictability*. However, only a few studies have analyzed dyadic relational information at this level of complexity.

Episodes. A more common and feasible analysis of complex patterns of interaction involves defining specific interaction sequences consisting of more than two codes/messages/behaviors configuring a particular relational meaning. These types of patterns were referred by Escudero and Rogers (2004a) as *episodes*, in the sense that they are communicative configurations depicting particular forms of the interaction process.

One example of this pattern is the *conflict episode* (Bavelas, Rogers, & Millar, 1985; Escudero et al., 1997; Millar, Rogers, & Bavelas, 1984), which is defined by the occurrence of at least three consecutive speech turns coded as competitive types of interchange (person *A* asserts a definitional claim, which is rejected by person *B*, which, in turn, is opposed by person *A*). The dialogue between Chrissy and her mother at the beginning of this chapter offers a specific example of a conflict episode.

Representative Research

Various observer-rated coding systems of dyadic interaction have been used to investigate relational communication between (a) spouses/romantic partners, (b) psychotherapist and client, (c) physician and patient, and (d) leader and subordinate. This section synopsizes the literature on verbal interactions in each of these types of dyadic relationships. Although we focus primarily on research with the RCCCS (Ericson & Rogers, 1973; Rogers & Farace, 1975), which has been used in all four topic areas, we also summarize representative studies with other dyadic coding systems. The review is not meant to be exhaustive but rather offers an overview of the kinds of dyadic interaction studies published to date.

Dyadic Interactions between Spouses/Romantic Partners

The RCCCS has been widely used to study communication patterns within romantic relationships. Additionally, the past 35 years have seen a proliferation of other dyadic coding systems: the Couple Interaction Coding System (CISS; Gottman, 1979; Notarius & Markman, 1981; Notarius, Markman, & Gottman, 1983) or Rapid Couple Interaction Scoring System (RCISS; Gottman, 1996); the Marital Interaction Coding System (MICS; Patterson, Weiss, & Hops, 1976); the Specific Affect Coding System (SPAFF; Gottman & Krokoff, 1989); the Couples Rating System Short Form (CRSSF; Heavey, 1991, as cited in Baucom et al., 2011) and the Couple Interaction Rating System-2nd Edition (CIRS-2; Heavey, Gill, & Christensen, 2002, as cited in Baucom et al., 2011).

These observer-rated coding systems have been used to examine how partners navigate mundane and conflictual discussions and whether different types of interactions predict marital outcomes and characterize different kinds of couples. Among the types of couples studied are those who are coping with infidelity (Allen et al., 2008); couples with a depressed spouse (Johnson & Jacob, 2000); heterosexual, gay, and lesbian couples (Gottman et al., 2003); middle-aged and older couples in long-term relationships (Cartensen, Gottman, & Levenson, 1995); couples in different cultural contexts (Rehman & Holtzworth-Munroe, 2006); and couples who vary along the dimensions of interdependence and ideology (Williamson & Fitzpatrick, 1985).

Across studies, results indicate that couples' dyadic interaction patterns, kinds of messages, as well as types of emotional interchange predict relationship satisfaction and stability (Buehlman, Gottman, & Katz, 1992; Clements, Stanley, & Markman, 2004; Courtright, Millar, & Rogers-Millar, 1979; Gottman & Levenson, 2000). With respect to satisfaction, Courtright et al. (1979), for example, used the RCCCS to investigate domineeringness (frequency or proportion of ↑ messages in a conversation) versus dominance (frequency or proportion of ↑ followed by ↓). Results showed that the two constructs are distinct but related; domineeringness was a better predictor of dissatisfaction than dominance. Similarly, Escudero et al. (1997) used the RCCCS to compare the communication of nondistressed couples in the community with distressed couples seeking therapy in a family clinic. Consistent with Courtright et al.'s (1979) results, domineeringness was inversely related to marital satisfaction. Whereas competitive symmetry was observed in both groups during conflictual discussions, the nonclinic group engaged in more counterbalancing symmetrical interactions with neutral emotion.

Gender has been examined in several RCCCS studies of couples. Courtright et al. (1979), for example, found that the wife's domineeringness was negatively associated with her own marital satisfaction but not her husband's, whereas the husband's domineeringness was negatively associated with the reported satisfaction of both spouses. Gender also played a role in how ↑ messages from one partner were responded to by the other partner in a study of engaged couples (Heatherington, Escudero, & Friedlander, 2005). Specifically, the male partner's ↑ messages tended to activate both competitive (↑↑) and complementary (↑↓) exchanges, whereas the female partner's ↑ messages only activated complementary exchanges.

Several studies focused on conflict and aggression in couple relationships. Among the studies on conflict, Clements et al. (2004) used the CISS to examine whether problem-solving facilitation (constructive behavior, such as planning or discussing a problem with positive emotion) and emotional invalidation (insulting or sarcastic remarks with negative emotion) would predict marital satisfaction and stability. Emotional invalidation was found to distinguish among (a) happily married, (b) married but distressed, and (c) divorced couples. In the studies on aggression (Cordova, Jacobson, Gottman, Rushe, & Cox, 1993; Rogers, Castleton, & Lloyd, 1996; Sabourin, 1995), results suggest that compared to nonviolent couples, couples with a violent husband tend to exhibit greater competitive symmetry and negative reciprocity.

Another line of research on couples' conflict involves the pattern of demand (pursuing with complaints and emotional pleas) and withdraw (retreating with passivity and defensiveness). In Gottman and Levenson's (2000) study with the RCISS and the SPAFF, for example, the demand-withdraw pattern predicted divorce both early on and later in marriage. Demand-withdraw interactions have also been investigated with the CIRS-2 and the CRSSF (Baucom et al., 2011). Results showed that this specific interaction pattern was associated with emotional arousal and occurred in nondistressed as well as distressed couples.

Finally, dyadic analyses also have been conducted to examine changes in partners' communication as a result of different approaches to couple therapy (Baucom, Baucom, & Christensen, 2015; Baucom, Sevier, Eldrigde, & Doss, 2011). Whereas one approach was superior to the other posttreatment (in effecting a decrease in partners' negativity, in couples' negative reciprocity, and in wife-demand/husband-withdraw behaviors, along with an increase in couples' positive reciprocity and vulnerability/empathy), the other approach was superior at the two-year follow-up. Not surprisingly, in both approaches changes in couples' communication patterns were associated with changes in their self-reported relationship satisfaction.

Dyadic Interactions in Psychotherapy

The use of observational dyadic coding systems has enabled psychotherapy researchers to study the overt communication patterns of therapist and client. Overall, results have been inconsistent. In the first RCCCS study of psychotherapy, Lichtenberg and Barké (1981) found that symmetrical transitory patterns ($\rightarrow$ $\rightarrow$) were more characteristic of therapeutic relationships than complementary ($\uparrow\downarrow$ and $\downarrow\uparrow$) patterns. Similarly, Heatherington and Allen (1984) found that complementarity in which the therapist assumes a $\uparrow$ position in relation to the client tended to occur infrequently. On the other hand, since dyadic patterns may differ depending on how relational control is operationalized, Tracey and Miars (1986) compared the behavior of client and therapist using the RCCCS and a coding system that analyzes topic initiation $\uparrow$ versus topic following $\downarrow$ (Tracey & Ray, 1984). Results showed different patterns of control across the two systems, with client-initiated $\uparrow$ complementarity characterizing the RCCCS analysis and therapist-initiated $\uparrow$ complementarity characterizing the topic control analysis.

Arguably the most important research on the process of psychotherapy involves comparing interactions in successful versus unsuccessful cases. Summarizing the literature in this area, Friedlander (1993) reviewed studies of complementarity and symmetry from two theoretical perspectives: interpersonal personality theory (IPT; Sullivan, 1953) and the circumplex model of interpersonal behavior (Leary, 1957) based on the theory, and relational control theory (RCT; Bateson, Jackson, Haley, & Weakland, 1956; Haley, 1963), which is based on communication theory (Bateson, 1958). Although some inconsistencies were noted and fewer RCT studies were available for review, Friedlander (1993) concluded that from an IPT perspective, complementary interactions in the initial stage of therapy, with the therapist in a friendly dominant position, tend to characterize successful therapy cases, whereas in the middle phase of therapy, noncomplementary interactions, such as responding to a client's question with another question *rather than a response*, may promote client change.

These results differ from the results of two studies conducted subsequent to Friedlander's (1993) review. Lichtenberg and Tracey (2003) found that psychotherapy interactions were characterized by complementarity across sessions, with either the therapist or the client in the dominant position, whereas Lichtenberg et al. (1998) concluded that patterns of relational control did not play a role in therapists' evaluations of their clients' clinical success.

Complementarity may be negative or positive in tone. Using Benjamin's (1974) Structural Analysis of Social Behavior (SASB) which is based on the circumplex model of interpersonal behavior (Leary, 1957), Henry, Schacht, and Strupp (1986) found that compared with unsuccessful cases, the successful ones were characterized by greater positive complementarity, i.e., "affiliative and autonomy-enhancing reciprocal interchanges" (p. 29), than negative complementarity, i.e., "hostile or controlling interchanges" (p. 29). In a later SASB study, Coady and Marziali (1994) reported that hostile controlling behaviors by the therapist and walling-off and distancing behaviors by the client were characteristic of a weak working alliance in the early phase of psychotherapy.

Examining clinical outcomes from the perspective of dropout versus continuation in treatment, Beyebach and Escudero (1997) used the RCCCS to compare (1) dyads with successful or (2) unsuccessful terminations (i.e., dropouts when the client's problems remained unresolved), and (3) dyads in which the client continued in therapy. Significant differences were found between the dropout and the continuation dyads, with greater competitive symmetry observed in the dropout cases.

Control patterns have also been studied in specific therapist-client dyads in the context of family therapy (Muñiz de la Peña, Friedlander, Escudero, & Heatherington, 2012; Raymond et al., 1993). For example, Muñiz de la Peña and colleagues studied communication control in relation to the working alliance between therapist and adolescent in early sessions. Competitive symmetry was observed more often in bad versus good alliance sessions and in sessions with deteriorating rather than stable alliances. Taken together with Beyebach and Escudero's (1997) findings, these results support the idea that problems in the working alliance between therapist and client are reflected in competitive symmetry.

An interesting application of the behavioral observation of dyads has been to the phenomenon of parallel process in the clinical supervision of novice therapists. With origins in psychoanalytic theory, *parallel process* refers to ways in which the kinds of communication patterns that characterize a therapy relationship with a client are reflected in the supervisory relationship, and vice versa (e.g., Ladany, Friedlander, & Nelson, 2005). Two studies of parallel processes using the Interpersonal Communication Rating System (ICRS; Strong et al., 1988) demonstrated the presence of parallel processes in supervisory and therapy dyads

(Friedlander, Siegel, & Brenock, 1989; Tracey, Bludworth, & Glidden-Tracey, 2012). Friedlander et al. (1989), who used the RCCCS and the ICRS, found a predominance of complementarity in both coding systems in a case study with a female client, female therapist, and female supervisor. In general, results supported the parallel process phenomenon. For example, the therapist tended to be more ↑ or leading when interacting with her client but more ↓ or cooperative when interacting with her supervisor.

Dyadic Interactions between Physician and Patient

The medical literature has increasingly come to acknowledge the importance of studying physician-patient interactions (Heritage & Maynard, 2006) in order to promote shared decision making. In an exploratory study with the RCCCS, O'Hair (1989) examined relational control in physician-patient interactions. Results showed competitive symmetry to be the most frequent pattern, followed by complementarity, in which patients were more likely to submit to a ↑ move by the physician and physicians were more likely to assume control (↑) when the patient assumed a submissive ↓ position.

These results were partially confirmed by von Friederichs-Fitzwater, Callahan, Flynn, and Williams (1991), who found that physicians tended to assume a ↑ position when the patient assumed a ↓ position. However, the most frequent pattern found in physician-patient interaction was neutralized symmetry. Similarly, von Friederichs-Fitzwater and Gilgun (2001) reported that physicians were more likely to assume control when the patient offered control. However, the most frequent pattern of interaction in this study was transitory submission. A transitory exchange was also the most frequent pattern between physician and patient in a study by Wigginton Cecil (1998). More notably, an inverse relation was found between physician domineeringness and patient compliance.

Despite evidence supporting a general pattern of transitory or neutralized physician-patient interactions, researchers have also been interested in circumstances surrounding competitive symmetry (↑↑) in physician-patient exchanges. For example, Eggly and Tzelepis (2001) examined RCCCS patterns in difficult encounters between medical residents and patients being seen in a pain clinic. The difficult encounters were identified based on the residents' expressed frustration after the encounter due to the patients' requests for pain medication. Not surprisingly, the most frequent pattern of transaction was competitive symmetry, with both physician and patient attempting to take control and rejecting the other's bid for control.

Research on physician-patient interactions has also attended to other aspects of emotional, and more broadly psychosocial, communication in medical encounters. Eide, Quera, Graugaard, and Finset (2003) used the Roter Interaction Analysis System (RIAS; Roter, 1977) to examine patterns of communication between physicians and patients before and after patients' emotional cues. Results showed that physicians' silence, minimal encouragers, and affirmations were most common preceding patient's emotional cues, whereas patients' silence or expression of concern tended to precede their emotional cues. Physicians most commonly followed patients' emotional cues with minimal encouragers and affirmations. Interestingly, Roter and Larson (2002) compared the communication patterns of patients with residents versus attending physicians. The resident-patient exchanges were dominated by a biomedical focus; the attending physicians were also much more biomedically focused, with few psychosocial interactions. The latter finding was unexpected, since the authors had predicted that experienced physicians would model a more inclusive approach that attends to psychosocial factors.

Dyadic Interactions of Leader and Subordinate

The analysis of relational control in the organizational literature brought a much-needed focus to the jointly produced, dyadic nature of leadership (Fairhurst, 2004), highlighting the multiple factors that influence leader-subordinate exchange patterns. Watson (1982), for example, used an analogue of leader-subordinate relationships with undergraduate and MBA graduate students to show that leader-initiated dominance more frequently led to RCCCS complementarity whereas subordinate-initiated dominance was more likely to lead to competitive symmetry. Leader-initiated exchanges led to more structured and predictable responses from subordinates, whereas leaders exercised more options in subordinate-initiated communications. Overall, these findings are consistent with the power dynamics that one would expect to occur between leader and subordinate in a work setting.

Although Watson's (1982) study lent support to the significance of roles in structuring communications, subsequent research showed that leader-subordinate communication is also a function of the type of organizational system and leadership style. Courtright, Fairhurst, and Rogers (1989), for example, compared leader-subordinate communication patterns in *organic organizations*, which are "characterized by dispersed control" (p. 773), and *mechanistic organizations*, which are "characterized by hierarchical control" (p. 773). Leader-subordinate exchanges in organic organizations showed greater neutralized symmetry and leader-initiated ↓complementarity, whereas communications in mechanistic organizations exhibited greater competitive symmetry and competitive transitions.

In a follow-up study, Fairhurst, Green, and Courtright (1995) compared leader-subordinate communication within four types of dyads: (1) dyads with an autocratic manager in a plant that was converting from a traditional, top-down decision-making system to a socio-technical system (STS) that values bottom-up decision-making; (2) dyads with a participative manager in a conversion plant; (3) dyads with an autocratic manager in an STS start-up plant; and (4) dyads with a participative manager in an STS start-up plant. Results were generally supportive of the hypothesis that autocratic-manager dyads would show less participative communication. In conversion plants, these dyads showed more manager-initiated discussions and more approval-seeking behaviors on the part of subordinates. In startup plants, participative-manager dyads showed more competitive symmetry and neutralized symmetry, indicative of a less hierarchical leader-subordinate relationship.

Since the early studies by Fairhurst and colleagues (Courtright, Fairhurst, & Rogers, 1989; Fairhurst, Green, & Courtright, 1995), there have been few studies on leader-subordinate relational control. Recently, Fairhurst, and Uhl-bien (2012) emphasized the importance of studying interactional communication within organizations and called for the use of sequential analysis of verbal interaction data.

Conclusion and Future Directions

In the past three decades of interaction research in general, and of dyadic interaction analysis in particular, there have been impressive developments in the methods for recording and analyzing observational data. As shown in our review of representative research, interaction analysis is an established method for studying diverse interpersonal relationships.

The analysis of dyadic interaction is, in our view, closely connected with an important epistemological issue in that dyadic methodology allows for a theoretical and analytical shift of focus from individual behavior to relational interaction. The seemingly simple idea of switching from the study of action to the study of interaction, and the consequent notion of *relational information*, has had relevant theoretical implications, including an emphasis on sequential processes, co-constructed patterns, and systemic level analyses.

The review of representative research on interaction analysis indicates that the development and application of different sequential analytical techniques have allowed researchers to investigate complex interaction patterns and their impact on important outcomes (such as predicting divorce or psychotherapeutic success). Studies on dyadic interaction have been conducted on different types of relationships, and included a diversity of contextual, social, and cultural variables.

Of note, despite the challenges of collecting observational data, most of the studies reviewed in this chapter have been based on data gathered in naturalistic settings (couples discussing their own problems, psychotherapy and medical settings, organizational environments, etc.). Nonetheless, practical applications of dyadic interaction analysis pose a continual challenge for researchers. We need a renewed focus on methods that facilitate the direct application of interaction analysis to the assessment of practical interventions (e.g., therapeutic interventions, conflict negotiation, shared decision making in health care management, and so on). The development of methods that are more accessible in applied settings will further the practical relevance of dyadic interaction analysis.

Another challenge for future research is the integration of subjective with objective perspectives on the relational process. Some of the research reviewed in this chapter has considered dyadic interaction analyses along with participants' subjective perceptions, such as spouses' satisfaction with their marriage or therapists' and clients' perceptions of their working relationship. On the other hand, participants' interpretations of their communication process have yet to be fully explored. Just a few of the observational methods have been adapted to investigate the affective and cognitive aspects of interaction from the participants' point of view; a pioneer example would be Gottman's (1994) strategy of having each member of a couple evaluate their communication while they observe a videotape of their interaction.

So where are we headed in the next decade? Considering the advances in video recording and coding methodologies, as well as the capability of obtaining sequential statistical analyses to visualize patterns of interaction, we expect to see an increase in dyadic interaction analysis in applied settings. We also anticipate a greater integration of observation with interpretive perspectives on relationships by the interactors themselves and by expert observers.

References

Allen, E. S., Rhoades, G. K., Stanley, S. M., Markman, H. J., Williams, T., Melton, J., & Clements, M. L. (2008). Premarital precursors of infidelity. *Family Process, 47*, 243–259. doi:10.1111/j.1545-5300.2008.00251.x

Bakeman, R., McArthur, D., & Quera, V. (1996). Detecting group differences in sequential association using sampled permutations: Log odds, kappa, and phi compared. *Behavior Research Methods, Instruments, and Computers, 28*, 446–457. doi:10.3758/BF03200524

Bakeman, R., & Quera, V. (1992). SDIS: A sequential data interchange standard. *Behavior Methods, Instruments, and Computers, 24*, 554–559. doi:10.3758/BF03203604

Bakeman, R., & Quera, V. (1995a). *Analyzing interaction: Sequential analysis with SDIS and GSEQ*. New York, NY: Cambridge University Press.

Bateson, G. (1958). *Naven*. London, UK: Cambridge University Press. (Original work published in 1936).

Bateson, G. (1979). *Mind and nature: A necessary unity*. New York, NY: Bantam Books.

Bateson, G., Jackson, D. D., Haley, J., & Weakland, J. H. (1956). Toward a theory of schizophrenia. *Behavioral Science, 1*, 251–264. doi:10.1002/bs.3830010402

Baucom, K. J. W., Baucom, B. R., & Christensen, A. (2015). Changes in dyadic communication after traditional and integrative behavioral couple therapy. *Behaviour Research and Therapy, 65*, 18–28. doi:10.1016/j.brat.2014.12.004

Baucom, K. J. W., Sevier, M., Eldrigde, K. A., & Doss, B. D. (2011). Observed communication in couples two years after integrative and traditional behavioral couple therapy: Outcome and link with five-year follow-up. *Journal of Consulting and Clinical Psychology, 79*, 565–576. doi:10.1037/a0025121

Bavelas, J. B., Rogers, L. E., & Millar, F. E. (1985). Interpersonal conflict. In T. A. van Dijk (Ed.), *Handbook of discourse analysis* (Vol. 4, pp. 9–26). New York, NY: Academic Press.

Benjamin, L. S. (1974). Structural analysis of social behavior. *Psychological Review, 81,* 392–423. doi.org/10.1037/h0037024

Beyebach, M., & Escudero Carranza, V. (1997). Therapeutic interaction and dropout: Measuring relational communication in solution-focused therapy. *Journal of Family Therapy, 19,* 173–212. doi:10.1111/1467-6427.00047

Buehlman, K. T., Gottman, J. M., & Katz, L. F. (1992). How a couple views their past predicts their future: Predicting divorce from an oral history interview. *Journal of Family Psychology, 5,* 295–318. doi:10.1037/0893-3200.5.3-4.295

Cartensen, L. L., Gottman, J. M., & Levenson, R. W. (1995). Emotional behavior in long-term marriage. *Psychology and Aging, 10,* 140–149. doi:10.1037/0882-7974.10.1.140

Clements, M. L., Stanley, S. M., & Markman, H. J. (2004). Before they said "I do": Discriminating among marital outcomes over 13 years. *Journal of Marriage and Family, 66,* 613–626. doi:10.1111/j.0022-2445.2004.00041.x

Coady, N. F., & Marziali, E. (1994). The association between global and specific measures of the therapeutic relationship. *Psychotherapy: Theory, Research, Practice, Training, 31,* 17–27. doi:10.1037/0033-3204.31.1.17

Cordova, J. V., Jacobson, N. S., Gottman, J. M., Rushe, R., & Cox, G. (1993). Negative reciprocity and communication in couples with a violent husband. *Journal of Abnormal Psychology, 102,* 559–564. doi:10.1037/0021-843X.102.4.559

Courtright, J. A., Fairhurst, G. T., & Rogers, L. E. (1989). Interaction patterns in organic and mechanistic systems. *Academy of Management Journal, 32,* 773–802. doi:10.2307/256568

Courtright, J. A., Millar, F. E., & Rogers-Millar, L. E. (1979). Domineeringness and dominance: Replication and expansion. *Communication Monographs, 46,* 179–192. doi:10.1080/03637757909376005

Eggly, S., & Tzelepis, A. (2001). Relational control in difficult physician-patient encounters: Negotiating treatment for pain. *Journal of Health Communication, 6,* 323–333. doi:10.1080/108107301317140814

Eide, H., Quera, V., Graugaard, P., & Finset, A. (2003). Physician-patient dialogue surrounding patients' expression of concern: Applying sequence analysis to RIAS. *Social Science and Medicine, 59,* 145–155. doi:10.1016/j.socscimed.2003.10.011

Ericson, P. M., & Rogers, L. E. (1973). New procedures for analyzing relational communication. *Family Process, 12,* 245–267. doi:10.1111/j.1545-5300.1973.00245.x

Escudero, V., & Rogers, L.E. (2004a). Observing relational communication. In L. E. Rogers & V. Escudero (Eds.), *Relational communication: An interactional perspective to the study of process and form* (pp. 3–21). Mahwah, NJ: Lawrence Erlbaum Associates.

Escudero, V., & Rogers, L. E. (2004b). Analyzing relational communication. In L. E. Rogers & V. Escudero (Eds.), *Relational communication: An interactional perspective to the study of process and form* (pp. 3–21). Mahwah, NJ: Lawrence Erlbaum Associates.

Escudero, V., Rogers, L. E., & Gutierrez, E. (1997). Patterns of relational control and nonverbal affect in clinic and nonclinic couples. *Journal of Social and Personal Relationships, 14,* 5–29. doi:10.1177/0265407597141001

Fairhurst, G. T. (2004). Organizational relational control research: Problems and possibilities. In L. E. Rogers & V. Escudero (Eds.), *Relational communication: An interactional perspective to the study of process and form* (pp. 197–215). Mahwah, NJ: Erlbaum.

Fairhurst, G. T., Green, S., & Courtright, J. (1995). Inertial forces and the implementation of a socio-technical systems approach: A communication study. *Organization Science, 6,* 168–185. doi:10.1287/orsc.6.2.168

Fairhurst, G. T., & Uhl-Bien, M. (2012). Organizational discourse analysis (ODA): Examining leadership as a relational process. *The Leadership Quarterly, 23,* 1043–1062. doi:10.1016/j.leaqua.2012.10.005

Friedlander, M. L. (1982). Counseling discourse as a speech event: Revision and extension of the Hill Counselor Verbal Response Category System. *Journal of Counseling Psychology, 29,* 425–429. doi:10.1037/0022-0167.29.4.425

Friedlander, M. L. (1993). Does complementarity promote or hinder client change in brief therapy?: A review of the evidence from two theoretical perspectives. *The Counseling Psychologist, 21,* 457–486. doi:10.1177/0011000093213010

Friedlander, M. L., Siegel, S. M., & Brenock, K. (1989). Parallel processes in counseling supervision: A case study. *Journal of Counseling Psychology, 36,* 149–157. doi:10.1037/0022-0167.36.2.149

Gottman, J. M. (1979). *Marital interaction: Experimental investigations.* New York, NY: Academic Press.

Gottman, J. M. (Ed.). (1996). *What predicts divorce?: The measures.* Hillsdale, NJ: Erlbaum.

Gottman, J. M., & Krokoff, L. J. (1989). Marital interaction and satisfaction: A longitudinal view. *Journal of Consulting and Clinical Psychology, 57,* 47–52. doi:10.1037/0022-006X.57.1.47

Gottman, J. M., & Levenson, R. W. (2000). The timing of divorce: Predicting when a couple will divorce over a 14-year period. *The Journal of Marriage and Family, 62,* 737–745. doi:10.1111/j.1741-3737.2000.00737.x

Gottman, J. M., Levenson, R. W., Swanson, C., Swanson, K., Tyson, R., & Yoshimoto, D. (2003). Observing gay, lesbian, and heterosexual couples' relationships: Mathematical modeling of conflictual interaction. *Journal of Homosexuality, 45,* 65–91. doi:10.1300/J082v45n01_04

Gottman, J. M., & Roy, A. K. (1990). *Sequential analysis: A guide for behavioral researchers.* Cambridge, UK: Cambridge University Press.

Haberman, S. J. (1978). *Analysis of qualitative data*: Vol. 1. New York: Academic Press.

Haley, J. (1963). *Strategies of psychotherapy.* Orlando, FL: Grune & Stratton.

Heatherington, L., & Allen, G. J. (1984). Sex and relational communication patterns in counseling. *Journal of Counseling Psychology, 31,* 287–294. doi:10.1037//0022-0167.31.3.287

Heatherington, L., Escudero, V., & Friedlander, M. L. (2005). Couple interaction during problem discussions: Toward an integrative methodology. *Journal of Family Communication, 5,* 191–207. doi:10.1207/s15327698jfc0503_2

Henry, W. P., Schacht, T. E., & Strupp, H. H. (1986). Structural analysis of social behavior: Application to a study of interpersonal process in differential psychotherapeutic outcome. *Journal of Consulting and Clinical Psychology, 54,* 27–31. doi:10.1037/0022-006X.54.1.27

Heritage, J., & Maynard, D. W. (2006). Problems and prospects in the study of physician-patient interactions: 30 years of research. *Annual Review of Sociology*, *32*, 351–374. doi.org/10.1146/annurev.soc.32.082905.093959

Johnson, S. L., & Jacob, T. (2000). Sequential interactions in the marital communication of depressed men and women. *Journal of Consulting and Clinical Psychology*, *68*, 4–12. doi:10.1037/0022-006X.68.1.4

Ladany, N., Friedlander, M. L., & Nelson, M. L. (2005). *Critical events in psychotherapy supervision: An interpersonal approach*. Washington, DC: American Psychological Association.

Leary, T. (1957). *Interpersonal diagnosis of personality: A functional theory and methodology for personality evaluation*. New York, NY: Ronald Press.

Lichtenberg, J. W., & Barké, K. H. (1981). Investigation of transactional communication relationship patterns in counseling. *Journal of Counseling Psychology*, *28*, 471–480. doi:10.1037/0022-0167.28.6.471

Lichtenberg, J. W., & Tracey, J. G. (2003). Interaction rules and strategies in psychotherapy. *Journal of Counseling Psychology*, *50*, 267–275. doi:10.1037/0022-0167.50.3.267

Lichtenberg, J. W., Wettersten, K. B., Mull, H., Moberly, R. L., Merkley, K. B., Corey, A. T. (1998). Relationship formation and relational control as correlates of psychotherapy quality and outcome. *Journal of Counseling Psychology*, *45*, 322–337. doi:10.1037/0022-0167.45.3.322

Millar, F. E., & Rogers, L. E. (1887). Relational dimensions of interpersonal dynamics. In M. Roloff & G. R. Miller (Eds.), *Explorations in interpersonal processes: New directions in communication research* (pp. 117–139). Newbury Park, CA: Sage.

Millar, F. E., Rogers, L. E., & Bavelas, J. B. (1984). Identifying patterns of verbal conflict in interpersonal dynamics. *Western Journal of Speech Communication*, *48*, 232–246.

Muñiz de la Peña, C., Friedlander, M. L., Escudero, V., and Heatherington, L. (2012). How do therapists ally with adolescents in family therapy? An examination of relational control communication in early sessions. *Journal of Counseling Psychology*, *59*, 339–351. doi:10.1037/a0028063

Notarius, C. I., & Markman, H. J. (1981). The Couples Interaction Scoring System. In E. Filsinger & R. Lewis (Eds.), *Assessing marriage: New behavioral approaches* (pp. 112–127). Beverly Hills, CA: Sage.

Notarius, C. I., Markman, H. J., & Gottman, J. M. (1983). The Couples Interaction Scoring System: Clinical issue. In E. Filsinger (Ed.), *Marriage and family assessment: A sourcebook for family therapy* (pp. 117–136). Beverly Hills, CA: Sage.

O'Hair, D. (1989). Dimensions of relational communication and control during physician-patient interactions. *Health Communication*, *1*(2), 97–115. doi:10.1207/s15327027hc0102_2

Patterson, G. R., Weiss, R. L., & Hops, H. (1976). Training of marital skills: Some problems and concepts. In H. Leitenberg (Ed.), *Handbook of behavior modification and behavior therapy* (pp. 242–254). Englewood Cliffs, NJ: Prentice-Hall.

Quera, V., & Bakeman, R. (2000). Quantification strategies in behavioral observation research. In T. Thompson, D. Felce, & F. J. Symons (Eds.), *Behavioral observation: Technology and applications in developmental disabilities* (pp. 297–315). Baltimore, MD: P. H. Brookes.

Raymond, L., Friedlander, M. L., Heatherington, L., Ellis, M. V., & Sargent, J. (1993). Communication processes in structural family therapy: Case study of an anorexic family. *Journal of Family Psychology, 6,* 308–326. doi:10.1037/0022-0167.29.4.425

Rehman, U. S., & Holtzworth-Munroe, A. (2006). A cross-cultural analysis of the demand-withdraw marital interaction: Observing couples from a developing country. *Journal of Consulting and Clinical Psychology, 4,* 755–766. doi:10.1037/0022-006X.74.4.755

Rogers, L. E., Castleton, A., & Lloyd, S. A. (1996). Relational control and physical aggression in satisfying marital relationships. In D. D. Cahn & S. A. Lloyd (Eds.), *Family violence from a communication perspective* (pp. 218–239). Thousand Oaks, CA: Sage.

Rogers, L. E., & Escudero, V. (2004). Theoretical foundations. In L. E. Rogers & V. Escudero (Eds.), *Relational communication: An interactional perspective to the study of process and form* (pp. 3–21). Mahwah, NJ: Lawrence Erlbaum Associates.

Rogers, L. E., & Farace, R. V. (1975). Analysis of relational communication in dyads: New measurement procedures. *Human Communication Research, 1,* 222–239. doi:10.1111/j.1468-2958.1975.tb00270.x

Roter, D. (1977). Patient participation in the patient-provider interaction: The effects of patient question-asking on the quality of interaction, satisfaction, and compliance. *Health Education Monographs, 5,* 281–330. doi:10.1177/109019817700500402

Roter, D., & Larson, S. (2002). The Roter Interaction Analysis System: Utility and flexibility for analysis of medical interactions. *Patient Education and Counseling, 46,* 243–251. doi:10.1016/S0738-3991(02)00012-5

Sabourin, T. C. (1995). The role of negative reciprocity in spouse abuse: A relational control analysis. *Journal of Applied Communication Research, 23,* 271–283. doi:10.1080/00909889509365431

Simmel, G. (1950). *The sociology of Georg Simmel.* New York, NY: Free Press.

Strong, S. R., Hills, H. I., Kilmartin, C. T., DeVries, H., Lanier, K., Nelson, B. N., Strickland, D., & Meyer III, C. W. (1988). The dynamic relations among interpersonal behaviors: A test of complementarity and anticomplementarity. *Journal of Personality and Social Psychology, 54,* 798–810. doi:10.1037/0022-3514.54.5.798

Sullivan, H. S. (1953). *The interpersonal theory of psychiatry.* New York, NY: Norton.

Tomm, K. (2014). Introducing the IPscope: A systematic assessment tool for distinguishing interpersonal patterns. In K. Tomm, S. St. George, D. Wulff, & T. Strong (Eds.), *Patterns in interpersonal interactions: Inviting relational understandings for therapeutic change* (pp. 13–35). New York, NY: Routledge.

Tracey, J. G., Bludworth, J., & Glidden-Tracey, C. E. (2012). Are there parallel processes in psychotherapy supervision: An empirical examination. *Psychotherapy, 49,* 330–343. doi:10.1037/a0026246

Tracey, T. J., & Miars, R. D. (1986). Interpersonal control in psychotherapy: A comparison of two definitions. *Journal of Clinical Psychology, 42,* 585–592. doi:10.1002/1097-4679(198607)42:4<585::aid-jclp2270420407>3.0.CO;2-L

Tracey, T. J., & Ray, P. B. (1984). Stages of successful time-limited counseling: An interactional examination. *Journal of Counseling Psychology, 31,* 13–27. doi:10.1037/0022-0167.31.1.13

von Friederichs-Fitzwater, M. M., Callahan, E. J., Flynn, N., & Williams, J. (1991). Relational control in physician-patient encounters. *Health Communication, 3,* 17–36. doi:10.1207/s15327027hc0301_2 von Friederichs-Fitzwater, M. M., & Gilgun, J. (2001). Relational control in physician-patient encounters. *Health Communication, 13*, 75–87. doi:10.1207/S15327027HC1301_07

Wampold, B. E. (1989). Kappa as a measure of pattern in sequential data. *Quality and Quantity, 23*, 171–187. doi:10.1007/BF00151902

Wampold, B. E. (1992). The intensive examination of social interaction. In T. R. Kratochvill & J. R. Levin (Eds.), *Single-case research design and analysis: New directions for psychology and education* (pp. 93–131). Hillsdale, NJ: Lawrence Erlbaum Associates.

Watson, K. M. (1982). An analysis of communication patterns: A method for discriminating leader and member roles. *Academy of Management Journal, 25*, 107–120. doi:10.2307/256027

Watzlawick, P., Bavelas, J. B., & Jackson, D. D. (1967). *Pragmatics of human communication: A study of interactional patterns, pathologies, and paradoxes*. New York, NY: Norton.

Wigginton Cecil, D. (1998). Relational control patterns in physician-patient clinical encounters: Continuing the conversation. *Health Communication, 10*, 125–150. doi:10.1207/s15327027hc1002_2

Williamson, R. N., & Fitzpatrick, M. A. (1985). Two approaches to marital interaction: Relational control patterns in marital types. *Communication Monographs, 52*, 236–252. doi:10.1080/03637758509376108

Yoder, P. J., & Feurer, I. D. (2000). Quantifying the magnitude of sequential association between events of behaviors. In T. Thompson, D. Felce, & F. J. Symons (Eds.), *Behavioral observation: Technology and applications in developmental disabilities* (pp. 317–333). Baltimore, MD: P. H. Brookes.

4 Observing Group Interaction

The Benefits of Taking Group Dynamics Seriously

Michaela Kolbe and Margarete Boos

Groups – in various forms – are the building blocks of modern organizations (Edmondson, 2012; Mathieu, Tannenbaum, Donsbach, & Alliger, 2014; Salas, Tannenbaum, Cohen, & Latham, 2013). How groups create and maintain high performance and satisfy their members' needs has been the focus of group research for decades. Remarkably, high group performance is not so much predicted by how competent the individual group members are but by the way they interact with one another, that is, the group process (Woolley, Aggarwal, & Malone, 2015; Woolley, Chabris, Pentland, Hashmi, & Malone, 2010). Group process is defined as "members' interdependent acts that convert inputs to outcomes through cognitive, verbal, and behavioral activities directed toward organizing taskwork to achieve collective goals" (Marks, Mathieu, & Zaccaro, 2001, p. 357). This definition implies that group processes are dynamic, which means not only unfolding over time but also continuously changing their patterns. Most empirical group research, however, has been static rather than dynamic; it has focused on describing group states rather than on investigating how group processes dynamically unfurl over time and how these dynamics predict group performance and other outcomes (Cronin, Weingart, & Todorova, 2011; Kozlowski, 2015; Mathieu et al., 2014; Roe, 2008). A main reason for this limitation lies in the reliance on self-reported, cross-sectional data and the associated neglect of meaningful behavioral data. A variety of psychological disciplines have been criticized for not giving sufficient attention to the temporal aspects of behavior (Baumeister, Vohs, & Funder, 2007; Roe, 2008). A recent review of group research literature pointed to a considerable absence of empirical studies analyzing behavioral dynamics predicted by existing theory (Mathieu et al., 2014). Whereas the body of theoretical contributions integrating time and temporal dynamics in group research is growing (Ballard, Tschan, & Waller, 2008; Lehmann-Willenbrock, 2017; McGrath, & Tschan, 2004), and some empirical research on temporal dynamics in groups was published recently (Boos, Pritz, Lange, & Belz, 2014; Grote, Kolbe, Zala-Mezö, Bienefeld-Seall, & Künzle, 2010; Kolbe et al., 2014; Lehmann-Willenbrock, Allen, & Kauffeld, 2013; Lehmann-Willenbrock, Meyers, Kauffeld, Neininger, & Henschel, 2011; Lei, Waller, Hagen, & Kaplan, 2016; Stachowski, Kaplan, & Waller, 2009; Tschan et al., 2015; Tschan et al., 2009; Zijlstra, Waller, & Phillips, 2012), the overall amount of this research is small considering for how long and how urgently it has been requested. Already in 1979, Graumann stated the "unease of the psychologist" in the face of interaction and criticized psychology for avoiding interaction research entirely (Graumann, 1979). Also, studies on group processes are usually limited to small samples and short observational periods. The neglect of groups' dynamic nature is problematic because recent group research has shown that patterns of behaviors among group members – rather than frequencies of individual group members' actions – are what discriminates high- from low-performing groups (Kim, McFee, Olguin Olguin, Waber, & Pentland, 2012; Kolbe et al., 2014; Lei et al., 2016; Zijlstra et al., 2012). These complex group dynamics that distinguish high-performing groups from low-performing groups cannot be uncovered with static group research. This is particularly problematic in light of the growing evidence demonstrating that poor teamwork in health care, for instance, can result even in the loss of a patient's life, thus emphasizing how critical it is to understand how group processes unfold and change over time (Cooper, Newbower, & Kitz, 1984; Fernandez Castelao et al., 2011; Flin & Mitchell, 2009; Reynard, Reynolds, & Stevenson, 2009). It is pivotal for this research to understand what groups need, and do, to perform well (Salas & Frush, 2013; Salas et al., 2013). In this chapter, we discuss (1) three group processes and respective examples we consider particularly noteworthy, (2) how these dynamic phenomena of interest are typically measured, and (3) how a methodical approach that takes dynamics into account contributes to knowledge gain.

Noteworthy Group Processes

How Groups Make Good Decisions

In organizations, problem-solving and decision-making tasks are often allotted to heterogeneous groups based on the assumption that such groups have a large and diverse knowledge base and can thus reach sound solutions (Brodbeck, & Greitemeyer, 2000). This advantage can only be realized if, during the process of task accomplishment, each member is willing to communicate information that is known only to her or him. Research on information exchange in groups, however, has shown that groups often fail to benefit from their theoretically expected advantage: They tend to discuss information known to all members (shared information) more extensively than information known by only one member (Larson, Sargis, Elstein, & Schwartz, 2002; Mesmer-Magnus & DeChurch, 2009). The Collective Information Sampling model of Stasser and Titus (1985, 1987) gives a probabilistic explanation for this bias toward shared information. The probability that an item of information will be mentioned during a group discussion depends on both the number of individuals knowing it and the probability that an individual possessing it will mention it.

A huge bulk of empirical studies is trying to identify psychological factors suitable to reduce the sampling advantage of shared information and to enforce the sampling of unshared information respectively (Wittenbaum, Bowman, & Hollingshead,

2003). Besides input variables such as task type (Stasser & Stewart, 1992) or familiarity of the team members (Gruenfeld, Mannix, Williams, & Neale, 1996), there are many process-oriented interventions, such as participative leadership behavior (Larson, Foster-Fishman, & Franz, 1998) or structuring of the decision-making process (Kolbe, 2007) that can enhance the exchange of unshared information and thus let the group profit from its combined expertise.

Example – Multidisciplinary Tumor Boards. As a prototypical example of a heterogeneous group for which the successful exchange of expertise should be vital is the discussion of individual patient cases in multidisciplinary tumor boards (MDT; Homayounfar, Mey, Boos, Gaedcke, & Ghadimi, 2015). MDT have become an international standard of cancer care (Pox et al., 2013). The implementation of tumor boards arises from the increasing complexity of treatment options and seeks to provide patients with the most effective treatment. MDT are not only associated with high organizational and personnel costs, they also include characteristics that can significantly stand in the way of effective discussion (e.g., high importance of status and hierarchy, conflicting personal interests, time pressure). Whereas effectiveness factors such as optimal team composition, infrastructure, and database logistics are already well investigated, there are less data on the most advantageous interaction and communication processes before and during MDT meetings. Communication rules, professional facilitation, and leadership behavior that take into account the complexity of the task, potential conflicting individual goals, hierarchical organizational structure, and time pressure must be designed and evaluated on the basis of a dynamic conceptualization of MDT functioning to allow for synergy during MDT.

How Groups Coordinate Actions

Coordination can be viewed as the synchronization of actions (behaviors) in time and space – the orchestration of the sequence and timing of interdependent actions (Boos, Kolbe, & Strack, 2011, p. 19). In the operating theatre, for example, group members each fulfill different roles that are defined by task responsibilities during anesthesia and surgery. They must coordinate their actions to successfully accomplish their group task, involving both explicit and implicit coordination mechanisms appropriate to the subtask at hand and the current situation of the patient (Kolbe, Burtscher, Manser, Künzle, & Grote, 2011; Zala-Mezö, Wacker, Künzle, Brüesch, & Grote, 2009). Effective synchronization of behaviors equates with the group doing the right things in the right order and at the right time. For example, anesthesia teams have been shown to perform better when their members monitored each other's performance and subsequently either provided back-up behavior or spoke up (Kolbe et al., 2014). Similarly, "closed-loop communication" involving the receiver of the message acknowledging its receipt was found to improve group performance (Salas, Sims, & Burke, 2005; Schmutz, Hoffman, Heimberg, & Manser, 2015).

Example – Managing Medical Emergencies. During the management of medical emergencies, the importance of leadership as a specific form of coordination has been shown (Tschan et al., 2014). Here, leadership is not just a role that is furnished with specific behavioral expectations towards the holder of this role by her or his followers, but consists of concrete behavior such as giving instructions, providing feedback, and maintaining overall situation awareness to reach a goal. In cardiopulmonary resuscitation (CPR), for example, effective leadership is positively related to patient outcome (Fernandez Castelao, Russo, Riethmüller, & Boos, 2013; Hunziker et al., 2011; Künzle, Zala-Mezö, Wacker, Kolbe, & Grote, 2010; Tschan et al., 2014). That is why both the European Resuscitation Council (ERC) and the American Heart Association (AHA) strongly recommend integrating teamwork trainings, including leadership as a key skill, into advanced life support education (Bhanji et al., 2010; Soar et al., 2010).

How Groups Learn

Learning involves the detection and correction of error (Argyris, 2002). Ideally, it involves correcting error by changing the mental models (i.e., frames, governing values) that have driven the previously erroneous actions, and then changing the actions (i.e., double-loop learning), rather than correcting error without changing the mental models (i.e., single-loop learning; Argyris, 2002). This requires reflective practice, that is the exploration of one's mental routines, taken-for-granted assumptions, and their behavioral consequences (Schön, 1983). Team learning in particular has been described as "a process and attempt to articulate the behaviors through which such outcomes as adaptation to change, greater understanding, or improved performance in teams can be achieved" (Edmondson, 1999, p. 353). Team learning involves not only identifying and correcting errors in one's own performance but also those in interactions with other team members (Edmondson, 2012; Gurtner, Tschan, Semmer, & Naegele, 2007). Modern forms of less stable and more dynamic teams (Tannenbaum, Mathieu, Salas, & Cohen, 2012) have particular learning needs because learning from shared experiences as a group is almost impossible, and their temporal instability limits the development of shared insights (Vashdi, Bamberger, & Erez, 2013). Brief and repeated reflections on teamwork and task work have been suggested as learning infrastructure (Konradt, Schippers, Garbers, & Steenfatt, 2015; Schmutz, & Eppich, 2017; Vashdi et al., 2013).

Example – Team Debriefing. Also called *after action reviews*, debriefings are guided conversations that facilitate the understanding of the relationship among events, actions, thoughts, and feelings, processes, and performance outcomes (Rudolph, Simon, Rivard, Dufresne, & Raemer, 2007). Reflections such as debriefings have to be explicitly initiated because groups do not naturally engage in shared reflective experiences (Tannenbaum, Beard, & Cerasoli, 2013). While the number of debriefing approaches is growing (Eppich, Mullan, Brett-Fleegler, & Cheng, 2016; Kessler, Cheng, & Mullan, 2015; Kolbe, Marty, Seelandt, & Grande, 2016;

Mullan, Kessler, & Cheng, 2014; Weiss, Kolbe, Grote, Spahn, & Grande, 2016), empirical insights into debriefing interaction patterns are scarce (Cheng et al., 2014). Few studies have examined actual debriefing conversations and how differences in debriefers' communication influence learners' outcomes (Husebø, Dieckmann, Rystedt, Søreide, & Friberg, 2013). More knowledge on debriefing interactions is important for obtaining insights into associations between debriefing, reflection, and learning, for comparing different debriefing approaches, and for gaining knowledge on what modern forms of teams should do to learn.

How Group Phenomena are Typically Measured – And How They Should Be Measured to Capture Dynamics

In this section, we will use the examples introduced above and describe how they are typically studied (i.e., treating group process as static) and how, from our point of view, they should be studied (i.e., treating group process as dynamic) to gain new knowledge about group functioning.

How Groups Make Good Decisions: Multidisciplinary Tumor Boards

A number of studies have been conducted to investigate the effectiveness of MDT. Using mainly surveys or database reviews, they have typically focused on inputs and outputs such as (1) the actual presence of MDT (Keating et al., 2013), (2) whether the conduct of MDT leads to a change in management plan (Brauer et al.; Tafe et al., 2015; Thenappan et al., 2017), (3) the content that is discussed (Snyder, Schultz, & Walbert, 2017), (4) the feasibility (e.g., use of technology, duration, Marshall et al., 2014), (5) to what degree the discussion is valued by participants (Snyder et al., 2017), or more specifically at participation (attendance) in (Kehl et al., 2015) and documentation during the MDT (Farrugia, Fischer, Delitto, Spiguel, & Shaw, 2015). Whereas these studies provide valuable information on the context and conditions of MDT, they do not yet provide insights into the process of information sharing and decision making during the MDT and the quality of treatment recommendations.

Studies explicitly addressing decision making in MDT have relied on rating tools such as the Multidisciplinary Team Metric for Observation of Decision-Making (MDT-MODe; Lamb et al., 2013; Shah et al., 2014) and self-reports (Lamb, Sevdalis, Mostafid, Vincent, & Green, 2011). They have provided valuable knowledge on MDT's ability to reach decisions (e.g., 82.2 percent to 92.7 percent; Lamb et al., 2013), on duration, attendance rate, and duration of case review (e.g., three minutes per case; Shah et al., 2014), on estimates of the (poor) quality of presented information (e.g., 29.6 percent to 38.3 percent; Lamb et al., 2013) and of teamwork (e.g., 37.8 percent to 43.0 percent; Lamb et al., 2013), on the comparative quality of team members' contributions (e.g., highest from surgeons; Shah et al., 2014), and on barriers to reaching decisions (e.g., inadequate information; Lamb et al., 2013).

However, although the authors of these studies conclude that applied rating and self-report tools allow for reliably assessing the quality of teamwork and decision making (Lamb et al., 2011), the methodology of these studies does not allow for insights into the actual, dynamic process of information sharing and decision making: How are contributions shared among board members of different levels of hierarchy? Who actually contributes when and with which information? How do other MDT members react? How do individual contributions (not) influence the decision recommendation? How does dissent about evaluations and recommendations emerge and dissolve? Not looking at these important aspects of the decision-making process is somewhat comparable to a patient undergoing surgery while his or her condition is judged using a rating scale from 1 (*bad*) to 5 (*good*) instead of using continuous, machine-based monitoring of heartbeat, breathing, blood pressure, body temperature, and other body functions.

To complement existing studies on MDT effectiveness we recommend using behavior observation by means of event-based or time-based sampling and using coding systems that have been designed to help uncovering group decision processes. For example, using the act4teams coding system (Kauffeld, Lehmann-Willenbrock, & Meinecke, this volume, Chapter 21) could provide important insights into the optimal sequence of voicing information on the patients' conditions versus introducing treatment decision preferences (Mojzisch & Schulz-Hardt, 2010) and into the impact of leaders' statements on the discussion (Lehmann-Willenbrock, Meinecke, Rowold, & Kauffeld, 2015). It would also allow for insights into the emergence and impact of counterproductive meeting behaviors (e.g., arriving late, complaining, engaging in irrelevant discussions; Allen, Yoerger, Lehmann-Willenbrock, & Jones, 2015), and into the role of solution-focused meeting behavior (Lehmann-Willenbrock, Chiu, Lei, & Kauffeld, 2017). Similarly, applying aspects of the Hidden Profile Coding scheme (Thürmer, Wieber, Schultz, & Schulz-Hardt, this volume, Chapter 37) or MICRO-CO (Kolbe, Strack, Stein, & Boos, 2011) would allow for tracing information processing during the meeting and reveal insights into what and how expert information is actually processed (or not processed) and integrated into decisions. Likewise, continuously coding actual participation (rather than just attendance) in the meeting would allow for insights into the balance of speaker switches, which has been found to be an indicator of good team performance (Lehmann-Willenbrock et al., 2017; Woolley et al., 2010).

How Groups Coordinate Actions: Managing Medical Emergencies

A variety of studies have been performed to analyze how healthcare teams manage emergencies. For this purpose, various methods have been applied ranging from surveys (Valentine, Nembhard, & Edmondson, 2015), to rating tools (e.g., Couto, Kerrey, Taylor, FitzGerald, & Geis, 2015; Undre, Sevdalis, & Vincent, 2009), and to event- and time-based observation tools (e.g., Riethmüller, Fernandez Castelao, Eberhardt, Timmermann, & Boos, 2012; Schmutz et al., 2015; Su et al., 2017).

Researchers have invested considerable effort in the development of respective teamwork observation measures (e.g., Fletcher et al., 2004; Kemper et al., 2013; Kolbe, Burtscher, & Manser, 2013; Kolbe, Künzle, Zala-Mezö, Wacker, & Grote, 2009; Manser, Howard, & Gaba, 2008; Robertson et al., 2014; Seelandt et al., 2014; Tschan et al., 2011; Yule, Flin, Paterson-Brown, Maran, & Rowley, 2006). These observation tools fall into two main categories: behavioral marker systems (e.g., Fletcher et al., 2004; Jones, Rosen, Duval-Arnould, & Hunt, 2014; Kemper et al., 2013; Robertson et al., 2014; Undre et al., 2009; Yule et al., 2006) and coding schemes (e.g., Kolbe et al., 2013; Kolbe et al., 2009; Manser et al., 2008; Seelandt et al., 2014; Tschan et al., 2011). Both categories of tools include a number of advantages and disadvantages (Table 4.1). For example, using a behavioral marker system at three designated times during 50 surgical procedures, Undre and colleagues found that teamwork behavior could be compared between members of different operating room subteams, and surgeons' teamwork score deteriorated towards the end of procedures (Undre, Sevdalis, Healey, Darzi, & Vincent, 2007). Whereas these results provide valuable knowledge of teamwork estimates and perceived quality, they do not provide insights into the actual operating room team interaction process. This insight is possible only with behavior coding. For example, Tschan and colleagues continuously coded communication of 167 surgical procedures and found, among other results, that particularly case-irrelevant communication during the closing phase of the procedure was associated with higher rates of surgical site infections – providing very specific insights into the relationship between team dynamics and outcomes (Tschan et al., 2015). Thus, investing time and resources in coding of actual group interaction allows for obtaining insights into group dynamics that would otherwise remain hidden.

How Groups Learn: Debriefings

The empirical analysis of group reflexivity, particularly debriefings, is relatively new. It involves experiments (e.g., DeRue, Nahrgang, Hollenbeck, & Workman, 2012; Eddy, Tannenbaum, & Mathieu, 2013; Ellis, Ganzach, Castle, & Sekely, 2010; Ellis, Mendel, & Aloni-Zohar, 2009; Gurtner et al., 2007; Konradt et al., 2015) and field studies (Vashdi et al., 2013; Weiss et al., 2017) in which the impact of reflexivity interventions on defined outcomes is tested or different debriefing approaches are compared. The actual process of reflection (e.g., verbal communication among group members) during these interventions is rarely investigated at all. However, tools for observing group debriefings have been developed: the Debriefing Assessment for Simulation in Healthcare (DASH; Brett-Fleegler et al., 2012; The Center for Medical Simulation, 2010) and the Objective Structured Assessment of Debriefing (OSAD; Arora et al., 2012). Both are behavioral marker systems. In a recent study investigating the value of a 360°-OSAD-based evaluation of debriefings by examining expert debriefing evaluators, debriefers, and learners (i.e., group members), significant differences among these groups were found: Debriefers

Salas, E., & Frush, K. (Eds.). (2013). *Improving patient safety through teamwork and team training*. New York, NY: Oxford University Press.

Salas, E., Sims, D. E., & Burke, C. S. (2005). Is there a "big five" in teamwork? *Small Group Research, 36*, 555–599. doi:10.1177/1046496405277134

Salas, E., Tannenbaum, S., Cohen, D., & Latham, G. (Eds.). (2013). *Developing and enhancing teamwork in organisations: Evidence-based best practices and guidelines*. San Francisco, CA: Jossey-Bass.

Schmutz, J., Hoffman, F., Heimberg, E., & Manser, T. (2015). Effective coordination in medical emergency teams: The moderating role of task type. *European Journal of Work and Organization Psychology, 24*, 761–776. doi:10.1080/1359432X.2015.1018184

Schmutz, J. B., & Eppich, W. J. (2017). Promoting learning and patient care through shared reflection: A conceptual framework for team reflexivity in health care. *Academic Medicine*. Advance online publication. doi:10.1097/acm.0000000000001688

Schön, D. A. (1983). *The reflective practitioner: How professionals think in action*. New York: Basic Books.

Seelandt, J., Grande, B., Kriech, S., & Kolbe, M. (2017). DE-CODE: A coding scheme for assessing debriefing interactions. *BMJ Simulation and Technology Enhanced Learning*. doi:10.1136/bmjstel-2017-000233

Seelandt, J. C., Kolbe, M., Heckel, H., & Grande, B. (2016). *Enhancing team learning in acute care team by using debriefings*. Paper presented at the SESAM, Lisbon, Portugal.

Seelandt, J. C., Tschan, F., Keller, S., Beldi, G., Jenni, N., Kurmann, A., . . . Semmer, N. K. (2014). Assessing distractors and teamwork during surgery: developing an event-based method for direct observation. *BMJ Quality & Safety, 23*, 918–929. doi:10.1136/bmjqs-2014-002860

Shah, S., Arora, S., Atkin, G., Glynne-Jones, R., Mathur, P., Darzi, A., & Sevdalis, N. (2014). Decision-making in colorectal cancer tumor board meetings: Results of a prospective observational assessment. *Surgical Endoscopy, 28*, 2783–2788. doi:10.1007/s00464-014-3545-3

Snyder, J., Schultz, L., & Walbert, T. (2017). The role of tumor board conferences in neuro-oncology: a nationwide provider survey. *Journal of Neuro-Oncology, 133*(1), 1–7. doi:10.1007/s11060-017-2416-x

Soar, J., Mancini, M. E., Bhanji, F., Billi, J. E., Dennett, J., Finn, J., . . . Morley, P. T. (2010). *Part 12: Education*, implementation, and teams. *Resuscitation, 81*(1), e288–e332. doi:10.1016/j.resuscitation.2010.08.030

Stachowski, A. A., Kaplan, S. A., & Waller, M. J. (2009). The benefits of flexible team interaction during crisis. *Journal of Applied Psychology, 94*, 1536–1543. doi:10.1037/a0016903

Stasser, G., & Stewart, D. (1992). Discovery of hidden profiles by decision-making groups: Solving a problem versus making a judgment. *Journal of Personality and Social Psychology, 63*, 426–434. doi:org/10.1037/0022-3514.63.3.426

Stasser, G., & Titus, W. (1985). Pooling of unshared information in group decision making: Biased information sampling during discussion. *Journal of Personality and Social Psychology, 48*, 1467–1578. doi:10.1037/0022-3514.48.6.1467

Stasser, G., & Titus, W. (1987). Effects of information load and percentage of shared information on the dissemination of unshared information during group discussion. *Journal of Personality and Social Psychology*, *53*, 81–93. doi:10.1037/0022-3514.53.1.81

Su, L., Kaplan, S., Burd, R., Winslow, C., Hargrove, A., & Waller, M. (2017). Trauma resuscitation: can team behaviours in the prearrival period predict resuscitation performance? *BMJ Simulation and Technology Enhanced Learning*, *3*, 106–110. doi:10.1136/bmjstel-2016-000143

Tafe, L. J., Gorlov, I. P., de Abreu, F. B., Lefferts, J. A., Liu, X., Pettus, J. R., ... Chamberlin, M. D. (2015). Implementation of a molecular tumor board: The impact on treatment decisions for 35 patients evaluated at Dartmouth-Hitchcock Medical Center. *The Oncologist*, *20*, 1011–1018. doi:10.1634/theoncologist.2015-0097

Tannenbaum, S. I., Beard, R. L., & Cerasoli, C. P. (2013). Conducting team debriefings that work: Lessons from research and practice. In E. Salas, S. I. Tannenbaum, D. Cohen, & G. Latham (Eds.), *Developing and enhancing teamwork in organizations: Evidence-based best practices and guidelines* (pp. 488–519). San Francisco, CA: Jossey-Bass.

Tannenbaum, S. I., Mathieu, J. E., Salas, E., & Cohen, D. (2012). Teams are changing: Are research and practice evolving fast enough? *Industrial and Organizational Psychology*, *5*(1), 2–24. doi:10.1111/j.1754-9434.2011.01396.x

The Center for Medical Simulation. (2010). *Debriefing Assessment for Simulation in Healthcare (DASH)©. Rater's Handbook*. Retrieved September 23, 2013, from www.harvardmedsim.org/_media/DASH.handbook.2010.Final.Rev.2.pdf.

Thenappan, A., Halaweish, I., Mody, R. J., Smith, E. A., Geiger, J. D., Ehrlich, P. F., ... Newman, E. A. (2017). Review at a multidisciplinary tumor board impacts critical management decisions of pediatric patients with cancer. *Pediatric Blood & Cancer*, *64*, 254–258. doi:10.1002/pbc.26201

Tschan, F., Seelandt, J. C., Keller, S., Semmer, N. K., Kurmann, A., Candinas, D., & Beldi, G. (2015). Impact of case-relevant and case-irrelevant communication within the surgical team on surgical-site infection. *British Journal of Surgery*, *102*, 1718–1725. doi:10.1002/bjs.9927

Tschan, F., Semmer, N. K., Gautschi, D., Hunziker, P., Spychiger, M., & Marsch, S. U. (2006). Leading to recovery: Group performance and coordinative activities in medical emergency driven groups. *Human Performance*, *19*, 277–304. doi:10.1207/s15327043hup1903_5

Tschan, F., Semmer, N. K., Gurtner, A., Bizzari, L., Spychiger, M., Breuer, M., & Marsch, S. U. (2009). Explicit reasoning, confirmation bias, and illusory transactive memory. A simulation study of group medical decision making. *Small Group Research*, *40*, 271–300. doi:10.1177/1046496409332928

Tschan, F., Semmer, N. K., Hunziker, S., Kolbe, M., Jenni, N., & Marsch, S. U. (2014). Leadership in different resuscitation situations. *Trends in Anaesthesia and Critical Care*, *4*, 32–36. doi:org/10.1016/j.tacc.2013.12.001

Tschan, F., Semmer, N. K., Vetterli, M., Gurtner, A., Hunziker, S., & Marsch, S. U. (2011). Developing observational categories for group process research based on task and coordination-requirement analysis: Examples from research on medical emergency-driven teams. In M. Boos, M. Kolbe, P. Kappeler, & T. Ellwart (Eds.), *Coordination in human and primate groups* (pp. 93–118). Heidelberg, Germany: Springer.

Undre, S., Sevdalis, N., Healey, A. N., Darzi, A., & Vincent, C. A. (2007). Observational Teamwork Assessment for Surgery (OTAS): Refinement and application in urological surgery. *World Journal of Surgery, 31*, 1373–1381. doi:10.1007/s00268-007-9053-z

Undre, S., Sevdalis, N., & Vincent, C. (2009). Observing and assessing surgical teams: The Observational Teamwork Assessment for Surgery (OTAS). In R. Flin & L. Mitchell (Eds.), *Safer surgery. Analysing behaviour in the operating theatre* (pp. 83–101). Aldershot, UK: Ashgate.

Valentine, M. A., Nembhard, I. M., & Edmondson, A. C. (2015). Measuring teamwork in health care settings: A review of survey instruments. *Medical Care, 53*, e16–e30. doi:10.1097/MLR.0b013e31827feef6

Vashdi, D. R., Bamberger, P. A., & Erez, M. (2013). Can surgical teams ever learn? The role of coordination, complexity, and transitivity in action team learning. *Academy of Management Journal, 56*, 945–971. doi:10.5465/amj.2010.0501

Weiss, M., Kolbe, M., Grote, G., Dambach, M., Marty, A., Spahn, D. R., & Grande, B. (2014). Agency and communion predict speaking up in acute care teams. *Small Group Research, 45*, 290–313. doi:10.1177/1046496414531495

Weiss, M., Kolbe, M., Grote, G., Spahn, D. R., & Grande, B. (2017). Why didn't you say something? Using after-event reviews to affect voice behavior and hierarchy beliefs in multi-professional action teams. *European Journal of Work and Organization Psychology, 26*(1), 66–80. doi:org/10.1080/1359432X.2016.1208652

Wittenbaum, G. M., Bowman, J. M., & Hollingshead, A. B. (2003). *Strategic information sharing in mixed-motive decision-making groups.* Paper presented at the Small Group Division of the National Communication Association. Miami, FL.

Woolley, A. W., Aggarwal, I., & Malone, T. W. (2015). Collective intelligence and group performance. *Current Directions in Psychological Science, 24*, 420–424. doi:10.1177/0963721415599543

Woolley, A. W., Chabris, C. F., Pentland, A., Hashmi, N., & Malone, T. W. (2010). Evidence for a collective intelligence factor in the performance of human groups. *Science, 330*, 686–688. doi:10.1126/science.1193147

Yule, S., Flin, R., Paterson-Brown, S., Maran, N., & Rowley, D. (2006). Development of a rating system for surgeons' non-technical skills. *Medical Education, 40*, 1098–1104. doi:10.1111/j.1365-2929.2006.02610.x

Zala-Mezö, E., Wacker, J., Künzle, B., Brüesch, M., & Grote, G. (2009). The influence of standardisation and task load on team coordination patterns during anaesthesia inductions. *Quality and Safety in Health Care, 18*, 127–130. doi:10.1136/qshc.2007.025973

Zijlstra, F. R. H., Waller, M. J., & Phillips, S. I. (2012). Setting the tone: Early interaction patterns in swift-starting teams as a predictor of effectiveness. *European Journal of Work and Organizational Psychology, 21*, 749–777. doi:10.1080/1359432X.2012.690399

5 Unpacking the Structures of Team Interaction Patterns

Zhike Lei

As much work in today's organizations is accomplished through teams, team interaction patterns are considered as a necessary dimension for understanding the complexity of team processes and outcomes in the real world (Katz & Kahn, 1978; Marks, Mathieu, & Zaccaro, 2001). In particular, a growing number of team researchers are engaging in a dynamic approach to team interaction patterns (e.g., Lehmann-Willenbrock, Chiu, Lei, & Kauffeld, 2017; Lei, Waller, Hagen, & Kaplan, 2016; Stachowski, Kaplan, & Waller, 2009), in which interaction patterns are conceptualized and studied as dynamic processes that manifest in forms of structure variability, trajectories, and cyclical fluctuations over time (Cronin, Weingart, & Todorova, 2011; Lei & Lehmann-Willenbrock, 2015). Moreover, innovations in research designs, analyses, and technology have provided empirical rigor in testing and analyzing these theories and research (Cronin et al., 2011; Kozlowski, 2015). Although the potential contribution of a dynamic approach to interaction patterns is motivating, the research journey can be inefficient and challenging, fraught with methodological hurdles and unknowns. The overarching goal of this chapter is to provide guidelines for better understanding how team interaction patterns in real time can be analyzed in a dynamic way, what relevant foci are involved in research design and testing, and which frontier technology and directions team scholars can take for advancing knowledge.

Team interaction patterns are discussed in this chapter both as overarching behavioral themes and as emergent processes that affect team performance and organizational outcomes (Kozlowski & Bell, 2008). Emergence is a bottom-up and interactive process that is shaped by organizational and team task contexts and can be patterned in different forms (see Kozlowski & Klein, 2000). From this vantage point, an emergence view of team interaction patterns necessitates a multilevel perspective that "simultaneously considers individuals; the team, its embedding task, and organizational contexts; and the interplay among these multiple levels over time" (Kozlowski & Bell, 2008, p. 3). This view also entails a temporal perspective because team members' individual or collective experiences in a team are time bounded and ever changing. Together, I interweave multilevel and temporal dynamic lenses in this chapter to highlight the key methodological and analytical considerations that allow a more integrative, dynamic approach to team interactions.

I begin the chapter with defining team interaction patterns and then describe some exemplar studies that inform interaction pattern analysis according to different levels of analysis. I pay particular attention to key methodological features of team interaction coding and analysis in describing these studies. I next discuss research needs and opportunities of team interaction patterns, and suggest technological and analytical frontiers that can advance our knowledge.

Structure of Team Interactions Across Different Levels of Analysis

Team interaction patterns are defined as regular sets of coordinated behavior in teams (i.e., verbalizations and nonverbal actions), repeated over time, occurring more often than could be expected on a random basis (Stachowski et al., 2009; Zellmer-Bruhn, Waller, & Ancona, 2004). Based on different levels of analysis, team interaction patterns can be characterized in three basic ways: observed outward-focused collective patterns *across teams*, inward-focused interaction themes emerging *within a team* or in a social network, and *micro* team processes of discrete interactions occurring within and across individuals.

Interaction Patterns Across Teams: Adaptive and Nested Structuration Approach

Studies of interaction patterns across team boundaries originated with research that is so-called "meso" in nature. One of the well-studied structures of collective team interaction patterns across team boundaries has been examined in the context of virtual teams or geographically dispersed teams, which are groups of people with a common purpose who carry out interdependent tasks across locations and time, using technology to communicate much more than they use face-to-face meetings (Cramton, 2001). Largely using adaptive structuration theory (DeSanctis & Poole 1994) as a template for organizing and interpreting qualitative and quantitative data, this research stream offers an important view of how effective global teams structure their team interactions and processes (Maznevski & Chudoba, 2000; Perlow, Gittell, & Katz, 2004). In particular, Maznevski and Chudoba (2000) identified and analyzed the appropriate patterns for global virtual team effectiveness for three global virtual teams. They collected longitudinal data over 21 months using multiple methods, including interviews (with senior team members, managers to whom the teams reported, and key personnel), observations (of face-to-face meetings and conference calls), communication logs, questionnaires, and company documentation for additional assessments of team processes, some structural characteristics, and team outcomes and mandates. Maznevski and Chudoba followed King's (1998) coding procedures that begin with template coding based on a research template (i.e., an already-produced list of codes or categories representing themes identified in their data and study contexts), rather than with open coding (without an a priori idea of what the categories should be; see Corbin & Strauss, 1990). Following template coding, they conducted axial coding (Corbin & Strauss, 1990) to disaggregate core themes to generate theory and uncover relationships among identified categories and subcategories. Once having captured the general relationships among concepts within and across three teams, they looked for larger patterns over time and pattern changes, adaptations, and evolutions associated with global virtual team effectiveness. Similar coding and analysis procedures were also used by Perlow, Gittell, and Katz (2004).

The direct implication of these research findings in the contexts of cross-team boundaries is that individual actions and patterns of interaction mutually reinforce each other, and further are part of a mutually reinforcing relationship with elements of the organizational context and the larger institutional context. From this vantage point, to better understand team functions and interactions such as coordination, collaboration, and task completion, it is insufficient to explore these patterns in isolation, given that today's team activities in organization life often occur beyond team boundaries. These findings point toward a nested theory of structuration for team interaction research, expanding structuration theory (DeSanctis & Poole 1994) to multiple levels simultaneously (see also Poole, this volume, Chapter 18). Such a multilevel exploration of the interconnections that exist across team interaction patterns and elements of the organizational context may prove fruitful in understanding the forces in play in teams and organizations, as well as broader institutional contexts that sustain or change team effectiveness (Arrow, McGrath, & Berdahl, 2000). As such, research efforts to develop and validate coding themes and procedures may be broadened by including coding themes coming both from the data themselves (an inductive approach) and from researchers' prior theoretical knowledge of team and organizational contexts (an a priori approach). Together, a multilevel exploration and a nested theory of structuration of team interactions help researchers gain additional insights on how and why specific interactions occur and matter for each context (Waller & Kaplan, 2016). Also importantly, this nested structuration approach may raise additional methodological questions for studying team interaction patterns. For example, are there cyclic relationships between patterns of interactions and organizational, institutional, and cultural contexts? If so, how should we best investigate and model these relationships?

An additional implication of the studies focusing on patterns across teams is – although the research findings themselves may not seem "novel" today – that a mixed method design and a temporal emphasis used in these studies provide a larger toolbox with which researchers aim to expand research questions and advance the field. For example, an emerging methodological trend suggests that adopting a mixed-methods approach (e.g., integrating qualitative and quantitative methods in the same study) can provide the necessary empirical rigor to capture the complexities of organizational phenomena (Edmondson & McManus, 2007; Gibson, 2017). This is particularly true because team dynamics and changes associated with team interactions cannot be fully captured using cross-sectional designs, or minimalist longitudinal designs with three measurement periods, or purely behavioral observations. As such, hybrid methods can be "combined successfully in cases where the goal is to increase validity of new measures through triangulation and/or to generate greater understanding of the mechanisms underlying quantitative results in at least partially new territory" (Edmondson & McManus, 2007, p. 1157). Also, to answer the questions raised above concerning the cyclic relationships, hybrid methods including qualitative and quantitative methods and longitudinal design may provide a promising first step in this direction.

Interaction Patterns Within a Team: A Dynamic Network Perspective

Recent research on team social networks has opened additional promising directions for theory and research on team interaction patterns because a network approach captures patterned relational aspects of social interactions among team members that determine the flow of resources and information among teammates (Schulte, Cohen, & Klein, 2012; Sparrowe, Liden, Wayne, & Kraimer, 2001; Tröster, Mehra, & van Knippenberg, 2014). As a case in point, Schulte, Cohen, and Klein (2012) took a more temporal approach to investigate how the changes in team members' perceptions of their teams (e.g., psychological safety) and the changes in the team network influence team members' social interactions over time. Schulte et al. (2012) used survey data from 80 residential, federally funded, and managed national service teams in the United States at three time points to generate the network data. The authors used SIENA (Simulation Investigation for Empirical Network Analysis; Snijders, Steglich, & Schweinberger, 2007) to identify six *reciprocal* mechanisms through which individual team members' team perceptions and their social network ties coevolve. The notable contribution of this study is its analytical SIENA modeling that is specifically geared towards a dynamic investigation of changing relational and structural aspects of social interactions between team members. SIENA is an actor-oriented, dynamic model (i.e., a stochastic actor-based model), meaning that the social actors (e.g., a focal team member) in a network are deemed to play a crucial role in changing their relationship to, or behavior toward, other actors. For example, teammate A initially directs all his or her questions to teammate B, but later stops doing so and asks questions to the entire group. Based on the amount of information coming from the number of actors in a network, the number of observation moments ("panel waves"), and the total number of changes between consecutive observations (e.g., new team members come in or exit, some team members become silent), SIENA simulates potential coevolution of networks and behaviors and then determines the most likely sequence of changes given the observed data at the different points of measurement (see Snijders, 2005; Ripley & Snijders 2009; for detailed explanations).

Although a large amount of social network data is collected from self-reported surveys, applying a SIENA analytical approach to team interaction analysis provides new ways to dynamically map social interactions between team members. In particular, once all team interaction behaviors or utterances are coded into different categories (e.g., asking for help, providing support, giving sense, suggesting solutions) and coded directionally (e.g., member A is talking to B, and/or C and D; similarly, member B is directing actions to C and/or E), SIENA modeling can provide rich illustrations – both graphic and statistical – of the structural patterns of communication flow within a team. For example, SIENA can calculate standard structural measures of a social network (see Wasserman & Faust, 1994 for detailed explanation), such as network density (i.e., how close-knit the members of the team are; often referred to as an overall measure of social interaction), centralization (i.e., the concentration of communication in the network, which is analogous to variance or a measure of dispersion), and in-degree centralization (i.e., the rank or importance of individuals based on their positioning/influence in the network). While these network characteristics do not describe the exact content of team communication or interaction exchanged, they provide a high-level view of structural relationships between or among teammates. More importantly, stochastic actor-based models in SIENA can be used to analyze longitudinal data on social networks including paneled interactions (over a period time), jointly with changing attributes of team members such as member perceptions and social relationships with each other (Snijders et al., 2007). The SIENA program and documentation can be downloaded free from the SIENA web page.[1] The method can be implemented in the R package *RSiena* and the more experimental version *RSienaTest*.

Discrete Behavioral Patterns Within a Team: Microcoding and Pattern Characteristics

Recording, coding, and interpreting occurrences and patterns of specific discrete behaviors have long been established in the group dynamics literature to understand observational team interactions in organizations (Waller & Kaplan, 2016). The timing and frequency of certain interaction behaviors are also captured in the coding process (i.e., microcoding,[2] see Stoolmiller, Eddy, & Reid, 2000). Compared to interaction themes or network properties as unit of analysis explained previously, focusing on specific interactions as the critical unit of analysis adds nuances in our understanding of both cognitive and emotional elements that pervade social interactions (Collins, 2004). For example, Gibson (2003; 2005)

---

[1] www.stats.ox.ac.uk/siena.
[2] Note that others may use different terminology, such as moment-to-moment coding or microprocesses, for the same process (see Collins, 2004; Lehmann-Willenbrock, Meyers, Kauffeld, Neininger, & Henschel, 2011; Lehmann-Willenbrock, Chiu, Lei, & Kauffeld, 2017; Riethmüller, Fernandez, Eberhardt, Timmermann, & Boos, 2012).

proposes a framework of participation shift for the analysis of conversational sequences that captures the moment-by-moment shuffling of individuals between the "participation statuses" of speaker, target, and unaddressed recipient. His analysis of participation shifts in team meetings bridges conversation-analytic concerns with the sequential production of talk and small-group researchers' interest in interaction patterns and points to several new lines of microsociological research.

Lehmann-Willenbrock and colleagues (2017) studied how positivity dynamically unfolds within the flow of team interactions in problem-solving teams. The study data included both survey responses and videos of meetings from 43 problem-solving teams involving 259 line technicians in two medium-sized companies in Germany. The authors and trained coders used INTERACT software (Mangold, 2010) and unitized each team's entire meeting conversation into individual utterances or sense unit (i.e., several utterances demonstrate a set of behaviors), or a particular form of moment-to-moment microprocess. Based on the act4teams scheme (see Kauffeld & Lehmann-Willenbrock, 2012; Kauffeld, Lehmann-Willenbrock, & Meinecke, this volume, Chapter 21), the research team then categorized each individual utterance to some specific discrete interaction behavior (e.g., identifying a problem, suggesting a solution, or demonstrating positivity). Throughout the coding process, the researchers preserved the temporal order of the individual utterances within the meeting conversation. A total of 43,139 utterances were obtained. This study has several important implications for our discussions here. First, it timely responds to a recurring call for a temporal approach to team interactions and processes (Cronin et al., 2011; McGrath & Tschan, 2004; Gevers, van Eerde, & Roe, 2014) by conceptualizing positivity as an emerging behavioral construct embedded in team microprocesses (i.e., preceding utterances/behaviors within a team's interaction stream). Furthermore, as most team interaction behaviors are dynamic by nature, analyses of team interactions should examine how recent discrete behaviors affect the likelihood of a target behavior (e.g., positivity in Lehmann-Willenbrock et al.'s 2017 study) at each moment in time. Therefore, by modeling the microtime context (i.e., the surrounding time period, such as earlier or later phases within a team meeting) and showing how distinct moments tap into different affective components of team interactions (e.g., the moderating effects of speaker switches), this study helps capture both the temporal complexity and nuances of team interaction processes.

A different line of work on team adaptation also advocates using a temporal lens and a microcoding approach to more fully explicate the emergent dynamics of team behavior (Marks et al., 2001). For example, Kolbe et al. (2014) examined two implicit coordination behaviors that tend to emerge autochthonously within high-risk anesthesia teams performing an induction of general anesthesia in a natural setting: team member monitoring and talking to the room. In this study, teamwork interactions, such as speaking up, monitoring, gathering information, talking to the room, were assessed with Co-ACT (Kolbe, Burtscher, & Manser, 2013), a coding framework capturing task-relevant verbal and nonverbal team interactions in acute care teams. Using coded verbal and nonverbal behaviors of 27 anesthesia teams, the research team conducted lag sequential analyses to examine sequential patterns of team member monitoring and talking to the room. Lag sequential analysis asks whether the presence of a "given" code (e.g., monitoring) increases the probability that another "target" code (e.g., talking to the room) will occur. In determining whether there is cross-dependency between "given" and "target" behaviors, lag sequential methods identify contingencies and the sequential flow (or temporal patterns) in sequentially coded interaction activities, which occur significantly more often than expected (Kolbe et al., 2014; Kauffeld & Meyers, 2009). Although this analysis does not permit causal conclusions, it does provide us more information about the temporal contingency between different specific team interaction behaviors.

Team interaction patterns can also be abstracted and conceptualized as more universal characteristics such as length, complexity, or variety of interaction patterns. For example, Stachowski et al. (2009) explored whether high- versus average-performing teams can be distinguished on the basis of the number and complexity of their interaction patterns. The authors collected behavioral data through videotaping 14 nuclear power plant control room crews who responded to a simulated crisis. Using a validated coding theme (e.g., Stout, Cannon-Bowers, Salas, & Milanovich, 1999), Stachowski and colleagues coded discrete verbal and nonverbal behaviors of these crews during nonroutine and complex situations. Because patterns of specific interactions can be extremely difficult to detect by simply looking at sequential strings of coded data, the authors used the THEME algorithm to identify patterns by using three steps (Magnusson, 2016, 2017, this volume, Chapter 16). First, the algorithm identifies simple temporal patterns – or "T-patterns" – consisting of two behaviors that sequentially occur significantly more often than by chance. For instance, a T-pattern of "Question (A)–Answer (B)", consisting of two behaviors (Question and Answer), occurs in this order more often than by chance. Second, after the significant two-behavior T-patterns are identified, THEME cycles through the data potentially hundreds of thousands of times to identify more complex hierarchical patterns of relationships among T-patterns. For example, a T-pattern of "Question (A)–Answer (B)" and a T-pattern of "Command (A)–Debrief (C)" may coexist, forming a longer, more complex pattern. Finally, THEME generates pattern statistics such as the duration (length) of an interaction pattern, a pattern complexity measure based on the number of nested sets of behaviors within a pattern, and "turn taking" between actors within a pattern (i.e., actor switches). Researchers can then submit these data of pattern characteristics for further analysis and formally test their hypotheses and research questions. The THEME algorithm[3] is extremely helpful as it is able to identify a pattern of behaviors that occurs above and beyond chance and generate pattern data for further analysis (Magnusson, this volume, Chapter 16).

---

[3] www.patternvision.com.

Zijlstra, Waller, and Phillips (2012) also used THEME for pattern analysis when they videotaped and analyzed observation data from newly formed flight crews during their first interactions together (i.e., the flight preparation phase, lasting approximately 15 to 20 minutes) in flight simulator training sessions. Lei et al. (2016) also used THEME to explore the nature of over 3,000 audiotaped behavioral interactions from 11 professional airline flight crews who were engaged in realistic, interactive flight simulation sessions.

The core of using pattern recognition algorithms such as THEME is its "bottom-up" approach of pattern detection that allows for identifying simple patterns first and then detecting larger patterns as a combination of the simpler ones. Doing so, researchers not only develop a fine-grained understanding of specific interaction patterns but also gain the opportunity to investigate questions such as whether and how these various patterns link and operate across different situations.

As manifested in the studies mentioned above (e.g., Kolbe et al., 2014; Lehmann-Willenbrock et al., 2017; Lei et al., 2016; Stachowski et al., 2009), focusing on specific discrete behavioral patterns in exploring team interactions provides a promising direction to capture the fluid, dynamic nature of team interactions and their effects on team life. For example, one process that emerges temporarily in interaction episodes (e.g., suggesting a solution, monitoring) can have more prolonged effects on subsequent team interactions (e.g., positivity, talking to the room at a later point) as the outcome of these interactions feeds into future interactions. To advance future research in this direction, the "Holy Grail" seems to be a research program that incorporates systematic methodologies to code interaction data reliably with increasingly sophisticated technology and analytical methods to analyze the resultant coding (Waller & Kaplan, 2016), which may lead to innovative questions and enlightening conclusions.

Research Knowns and Needs

Here I reflect on the implications of the review of the team interaction research, highlighting both cumulative knowledge (i.e., the "research knowns") and opportunities (i.e., the "research needs") for further research and analysis.

Research Knowns

One of the most consistent themes that has received the widespread attention is that the structure of team interaction patterns – be it at the meso level across team boundaries or at the microprocess level – plays an important role in predicting team performance (Lehmann-Willenbrock et al., 2017; Stachowski et al., 2009; Zijlstra et al., 2012). Despite these consistent findings, quantitative evidence such as a meta-analysis on this relationship is needed to substantiate the claim that structured team interaction patterns have an important impact on team effectiveness and performance, especially when taking other factors such as team composition and other emergent states (e.g., climate) into consideration. Moreover, psychological mechanisms underlying the relationship between interaction patterns and team outcomes have yet to be specified in extant research. This means that more nuanced coding themes should be adopted to capture the contexts and psychological mechanisms. For example, more content coding can be combined with behavioral observation coding for a richer account of the mechanisms through which interaction patterns play a role in team processes and outcomes.

A second "known" theme emerging from empirical research on team interactions is that there are an increasing number of studies that examine specific discrete team interactions as micro team processes (e.g., Kolbe et al., 2014; Lehmann-Willenbrock et al., 2017; Lei et al., 2016; Riethmüller et al., 2012). These studies also begin to integrate advanced analytical models to explore more complex dynamics of team interactions. For example, how do different microprocesses (e.g., in-process planning, speaker switches) interplay to achieve team performance and desirable outcomes (e.g., positivity) over time (see Lehmann-Willenbrock et al., 2017; Lei et al., 2016)? Moreover, pattern structures (e.g., pattern length, pattern complexity) detected through pattern recognition algorithms such as THEME transcend the limits of specific study settings and bridge diverse disciplinary backgrounds to provide more generalizable findings.

Finally, a recurrent theme in extant research shows a somewhat singular approach to abstracting the structure of team interactions – being either context-specific or context-independent. On one hand, context-specific pattern analysis is consistent with the classic view that highlights the role of context in group development (Hackman, 2002; Sterman, 1989). On the other, it may be difficult to generalize the findings based on interaction patterns embedded in specific contexts. In contrast, a second stream of recent research on team social networks (Schulte et al., 2012) and software-recognized pattern analysis (Lei et al., 2016; Stachowski et al. 2009; Zijlstra et al. 2012), as explained above, exemplified team interaction patterns as network features, or as structure characteristics such as pattern length and complexity without considering specific contexts. The limitation of this approach is a lack of the nuanced explanation offered by the specific content of team interactions that can profoundly influence team performance. How to incorporate the role of study contexts thus remains a key decision area for team researchers, which will be further discussed in the next section.

Research Needs

As team research is entering the exciting area of coping with the complex, fluid structures of team interactions in organizations, additional research is needed to significantly advance our understanding of how team interactions can work in concert to help teams achieve their goals and objectives (Arrow et al., 2000).

Here I highlight several theoretical and methodological issues for future research attention.

First, further advance our dynamic approach to studying team interactions. Specifically, the following areas present fruitful research opportunities (Cronin et al., 2011):

(1) dynamic team profiles – extreme action teams comprised of fluid team members versus stable teams evolving over time – are still underrepresented;
(2) cause–effect relationships are still largely unspecified or unidirectional;
(3) evolutionary states within the change processes (i.e., using change to predict change) are still underutilized in empirical testing.

I explain each point in detail below.

To generalize our extant research findings, both fluid and stable team profiles need to be included in our investigation. For example, many interaction studies were based on a stable team in which team boundary is clearly defined and fixed. However, work teams nowadays can be transitory and ephemeral, such as when their members come together just for a few minutes and then disband, or when they are operating in a multiteam system where "two or more teams that interface directly and interdependently in response to environmental contingencies toward the accomplishment of collective goals" (Mathieu, Marks, & Zaccaro, 2001, p. 290). Or, team members may enter or exit team interactions at different time points. Addressing the fluidness or stableness of team profiles may open up new research avenues. Doing so, a priori knowledge of a fluid team profile should be considered in both interaction coding and statistical modeling (e.g., membership as control variables or moderators, depending on research question).

Regarding cause-effect relationships, researchers should make efforts in this direction by first proposing well-thought-out theorizing that specifies the causal links and feedback loops that are central to team interaction dynamics. A framework of system dynamics (cf. Sterman, 1989) may help in this capacity as it highlights temporal dependence under conditions of feedback. This theorizing is important as it will guide researchers' study design, coding themes, and analytical procedures. For example, a longitudinal and dynamic design, with particular attention to recursive relationships and feedback loops, may be a first step forward. Because reciprocal models filled with feedback loops are extremely challenging to test in real time, I also suggest simulated studies as a feasible means in this direction (Waller, Lei, & Pratten, 2014). Moreover, meta-analytic reviews also provide a quantitative foundation for some of the most forceful conclusions and recommendations.

Research using change to predict change or studying trajectories of both independent variables and dependent variables is rarely found in the team literature and empirical investigations. A lack of specification or misspecification of such changes in a predicting construct can be problematic. For example, group affective tone at one time point may help elevate team effectiveness, but such shared affective tone may change at a later time, which has no effect on team outcomes. Failure to recognize this can lead to some misleading or wrong conclusions. I thus encourage scholars to take this changing nature of evolutionary states into consideration in both research design and hypothesis testing. Recent advances in data modeling such as multilevel structural equation modeling, Random Coefficient Modeling (Bliese & Ployhart, 2002), and Hierarchical Linear Modeling (HLM, Raudenbush & Bryk, 2002) can help test hypotheses on the relationships between the changes of emergent states and process changes on multiple levels of analysis over time. Team interaction data are multilevel, multiwave by nature and present exciting research opportunities in this direction.

Second, move beyond the structural perspective and explore the relational, psychological, or even biological mechanisms that undergird the effective interaction process. For example, affective components of team interactions – such as laughter, voice pitch, and intensity (see Burgoon & Dunbar, this volume, Chapter 6) – can be captured and integrated in the research questions and statistical modeling to add an additional layer of various paralingual and structural aspects of team interactions. Future research might also explore alternative models of interrelating in teams that are less instrumental for understanding something as basic and human as the dynamics of collaboration at work. For example, recent work in organizational compassion and positivity models points to how human beings' biological systems are exquisitely designed to detect and respond to one another's changes in moods without cognitive mediation or calculation of what is given or received in interaction (Dutton, Workman, & Hardin, 2014; Fredrickson, 2013). Although these examples may appear remotely related on surface, the general point is that we need richer accounts of the relational and psychological mechanisms underlying team member interactions. Doing so, observing, coding, and analyzing team interactions may become more precise, rigorous, and complete.

Third, better understand boundary conditions for the effects of different interaction patterns on team processes and outcomes. Therefore, moderation relationships, rather than sequential or mediation effects, between microprocesses and team outcomes should be tested and modeled. For example, Lehmann-Willenbrock et al. (2017) found that speaker switches (i.e., speaking turns) can enhance the positive effects of suggesting a solution on subsequent positivity during team interactions. Future research can examine how a variety of organizational and team contextual variables (e.g., team climate, leader-member exchange relationships) affect team member exchanges and responses across different time points. For example, Lei et al. (2016) illustrated that different interaction pattern characteristics interact with varying workloads (i.e., routine vs. nonroutine situations) to affect team adaptiveness. Researchers can also synthesize knowledge from multiple industrial (e.g., efficiency-, safety- or innovation-driven industries) contexts so that we can understand variations in team interactions not just across individuals and work groups, but also across organizations, industries, and geographical locations.

Finally, employ a mixed-methods approach to capture the complexities of the phenomena of team interactions. To extend what has been discussed previously, here I focus on specific design issues – data collection and analysis tools. Specifically, qualitative data are data that were originally observed (e.g., author notes, log entries, videos) or orally communicated (e.g., in interviews) and subsequently transcribed into text and image-based form. Qualitative analysis techniques entail a set of processes for making sense of such data, which include (but are not limited to) deriving categories for sets of codes and themes and describing and interpreting the meaning, the relationships, patterns, or trajectories based on interpretive comparison of themes or events. In contrast, quantitative data are numeric representation of concepts, such as that based on survey scores, employee or manager ratings, or evaluations. Quantitative analysis techniques involve a set of processes for making sense of numeric data (e.g., descriptive statistics) and obtaining predictive statistics (e.g., correlation, regression, or structural equation model; network analysis). Given that different methods have different weaknesses and strengths, the triangulation between qualitative and quantitative methods offers the potential integration of the strength of any single method in a mixed methods approach (Edmondson & McManus, 2007; Gibson, 2017). Qualitative and quantitative methods are used simultaneously in a study in which qualitative data demonstrate or inform quantitative relationships. For example, Lehmann-Willenbrock et al. (2017) and Lei et al. (2016) attached the transcripts of member dialogue excerpts to illustrate their quantitative findings.

Moreover, mixed methods also involve considering multiple sources of data (i.e., where data have come from), including observation logs, employee ratings, and company reports (Gibson, 2017) to avoid what is often referred to as single-source bias (Campbell & Fiske, 1959). In addition, mixed qualitative and quantitative data can also be obtained from both field studies and laboratory research to ensure research richness and rigor. In sum, I do not advocate one method or data source over others but, rather, call for leveraging a mix of qualitative and quantitative data to develop new constructs in team interaction research and powerfully demonstrate the plausibility of new relationships (Edmondson & McManus, 2007; Gibson, 2017).

Research Frontiers

As our discussion above suggests, there are exciting conceptual and methodological opportunities and developments that offer team researchers some novel, interesting lenses through which they can examine the emergence of team interactions in groups and teams. Here I highlight some research technological and methodological tools that may give help to group researchers for understanding team interactions over time.

First, systematic methodologies to code behavior-based data and sophisticated statistical programs to analyze the resultant coding are leading interaction research into an exciting era. For example, as previously explained, lag sequential analysis (see Bakeman & Gottman, 1997; Kolbe et al., 2014; Quera, this volume, Chapter 15) or the THEME algorithm can be used to identify sequential patterns of coded interactions. In this direction, Waller and Kaplan (2016) provide insightful guidance for various methodological approaches to using video or audio recorded behavior as a source of quantitative data. While using video- or audio-based data is not new, subsequent statistical analyses such as conditional likelihood logit models, lag sequential analyses, the neural network approach, and software pattern recognition algorithm outlined by Waller and Kaplan (2016) help us consider innovative questions for future research. Another notable statistical technology is mixed-effects growth models (also known as random coefficient or hierarchical linear models, or RCM, Bliese & Ployhart, 2002) that can be used to understand change and transitions of team interactions over time. The core of RCM models is to describe temporal change as a slope (flat, increasing, or decreasing) that is calculated from the empirical Bayes slope estimates across at least three measurement times. The advantage to using empirical Bayes estimates is that values generated for a specific entity (e.g., an individual) are more precise (Bliese & Ployhart, 2002). As such, applying RCM in team interaction analysis can help demonstrate the trajectories of ever changing interaction behaviors over time or test hypotheses concerning ever changing, emergent states of team interactions; in fact, coded interaction data over time can be readily formatted for using RCM.

Second, in the blossoming field of technology advances and data computing, researchers from computer science and engineering, machine learning, biology, and psychology are collaborating to design and implement novel methods for measuring and modeling individuals' behaviors and interactions over time (Boos, Pritz, Lange, & Belz, 2014). In particular, Picard and her colleagues have developed wireless, unobtrusive sensors that measure activation of the sympathetic nervous system – a correlate of affective arousal or activation (Picard, Vyzas, & Healey, 2001; Poh, Swenson, & Picard, 2010; see also Rosen, Dietz, and Kazi, this volume, Chapter 8). Similarly, using web cams helps track and continuously monitor individual emotions and interaction utterance. In terms of generating more information, programs such as Linguistic Inquiry and Word Count[4] can help add content coding to behavioral observation coding (Pennebaker, Francis, & Booth, 2001). As another example, PRAAT, a free downloadable paralanguage system, analyzes features of speech such as pitch, intensity, and voice breaks.[5] These innovations in equipment and software

---

[4] LIWC; http://liwc.wpengine.com.   [5] www.fon.hum.uva.nl/praat/.

provide additional data at multiple time points that are often extremely difficult to obtain, complementing behavioral observations and allowing for some more sophisticated analyses.

Moreover, the promise of "big data" has yet to be applied to team research in general and interaction research in particular. Big data refers to large volumes of high-velocity, complex, and variable data that require advanced techniques and technologies to enable the capture, storage, distribution, management, and analysis of the information (Schneeweiss, 2014). Large-scale integration of "big data," coming from sensors, devices, video or audio, networks, log files, transactional applications, web, and social media – much of it generated in real time and on a very large scale (e.g., aviation records, images from patient scans, information from wearable and other monitoring devices) – can boost the generation of high-quality, rich evidence on team interactions that was previously inaccessible or unusable (Schneeweiss, 2014). Moreover, using advanced analytics techniques such as text analytics, machine learning, predictive analytics, and data mining, researchers can potentially uncover hidden patterns, perform more advanced analyses such as stochastic shocks, recursive and cyclical relationships, and path dependence, and gain new insights resulting in significantly more accurate predictions. Despite its overwhelming power and potential, the big data approach has some challenging limitations, such as how to ensure data quality, understand the data, and meaningfully make sense of the analytical results. Moreover, data integration presents a key operational challenge, as different sources of data – sensor information of team member movement and team meeting transcripts – often exist in silos in large organizations. That is, different sources of data may not be coded consistently or accessible across different functional departments, making data integration challenging or unfeasible. In order to benefit from these data, team scholars need to gain deep contextual knowledge and develop close working relationships with participating organizations. Although theoretical and practical knowledge on using big data is limited, its promise remains significant. Indeed, a priori coding themes developed by team scholars may serve as valuable resources for big data scientists because these themes shed light on the architecture and integration of big data. Together, team interaction research presents an exciting research area for all audiences beyond team scholars.

References

Arrow, H., McGrath, J. E., & Berdahl, J. L. (2000). *Small groups as complex systems: Formation, coordination, development, and adaptation.* Thousand Oaks, CA: Sage Publications.

Bakeman, R., & Gottman, J. M. (1997). *Observing interaction: An introduction to sequential analysis.* Cambridge, UK: Cambridge University Press.

Bliese, P. D., & Ployhart, R. E. (2002). Growth modeling using random coefficient models: Model building, testing, and illustrations. *Organizational Research Methods*, *5*, 362–387. doi:10.1177/109442802237116

Boos M., Pritz J., Lange S., & Belz, M. (2014). Leadership in moving human groups. PLoS *Computational Biology*, *10*(4), e1003541. doi:10.1371/journal.pcbi.1003541

Campbell, D. T., & Fiske, D. W. (1959). Convergent and discriminant validation by the multitrait-multimethod matrix. *Psychological Bulletin*, *56*(2), 81–105.

Collins, R. (2004). *Interaction ritual chains*. Princeton, NJ: Princeton University Press.

Corbin, J. M., & Strauss, A. (1990). Grounded theory research: Procedures, canons, and evaluative criteria. *Qualitative Sociology*, *13*(1), 3–21. doi:10.1007/BF00988593

Cramton, C. D. (2001). The mutual knowledge problem and its consequences in geographically dispersed teams, *Organization Science*, *12*, 346–371. doi.10.1287/orsc.12.3.346.10098

Cronin, M. A., Weingart, L. R., & Todorova, G. (2011). Dynamics in groups: Are we there yet? *The Academy of Management Annals*, *5*, 571–612. doi:10.1080/19416520.2011.590297

DeSanctis, G., & Poole, M. S. (1994). Capturing the complexity in advanced technology use: Adaptive structuration theory. *Organization science*, *5*(2), 121–147. doi:10.1287/orsc.5.2.121

Dutton, J., Workman, K., & Hardin, A. (2014). Compassion at Work. *Annual Review of Organizational Psychology and Organizational Behavior*, *1*, 277–304. doi:10.1146/annurev-orgpsych-031413-091221

Edmondson, A. C., & Lei, Z. (2014). Psychological safety: The history, renaissance, and future of an interpersonal construct. *Annual Review of Organizational Psychology and Organizational Behavior*, *1*, 23–43. doi:10.1146/annurev-orgpsych-031413-091305

Edmondson, A. C., & McManus, S. E. (2007). Methodological fit in management field research. *Academy of Management Review*, *32*(4), 1246–1264. doi:10.5465/amr.2007.26586086

Fredrickson, B. L. (2013). Positive emotions broaden and build. In P. Devine, & A. Plant (Eds.), *Advances in experimental social psychology*, Vol. 47 (pp. 1–54). San Diego, CA: Academic Press.

Gevers, J. M., van Eerde, W., & Roe, R. (2014). The relevance of time in organizations and organizational studies: Introduction to the special issue. *Gedrag & Organisatie*, *27* (1), 5–18.

Gibson, C. B. (2017). Elaboration, generalization, triangulation, and interpretation: On enhancing the value of mixed method research. *Organizational Research Methods*, *20*(2), 193–223. doi:10.1177/1094428116639133

Gibson, D. R. (2003). Participation shifts: Order and differentiation in group conversation. *Social Forces*, *81*, 1335–1381. doi:10.1353/sof.2003.0055

Gibson, D. R. (2005). Taking turns and talking ties: Network structure and conversational sequences. *American Journal of Sociology*, *110*, 1561–1597. doi:10.1086/428689

Hackman, J. (2002). *Leading teams: Setting the stage for great performances*. Boston, MA: Harvard Business School Press.

Katz, D., & Kahn, R. L. (1978). *The social psychology of organizations* (2nd edn.), New York, NY: Wiley.

Kauffeld, S., & Lehmann-Willenbrock, N. (2012). Meetings matter: Effects of team meetings on team and organizational success. *Small Group Research*, *43*(2), 130–158. doi:10.1177/1046496411429599

Kauffeld, S., & Meyers, R. A. (2009). Complaint and solution-oriented circles in work groups. *European Journal of Work and Organizational Psychology*, *18*, 267–294. doi:10.1080/13594320701693209

King, N. (1998). Template analysis. In C. Cassell & G. Symon (Eds.) *Qualitative methods and analysis in organizational research: A practical guide*. Thousand Oaks, CA: Sage Publications.

Kolbe, M., Burtscher, M., & Manser, T. (2013). Co-ACT – A framework for observing coordination behavior in acute care teams. *BMJ Quality & Safety*, *22*, 596–605. doi:10.1136/bmjqs-2012-001319

Kolbe, M., Grote, G., Waller, M. J., Wacker, J., Grande, B., Burtscher, M. & Spahn, D. R. (2014). Monitoring and talking to the room: Autochthonous coordination patterns in team interaction and performance. *Journal of Applied Psychology*, *99*, 1254–1267. doi:10.1037/a0037877

Kozlowski, S. W. (2015). Advancing research on team process dynamics. *Organizational Psychology Review*, *5*(4), 270–299. doi:10.1177/2041386614533586

Kozlowski, S. W. J., & Bell, B. S. (2008). Team learning, development, and adaptation. In V.I. Sessa & M. Lonson (Eds.), *Work group learning* (pp. 15–44). Mahwah, NJ: Lawrence Erlbaum Associates.

Kozlowski, S. W. J., & Klein, K. J. (2000). A multilevel approach to theory and research in organizations: Contextual, temporal, and emergent processes. In K. J. Klein & S. W. J. Kozlowski (Eds.), *Multilevel theory, research and methods in organizations: Foundations, extensions, and new directions* (pp. 3–90). San Francisco, CA: Jossey-Bass.

Lehmann-Willenbrock, N., Chiu, M. M., Lei, Z., & Kauffeld, S. (2017). Understanding positivity within dynamic team interactions. *Group & Organization Management*, *42*(1), 39–78. doi:10.1177/1059601116628720

Lehmann-Willenbrock, N., Meyers, R. A., Kauffeld, S., Neininger, A., & Henschel, A. (2011). Verbal interaction sequences and group mood: Exploring the role of planning communication. *Small Group Research*, *42*, 639–668. doi:10.1177/1046496411398397

Lei, Z., & Lehmann-Willenbrock, N. (2015). Affect in meetings: An interpersonal construct in dynamic interaction processes. In J. A. Allen, N. Lehmann-Willenbrock, & S. G. Rogelberg (Eds.), *The Cambridge handbook of meeting science* (pp. 456–482). New York, NY: Cambridge University Press.

Lei, Z., Waller, M. J., Hagen, J., & Kaplan, S. (2016). Team adaptiveness in dynamic contexts: Contextualizing the roles of interaction patterns and in-process planning. *Group & Organization Management*, *41*(4), 491–525. doi:10.1177/1059601115615246

Magnusson, M. S. (2016). Time and self-similar structure in behavior and interactions: From sequences to symmetry and fractals. In M. S. Magnusson et al. (Eds.), *Discovering Hidden Temporal Patterns in Behavior and Interaction: T-Pattern Detection and Analysis with THEME™*, 3–35. New York, NY: Springer.

Magnusson, M. S. (2017). Why search for hidden repeated temporal behavior patterns: T-pattern analysis with theme. *International Journal of Clinical Pharmacology & Pharmacotherapy*, *2*, 128. https://doi.org/10.15344/2017/2456-3501/128.

Mangold, P. (2010). INTERACT quick start manual V2. 4. www. mangold-international.com.

Marks, M. A., Mathieu, J. E., & Zaccaro, S. J. (2001). A temporally based framework and taxonomy of team processes. *Academy of Management Review*, *26*(3), 356–376. doi:10.5465/AMR.2001.4845785

Mathieu, J. E., Marks, M. A., & Zaccaro, S. J. (2001). Multi-team systems. In N. Anderson, D. Ones, H. K. Sinangil, & C. Viswesvaran (Eds.), *International handbook of work and organizational psychology* (pp. 289–313). London, UK: Sage.

Maznevski, M. L., & Chudoba, K. M. (2000). Bridging space over time: Global virtual team dynamics and effectiveness. *Organization Science*, *11*(5), 473–492. doi:10.1287/orsc.11.5.473.15200

McGrath, J. E., & Tschan, F. (2004). *Temporal matters in social psychology: Examining the role of time in the lives of groups and individuals*. Washington, DC: American Psychological Association.

Pennebaker, J. W., Francis, M. E., & Booth, R. J. (2001). *Linguistic inquiry and word count: LIWC 2001*. Mahwah, NJ: Lawrence Erlbaum Associates.

Perlow, L., Gittell, J. H., Katz, N. (2004). Contextualizing patterns of work group interaction: Toward a nested theory of structuration. *Organization Science*, *15* (5), 520–536. doi:10.1287/orsc.1040.0097

Picard, R. W., Vyzas, E., & Healey, J. (2001). Toward machine emotional intelligence: Analysis of affective physiological state. *IEEE Transactions on Pattern Analysis and Machine Intelligence*, *23*, 1175–1191. doi:10.1109/34.954607

Poh, M., Swenson, N. C., & Picard, R. W. (2010). A wearable sensor for unobtrusive, long-term assessment of electrodermal activity. *IEEE Transactions on Biomedical Engineering*, *57*, 1243–1252. doi:10.1109/TBME.2009.2038487

Raudenbush, S. W., & Bryk, A. S. (2002). *Hierarchical linear models: Applications and data analysis methods* (2nd edn.). Newbury Park, CA: Sage.

Ripley, R., & Snijders, T. A. B. (2009). *Manual for SIENA Version 4.0. Department of Statistics*, Nufield College, University of Oxford, UK.

Riethmüller, M., Fernandez C. E., Eberhardt, I., Timmermann, A., & Boos, M. (2012). Adaptive coordination development in student anaesthesia teams: a longitudinal study. *Ergonomics*, *55*(1), 55–68. doi:10.1080/00140139.2011.636455

Schneeweiss, S. (2014). Learning from big health care data. *New England Journal of Medicine*, *370*(23), 2161–2163. doi:10.1056/NEJMp1401111

Schulte, M., Cohen, N. A., & Klein, K. J. (2012). The coevolution of network ties and perceptions of team psychological safety. *Organization Science*, *23*(2), 564–581. doi:10.1287/orsc.1100.0582

Snijders, T. A. B. (2005). Models for longitudinal network data. In P. J. Carrington, J. Scott, S. Wasserman (Eds)., *Models in social network analysis* (pp. 215–247). Cambridge, UK: Cambridge University Press.

Snijders, T. A. B., Steglich, C. E. G., & Schweinberger, M. (2007). Modeling the co-evolution of networks and behavior. In van Montfort, K., Oud, H., Satorra, A. (Eds.), *Longitudinal models in the behavioral and related sciences* (pp. 41–71). Mahwah, NJ: Lawrence Erlbaum Associates.

Sparrowe, R. T., Liden, R. C., Wayne, S. J., & Kraimer, M. L. (2001). Social networks and the performance of individuals and groups. *Academy of Management Journal*, *44*, 316–325. doi:10.2307/3069458

Stachowski, A. A., Kaplan, S. A., & Waller, M. J. (2009). The benefits of flexible team interaction during crises. *Journal of Applied Psychology*, *94*(6), 1536–1543. doi:10.1037/a0016903

Sterman, J. D. (1989). Misperceptions of feedback in dynamic decision making. *Organizational Behavior and Human Decision Processes*, *43*, 301–335. doi:10.1016/0749-5978(89)90041-1

Stoolmiller, M., Eddy, J. M., & Reid, J. B. (2000). Detecting and describing preventive intervention effects in a universally school-based randomized trial targeting delinquent and violent behavior. *Journal of Consulting and Clinical Psychology*, *68*(2), 296–306.

Stout, R. J., Cannon-Bowers, J. A., Salas, E., & Milanovich, D. M. (1999). Planning, shared mental models, and coordinated performance: An empirical link is established. *Human Factors*, *41*(1), 61–71. doi:10.1518/001872099779577273

Tröster, C., A. Mehra, & D. van Knippenberg. (2014). Structuring for team success: the interactive effects of network structure and cultural diversity on team potency and performance. *Organizational Behavior and Human Decision Processes*, *124*, 245–255. doi:10.1016/j.obhdp.2014.04.003

Waller, M. J., & Kaplan, S. (2016). Systematic behavioral observation for emergent team phenomena: Key considerations for quantitative video-based approaches. *Organizational Research Methods*. Advance online publication. doi: 10.1177/1094428116647785

Waller, M. J., Lei, Z., & Pratten, R. (2014). Focusing on teams in crisis management education: An integration and simulation-based approach. *Academy of Management Learning & Education*, *13*, 208–221. doi:10.5465/amle.2012.0337

Wasserman, S., & Faust, K. (1994). *Social network analysis: Methods and applications*. Vol. 8. Cambridge, UK: Cambridge University Press.

Weingart, L. R. (2012). Studying dynamics within groups. In M. A. Neale & E. A. Mannix (Eds.), *Looking back, moving forward: A review of group and team-based research* (pp. 1–25). Bingley, UK: Emerald.

Zellmer-Bruhn, M., Waller, M. J., & Ancona, D. (2004). *The effect of temporal entrainment on the ability of teams to change their routines*. Oxford, UK: Elsevier Science Press.

Zijlstra, F. R. H., Waller, M. J., & Phillips, S. I. (2012). Setting the tone: Early interaction patterns in swift-starting teams as a predictor of effectiveness. *European Journal of Work and Organizational Psychology*, *21*, 749–777. doi:10.1080/1359432X.2012

6 Coding Nonverbal Behavior

Judee K. Burgoon and Norah E. Dunbar

Imagine a group of coworkers gathered around a conference room table in the workplace. It's a typical office meeting. They might be trying to solve a problem, design a new product, manage a crisis, hire a new employee, or decide who to lay off during a budget shortfall. It's the kind of situation that is repeated over and over again every day in conference rooms around the world. And, while the verbal content of the messages exchanged may seem to be the most telling aspect of the communication taking place, it is the nonverbal signals that may carry even greater import. It has been said that nearly two-thirds of the meaning in any human interaction are conveyed by nonverbal rather than verbal signals (Burgoon, 1985). Consequently, understanding group interaction requires understanding the rich implicit dialogue taking place in the nonverbal modalities.

Analyzing the nonverbal exchanges is made complex by the fact that the people gathered in the room might have different personalities, skills, and roles within the organization that all direct their behavior. The status of the various coworkers, their personal histories working together, and their history with the company can all affect the way they communicate during the meeting. These challenges notwithstanding, meetings are an excellent site for investigating all manner of research questions regarding group contexts because everyday interactions reveal a great deal about people's attitudes and relationships with one another. A researcher who wants to study gender bias in the workplace, for example, might examine the amount of participation offered by men and women in the meeting, the number of times each sex is interrupted, how dominant each participant appears, whether others in the meeting synchronize their behaviors with the leader depending on the leader's gender, how co-workers react to the suggestions made by males versus females, and many other possible cues to bias or acceptance.

Using the meeting scenario as an example, we will discuss what nonverbal cues are and how they are generally collected and coded by behavioral researchers; what choices researchers must make when collecting data depending on their research question; what sampling units are available when coding nonverbal cues for fine-grained analysis; and how the codes can be used to understand the patterns of cues observed and their interrelatedness in the total communication picture.

Structure, Function, and Meaning of Nonverbal Communication

The study of nonverbal communication involves examining all the parts of a message other than the language itself. It is often organized around what are variously called codes, channels, or modalities. These are the means by which messages are transmitted other than through words.

Nonverbal Codes

The seven most commonly recognized codes are listed in Table 6.1 along with definitions and examples of their use in groups (see Burgoon, Guerrero, & Floyd, 2010, for an in-depth review of all the codes).

Table 6.1 *Seven nonverbal communication codes*

Codes	Definition	Example
Kinesics	All forms of body movement, including head, face, eyes, torso, limbs, gestures, posture, and gait. What is typically thought of as "body language."	Eye contact and smiling toward other group members to signal approval.
Proxemics	Use, arrangement, and perception of space, including personal space around the body, distancing between people, and creation and management of territories.	Seating arrangement with leader at head of conference table or opposite most of the others.
Haptics	Use and perception of all the ways touch can be used as a message, such as hugging, grasping, poking, or patting.	Congratulatory arm around another group member's shoulders after winning an election.
Vocalics	All facets of the voice, other than words themselves, used as part of a message. Also called paralanguage or prosody.	High-pitched, rapid speech during a heated exchange.
Chronemics	Use and perception of time as a message system, such as urgency, punctuality, waiting time, lead time or multi-tasking.	Engaging in texting and doodling during a serious group discussion.
Physical appearance	Features of the body such as physical attractiveness, body features, adornment, clothing, hair styles, tattoos and even scent. Scent is sometimes called olfactics (see Haviland-Jones, Wilson & Freyberg, 2016).	Dressing in a uniform or formal attire to signify the formality of a meeting.
Environment and artifacts	Physical objects as conveyors of messages, including built space (e.g., lighting, temperature, texture, architecture, decorations) and personal artifacts such as one's automobile.	Award plaques on a conference room wall that are status reminders of the space's owner/occupant.

A researcher interested in studying the aforementioned conference room meeting of coworkers would first decide which codes are of interest and whether multiple codes should be examined simultaneously. If the question of interest is how dominance and status are played out in groups, for example, all of the nonverbal codes would be relevant – posture, eye contact, gestural animation, body orientation, seating arrangement, initiation of touch, vocal amplitude and pitch, arrival time, polychronic activity (doing multiple things at once), casual or formal attire, and presence of status symbols such as the latest smartphones and smartwatches might all be relevant to observe. In other cases, such as understanding how groups negotiate turn taking, only kinesics, proxemics, and vocalics might be of interest. Or environmental features might be examined for the ways in which they dictate or constrain communication.

Nonverbal Functions

While the emphasis on codes looks at particular nonverbal cues and examines them independently, a *functional approach* presumes that the codes work together to exchange messages relating to identities, emotional states, interpersonal relationship states (e.g., liking, trust), management of the conversational turn taking, persuasion, deception, or other meanings (Burgoon, Buller, & Woodall, 1996; Patterson, 1994). For example, an investigation of a team leader's dominance would be best served by incorporating several codes and cues, inasmuch as dominance is multifaceted and cannot be easily or adequately captured by one single code (Dunbar & Burgoon, 2005). Different researchers have generated different lists of functions that are typically of interest in nonverbal communication but, in reality, anytime a group of nonverbal cues comes together to form a recognizable pattern of behavior, then an examination of what function that pattern serves is potentially interesting. Several coding schemes intended to capture the various codes and functions can be found in Manusov's (2005) *Sourcebook of Nonverbal Measures*.

Taxonomies and their Moderators

Ideally, one could enumerate the lexicon of nonverbal behavior in the form of a dictionary, with each nonverbal behavior having a single, or limited, set of definitions. When one considers, however, the full gamut of unique nonverbal behaviors that could be catalogued – over 700,000 different body movements alone – the task becomes extremely daunting. In an effort to simplify the labeling of behaviors, various systems have been put forward to reduce the nearly infinite number of possibilities to small and manageable categories, such as the set of 50 to 60 kinemes – the building blocks of kinesics identified by Birdwhistell (1970), the catalogue of 1,000 postures used around the world (Hewes, 1957), or the features of the voice that can disambiguate discourse (Shriberg et al., 1998). In fact, several efforts have been made along those lines. For example, Bavelas and

Chovil (2000, 2006) and McNeill (1992) created taxonomies of gestural and facial displays. Jones (1994) did the same for touch. And, Poggi (2002) created a multimodal gestionary – an alphabet and lexicon of gaze, gestures, vocalizations, and touches that indicate a speaker's thoughts, goals, plans, and emotions.

Throughout these efforts, there has been strong recognition that no taxonomy is universal. Although emotional displays, touches, gaze patterns, and gestures may look alike, what is evident on the surface may be very misleading about what is being expressed. Thus, any coding system must be tailored to take into account key moderators that alter how the behaviors are performed and what they mean. The three most important moderators we will highlight here are culture, relationship, and gender.

Culture. Cultures may be classified as high or low frequency in the amount and complexion of their nonverbal expressivity (Kendon, 1981; Pika, Nicoladis, & Marentette, 2006). In our office meeting example, group members from Italy, France, and Israel will likely be far more gestural than those from England or the United States. But even more important, from the standpoint of behavioral coding, the gestures may look alike but have very different meanings, depending on where the speakers originate geographically, or they may look different but have the same meaning (Kendon, 1981; Morris, Collett, Marsh, & O'Shaughnessy, 1979). What is an "AOK" gesture (thumb and index finger making a circle with the other fingers extended) in the United States means "worthless" in Belgium. Additionally, nonverbal behaviors may follow different culturally defined display rules for when they can and should or should not be displayed and with what consequences (Ekman & Friesen, 1969). A Saudi Arabian, when questioned by another meeting attendee, may return the questioner's direct gaze, whereas a Japanese attendee may avoid direct gaze out of respect for the questioner. There may also be differences within each culture that make it difficult to generalize what one member of a culture will do in any given circumstance. It is therefore insufficient to just describe the form of nonverbal behaviors; one must know their functions and interpretations. This requires having some kind of knowledge not only of the structural characteristics of a behavior that cultural outsiders might observe (what linguists refer to as the etic approach) but also what the behavior means to cultural insiders (what linguists refer to as the emic approach; Harris, 1976). The key point here is that however the coding and ratings are conducted, they need to be tailored to the culture in which the observations are taking place. A coding system that is suited to interaction in Thailand may be inappropriate for Finland.

Relationship. More difficult in some ways than adapting behavioral coding for cultural differences is adapting it for relationship differences because there are many relationship features that could be taken into account, among them power, status equality, familiarity, liking, age similarity, trust, and group membership.

To illustrate, if our office meeting group has an acknowledged leader, some behaviors exhibited by that individual may be intended to reinforce one's role (what is called a status reminder). Leaders often engage in nonreciprocal touch, are the recipient rather than the sender of the most frequent gaze, sit across from most group members, are more relaxed than other group members, smile less than others, and use a deeper, faster, and more fluent voice than others (Burgoon & Dunbar, 2006). If one's purpose is to identify who is the leader of the group, these dominance behaviors would all be candidates for observation to validate or identify who is in a leadership role. However, if group members are relatively equal in status, then these behaviors might take on different meanings, such as the sender trying to persuade or intimidate the group. Postural mirroring of a powerful leader could signify deference, whereas mirroring of another in a more egalitarian group could signify liking and admiration. The lack of mirroring in a conflict-ridden group could signify disagreement, whereas the lack of mirroring in a newly formed group might merely signify that the members were unfamiliar with one another and had not yet settled into a group interaction style. And, the observed patterns would likely be moderated by gender, with women exhibiting a more affiliative demeanor than men (Canary & Dindia, 1998).

Fortunately, the nonverbal literature is replete with data on how different relational states can be signaled, thereby reducing the "degrees of freedom" in assigning function and meaning to behaviors (e.g., Burgoon et al., 2010; Hale, Burgoon, & Householder, 2005). In a group context, for instance, nodding by listeners (what is known as back-channel nodding) is usually taken as a sign of agreement with the speaker rather than a bid for a speaking turn. However, combinations of behaviors can assist in clarifying function and meaning. The head nod accompanied by audible inhalation and direct eye contact with the speaker is likely to be viewed as a request for the next speaking turn. Research on some of the behaviors like gaze avoidance that have multiple meanings can help sort out the potential meanings that could be assigned to a given behavior and what other accompanying behaviors might disambiguate the meaning (Kleinke, 1986). This is one reason why we advocate aggregating multiple behaviors into composite measures.

Gender. As with relationship differences, men and women also have some different nonverbal behavior patterns. A high-pitched voice by a woman might be regarded as normative whereas by a man might express excitement or hysteria. Touch to a woman's forearm by another woman might be seen as affection whereas the same touch by a man might be seen as an intimate overture or attempt to intimidate. Given differences in some men's and women's non-verbal behaviors, one solution to accommodate behavioral coding to this is to first identify what is normative for women versus men then measure individual behaviors according to their deviations from the gender norms. For example, if on average women have shorter speaking turns in groups than do men, it may be more informative to compute difference scores for the group members – how less often Woman A speaks than the average woman in the group or how more often Man B talks than the average of the men. This same strategy can also be used for relationship differences, although it is easiest when the variable has only two categories.

Coding Unit Decisions

We have already alluded to some of the decisions that must be made when developing a coding system, such as nonverbals that need to be captured and concerns such as camera angles and seating arrangements. Here we consider some of the central decisions in more detail.

Sampling Unit

Interaction data lend themselves to a variety of options regarding the sampling unit for data observation and analysis. The first decision is whether observations are going to be based on individual behaviors, adjacent pairs of behaviors that form what are called interacts, or patterns themselves. The most common approach is to measure individual behaviors then aggregate across individuals or groups. But an alternative would be to analyze pairs of individuals, with all possible pairings being studied, such as when identifying clique groups and the nonverbal tie signs that symbolize their membership in the clique. A third alternative – if one is studying multiple groups that differ on some variable of interest, such as comparing all-female and all-male groups on the amount of interruptions and overlapped speech – is to take the groups themselves as the unit of analysis. Of course, all three approaches can be combined. For example, Burgoon, Wilson, Hass, and Schuetzler (2015) conducted an experiment with three-person groups in which one person was naïve, one was deceptive, and one was suspicious. Using a split screen showing all three group members simultaneously, it was possible to record not only use of adaptor and illustrator gestures by each role but also instances of mirroring (showing identical simultaneous postures and behaviors) between pairs of people and overall degree of nonverbal involvement for groups as a whole.

Alternatively, the messages themselves can be selected as the unit of measure. This is usually operationalized as turns at talk – from the moment Speaker A begins solo speaking to when Speaker B begins solo speaking (with interruptions and overlapped speech assigned to the person who holds the floor). If Speaker A has twice as many speaking turns as Speaker B, then there will be twice as many data points from Speaker A as from Speaker B (which can be an argument for using individuals rather than messages as the unit of analysis because of the disproportionate representation it gives to more talkative speakers).

Temporal Units

The dynamic quality of group interaction also invites consideration of how to handle time. Should an interaction be divided into phases, topics, turns at talk, sentences, or phrases within speaking turns, or nonverbal events (which might occur frequently within a single speaking turn)? We have argued elsewhere that the size of a temporal unit should be small enough to detect meaningful changes and yet not so large that it glosses over important dynamics (Burgoon & Baesler, 1991). For example, if a speaker has been talking in a quiet voice and suddenly becomes very loud and belligerent, measurement at the turn level may miss this change. However, acoustic measurements at the level of 48,000 Hz (48,000 measurements per second) would be unnecessarily granular to detect changes in loudness and voice quality. The research question and behaviors of interest should dictate how large or small to make the time divisions. For example, in the Burgoon et al. (2015) experiment, analysis considered how much naïve members entrained to the deceiver's behavioral lead during each phase of the game. An analysis of group synchrony could examine junctures at which synchrony waxed and waned and who became the zeitgeber (time-giver) setting the tempo for the team nonverbal coordination.

Micro versus Macro Behaviors

A commonly encountered decision when performing nonverbal interaction coding is whether to measure a given behavior at a microscopic, midi-level or macroscopic level (Baesler & Burgoon, 1987). Microscopic behaviors are those that change rapidly and could be measured at a high rate of frequency, eye blinks being a good example. At the other end of the spectrum are behaviors that are relatively unchanging over a period of time, such as body posture, and so could be measured over a long time interval.

Highly granular measurement offers the advantage of high precision and is ideally suited to capturing the dynamics of nonverbal behavior (Bakeman & Gottman, 1997). But such measurement is also costly and often unnecessary to collect. Seating position (e.g., head of table) and body lean (e.g., forward) are two good examples of static behaviors that would not benefit from second-by-second measurement. It also may be too small to be meaningful. Midi-level (intermediate) observations are ones that more closely approximate the level of observation used by untrained raters (Boice & Monti, 1982). Matching measurement with the phenomenological experience of human communicators makes good sense. If an observer would not notice a stare until it had lasted more than three seconds, it would not be productive to ask observers to record eye behavior at the millisecond level. Finally, macroscopic measurements are more global judgments that cover longer time frames and/or constellations of behavior. Macroscopic measures offer the advantages of economy and parsimonious interpretation but are not easily decomposed into their constituent elements.

Table 6.2 *Recommended level of measurement for various nonverbal behaviors (from Burgoon & Baesler, 1991)*

	Macroscopic (molar) coding only	Microscopic (molecular) coding only	Leaning toward macroscopic	Leaning toward microscopic	Either acceptable/ mixed findings
Kinesic behaviors	Gestural animation			Nodding	Self- and object-adaptors duration or frequency
				Illustrator frequency	Smiling
				Emblem frequency	Gaze direction/ Facial orientation
Vocalic behaviors	Pitch variety	Tempo	Vocal rhythm	Silences (pauses, response latencies)	Tempo variety
	Vocal tension	Pitch Vocal intensity		Loudness	Fluency Vocal pleasantness Vocal warmth Resonance

In an analysis of macroscopic and microscopic measurement of 20 kinesic and vocalic behaviors, Burgoon and Baesler (1991, p. 77) identified which levels of measurement would achieve better reliability and validity for specific behaviors or behavioral composites. Their conclusions are summarized in Table 6.2. For some nonverbal behaviors, either fine-grained molecular or gross level molar measurement can be suitable, but in other cases, especially slow-changing signals or highly dynamic ones, one approach is superior to the other.

Objective versus Subjective Measurement

A major decision point closely related to the micro-macro decision is whether measures will be objective or subjective, inasmuch as objective measures are almost invariably measured at a more granular level and subjective ones, at a more global level (see Baesler & Burgoon, 1987, for a more detailed definition). Objective measures are those that Ekman (1982) referred to as descriptive sign vehicles. These are straightforward observables upon which there is usually high agreement (and therefore high reliability) on what they are. No inferences are needed. In our office meeting example, observers could easily record who sat where around a conference table, who spoke the most often, how frequently people gestured, and so on. Subjective measures, by contrast, require some mental synthesis of multiple indicators of an inferred state such as involvement or attempted provocation of conflict. In our office example, the degree of nonverbal pleasantness and harmony in a group could be based on untrained or trained judgments, depending on whether the naïve scientist or informed perspective is preferred.

How to address this issue from a behavioral observation standpoint? One option is to have observations based strictly on form and assign meanings on a post hoc basis. For example, coders might record how many times each group member gestures or what distances people sit from one another. This kind of objective coding has the virtues of being easy to train, easy to conduct, and easy to achieve high reliability among coders. But the meaningfulness of the behaviors is left to be resolved after the fact by participant self-reports, trained observers, cultural informants, or other subject matter experts. From the standpoint of capturing cultural nuances, this approach may lead to the mistaken assumption that surface similarities across cultures reflect the same "deep structure" meanings when in fact the behaviors may have different antecedents, different rules for when the behaviors are permissible or impermissible to display, and what the consequences are for their display. For example, an audible belch may be regarded as rude after a dinner meeting in the United States, Russia, or France, but expected as a show of appreciation for a fine meal in Turkey, Saudi Arabia, or India.

A second approach is to use more subjective coding, such as training coders to judge participants' levels of involvement, dominance, and such. For example, the Specific Affect Coding Scheme (SPAFF) requires coders to act as "cultural informants" to decode meaning behind the observed behavior (Coan & Gottman, 2007). These kinds of global judgments can then be correlated with more granular and objective observations.

Yet a third approach is to have participants review their own recorded interactions afterward and assign meanings using what is sometimes called retrospective verbalization (Ericsson & Simon, 1980) or "stimulated recall" (Bonito, Ruppel, DeCamp, & Garreaud de Mainvilliers, 2011; Waldron, 1997). In the latter case, group members watch a video-recording of a just-completed interaction and make periodic assessments of themselves, other group members, and the interaction itself. This means that the meanings of the behaviors can be judged by the participants themselves and not by third-party observers who might lack the context to understand the complexity of the behaviors being shown. This subjective approach tailors interpretation not only to culture but also to an individual's gender and personality. This approach has the benefit of refreshing participants' memory of what took place. Absent this "boost," providing ratings and commentary on several participants can be challenging and can be colored by halo effects and other perceptual biases. Pausing the recording at various junctures to ask questions also helps respondents overcome memory lapses.

Each approach has its own advantages and drawbacks. Objective coding is straightforward to define, easy to train, easy to conduct, and easy to achieve high reliability. Additionally, a variety of software packages are available to facilitate behavioral coding by humans, among them *CBAS* (version 2.0 available from Meservy, 2010), *Interact* (commercially available from Mangold[1]), and the *Observer* (commercially available from Noldus, 2013). Other tools are also available to remove the human coder altogether and conduct automated annotation and tracking. The sociometric badges used by Kim, McFee, Olguin Olguin, Waber, and Pentland (2012) are an example (see also Rosen, Dietz, and Kazi, this volume, Chapter 8). Sociometric badges use an accelerometer to record degree of movement, microphones to capture a variety of prosodic speech features, and GPS and Bluetooth to record spatial proximity. An entire corpus of sociometric badge and self-report data is available for analysis (Lepri et al., 2012). Other open-source and proprietary tools (that are beyond the scope of this chapter) such as Visage, Affectiva, and Intraface are available for capturing and tracking facial emotions and head positions.

As for subjective coding, because such measures require drawing inferences, and because observers' judgments will be influenced by their own idiosyncratic experiences, subjective judgments are most successful when judgments from multiple observers are pooled rather than rely on a single observer who may be biased or mistaken. Reliably assessing whether a group member is being domineering is better accomplished with multiple judges making ratings; the more raters, the higher the reliability. Additionally, coding at the functional level – such as recording the kinesic, vocal, and proxemic behaviors that comprise greetings and leave taking – save the researcher from determining how best to integrate and weight different codes and indicators.

Finally, combined methods such as retrospective video reviews by participants and trained observer judgments offer the richest assessment of group behavior but may introduce their own challenges when trying to triangulate conflicting conclusions.

Frequency versus Duration versus Rating Measures

A final decision point is whether to collect measurement as frequency counts, durations, or subjective ratings. Our experience has been that rather than select one approach, sometimes it is advisable to use two or three measurement strategies. A prime example is adaptor gestures – self-manipulations such as scratching, rubbing, or picking that are usually done in private and intended to alleviate psychological or physical discomfort. If a group member exhibits many hand-to-face touches, the average duration of each may be short. Conversely, if a group member engages in extended face rubbing, the duration measure will be high but the frequency count will be low. That is, the two measures will be inversely correlated. An investigator's research questions will dictate which measure is more likely to be meaningful. Finally, a rating of the individual's level of

---

[1] www.mangold-international.com.

discomfort may add useful information by clarifying whether the gesturer appears uneasy or merely bored. In a team setting, a behavior performed by one team member might be mirrored by others, so knowing which behaviors to capture and how to track them across time for all team members will be an important part of the decision-making process for the researcher.

Nonverbal Communication in a Group Context

Coding Unique Features of Groups

The study of nonverbal communication has overwhelmingly emphasized the study of individuals by examining the nonverbal cues of one particular actor or perhaps a pair of actors, but very little research has examined nonverbal behavior in groups, probably because of the complexity of doing so (see Heath, Sanchez Svensson, Hindmarsh, Luff, & vom Lehn, 2002; Kim et al., 2012; and Kolbe et al., 2014, for notable exceptions). In a typical dyadic study of nonverbal behavior, Afifi and Johnson (1999) recorded the publicly displayed haptic behaviors of friends and cross-sex dating partners. Trained coders recorded the different types of touches they saw from the dyads. They then interviewed the pairs in order to ascertain the functional meaning behind their touch displays. By measuring behavior for each person individually, Afifi and Johnson had the flexibility to test hypotheses at both the individual (such as comparing males and females) and the dyad level (such as comparing dating couples and friends). If such a study were conducted in a group conversation, it would become exponentially more complex with the addition of more people to the interaction.

One example of an early pioneer in the study of nonverbal group dynamics is LaFrance and Broadbent's (1976) study of postural mirroring as a sign of rapport in small group discussions. The researchers coded the posture of students in small seminars and then analyzed how often their posture mirrored that of the instructor in the class. In a more recent example, Koch, Baehne, Kruse, Zimmermann, and Zumbach (2010) investigated the role of gaze behavior in group discussions in revealing sex differences in egalitarianism. They created a method for establishing the visual dominance of the team members by examining the visual attention that a person pays to team members while speaking or listening. When coding each group member individually, it is easy to see how the amount of data that is gathered can proliferate, especially if many codes are examined or data are gathered over a period of time.

Another consideration in coding groups rather than dyads is to identify and record unique aspects of group interaction, such as individuals who are central, who are isolated, and who are parts of clique groups. In the office example, tracking who initiates turns at talk, who talks to whom and for how long can reveal those who are more dominant and influential in the organization versus those who are largely excluded from group interaction and may be apprehensive, detached, or disaffected. Coding the relational messages being exchanged may reinforce the conclusions drawn from the simple sociometry of talk.

Patterns of Group Behavior

An approach to make the coding more manageable is to code at the group or dyad level rather than aggregating the behaviors of individuals. An example of coding that is truly dyadic is synchrony coding. Synchrony refers to the behavioral coordination of two people in an interaction and is an indicator of influence, liking, or rapport. We conducted a study of interviews in which we trained coders to look for instances of synchrony during the interactions. Whenever coders saw what we defined as behaviors that mirrored or synchronized with one another, they made a notation of the type of synchrony according to our coding scheme (Dunbar, Jensen, Tower, & Burgoon, 2014). The same type of coding could be extended to the group level by having coders observe the behavior of a group as a whole rather than individuals within the group. For example, Kim et al. (2012) examined the mirroring and turn taking of different group members collected via sociometric badges. Although not a face-to-face setting, Boos, Pritz, Lange, and Belz (2014) examined how groups of ten players coordinated locomotion in the pathways and direction of avatars they moved on a game board to see if humans exhibited the same "swarming behavior" shown by nonhuman animals.

In addition to examining the synchrony and coordination of two or more speakers, nonverbal coding can also be used to examine the sequences of behaviors over time during an interaction. This demonstrates how behavior evolves over time and tracks what is occurring moment to moment. One illustration is the Kolbe et al. (2014) investigation of sequential nonverbal and verbal patterns in lower-performing and higher-performing anesthesia teams. The authors make the case for examining patterns rather than just frequencies of behaviors. Bakeman and Gottman (2009) explain the statistical analyses that are available, such as time-series analysis, which allows researchers to examine the ebb and flow of contingencies within interactions. Categorical coding systems, like those discussed here, are ideal for examining cycles of interactions within a group system. For example, in our meeting of coworkers, there might be a process in which the team leader asks a question and uses long pauses to encourage other group members to speak before jumping in and offering his or her own opinions. Categorical coding of events doesn't capture the cyclical nature of such an interaction but knowing the sequence of behaviors will demonstrate how the leader responds to challenges, when the leader decides to express himself or herself, and what the reaction is to the leader's expressions.

One commercially available software program that can be used to uncover such sequences and patterns of behavior in groups is Theme, developed by Magnusson (2005; Magnusson, Burgoon, & Casarrubea, 2016) to detect subtle but recurrent temporal patterns in a dataset. Theme can discover and analyze patterns in any data that are discrete events arranged in a temporal fashion. For example, in an analysis of a decision-making simulation during which some group members were deceptive, Burgoon, Wilson, Hass, and Schuetzler (2015) coded several different nonverbal behaviors across the course of six phases of the group discussion. Theme identified anywhere from a low of 48 to over 1,600 patterns among the nonverbal behaviors, with 373 unique patterns but 89% of all interaction behaviors falling into repeated patterns. The highly contingent nature of nonverbal behaviors in this investigation speaks to the importance of multimodal and longitudinal coding. Coding patterns of behavior is consistent with the functional approach to nonverbal communication because it examines the meaning of many nonverbal cues rather than examining behavior on a code-by-code basis. A single nonverbal cue rarely has particular meanings without taking into account the context in which it occurs or the other nonverbal cues that accompany it. For example, if our coworkers suspect that one member of the group is being deceptive, should they focus in on one particular code such as the face, voice, or gestures? Decades of research into deception detection, for example, has found that no one cue represents a "Pinocchio's nose" and so the structural approach examining particular codes or cues will be less successful than one that examines a host of nonverbal cues working together to give a pattern of deceptiveness (Vrij, 2008). This is likely true for other functions as well, but investigating one code at a time will not reveal the intricacies of communication nor the depth of meaning that is conveyed. Using the functional approach instead will allow for more close analysis of the various cues and how they work together to send messages.

Conclusion

Much of the communicative meaning exchanged in groups derives from nonverbal signals. Group members rely substantially on nonverbal behaviors to convey their identities, express their emotions, define the character of their interpersonal relationships, regulate the flow of conversation, and influence one another, among other communication functions. They do so by enlisting interconnected kinesic, vocalic, proxemic, haptic, appearance, chronemic, and artifact-based signals. Although capturing these implicit messages through behavioral observation and coding is challenging, particularly when the interchanges are occurring not just between pairs of people but groups of varying sizes, the challenges are not insurmountable.

A first and foremost consideration is the research question being investigated, which will dictate answers to many of the decision points a researcher faces. A good place to start is to characterize the communication context. What communication functions are at stake? How does the culture of the group members affect the communication expectations and processes? What are the relationships among group members – acquainted or strangers? Congenial or adversarial? Status equal or unequal? And, what role does gender play – is the group same- or mixed-sex and are there gender-linked roles in play? The variables of culture, relationship, and gender are especially likely to moderate what nonverbal behaviors will be observed.

A next step in decision making is what nonverbal codes and functions to measure. Some codes may be more salient than others and some more accessible to observation than others. Similarly, research questions centering on a communication function may widen or narrow the observational scope. Questions related to leadership and dominance behavior in a group, for instance, may implicate all seven nonverbal codes whereas research questions related to expressions of positive and negative affect may direct the researcher to coding only kinesic and vocalic behaviors. Choosing a functional approach, however, will typically entail multimodal observation.

Other coding decisions include (1) choosing the sampling unit as the individual, dyad, or group, (2) selecting what time scale to adopt that best approximates group members' phenomenological experience while being manageable for human coders, (3) designing coding templates that measure behaviors at a microscopic, midi-, or macroscopic level or a combination of these, (4) conducting objective recordings or subjective ratings, (5) whether to measure frequencies or durations or both, (6) whether to examine features that are unique to groups, such as the presence of clique groups, (7) whether to analyze sequences and patterns of behavior, and (8) whether to rely on manual coding or employ advanced software packages to augment or replace human coders.

These various decision points make plain that much forethought should go into planning investigations that will entail nonverbal coding. Although analysis of group communication through nonverbal behaviors is complex and time consuming, the yield in terms of the depth of understanding that can be achieved for the effort invested can be richly rewarding.

References

Afifi, W. A., & Johnson, M. L. (1999). The use and interpretation of tie signs in a public setting: Relationship and sex differences. *Journal of Social and Personal Relationships*, *16*(1), 9–38. doi:10.1177/0265407599161002

Baesler, E. J., & Burgoon, J. K. (1987). Measurement and reliability of nonverbal behavior and percepts. *Journal of Nonverbal Behavior*, *11*, 205–233. doi:10.1007/BF00987254

Bakeman, R., & Gottman, J. M. (2009). *Observing interaction: An introduction to sequential analysis* (2nd edn.). New York, NY: Cambridge University Press.

Bavelas, J. B., & Chovil, N. (2000). Visible acts of meaning: An integrated message model of language in face-to-face dialogue. *Journal of Language and Social Psychology*, *19*, 163–194. doi:10.1177/0261927X00019002001

Bavelas, J. B., & Chovil, N. (2006). Hand gestures and facial displays as part of language use in face-to-face dialogue. In V. Manusov & M. L. Patterson (Eds.), *The Sage handbook of nonverbal communication* (pp. 97–115). Thousand Oaks, CA: Sage.

Birdwhistell, R. (1970). *Kinesics and context: Essays on body motion communication.* Philadelphia, PA: University of Pennsylvania Press.

Boice, R., & Monti, P. M. (1982). Specification of nonverbal behaviors for clinical assessment. *Journal of Nonverbal Behavior, 7,* 79–94. doi:10.1007/BF00986870

Bonito, J. A., Ruppel, E. K., DeCamp, M. H., & Garreaud de Mainvilliers, I. (2011). Evaluating participation in small groups: Stimulated recall, self-ratings, and their effects on task-relevant judgments. *Communication Methods and Measures, 5,* 28–47. doi:10.1080/19312458.2010.527873

Boos, M., Pritz, J., Lange, S., & Belz, M. (2014). Leadership in moving human groups. *PLOS Computational Biology, 10*(4), e1003541. doi:10.1371/journal.pcbi.1003541

Burgoon, J. K. (1985). The relationship of verbal and nonverbal codes. In B. Dervin & M. J. Voight (Eds.), *Progress in communication sciences* (Vol. 6, pp. 263–298). Norwood, NJ: Ablex.

Burgoon, J. K., & Baesler, E. J. (1991). Choosing between micro and macro nonverbal measurement: Application to selected vocalic and kinesic indices. *Journal of Nonverbal Behavior, 15,* 57–78. doi:10.1007/BF00997767

Burgoon, J. K., Buller, D. B., & Woodall, W. G. (1996). *Nonverbal communication: The unspoken dialogue.* New York, NY: McGraw-Hill.

Burgoon, J. K., & Dunbar, N. E. (2006). Dominance, power and influence. In V. Manusov & M. Patterson (Eds.), *The SAGE handbook of nonverbal communication* (pp. 279–298). Thousand Oaks, CA: Sage.

Burgoon, J. K., Guerrero, L. K., & Floyd, K. (2010). *Nonverbal communication.* New York, NY: Routledge.

Burgoon, J. K., Wilson, D., Hass, M., & Schuetzler, R. (2015). Interactive deception in group decision-making: New insights from communication pattern analysis. In M. S. Magnusson, J. K. Burgoon, & M. Casarrubea (Eds.), *Discovering hidden temporal patterns in behavior and interaction: T-pattern detection and analysis with THEME.* New York, NY: Springer.

Canary, D., & Dindia, K. (Eds.) (1998). *Sex differences and similiarities in communication.* Mahwah, NJ: LEA.

Coan, J. A., & Gottman, J. M. (2007). The specific affect coding system (SPAFF). In J. A. Coan & J. A. Allen (Eds.), *Handbook of emotion elicitation and assessment* (pp. 267–285). Oxford, UK: Oxford University Press.

Dunbar, N. E., & Burgoon, J. K. (2005). Nonverbal measurement of dominance. In V. Manusov (Ed.), *The sourcebook of nonverbal measures: Going beyond words* (pp. 361–374). Hillsdale, NJ: Erlbaum.

Dunbar, N. E., Jensen, M. L., Tower, D. C., & Burgoon, J. K. (2014). Synchronization of nonverbal behaviors in detecting mediated and non-mediated deception. *Journal of Nonverbal Behavior, 38,* 355–376. doi:10.1007/s10919-014-0179-z

Ekman, P. (1982). Methods for measuring facial action. In K. R. Scherer & P. Ekman (Eds.), *Handbook of methods in nonverbal behavior research* (pp. 45–90). Cambridge, UK: Cambridge University.

Ekman, P., & Friesen, W. V. (1969). The repertoire of nonverbal behavior: Categories, origins, usage, and coding. *Semiotica, 1,* 49–98. doi:10.1515/semi.1969.1.1.49

Ericsson, K. A., & Simon, H. A. (1980). Verbal reports as data. *Psychological Review, 87*, 215–251. doi:10.1037/0033-295X.87.3.215

Hale, J. L., Burgoon, J. K., & Householder, B. (2005). Nonverbal measurement of relational communication. In V. Manusov (Ed.), *The sourcebook of nonverbal measures: Going beyond words* (pp. 127–139). Hillsdale, NJ: Erlbaum.

Harris, M. (1976). History and significance of the emic/etic distinction. *Annual Review of Anthropology, 5*, 329–350.

Haviland-Jones, J., Wilson, P. & Freyberg, R. (2016). Signs, signals, and symbols in olfactics. In Matsumoto, D., Hwang, H. C., & Frank, M. G. (Ed). *APA handbook of nonverbal communication* (pp. 363–385). Washington, DC: American Psychological Association.

Heath, C., Sanchez Svensson, M., Hindmarsh, J., Luff, P., & vom Lehn, D. (2002). Configuring awareness. *Computer Supported Cooperative Work, 11*, 317–347. doi:10.1023/A:1021247413718

Hewes, G. W. (1957). The anthropology of posture. *Scientific American, 196*, 123–132. doi:10.1038/scientificamerican0257-122

Jones, S. E. (1994). *The right touch: Understanding and using the language of physical contact.* Cresshill, NJ: Hampton Press.

Kendon, A. (1981). Geography of gesture. *Semiotica, 37*, 129–163.

Kim, T., McFee, E., Olguin Olguin, D., Waber, B., & Pentland, A. (2012). Sociometric badges: Using sensor technology to capture new forms of collaboration. *Journal of Organizational Behavior, 33*, 412–427. doi:10.1002/job.1776

Kleinke, C. L. (1986). Gaze and eye contact: a research review. *Psychological Bulletin, 100* (1), 78–100. doi:10.1037/0033-2909.100.1.78

Koch, S. C., Baehne, C. G., Kruse, L., Zimmermann, F., & Zumbach, J. (2010). Visual dominance and visual egalitarianism: Individual and group-level influences of sex and status in group interactions. *Journal of Nonverbal Behavior, 34*(3), 137–153. doi:10.1007/s10919-010-0088-8

Kolbe, M., Grote, G., Waller, M. J., Wacker, J., Grande, B., Burtscher, M., & Spahn, D. (2014). Monitoring and talking to the room: Autochthonous coordination patterns in team interaction and performance. *Journal of Applied Psychology, 99*, 1254–1267. doi:org/10.1037/a0037877

LaFrance, M., & Broadbent, M. (1976). Group rapport: Posture sharing as a nonverbal indicator. *Group & Organization Management, 1*(3), 328–333. doi:10.1177/105960117600100307

Lepri, B., Staiano, J., Rigato, G., Kalimeri, K., Finnerty, A., Pianesi, F., Sebe, N. & Pentland, A. (2012, September). The sociometric badges corpus: A multilevel behavioral dataset for social behavior in complex organizations. In *Privacy, Security, Risk and Trust (PASSAT), 2012 International Conference on and 2012 International Conference on Social Computing (SocialCom)* (pp. 623–628). IEEE.

Magnusson, M. S. (2005). Understanding social interaction: Discovering hidden structure with model and algorithms. In L. Anolli, S. Duncan Jr., M. S. Magnusson, & G. Riva (Eds.), *The hidden structure of interaction: From neurons to culture patterns* (pp. 3–22). Amsterdam, The Netherlands: IOS Press.

Magnusson, M., Burgoon, J. K., & Casarrubea, M. (Eds.) (2016). *Discovering hidden temporal patterns in behavior and interaction: T-pattern detection and analysis with THEME.* New York, NY: Springer.

Manusov, V. (2005) (Ed.). *The sourcebook of nonverbal measures: Going beyond words.* Hillsdale, NJ: Erlbaum.

McNeill, D. (1992). *Hand and mind.* Chicago, IL: University of Chicago Press.

Meservy, T. O. (2010). *CBAS 2.0.* University of Arizona, AZ: Center for Identification Technology Research.

Morris, D., Collett, P., Marsh, P., & O'Shaughnessy, M. (1979). *Gestures, their origins and distribution.* New York, NY: Stein & Day.

Noldus (2013). *The Observer.* Noldus Information Technology.

Patterson, M. L. (1994). Strategic functions of nonverbal exchange. In Daly, J. A. & Wiemann, J. M. (Eds.), *Strategic interpersonal communication* (pp. 273–293). Hillsdale, NJ: Lawrence Erlbaum Associates.

Pika, S., Nicoladis, E., & Marentette, P. F. (2006). A cross-cultural study on the use of gestures: Evidence for cross-linguistic transfer? *Bilingualism: Language and Cognition, 9,* 319–327. doi:10.1017/S1366728906002665

Poggi, I. (2002). Symbolic gestures: The case of the gestionary. *Gesture, 2,* 71–98. doi:10.1075/gest.2.1.05pog

Shriberg, E., Stolcke, A., Jurafsky, D., Coccaro, N., Meteer, M., Bates, R., . . . & Van Ess-Dykema, C. (1998). Can prosody aid in automatic classification of dialog acts in conversational speech? *Language and Speech, 41,* 439–487. doi:10.1177/002383099804100410

Vrij, A. (2008). *Detecting lies and deceit: Pitfalls and opportunities.* Chichester, UK: John Wiley & Sons.

Waldron, V. R. (1997). Toward a theory of interactive conversational planning. In J. O. Greene (Ed.), *Message production: Advances in communication theory* (pp. 195–220). Mahwah, NJ: Erlbaum.

7 Behavioral Coding in Animals

Joanna M. Setchell

Why We Study Animal Behavior

The study of animal behavior helps us to understand why animals behave as they do, to understand our own behavior, and to conserve or control other species (Lehner, 1998; Drickamer & Vessey, 2001). Animal behavior is also often integrated with other approaches, resulting in fields such as behavioral ecology, behavioral genetics, and behavioral endocrinology (Martin & Bateson, 1994). For example, my own work combines observations of mandrill behavior with demography, genetics, morphology, semiochemistry (the chemistry of communication), immune response, and parasite analysis (Setchell, 2016).

Animal interactions can be affiliative and cooperative, competitive and sexual (which may be cooperative or coercive). Interactions occur among females, among males, between the sexes, and across age classes. Animals interact with other members of their social group (if they are social) and with members of other social groups, as well as with other species. Interactions occur between close kin (e.g., mothers and infants), more distant kin (e.g., cousins), and with unrelated individuals. Variation in the nature, frequency, and intensity of interactions between individuals forms the basis of social relationships, which, in turn, result in the social structure of a society (Hinde, 1976; Kappeler & van Schaik, 2002).

Major research questions concerning animal interactions include the adaptive value of sociality, how social relationships are regulated and maintained, and who mates with whom. The adaptive value of sociality asks how social bonds influence individual survival and reproductive success (Silk, 2012). How social relationships are regulated and maintained includes the roles of affiliation and aggression, and how conflicts are resolved (Aureli, Fraser, Schaffner & Schino, 2012). Individuals compete over access to resources, and aggression can incur substantial costs to both participants. Who mates with whom includes both competition for access to mates (e.g., the relationship between dominance rank and reproductive success) and attraction (Darwin, 1871; Andersson, 1994; Setchell & Kappeler, 2003).

The majority of the approximately 450 living primate species are highly social, but social behavior is highly variable across species (Mitani, Call, Kappeler,

I am grateful to the editors for the invitation to contribute to this volume and for their highly constructive comments on the first draft of this chapter, and to Primatology@Durham for their very helpful comments.

Palombit, & Silk 2013). For example, galagos and orangutans are usually described as solitary, whereas baboons and macaques often live in large multimale, multifemale groups. As a result of this diversity, there is no single established protocol for describing primate interactions. Instead, the methods used depend on the specific research question under study.

Asking Questions about Animal Behavior

Nikolaas Tinbergen set out four questions that underpin the understanding of any animal behavior, including interactions (Tinbergen, 1963). Based on Aristotle's "Four Causes," these questions are the foundation of "ethology," or the scientific study of animal behavior. The questions combine the proximate causation versus the ultimate evolutionary explanations of a behavior on one axis, with the current utility versus historical origins of the behavior on the other (Table 7.1). Together, these distinct levels of enquiry allow a holistic understanding of a particular behavior. Table 7.1 illustrates this approach with one of the most frequently observed behaviors in many primate species, allo-grooming, in which one animal parts another animal's fur with one or both hands, picking at the skin and transferring particles to his mouth (Figure 7.1).

From Preliminary Observations to Hypotheses and Predictions

Studies of animal interactions follow *the scientific method* (Figure 7.2). The first step is to make *preliminary observations* (Figure 7.2, step 1) to familiarize yourself with the species, its behavior, and the environment. Spending time with animals gives you the raw material to develop a research question and helps to identify feasible methods. Reviewing the literature that reports previous research on the subject you are interested in will allow you to assess the current understanding of the question that you wish to address, identify important issues and what is not yet known, and understand and build on existing methods. Reading more generally about your study species will help you to determine whether it is a suitable choice to advance our knowledge of the question in hand. This will focus your attention onto a *research question* (Figure 7.2, step 2).

An example research question, based on a study of dominance hierarchies and secondary sexual coloration (red noses) in male mandrills (Setchell & Wickings, 2005), would be:

Question: What is the relationship between male-male interactions and secondary sexual coloration in male mandrills?

A thorough understanding of previous work, combined with your own preliminary observations, will allow you to formulate your *hypotheses* and make

Table 7.1 *Tinbergen's four questions (modified from Tinbergen, 1963), with examples for allo-grooming in primates*

	Current utility questions	Historical origins questions
Proximate (how?) questions	**Causation**	**Ontogeny**
	The mechanisms that underlie the behavior, or how it works	*The development of the behavior over the life course of an individual, including the roles of maturation and learning*
	Primates are motivated to groom because grooming is linked to reduction of stress hormone levels in the giver (Shutt, McLarnon, Heistermann, & Semple, 2007) and reduction of heart rate in the receiver (Aureli, Preston, & de Waal, 1999).	Grooming differs between sexes and varies with life history stage. In female-philopatric species, a female-bias in grooming is established during the first year of life (Simonds, 1974; Young, Coelho, & Bramblett, 1982; Saunders & Hausfater, 1988).
Ultimate (why?) questions	**Function**	**Evolution**
	The adaptive significance of the behavior, or how it increases the fitness of the animal	*The evolutionary history of the behavior, based on a phylogenetic comparative approach*
	Grooming serves a hygiene function (Akinyi et al., 2013) and sustains and regulates social relationships (e.g., Dunbar, 1988; Silk, Altmann, & Alberts, 2006).	Grooming occurs in many species, including insects, fish, birds, and mammals. The evolutionary transition from a hygienic purpose to a social purpose is likely to have co-occurred with the transition to living in large social groups (Dunbar, 1988, 2010).

predictions (Figure 7.2, step 3). Competing hypotheses that make different predictions will help to determine the best explanation for the patterns of behavior you observe.

In the study of animal behavior, a hypothesis is a tentative explanation for an observed phenomenon. For the example research question above, the hypothesis might be:

Hypothesis: Red coloration functions as a badge of status, signaling the dominance rank of the bearer, so that males don't need to fight to determine who is stronger.

From your hypothesis, you can derive predictions about what you will actually observe. These are often formulated as "if . . . then . . . " statements. For example, based on the hypothesis above:

Figure 7.1 *An adult female mandrill grooms an adult male at the Centre International de Recherches Médicales, Franceville, Gabon.*

Prediction 1: If red coloration functions as a badge of status, then red coloration should increase with dominance rank.

Prediction 2: If red coloration functions as a badge of status, then where one male is much more colorful than another, the less colored male should avoid escalation by showing submission in potentially aggressive interactions.

Prediction 3: If red coloration functions as a badge of status, then aggression should occur more often between males that are similar in color, and thus unable to determine encounter outcome on the basis of simple rules.

Predictions, if well formulated, tell you which animals you need to study and what you need to measure (*variables*) to test your hypothesis(es) as well as how to test them. Thinking this through in detail at this stage is very important, and it is very useful to consult with a statistician with a good understanding of animal behavior. A detailed consideration of the response variable of interest, the predictor variables, any control variables that, if not accounted for, might prevent you from observing the predicted effect, and potential interactions between variables is vital for the success of your study. In our example, the study subjects would be adult males. Key variables to measure would be male color and the occurrence of submission and aggression in male-male dyads.

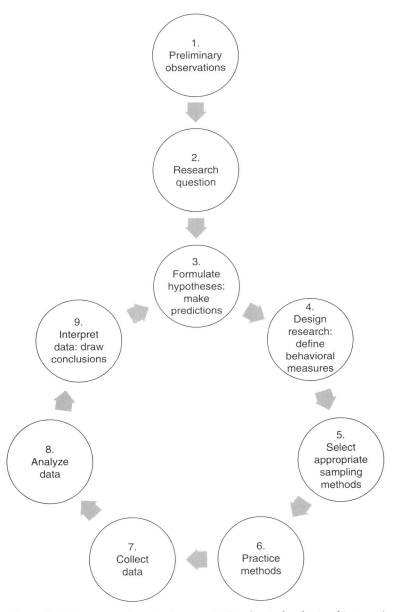

Figure 7.2 *The scientific method, as applied to the study of animal interactions.*

Designing Your Research and Defining Your Behavioral Measures

The next step in studying animal interactions is to design your research and define your behavioral measures (Figure 7.2, Step 4). In experimental research, the researcher manipulates variables of interest and holds others constant to test hypothesized causal relationships. In observational research, observers measure natural variation in the variables of interest, without manipulation. This can range from opportunistic observations to systematic observations that focus on one or a few specific variables (quasi-experiments; Janson, 2012).

When to Observe Animals

Behavior varies with season and through the day, so you need to ensure that each time period is equally represented (if possible) or that you do not generalize beyond the data you collect. The timing of observation sessions should be predetermined to avoid bias, except where your aim is specifically focused on what happens after a particular event. For example, you might use a play-back design, in which the researcher broadcasts a prerecorded sound from a hidden speaker or presents an object to animals, and records their reactions (Zuberbühler & Wittig, 2011). Some research questions employ a matched controls paradigm, in which behavior is measured directly following an event, such as a conflict, and compared with behavior during "control" observations. For example, matched control observations might be made at the same time on the next observation day, to control for diurnal and seasonal variation in behavior (Veenema, 2000).

Finding and Habituating Animals

Animals can be difficult to find and observe in the wild, and the presence of observers will alter the behavior of animals unused to being observed. For example, animals may flee from observers (Williamson & Feistner, 2011). Habituation, in which repeated neutral contacts eventually lead to animals ignoring the observer, facilitates observation, although observer presence may affect behavior even if study animals are well habituated (Williamson & Feistner, 2011). For example, the presence of human observers influences foraging in samango monkeys (*Cercopithecus mitis erythrarcus*; Nowak, le Roux, Richards, Scheijen, & Hill, 2014).

Ethics

Students of animal behavior should abide by the guidelines for the use of animals developed by their discipline, such as the *Animal Behavior Society* or the *Association for the Study of Animal Behaviour*. Field projects are subject to additional ethical considerations in relation to both the study animals and the local human communities that surround them (Fedigan, 2010; MacKinnon & Riley, 2010; Malone, Fuentes, & White, 2010; Curtis, Setchell, & Talebi, 2011). The *International Primatological Society* have formulated a code of best practices to highlight the ethical issues that should be considered when conducting field research in primatology (MacKinnon, Riley, Garber, Setchell, & Fernandez-Duque, 2014).

Defining Your Behavioral Measures

At first glance it may seem simple to describe animal behavior. However, as students learn quickly when asked to write down everything that happens in a group of primates, it is not easy to describe behavior in a systematic, replicable manner. To achieve this, we organize the continual stream of animal behavior into categories in an *ethogram*. An ethogram is a catalog of the behaviors shown by a species, with clear, concise, and unambiguous descriptions of each behavior. These should be clear to other observers. The precision varies with the specific study. For example, "foraging" may suffice to describe the act of searching for and ingesting food, but a fine-grained study of dietary ecology might split this behavior into many categories. If behaviors are to be used to determine time budgets (the percentage of time spent in each behavior), then they should be mutually exclusive and exhaustive, but otherwise behaviors may be simultaneous, as animals often perform more than one behavior at a time (e.g., approach with bared teeth).

Ethograms describe what the observer sees, in neutral terms, rather than attributing meaning or function to a behavior. Functional descriptions can be misleading unless they are based on careful analysis of the reaction to a behavior. Facial expressions can be a particular problem, for example. Physical similarities between animal and human expressions do not necessarily indicate functional similarity. For example, humans use a bared-teeth face, the smile, to indicate appeasement and reassurance, and to facilitate social bonding (Preuschoft & van Hooff, 1997). Other primates also use a bared-teeth face, but the function of this expression ranges from submission to affiliation, depending on the species (Preuschoft & van Hooff, 1997; Parr & Waller, 2006). Close examination of the context of a behavior can help to understand the function. For example, the mandrill's "grin,"[1] a facial expression in which the corners of the mouth are open wide but the middle is closed (Figure 7.3), has been described as aggressive (Jouventin, 1975). However, grins are usually bidirectional (both individuals grin in the majority of encounters), and occur far more often in approach or mild threat encounters than in severe agonistic encounters, suggesting that it is actually an appeasement behavior (Setchell & Wickings, 2005).

Table 7.2 gives an example of a partial ethogram for male mandrills, concentrating on agonistic behaviors (modified from Setchell & Wickings, 2005). Social behaviors are usually dyadic in nature, with an actor and a receiver. Recording a reaction results in a sequence, for example "A approached B who fled from A." For behavioral recording, behaviors are reduced to short codes (e.g., HB for Head-bob). It is essential to keep a record of these codes with the data, as they are easily forgotten, rendering raw data meaningless.

States and Events

Behaviors are divided into states and events (Altmann, 1974). A *state* is a behavior that occurs for an extended period of time, such as sitting, foraging, or sleeping, and

---

[1] A poor choice of term, as it implies function by analogy with humans.

Figure 7.3 *An adult male mandrill at the Centre International de Recherches Médicales, Franceville, Gabon, showing the "grin" face.*

is generally measured in terms of *duration* (the length of time that a single behavior lasts). *Events* are of short duration, such as a yawn, a vocalization, or a bite, and are generally measured as a number of events per unit of time (i.e., a *rate*). In Table 7.2, "stand-off" is a state, while the putative threats, chases, and contact aggression are all examples of events. Events may be repeated in bouts, in which case you need rules for what to measure (do you need to score each event, or just each bout? How do you define a bout, exactly?). Similarly, states may be interrupted briefly, then resumed and, again, you need rules for what constitutes a new session rather than an interrupted session. Other measures include the *total time* spent in a behavior during a given period, or the *proportion* of time spent in a behavior during a given period.

Identifying Individuals

Studies of social behavior often rely on individual identification. Animals often have distinguishing marks, such as broken tails, scars, or facial characteristics (e.g., "nose prints" in gorillas). In other cases, marking requires capture and restraint to apply dye, tags, collars, radiotransmitters, or other identification

Table 7.2 *Partial ethogram for male mandrills, concentrating on agonistic behaviors recorded in a study of dominance and signaling in males (modified from Setchell & Wickings, 2005)*

Behavior	Description
Putative facial and gestural threats	
Stare	Male looks fixedly at another male.
Head-bob	Male stares at another male and jerks his head down and forwards rapidly. Can be repeated.
Ground-slap	Male hits one or both hands on the ground in a fast movement, while staring at another male.
Threat grunt	A short bark directed towards another male.
Lunge	Male suddenly launches himself towards another male, but does not follow up with a chase.
Chases and contact aggression	
Chase	Male runs rapidly after another male.
Hit	Male brings his hand into contact with another male suddenly and forcefully.
Grab	Male grasps another male suddenly and roughly.
Fight	Reciprocal contact aggression. Males grapple with one another physically, usually face to face.
Submission	
Avoid	Male moves away at least 1 m in reaction to an approach or threat by another male.
Flee	Male runs away fast from another male.
Presentation	Male approaches another male and turns to place his rump in the other's line of vision. Can be accompanied by a crouch.
Scream	Sharp, sometimes repeated scream, with wide-open mouth and retracted lips. Directed visually at another animal.
Other	
Approach	Male moves to within 2 m of another male, passing him, or standing near him.
∞ face	Male's mouth retracted horizontally and vertically at the corners, but remains closed centrally, resulting in a '∞' shape.
Head-shake	Male shakes his head one or more times sideways in a '∞' motion.
Lip-smack	Male smacks his lips together audibly, and moves his tongue back and forward in and out of the mouth
Crest-raise	The crest of hair on the nape of the neck and top of the skull is vertically erected.
Stand-off	Two males stand side by side or at right angles to one another, generally within reach of one another, for several minutes. Males avoid one another's gaze, shift position frequently, and occasionally defecate. They also exhibit self-directed behavior, including scratching, body-shaking, auto-grooming, and grooming the ground. Males may also show other signs of extreme arousal, including raised nuchal crests, and the tail is directed forwards and laid flat along the spine. Males may also yawn, showing their canines, but direct yawns away from the other male. Stand-offs can include stares, head-bobs, or ground-slaps to the other male, to surrounding individuals, or at no obvious target. Stand-offs can also be associated with reciprocal contact aggression prior to, during, or following the stand-off.
Roar	One syllable, energetic, low, groaning sound emitted once or a few times.
Two-phase grunt	Two-syllable energetic, low, groaning sound. Continuous and regular.

methods, and therefore reflection on ethical considerations (Honess & MacDonald, 2013).

Selecting Appropriate Sampling Methods

It is simply not possible to observe and record all the behavior of all the animals in a group. As observers, we must, therefore, content ourselves with a partial record. To make this record representative, we must select appropriate sampling methods (Figure 7.2, Step 5). The choice of sampling methods depends on what you want to measure (Table 7.3). In other words, there is no simple protocol, but the methods depend on your predictions and the variables required to test your hypotheses. Altmann (1974) examines sampling alternatives and provides guidelines for choosing among them. Different texts split these choices up in different ways (Altmann, 1974; Martin & Bateson, 1994; Lehner, 1998). Here, I follow Martin and Bateson in differentiating between *sampling rules* and *recording rules*.

Table 7.3 *Combinations of sampling and recording rules and what they can be used to measure*

Sampling rule	Recording rule		
	Continuous	Instantaneous	One-zero
Ad libitum	No systematic data on frequency, duration, or sequence of behaviors. Useful for preliminary observations and developing your ethogram	N/A	N/A
Focal animal	Complete and accurate record of the frequency, duration, and sequence of all behaviors. Can underestimate duration	Proportion of time spent in particular behaviors, such as in proximity to other animals, basic activity budgets	Not usually useful
Behavior sampling	Frequency of particular behaviors. Can be biased towards highly visible animals. Useful for rare events such as fights and copulations	N/A	N/A
Scan sampling	N/A	Proportion of time spent in particular behaviors, such as basic activity budgets	N/A

Note: N/A indicates combinations that are not used

Sampling Rules

The first choice to make is which animals to watch, and when. Here, there are four choices: ad libitum sampling, focal sampling, all animal sampling, and scan sampling.

Ad libitum sampling involves making opportunistic notes of behavior. It is very useful for preliminary observations. However, it is not systematic and can easily lead to problems of bias towards more conspicuous individuals and behaviors.

Focal sampling involves observing one individual for a defined period of time. It can provide accurate data on the frequency and duration of the behaviors of an individual. Focal samples can also provide information about the animals that interact with the focal individual, although you may miss some if your focal subject does not react. Focal samples range in length from 10 mins (e.g., Silk, Altmann, & Alberts, 2006) to full days or occasionally multiday follows (Johnson, Raubenheimer, Rothman, Clarke & Swedell, 2013). You will need to balance the schedule of individuals observed carefully to ensure equal representation of individuals and across time, and to ensure that samples of the same individual are independent of one another (e.g., only one sample per individual per day). Animals often go out of sight during a focal sample, so you also need rules to address this systematically, for example by abandoning a sample if the animal disappears within a set time period of the start and noting the exact time an animal spends in view during a focal sample.

Behavior sampling (or all animal sampling) involves recording a few behaviors in a larger number of animals. For example, you might scan all animals for general activity or record all occurrences of fights. As with focal sampling, animals moving out of your view pose a problem, particularly where animals differ systematically in how often they do this. For example, subordinate males may be more likely to mate surreptitiously, while dominant males mate in full view of the group, biasing your observations of copulations towards dominant males.

Scan sampling involves recording the behavior of all individuals present by scanning the group rapidly. Ideally, this follows a predetermined order (e.g., left to right). Scan sampling is useful for obtaining simple data on general activity and spatial location. It can be biased by the relative visibility of individuals and behaviors (e.g., fights may capture your attention more than resting animals).

Recording Rules

The next decision is how to record behavior. The choice depends on a trade-off of information recorded vs. the number of subjects studied, and will depend on the variables you need to measure.

Continuous recording involves recording each occurrence of a behavior with the time at which it occurred for events, or the times of onset and end for states. It provides a complete and accurate record of the frequency, duration, and sequence of all behaviors. However, it can underestimate duration if a focal sample ends before a bout of behavior finishes (Martin & Bateson, 1994). It is suitable where animals can be observed easily. Continuous recording pairs well with focal animal sampling and students often confuse the two, although focal sampling can also be used with other recording rules.

The two alternatives to continuous recording, instantaneous recording and one-zero-recording, involve recording behavior at predetermined intervals. These intervals must be spaced over time if they are to provide independent data (e.g., two animals sitting in contact with one another at 0 min may well still be together at 1 min). The appropriate time interval requires careful consideration.

Instantaneous recording involves scoring behavior at a particular instant in time (on the "beep" when using an electronic timer). This is useful for states but not for events, as the point sample is unlikely to coincide with an event. It is commonly used to estimate the proportion of time spent in each activity (the time budget), but does not measure the true frequency or duration of behavior, unlike continuous recording. Instantaneous recording cannot be used to record sequences. It is particularly useful for recording an animal's spatial relationships and proximity to other animals, for example, the nearest neighbor(s) with the distance between them, the identity of animals in contact, within arm's reach (a potential danger zone!), or within a defined distance. Some authors refer to instantaneous recording as scan sampling, creating confusion between sampling and recording rules.

One-zero recording records whether a behavior occurs (score 1) or does not occur (score 0) in a specified time window (rather than at a time point, as in instantaneous recording). It is useful for collecting data on relatively few behaviors for a relatively large sample of subjects simultaneously. It does not yield frequencies of behavior. One-zero recording is limited in application as it often yields a biased estimate of duration and frequency. It is recommended only for very specific circumstances (Altmann, 1974), but may provide a useful index of behavior in some cases (Martin & Bateson, 1994).

You can combine sampling and recording rules in various ways, depending on the variables you need to record, but some combinations are not useful (Table 7.3). Lehner (1998, p. 192) provides a flow chart that also aids the selection of methods (but uses a slightly different scheme). You can also employ more than one combination of sampling rule and recording rule simultaneously. For example, 10-minute focal samples with continuous recording of social interactions might be combined with 1-minute instantaneous samples of proximity scans on the focal subject, ad libitum records of agonistic encounters in all visible animals, and group scans every 30 minutes for general activity and location. Your pilot study will tell you what is feasible.

You also need to record the date and time of observation sessions, along with other contextual information (e.g., habitat, weather).

Practicing Methods

The next step is to *practice your methods* in a pilot study and refine them until they are repeatable, consistent, and accurate (Figure 7.2, Step 6). Keep a good eye on your priorities – it is easy to concentrate on what is easy to do rather than on the data you need to address your hypotheses. Check that the data you are collecting will allow you to test your predictions by setting up your data analysis spreadsheet, entering your pilot data into it, and computing your summary variables to check for any gaps. It can be very easy to jump into data collection with enthusiasm, only to realize later that a crucial variable is missing from your analyses.

Traditionally, behavior is recorded using pen and paper, often with preprepared checksheets (Lehner, 1998, gives many examples) and a stopwatch. This requires a manual "timestamp" and is limited by the need to combine observing (often with binoculars) with writing and checking the time. Checksheets can be laborious to transcribe (e.g., Wilson, 2012), rot in the field, be eaten by animals, or end up at the bottom of a river (I have known all these to happen). Handheld electronic data collection devices with dedicated software packages for data collection and mobile or tablet applications (e.g., McDonald & Johnson, 2014) are fast, accurate, and efficient, and can export timestamped data directly to a computer for analysis. These data can be backed up, ideally to a remote server, but the hardware is expensive. Where animals move fast, you can use a voice recorder (e.g., Perry, Godoy, & Lammers, 2012). This has the advantage of an integral timestamp and removes the need to look at a checksheet but you will need to transcribe the records for analysis. Filming animal interactions gives a permanent record of behavior, but postpones the actual observation, more than doubling the time required for coding. It permits frame-by-frame analysis of fast and complex events. It is limited by filming conditions, and to the camera's field of view. It is useful in experimental conditions, where you want to record the behavior of multiple individuals simultaneously. You will need to record a running commentary, including the identities of the individuals entering and leaving the field of view. Equipment can (and will) fail under difficult field conditions. Finally, animals can record their own data using automated proximity loggers, similar to the "sociometric badges" used in human social interaction analyses. This involves attaching a device to the animal subjects using a collar, harness, or tag. The device records the frequency and duration of contacts with other devices, and, thus, other animals (e.g., Ji, White, & Clout, 2005). Studies using these devices require careful attention to variation in logging performance (Boyland, James, Mlynski, Madden, & Croft, 2013; Rosen, Dietz, & Kazi, this volume, Chapter 8), as well as to ethical considerations.

Data Collection

Once you are satisfied that your methods are appropriate and will allow you to test your predictions, collect the data (Figure 7.2, Step 7). Do not alter the methods after this stage, otherwise your data will not be comparable over time. Practice reduces observer error related to inexperience, but observer error can also include drift in methods over time and mental lapses. You can check for this by observing filmed behavior periodically and comparing the observations you record. You will also need to check inter-observer reliability by measuring the same behavior and checking for agreement (see Lehner, 1998; Martin & Bateson, 1994, for methods).

Analyzing Data

Once you have collected your behavioral data, you will need to summarize and analyze them to test your predictions (Figure 7.2, Step 8). Your predictions will guide this analysis and determine the exact statistical models required.

Interactions can be summarized in dyadic interaction matrices, in which each individual is listed along each axis. These matrices can be assessed on coverage, including the percentage of dyads in which no act occurred, the percentage in which only one animal in the dyad performed the action (one-way relationships), and the percentage in which both animals performed the action (two-way relationships) (van Hooff & Wensing, 1987). Tied relationships are those in which both animals perform the action the same number of times. For example, Table 7.4 shows a matrix of 55 dyadic male-male relationships, in which coverage is 100% (no dyads have no

Table 7.4 *Matrix of avoids and flees made by males in one group of mandrills at the Centre International de Recherches Médicales, Franceville, Gabon, in 1996–1997*

Actor	Recipient										
	2E	18	12E	12A1	5C	2C1	5E	2G	2F	5D1	12C1
2E	*	9	0	0	2	2	1	0	0	0	0
18	85	*	34	0	3	1	2	2	1	0	1
12E	67	49	*	7	8	2	0	1	2	0	0
12A1	11	12	10	*	7	0	0	1	0	1	0
5C	29	22	18	7	*	0	0	1	0	0	3
2C1	16	41	10	8	7	*	0	1	1	0	0
5E	31	35	29	4	15	20	*	5	0	0	0
2G	47	51	34	18	19	42	22	*	7	1	1
2F	42	52	47	12	23	30	34	25	*	1	0
5D1	20	12	38	3	23	13	23	37	40	*	7
12C1	15	17	14	1	2	10	3	14	27	37	*

Note: Males listed down the table avoided or fled from males listed across the table (Table 3 from Setchell & Wickings, 2005)

act), 25 dyads were one-way (45%), with all avoids and flees made by the same male, and 30 were two-way (55%). One relationship (5C/12A1) was tied, with five acts each.

The directional consistency index (DCI) of a matrix is calculated as the total number of times that a behavior occurred in the direction of higher frequency in a dyad (H) minus the total number of times it occurred in the direction of the lower frequency in a dyad (L), divided by the total number of times the behavior was performed by all individuals: $DCI = (H - L) / (H + L)$. This score varies from 0 (completely equal exchange) to 1 (complete unidirectionality) (van Hooff & Wensing, 1987). For example, the DCI for Table 7.4 is .85 (Setchell & Wickings, 2005), indicating high unidirectionality of submissive behavior in males in this group at this time.

Table 7.4 is a dominance matrix, a common example of a dyadic interaction matrix in which one axis lists winners and the other losers. These depend on unambiguous win/lose criteria. For example, if A approaches B and B avoids A, the avoid indicates a win for A and a loss for B. Similarly, if A threatened B and B fled, we could score a win for A and loss for B. However, if A were to threaten B, but B did not react, we can draw no conclusion about their relative ranks, as the interaction includes no submissive behavior.

Dominance matrices yield a rank order. In Table 7.4, male 2E is the most dominant and male 12C1 the most subordinate male. You can also calculate continuous variables to describe rank positions in more detail (e.g., Neumann, Duboscq, Dubuc, Ginting, Irwan, Agil, Widdig, & Engelhardt, 2011). Dominance hierarchies can be further characterized in terms of linearity and steepness. In a linear hierarchy the dominance relationships are transitive. In other words, if A dominates B and B dominates C, then A will also dominate C. Landau's index of linearity (h') orders animals into a dominance hierarchy by minimizing the number of inconsistencies and accounting for tied or unknown relationships (de Vries, 1995). A value of 1 indicates a completely linear hierarchy, while a value of 0 indicates that individuals each dominate an equal number of other animals. For example, h' is .88 for Table 7.4, indicating a highly, but not completely, linear hierarchy (Setchell & Wickings, 2005). You can use randomization procedures to test whether a hierarchy is more linear than expected due to chance given the number of individuals in the group (de Vries, 1995). Running this test for Table 7.4 shows that the linearity of the hierarchy is significant (Setchell & Wickings, 2005).

Other indices measure affiliative dyadic relationships. For example, Martin and Bateson (1994) provide a simple index of association, as $N_{ij}/(N_i+N_j+N_{ij})$ where N_{ij} is the number of occasions i and j are observed together, N_i is the number of times i is seen without j, and N_j is the number of times j is seen without i. A score of .5 indicates that the animals are seen apart as often as they are seen together. You can compare these scores across categories of dyad, for example to compare whether females associate more with one another than do males. Joan Silk and her collea-gues created a composite sociality index that combined grooming and proximity in dyads of baboons, adjusted for the frequency of each variable for all dyads in group x in year y (Silk, Alberts, & Altmann 2006; Silk, Altmann, & Alberts 2006). High values of the sociality index represent dyads that had stronger bonds than the average dyad in that group in that year, while low values represent dyads that had weaker bonds. Such analyses have been used, for example, in studies showing that individuals with stronger strong bonds have higher infant survival (Silk, Alberts, & Altmann, 2003), and that such bonds endure over time (e.g., Silk, Beehner, Bergman, Crockford, Engh, Moscovice, Wittig, Seyfarth, & Cheney, 2010).

Hinde and Atkinson (1970) proposed an index to measure the responsibility for maintaining spatial proximity in a dyad. It is calculated as $[A_i/(A_i+A_j)] - [L_i/(L_i+L_j)]$ where A_i is the number of approaches made by individual i to individual j, A_j is the number of approaches made by individual j to individual i, L_i is the number of times individual i moved away from (left) individual j, and L_j is the number of times individual j left individual i. Values range from -1 (animal j is entirely responsible for maintaining proximity) to $+1$ (animal i is entirely responsible for maintaining proximity).

Silk, Cheney, and Seyfarth (2013) review further methods for quantifying social relationships. For example, an index of grooming equality can be calculated as $1 - abs [(D_{ij} - D_{ji})/ D_{ij} + D_{ji})]$ where D_{ij} is the number of minutes per hour that animal i groomed j, and D_{ji} is the number of minutes that animal j groomed i (Silk, Alberts, & Altmann, 2006). The value of this grooming index equals 1 when grooming is evenly balanced within the dyad and 0 when grooming is completely one sided. This can be extended to measure the equality of any behavior.

Simple sequences can be used to examine responses to behaviors. For example, analysis of approaches and putative threat behaviors in male mandrills (Setchell & Wickings, 2005) showed that males showed no reaction to the majority of approaches, which also showed very low directional consistency, and a low degree of linearity. Males also often made no response to head-bobs, stares, ground-slaps, and threat-grunts (see Table 7.2). Head-bobs, stares, and ground-slaps had low directional consistency, but threat-grunts were more directional. Thus, although a naïve observer might assume we could assign ranks to males based on head-bobs given, this analysis shows that head-bobs are in fact largely uninformative as to dominance rank. Instead, we need to look at submission to determine dominance rank (Table 7.4).

The patterns of dyadic relationships discussed above scale up to relationships among all group members, or social structure (Hinde, 1976). These can be analyzed using social network analysis (Krause, Croft, & James, 2007; Croft, James, & Krause, 2008; Kurvers, Krause, Croft, Wilson, & Wolf 2014). As with dyadic analysis, social networks investigate the intensity, frequency, and directedness of affiliative, agonistic, and other interactions, and are constructed from matrix data. Networks put interactions into the context of the wider social context, describing who is connected to whom and in what way. They can be used to identify individual roles (e.g., Lusseau & Newman, 2004), sub-groups (Clark, 2011), and the transmission of information or disease (Hobaiter, Poisot, Zuberbuhler, Hoppitt, & Gruber,

2014; Rushmore, Caillaud, Matamba, Stumpf, Borgatti, & Altizer, 2013). They also permit virtual and empirical experiments to predict how removal of an individual might affect network structure (e.g., Flack, Girvan, de Waal, & Krakauer, 2006), and comparison across groups, populations, and species (Sueur, Jacobs, Amblard, Petit, & King, 2011).

Having summarized your data, you can use them to test the theoretical framework that you defined before making your observations. The precise details of the statistical analysis are beyond the scope of this chapter, but the advent of general linear mixed models (Bolker, Brooks, Clark, Geange, Poulsen, Stevens, & White, 2009) provides an important improvement to inferential tests of hypotheses in studies that include repeated measures on focal individuals, as well as other repeated measures, such as study groups (Janson, 2012).

Interpreting Your Data and Drawing Conclusions

Finally, having analyzed your data you can interpret your findings and draw conclusions about the hypotheses that you tested (Figure 7.2, Step 9). These conclusions, in turn, will lead you to generate new hypotheses, and to continue your study of animal interactions, taking you back to step 3 in the process (Figure 7.2).

Summary

The study of animal interactions requires considerable thought and a scientific approach. Studies often start with a broad question based on preliminary observations and existing knowledge, then focus on a specific hypothesis or set of hypotheses. Carefully formulated hypotheses and the predictions that arise from them determine the nature of the data you need to collect. Ethical considerations and pilot studies determine the practicality of data collection and help to refine the methods. This preliminary work, prior to data collection, is crucial, as poorly designed studies can be a sad waste of time and effort. In carefully designed studies, data collection followed by analysis allows you to test our hypotheses and draw conclusions about the behavior you wish to understand, and to propose new explanations.

References

Akinyi, M. Y., Tung, J., Jeneby, M., Patel, N. B., Altmann, J., & Alberts, S. C. (2013). Role of grooming in reducing tick load in wild baboons (*Papio cynocephalus*). *Animal Behavior*, *85*, 559–568. doi:10.1016/j.anbehav.2012.12.012

Altmann, J. (1974). Observational study of behavior: Sampling methods. *Behaviour*, *49*, 227–263.

Andersson, M. (1994). *Sexual selection*. Princeton, NJ: Princeton University Press.

Aureli, F., Fraser, O. N., Schaffner, C. M., & Schino, G. (2012). The regulation of social relationships. In J. C. Mitani, J. Call, P. M. Kappeler, R. A. Palombit, & J. B. Silk (Eds.), *Evolution of primate societies* (pp. 531–550). Chicago, IL: Chicago University Press.

Aureli, F., Preston, S. D., & Waal, F. d. (1999). Heart rate responses to social interactions in free-moving rhesus macaques (*Macaca mulatta*): A pilot study. *Journal of Comparative Psychology, 113*(1), 59–65.

Bolker, B. M., Brooks, M. E., Clark, C. J., Geange, S. W., Poulsen, J. R., Stevens, M. H., & White, J. S. (2009). Generalized linear mixed models: a practical guide for ecology and evolution. *Trends in Ecology & Evolution, 24*(3), 127–135. doi:10.1016/j.tree.2008.10.008

Boyland, N. K., James, R., Mlynski, D. T., Madden, J. R., & Croft, D. P. (2013). Spatial proximity loggers for recording animal social networks: consequences of inter-logger variation in performance. *Behavioral Ecology and Sociobiology, 67*(11), 1877–1890. doi:10.1007/s00265-013-1622-6

Clark, F. E. (2011). Space to choose: network analysis of social preferences in a captive chimpanzee community, and implications for management. *American Journal of Primatology, 73*(8), 748–757.

Croft, D. P., James, R., & Krause, J. (2008). *Exploring animal social networks*. Princeton, NJ: Princeton University Press.

Curtis, D. J., Setchell, J.M., & Talebi, M. (2011). Introduction. In J. M. Setchell & D. J. Curtis (Eds.), *Field and laboratory methods in primatology: A practical guide* (2nd edn., pp. 1–20). New York, NY: Cambridge University Press.

Darwin, C. (1871). *The descent of man and selection in relation to sex*. London, UK: John Murray.

de Vries, H. (1995). An improved test of linearity in dominance hierarchies containing unknown or tied relationships. *Animal Behavior, 50*, 1375–1389.

Drickamer, L. C., & Vessey, S. H. (2001). *Animal behavior: Mechanisms, ecology, evolution* (5th edn.). Dubuque, IA: McGraw-Hill Higher Education.

Dunbar, R. I. M. (1988). *Primate social systems*. Ithaca, NY: Comstock Press.

Dunbar, R. I. M. (2010). The social role of touch in humans and primates: Behavioural function and neurobiological mechanisms. *Neuroscience & Biobehavioral Reviews, 34*(2), 260–268. doi:10.1016/j.neubiorev.2008.07.001

Fedigan, L. M. (2010). Ethical issues faced by field primatologists: Asking the relevant questions. *American Journal of Primatology, 72*(9), 754–771. doi:10.1002/ajp.20814

Flack, J. C., Girvan, M., de Waal, F. M., & Krakauer, D. C. (2006). Policing stabilizes construction of social niches in primates. *Nature, 439*(7075), 426–429. doi:10.1038/nature04326

Hinde, R. A. (1976). Interactions, relationships and social structure. *Man, 11*, 1–17.

Hinde, R. A., & Atkinson, S. (1970). Assessing the roles of social partners in maintaining mutual proximity, as exemplified by mother-infant relations in rhesus monkeys. *Animal Behaviour, 18*, 169–176.

Hobaiter, C., Poisot, T., Zuberbühler, K., Hoppitt, W., & Gruber, T. (2014). Social network analysis shows direct evidence for social transmission of tool use in wild chimpanzees. *PLoS Biology, 12*(9), e1001960. https:doi.org/10.1371/journal.pbio.1001960

Honess, P. E., & MacDonald, D. W. (2013). Marking and radio-tracking primates. In J. M. Setchell & D. J. Curtis (Eds.), *Field and laboratory methods in primatology: A practical guide* (2nd edn., pp. 189–206). Cambridge, UK: Cambridge University Press.

van Hooff, J. M., & Wensing, J. B. (1987). Dominance and its behavioral measures in a captive wolf pack. In H. Frank & H. Frank (Eds.), *Man and wolf: Advances, issues, and problems in captive wolf research* (pp. 219–252). Dordrecht, The Netherlands: Dr W Junk Publishers.

Janson, C. (2012). Reconciling rigor and range: Observations, experiments, and quasi-experiments in field primatology. *International Journal of Primatology, 33* (3), 520–541. doi:10.1007/s10764-011-9550-7

Ji, W., White, P. L., & Clout, M. N. (2005). Contact rates between possums revealed by proximity data loggers. *Journal of Applied Ecology, 42*(3), 595–604. doi:10.1111/j.1365-2664.2005.01026.x

Johnson, C. A., Raubenheimer, D., Rothman, J. M., Clarke, D., & Swedell, L. (2013). 30 days in the life: Daily nutrient balancing in a wild chacma baboon. *Plos One, 8*(7), e70383. doi:10.1371/journal.pone.0070383

Jouventin, P. (1975). Les rôles des colorations du mandrill (*Mandrillus sphinx*). *Zeitschrift Für Tierpsychologie, 39, 455–462.*

Kappeler, P. M., & van Schaik, C. P. (2002). Evolution of primate social systems. *International Journal of Primatology, 23*(4), 707–740. doi:10.1023/A:1015520830318

Krause, J., Croft, D. P., & James, R. (2007). Social network theory in the behavioural sciences: Potential applications. *Behavioral Ecology and Sociobiology, 62*(1), 15–27. doi:10.1007/s00265-007-0445-8

Kurvers, R. M., Krause, J., Croft, D. P., Wilson, A. M., & Wolf, M. (2014). The evolutionary and ecological consequences of animal social networks: Emerging issues. *Trends in Ecology & Evolution, 29*(6), 326–335. doi:10.1016/j.tree.2014.04.002

Lehner, P. N. (1998). *Handbook of ethological methods* (2nd edn.). Cambridge, UK: Cambridge University Press.

Lusseau, D., & Newman, M. J. (2004). Identifying the role that animals play in their social networks. *Proceedings: Biological Sciences, 271,* S477–S481. doi:10.1098/rsbl.2004.0225

MacKinnon, K. C., Riley, E. P., Garber, P. A., Setchell, J. M., & Fernandez-Duque, E. (2014). *Code of best practices for field primatology.* www.internationalprimatologicalsociety.org/policy.cfm.

MacKinnon, K. C., & Riley, E. P. (2010). Field primatology of today: Current ethical issues. *American Journal of Primatology, 72*(9), 749–753. doi:10.1002/ajp.20836

Malone, N. M., Fuentes, A., & White, F. J. (2010). Ethics commentary: Subjects of knowledge and control in field primatology. *American Journal of Primatology, 72*(9), 779–784. doi:10.1002/ajp.20840

Martin, R. D., & Bateson, P. P. G. (1994). *Measuring behaviour: An introductory guide* (2nd edn.). Cambridge, UK: Cambridge University Press.

McDonald, M. M., & Johnson, S. (2014). 'There's an app for that': a new program for the collection of behavioural field data. *Animal Behaviour, 95,* 81–87. doi:10.1016/j.anbehav.2014.06.009

Mitani, J. C., Call, J., Kappeler, P. M., Palombit, R. A., & Silk, J. B. (Eds.) (2013). *The evolution of primate societies*. Chicago, IL: Chicago University Press.

Neumann, C., Duboscq, J., Dubuc, C., Ginting, A., Irwan, A. M., Agil, M., … Engelhardt, A. (2011). Assessing dominance hierarchies: Validation and advantages of progressive evaluation with Elo-rating. *Animal Behaviour, 82*(4), 911–921. doi:10.1016/j.anbehav.2011.07.016

Nowak, K., le Roux, A., Richards, S. A., Scheijen, C. J., & Hill, R. A. (2014). Human observers impact habituated samango monkeys' perceived landscape of fear. *Behavioral Ecology, 25*(5), 1199–1204. doi:10.1093/beheco/aru110

Parr, L. A., & Waller, B. M. (2006). Understanding chimpanzee facial expression: Insights into the evolution of communication. *Social Cognitive & Affective Neuroscience, 1*(3), 221–228. doi:10.1093/scan/nsl031

Perry, S., Godoy, I., & Lammers, W. (2012). The Lomas Barbudal Monkey Project: Two decades of research on *Cebus capucinus*. In P. M. Kappeler & D. P. Watts (Eds.), *Long-term field studies of primates* (pp. 141–163). Berlin, Germany: Springer.

Preuschoft, S., & van Hooff, J. (1997). The social function of "smile" and "laughter": Variations across primate species and societies. In U. Segerstrale & P. Mobias (Eds.), *Nonverbal communication: Where nature meets culture* (pp. 252–281). Mahwah, NJ: Erlbaum.

Rushmore, J., Caillaud, D., Matamba, L., Stumpf, R. M., Borgatti, S. P., & Altizer, S. (2013). Social network analysis of wild chimpanzees provides insights for predicting infectious disease risk. *Journal of Animal Ecology, 82*(5), 976–986. doi:10.1111/1365-2656.12088

Saunders, C. D., & Hausfater, G. (1988). The functional significance of baboon grooming behavior. *Annals of the New York Academy of Sciences, 525*, 430–432.

Setchell, J. M. (2016). Sexual selection and the differences between the sexes in mandrills (*Mandrillus sphinx*). *American Journal of Physical Anthropology, 159*(Suppl 61), S105–S129. doi:10.1002/ajpa.22904

Setchell, J. M., & Kappeler, P. M. (2003). Selection in relation to sex in primates. *Advances in the Study of Behavior, 33*, 87–173. doi:10.1016/S0065-3454(03)33003-7

Setchell, J. M., & Jean Wickings, E. (2005). Dominance, status signals and coloration in male mandrills (*Mandrillus sphinx*). *Ethology, 111*(1), 25–50. doi:10.1111/j.1439-0310.2004.01054.x

Shutt, K., MacLarnon, A., Heistermann, M., & Semple, S. (2007). Grooming in Barbary macaques: Better to give than to receive?. *Biology Letters, 3*(3), 231–233. doi:10.1098/rsbl.2007.0052

Silk, J., Cheney, D., & Seyfarth, R. (2013). A practical guide to the study of social relationships. *Evolutionary Anthropology, 22*(5), 213–225. doi:10.1002/evan.21367

Silk, J. B. (2012). The adaptive value of sociality. In J. C. Mitani, J. Call, P. M. Kappeler, R. A. Palombit, & J. B. Silk (Eds.), *Evolution of primate societies* (pp. 552–564). Chicago, IL: Chicago University Press.

Silk, J. B., Alberts, S. C., & Altmann, J. (2003). Social bonds of female baboons enhance infant survival. *Science, 302*, 1231–1234.

Silk, J. B., Alberts, S. C., & Altmann, J. (2006). Social relationships among adult female baboons (*Papio cynocephalus*) II. Variation in the quality and stability of social bonds. *Behavioral Ecology and Sociobiology, 61*(2), 197–204. doi:10.1007/s00265-006-0250-9

Silk, J. B., Altmann, J., & Alberts, S. C. (2006). Social relationships among adult female baboons (*Papio cynocephalus*) I. Variation in the strength of social bonds. *Behavioral Ecology and Sociobiology, 61*(2), 183–195. doi:10.1007/s00265-006-0249-2

Silk, J. B., Beehner, J. C., Bergman, T. J., Crockford, C., Engh, A. L., Moscovice, L. R., . . .Cheney, D. L. (2010). Female chacma baboons form strong, equitable, and enduring social bonds. *Behavioral Ecology and Sociobiology, 64* (11), 1733–1747. doi:10.1007/s00265-010-0986-0

Simonds, P. E. (1974). Sex differences in bonnet macaque networks and social structure. *Archives of Sexual Behavior, 3*(2), 151–166.

Sueur, C., Jacobs, A., Amblard, F., Petit, O., & King, A. J. (2011). How can social network analysis improve the study of primate behavior? *American Journal of Primatology, 73*(8), 703–719. doi:10.1002/ajp.20915

Tinbergen, N. (1963). On aims and methods in ethology. *Zeitschrift für Tierpsychologie, 20*, 410–433.

Veenema, H. (2000). Methodological progress in post-conflict research. In F. Aureli (Ed.), *Natural Conflict Resolution* (pp. 21–23). Berkeley, CA: University of California Press.

Williamson, E. A., & Feistner, A. T. C. (2011). Habituating primates: Processes, techniques, variables and ethics. In J. M. Setchell, & D. J. Curtis (Eds.), *Field and laboratory methods in primatology: A practical guide* (2nd edn., pp. 33–50). Cambridge, UK: Cambridge University Press.

Wilson, M. L. (2012). Long-term field studies of the chimpanzees of Gombe National Park, Tanzania. In P. M. Kappeler, & D. P. Watts (Eds.), *Long-term field studies of primates* (pp. 357–384). Berlin, Germany: Springer.

Young, G. H., Coelho, A. M., & Bramblett, C. A. (1982). The development of grooming, sociosexual behavior, play and aggression in captive baboons in their first two years. *Primates, 23*(4), 511–519. doi:10.1007/BF02373962

Zuberbühler, K., & Wittig, R. M. (2011). Field experiments with non-human primates: A tutorial. In J. M. Setchell & D. J. Curtis (Eds.), *Field and laboratory methods in primatology: A practical guide* (2nd edn., pp. 207–224). Cambridge, UK: Cambridge University Press.

8 Beyond Coding Interaction

New Horizons in Interaction Analysis

Michael A. Rosen, Aaron S. Dietz, and Sadaf Kazi

In this chapter, we attempt to synthesize what is known, broadly, about emerging methods of team interaction analysis. We focus on alternative and complementary methods to traditional interaction coding, survey, and observational rating. This review is not exhaustive, but integrative and representative of the increasingly wide range of possibilities in designing measurement systems for team or group research. We organize our review around three fundamental domains of interaction measurement – collections of knowledge and decisions that must be addressed when developing a team interaction measurement system. Specifically, we address the following three domains of interaction analysis: (1) the *conceptual domain* concerning the nature and attributes of the phenomenon of interest; (2) the *data acquisition and measurement method domain* concerning the processes of collecting data, and assigning numbers or categories to the object(s) of measurement; and (3) the *analysis domain* concerning approaches to testing relationships between measured phenomena. For each of these domains, we discuss the state of the science and recent advancements, key decisions to make when designing a measurement system, and common tradeoffs to consider. We conclude with a discussion of future directions in the measurement of team interaction.

Overview of the Domains of Team Interaction Measurement

In this section, we introduce three domains involved in designing measurement systems for team interaction. Throughout this chapter, we will use this framework to discuss linkages between the different types of decisions made while developing a measurement system.

First, the *conceptual domain* involves articulating a theoretical description of the phenomenon of interest. All measurement systems should be grounded in theory. Development of a team interaction measurement system should be driven by relevant theory or theories of teams, teamwork, team interaction, team process, and the like. Over the years and across disciplines, researchers have focused on diverse aspects of interaction, including the overall amount of information sharing

This work was partially supported by a grant from the National Aeronautics and Space Administration (NNX17AB55G, PI: M.A. Rosen).

(Mosier & Chidester, 1991), the content of what is communicated (Orlitzky & Hirokawa, 2001), the temporal dynamics or flow of interaction (Bowers, Jentsch, Salas, & Braun, 1998; Tschan, 2002), or the form or quality of communication (Smith-Jentsch, Cannon-Bowers, Tannenbaum, & Salas, 2008) among others. Different theories underlie the rationales for why these different aspects of inter-action should be important, and a first step in developing a measurement system is to choose theory to guide decisions on how to focus measurement. In this chapter, we will use the Input–Mediator/Process–Output framework to discuss the range of possibilities (Ilgen, Hollenbeck, Johnson, & Jundt, 2005).

Second, the *data acquisition and measurement method domain* involves deci-sions about the source of data, processes for capturing data, and methods for assigning values to observations. Typical data sources include team members or external observers, and methods include self-report surveys, observational rating forms, and communication or interaction coding. However, advancements in wearable and environmental sensors create new options for interaction measure-ment methods (Onnela, Waber, Pentland, Schnorf, & Lazer, 2014). In principle, these types of data collection methods may reduce respondent, observer, and coder burden, and enable large-scale data collection of team interaction in a variety of settings (Kozlowski, Chao, Chang, & Fernandez, 2015). As speech recognition and natural language processing methods mature, these platforms may even augment functional or speech coding as well (see also Bonito & Keyton, this volume, Chapter 19). However, each method introduces its own bias and will be more or less practical in any given study context.

Third, the *data analysis domain* includes an increasingly large, varied, and powerful set of approaches for testing relationships between different constructs (Kozlowski et al., 2015). In addition to traditional applications of the General Linear Model to test differences in group means or associations between variables, network analysis, sequential analysis, and nonlinear dynamical modeling are becoming more widely used in team interaction research.

Each of these three domains represents a unique knowledge base and set of techniques, methods, and tools for supporting decisions about what data should be collected, and how they should be collected and analyzed for a given context and purpose. The idealized movement through these domains is typically outlined as follows: (1) research questions are formulated from theory; (2) theory specifies the content of measurement, and measures are chosen or developed that best capture this content; and, (3) an analytic technique is chosen appropriate to the research question and data characteristics (e.g., type, distribution, and sample size). However, this is not always the case. Decisions made or actions taken within one domain have consequences for what can be done within the other domains. The context in which a measurement system is developed will place constraints on choices between data acquisition and measurement methods. For example, heeding the repeated call for more studies of teams "in the wild" (i.e., real teams performing actual work vs. contrived laboratory studies) means accepting limitations on data collection methods (e.g., observation may not be a feasible strategy if the work environment poses risks to observers, or observers pose risks within the work environment) and sampling (e.g., members of functioning teams within organizations are typically time constrained and repeated surveys may not be feasible). In the following sections we will discuss more of these tradeoffs and constraints for decisions within and across these three domains.

The Conceptual Domain: What Is the Nature of the Phenomena of Interest?

Navigating the conceptual domain requires articulating the content of measurement as well as specifications of levels of analysis and time. The following sections provide a summary of key conceptual issues in team interaction and their implications for measurement and analysis.

The Content of Measurement

Most fundamentally, an interaction measurement system must define the social unit of interest, be it a group, team, or other form of collective. Here, we consider work teams – two or more individuals who must interact interdependently and adaptively to achieve a shared goal (Salas, Dickinson, Converse, & Tannenbaum, 1992). Team members may perform specialized roles and possess different characteristics and capabilities. Interdependence exists between team members because, although some tasks can be accomplished as an individual, some sets of tasks require inputs from multiple team members or can only be performed by collaborating with other members. This interdependence is essential for work teams, as achieving the shared goal of the team is beyond any single member (Dietz, Pronovost, Benson, Mendez-Tellez, Dwyer, Wyskiel, & Rosen, 2014; Marks, Mathieu, & Zaccaro, 2001; see also Bonito & Staggs, this volume, Chapter 17).

After defining and bounding the social unit of interest, relevant theories can be drawn upon for measure development. The Input–Mediator/Process–Output framework is the dominant theory that helps organize how relatively stable team characteristics (i.e., inputs) are converted into outcomes through dynamic interactions between team members (Dietz et al., 2014; McGrath, 1964; Rosen, Dietz, Yang, Priebe, & Pronovost, 2015).

Levels of Analysis and Time

Team performance processes are multilevel and dynamic (Rosen, Schiebel, Salas, Wu, Silvestri, & King, 2012), which can complicate the measurement of team processes in two central ways. This first issue relates to whether team attributes are measured at the team or individual level of analysis. The measurement of global properties (e.g., the purpose of the team, the size of the team) occurs at the team level of analysis (Kozlowski & Klein, 2000). Interaction can also be measured at the team level. For example, network measures of the distribution of leadership functions across members within a team are common (D'Innocenzo, Mathieu, & Kukenberger, 2016). Frequently, measurement systems rely on the aggregation of individual scores to draw inferences about teamwork processes and emergent states (e.g., leadership, Schaubroeck, Lam, & Cha, 2007; cohesion, Gully, Devine, & Whitney, 1995; team workload, Funke, Knott, Salas, Pavlas, & Strang, 2012). The aggregation of individual-level properties, however, does not unequivocally translate into accurate representations of teamwork constructs. It is essential to motivate these constructs by teamwork theories, use suitable statistical methods of aggregation, and be cognizant about confounds while interpreting relationships (e.g., shared history, strong organizational culture, Tesluk, Mathieu, Zaccaro, & Marks, 1997; for aggregation of multiple levels of interaction analysis, see also Poole, this volume, Chapter 18).

The second challenge considers the temporal aspect of team performance measurement. A single sample of performance provides limited insight into a particular team. While repeated measurement is the ideal practice (both in terms of process measurement and capturing multiple episodes of a team's performance over time), more measurements increase the burden on participants in the case of survey research, or require additional labor costs for raters in the case of observation. Exciting developments in the areas of physiological measurement (e.g., Stevens, Gorman, Amazeen, Likens, & Galloway, 2013), interaction and activity detection (e.g., Rosen et al., 2015), and other novel approaches described later in this chapter and elsewhere (Mehl & Conner, 2012) have great promise for realizing a compromise between continuous measurement as a best practice and logistical considerations associated with data collection.

The Data Acquisition and Measurement Domain: How Are Numbers and Categories Assigned to a Phenomenon of Interest?

In this section, we provide an overview of two emerging categories of methods used to study teams and groups: physiology, and social interaction sensing and activity traces. Table 8.1 provides an overview of these approaches.

Physiology

There is a long tradition of using physiological measurement to understand and analyze interaction data. Seminal work by Levenson and Gottman (1983) investigated the extent to which physiological responses during husband-wife interactions explained marital satisfaction during a conversation. Four physiological systems were measured to investigate the physiological linkage among couples (i.e., whether elevated physiological indicators from one partner elicited synchronous physiological patterns in the other), including cardiovascular (heart rate), vascular (pulse transmission time), sweat glands (skin conductance level), and muscle

Table 8.1 *Overview of physiological, social sensing, and activity trace measurement methods for team and group research*

Measurement approach	Description	Example measures	Benefits and challenges
Physiology	• Capturing continuous measures of physiological dynamics of two or more people interacting in a social situation • Assessing overall levels of physiological activation or the relationship between team members' physiological dynamics over time • Measures of autonomic and central nervous systems are used	• The degree of physiological synchrony within a team using individual measures of electrodermal activity or cardiac functioning (Walker et al., 2013) • The degree of stability in patterns of brain activation across team members over time (Stevens et al., 2013) • The degree to which individual team members' physiology drives, or is driven by other team members' changes in physiology (Guastello & Peressini, 2017)	• Provides information about otherwise unobservable, internal responses of team members to social interaction • Captures dynamic phenomena at a high time resolution, allowing for the development and testing of more temporal theories of group interaction • Data collection and processing requires specialized skills and equipment • Currently there are few connections between interpersonal physiological dynamics and theories of groups or team performance
Social sensing and activity traces	• Use of wearable and environmental sensors to capture data related to social interaction • Application of algorithms to extract indicators of verbal and nonverbal behavior • Use of the byproducts of interaction captured through information systems used for collaboration (e.g., email, paging, electronic document repositories)	• Paralinguistic components of communication including voice quality, prosody, pitch, gesture, facial expressions, eye gaze and posture (Vinciarelli, Pantic, & Bourlard, 2009) • Patterns of interactions extracted from proximity sensors (Isella et al., 2011) or information systems (de Montjoye et al., 2014)	• Provides low-cost data collection in field settings • Does not require coders, raters, or responses from participants • Unknown error structure (reliability and bias) to many of the data collection methods • Data can be information rich, but difficult to interpret without contextual information

(somatic) activity. When couples discussed problems, these measures explained 60 percent of the variance in marital satisfaction. This research area has grown dramatically over the past decades to include a wide range of measures, study samples, and outcomes. Broadly, this area has been defined as the study of Interpersonal Autonomic Physiology (IAP): "the relationship between people's physiological dynamics, as indexed by continuous measures of the autonomic nervous system (ANS)" (Palumbo, Marraccini, Weyandt, Wilder-Smith, McGee, Liu, & Goodwin, 2017, p. 99). IAP uses measures of the sympathetic (i.e., the system associated with increased arousal and "fight" or "flight" responses) and parasympathetic (i.e., the system associated with decreasing arousal and promoting rest and repair) nervous systems captured during social interactions to provide information about the internal and covert responses of participants in that interaction. An advantage of employing this measurement strategy is to objectively capture information in real time, even fluctuations that occur over a matter of seconds. Physiological measurement also has the potential to investigate dynamic changes in teamwork without having to rely on overt ratings of behavior by external raters. Observational ratings rely on some level of subjective judgment. Physiological data can be captured more objectively, but the data can be more effortful to interpret. In addition to measures of the autonomic system, recent work in teams and group settings has expanded to include measures of central nervous system functioning.

Much of the literature employing physiological measures in team research centers on the idea of physiological synchrony. Physiological synchrony is broadly defined as interdependence, linkage, or association between the physiological dynamics of two or more people (Palumbo et al., 2017; Guastello & Peressini, 2017). This is related to the more general idea of temporal entrainment explored in team science (Harrison, Mohammed, McGrath, Florey, & Vanderstoep, 2003). Exploratory work by Elkins and colleagues (2009) examined the association between physiological synchrony and team performance in a simulated military task. Four-person teams were tasked with clearing a building of enemy combatants while correctly identifying noncombatants. The physiological synchrony of heart rate variability was explored relative to performance. Findings from their analysis revealed a positive relationship between the physiological synchrony of heart rate variability and team performance. Similarly, Walker and colleagues (2013) examined two-person teams managing a simulated chemical plant. During this process control task, electrocardiogram and impedance cardiogram data were collected to measure cardiovascular activity. They found that physiological synchrony predicted 10 percent of the variance in team performance outcomes. This effect is much smaller than that found by Levenson and Gottman (1983) investigating satisfaction in married couples. This is likely due to the nature of the outcomes studied. Walker and colleagues were investigating a task performance outcome, whereas Levenson and Gottman were investigating an interpersonal affective outcome (i.e., satisfaction with the relationship). Physiological responses are logically more directly tied to experiences of affective constructs, therefore a smaller effect on task performance outcomes is not surprising. However, the effect found by Walker and colleagues is in line with meta-analytic estimates of the overall effect of team process on task performance outcomes (Lepine, Piccolo, Jackson, Mathieu, & Saul, 2008). This suggests that physiological synchrony captures meaningful information about social interaction. However, it is not clear at the present time how physiological synchrony is causally related to social interaction and team outcomes or if it captures information about the team's performance that is unique or different from more traditional measures of interaction employing coding, observational rating, or survey methods.

Historically, much of the physiological synchrony research has focused on dyads, with little formal guidance on constructing measures of synchrony for larger groups or teams. Recently, Guastello and Peressini (2017) have proposed a framework and process for generating a group synchronization coefficient (S_E). Their approach builds from pairwise correlations between all possible dyads in the team and provides an index of overall synchronization for the team as well as indices for each member of the team. Specifically, Guastello and Peressini define metrics for identifying "drivers" (i.e., team members most responsible for moving the team's responses) and "empaths" (i.e., team members most moved by the team's responses). If an individual member of the team is a "driver," this means that, on average, other members of the team are synchronizing their physiological patterns to this driving team member. If an individual is an "empath," they are primarily synchronizing their physiological dynamics to other members of the team. In a small study of 11 three- to four-member teams completing emergency response simulations, peer ratings of contributions to the problem-solving process indicated that empaths were viewed more positively than the drivers (Guastello, Marra, Perna, Castro, Gomez, & Peressini, 2016). This exciting development allows for viewing IAP in larger group or team settings of up to 16 members in a multilevel manner (Guastello & Peressini, 2017).

Other researchers have examined patterns of brain activation among team members during task performance. Specifically, patterns of team member neurophysiological activation are measured by an electroencephalography (EEG) and represent the concurrent levels of team members' cognitive engagement across time (see Stevens, Galloway, & Berka, 2007; Stevens, Galloway, Wang, & Berka, 2012; Stevens, Gorman, Amazeen, Likens, & Galloway, 2013). These patterns were investigated in twelve-person US submarine teams during a submarine simulation that involved three tasks. First, teams conducted a briefing to review goals and discuss positional, meteorological, and other relevant information. Next, teams engaged in the scenario, which involved routine team processes related to navigating and providing updates on the team's position and responding to perturbations. Last, the simulation session ended with a team debriefing. A wireless EEG system was employed to assess the cognitive engagement of six of the team members. EEG-Engagement (EEG-E) is derived from an algorithm based on the placement of EEG electrodes to reflect high probabilities of cognitive engagement (i.e., cognitive processes involved with information retrieval, search, and attention allocation). Low and high EEG-E levels are compared to an individual's average EEG-E and whether or not the entire team was experiencing high or low EEG-E levels. Findings from a series of analyses revealed the organization of brainwave patterns varied as teams switched from briefing, scenario, and debriefing segments of the simulation and in response to task perturbations (Stevens et al., 2012; 2013). Further, overall entropy profiles of brainwave patterns were higher for expert teams compared to novice teams, though periods of cognitive reorganizations occurred less frequently for expert teams. These findings may suggest that expert teams are more flexible in terms of their cognitive processing than novice teams (Stevens et al., 2013).

The measurement of physiological systems to quantify teamwork and team performance holds great potential. Synchronies exhibited in cardiovascular and neurophysiological patterns between team members have been linked to cognitive mechanisms, expert novice differences, and performance outcomes as described above. However, results have not always replicated, and there is a need for continued refinement in theory and methods for physiological synchrony within team contexts (Palumbo et al., 2017). Much conceptual and empirical work remains to be done to truly capitalize on these technologies, but the benefits include: (1) access to otherwise unobservable internal responses to social interaction; (2) more nuanced, higher time resolution data about a team's interaction; and (3) as data acquisition, processing, storage, and analysis methods mature, low levels of burden on researchers and participants in research. These benefits, however, are not without tradeoffs. Funke et al. (2012) outlined conceptual and logistical challenges for using physiological measures in team research. For instance, physiological measures may interfere with ordinary behavior given that team members are "wired" to equipment that may restrict their movement. As mobile sensing technology evolves, this limitation will lessen. Establishing baseline levels of physiological activity also depends on individual differences of each team member and their current psychophysiological state at the time of data collection. Currently, the interpretation of meaning for physiological data in team settings remains challenging, as there are few direct linkages between established theories of team interaction and physiology. Resolving this challenge is a great opportunity to advance conceptual models of interaction.

In addition to these concerns, physiological measures currently seem better suited for smaller teams. The submarine simulation captured data from six members from a twelve-person team (Stevens et al., 2012). In the absence of other physiological data sources, usable data were only collected for two members of the four-person building-clearing teams (Walker et al., 2013). Last, it may be difficult to parse meaning from physiological signals in the absence of other measurement approaches. Whereas changes in physiological state can be interpreted in real time, it may be less clear why they are occurring or which team processes are engaged without other contextual information.

Social Interaction Sensing and Activity Traces

The recent and rapid development of a range of wearable and environmental sensors has created the opportunity to dramatically expand the team process measurement toolbox. In this section, we discuss two related approaches for capturing information about social interaction: social interaction sensing and activity traces.

First, social interaction sensing involves the use of sensor technologies to capture data streams related to team interaction and the application of algorithms to extract verbal and nonverbal behavior (Pentland & Heibeck, 2010). The types of sensor inputs to this process vary widely and include video and computer vision for capturing behavioral coordination and paralinguistic aspects of communication, proximity detecting systems for identifying co-location and team interaction (i.e., infrared, radio frequency identification, and GPS sensors), and microphones for extracting noncontent features of speech (e.g., volume, pitch, turn taking, prosody). Integrated wearable sensor packages (e.g., sociometric badges; Olguín Olguín, Waber, Kim, Mohan, Ara, & Pentland, 2009) combine these methods and are becoming more commonplace as is the use of smartphones as data collection devices (Miller, 2012). Unique examples making use of these technologies include:

- Image-based behavioral tracking methods drawing on video recordings of crowds to study the formation and evolution of small groups (Halberstadt, Jackson, Bilkey, Jong, Whitehouse, McNaughton, & Zollman, 2016) and the propagation of visual attention (Gallup, Hale, Sumpter, Garnier, Kacelnik, Krebs, & Couzin, 2012);
- The use of location detection systems to study patterns of coordination among staff members and their relationship to infection transmission in hospital settings (Isella, Romano, Barrat, Cattuto, Colizza, Van den Broeck, Gesualdo, Pandolfi, Rava, Rizzo, & Tozzi, 2011);
- Classifying team members' body language to indicate emotional state using video and machine learning (Behoora & Tucker, 2015).

For detailed reviews of these and other technologies and how they have been applied to interaction research, see Vinciarelli, Pantic, and Bourlard (2009); Miller (2012); Rosen et al. (2015); and Schmid Mast, Gatica-Perez, Frauendorfer, Nguyen, and Choudhury (2015), Schuller and Batliner (2013).

Second, activity traces involve measures developed from "information collected about team member interaction as a byproduct of task completion" (Rosen et al., 2015, p. 11). Modern work teams increasingly use technology to mediate their interactions. These teams generate a record of their interaction through the tools they use including email, paging, phone, electronic record, and document repository systems. Activity traces are not new, and have been employed in laboratory team studies for some time. For example, Cooke and colleagues employed an experimental paradigm using a push button to talk paradigm to track conversational flow (Gorman, Hessler, Amazeen, Cooke, & Shope, 2012). They used information from the communication device (who was selecting to talk to whom, and when) as a measure of important information about team interaction.

Both social interaction sensing and activity traces are exciting (and challenging) for similar reasons. They promise lower researcher and respondent burden and therefore are more scalable. These methods do not require the active response of research participants (i.e., no time spent completing surveys) or the ever present eye of well-trained observers or diligence of communication coders. These methods also provide higher time resolution data (near continuous capture of data in many cases), allowing for the development and testing of more dynamic theories of team interaction. Taken together, these would indicate that sensor measures enable larger field data collections in a manner allowing for testing more advanced theories of team interaction. However, there are several key challenges, mostly related to the novelty of these measurement methods. First, unlike traditional measurement methods, the error structure of these methods is not known. For example, Chaffin and colleagues (2017) performed a systematic evaluation of the basic psychometric properties of a wearable social sensing system, and highlighted the need for caution and rigor in establishing the reliability and validity of these new measurement methods. Second, these methods can be information rich (i.e., generate a large volume of data points), but context lean. Interpreting signals in sensor data without knowledge of what is happening (e.g., what task is the team performing, or what situational factors are present) can be challenging. In this way, interaction coding and social sensing data may complement one another. Interaction coding can add the contextual information necessary to better make use of social sensing data. For example, physiology or paralinguistic content derived from sensors can be better interpreted with an understanding of what group process behaviors were occurring at the time that pattern was detected. Third, there are issues with levels of abstraction in that there are not always clear methods for mapping the types of discrete behaviors captured in proximity detection or video data to higher level constructs. Fourth, when employed in work environments, sensors for tracking social interaction can be met with suspicion. There can be a lack of trust that the data will be kept confidential, or not used against participants in some way by the organization. This can most directly lead to a lack of participation in studies, or noncompliance with study procedures (e.g., not wearing sensors, or interfering with their functioning). While collection of social sensing data within a given study should occur under the protections of an Institutional Review Board and informed consent practices, many organizations are collecting these data about their staff for management purposes. There is currently a debate over the legal and ethical issues associated with "employee surveillance" that includes the types of social sensing and activity trace data discussed here (Wild, 2017).

The Analysis Domain: How Are Relationships Between Phenomena of Interest Tested?

Ultimately, team interaction is measured for a purpose – to answer some type of question. Decisions made in the conceptual domain to frame the question, along with decisions in the measurement domain to produce data, will shape the analysis. Here, we focus on three core approaches to analysis in team interaction using physiological or social sensing data: the General Linear Model (GLM), Network Analysis, and Nonlinear Dynamical Systems. Below, we describe each method briefly and provide examples of its application to physiological or social sensing data in team research.

General Linear Model (GLM)

Analytic approaches rooted in the GLM dominate much of the research in behavioral, cognitive, social, and organizational sciences and include a broad array of specific techniques including testing for differences in group means (e.g., using a t-test or ANOVA to test differences between teams in different experimental conditions) or the strength of a relationship between two or more variables. Hierarchical linear modeling (HLM) is a GLM method uniquely suited to the multilevel nature of teams as it provides a means to account for the nonindependence of observations of individuals nested within teams (Woltman, Feldstain, MacKay, & Rocchi, 2012). Relationships between variables can be modeled at individual, team, and other levels (e.g., cohorts, organizations, settings), including cross-level interactions (e.g., the effects of an individual on a team-level outcome). GLM methods have numerous advantages including their commonality (i.e., they are the de facto standard approach for many social sciences), maturity, and diversity of specific techniques. However, GLM methods do have weaknesses related to their ability to represent time at high resolutions, and their assumptions of independence of observations are violated when measures are taken at the individual level within team settings. As mentioned, HLM techniques address this last issue, but meeting sample size requirements for this method can be challenging.

A common application of GLM techniques in team research using physiological or social sensing applications is to first calculate measures of synchrony or physiological compliance using autocorrelation of physiological signals, then cross correlation between the physiological signals of team members. GLM methods are then used on these measures of synchrony to test differences between conditions, as a dependent variable for individual or team predictors, or as an independent variable to predict team outcomes using regression analyses. For example, in the Elkins and colleagues (2009) study discussed above, groups were created based on their performance in a room clearing task and simple t-tests used to test the hypothesis that physiological synchrony was related to team performance. Higher performing teams had higher levels of physiological synchrony.

Similarly, Moya-Albiol and colleagues (2013) used ANOVA procedures to investigate gender differences in the impact of successful and unsuccessful cooperation on individual physiological responses, and Fusaroli and colleagues (2016) used linear regression to demonstrate that physiological synchrony in heart rate within a team was predicted by patterns of speech and behavioral coordination.

Network Analysis

In contrast to GLM methods that assume independence of observations, network analysis methods directly model dependencies (or relations) between observations. These relational data are analyzed in terms of their structure (e.g., the density of connections, the centrality of individuals within a network), and the observed structure of a network can be statistically tested against distribution of possible network structures using methods of Exponential Random Graph Models (ERGMs; Robins, Snijders, Wang, Handcock, & Pattison, 2007). A recent advancement in network analysis methods that includes temporal information – Relational Event Networks (Butts, 2008) – has been proposed as a viable and productive approach to analyzing team interaction. Specifically, Leenders and colleagues (2016) articulate how team processes can be represented as relational events. Relational events refer to an "interaction initiated by one team member to one or more other team members at a particular point in time" (p. 97). In addition to capturing information about which team member initiates the interaction, towards which other member, and details about the content and function of the interaction, perhaps the greatest contribution of relational events is on the measurement of the *rate* of interactions. Capturing continuous data about how often particular team members initiate interactions towards which other members based on their prior interactions can be used to understand how interactions evolve over time and may be changed after important events. Sequential structure signatures (SSS) such as reciprocity, transitivity, and participation shift, for example, can then be used to study the specific patterns in which the interactions unfold. This approach holds great potential as an analytic framework capable of making use of the high temporal frequency data collected through social sensing systems.

While Relational Event Networks are relatively new, researchers more commonly use general network analysis techniques to characterize social interactions measured through social sensing and activity trace data. For example, Chancellor and colleagues (2017) provide a novel application of network methods and social sensing data to answer questions about the drivers of socialization in workplace settings. Specifically, they captured both self-report measures of with whom people socialized and behavioral data over a two-week period (i.e., sensors tracking physical proximity in the workplace). Using network methods to cluster self-report and social sensing data, they found that individuals formed groups based on similarity in wellbeing. Activity traces generated from cell phone and computer access logons to a Wi-Fi network were used to generate proxy measures of instrumental ties in student teams engaged in projects throughout a course. Network measures derived from patterns of co-location in university buildings were used to predict team outcomes (i.e., grades on course projects) above and beyond personality or task competency variables (de Montjoye, Stopczynski, Shmueli, Pentland, & Lehmann, 2014).

Systems Dynamics

Teams have long been viewed through the lens of complex, nonlinear systems (Arrow, McGrath, & Berdahl, 2000), but only recently are team interaction data being analyzed using systems dynamics methods. Systems dynamics includes a broad variety of methods for mathematically modeling complex phenomena (for general introductions see Guastello, 2013; Nowak & Vallacher, 1998). In teams research, recurrence analysis is one such tool that is increasingly being used. Recurrence analysis uncovers underlying structure in temporal aspects of variables, and can answer questions about whether nonlinear dynamic systems return to similar states at different points in their lifecycle. Knight, Kennedy, and McComb (2016) describe how recurrence analysis can be used to investigate longitudinal team dynamics. The progression of team dynamics through different states over time for each interaction episode can be captured through time-series data. Time-series data from each interaction episode can then be converted into a recurrence plot highlighting times at which the system returns to a previous state. Owing to the difficulty inherent in reaching high-level conclusions about the system from multiple recurrence plots, it is recommended that each plot be converted to standardized metrics. Metrics such as the rate of recurrence of particular states, determinism or predictability of the system, and entropy or the complexity of the deterministic structure of the system can be used to obtain a nuanced understanding of team dynamics. In this way, data from recurrence analysis can be used to study a variety of team dynamics variables such as emergence of team processes over time, the timing of transitions within teams, and their effect on important outcomes.

There have been several studies comparing linear and nonlinear approaches to generating measures of synchrony. Strang and colleagues (2014) evaluated linear and nonlinear methods of analyzing physiological and behavioral data within teams including postural sway and cardiac interbeat intervals (IBI). Specifically, they collected these measures within an experimental dyadic puzzle-solving task that required role differentiation. The linear method of cross-correlation (CC) and the nonlinear method of cross-recurrence quantification analysis (CRQA) were used to generate measures of synchrony. CRQA measures were more consistently related to team performance than CC. The authors suggest that whereas nonlinear measures are better for capturing coupling between members of teams with high degrees of role differentiation, linear methods are most effective at detecting true "phase locked" synchrony, but teams with role diversity may not exhibit such tightly coupled behavior. These teams may engage in complementary behaviors, and nonlinear methods may be more suited for detecting these more complex patterns of coordination. Guastello (2016) compared linear and nonlinear methods for generating measures of physiological synchrony in dyads performing a vigilance task. Both approaches could detect synchrony, but nonlinear methods exhibited a stronger relationship with team performance outcomes and psychological variables such as perceived workload and empathy.

Each of these methodological approaches may be more or less suitable to a given dataset and research questions, and they are often not mutually exclusive. For example, it is common currently for researchers to generate measures of social interaction using network or systems dynamics approaches and then test differences between experimental conditions or associations with team outcomes using GLM methods. This is an exciting time for methodologists as new technologies afford larger datasets, and increasingly accessible and affordable computational power enables processing using sophisticated approaches.

Future Directions

The foundations of team interaction measurement are firmly in place, but advances in the conceptual, measurement, and analytic domains continue to accelerate. Here, we discuss how three themes describe trends in this development: multilevel, multi–time scale, and multimethod measurement.

First, team interaction measurement practices will grow in their capacity to meaningfully capture information from different levels of analysis. Team interaction arises across individual, team, multiteam, and organizational levels. The team level is the focal level of interest, but important causal mechanisms often lie at levels above or below the primary unit of analysis of interest (Hackman, 2003; Kozlowski, 2015). Multilevel GLM analysis approaches have existed for some time, and multilevel network analysis approaches are maturing (Lazega & Snijders, 2015).

Second, team interaction measurement will progress in its ability to manage multiple time scales. Team interaction is clearly dynamic, unfolding over time. However, current interaction measurement approaches tend to rely on relatively low-temporal resolution measurements (Kozlowski, Chao, Grand, Braun, & Kuljanin, 2013). There have been frequent calls in the literature to focus on more micro time scales (e.g., Humphrey & Aime, 2014). Advancing temporality in team interaction measurement requires advancements in conceptual, measurement, and analytic domains. Currently, the capabilities of measurement methods (e.g., sensors and activity traces) are outpacing the application of sophisticated temporal analysis methods and clearly run in advance of robust temporal theorizing on team interaction. The technical infrastructure for high temporal resolution team interaction measurement exists, but the conceptual drivers behind decisions about the content of measurement and how to map measures to constructs are limited. This gap between measurement and analysis capabilities and theory can be closed by employing both bottom-up and top-down approaches. Bottom-up approaches involve exploratory work where patterns within and across different social sensing data streams predictive of other constructs of interest (e.g., group task or affective outcomes, functional codings of group process) are discovered. Outputs of this process should be subjected to prospective confirmatory research and theory building to determine which, if any, are generalizable and meaningful. The top-down approaches involve a more rigorous application of known psychometric test development processes to these novel data types. For example, when developing a survey, the item generation step involves creating a large set of potential test items based on theoretical definitions. This initial item pool is piloted and refined based on the statistical performance of items and scales. Specific patterns in social sensing system data could be generated in a way analogous to a test item pool (i.e., creating a large bank of potential indicators of constructs of interest) and refined through well-established psychometric practices and guidelines. Observational rating tools are often generated using a team task analysis, which could also be used to generate candidate patterns of social sensing data.

Third, team interaction measurement practices will continue to include multiple methods. All methods introduce bias and have unique constraints, benefits, and limitations. While this is commonly recognized, there is a gap in formalized frameworks for guiding the integration of multiple methods of measurement. For example, there is a need for integrating social sensing and activity trace methods with traditional task analysis to better understand how different patterns of sensor data may represent meaningful information about team interaction under different task conditions or team configurations.

Each of these themes of levels, time scales, and measurement methods provide exciting opportunities for researchers to progress the field. Applying and maturing the existing approaches will advance team interaction research as a truly multilevel integrative discipline (Cacioppo, Berston, Sheridan, & McClintock, 2000).

Concluding Remarks

There has never been a more exciting time to be a teams or groups researcher. The practical need for knowledge on teams and groups is more salient than ever. New technologies and data analysis capabilities open the door for new approaches not only to developing measurement systems, but to conceptualizing what team interaction is, and how to improve it.

References

Arrow, H., McGrath, J. E., & Berdahl, J. L. (2000). *Small groups as complex systems: Formation, coordination, development, and adaptation.* Thousand Oaks, CA: Sage Publications.

Behoora, I., & Tucker, C. S. (2015). Machine learning classification of design team members' body language patterns for real time emotional state detection. *Design Studies*, *39*, 100–127. http://dx.doi.org/10.1016/j.destud.2015.04.003

Bowers, C. A., Jentsch, F., Salas, E., & Braun, C. C. (1998). Analyzing communication sequences for team training needs assessment. *Human Factors*, *40*(4), 672–679. http://dx.doi.org/10.1518/001872098779649265

Butts, C. T. (2008). A relational event framework for social action. *Sociological Methodology*, *38*(1), 155–200. http://dx.doi.org/10.1111/j.1467-9531.2008.00203.x

Cacioppo, J. T., Berntson, G. G., Sheridan, J. F., & McClintock, M. K. (2000). Multilevel integrative analyses of human behavior: Social neuroscience and the complementing nature of social and biological approaches. *Psychological Bulletin*, *126*(6), 829–843. http://dx.doi.org/10.1037/0033-2909.126.6.829

Chaffin, D., Heidl, R., Hollenbeck, J. R., Howe, M., Yu, A., Voorhees, C., & Calantone, R. (2017). The promise and perils of wearable sensors in organizational research. *Organizational Research Methods*, *20*(1), 3–31. http://dx.doi.org/10.1177/1094428115617004

Chancellor, J., Layous, K., Margolis, S., & Lyubomirsky, S. (2017, March 30). Clustering by well-being in workplace social networks: Homophily and social contagion. *Emotion*. Advance online publication. http://dx.doi.org/10.1037/emo0000311

de Montjoye, Y. A., Stopczynski, A., Shmueli, E., Pentland, A., & Lehmann, S. (2014). The strength of the strongest ties in collaborative problem solving. *Scientific Reports*, *4*, 5277. http://dx.doi.org/10.1038/srep05277

Dietz, A. S., Pronovost, P. J., Benson, K. N., Mendez-Tellez, P. A., Dwyer, C., Wyskiel, R., & Rosen, M. A. (2014). A systematic review of behavioural marker systems in healthcare: What do we know about their attributes, validity and application? *BMJ Quality & Safety*, *23*, 1031–1039. http://dx.doi.org/10.1136/bmjqs-2013-002457

D'Innocenzo, L., Mathieu, J. E., & Kukenberger, M. R. (2016). A meta-analysis of different forms of shared leadership–team performance relations. *Journal of Management*, *42*(7), 1964–1991. https://doi.org/10.1177/0149206314525205

Elkins, A. N., Muth, E. R., Hoover, A. W., Walker, A. D., Carpenter, T. L., & Switzer, F. S. (2009). Physiological compliance and team performance. *Applied Ergonomics*, *40*(6), 997–1003. http://dx.doi.org/10.1016/j.apergo.2009.02.002

Funke, G. J., Knott, B. A., Salas, E., Pavlas, D., & Strang, A. J. (2012). Conceptualization and measurement of team workload: A critical need. *Human Factors*, *54*(1), 36–51. http://dx.doi.org/10.1177/0018720811427901

Fusaroli, R., Bjørndahl, J. S., Roepstorff, A., & Tylén, K. (2016). A heart for interaction: Shared physiological dynamics and behavioral coordination in a collective, creative construction task. *Journal of Experimental Psychology: Human Perception and Performance*, *42*(9), 1297–1310. http://dx.doi.org/10.1037/xhp0000207

Gallup, A. C., Hale, J. J., Sumpter, D. J., Garnier, S., Kacelnik, A., Krebs, J. R., & Couzin, I. D. (2012). Visual attention and the acquisition of information in human crowds. *Proceedings of the National Academy of Sciences*, *109*(19), 7245–7250. http://dx.doi.org/10.1073/pnas.1116141109

Gorman, J. C., Hessler, E. E., Amazeen, P. G., Cooke, N. J., & Shope, S. M. (2012). Dynamical analysis in real time: Detecting perturbations to team communication. *Ergonomics*, *55*(8), 825–839. http://dx.doi.org/10.1080/00140139.2012.679317

Guastello, S. J. (2013). *Chaos, catastrophe, and human affairs: Applications of nonlinear dynamics to work, organizations, and social evolution.* Mahwah, NJ: Lawrence Erlbaum Associates, Inc.

Guastello, S. J. (2016). Physiological synchronization in a vigilance dual task. *Nonlinear Dynamics, Psychology, and Life Sciences*, 20(1), 49–80.

Guastello, S. J., Marra, D. E., Perna, C., Castro, J., Gomez, M., & Peressini, A. F. (2016). Physiological synchronization in emergency response teams: Subjective workload, drivers and empaths. *Nonlinear Dynamics, Psychology, and Life Sciences*, 20(2), 223–270.

Guastello, S. J., & Peressini, A. F. (2017). Development of a synchronization coefficient for biosocial interactions in groups and teams. *Small Group Research*, 48(1), 3–33. http://dx.doi.org/10.1177/1046496416675225

Gully, S. M., Devine, D. J., & Whitney, D. J. (1995). A meta-analysis of cohesion and performance effects of level of analysis and task interdependence. *Small Group Research*, 26(4), 497–520. https://doi.org/10.1177/1046496495264003

Hackman, J. R. (2003). Learning more by crossing levels: Evidence from airplanes, hospitals, and orchestras. *Journal of Organizational Behavior*, 24(8), 905–922. http://dx.doi.org/10.1002/job.226

Halberstadt, J., Jackson, J. C., Bilkey, D., Jong, J., Whitehouse, H., McNaughton, C., & Zollmann, S. (2016). Incipient social groups: An analysis via in-vivo behavioral tracking. *PloS ONE*, 11(3), e0149880. http://dx.doi.org/10.1371/journal.pone.0149880

Harrison, D. A., Mohammed, S., McGrath, J. E., Florey, A. T., & Vanderstoep, S. W. (2003). Time matters in team performance: Effects of member familiarity, entrainment, and task discontinuity on speed and quality. *Personnel Psychology*, 56(3), 633–669. http://dx.doi.org/10.1111/j.1744-6570.2003.tb00753.x

Humphrey, S. E., & Aime, F. (2014). Team microdynamics: Toward an organizing approach to teamwork. *Academy of Management Annals*, 8(1), 443–503. http://dx.doi.org/10.1080/19416520.2014.904140

Ilgen, D. R., Hollenbeck, J. R., Johnson, M., & Jundt, D. (2005). Teams in organizations: From input-process-output models to IMOI models. *Annual Review of Psychology*, 56, 517–543. http://dx.doi.org/10.1146/annurev.psych.56.091103.070250

Isella, L., Romano, M., Barrat, A., Cattuto, C., Colizza, V., Van den Broeck, W., ... Tozzi, A. E. (2011). Close encounters in a pediatric ward: Measuring face-to-face proximity and mixing patterns with wearable sensors. *PloS ONE*, 6(2), e17144. http://dx.doi.org/10.1371/journal.pone.0017144

Knight, A. P., Kennedy, D. M., & McComb, S. A. (2016). Using recurrence analysis to examine group dynamics. *Group Dynamics: Theory, Research, and Practice*, 20(3), 223–241. http://dx.doi.org/10.1037/gdn0000046

Kozlowski, S. W. (2015). Advancing research on team process dynamics: Theoretical, methodological, and measurement considerations. *Organizational Psychology Review*, 5(4), 270–299. http://dx.doi.org/10.1177/2041386614533586

Kozlowski, S. W., Chao, G. T., Chang, C. H., & Fernandez, R. (2015). Team dynamics: Using "big data" to advance the science of team effectiveness. *Big data at work: The data science revolution and organizational psychology.* New York, NY: Routledge Academic.

Kozlowski, S. W., Chao, G. T., Grand, J. A., Braun, M. T., & Kuljanin, G. (2013). Advancing multilevel research design: Capturing the dynamics of emergence. *Organizational Research Methods*, *16*(4), 581–615. http://dx.doi.org/10.1177/1094428113493119

Kozlowski, S. W. J., & Klein, K. J. (2000). A multilevel approach to theory and research in organizations: Contextual, temporal, and emergent processes. In K. J. Klein & S. W. J. Kozlowski (Eds.), *Multilevel theory, research, and methods in organizations: Foundations, extensions, and new directions* (pp. 3–90). San Francisco, CA: Jossey-Bass.

Lazega, E., & Snijders, T. A. B. (Eds.). (2015). *Multilevel network analysis for the social sciences: Theory, methods and applications* (Vol. 12). New York, NY: Springer International Publishing.

Leenders, R. T. A., Contractor, N. S., & DeChurch, L. A. (2016). Once upon a time: Understanding team processes as relational event networks. *Organizational Psychology Review*, *6*(1), 92–115. http://dx.doi.org/10.1177/2041386615578312

LePine, J. A., Piccolo, R. F., Jackson, C. L., Mathieu, J. E., & Saul, J. R. (2008). A meta-analysis of teamwork processes: Tests of a multidimensional model and relationships with team effectiveness criteria. *Personnel Psychology*, *61*(2), 273–307. http://dx.doi.org/10.1111/j.1744-6570.2008.00114.x

Levenson, R. W., & Gottman, J. M. (1983). Marital interaction: Physiological linkage and affective exchange. *Journal of Personality and Social Psychology*, *45*(3), 587–597. http://dx.doi.org/10.1037/0022-3514.45.3.587

Marks, M. A., Mathieu, J. E., & Zaccaro, S. J. (2001). A temporally based framework and taxonomy of team processes. *Academy of Management Review*, *26*(3), 356–376. http://dx.doi.org/10.2307/259182

McGrath, J. E. (1964). *Social psychology: A brief introduction*. New York, NY: Holt, Rinehart, and Winston.

Mehl, R. M. & Conner, T. S. (Eds.) (2012). *Handbook of research methods for studying daily life*. New York, NY: The Guilford Press.

Miller, G. (2012). The smartphone psychology manifesto. *Perspectives on Psychological Science*, *7*(3), 221–237. http://dx.doi.org/10.1177/1745691612441215

Mosier, K. L., & Chidester, T. R. (1991). Situation assessment and situation awareness in a team setting. In Y. Queinnec and F. Daniellou (Eds.), *Designing for Everyone* (pp. 798–800). London, UK: Taylor & Francis.

Moya-Albiol, L., Andrés-García, D., Sanchis-Calatayud, M. V., Sariñana-González, P., Ruiz-Robledillo, N., Romero-Martínez, Á., & González-Bono, E. (2013). Psychophysiological responses to cooperation: The role of outcome and gender. *International Journal of Psychology*, *48*(4), 542–550. http://dx.doi.org/10.1080/00207594.2012.666552

Nowak, A., & Vallacher, R. R. (1998). *Dynamical social psychology* (Vol. 647). New York, NY: Guilford Press.

Olguín Olguín, D., Waber, B. N., Kim, T., Mohan, A., Ara, K., & Pentland, A. (2009). Sensible organizations: Technology and methodology for automatically measuring organizational behavior. *IEEE Transactions on Systems, Man, and Cybernetics, Part B (Cybernetics)*, *39*(1), 43–55. http://dx.doi.org/10.1109/TSMCB.2008.2006638

Onnela, J. P., Waber, B. N., Pentland, A., Schnorf, S., & Lazer, D. (2014). Using sociometers to quantify social interaction patterns. *Scientific Reports*, *4*, 5604. http://dx.doi .org/10.1038/srep05604

Orlitzky, M., & Hirokawa, R. Y. (2001). To err is human, to correct for it divine: A meta-analysis of research testing the functional theory of group decision-making effectiveness. *Small Group Research*, *32*(3), 313–341. http://dx.doi.org/10.1177/ 104649640103200303

Palumbo, R. V., Marraccini, M. E., Weyandt, L. L., Wilder-Smith, O., McGee, H. A., Liu, S., & Goodwin, M. S. (2017). Interpersonal autonomic physiology: A systematic review of the literature. *Personality and Social Psychology Review*, *21*(2), 99–141. http://dx.doi.org/10.1177/1088868316628405

Pentland, A., & Heibeck, T. (2010). *Honest signals: How they shape our world*. Cambridge, MA: MIT Press.

Robins, G., Snijders, T. A. B., Wang, P., Handcock, M., & Pattison, P. (2007). Recent developments in exponential random graph (p*) models for social networks. *Social Networks*, *29*(2), 192–215. http://dx.doi.org/10.1016/j.socnet.2006.08.003

Rosen, M. A., Dietz, A., Yang, T., Priebe, C. E., & Pronovost, P. J. (2015). An integrative framework for sensor-based measurement of teamwork in healthcare. *Journal of the American Medical Informatics Association*, *22*(1), 11–18. http://dx.doi.org/ 10.1136/amiajnl-2013-002606

Rosen, M. A., Schiebel, N., Salas, E., Wu, T., Silvestri, S., & King, H. (2012). How can team performance be measured, assessed, and diagnosed? In E. Salas & K. Frush (Eds.), *Improving patient safety through teamwork and team training* (pp. 59–79). New York, NY: Oxford University Press.

Salas, E., Dickinson, T. L., Converse, S. A., & Tannenbaum, S. I. (1992). Toward an understanding of team performance and training. In R. W. Swezey & E. Salas (Eds.), *Teams: Their training and performance* (pp. 3–29). Westport, CT: Ablex Publishing.

Schaubroeck, J., Lam, S. S., & Cha, S. E. (2007). Embracing transformational leadership: team values and the impact of leader behavior on team performance. *Journal of Applied Psychology*, *92*(4), 1020. http://dx.doi.org/10.1037/0021-9010.92.4.1020

Schmid Mast, M., Gatica-Perez, D., Frauendorfer, D., Nguyen, L., & Choudhury, T. (2015). Social sensing for psychology: Automated interpersonal behavior assessment. *Current Directions in Psychological Science*, *24*(2), 154–160. http://dx.doi.org/ 10.1177/0963721414560811

Schuller, B., & Batliner, A. (2013). *Computational paralinguistics: Emotion, affect and personality in speech and language processing*. West Sussex, UK: John Wiley & Sons.

Smith-Jentsch, K. A., Cannon-Bowers, J. A., Tannenbaum, S. I., & Salas, E. (2008). Guided team self-correction: Impacts on team mental models, processes, and effectiveness. *Small Group Research*, *39*(3), 303–327. http://dx.doi.org/10.1177/ 1046496408317794

Stevens, R. H., Galloway, T., & Berka, C. (2007). EEG-related changes in cognitive workload, engagement and distraction as students acquire problem solving skills. In C. Conati, K. McCoy & G. Paliouras (Eds.), *User modeling 2007. UM 2007. Lecture Notes in Computer Science, Vol. 4511*. Berlin, Germany: Springer. https://doi.org/ 10.1007/978-3-540-73078-1_22

Stevens, R. H., Galloway, T. L., Wang, P., & Berka, C. (2012). Cognitive neurophysiological synchronies: What can they contribute to the study of teamwork? *Human Factors*, *54*(4), 489–502. https://doi.org/10.1177/0018720811427296

Stevens, R., Gorman, J. C., Amazeen, P., Likens, A., & Galloway, T. (2013). The organizational neurodynamics of teams. *Nonlinear Dynamics, Psychology, and Life Sciences*, *17*(1), 67–86.

Strang, A. J., Funke, G. J., Russell, S. M., Dukes, A. W., & Middendorf, M. S. (2014). Physio-behavioral coupling in a cooperative team task: Contributors and relations. *Journal of Experimental Psychology: Human Perception and Performance*, *40*(1), 145–158. http://dx.doi.org/10.1037/a0033125

Tesluk, P., Mathieu, J. E., Zaccaro, S. J., & Marks, M. (1997). Task and aggregation issues in the analysis and assessment of team performance. In M. T. Brannick, E. Salas, & C. W. Prince (Eds.). *Team performance assessment and measurement: Theory, methods, and applications* (pp. 197–224). New York, NY: Taylor & Francis.

Tschan, F. (2002). Ideal cycles of communication (or cognitions) in triads, dyads, and individuals. *Small Group Research*, *33*(6), 615–643. http://dx.doi.org/10.1177/1046496402238618

Vinciarelli, A., Pantic, M., & Bourlard, H. (2009). Social signal processing: Survey of an emerging domain. *Image and Vision Computing*, 27(12), 1743–1759. http://dx.doi.org/10.1016/j.imavis.2008.11.007

Walker, A. D., Muth, E. R., Switzer, F. S., & Rosopa, P. J. (2013). Predicting team performance in a dynamic environment: A team psychophysiological approach to measuring cognitive readiness. *Journal of Cognitive Engineering and Decision Making*, *7*(1), 69–82. http://dx.doi.org/10.1177/1555343412444733

Wild, J. (2017, February 28). Wearables in the workplace and the dangers of staff surveillance. *Financial Times*. Retrieved February 16, 2018, from https://www.ft.com/content/089c0d00-d739-11e6-944b-e7eb37a6aa8e

Woltman, H., Feldstain, A., MacKay, J. C., & Rocchi, M. (2012). An introduction to hierarchical linear modeling. *Tutorials in Quantitative Methods for Psychology*, *8*(1), 52–69. http://dx.doi.org/10.20982/tqmp.08.1.p052

PART III

Methodology and Procedures of Interaction Analysis

observer inference than activity-focused systems but with good definitions of the categories, these systems are relatively easy to apply and to train. An example would be Axelrod's (1976) *cognitive mapping* that sorts ideas into abstract categories based on their content and classifies relations between these ideas (e.g., causal, connotative, subordinate). Then, content mentioned in discussions can be drawn as signed graphs where nodes represent ideas and edges (or vertices) denote (weighted) relations (e.g., Eden, 2004; see also Beck & Orth, 1995; Brauner & Orth, 2002).

The third dimension of interaction is the intent of a message: *what is meant*. Bühler (1934/1982) calls this the conative function (*Appell*), the intended goal of the utterance. For Austin (1975), it is the illocutionary act, such as asking questions, giving information, or issuing a warning (p. 98). Schulz von Thun (1981/1994) follows Bühler and calls it appeal. McGrath and Altermatt (2003, p. 535) use the term *process-focused*: "it defines the acts in terms of what kind of contribution the act makes to the group's task performance, group functioning, and interpersonal relationships." As examples, they list Bales' (1950) IPA or SYMLOG (Bales & Cohen, 1979). Many of the coding schemes in Part V of this volume code for intent, for instance, Stiles' Verbal Response Modes (Chapter 44) or Paletz or Schunn's Micro-Conflict Coding Scheme (Chapter 27). To code intent, it is necessary for an observer to exercise much more judgment than in the previous two dimensions. Intent needs to be defined very thoroughly so that categories are clearly mutually exclusive and observers are provided with sufficient examples showing potential conflict.

The final two dimensions of interaction address *how* something is being said. This can express how the speaker sees own self (fourth dimension) and how the speaker perceives the conversation partner (fifth dimension). Watzlawick and Beavin (1967, p. 5) call both the relationship *aspect*: "There are many levels of information in every communication, and one always pertains to the relationship in which the communication occurs." As examples of such relationship statements, Watzlawick et al. (1967) list how speakers see themselves, how they see the other person, how they think the other sees them, etc. The relationship aspect "classifies" the content of a communication and is therefore a *metacommunication* (Watzlawick et al., 1967, p. 54; see also Brauner, 1998).

Schulz von Thun (1981/1994) – following Watzlawick but differentiating two separate parts – defines one aspect as *self-disclosure* (I-messages) and the other as *relationship definition* (You-messages). I-messages disclose what speakers think about themselves, whereas You-messages disclose how speakers view other or their relationship with other. Although Watzlawick et al. (1967) do not distinguish two separate aspects explicitly, they are important to differentiate because messages can contain both aspects at the same time.[7] I will call the fourth dimension *self-perception of the speaker* and the fifth dimension *other-perception of the*

---

[7] This is why Schulz von Thun (1981/1994) calls his model the four sides of a message: content, intent, self-disclosure, and relationship definition.

speaker because we learn something about speaker's self from the former, and we learn something about the speaker's view of other from the latter. It is important to note that self-perception and other-perception are predominantly communicated implicitly. If communicated explicitly, they would indicate what speakers *intend* to convey rather than *how* they convey it. Examples for codes relating to these aspects are those addressing the valence of utterances, such as showing contempt, conveying praise, expressing dominance, or voicing insecurity. Research questions focusing on any socioemotional aspects would use these codes and coding schemes. For both self-perception and other-perception, a considerable amount of inference is required. Here, it is particularly important that observers have access to the maximum possible information about the conversation. Coding these levels from a transcript alone will be impossible. If video is available, it is preferable to only audio, because information about kinesics and proxemics (e.g., eye gaze or body posture) can provide valuable information about how speakers view themselves or other, in addition to vocalics (see Burgoon & Dunbar, this volume, Chapter 6).

Thus, five dimensions of interaction can be distinguished: action, content, intent, self-perception, and other-perception.[8] The amount of inference needed when coding these aspects increases with each dimension. It is lower when coding actions and content, but significantly higher for coding the intent and the *how* of the interaction. Problems arise when the distinction among these dimensions is not explicitly made. Often, how-categories are added to coding schemes that address content or intent because researchers realize that this aspect is important for understanding interactive processes, particularly in contentious groups or relationships. Consequently, however, the distinction between categories becomes fuzzy, codes become not mutually exclusive, and observers get confused. For instance, a coding scheme could contain a code for *solution* (intent) and for *positive evaluation-other* (other-perception). An utterance can be both of these at the same time, which presents a coding dilemma. Defining priority rules may help although at the expense of information loss. Therefore, it is important for researchers to be mindful of coding schemes that address two or multiple dimensions.

Granularity of Observation. The third and last leg of the triumvirate of coding scheme properties addresses the level of detail at which the interaction will be observed, which can range from fine-grained (or molecular) to coarse-grained (or molar) (Bakeman & Quera, 2011). Burgoon and Baesler (1991) discuss micro and macro measurement specifically for nonverbal interaction. Micro-analytic systems allow fine-grained observation and macro-analytic systems allow coarse-grained

---

[8] Austin's (1975) perlocutionary act, the actual effect on other, is not listed here. The perlocutionary effect is not part of a message and therefore cannot be derived from one utterance alone. It can only become part of a coding category if the unit of analysis is not the utterance or thought unit or speaker turn but rather the interact, i.e., an utterance by one person followed by an utterance or action of another person.

observation (Lindahl, 2009). For micro-level observation, interaction is segmented into smaller units, whereas for macro-level observation, larger units are being observed (Lindahl, 2009). For instance, affect during an interpersonal exchange can be studied by coding prosody (micro-level) or by rating global affect (macro-level) (see Table 9.1). The appropriate level of measurement somewhat depends on the construct of interest, although most constructs can be measured at various levels. Bakeman and Quera (2011) recommend choosing a finer-grained level when in doubt because retroactively aggregating is simple whereas parsing is impossible (see also Saldana, 2009).

Summary. Concreteness of the observed construct and granularity of the observations are mostly independent in that many constructs can be measured at lower or higher levels of granularity. Moreover, some constructs, although not all, can be defined at concrete or abstract levels. Figure 9.3 illustrates the relation between concreteness of a construct and granularity of its observation and provides several examples of coding schemes and their approximate location in this graph. The diagonal indicates the increasing degree of inference needed to interpret and code observed interaction. Whereas these two properties of the *What* being coded are variable, the third property, interactional dimension, comprises five discrete and independent dimensions of interaction and communication.

Different coding systems thus focus on different kinds of constructs (from concrete to abstract), different dimensions of the interaction (action, content, intent, self-perception, other-perception), and varying granularity of the observation (from micro to macro). Which type of coding system a researcher chooses depends entirely on the research question and the related construct. They determine which property of the conversation should be coded and at which level of detail. When research questions address multiple dimensions, researchers need to choose coding schemes that were constructed to assess those dimensions. Otherwise, problems with competing alternatives while coding will ensue (see below on coding conflicts) and researchers will experience difficulties when analyzing the data (see also Poole, this volume, Chapter 18).

The How: Which Type of Coding System to Use?

With regard to *How* coding is done, Faßnacht (1982, p. 83ff.) distinguishes verbal (e.g., descriptions), nominal (e.g., categorical), dimensional (e.g., ordinal), and structural systems (e.g., generative syntax of behavior). Sillars and Overall (2017) distinguish discrete, categorical systems from rating systems. These systems mainly differ with regard to the measurement level of observations. Different types of coding systems at different levels of measurement yield different kinds of data, which entail different potential for data analyses. I will build on both systemizations.

Table 9.1 *Examples for measuring positive emotion at different levels of behavior granularity and construct concreteness*

Coding scheme	Construct definition	Examples of indicators	Construct	Observation
The Specific Affect Coding System (The SPAFF, Coan and Gottman, 2007)	Positive affects, e.g., affection, enthusiasm, humor, interest, validation (p. 272)	*Social cues*: e.g., caring statements (affection); anticipation (enthusiasm); wit and silliness (humor); elaboration and clarification seeking (interest); back channels, paraphrasing (validation). *Physical cues*: e.g., AU 1, 2, 1+2, 5, 6, 12, 6+12, 23, 24, 25–27 (p. 272ff).	Concrete to abstract	Micro- to meso-level
System for Coding Interactions and Family Functioning (SCIFF, Lindahl & Malik, 2000)	Child code – positive affect: "positiveness of the child's tone of voice, facial expressions, and body language …" (p. 33)	*Nonverbal cues*: may be expressed through behaviors such as affection, laughter, and smiling (p. 33)	Rather concrete	Meso-level
Global responsive behaviors coding[b] (Maisel, Gable, & Strachman, 2008)	Perceived responsiveness: "the process by which individuals come to believe that relationship partners both attend to and react supportively to central, core defining features of the self." (Reis, Clark, & Holmes, 2004, p. 203)	*Behavioral cues*: Understanding (e.g., attentive listening, information gathering, asking relevant questions) Validation (e.g., expressing respect towards other, communicate acceptance, support, taking side of other) Caring (e.g., expressing love and affection, showing concern, offering support, offering help, expressing empathy)	Abstract	Macro-level

Note. Due to space reasons, some detail omitted.
[a] These codes are from the Facial Action Coding System (FACS, Ekman & Friesen, 1978).
[b] Maisel et al. (2008) also describe a microanalytic coding system omitted here.

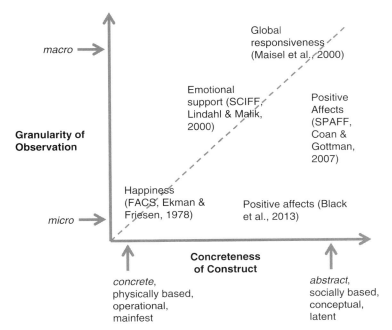

Figure 9.3 *Examples of coding techniques based on level of granularity of the observation and level of concreteness of the construct. The diagonal dotted line indicates that the degree of inference needed while coding increases as a function of granularity of the observation and abstractness of the construct.*

Categorical Coding Systems. Most behavioral researchers understand coding systems as categorical (or nominal) systems. This means that a category is assigned to a behavior (or more specifically, to a coding unit). First, in a *qualitative process* a qualitative, abstract characteristic (e.g., supportive remark; Sillars, this volume, Chapter 29) is assigned to a qualitative, concrete event (e.g., the utterance "I see why you would be upset"; ibid.). Second, in a process of *quantification*, an arbitrary numeric value is assigned to the abstract characteristic (e.g., 23, ibid.). That the value is arbitrary means that it does not matter whether it is 23 or 5795. The number itself is meaningless other than that it makes it somewhat easier to count how many 23s occurred as opposed to counting how many supportive remarks occurred, particularly when using computer programs. The only permitted statistics are counting numbers of cases in the same category, calculating mode, and computing contingency correlation (Stevens, 1946). Assigning numeric values to represent characteristics of reality is considered the most elementary form of measurement (although Michell, 1990, discusses why it is controversial; see also Rack, Zahn, & Mateescu, this volume, Chapter 14).

Rules for creating categorical coding systems are: First, they should be *exhaustive*, which means that categories should cover all instances of possible relevant behavior. Second, categories should be *mutually exclusive*, which means that only one category should be assigned to an utterance. In other words, coding systems should not cover multiple dimensions of interaction, such as content and emotional aspects (see also Tschan et al., this volume, Chapter 10). This will be relevant further below when I discuss potential conflicts while coding.

Magnitude Coding. Magnitude coding systems use categories for coding behavior; however, categories are defined hierarchically and a value is added to each code (Saldana, 2009, p. 58). This means that one type of behavior is considered to show more evidence of the construct of interest than other types of behavior. For instance, Furtak and Kiemer (this volume, Chapter 36), define teacher utterances as showing more or less evidence of eliciting students' independent thought processes; utterances showing more evidence receive a higher score. Summative scores then indicate the quality of a category rather than just the quantity; depending on the anchors, they can be analyzed like ordinal or Likert-type scales.

Process Rating Systems. Rating systems (or dimensional systems) usually assess shorter segments of interaction. Observers rate the interaction along the dimensions of the system. For instance, Wildey and Burt (this volume, Chapter 42) ask raters to judge the frequency of utterances of positive reciprocity during 10 minutes of a couple's interaction. Judgments are made on a scale from *None* to *Constantly throughout the interaction*. Although some grain of detail may be lost, comparisons between process rating systems and categorical systems show that for shorter interactive sequences, rating may be a valid, reliable, and most importantly faster alternative (see Sillars & Overall, 2017).

Mixed Coding and Rating Systems. Some interaction analysis systems contain categories as well as items that are being coded and rated by observers, thus permitting different aspects and levels of the interaction to be assessed. For instance, Grünberg, Mattern, Geukes, Küfner, and Back (this volume, Chapter 41) assess individual differences in interactions. At the micro-level, expressiveness is coded using paraverbal behavior, by counting number of cheerful laughter, giggles, etc. At the meso-level and macro-level, it is recorded by raters assessing nonverbal behavior such as "expressive lively facial expressions" and "shows expressive behavior" respectively.

Checklists. Checklists are lists of all behavior potentially relevant for the research question and the construct of interest. The advantage of checklists is that they do not have to follow the above principles of exhaustiveness and exclusiveness. The same range of coding units as in categorical coding systems can be used (thought units, speaking turns, specified time intervals) although somewhat larger units may make more sense. For each unit, coders check all codes (or items) that are represented in the coding unit; thus resulting scores are ordinal rather than categorical. Reliability is assessed globally rather than at the unit-level (Sillars & Overall, 2017).

Duration Coding. Rather than categorizing momentary, discrete behavior, researchers can also code the duration of the behavior[9] (Bakeman & Gottman, 1997, p. 38f.). Many coding schemes can be used either way. Adapting is easily possible for coding schemes that address the dimensions *action* or *content* but less feasible for the dimensions *intent, self-perception,* or *other-perception*, because the latter tend to be discrete or rather fleeting events (e.g., the expression of contempt on an interactant's face). For instance, a coder can record *when* a person smiles (discrete behavior) or they can code when the person *begins and ends* smiling (duration). Or, if they are interested in content, they could either record *that* a group mentions a subject (e.g., weather) or record *when* the group begins and ends talking about the subject (i.e., change of subject). Other examples for such behaviors are grooming in animal research, cooperative play of children, or discussions of themes in groups (Bakeman & Gottman, 1997). Duration coding is particularly suitable if behaviors last a significant amount of time and therefore would need to be coded repeatedly over multiple units of analysis, which increases both frequency count and impact on sequential results, thus distracting from potentially more important behaviors of shorter duration.

Questions to Ask Before Coding

Before starting the actual coding process, researchers need to clarify three issues: What will be the unit of analysis, should coding software be used, and which data analyses will be conducted? Although I am presenting these questions in the logical place where they occur in the research process, they need to be decided right after the research question is formulated.

What Unit of Analysis to Code?

Unitizing is thoroughly discussed in Tschan et al. (Chapter 10) and Reed et al. (Chapter 11) (both this volume). In part, units of analysis are dictated by the coding scheme. Some coding schemes require using specific units of analysis, otherwise coding may not be possible or data may not make sense. For instance, a coding scheme that requires speaking turns as unit of analysis is the (F)RCCCS coding system (see Friedlander, Escudero, & Heatherington, this volume, Chapter 43). Other coding schemes give researchers some degrees of freedom to make decisions based on their research question and based on their resources (e.g., Lindahl, 2009; Krippendorff, 2004; Faßnacht, 1982; Bakeman & Gottman, 1997).

---

[9] Note that this should not be confused with time sampling. Whether discrete or duration behavior is coded, both types fall into the event-sampling method.

When to Use Coding Software?

Bakeman and Gottman (1997) raved about the "pleasures of pencil and paper" that give researchers a better feel for their data and come with fewer technology-based tragedies. Although still true 20 years and significant technology advances later, data transfer by hand from paper to computer (which also gives better feel for data) is tedious and time consuming. Coding software makes further analyses easier, because once data are in electronic format, importing into other software is simple. Innovations involving tablets or smartphone apps allow easy application in the field. In some situations, tablets or other supportive devices are indispensable. As soon as a dataset is sufficiently large, and further data analyses are planned, coding software makes the life of an already pained interaction researcher somewhat easier (see Glüer, this volume, Chapter 13).

Which Data Analyses to Conduct?

Data analyses, too, depend on the research question. Some questions require frequency calculations, others require sequential analyses, whereas others require pattern detection. The kinds of analyses to be conducted will further influence whether the interaction needs to be recorded, whether it needs to be transcribed, and what kind of coding scheme can be applied. For instance, if a researcher is interested in frequencies without sequential information, recording and transcribing are not necessarily required if the coding scheme is not too complex. Therefore, to ensure that the right data are collected, it is imperative that researchers plan the data analyses right after formulating the research question.

Conflicts to Solve While Coding

During the coding process, coders may encounter situations in which it is difficult to decide which code to use. Whereas many coding conflicts specific to a coding scheme should be covered in the coding manual and discussed during training (see Seelandt, this volume, Chapter 12), some conflicts occur based on general rules associated with human communication. Keyton (this volume, Chapter 1) notes that coding is a social skill and more or less well developed in different people. When coding affective behaviors, Coan and Gottman (2007) require that coders are flexible in terms of integrating a large number of cues as well as their own history of affective communication. Stiles (1992, p. 21) lists as coder qualifications for the Verbal Response Modes system: "high verbal aptitude, interest in interpersonal communication, patience with details, and intensive training and practice. Competence in basic grammar is essential. Psychological-mindedness is helpful but professional training in psychology is not required." Saldana (2009, p. 28f.) lists seven personal attributes that successful coders need to have: organization, perseverance, tolerance for ambiguity, flexibility, creativity, rigorous ethics, and extensive vocabulary.

The main reason for these long lists of qualifications and interpersonal competencies is that coding generally requires inferences. Depending on the concreteness of the construct, the dimension coded, and the granularity of the observation, less or more inference is required of a coder. The more inference is necessary for coding a dimension, the more critical will be the above competencies. Although the following recommendations will not solve the general issue, they are intended to engage researchers and coders in explicit reflection on intricacies of the communicative process and thus help improve coding.

Multiple Aspects of Messages

Above I discussed five dimensions of messages. Generally, coding schemes should be constructed so that categories are mutually exclusive, i.e., only address one of these dimensions to not create conflicts while coding. However, if a coding scheme contains categories, for instance, for the content as well as the relationship dimension, coders can experience conflicts as soon as both dimensions become simultaneously salient in an utterance. Dilemmas can be resolved by providing priority coding rules that will give preference to one dimension over the other or by coding such utterances twice. But both solutions will have a negative impact on interrater reliability and they introduce measurement error because they duplicate coding units. One remedy is to separate out categories addressing different dimensions and using one coding scheme first, then the other. Some researchers recommend creating a new code that would reflect the quality of both aspects (Hewes, 1979), which can potentially lead to large numbers of codes and bulky coding schemes. If the research question indeed requires addressing different aspects of the interaction, a better solution is to use two intact coding schemes that have been developed conceptually to fit each purpose and adequately reflect each desired dimensions of the interaction. Then, researchers should use them consecutively, resulting in separate tracks. If dimensions are coded separately, the information has to be combined in the data analyses to be interpretable (see Poole, this volume, Chapter 18).

One Cannot Not Communicate

Watzlawick and Beavin (1967) write: "In the presence of another, all behavior is communicative" (p. 4). The first part of this statement often gets overlooked: A behavior only becomes communication if, and when, there is another person to observe it. And this includes not only verbal and nonverbal behavior but also signals (as defined by semiotics, in contrast to signs, e.g., Nöth, 1995). A mandrill's red coloration is signaling an animal's dominance rank (see Setchell, this volume, Chapter 7); but it will become communication only if other animals observe the signal. As for the second part, Watzlawick et al. (1967, p. 48) note that behavior does not have an opposite: There is no "nonbehavior." Activity is behavior but nonactivity is also behavior. Both can be interpreted by a communication partner.

Therefore, coders need to be aware that sometimes, no action or no words can carry meaning for both interactants and may affect all further interaction between them. Moreover, coders need to be aware that interactants could miss a message or an action (that the coder did note), which can also influence all further interactions. Thus, if behavior other than verbal behavior could be relevant to the research question, and more often than not it is, coders need to be vigilant.

Explicit and Implicit Messages

Schulz von Thun (1981/1994, p. 33) distinguishes between explicit and implicit messages. All aspects of messages can be communicated either explicitly or implicitly. In some cases, implicit information is communicated nonverbally (e.g., responding to someone's request but showing disdain while doing it). In other cases, implicit information can be communicated verbally (e.g., "I have no spoon"). Particularly in the latter case, it is important for coders to be aware that not the explicit content (no spoon) but rather the implicit intent (bring me a spoon) is relevant (see also Kolbe, Strack, Stein, & Boos, 2011).

Congruent and Incongruent Messages

With a happy smile, one of our doctoral students once said: "My passport was stolen." Obviously, she could not have been happy about the stolen passport. Because communication is always also metacommunication (Watzlawick et al., 1967), one dimension of a message qualifies another dimension of the message. Messages are congruent if both dimensions – content and relationship aspect – point in the same direction. If they are incongruent, both dimensions are mutually exclusive (Watzlawick et al., 1967, p. 212). Incongruent messages can be double-bind messages, indicating confusion within the speaker. This confusion can lead coders to experience conflict as to which aspect of the message they should attend. Paying attention to other qualifying information is crucial in this case. Messages are qualified by context (e.g., situational circumstances), wording (e.g., exaggerations), and nonverbal expression (e.g., kinesics, proxemics, vocalics, etc.; see Burgoon & Dunbar, this volume, Chapter 6) (Schulz von Thun, 1981/1994, p. 36ff.). This is particularly relevant in relationship research and all conflict-laden groups or dyads where the emotional and relationship aspect is in the foreground, but it can become relevant even in work teams, particularly under stress conditions. As for the stolen passport, context – in this case prior knowledge of a person's personality – explains the incongruence.

Literal and Implied Meaning of Messages

Implicature (implying) and *implicatum* (what is implied) (Grice, 1989, p. 24ff.) means that what is said is not always what is being meant. This seems related to the distinction between implicit and explicit messages but it poses a different problem. Grice (p. 26) describes communication as a cooperative effort, based on the cooperative principle: "Make your conversational contribution such as is required at the stage at which it occurs, by the accepted purpose or direction of the talk exchange in which you are engaged." Moreover, he formulates four maxims, quantity, quality, relation, and manner. These maxims help communicators deci-pher *implicature*. For instance, a speaker observing the maxim of quantity will provide just enough information so that a hearer will understand what is being communicated. If seemingly too much information is being provided, the hearer will still assume (applying Wilson's and Quine's Principle of Charity; Quine, 1960/2013; Wilson, 1959) that there is a reason for all that information rather than that the maxim of quantity is being violated (or assuming silliness of the speaker, Quine, 1960/2013, p. 54). The hearer will infer that the seemingly superfluous information was included purposefully because the hearer indeed needs to know it. Observing the maxim of relation ("Be relevant") means that the hearer's response to the speaker's utterance will be relevant in the sense that it will be useful to the speaker. Grice (p. 32) uses this example: A: "I am out of petrol." B: "There is a garage around the corner." Although it was not said, it is implied that A can walk over or push the car around the corner to the garage, that the garage will be open, and that A will most likely be able to get gas there.

The conversational maxims are a form of implicit metacommunicative device (see also Watzlawick et al., 1967, p. 42). Communicators are actively using them, albeit most are not conscious of their use.[10] For behavioral observers, knowing the maxims explicitly, being aware of them during the coding process, and being aware of flouting of maxims will allow for more accurate categoriza-tions of utterances. Thus, teaching conversational rules should be part of any coder training.

Indexical Utterances

Communication among members of the same culture or in close relationships is often indexical (Garfinkel, 1967). The term "indexical" means that over the process of many interactions, communicators have reached common ground and have created short forms of referencing shared experiences, that is, an index. This occurs in close relationships as it does in cultural communities. An observer may have difficulties deciphering such indexicalized messages because they are not privy to the shared history. Contextual knowledge (e.g., knowing the cultural background of a speaker) will help coders to

---

[10] Although sometimes misunderstood, Grice (1989) formulated these maxims descriptively rather than prescriptively.

categorize such messages. Often, it helps to listen to a conversation over again, which requires recording of the conversation. Therefore, it is recommendable to record conversations that are potentially high in indexical expressions. Cultural knowledge and awareness are indispensable for correct coding of indexical messages as well (see also Seelandt, this volume, Chapter 12, on how to write coding manuals).

Indexicality is related to Grice's (1989, p. 270) idea of implicature, although the consequence for coding and categorizing conversational utterances is different. Whereas implicature generally follows culturally shared conversational principles, indexicality can be a private, interpersonal process, shared only among conversational partners with significant interactive history.

Illocutionary Force and Perlocutionary Effect

Stiles (1981) describes communicative acts as attempts of one person to make an impact on another person. However, he points out (p. 228): "The *illocutionary* force on the recipient is entirely determined by the speaker and is distinct from the *perlocutionary* effect" (original emphasis). For instance, the sentence "it is cold in here" uttered by a guest may lead the host to close the window or turn on the heater. But although it creates *Aufforderungscharakter* (valence, or affordance; Lewin, 1969), and although the guest may *want* the host to close the window (illocutionary force), nothing about the effect on the host (perlocutionary effect) can be determined from the message of the guest. When coding from a recording, coders might listen to the same passage repeatedly, thus knowing what reaction from the hearer will come next. Coders need to ascertain that the hearer's behavior does not influence their judgment of the speaker's behavior. Thus, observers need to be aware not to confuse illocutionary force and perlocutionary effect when coding.

Presumptions and Implicit Theories of Coders

Context (e.g., Cicourel, 1985), frame (Bateson, 1972; Goffman, 1974), or social construction of reality (e.g., Berger & Luckmann, 1966) will influence understanding in interaction (see also Jordan & Henderson, 1995). The same utterance will mean something different in different contexts. Tannen and Wallat (1987) as well as Cicourel (1987) apply this to interactions in the medical context. Mostly, this is discussed with regard to interactants, but it applies just as much, if not more, to coders and observers. Coders and observers must be completely aware of their expectations and implicit assumptions about the interactions they are about to observe. They need to be directed and instructed appropriately during the training process. Observers need to be fully aware of the cultural, contextual, and situational circumstances and constantly reflect on those while categorizing utterances.

Addressees and Overhearers

A final complicating factor during the coding process was shown in research by Krauss (1987) and Schober and Clark (1989). Speakers tailor their messages towards their addressees, and addressees give feedback (uhm, hm) when they understood what was said, thus indicating that the conversation can move along. Overhearers, which observers and coders are, can face difficulties understanding messages because they are not directly involved in the conversational grounding process (Clark & Brennan, 1991). Observers need to pay very close attention to such micro-processes; otherwise they might miss the moment of grounding, and potentially critical information about how the conversation develops will be lost.

And Now What? Aggregation and Analyses

Interaction coding usually yields immense amounts of data, especially if interactions are coded at micro-level and if these interactions are long (e.g., group meetings, therapy sessions). Bakeman and Gottman (1997, p. 24f.) and Saldana (2009, p. 19f.) discuss "splitting and lumping," which means that once a concept is originally assessed at the micro- (or molecular) level, further data processing can include summarizing multiple codes to represent the same construct at the macro-level. Lumping can be done on the basis of conceptual considerations or based on empirical considerations. Categories can be aggregated across the entire interaction, for multiple shorter time intervals, across speakers, speaking turns, subsections larger than the unit of analysis (e.g., Stiles, 1992, p. 20), or across dimension, and then used for further analyses. Thus, coding at a lower level of analysis allows more opportunities for later data analysis and exploration.

Depending on the type of coding scheme, data resulting from interaction coding are most often nominal (when categorical coding schemes are used) or ordinal (when process rating schemes are used) (Faßnacht, 1982). When nominal codes are summarized into scores (e.g., sums of individual categories), the measurement level changes to interval and ratio scale. The scores give an absolute count of each category, with an occurrence of 0 meaning the complete absence of the category. These *aggregated* values have ratio scale level. Part IV of this handbook presents various data analysis and statistics techniques for interaction data. Rack et al. (Chapter 14) present how frequency analyses can be used to analyze data (particularly in the absence of sequential information), Quera (Chapter 15) and Magnusson (Chapter 16) show different techniques for sequential analyses, Bonito and Staggs (Chapter 17) discuss issues of dependence in interaction data, and Poole (Chapter 18) covers the problem of multiple levels of analysis. Bonito and Keyton (Chapter 19) review how computers can be used for coding interaction data. Finally, Koch, Ritz, Kleindienst, and Brüngger (Chapter 20) introduce one method of visualizing team processes (all chapters this volume).

Epilogue: Why Is Studying Interaction Processes so Difficult?

If we believe Yogi Berra, "[y]ou can observe a lot by watching" (Berra, 2008), why, then, is it so difficult to study interaction processes? As humans, we are experts in people watching, which may be part of the reason why it is difficult. Coan and Gottman (2007) give three rules for people watching: (1) View observed behavior as if it is one of many different alternatives, (2) view behavior as if it was part of a movie script, and (3) watch as if you had to play that person in a movie. These rules aim to avoid some of the implicit biases humans submit to when watching others (e.g., correspondence bias, actor-observer bias).

A lot of expertise, practice, and, in part, talent go into the analysis of social interaction. But even with all the expertise, practice, and talent, it still proves difficult to achieve meaningful results. Many decisions need to be made *before conducting* the observation, and more decisions need to be made *while coding* interaction. But after coding is done, and all codes lined up, interaction researchers sometimes tend to think the trees *are* the forest. Making sense of statistical analyses can be difficult, because often, theoretical implications are neglected. Thus, researchers should strive to understand the various dimensions reflected and contained in their data; they should not only rely on statistical aggregation but think conceptually, thus addressing the latent constructs (whether concrete or rather abstract) that are implicit in their data. Combining empirical with theoretical and conceptual analyses is therefore crucial for advancing the field.

Yet some difficulties may result from the highly interwoven nature of interaction where "the behavior of one person [is] a function of the behavior of the other person" (Laing, Phillipson, & Lee, 1966, p. 8). Or as Mead (1934/1967, p. 226) states in his social theory of mind, "But there is nothing odd about a product of a given process contributing to, or becoming an essential factor in, the future development of that process." While coding interaction and analyzing respective data, we attempt to capture some aspects of these recursive processes. A further complicating factor is that we are using communication to study communication, thus studying the tool while using it to study it. Future methodological developments will have to attempt to capture some of the recursivity expressed in Mead's quote. Only then will we be able to capture the dynamic, time-bound essence of the reality of social systems.

References

Arrow, H., McGrath, J. E., & Berdahl, J. L. (2000). *Small groups as complex systems: Formation, coordination, development, and adaptation*. Thousand Oaks, CA: Sage.

Austin, J. L. (1975). *How to do things with words*. Cambridge, MA: Harvard University Press.

Axelrod, R. (Ed.) (1976). *Structure of decision. The cognitive maps of political elites*. Princeton, NJ: Princeton University Press.

Bakeman, R., & Gottman, J. M. (1997). *Observing interaction: An introduction to sequential analysis* (2nd edn.). Cambridge, UK: Cambridge University Press.

Bakeman, R., & Quera V. (1995). *Analyzing interaction: Sequential analysis with SDIS and GSEQ*. New York, NY: Cambridge University Press.

Bales, R. F. (1950). *Interaction process analysis: A method for the study of small groups*. Cambridge, MA: Addison-Wesley.

Bales, R. F., & Cohen, S. P. (1979). *SYMLOG: A system for the multiple level observation of groups*. New York, NY: Free Press.

Bateson, G. (1972). *Steps to an ecology of mind*. New York, NY: Ballantine.

Beck, D., & Orth, B. (1995). Wer wendet sich an wen? – Muster in der Interaktion kooperierender Kleingruppen [Who addresses whom? Interaction patterns in cooperating small groups]. *Zeitschrift für Sozialpsychologie*, *26*, 92–106.

Belar, C. D., & Perry, N. W. (1992). The National Conference on Scientist-Practitioner education and training for the professional practice of psychology. *American Psychologist*, *47*(1), 71–75. Retrieved February 22, 2016, from http://dx.doi.org /10.1037/0003-066X.47.1.71

Berger, P. L., & Luckmann, T. (1966). *The social construction of reality. A treatise in the sociology of knowledge*. Garden City, NY: Doubleday.

Berra, Y. (with Kaplan, D. H.) (2003). *What time is it? You mean now? Advice for life from the Zennest Master of them all*. New York, NY: Simon & Schuster.

Berra, Y. (with Kaplan, D. H.) (2008). *You can observe a lot by watching. What I've learned about teamwork from the Yankees and life*. Hoboken, NJ: Wiley & Sons.

Black, M. P., Katsamanis, A., Baucom, B. R., Lee, C-C., Lammert, A. C., Christensen, A., . . . Narayanan, S. S. (2013). Toward automating a human behavioral coding system for married couples' interactions using speech acoustic features. *Speech Communication*, *55*, 1–21. http://dx.doi.org/10.1016/j.specom.2011.12.003

Bonito, J. A., & Hollingshead, A. B. (1997). Participation in small groups. In B. R. Burleson (Ed.), *Communication yearbook 20* (pp. 227–261). Thousand Oaks, CA: Sage.

Brauner, E. (1998). Die Qual der Wahl am Methodenbuffet—oder: Wie der Gegenstand nach der passenden Methode sucht [Tough choices at the methods buffet—or: How a construct is searching for the appropriate method]. In E. Ardelt, H. Lechner, & W. Schloegl (Eds.), *Neue Gruppendynamik. Theorie und Praxis, Anspruch und Wirklichkeit* [New Group dynamics. Theory and practice, desiderata and reality] (S. 176–193). Göttingen, Germany: Verlag für Angewandte Psychologie.

Brauner, E., & Orth, B. (2002). Strukturen von Argumentationssequenzen in Gruppen [Structures of sequences of argumentation in groups]. *Zeitschrift für Sozialpsychologie*, *33*, 65–81. https://doi.org/10.1024//0044-3514.33.2.65

Bühler, K. (1934/1982). *Sprachtheorie. Die Darstellungsfunktion der Sprache*. [Language theory: The representative function of language]. Stuttgart, Germany: Fischer.

Burgoon, J. K., & Baesler, E. J. (1991). Choosing between micro and macro nonverbal measurement: Application to selected vocalic and kinesic indices. *Journal of Nonverbal Behavior*, *15*, 57–78. doi:10.1007/BF00997767

Cheng, A., Kessler, D., Mackinnon, R., Chang, T. P., Nadkarni, V. M., Hunt, E. A., . . . Auerbach, M. (2016). Reporting guidelines for health care simulation research: Extensions to the CONSORT and STROBE statements. *BMJ Simulation and Technology Enhanced Learning*, *2*(3), 51–60. doi:10.1136/bmjstel-2016-000124

Cicourel, A. V. (1985). Text and discourse. *Annual Review of Anthropology*, *14*, 159–185. https://doi.org/10.1146/annurev.an.14.100185.001111

Cicourel, A. V. (1987). The interpretation of communicative contexts: Examples from medical encounters. *Social Psychology Quarterly*, *50*(2), 217–226. http://dx.doi.org/10.2307/2786753

Cicourel, A. V. (1985). Text and discourse. *Annual Review of Anthropology*, *14*, 159–185. https://doi.org/10.1146/annurev.an.14.100185.001111

Clark, H. H., & Brennan, S. E. (1991). Grounding in communication. In L. B. Resnick, J. M. Levine, & S. D. Teasley (Eds.), *Perspectives on socially shared cognition* (pp. 127–149). Washington, DC: American Psychological Association.

Coan, J. A., & Gottman, J. M. (2007). The specific affect coding system (SPAFF). In J. A. Coan & J. J. B. Allen (Eds.), *Handbook of emotion elicitation and assessment* (pp. 106–123). New York, NY: Oxford University Press.

Duck, S., & Montgomery, B. M. (1991). The interdependence among interaction substance, theory, and methods. In B. M. Montgomery & S. Duck (Eds.), *Studying interpersonal interaction* (pp. 3–15). New York, NY: Guilford.

Eden, C. (2004). Analyzing cognitive maps to help structure issues or problems. *European Journal of Operational Research*, *159*, 673–686. http://dx.doi.org/10.1016/S0377-2217(03)00431-4

Edmondson, A. C., & McManus, S. E. (2007). Methodological fit in management field research. *The Academy of Management Review*, *32*, 1155–1179. http://dx.doi.org/10.5465/AMR.2007.26586086

Ekman, P., & Friesen, W. (1978). *The facial action coding system*. Palo Alto, CA: Consulting Psychologists Press.

Faßnacht, G. (1982). *Theory and practice of observing behavior (C. Bryant, Trans.)*. London, UK: Academic Press.

Garfinkel, H. (1967). *Studies in ethnomethodology*. Englewood Cliffs, NJ: Prentice-Hall.

Goffman, E. (1974). *Frame analysis*. New York, NY: Harper.

Grice, P. (1989). *Studies in the way of words*. Cambridge, MA: Harvard University Press.

Heatherington, L., & Friedlander, M. L. (2004). From dyads to triads, and beyond: Relational control in individual and family therapy. In L. E. Rogers & V. Escudero (Eds.), *Relational communication: An interactional perspective to the study of process and form* (pp. 103–129). Mahwah, NJ: Lawrence Erlbaum Associates.

Heine, S. J. (2011). *Cultural psychology* (2nd Ed.). New York, NY: Norton.

Hewes, D. E. (1979). The sequential analysis of social interaction. *The Quarterly Journal of Speech*, *65*, 56–73. http://dx.doi.org/10.1080/00335637909383458

Jordan, B., & Henderson, A. (1995). Interaction analysis: Foundations and practice. *The Journal of the Learning Sciences*, *4*, 39–103. http://dx.doi.org/10.1207/s15327809jls0401_2

Kolbe, M., Strack, M., Stein, A., & Boos, M. (2011). Effective coordination in human group decision making: MICRO-CO: A micro-analytical taxonomy for analysing explicit coordination mechanisms in decision-making groups. In M. Boos, M. Kolbe, P. M. Kappeler, & T. Ellwart (Eds.), *Coordination in human and primate groups* (pp. 199–219). Heidelberg, Germany: Springer.

Krauss, R. M. (1987). The role of the listener: Addressee influences on message formulation. *Journal of Language and Social Psychology*, *6*, 81–98. http://dx.doi.org/10.1177/0261927X8700600201

Krippendorff, K. (2004). *Content analysis: An introduction to its methodology* (2nd edn.). Thousand Oaks, CA: Sage.

Laing, R. D., Phillipson, H., & Lee, A. R. (1966). *Interpersonal perception*. New York, NY: Springer.

Lewin, K. (1969). *Grundzuege der topologischen Psychologie* [Principles of topological psychology]. Bern: Huber.

Lindahl, K. M. (2009). Coding systems for observing interaction. In H. T. Reis & S. Sprecher (Eds.) *Encyclopedia of human relationships* (pp. 219–222). Thousand Oaks, CA: Sage.

Lindahl, K. M., & Malik, N. M. (2000). *System for coding interactions and family functioning (SCIFF): A coding system for family problem discussions*. Available at http://www.psy.miami.edu/faculty/klindahl/

Maisel, N. C., Gable, S. L., & Strachman, A. (2008). Responsive behaviors in good times and bad. *Personal Relationships*, *15*, 317–338. http://dx.doi.org/10.1111/j.1475-6811.2008.00201.x

McGrath, J. E. (1984). *Groups: Interaction and performance*. Englewood Cliffs, NJ: Prentice Hall.

McGrath, J. E., & Altermatt, T. W. (2003). Observation and analysis of group interaction over time: Some methodological and strategic choices. In M. A. Hogg & S. Tindale (Eds.), *Blackwell handbook of social psychology: Group processes* (pp. 525–556). Oxford, UK: Blackwell.

Mead, G. H. (1934/1967). *Mind, self, and society. From the standpoint of a social behaviorist*. Chicago, IL: The University of Chicago Press.

McGrath, J. E., & Tschan, F. (2004). *Temporal matters in social psychology: Examining the role of time in the lives of groups and individuals*. Washington, DC: APA Publications.

Michell, J. (1990). *An introduction to the logic of psychological measurement*. New York, NY: Lawrence Erlbaum.

Nöth, W. (1995). *Handbook of semiotics*. Bloomington, IN: Indiana University Press.

Poole, M. S., & Hewes, D. E. (2017). Reliability and validity in the measurement of social interaction. In C. A. VanLear & D. J. Canary (Eds.), *Researching interactive communication behavior. A sourcebook of methods and measures* (pp. 217–233). Los Angeles, CA: Sage.

Quine, W. V. (1960/2013). *Word and object*. Cambridge, MA: The MIT Press.

Reis, H. T., Clark, M. S., & Holmes, J. G. (2004). Perceived partner responsiveness as an organizing construct in the study of intimacy and closeness. In D. J. Mashek & A. P. Aron (Eds.), *Handbook of closeness and intimacy* (pp. 201–225). Mahwah, NJ: Lawrence Erlbaum.

Salas, E., Paige, J. T., & Rosen, M. A. (2013). Creating new realities in healthcare: the status of simulation-based training as a patient safety improvement strategy. *BMJ Quality & Safety*, *22*(6), 449–452. doi:10.1136/bmjqs-2013-002112

Saldana, J. (2009). *The coding manual for qualitative researchers*. London, UK: Sage.

Schober, M. F., & Clark, H. H. (1989). Understanding by addressees and overhearers. *Cognitive Psychology*, *21*, 211–232. http://dx.doi.org/10.1016/0010-0285(89)90008-X

Schulz von Thun, F. (1981/1994). *Miteinander Reden 1. Störungen und Klärungen. Allgemeine Psychologie der Kommunikation* [Talking to each other 1.

Disruptions and clarifications. General psychology of communication]. Reinbek bei Hamburg, Germany: Rowohlt.

Sillars, A. (1991). Behavioral observation. In B. M. Montgomery & S. Duck (Eds.), *Studying interpersonal interaction* (pp. 197–218). New York, NY: Guilford.

Sillars, A. L., & Overall, N. C. (2017). Coding observed interaction. In C. A. VanLear & D. J. Canary (Eds.), *Researching interactive communication behavior. A sourcebook of methods and measures* (pp. 199–215). Los Angeles, CA: Sage.

Stevens, S. S. (1946). On the theory of scales of measurement. *Science, 103*, 677–680. http://dx.doi.org/10.1126/science.103.2684.677

Stiles, W. B. (1981). Classification of intersubjective illocutionary acts. *Language in Society, 10*(2), 227–249. http://dx.doi.org/10.1017/S0047404500008654

Stiles, W. B. (1992). *Describing talk: A taxonomy of Verbal Response Modes*. Newbury, CA: Sage.

Swaab, R. I., Schaerer, M., Anicich, E. M., Ronay, R., & Galinsky, A. D. (2014). The too-much-talent effect: Team interdependence determines when more talent is too much or not enough. *Psychological Science, 25*(8), 1581–1591. doi:10.1177/0956797614537280

Tannen, D., & Wallat, C. (1987). Interactive frames and knowledge schemas in interaction: Examples from a medical examination/interview. *Social Psychology Quarterly, 50* (2), 205–216. http://dx.doi.org/10.2307/2786752

Tomasello, M. (2000). *The cultural origins of human cognition*. Cambridge, MA: Harvard University Press.

Tomasello, M., Carpenter, M., Call, J., Behne, T., & Moll, H. (2005). Understanding and sharing intentions: The origins of cultural cognition. *Behavioral and Brain Sciences, 28*, 675–735. doi:10.1017/S0140525X05000129

Trujillo, N. (1986). Toward a taxonomy of small group interaction-coding systems. *Small Group Behavior, 17*(4), 371–394. http://dx.doi.org/10.1177/104649648601700401

Tschan, F. (2002). Ideal cycles of communication (or cognitions) in triads, dyads, and individuals. *Small Group Research, 33*, 615–643. doi:10.1177/1046496402238618

Salas, E., Maurino, D., & Curtis, M. (2010). Human factors in aviation: An overview. In E. Salas & D. Marino (Eds.), *Human factors in aviation* (2nd edn., pp. 3–19). Oxford, UK: Oxford University Press.

Watzlawick, P. & Beavin, J. (1967). Some formal aspects of communication. *American Behavioral Scientist, 10*(8), 4–8. http://dx.doi.org/10.1177/0002764201000802

Watzlawick, P., Beavin, J., & Jackson, D. D. (1967). *Pragmatics of human communication. A study of interactional patterns, pathologies, and paradoxes*. New York, NY: Norton.

Weingart, L. R. (1997). How did they do that? The ways and means of studying group processes. *Research in Organizational Behavior, 19*, 189–239.

Wilson, N. L. (1959). Substances without substrata. *The Review of Metaphysics, 12*(4), 521–539.

10 Rules for Coding Scheme Development

Franziska Tschan, Jasmin Zimmermann, and Norbert K. Semmer

This chapter is intended for group researchers interested in assessing group processes through behavioral observation. We assume that the researcher sees this as the best way to proceed (Weingart, 1997) and either has access to the group process in vivo, or has video or audio recordings. We further assume that the researcher contemplates developing a specific coding scheme for the group process. We will guide through the process of developing such a coding scheme and illustrate the development steps with examples of our work: We observe real surgical teams in vivo, and we code behaviors of medical teams performing tasks in simulators from recorded video tapes.

We will concentrate on how to develop a coding scheme that can be used for quantitative analyses. We therefore refrain from discussing methods based on qualitative approaches. This does not imply, however, that ethnomethodological or other qualitative approaches are problematic. Some of the most interesting group process analyses – for example, of surgical teams – are based on field notes observers took during observations (Cristancho et al., 2013; Lingard et al., 2004; Lingard, Reznick, Espin, Regehr, & DeVito, 2002). We also do not discuss behavioral rating scales or checklists that are used to assess the group process as a whole or in large chunks, such as the behavioral rating scales for observing nontechnical skills during surgeries (NOTTS) (Yule et al., 2008).

We start the chapter by outlining three general rules that help in deciding whether, and to what extent, a researcher should develop a coding scheme (General Rules 1 to 3). We then describe the development of a coding scheme in six steps.

Three General Rules to Consider Before Developing Your Own Coding Scheme

General Rule 1: Do Not Develop Your Own Scheme, Unless You Have To

Coding schemes for assessing group process behaviors have a long tradition. Carr suggested analyzing group discussions using categories such as suggestion, opposition to, or acceptance of solutions, questions, and replies as early as 1930 (Carr, 1929). Since then, numerous coding schemes have been developed; the best known is Bales' interaction process analysis (Bales, 1950). Part V of this book presents the IPA coding scheme as well as a representative selection of classic as well as newer coding schemes. Thus, before developing a new scheme, we urgently recommend consulting these as well as method sections of papers that use behavioral coding, because many excellent schemes have not been published separately.

There are two main arguments for this position: First, developers of schemes have made the effort to go through all the steps, and they have dealt with most of the mistakes one is likely to commit when developing a new coding scheme. They have tested feasibility and addressed validity and reliability issues. So, it simply saves time and effort to adopt a previously developed scheme. Second, and more importantly, using an existing scheme has the advantage of making one's research comparable with previous research. This facilitates reviews and meta-analyses (Bakeman, 2000; McGrath & Altermatt, 2001; Waller & Kaplan, 2016; Weingart, 1997).

The first general rule in coding scheme development is thus to carry out a thorough literature search with the aim to find an already developed and tested, suitable coding scheme. It may also be worth extending the literature search to other fields than small group or team research. Schemes exist for coding marital interactions (Bakeman, 2000; Filsinger, 1983), interactions between patients and caretakers (Roter & Larson, 2002), medical teamwork (Kolbe, Künzle, Zala-Mezö, Wacker, & Grote, 2009), and negotiations (Brett, Weingart, & Olekalns, 2004; Weingart, Olekalns, & Smith, 2004), to name just a few. However, consider also General Rule 2.

General Rule 2: Do Not Just Take a Coding Scheme from Somebody Else, Unless It Is Perfect for the Task and the Research Question

Coding schemes need to be based on theoretical considerations and have to be adapted to the type of task, the type of group, and the situation to be studied, because the researcher needs to be sure to capture all relevant behavior. Using an existing coding scheme is only recommended if it is compatible with these requirements. If this is not the case, it bears the risk of missing important behaviors, or of coding behaviors that are not important for the research question. However, beware of the narcissism of small differences: At first, no scheme may look like it fits the researcher's purpose really well, for instance because one uses somewhat different terms or distinguishes between subtypes of a given category. However, the similarities may be much more striking than the differences. Even if the researcher decides that a new scheme has to be developed, existing schemes can be adapted, combined, or used as inspirations for the new scheme; properly citing resources and documenting the adaptations is mandatory.

General Rule 3: Know Very Well What You Want

Some scholars fascinated with group processes may be tempted to start their research and collect data with only a vague idea about which aspects of the group process they eventually want to assess (e.g., "coordination") and how. Others start developing a coding scheme before deciding which behaviors are of interest and thus include "all possible" behaviors. These strategies often backfire and lead to unnecessary work. Developing the coding scheme is part of the operationalization and measurement process: One translates a concept into observable (behavioral) indicators and decides how these indicators are to be measured. The main challenge of a good operationalization is its fit with the concept it is supposed to represent. The better and the more precisely researchers know what they want, the more focused the coding scheme will be. It is therefore useful to develop the coding scheme on pilot data.

It is also important to have an informed idea – before the coding scheme is developed – of how the data will be analyzed. Behavioral data can simply be aggregated (e.g., how many questions were asked during a process); they may be expressed as proportions (e.g., of all the questions asked, what proportion was asked by nurses or physicians), as density (e.g., how many questions per minute), but also as sequences (e.g., to what percentage of questions asked did someone provide an answer; what happened before or after a question was asked) or as regularities in the interaction process (e.g., is there a temporal regularity between questions and answers, etc.). Knowing how the data will be analyzed influences the construction of the coding scheme (see Part IV of this book for various options for data analysis).

How to: The Practical Steps

We suggest a six-step development procedure for the construction and testing of a self-developed coding scheme. For the presentation of the steps, we draw on our own experiences, and on publications describing this process in greater detail (Bakeman, 2000; Bakeman & Gottman, 1997; Brett et al., 2004; Chorney, McMurtry, Chambers, & Bakeman, 2015; Donohue, Diez, & Hamilton, 1984; Kerr, Aronoff, & Messé, 2000; McGrath & Altermatt, 2001; Meyers & Seibold, 2012; Weingart, 1997; Yoder & Symons, 2010). Coding scheme development is an iterative process, guided by theoretical aspects, and limited by practical feasibility. Once developed, schemes should be extensively pilot tested, and altered, if necessary, but finalized before the coding process starts (Kerr et al., 2000; McGrath & Altermatt, 2001; Weingart et al., 2004).

Step 1: Know Your Task – Task Analysis

When studying group processes, the task is often not in the center of interest, it is rather seen as a necessary condition to study a specific hypothesis: We can only observe group processes if the group is actually doing something. In experimental research, researchers often choose a task because it can be easily performed by groups of unacquainted people, does not need excessive preparation or material, is motivating, and can be completed within reasonable time, and furthermore allows an easy assessment of group performance – given the restrictions of subject pools and researcher's time. Things are different in applied research. There, task performance may be at the center of interest, for example, if process aspects related to performance are studied (Hunziker et al., 2010). However, real world tasks can be very complex, and it can be difficult to understand what the team is actually doing, and even more difficult from an outsider's perspective to know when and whether they are doing it well.

It is tempting to assume that we can ignore the task and – regardless of the task – expect that similar processes in groups are related to performance, and thus similar behaviors can be observed. However, group processes do not exist independently of the specific group task (Kerr, 2010; McGrath, 1984; Tschan, Semmer, Nägele, & Gurtner, 2000; Tschan & von Cranach, 1996), and a specific behavior may be positively related to performance for one task, but detrimental in another task (Tschan, Semmer, Hunziker, & Marsch, 2011). Tasks influence the group process (Hackman & Morris, 1975; McGrath, 1984). Morris (1966) compared the frequency of specific observational codes across tasks and showed that the type of task was the major influence on the frequency of most of the behaviors observed. Thus, the task has to be taken into account when developing a coding scheme, and existing coding schemes have to be adapted to the tasks used or studied. Such adaptations have been done for decision making tasks (Poole, 2009); in view of the structure of arguments in communication (Meyers, Seibold, & Brashers, 1991); with regard to problem solving in real meetings (Kauffeld & Lehmann-Willenbrock, 2011); and for negotiation tasks (Brett et al., 2004), to name only a few.

In order to tailor a coding scheme to a task, a task analysis can be helpful (Futoran, Kelly, & McGrath, 1989). In our research, we use a variant of the Hierarchical Task Analysis (HTA) technique (Gurtner, Tschan, Semmer, & Nägele, 2007; Tschan et al., 2011), a relatively straightforward method developed in ergonomics (Annett, 2003; Stanton, 2006) and also adapted for team tasks (Annett, Cunningham, & Mathias-Jones, 2000). The first step of a HTA consists of decomposing a task into parts by describing it as a structure of goals and subgoals. For a project investigating team performance in cardiopulmonary resuscitation (Tschan, Semmer, Hunziker, & Marsch, 2012; Tschan, Vetterli, Semmer, Hunziker, & Marsch, 2011), we identified the main goal "resuscitating the patient", with subgoals of diagnosing the cardiac arrest (assessing the patient), oxygenating the brain (cardiac massage and ventilation), and attempting to reestablish spontaneous circulation (defibrillation and medication). In a second step, we defined coordination-relevant criteria for each goal (e.g., interruptions should be minimized between cardiac massage and ventilation) and direct coordination requirements (i.e., for parts of the task where mutual adaptation of two or more team members is particularly important). An example of such a coordination requirement is that cardiac massage and ventilation should not be done at the same time, but rather in an alternating, gapless sequence (Tschan et al., 2011).

Analyzing the task and its coordination requirements helps to make an informed decision about the behaviors to be coded and serves as a base for identifying task phases, turning points, and other temporal aspects. In the resuscitation task, a turning point, for example, occurs when the team is sure that the patient has indeed a cardiac arrest. At this point, the team changes from deliberation to action (Gollwitzer, 2012), and team behaviors are very likely to change markedly. In sum, tasks influence, guide, and restrict the behavior of the team; this should be taken into account.

Step 2: Define the Data Source

Which type of coding can be done depends on the source of data. If the group process can be recorded, researchers can rewind, and thus observe the group interaction several times. This allows for multiple rounds of coding and allows for assessing more fine-grained aspects. If, however, recording is not possible and group interaction has to be coded in vivo, the coders have to assess the process as it occurs; this limits the number of codes to be included in the coding scheme. For example, in the coding scheme for in-vivo observations of surgical teams (Seelandt et al., 2014), we defined only four codes for communication: patient-relevant communication, teaching, problem solving, and nonpatient-relevant communication. For in-vivo observations, the coding scheme has to be adapted to the cognitive and attentional limits of observers: An observer may not see or hear in detail what is happening; team members may work or talk in parallel, and the density of actions to be coded may be very high (Seelandt et al., 2014).

Step 3: Unitize the Group Process

One of the first decisions in coding interactions is to decide on the start and the end of an observational unit (McGrath & Altermatt, 2001), and to assure that these units are comparable (see Reed, Metzger, Kolbe, Zobel, & Boos, this volume, Chapter 11). Which unitizing of the group process one chooses is crucial because it influences the coding and impacts the analyses.

When coding communication, unitizing can range from identifying "sentences" to speaking turns, or even longer phases. Some researchers choose turns as observational units. This has some disadvantages, because for longer turns, multiple coding categories may apply (McGrath & Altermatt, 2001). Often, a "spoken sentence" is chosen as a unit – also called "thought unit" – which is a "sequence of a few words containing a single thought" (Weldon, Jehn, & Pradhan, 1991, p. 559). Such a definition is useful, because people do not speak in whole sentences with correct grammar and punctuation, and incomplete sentences have to be considered for coding if they contain meaning (Meyers et al., 1991). In our research (Tschan, 1995), we segmented spoken language (of word-by-word transcripts) around the predicate (the main verb): We identified the verb as the center of meaning and considered everything directly linked to it as part of the thought unit. This method has the advantage that communication linked to manual tasks can be unitized. While performing a task, group members often use multiple channels of communication, and they often "substitute" the verb with an overt action (e.g., a communication such as "this ... here," accompanied by putting something on the table, substitutes the verb with an overt action, and can be interpreted as the unit "this [goes] here").

Defining units in terms of meaningful behavior or communication inevitably creates units of different length. An alternative way of unitizing is to divide the process into fixed time segments (for example, 10 seconds), and then code the time-based units (Hirokawa, 1983; Waller, 1999; Waller & Kaplan, 2016). The disadvantage of time-based unitizing is that the units most often do not coincide with the natural sequence of an interaction; coding thus requires very high concentration from coders, because they have to pay attention to the predefined time segment as well as to the natural flow of the interaction.

The decision about unitizing is very important. "Smaller" units allow for more precision, but coding is more labor intensive, thus limiting the number of interactions that can be coded, often resulting in small sample sizes and less generalizable results (Koeszegi & Vetschera, 2010). If larger units are chosen, several codes may be needed to describe a single unit, which, in turn, limits the possibility of expressing results in proportions or performing sequential analyses of the group process.

There is no general rule on how to unitize – it, again, depends on the research question and the theoretical background. Finally, the reliability of the unitizing process itself has to be assessed (for a short description on how to calculate unitizing reliability, see for example Weingart and colleagues, 2004).

Step 4: Develop Coding Contents

For this part, we adopt the framework laid out by McGrath and Altermatt (2001). They suggest considering the following aspects: (1) the time (when); (2) the actors – the group member(s) involved (who); (3) the behavior to be observed (what); and (4) (how much) whether the coding is nominal (a behavior is shown or not) or includes qualifiers, such as intensity ratings (Chorney et al., 2015).

Step 4.1: When – Coding Temporal Aspects. Group interactions develop over time, and coding is an excellent opportunity to capture temporal aspects of group processes (Ballard, Tschan, & Waller, 2008). However, if neither temporal location of behaviors, nor group interaction phases, duration of behaviors, behavior cycles, sequences, or behavioral density are of interest, temporal information can be neglected. If any of these aspects are of interest, the appropriate temporal information needs to be captured through coding.

How to include temporal information? A simple method is to project the actual time within the video frame of recordings. If this is not possible, video players display times, and time can be included as information, if transcripts of group communication are made. We write a transcript of communication into spreadsheets, using a separate row for each (thought) unit. We prepare these rows in advance and include time information (one row per second), and then transcribe the unit in the row with the appropriate onset time. Although this leads to many empty rows, it is a simple method that allows automatically preparing time information in advance instead of manually noting times – and empty rows are rapidly deleted. Note that the timing information using this method is not really precise; we actually accept a difference between the real and the coded onset time of a unit of up to five seconds, because more precise timing is not important for our research goals. Note too, that this method does not allow for capturing interruptions and parallel talk. If a higher level of precision of transcripts is necessary, we refer to the methods of transcription and timing developed in linguistics (Jefferson, 2004).

Coding programs (for example, CowLog[1]) that can be used to directly code recordings without transcripts usually automatically timestamp codes. For in-vivo observations, we use an application that automatically timestamps every event the moment we code it (Seelandt et al., 2014). Note that these time codes are not perfect representations of the time the behavior actually occurs. Such time stamps are always delayed and often indicate the end, rather than the beginning of a behavior or an event. This is because observers must first observe, interpret, and categorize the behavior in order to be able to choose the appropriate code. The coding of a behavior can well be delayed 30 seconds or more in comparison to its actual occurrence. For our research, this is accurate enough, but timings have to be adapted if more exact timing information (for example noise measures) are matched with observations (for an example, see Keller et al., 2016).

If we need to distinguish phases of the group interaction, and/or if specific turning points in the group process have to be considered, we define turning points or phases using specific codes. For example, we have codes indicating that a new surgeon joins the group or leaves the surgery. Such information can be used to segment the group process for analyses of different task phases.

Step 4.2: Who – Coding Actors. "Who" refers to the question to what extent actors will be coded. McGrath and Altermatt (2001) distinguish four possibilities: (1) If only the group behavior itself is of interest, information about individual actors does not need to be gathered; (2) actors are coded if the researcher is interested in the person who shows the behavior; (3) if action and reaction are of interest, the source and receiver or target of a behavior are coded (for example, who addresses whom with a communication, or who reacts to a specific communication), and finally (4) if joint activity is of interest, co-acting between different group members is coded. Again, it depends on the research question whether and which information about actors is included.

Whether actor information can be reliably coded depends on the group process and the quality of the data: If the group behavior is coded in vivo and the group has

---

[1] CowLog is an open-source software for coding behaviors from digital video (for more information go to http://cowlog.org/).

many members, it may be difficult to distinguish actors and co-acting. For example, during surgeries there are often ten or more people in the room, all wearing similar clothing, surgical caps, and face masks – in such a situation it is often impossible to determine who exactly is talking and to whom. A possible solution to this is to have people wear headsets and separate microphones. The participants in our patient simulator studies wear t-shirts with numbers printed on the back, front, and both arms to be able to identify them at any time while they are moving around the patient.

Step 4.3: What – Developing Content Coding Categories. Defining content coding categories is the most important part when developing a coding scheme. We first describe the process of defining coding categories, and then suggest considering content, process, and nontask-related categories as well as coding for task aspects. We then discuss issues related to interpretation of codes.

Defining the Categories. The choice of content coding categories will be influenced by theoretical considerations (e.g., theories about the group process, member behavior, and their relationship with the other variables to be studied). As described above, it will also be influenced by the task and the unitizing decisions taken in step 3. In addition to a top-down, theory-driven approach, some content categories are defined when trial material is coded because it may be difficult to conceptually foresee all relevant behaviors. Therefore, an initial, theory-driven coding scheme will likely be refined and changed during the development phase (Weingart et al., 2004). We used such a hybrid approach when developing the coding scheme for observing surgeries (Seelandt et al., 2014): We went to the operating room (OR) with codes derived theoretically and codes we thought to be important based on a literature review. As a next step, we conducted interviews with surgeons, nurses, and anesthetists, which led to a task analysis of the surgical process. This helped to refine the codes. In addition, we used codes adapted from another scheme (Healey, Sevdalis, & Vincent, 2006). We started in-vivo observations with this preliminary scheme, and adapted it during 15 pilot surgeries (about 60 hours of observation). The next five surgeries of the developing phase were used to pilot the final system and to assess initial interobserver agreement.

Consider Content, Process, Nontask-Related Categories, and Coding Task Aspects. There is a wide variety of possible content categories, because most observable behavior can be coded in some way. In groups, content categories can include verbal and nonverbal behavior, task handling, positional movements, and so on. As most group researchers code verbal behavior, we will concentrate our discussion on coding communication and contextual aspects.

For coding verbal behavior, McGrath and Altermatt (2001) and Futoran and colleagues (1989) suggest distinguishing between (1) task-related and (2) nontask-related communication, and (3) contextual aspects.

(1)   Within *task-related communication* Futoran and colleagues (1989) distinguish *content* and *process* categories. *Content categories* refer to functions related directly to the task (e.g., agree, clarify, modify), *process categories* refer to how the task is or should be done (for a similar distinction, see Weingart et al., 2004). Note that this differentiation is very compatible with conceptual frameworks that distinguish between taskwork and teamwork (e.g., Marks, Mathieu, & Zaccaro, 2001; McGrath & Tschan, 2004). The inclusion of process categories may easily be overlooked when developing a content coding scheme because process-related communication is often relatively rare (e.g., a group may distribute tasks among its members only once at the beginning of the process, and never afterwards), but such behavior may have a very important influence on the group process, so it is well worth coding it.

(2)   Group members do not always work on the task, they may digress; and even while working on the task, they may talk about other things (e.g., the schedule for the next day). Futoran and colleagues (1989) suggest different codes to capture such nontask-related communication; other researchers do not code such behavior. Again, the decision depends on the research purpose. In our surgery coding scheme, we measure nonpatient-related communication (i.e., talking about weekend activities), because we are interested in its effects on team performance (Seelandt et al., 2014; Tschan et al., 2015).

(3)   As groups work on different aspects of the task, it is often useful to code task content in parallel to communication as separate categories. Futoran and colleagues (1989) code cycles (changes in task content), which they defined as periods of working on the same aspect of a task; a new cycle indicates that the group turns its attention to a new part of the task. This scheme thus includes topic changes, but not the content of the topic. In our research (Tschan, 2002), we identified different task contents, and we coded for each unit to what part of the task it refers, as did other studies (Weingart, 1992; Weldon et al., 1991).

Interpretation of Codes. Some behaviors are easier to define and code than others. If visible behavior can be coded in clear-cut categories (points at the monitor; laughs; moves in the room), little interpretation is needed to code such behavior reliably. Other codes require more judgment because the coders have to interpret what the actor intends to communicate with an utterance or an action – this is what Bakeman and Gottman (1997) called socially based categories, and Ray and colleagues (2011) called functional categories. To be able to interpret the behavior of interest correctly, the specific situation and context may be important. Therefore, coders have to be familiar with the relevant aspects of the situation. Because one is often interested in categories that require a fair amount of interpretation, particular attention has to be given to clear and distinct definitions of the categories, an elaborate codebook, and extended coder training.

   Group process behavior is very rich and often much nuanced, and a great number of categories can potentially be developed and coded. However, coding has to be feasible. The number of different categories to be included in a coding scheme is limited by the coders' capability of reliably distinguishing different behaviors and by other aspects influencing the coder's cognitive load. To summarize this part, we cite a short checklist to consider when defining the coding categories, developed by Weingart and colleagues (2004, p. 446): "Can coders differentiate between the categories when applying them? Are there categories for all relevant behavior? Can the scheme be applied reliably?"

Step 4.4: How Much – Qualifying Codes. The simplest way to code a behavior is to indicate whether or not it has been observed within a predefined unit. This is a binary "present or absent" decision. If it is necessary to code more than whether a behavior has been shown, a qualifier can be added to a code. For example, an expressed "tension" (code) can be qualified as low, medium, or high intensity. Adding qualifiers makes coding more difficult, because the coder has to make two decisions – first, he or she has to indicate which behavior is shown, and second, he or she must evaluate an attribute of the behavior. Evidently, this takes more time and entails a higher cognitive load for the observer. As with any other coding, interobserver agreement has to be established for qualifiers.

Step 5: Writing the Coding Manual

During the development and testing of the coding scheme, the coding manual is written. It is a highly important document that describes the operationalization of the variables, serves as an extensive guideline on how to code the material, and is thus also a training manual. An optimal coding manual should be a specific enough instruction to allow a new coder to code the same or similar material reliably without further instruction.

The coding manual specifies all codes and describes in detail the coding process; it instructs on all steps of the coding. It starts with transcription rules, and explains unitizing rules. The most important part concerns the clear definitions and specific descriptions of each code. Examples are provided, and rules for using the context to interpret the meaning of a particular behavior are described (Brett et al., 2004; Weingart et al., 2004; Weingart, 1997; Yoder & Symons, 2010). It is useful to provide prototypical examples of behaviors for each code, but also to describe less typical as well as close nonexamples, including the rationale for their inclusion or exclusion for a specific code (Chorney et al., 2015). In our coding manuals, we also include the source if a code was adapted from another coding scheme.

Coding manuals are often changed and adapted during the development and piloting process to include solutions to problems detected during pilot coding. In our coding manuals, we note the solution to each problem coders bring up. Weingart (1997) called coding manuals "living documents" during the development and testing period that are closed once the final coding starts. The coding manual is the essential document for coder training; in addition, we ask the coders to reread the coding manual each time before they start coding – as additional reminder and training.

Step 6: Train Observers and Assure Interobserver Agreement

One of the most important aspects of a coding scheme is its reliability – independent coders have to code the same material in a similar way. Bakeman stated that "agreement is the sine qua non of observational research" (2000, p. 149). Interobserver agreement depends on clearly distinguishable codes and a good coding manual, but mostly it depends on coder training.

Training coders takes time. For example, for our in-vivo coding of surgeries, a minimum of 35 hours of (often one-to-one) training was needed to obtain acceptable reliability (Seelandt et al., 2014). Training time estimations are similar for other projects: 40 hours of training for a scheme containing 17 categories (Meyers et al., 1991), and 60 hours for a 14-category scheme (Weingart, 1997).

As an example, our procedure for training new observers to code surgeries in vivo has several steps. First, a theoretical training introduces to the task environment and to the codes. Observers then individually study and memorize the codes and the definitions; they then familiarize themselves with the coding technology with the goal to automatically localize the code on the tablet computer; this needs to be highly overlearned. After this phase, they accompany experienced observers to the operating room: In a first surgery, they mainly look over the observer's shoulders and start coding a subset of behaviors. In a second (and often third) surgery, the trainee and the experienced coder code shoulder to shoulder, which allows to compare codes on the spot. The next step is independent parallel observation – after which trainees compare the two codings line by line; systematic disagreements are discussed immediately after the coding phase, when memory is still relatively fresh. As a last step of training, trainee and expert code independently; observations are matched, and interobserver agreement is calculated for each code. Training is only completed if trainees code highly reliably.

The methods to assess coder reliability are discussed in Seelandt (this volume, Chapter 12). Coder agreement has to be assured for all steps – for unitizing, for content coding, and, if the data are used to do sequential analyses, also for sequences (Ray et al., 2011; Waller & Kaplan, 2016). Interobserver agreement based on previously unitized material can directly be calculated. Things are different with event-codes that are automatically timestamped, because time stamps for the same event between two coders are almost never exactly the same. To assess interobserver agreement, we manually align the events before calculating agreement. In the surgery study, we allowed for a time difference between the coders of up to 30 seconds for the same event. This is realistic if dense coding is necessary, and it is admissible because we do not analyze time segments shorter than five minutes.

Coder agreement needs to be assessed throughout the study because the interpretation of the codes can change over time. If specific circumstances can influence coding, interobserver agreement should be tested under these circumstances. For example, in the surgery study, we observed very long surgeries (several hours); we were thus concerned about observer fatigue. We therefore assessed coding reliability after three hours into the surgery between a tired coder (who had observed since the beginning) and a fresh coder who joined at this time (Seelandt et al., 2014).

Conclusions

Observing behavior is the gold standard to assess group processes. Retrospective reports of group members as well as generalized observer reports are likely to be biased (Guzzo, Wagner, Maguire, Herr, & Hawley, 1986; Staw, 1975). Developing a coding scheme corresponding to high methodological standards is a labor-intensive, nontrivial, multistep process. We therefore recall our first rule: Don't do it unless you have to. However, when creating a coding scheme from scratch, attention to the details outlined in this chapter can help to avoid excessive work and regrets when starting data analysis. Figure 10.1 gives a final overview of the coding scheme development process.

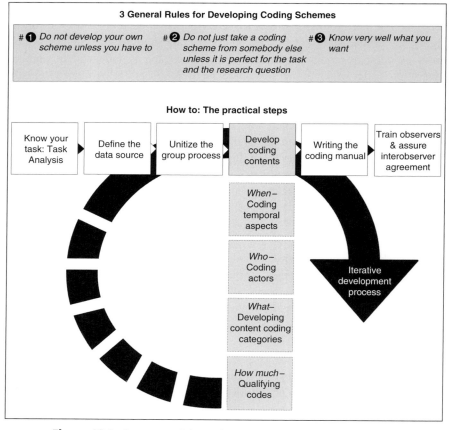

Figure 10.1 *Overview of the coding scheme development process.*

References

Annett, J. (2003). Hierarchical task analysis. In E. Hollnagel (Ed.), *Handbook of cognitive task design* (Vol. 2, pp. 17–35). Mahwah, NJ: Lawrence Erlbaum Associates. doi:10.1201/9781410607775

Annett, J., Cunningham, D., & Mathias-Jones, P. (2000). A method for measuring team skills. *Ergonomics, 43*(8), 1076–1094. doi:10.1080/00140130050084888

Bakeman, R. (2000). Behavioral observation and coding. In H. T. Reis & C. M. Judd (Eds.), *Handbook of research methods in social and personality psychology* (pp. 138–159). New York, NY: Cambridge University Press.

Bakeman, R., & Gottman, J. M. (1997). *Observing interaction: An introduction to sequential analysis.* New York, NY: Cambridge University Press. doi:10.1017/CBO9780511527685

Bales, R. F. (1950). *Interaction process analysis; a method for the study of small groups.* Reading, MA: Addison-Wesley.

Ballard, D. I., Tschan, F., & Waller, M. J. (2008). All in the timing – Considering time at multiple stages of group research. *Small Group Research, 39*(3), 328–351. doi:10.1177/1046496408317036

Brett, J., Weingart, L., & Olekalns, M. (2004). Baubles, bangles, and beads: Modeling the evolution of negotiating groups over time. In M. A. Neale, E. A. Mannix, & S. Bloung-Lyons (Eds.), *Research on managing groups and teams: Time in groups* (Vol. 6, pp. 39–64). New York, NY: Elsevier Science Press. doi:S0738-3991(02)00012-5/S1534-0856(03)06003-1

Carr, L. J. (1929). Experimental sociology: A preliminary note on theory and method. *Social Forces, 8,* 63–74. doi:10.2307/2570053

Chorney, J. M., McMurtry, C. M., Chambers, C. T., & Bakeman, R. (2015). Developing and modifying behavioral coding schemes in pediatric psychology: a practical guide. *Journal of Pediatric Psychology, 40*(1), 154–164. doi:10.1093/jpepsy/jsu099

Cristancho, S. M., Apramian, T., Vanstone, M., Lingard, L., Ott, M., & Novick, R. J. (2013). Understanding clinical uncertainty: What is going on when experienced surgeons are not sure what to do? *Academic Medicine, 88*(10), 1516–1521. doi:10.1097/ACM.0b013e3182a3116f

Donohue, W. A., Diez, M. E., & Hamilton, M. (1984). Coding Naturalistic Negotiation Interaction. *Human Communication Research, 10*(3), 403–425. doi:10.1111/j.1468-2958.1984.tb00025.x

Filsinger, E. E. (1983). Choices among marital observation coding systems. *Family Process, 22*(3), 317–335. http://dx.doi.org/10.1111/j.1545-5300.1983.00317.x

Futoran, G. C., Kelly, J. R., & McGrath, J. E. (1989). Tempo – a Time-Based System for Analysis of Group-Interaction Process. *Basic and Applied Social Psychology, 10*(3), 211–232. doi:10.1207/s15324834basp1003_2

Gollwitzer, P. M. (2012). Mindset theory of action phases. In P. A. van Lange, A. W. Kruglanski, & E. T. Higgins (Eds.), *Handbook of Theories in Social Psychology* (Vol. 1, pp. 526–545). Los Angeles, CA: Sage. doi:10.4135/9781446249215.n26

Gurtner, A., Tschan, F., Semmer, N. K., & Nägele, C. (2007). Getting groups to develop good strategies: Effects of reflexivity interventions on team process, team performance, and shared mental models. *Organizational Behavior and Human Decision Processes, 102*(2), 127–142. doi:S0738-3991(02)00012-5/j.obhdp.2006.05.002

Guzzo, R. A., Wagner, D. B., Maguire, E., Herr, B., & Hawley, C. (1986). Implicit theories and the evaluation of group-process and performance. *Organizational Behavior and Human Decision Processes, 37*(2), 279–295. doi:S0738-3991(02)00012-5/ 0749-5978(86)90056-7

Hackman, J. R., & Morris, C. G. (1975). Group tasks, group interaction process, and group performance effectiveness: A review and proposed integration. *Advances in Experimental Social Psychology, 8*, 45–99. doi:S0738-3991(02)00012-5/S0065-2601(08)60248-8

Healey, A. N., Sevdalis, N., & Vincent, C. A. (2006). Measuring intra-operative interference from distraction and interruption observed in the operating theatre. *Ergonomics, 49*(5–6), 589–604. doi:10.1080/00140130600568899

Hirokawa, R. Y. (1983). Group communication and problem-solving effectiveness: An investigation of group phases. *Human Communication Research, 9*(4), 291–305. doi:10.1111/j.1468-2958.1983.tb00700.x

Hunziker, S., Buhlmann, C., Tschan, F., Balestra, G., Legeret, C., Schumacher, C., Semmer, N. K., Hunziker, P., & Marsch, S. (2010). Brief leadership instructions improve cardiopulmonary resuscitation in a high-fidelity simulation: A randomized controlled trial. *Critical Care Medicine, 38*(4), 1086–1091. doi:10.1097/CCM.0b013e3181cf7383

Jefferson, G. (2004). Glossary of transcript symbols with an Introduction. In G. H. Lerner (Ed.), *Conversation Analysis. Studies from the first generation* (pp. 13–23). Philadelphia, PA: John Benjamins. doi:10.1075/pbns.125.02jef

Kauffeld, S., & Lehmann-Willenbrock, N. (2011). Meetings matter: Effects of team meetings on team and organizational success. *Small Group Research, 43*(2), 130–158. doi:10.1177/1046496411429599

Keller, S., Tschan, F., Beldi, G., Kurmann, A., Candinas, D., & Semmer, N. K. (2016). Noise peaks influence communication in the operating room. An observational study. *Ergonomics, 59*(12), 1541–1552. doi:10.1080/00140139.2016.1159736

Kerr, N. L. (2010). Group task. In J. M. Levine & M. A. Hogg (Eds.), *Encyclopedia of Group Processes & Intergroup Relations* (pp. 385–390). Thousand Oaks, CA: Sage. doi:10.4135/9781412972017.n116

Kerr, N. L., Aronoff, J., & Messé, L. A. (2000). Methods of small group research. In H. T. Reis & C. M. Judd (Eds.), *Handbook of research methods in social and personality psychology* (pp. 160–189). New York, NY: Cambridge University Press. doi:10.1017/CBO9780511996481.013

Koeszegi, S. T., & Vetschera, R. (2010). Analysis of negotiation processes. In D. M. Kilgour & C. Eden (Eds.), *Handbook of group decision and negotiation* (pp. 121–138). Dordrecht, The Netherlands: Springer. doi:10.1007/978-90-481-9097-3_8

Kolbe, M., Künzle, B., Zala Mezö, E., Wacker, J., & Grote, G. (2009). Measuring coordination behavior in anaesthesia teams during induction of general anaesthetics. In R. Flin & L. Mitchell (Eds.), *Safer surgery: Analysing behavior in the operating theatre* (pp. 203–221). London, UK: Ashgate. doi:10.7748/nm.17.8.9.s12

Lingard, L., Espin, S., Whyte, S., Regehr, G., Baker, G. R., Reznick, R., Bohnen, J., Orser, B., Doran, D., & Grober, E. (2004). Communication failures in the operating room: An observational classification of recurrent types and effects.

Quality and Safety in Healthcare, 13(5), 330–334. doi:10.1136/qshc.2003.008425

Lingard, L., Reznick, R., Espin, S., Regehr, G., & DeVito, I. (2002). Team communications in the operating room: Talk patterns, sites of tension, and implications for novices. *Academic Medicine, 77*(3), 232–237. doi:10.1097/00001888-200203000-00013

Marks, M. A., Mathieu, J. E., & Zaccaro, S. J. (2001). A temporally based framework and taxonomy of team processes. *Academy of Management Review, 26*(3), 356–376. doi:10.2307/259182

McGrath, J. E. (1984). *Groups: Interaction and performance.* Englewood Cliffs, NJ: Prentice-Hall.

McGrath, J. E., & Altermatt, W. T. (2001). Observation and analysis of group interaction over time: Some methodological and strategic consequences. In M. A. Hogg & R. S. Tindale (Eds.), *Blackwell handbook of social psychology: Group processes* (pp. 525–556). Oxford, UK: Blackwell Publishers. doi:10.1002/9780470998458

McGrath, J. E., & Tschan, F. (2004). Dynamics in groups and teams: Groups as complex action systems. In M. S. Poole & A. H. van de Ven (Eds.), *Handbook of organizational change and development* (pp. 50–73). Oxford, UK: Oxford University Press.

Meyers, R. A., & Seibold, D. R. (2012). Coding group interaction. In A. B. Hollingshead & M. S. Pool (Eds.), *Research methods for studying groups and teams, a guide to approaches, tools, and technologies* (pp. 329–357). New York, NY: Routledge.

Meyers, R. A., Seibold, D. R., & Brashers, D. (1991). Argument in initial group decision-making discussions: Refinement of a coding scheme and a descriptive quantitative analysis. *Western Journal of Speech Communication, 55*(1), 47–68. doi:10.1080/10570319109374370

Morris, C. G. (1966). Task effects on group interaction. *Journal of Personality and Social Psychology, 4*(5), 545–554. doi:10.1037/h0023897

Poole, M. S. (2009). Decision development in small groups II: A study of multiple sequences in decision making. *Communication Monographs, 50*(3), 206–232. doi:10.1080/03637758309390165

Ray, R. D., Ray, J. M., Eckerman, D. A., Milkosky, L. M., & Gillins, L. J. (2011). Operations analysis of behavioral observation procedures: A taxonomy for modeling in an expert training system. *Behavior Research Methods, 43*(3), 616–634. doi:10.3758/s13428-011-0140-6

Roter, D., & Larson, S. (2002). The Roter interaction analysis system (RIAS): Utility and flexibility for analysis of medical interactions. *Patient Education and Counseling, 46*(4), 243–251. https://doi.org/S0738-3991(02)00012-5/S0738-3991(02)00012-5

Seelandt, J. C., Tschan, F., Keller, S., Beldi, G., Jenni, N., Kurmann, A., Candinas, D., & Semmer, N. K. (2014). Assessing distractors and teamwork during surgery: Developing an event-based method for direct observation. *BMJ Quality & Safety, 23*(11), 918–929. doi:10.1136/bmjqs-2014-002860

Stanton, N. A. (2006). Hierarchical task analysis: developments, applications, and extensions. *Applied Ergonomics, 37*(1), 55–79. doi:S0738-3991(02)00012-5/j.apergo.2005.06.003

Staw, B. M. (1975). Attribution of the "causes" of performance: A general alternative interpretation of cross-sectional research on organizations. *Organizational*

Behavior and Human Performance, 13, 414–432. doi:S0738-3991(02)00012-5/ 0030-5073(75)90060-4

Tschan, F. (1995). Communication enhances small group performance if it conforms to task requirements: The concept of ideal communication cycles. *Basic and Applied Social Psychology, 17*(3), 371–393. https://doi.org/10.1207/s15324834basp1703_6

Tschan, F. (2002). Ideal cycles of communication (or cognitions) in triads, dyads, and individuals. *Small Group Research, 33*(6), 615–643. Retrieved from https://doi .org/10.1177/1046496402238618

Tschan, F., Seelandt, J., Keller, S., Semmer, N. K., Kurmann, A., Candinas, D., & Beldi, G. (2015). Impact of case-relevant and case-irrelevant communication within the surgical team on surgical site infection. *British Journal of Surgery, 102*(13), 1718– 25. doi:10.1002/bjs.9927

Tschan, F., Semmer, N. K., Hunziker, P., & Marsch, S. (2011). Decisive action vs. joint deliberation: Different medical tasks imply different coordination requirements. In V. G. Duffy (Ed.), *Advances in human factors and ergonomics in healthcare* (pp. 191–200). Boca Raton, FL: Taylor & Francis. doi:10.1201/ EBK1439834978

Tschan, F., Semmer, N. K., Hunziker, S., & Marsch, S. U. (2012). Group research using high-fidelity experimental simulations. In A. B. Hollingshead & M. S. Poole (Eds.), *Research methods for studying groups and teams: A guide to approaches, tools, and technologies* (pp. 58–78). New York, NY: Routledge. doi:10.1177/ 1046496412473662

Tschan, F., Semmer, N. K., Nägele, C., & Gurtner, A. (2000). Task adaptive behavior and performance in groups. *Group Processes & Intergroup Relations, 3*(4), 367–386. http://dx.doi.org/10.1177/1368430200003004003

Tschan, F., Semmer, N. K., Vetterli, M., Gurtner, A., Hunziker, S., & Marsch, S. U. (2011). Developing observational categories for group process research based on task and coordination-requirement analysis: Examples from research on medical emer-gency-driven teams. In M. Boos, M. Kolbe, P. Kappeler, & T. Ellwart (Eds.), *Coordination in Human and Primate Groups* (pp. 93–115). Berlin, Germany: Springer. doi:10.1007/978-3-642-15355-6

Tschan, F., Vetterli, M., Semmer, N. K., Hunziker, S., & Marsch, S. C. (2011). Activities during interruptions in cardiopulmonary resuscitation: A simulator study. *Resuscitation, 82*(11), 1419–1423. doi:10.1016/j.resuscitation.2011.06.023

Tschan, F., & von Cranach, M. (1996). Group task structure, processes and outcome. In M. West (Ed.), *Handbook of work group psychology* (pp. 95–121). Chichester, UK: Wiley.

Waller, M. J. (1999). The timing of adaptive group responses to nonroutine events. *Academy of Management Journal, 42*(2), 127–137. doi:10.2307/257088

Waller, M. J., & Kaplan, S. A. (2016). Systematic behavioral observation for emergent team phenomena: Key considerations for quantitative video-based approaches. *Organizational Research Methods, 21*(2), 1–16. doi:10.1177/1094428116647785

Weingart, L., Olekalns, M., & Smith, P. L. (2004). Quantitative coding of negotiation behavior. *International Negotiation, 9*, 441–455. doi:10.1163/1571806053498805

Weingart, L. R. (1992). Impact of group goals, task component complexity, effort, and planning on group performance. *Journal of Applied Psychology, 77*(5), 682–693. doi:10.1037/0021-9010.77.5.682

Weingart, L. R. (1997). How did they do that? The ways and means of studying group processes. In L. L. Cummings & B. M. Staw (Eds.), *Research in organizational behavior* (Vol. 19, pp. 189–239). Greenwich, CT: JAI Press.

Weldon, E., Jehn, K. A., & Pradhan, P. (1991). Processes that mediate the relationship between a group goal and improved group performance. *Journal of Personality and Social Psychology, 61*(4), 555–569. doi:10.1037/0022-3514.61.4.555

Yoder, P. J., & Symons, F. J. (2010). *Observational measurement of behavior*. New York, NY: Springer.

Yule, S., Flin, R., Maran, N., Rowley, D., Youngson, G., & Paterson-Brown, S. (2008). Surgeons' non-technical skills in the operating room: Reliability testing of the NOTSS behavior rating system. *World Journal of Surgery, 32*(4), 548–556. doi:10.1007/s00268-007-9320-z

11 Unitizing Verbal Interaction Data for Coding

Rules and Reliability

Natasha Reed, Yvonne Metzger, Michaela Kolbe, Sarah Zobel, and Margarete Boos

In micro-analysis of group interactions, categories are assigned to individual units of interaction for later analysis (Burtscher, Kolbe, Wacker, & Manser, 2011; Riethmüller, Fernandez Castelao, Eberhardt, Timmermann, & Boos, 2012; Tschan et al., 2015). Coding interaction data after the period of observation typically follows three distinct steps: (1) transcription and/or transfer of data into coding software (see Glüer, this volume, Chapter 13), (2) segmentation into codable units, also known as "unitizing," and (3) allocation of individual units to coding categories (see Kolbe, Boos, Stein, & Strack, 2016). Live coding of interaction data, in contrast, omits Step (1), and Steps (2) and (3) occur simultaneously. A coding unit may also be referred to as a "unit of analysis," a "scored unit," or a "codable unit" (e.g., Chi, 1997; Dollard & Auld, 1959; Duncan, 1975; Srnka & Koeszegi, 2007; Strijbos, Martens, Prins, & Jochems, 2005) and represents the smallest data component that is analyzed within an interaction (Bales, 1950; Mayring, 2003). Unit size can vary significantly (Guetzkow, 1950), for example, a time interval can be "a second, a day or a year" (Magnusson, 1996, p. 116). The focus of this chapter is placed on Step (2), unitizing.

The respective aims of a research project influence the choice of unit of analysis adopted by researchers, for example, due to the type of data required for later analysis (Hirokawa, 1988). When choosing the method for segmenting verbal data into coding units, the desired "grain size" of the unit must be identified (Chi, 1997). This involves a tradeoff between the informational content of a coding unit and the work involved in processing units of a specific size (Chi, 1997, p. 286).

The reliability of interaction coding is not only determined by the coder's accuracy in applying content or behavioral categories to the data but also their accuracy in segmenting observational data into codable units (Guetzkow, 1950). Such segmentation needs to provide an "intersubjective, transparent basis for forming coding units" (Bilandzic, Koschel, & Scheufele, 2001, p. 103, own translation) and thus allow assigning clearly defined, disjunct categories to each coding unit (Bakeman, 2000; Quera, Bakeman, & Gnisci, 2007).

This chapter is informed in content and structure by the article published by Kolbe et al. (2016). Some text extracts have been adapted and translated by permission from Springer Customer Service Centre GmbH: Springer Nature, Gruppe. Interaktion. Organisation. Zeitschrift fur Angewandte Organisationspsychologie (GIO) (SYNSEG – Eine Methode zur syntaxgeleiteten Segmentierung von Kodiereinheiten für die Analyse von Gruppenprozessen, Michaela Kolbe, Margarete Boos, Alexandra Stein, & Micha Strack), 47(4), 335–344. © Springer Fachmedien Wiesbaden 2016. https://link.springer.com/

The Difficulty with Defining Coding Units

Researchers are able to unitize data in differing ways, for example, according to the occurrence of a specific event or the lapse of a predetermined time interval (Bakeman & Gottman, 1997). Alternately, approaches can be thematically grouped into those unitizing according to theme, proposition, physical form, syntax, or reference, respectively (Krippendorff, 1981). The terms "unitizing" and "sampling" are sometimes used interchangeably within the literature, which can be misleading. These terms can, however, be differentiated: "Unitizing" refers to the process by which boundaries are defined for data units that should be segmented, and "sampling" refers to the identification process of a suitable size sample of data for analysis (Krippendorff, 1981).

The *time sampling* method enables researchers to capture the occurrence of a defined behavior within a specific, explicit time interval (Olson & Cunningham, 1934). It provides a "snapshot" of the observed behavior, which renders it particularly useful for researchers sampling behaviors occurring at high frequency (Langdridge & Hagger-Johnson, 2009). On the one hand, it is a reliable way of forming coding units (Faßnacht, 1995) and in some instances, such as the investigation of nonverbal micro-expressions, represents the only sampling technique which can be adopted. For example, time sampling could be used to segment an observed interaction into ten-second-long coding units (see Kolbe et al., 2016, p. 336; Waller, 1999). On the other hand, time sampling can yield a potentially unrepresentative portrayal of behavior if the period of observation is too long or too short (Langdridge & Hagger-Johnson, 2009) with respect to the construct under investigation. Moreover, time sampling limits the number of applicable data analysis methods (Kolbe et al., 2016).

Event sampling, in comparison, allows capturing preselected behaviors in a continuous, precise, and chronological manner (Bakeman & Quera, 2011; Quera, Bakeman, & Gnisci, 2007), thus permitting the application of many analytical methods (Kolbe et al., 2016). Despite event sampling often being adopted within psychological group research (e.g., Lehmann-Willenbrock, Meinecke, Rowold, & Kauffeld, 2015; Tschan, Rochat, & Zapf, 2005; Tschan et al., 2015), unitizing of verbal behavior recorded by continuous observation is particularly difficult (Guetzkow, 1950; Klonek, Quera, & Kauffeld, 2015). Group members' verbal input within a group tends to differ qualitatively and quantitatively; for example, Person A may utter two words, whereas Person B may speak for several minutes about multiple topics. Because the richness of verbal data provided by the speakers varies significantly, so too would the number of categories assigned to the individual turns, with Person B's verbal input perhaps being coded multiple times (Kolbe et al., 2016). Multiple coding would exclude the possibility of exploring the sequence of interaction using sequential analysis (Bakeman & Gottman, 1986; van Hooff, 1982).

This raises a significant dilemma: Whereas too large units would result in each unit being assigned to more than one category, too small units could mean many units are allotted to the *remainder* category (Guetzkow, 1950). When investigating interaction over time, speech should be divided into coding units that contain similar depth of content to avoid "losing" valuable richness of data. Equally, their size should be appropriate for measuring the construct under investigation (see Kolbe et al., 2016, p. 336).

Current Approaches to Unitizing

The following overview is based on a literature review that was conducted using Google Scholar and databases Psyndex and PsycArticles[1] to identify methods of unitizing transcribed English verbal interaction between two or more persons along semantic, pragmatic, and syntactic lines. The following discussion and Tables 11.1 and 11.2 present examples of literature meeting the following criteria: empirical studies in which authors explicitly refer to unitizing their data or methodological works outlining a unitizing procedure along semantic, pragmatic, or syntactic lines; unitizing is applied to transcribed English verbal interaction between two or more persons; primary, rather than secondary sources. Segmentation approaches for written texts based, for instance, solely on punctuation (Kramer, Kuo, & Dailey, 1997) are omitted from this overview. Additionally, we omit automatic-based segmentation procedures (e.g., Oh, Myaeng, & Jang, 2001) from discussion, since our aim was to create a methodology for manually segmenting transcripts of verbal interaction.

Searches yielded few explicitly outlined methods for manually segmenting transcribed dialogues intended for the purposes of interaction analysis. Consequently, we also drew upon unitizing approaches used for other analyses (e.g., content analysis, sequential analysis, and analysis within the field of psycholinguistics) to provide a selection of segmentation procedures and coding units currently applied by psychologists and psycholinguists to transcribed verbal interaction between two or more persons.

Semantic and Pragmatic Approaches to Unitizing

Russell and Staszewski (1988) noted that "the selection of units for study is infrequently carried out on a principled basis" (p. 191) and that the reliability of the adopted segmentation process is often not reported. They described seven dimensions, including *semantic and pragmatic* dimensions, according to which units can be defined.[2] The semantic dimension refers to the "use of aspects of

---

[1]   Search terms included, for example: "interaction analysis (and English language)," "syntactic units interaction analysis," "semantic units interaction analysis," "group interaction analysis," and "segmenting transcripts syntactic units."

[2]   The five additional dimensions described by Russell and Staszewski (1988) are: (1) temporal, (2) para/extralinguistic, (3) treatment process, (4) structural discourse, and (5) syntactic. Dimensions (1)–(3) are omitted from our discussion: (1) is analogue to the time sampling method, which presents the aforementioned analytical difficulties; (2) is not applicable for our purposes since we propose working solely with transcripts, excluding the requirement of phonological input; (3) is not applicable for our purposes since it relates specifically to psychotherapeutic process. (4) and (5) are discussed later in this chapter.

Table 11.1 *A selection of semantic and pragmatic unitizing approaches*

Author	Name of unit	Definition & IRR (if stated)	Example of a unitizing rule
Berkowitz & Gibbs (1983)	Statement	"A statement is a speech act defined by the speaker's intention . . . it is an act that serves a unitary goal, such as refining, analyzing, or integrating." (Berkowitz & Gibbs, 1983, p. 405)	Not stated
Crowell & Scheidel (1961)	Thought unit	Not stated	Not stated
Stinson, Milbrath, Reidbord, & Bucci (1994)	Thematic unit (TU)	A "complete thought or idea" (Stinson et al., 1994, p. 40).	"[The unitizers] inserted markers to divide the text into relatively small segments with each containing only a single idea, using their best intuitive understanding of what an 'idea' was and of what was being said" (Stinson et al., 1994, p. 40).
	Major thematic unit (MTU)	IRR = .56–.91 (M = .77) and .72–.95 (M = .87) (percent agreements), calculated using two formulas by Scott and Hatfield (1985, as cited in Stinson et al., 1994). "Macrostructures of meaning expressed in aggregates of one or more TUs" (Stinson et al., 1994, p. 41). IRR = .41–.43 ("predictive value in a positive test", p. 43); κ = .40–.42 and .90–.10 (specificity and sensitivity to major thematic shift, respectively) (Stinson et al., 1994)	"Judges read TU-segmented transcripts and divide the text into relatively large segments containing ideas unified under a common theme, using their best intuitive idea of what was being said and of what unified the separate ideas." (Stinson et al., 1994, p. 41).
Rosenberg & Bonoma (1974)	Intended speech sequence (ISS)	A "completed thought sequence" (Rosenberg & Bonoma, 1974, p. 1). IRR = .89	Not stated

Note. IRR = Inter-rater reliability. [a] Stinson et al. (1994) developed a training manual for TU and MTU segmentation.

Table 11.2 *A selection of syntax-based unitizing approaches*

Author	Unit name	Unit definition & IRR (if stated)	Example of a unitizing rule
Bales (1950)	Communication unit	"The unit to be scored is the smallest discriminable segment of verbal or nonverbal behavior to which the observer . . . can assign a classification under conditions of continuous serial scoring. This unit may be called an act, or more properly, a single interaction, since all acts in the present scheme are regarded as interactions. The unit as defined here has also been called the single item of thought or the single item of behavior." (Bales, 1950, p. 37.) IRR: 91.6% agreement (Inui, Carter, Kukull, & Haigh, 1982)	"If a series of predicates are asserted of a single subject, a separate score is given for each additional predicate on the reasoning that each one constitutes a new item of information or opinion" (Bales, 1950, p. 37).
Auld & White (1956)	Sentence	"The minimum utterance which can be understood by itself" (Fries, 1952, as cited in Auld & White, 1956, p. 273) "An independent linguistic form not included by virtue of any grammatical construction in any larger linguistic form" (Bloomfield, 1933, as cited in Auld & White, 1956, p. 273). IRR: .95–.99 and .93–.97, respectively.	"The unit consists of an independent clause, standing by itself or occurring alone with one or more dependent clauses" (Auld & White, 1956, p. 273).
Dollard & Auld (1959)	Sentence	"A sentence is a single free utterance – free in the sense that it is not included in any larger structure by means of any grammatical device" (Fries, 1952, as cited in Dollard & Auld, 1959, p. 12). Inter-rater reliability: 83–91% agreement (*M* = 86%).	"Some actor-action constructions which, if they stood alone, would be considered complete sentences are to be included with the sentence that surrounds them. These *parenthetic* clauses can be identified by the fact that they interrupt the surrounding sentence (Bloomfield, p. 186)" (Dollard & Auld, 1959, p. 17).
Stiles (1992)	Utterance	"An utterance is defined as a simple sentence, an independent clause, a nonrestrictive dependent clause, an element of a compound predicate, or a term of acknowledgment, evaluation, or address" (Stiles, 1992, p. 11).	"*Noun clauses* – clauses used as subjects or objects of other clauses – are not coded separately, though their content may influence the code for utterance intent" (Stiles, 1992, p. 112).

Table 11.3 (cont.)

| I just can't work out, **erm**, the best solution. @ | **you know**, the implications that this will have. |

Optional rules for specific phenomena within conversational group interaction

7. Separation of speech when addressing someone by name	• Segmentation of any form of address if this does not cause an incomplete coding unit on either side of it.
*E.g., If you'd like to leave, @ **ladies and gentlemen**, @= feel free to do so. @*	• Segmentation, marked by = and @ (@=), takes place after the part of speech that constitutes the form of address.
No separation if naming a person functions as the subject or object in a sentence	
*E.g., I will arrange a meeting with **Mrs Smith** for next week. @*	
Or when a coding unit is broken up by addressing someone by name (see Rule 6).	
E.g., If you, Mrs Smith, would like to address the issue … @	
8. Separation of diverse phenomena unique to spoken language:	• Phenomena unique to spoken language are segmented into standalone units *if this does not break up a syntactic unit* (see Rule 6)
Interjection: *Oh! @#, ahh @#, huh @#*	• @ and # (@#) are placed after these phenomena to mark the point of segmentation.
Pause/Hesitation: *Like @#, I mean @#, you see @#, erm @#, hmm @#, I'm not sure … @#*	
One-word constructions: *What? @#, No! @#, Good. @#*	• If these phenomena occur immediately after each other, they should be segmented separately, with the segmentation symbols @# placed after each phenomenon.
Ellipsis: *Sound good to you? @#*	
Introductory word: *Well @#, hey @#, anyway @#, Anyhow @#, Personally @#*	
Self-correction: *I thought it wasn't, @# it was booked today. @*	
Self-repetition: *Let's start, @# let's start with the agenda for today. @*	
Question tag: *will you? @#, don't you? @#, isn't it? @#*	
Invariant tag: *… right? @#, okay? @#*	
No separation of these phenomena if this would break up a syntactic unit (see Rule 6).	

This table has been adapted and translated by permission from Springer Customer Service Centre GmbH: Springer Nature, Gruppe. Interaktion. Organisation. Zeitschrift für Angewandte Organisationspsychologie (GIO) (SYNSEG – Eine Methode zur syntaxgeleiteten Segmentierung von Kodiereinheiten für die Analyse von Gruppenprozessen, Michaela Kolbe, Margarete Boos, Alexandra Stein, & Micha Strack), 47(4), 335–344. © Springer Fachmedien Wiesbaden 2016. https://link.springer.com/
Note. Symbols inserted during transcription should be ignored for unitizing. Boldface text within examples represents the rule-specific triggers for segmentation or non-segmentation, respectively. @ = symbol for the point at which a segmentation into a syntactically complete coding unit occurs (Rules 1–8); // = symbol representing the point at which a change in speaker occurs (Rule 1); == = symbol for separation of speech when addressing someone by name (Rule 7); # = symbol for separation of diverse phenomena unique to spoken language (Rule 8).

is available on request from the authors. The SynSeg rules are intended for unitizing verbal group communication. Their applicability does not encompass monologues, which lack unique interpersonal phenomena, such as people talking over each other (Gale et al., 2013; Poland, 1995), completing each other's sentences (Leech, 2000), and spontaneous development of conversation resulting from different group members' verbal input. The rules have been developed for spoken data that were transcribed because the grammatical and qualitative manifestation of speech differs significantly from that of written text (Kvale, 1988; Biber, 1991) through, for example, the inclusion of pauses/hesitations, self-corrections, and self-interruptions (Huddleston & Pullum, 2008; Kasper, 1998; Levelt, 1989, as cited in Leech, 2000). The rules can be applied to transcribed British and American English. In what follows we explain how to use SynSeg.

Practical Issues. Points of segmentation are represented by four symbols: @, //, =, or #, as well as possible combinations of these symbols. The @ symbol is used to mark the location at which segmentation into a syntactically complete coding unit occurs. It should be placed at the *end* of the unit to which it belongs. Any pre-existing symbols or punctuation in the transcript should be ignored during the segmentation process (Dollard & Auld, 1959). If a syntactically complete coding unit has been segmented and the following text presents a syntactically incomplete coding unit, the unitizer should continue reading through the transcript and segment the text after the next coding unit. Text that cannot be segmented remains connected to the beginning of the next coding unit. It is important to place all symbols that are relevant to the specific segmentation to enable automatic computer-based searches during later analysis.

Rules 1–6 represent core rules to be applied to a transcript, while the inclusion/omission of Rules 7 and 8 is optional according to the research project's requirements. For example, someone wishing to explore whether addressing someone by name evokes a difference in their contribution to a group activity could utilize Rule 7. In contrast, someone investigating how people use subordinate clauses as a way of strengthening their argument may omit Rules 7 and 8.

The SynSeg segmentation rules are as follows:

Rule 1 (*Separation at the point of change in speaker*) assists in the organization of the transcript in a straightforward way, since speech uttered by distinct speakers will have usually been placed on separate lines during the transcription process (Kolbe et al., 2016). By positioning different group members' speech on distinct lines and by placing the // symbol to mark speech turns, the analyst is able to easily identify the number of verbalizations per group member.

For the segmentation according to **Rule 2** (*Separation of adjacent main or subordinate clauses*), a clause must consist of at least two clausal elements: a subject and a predicate, if the predicate consists of an intransitively used verb, or a minimum of three clausal elements, a subject, a predicate, and an object, if the predicate consists of a transitively used verb (Dollard & Auld, 1959; Herbst et al., 2004; Downing, 2015; Huddleston & Pullum, 2008). The use of a predicate's transitivity to inform segmentation aims to keep together what belongs together semantically, without which it would be grammatically incomplete and uninterpretable, by using objective syntactic markers for unitizing. The verb-frame form is used as the root of the unit because the predicator is "the head [of a clause], with the subject a dependent of it" (Huddleston, 1984, p. 177) and "dependents, often optional, are syntactically subordinate elements" (Huddleston & Pullum, 2008, p. 24). The predicate is a syntactically more powerful element than the subject or object (Greenbaum & Nelson, 2002).

The verb-frame core of a unit is also required for segmentation according to **Rule 3** (*Separation of contracted coordinated clauses*). These are sentences used commonly within conversational speech in which the subject, predicate, or object are shared and implicitly repeated in multiple coordinated clauses. Because these clausal elements are explicitly omitted from the following clause, contracted coordinated clauses appear syntactically incomplete. Since the omitted elements are implicitly recoverable, however, they still syntactically function as separate main or subordinate clauses and express full, distinct clausal content. This mirrors Bales' (1950) rationale for segmenting compound sentences (which we define as "coordinated contracted clauses") with a shared subject and separate predicates into separate "communicative acts" because distinct ideas are tied to distinct predicates.

Rule 4 (*Separation of a participial-clause with its adjunct[s]*) addresses a further syntactic formation, which is not a subordinate clause in the literal sense, but is still regarded as in many cases replacing a subordinate clause in spoken English. Past and present participles can be used in the form of participial clauses, which may not immediately appear to meet objective prerequisites for syntactic completion, but should be segmented due to their clause-like function.

Rule 5 (*No separation of any relative clause from a main/subordinate clause*) and **Rule 6** (*No separation of a parenthesis when it splits up another coding unit*) provide explicit rules as to which syntactic elements should not be segmented. We argue that relative clauses and parentheses should not be unitized because their segmentation into separate coding units would often result in the text in which they are embedded being broken up into fragmented syntactic coding units. For instance, relative clauses are often placed directly following the expression (e.g., a subject or object) on which they provide additional (and in many cases essential) information. In these cases, they are syntactically considered to be constituent parts of the expression and should not be separated from them.

Rule 7 (*Separation of speech when addressing someone by name; utilizing the =symbol*) and **Rule 8** (*Separation of diverse phenomena unique to spoken language; utilizing the # symbol*) provide optional rules for phenomena unique to spoken English that may be useful for later analysis. With regard to **Rule 7**, participants in conversational group interaction will often address someone by name or by another form of address (e.g., nickname, endearment/disparagement, title, salutation). **Rule 8** provides segmentation criteria for ten phenomena unique to spoken English that one is highly likely to come across when unitizing a transcribed group interaction. We argue that these phenomena should form standalone coding units (albeit not syntactically complete coding units), due to their important communicative function (Leech, 2000; Holmes, 1987).

Evaluation

Applicability. An interdisciplinary group of experts developed SynSeg (i.e., psychologists, linguists) with considerable experience in analyzing group interaction data. We feel that this approach contributed to the comprehensive applicability of SynSeg for a variety of social interaction data.

Interrater Reliability. To test for interrater reliability (IRR), four researchers (a British-English native speaker, two German native speakers, and an American-English native speaker) segmented a six-page section of a British National Corpus transcript (2007, Transcript "JA6", Lines 58–192). Prior to segmenting, they familiarized themselves with the training manual. IRR was analysed by calculating a normalized Levenshtein Distance value (nD), which represents the lowest relative number of alterations needed to create a match between two segmented versions of identical text and the total number of operations required to make the two versions of segments match (Conroy, 2001; Levenshtein, 1966). The operations for the alterations needed are deletion, insertion, and substitution, the latter of which, also known as "Indel" (Levenshtein, 1966), refers to an exchange of one symbol in the place of another. The thresholds for determining IRR quality were used according to Kolbe et al. (2016): $nD < .10$: good; $.10 < nD < .20$: acceptable; $nD > .20$: critical; $nD > .30$: unacceptable. The initial IRR was deemed unsatisfactory.

Consequently, the rules and training manual were reviewed and adjusted. The final IRR analysis involved a British-English native speaker and a German native speaker segmenting a six-page section of a BNC transcript (2007, Transcript "F8U", Lines 567–775). The text was segmented into 314 and 309 units, respectively ($M = 311.50$ units), yielding an nD value of .05. Consequently, IRR between unitizers applying SynSeg is considered to reach a good level of reliability.

Conclusion

We have presented SynSeg, a syntax-based unitizing system for manually segmenting verbal group interaction data according to the syntactic function of its constituent elements. SynSeg aims to extend existing English syntax-based approaches to unitizing by offering easy-to-use, clearly defined rules for unitizing that do not require phonological input. SynSeg advocates the application of eight segmentation rules; six core rules and two optional rules which can be applied or omitted according to the research project's requirements. SynSeg was developed for unitizing verbal transcripts for use in group interaction analysis with the aim to facilitate transparency and reliability of analysis of social interaction data. Even though SynSeg offers clear and well-defined unitizing rules, with good IRR, their solely manual application could be argued to be effortful. However, in the future, we expect automated voice recognition methods to reduce annotation effort and to be fully compatible with the proposed approach.

References

Auld Jr., F., & White, A. M. (1956). Rules for dividing interviews into sentences. *The Journal of Psychology, 42*(2), 273–281. doi:10.1080/00223980.1956.9713040

Austin, J. L. (1962). *How to do things with words*. Cambridge, MA: Harvard University Press.

Bakeman, R. (2000). Behavioral observation and coding. In H. T. Reis & C. M. Judd (Eds.), *Handbook of research methods in social and personality psychology* (pp. 138–159). New York, NY: Cambridge University Press.

Bakeman, R., & Gottman, J. M. (1986). *Observing interaction: An introduction to sequential analysis*. Cambridge, UK: Cambridge University Press.

Bakeman, R., Quera, V., & Gnisci, A. (2009). Observer agreement for timed-event sequential data: A comparison of time-based and event-based algorithms. *Behavior Research Methods, 41*(1), 137–147. doi:10.3758/brm.41.1.137

Bales, R. F. (1950). *Interaction process analysis. A method for the study of small groups.* Addison-Wesley Press Inc. Retrieved February 16, 2018, from https://archive.org /stream/interactionproce00bale

Berg, D. M. (1967). A thematic approach to the analysis of the task-oriented, small group. *Communication Studies, 18*(4), 285–291. doi:10.1080/10510976709362891

Berkowitz, M. W., & Gibbs, J. C. (1983). Measuring the developmental features of moral discussion. *Merrill-Palmer Quarterly, 29*(4), 399–410.

Biber, D. (1991). *Variation across speech and writing*. Cambridge, UK: Cambridge University Press.

Bilandzic, H., Koschel, F., & Scheufele, B. (2001). Theoretisch-heuristische Segmentierung im Prozeß der empiriegeleiteten Kategorienbildung. In W. Wirth & E. Lauf (Eds.), *Inhaltsanalyse* (pp. 98–116). Köln, Germany: Herbert von Halem Verlag.

The British National Corpus. (2007). (Version 3, BNC XML Edition). *JA6*. Retrieved using BNCweb (CQP-edition), Lancaster University Computing Services, Lancaster, from http://bncweb.lancs.ac.uk

Burtscher, M. J., Kolbe, M., Wacker, J., & Manser, T. (2011). Interactions of team mental models and monitoring behaviors predict team performance in simulated anesthesia inductions. *Journal of Experimental Psychology: Applied, 17*(3), 257–269. doi:10.1037/a0025148

Chi, M. T. (1997). Quantifying qualitative analyses of verbal data: A practical guide. *The Journal of the Learning Sciences, 6*(3), 271–315. doi:10.1207/ s15327809jls0603_1

Conroy, R. (2001). *Spatial navigation in immersive virtual environments*. University College London, London.

Crookes, G. (1990). The utterance, and other basic units for second language discourse analysis. *Applied Linguistics*, *11*(2), 183–199. doi:10.1093/applin/11.2.183

Dollard, J., & Auld Jr., F. (1959). *Scoring human motives: A manual*. New Haven, CT: Yale University Press.

Downing, A. (2015). *English grammar: A university course* (3rd edn.). Abingdon, UK, and New York, NY: Routledge.

Duncan Jr, S. (1975). Interaction units during speaking turns in dyadic, face-to-face conversations. In A. Kendon, R. M. Harris, & M. R. Key (Eds.), *Organization of Behavior in Face-to-Face Interaction* (pp. 199–214). The Hague & Paris: Mouton Publishers.

Faßnacht, G. (1995). Systematische Verhaltensbeobachtung: Eine Einführung in die Methologie und Praxis [Systematic behavioral observation: An introduction into the methodology and practice] (2nd ed.). Munich: Reinhardt.

Foster, P., Tonkyn, A., & Wigglesworth, G. (2000). Measuring spoken language: A unit for all reasons. *Applied Linguistics*, *21*(3), 354–375. doi:10.1093/applin/21.3.354

Gale, N. K., Heath, G., Cameron, E., Rashid, S., & Redwood, S. (2013). Using the framework method for the analysis of qualitative data in multi-disciplinary health research. *BMC Medical Research Methodology*, *13*(117), 1–8. doi:10.1186/1471-2288-13-11

Gamsky, N. R., & Farwell, G. F. (1966). Counselor verbal behavior as a function of client hostility. *Journal of Counseling Psychology*, *13*(2), 184–190. doi:10.1037/h0023397

Gottman, J. M. (1979). *Marital interaction: Experimental investigations*. New York, NY: Academic Press, Inc.

Greenbaum, S., & Nelson, G. (2002). *An introduction to English grammar* (2nd edn.). Harlow, UK: Longman.

Guetzkow, H. (1950). Unitizing and categorizing problems in coding qualitative data. *Journal of Clinical Psychology*, *6*(1), 47–58. doi:10.1002/1097-4679(195001)6:1%3C47::AID-JCLP2270060111%3E3.0.CO;2-I

Hatfield, J. D., & Weider-Hatfield, D. (1978). The comparative utility of three types of behavioral units for interaction analysis. *Communications Monographs*, *45*(1), 44–50. doi:10.1080/03637757809375950

Herbst, T., Heath, D., Roe, I. F., & Götz, D. (2004). *A valency dictionary of English: A corpus-based analysis of the complementation patterns of English verbs, nouns and adjectives* (Vol. 40). Berlin, Germany: Walter de Gruyter.

Hiltz, S. R., Johnson, K., & Turoff, M. (1986). Experiments in group decision making communication process and outcome in face-to-face versus computerized conferences. *Human Communication Research*, *13*(2), 225–252. doi:10.1111/j.1468-2958.1986.tb00104.x

Hirokawa, R. Y. (1988). Group communication research: Considerations for the use of interaction analysis. In C. H. Tardy (Ed.), *A handbook for the study of human communication: Methods and instruments for observing, measuring, and assessing communication processes* (pp. 229–245). Norwood, NJ: Ablex Publishing Corporation.

Holmes, J. (1987). Hedging, fencing and other conversational gambits: An analysis of gender differences in New Zealand speech. In A. Pauwels (Ed.), *Women and language in Australian and New Zealand society* (pp. 59–79). Sydney, Australia: Australian Professional Publications.

Huddleston, R. (1984). *Introduction to the grammar of English*. Cambridge, UK: Cambridge University Press.

Huddleston, R., & Pullum, G. K. (2008). *The Cambridge grammar of the English language*. Cambridge, UK: Cambridge University Press.

Kasper, G. (1998). Analysing verbal protocols. *Tesol Quarterly*, *32*(2), 358–362. doi:10.2307/3587591

Keyton, J., & Beck, S. J. (2009). The influential role of relational messages in group interaction. *Group Dynamics: Theory, Research, and Practice*, *13*(1), 14–30. doi:10.1037/a0013495

Klonek, F. E., Quera, V., & Kauffeld, S. (2015). Coding interactions in Motivational Interviewing with computer-software: What are the advantages for process researchers? *Computers in Human Behavior*, *44*, 284–292. doi:org/10.1016/j .chb.2014.10.034

Klonek, F. E., Quera, V., Burba, M., & Kauffeld, S. (2016). Group interactions and time: Using sequential analysis to study group dynamics in project meetings. *Group Dynamics: Theory, Research, and Practice*, *20*(3), 209–222. doi:10.1037/ gdn0000052

Kolbe, M., Boos, M., Stein, A., & Strack, M. (2016). SYNSEG–Eine Methode zur syntax-geleiteten Segmentierung von Kodiereinheiten für die Analyse von Gruppenprozessen. *Gruppe. Interaktion. Organisation. Zeitschrift für Angewandte Organisationspsychologie (GIO)*, *47*(4), 335–344. doi:10.1007/ s11612-016-0345-3

Kramer, M. W., Kuo, C. L., & Dailey, J. C. (1997). The impact of brainstorming techniques on subsequent group processes: Beyond generating ideas. *Small Group Research*, *28*(2), 218–242. doi:10.1177/1046496497282003

Krippendorff, K. (1981). *Content analysis. An introduction to its methodology.* Beverly Hills, CA, and London, UK: Sage.

Kvale, S. (1988). The 1000-page question. *Phenomenology + Pedagogy*, *6*(2), 90–106.

Langdridge, D., & Hagger-Johnson, G. (2009). *Introduction to research methods and data analysis in psychology* (2nd edn.). Harlow, UK: Pearson Education Limited.

Leech, G. (2000). Grammars of spoken English: New outcomes of corpus-oriented research. *Language Learning*, *50*(4), 675–724. doi:10.1111/0023-8333.00143

Lehmann-Willenbrock, N., Allen, J. A., & Meinecke, A. L. (2014). Observing culture: Differences in US-American and German team meeting behaviors. *Group Processes & Intergroup Relations*, *17*(2), 252–271. doi:10.1177/ 1368430213497066

Lehmann-Willenbrock, N., Meinecke, A. L., Rowold, J., & Kauffeld, S. (2015). How transformational leadership works during team interactions: A behavioral process analysis. *The Leadership Quarterly*, *26*(6), 1017–1033. doi:10.1016/j. leaqua.2015.07.003

Levenshtein, V. I. (1966). Binary codes capable of correcting deletions, insertions and reversals. *Soviet Physics-Doklady*, *10*(8), 707–710.

Magnusson, M. S. (1996). Hidden real-time patterns in intra-and inter-individual behavior: description and detection. *European Journal of Psychological Assessment*, *12*(2), 112–123. doi:10.1027/1015-5759.12.2.112

Mayring, P. (2003). *Qualitative Inhaltsanalyse. Grundlagen und Techniken* (8th edn.). Weinheim and Basel, Switzerland: UTB.

Murphy, M. L., & Koskela, A. (2010). *Key terms in semantics*. London, UK, and New York, NY: Continuum International Publishing Group.

Oh, H. J., Myaeng, S. H., & Jang, M. G. (2007). Semantic passage segmentation based on sentence topics for question answering. *Information Sciences*, *177*(18), 3696–3717. doi:10.1016/j.ins.2007.02.038

Olson, W. C., & Cunningham, E. M. (1934). Time-sampling techniques. *Child Development*, *5*(1), 41–58. doi:10.2307/1125795

Poland, B. D. (1995). Transcription quality as an aspect of rigor in qualitative research. *Qualitative Inquiry*, *1*(3), 290–310. doi:10.1177/107780049500100302

Quera, V., Bakeman, R., & Gnisci, A. (2007). Observer agreement for event sequences: Methods and software for sequence alignment and reliability estimates. *Behavior Research Methods*, *39*(1), 39–49. doi:10.3758/bf03192842

Riethmüller, M., Fernandez Castelao, E., Eberhardt, D., Timmermann, A., & Boos, M. (2012). Adaptive coordination development in student anaesthesia teams: A longitudinal study. *Ergonomics*, *55*(1), 55–68. doi:10.1080/00140139.2011.636455

Rosenberg, H., & Bonoma, T. V. (1974). A social influence rating method for group interaction and some pilot results on group therapy process. *Proceedings of the Division of Personality and Society Psychology*, *1*(1), 259–262. doi:10.1177/014616727400100188

Russell, R. L., & Staszewski, C. (1988). The unit problem: Some systematic distinction and critical dilemmas for psychotherapy process research. *Psychotherapy: Theory, Research, Practice, Training*, *25*(2), 191–200. doi:10.1037/h0085333

Srnka, K. J., & Koeszegi, S. (2007). From words to numbers: how to transform qualitative data into meaningful quantitative results. *Schmalenbach Business Review*, *59*, 29–57.

Stiles, W. B. (1992). *Describing talk: A taxonomy of verbal response modes*. Newbury Park, CA: Sage Publications.

Stinson, C. H., Milbrath, C., Reidbord, S. P., & Bucci, W. (1994). Thematic segmentation of psychotherapy transcripts for convergent analyses. *Psychotherapy: Theory, Research, Practice, Training*, *31*(1), 36–48. doi:10.1037/0033-3204.31.1.36

Strijbos, J. W., Martens, R. L., Prins, F. J., & Jochems, W. M. (2006). Content analysis: What are they talking about? *Computers & Education*, *46*(1), 29–48. doi:10.1016/j.compedu.2005.04.002

Tschan, F., Rochat, S., & Zapf, D. (2005). It's not only clients: Studying emotion work with clients and co-workers with an event-sampling approach. *Journal of Occupational and Organizational Psychology*, *78*(2), 195–220. doi:10.1348/096317905X39666

Tschan, F., Seelandt, J. C., Keller, S., Semmer, N. K., Kurmann, A., Candinas, D., & Beldi, G. (2015). Impact of case-relevant and case-irrelevant communication within the surgical team on surgical-site infection. *British Journal of Surgery*, *102*(13), 1718–1725. doi:10.1002/bjs.9927

van Hooff, J. A. R. A. M. (1982). Categories and sequences of behavior: Methods of description and analysis. In K. R. Scherer & P. Ekman (Eds.), *Handbook of methods in nonverbal behavior research* (pp. 362–439). Cambridge, UK: Cambridge University Press.

Waller, M. J. (1999). The timing of adaptive group responses to nonroutine events. *Academy of Management Journal*, *42*(2), 127–137. doi:10.2307/257088

12 Quality Control

Assessing Reliability and Validity

Julia C. Seelandt

Behavioral observation is the method of choice for studying team processes and interactions. It allows researchers to assess behaviors as they happen and provides a measurement for not-readily-apparent team phenomena (e.g., conflicts) or phenomena that only become apparent over time (e.g., communication patterns) (Tschan et al., 2015). When using behavior observation, specific teamwork behavior can be associated with different outcomes (e.g., performance), allowing the comparison and understanding of differences between or within teams (e.g., high versus low performing teams) (Kolbe, Burtscher, & Manser, 2013; Weingart, 1997). Behavioral observation can be based on videotaped behaviors or on direct, on-site observations applying techniques such as coding systems or category systems.

In the absence of an appropriate coding system for the intended study purpose, researchers may have to develop a new one for their needs (see Tschan, Zimmermann, & Semmer, this volume, Chapter 10). However, developing a coding system to assess team interactions is a challenging and complex task because each tool for data collection has to meet distinct and precise methodological criteria for validity and reliability.

The objective of this chapter is to provide an overview of the concepts of reliability and validity as well as to give recommendations on how to satisfy these criteria when developing a new tool for behavioral observations or when applying an existing one and especially coding schemes. The chapter has three main objectives. First, I will provide information about the content of the behavior coding training procedure, what makes trainings effective, and what should be included in a coding manual. This is especially important because conducting behavioral observations usually requires extensive training since coders need a shared understanding of the instrument they are supposed to use and of the setting in which the coders will apply it. Second, I will describe the most commonly used indices for assessing interrater reliability because different coders should provide similar results regarding the categories of interest. Third, I will explain validity, its different types, and how these validities can be increased because in addition to being reliable, a method should also measure what it is intended to measure.

Training Coders to Use Coding Manuals

After having developed a coding scheme, inexperienced coders usually have to complete extensive training before they can use the coding scheme. Applying a coding scheme successfully requires familiarity with the coding system as well as familiarity with the setting in which the coding system will be applied (Weingart, 1997).

Coder Training

Helping new coders learn the coding scheme, use it properly, and improve the quality of their coding requires substantial preparation. Such preparation ideally contains theoretical information about the concepts of interest and the team(s) being examined (e.g., specific characteristics of ad hoc teams and their team members' roles and functions) as well as relevant information and useful pointers on the corresponding setting and context (e.g., formal work procedures, practical explanations of typical workdays, and typical working procedures). Behavioral guidelines for coders in the corresponding setting can be of additional benefit (e.g., how to conduct themselves in the operating room or intensive care unit, guidelines concerning the adherence to hygiene, etc.), as well as an explanation of the technical skills required for coding (e.g., guidance using coding software or other technical equipment). The preparation should also include training regarding the coding system used, which takes the vast majority of the time allocated to coder training because it needs to be learned in repeated trial and error and correction.

Table 12.1 outlines the content and typical procedures of training coders in using coding manuals and familiarizing them with the context, setting, and method. Training coders is an iterative process, and especially the fifth and sixth step of the procedure are recurring parts of the training procedure.

Using Field Notes, Rating Scales, Event Sampling, and Time Sampling

Field notes are notes that observers are taking in free text form without a predefined structure, typically of nonroutine situations or for explorative studies. Therefore, coders need an introduction to the general method, and they should well understand the context and setting they observe in order to not miss important behavior and events (Atkinson, Coffey, Delamont, Lofland, & Lofland, 2001; Emerson, Fretz, & Shaw, 2011; Hammersley & Atkinson, 2007).

When using *rating scales*, observers assign a value to an observed behavior (e.g., Yule et al., 2009). Observers assess the overall quality of an observed behavior permanently during the entire session, relate it to predefined behavioral categories, and merge it into a quality score for each of the behavioral categories (e.g., Yule et al., 2009). Using rating scales needs training because it is essential that observers know the behavioral categories, their corresponding examples of good and poor

Table 12.1 *Content and typical procedure of training coders using coding manuals*

General category	Subcategory	Example
1. Theoretical input	1.1. Theoretical input about the concepts of interest	Give information about why this study is conducted; discuss studies that have a similar structure or that investigate similar theoretical constructs; talk about the concepts of interest such as specific aspects of communication (what does verbalization/closed-loop communication mean?), teamwork skills, implicit/explicit coordination, situation awareness, etc.
	1.2. Theoretical background about the team being examined	Discuss what ad hoc team/crews/task forces means and talk about the difference regarding stable teams; provide information about the professionals with their different status, power, and professional background to give coders an idea of the observed setting
2. Provide background information about	2.1. Typical workdays	Since healthcare/police/fire service has to be provided 24/7, information about working hours and work shifts is helpful to understand why team members may not know each other and to understand why teamwork could be challenging
	2.2 Formal work procedures	Different phases of the task or procedure observed (e.g., main task, subtask, perioperative phase, intraoperative phase), give examples of routine and nonroutine situations
	2.3 Practical explanations of typical working procedures	Information about typical team compositions such as number of people working in the team; information about who does what to whom, when, why, and how
	2.4 Behavioral guidelines for coders in the corresponding setting	Guidelines concerning the adherence to hygiene or safety measures, how to conduct themselves when a person is aggressive during a police operation, how to react when teams refuse to be observed
3. Explain the method and technical equipment used in the study		Discuss the requirements for using field notes/rating scales/event sampling/time sampling; demonstrate the coding software (e.g., Interact; Mangold, 2014; Hyperresearch; Researchware, 2002 etc. – see Glüer, this volume, Chapter 13 on coding software); explain how to manage problems to avoid data loss; give an introduction on how to properly store data
4. Provide a structured introduction to the coding manual		Discuss each code, its explanation, and corresponding examples; provide background on how the coding scheme was developed or why an existing one was chosen; clarify questions regarding the coding manual and revise it if the categories are too broad/overlapping/when definitions are unambiguous/not sufficiently culturally sensitive (see also section about reliability); use short video clips or video-based data to practice the coding scheme

Table 12.1 (*cont.*)

General category	Subcategory	Example
5. Conduct observation and code under supervision		Coding of several units of observations under the direct supervision of an expert observer; review these codings and expert provides extensive feedback; resolve discrepancies by discussions and further explanations of the codes
6. Training is completed		Interrater reliabilities are seldom perfect; coder training is usually completed when interrater reliabilities are above an acceptable level, which will be discussed later in this chapter; if interrater reliabilities remain low after the coder training, the coding manual should either be reviewed and revised and/or more observations under the direct supervision of an expert observer are needed

behaviors, as well as the rating scales themselves (Carthey, de Leval, Wright, Farewell, & Reason, 2003; Crossley, Marriott, Purdie, & Beard, 2011; Hull, Arora, Kassab, Kneebone, & Sevdalis, 2011; Hull et al., 2013; Yule, Flin, Paterson-Brown, Maran, & Rowley, 2006).

Another methodological approach for observing behavior is *event sampling*, which is the coding of specific, predefined events. Since these predefined events are coded as they happen, little judgment from the observer is needed. However, event sampling methodology needs extensive observer training, and the predefined events should be described in a coding manual (McGrath & Altermatt, 1999; Seelandt et al., 2014; Weingart, 1997; Weingart, Olekalns, & Smith, 2004; Yoder & Symons, 2010).

During *time sampling*, coders observe specific behavior during predefined time intervals and record the absence or presence of this behavior (Martin & Bateson, 2007). Time sampling needs observer training because coders should know, and be able to recognize, the behavior of interest.

Coding Manuals

Coding manuals are necessary because different coders should provide similar results regarding the categories of interest. In addition, coding manuals help coders who were not included in the development process (e.g., students, research assistants) to gain an accurate and shared understanding about the coding scheme. Coding manuals ought to contain category names, definitions, and explanations, as well as specific examples for each category. Additionally, rules of thumb about allowing the interpretation of the context (see Table 12.2) are important for coders to know (Weingart, 1997) as well as guidelines for coding, such as clarifying which units are being coded, the beginning and end of the coding period, or remarks about

Table 12.2 *Required components of coding manuals*

Required component	Example
Category names	Leadership
Definitions and explanations	Leadership refers to a clear instruction on what to do or what not to do
Specific examples for each category	"Peter, please administer 20mg Buscopan"
Rules of thumb	Leadership that contains more than one word is coded; "knife" would not be coded as leadership
Guidelines for coding units	Clarifying which units are coded; e.g., coding different phases of a task or procedure, coding within a predefined time interval, etc. Beginning and end of the coding period; e.g., coding period during surgeries from incision to closure Remarks about whether assessing the duration or the occurrence of events; e.g., coding the beginning and end of a defined event. (see Reed, Kolbe, & Boos, this volume, Chapter 11)

whether coders are assessing the duration or solely the occurrence of events. Table 12.2 summarizes the required components for a coding manual with examples.

Understanding and memorizing the coding scheme and its corresponding coding manual takes up a significant amount of the training time. However, training observers should not be considered a burden that has to be performed as quickly as possible. Feedback from coders during training procedures is very valuable in detecting possible systematic problems with the coding scheme (e.g., identification of categories that are too broad) or with coders' current understanding of the coding scheme (e.g., poor understanding regarding the difference between two codes), which might indicate that additional training sessions are needed. Training observers is therefore an opportunity to reveal ambiguous or vague categories, to revise the coding manual, and to clarify definitions and explanations before its application (Weingart, 1997).

Another important part of the training procedure includes several coding trials that are accompanied by an expert. This approach allows calculating interrater reliabilities (discussed later in this chapter) between new coders and the expert (e.g., the developer of the coding scheme or someone with considerable experience with it). When using video-based coding, one option is commenting and explaining the coding of one or more observations in detail by an expert. Appropriately learning to apply the coding scheme is facilitated when the expert provides extensive feedback concerning missed codes or wrong categorization; discussions about discrepancies after each of these trial observations help coders improve as well. In addition, comparison of the codings of two observers – especially when using event sampling – helps identifying systematic coding errors such as constantly confusing two similar codes.

Training procedures are usually completed when interrater reliabilities are above an acceptable level.[1] Considering the different steps of the training procedure, it is not surprising that 25 hours (Seelandt et al., 2014) and up to 200 hours (Lehmann-Willenbrock, Meinecke, Rowold, & Kauffeld, 2015) are reported for coders to learn how to use a coding scheme and to obtain acceptable values of reliability indicating successful training completion.

Having a common understanding of the context and the codes essentially contributes to the quality of coding. It is very important to not consider training as a procedure that is successfully completed after a certain number of codes are logged. Rather, it should be considered a continuous process accompanying data collection and coding, respectively. Coding manuals and rules should be discussed with the coders not only during training but also on a regular basis during the whole phase of data collection. The rationale behind this is to monitor quality of data collection continuously and to avoid coders reinterpreting the coding scheme by developing their own subsystem containing their own exceptions and rules of thumb. In addition, reoccurring discussions of the coding scheme help avoid observer biases. Examples for biases are *observer drift* (when observers sharpen the definition of codes over time, Martin & Bateson, 2007), *the mere exposure effect* (repeated exposure enhances attitudes towards a person, Bornstein, 1993, and may result in over-coding of favorable behaviors), or *the self-fulfilling prophecy* (expectations about people that may affect their behavior in the way that these expectations will be fulfilled, Rosenthal & Jacobson, 1968, e.g., the observer rolls his/her eyes, which irritates the observed person and results in nonfavorable behavior confirming the observer's negative belief regarding the observed person).

Assessing Reliability

No measurement will ever represent reality perfectly because every measurement includes random measurement error referring to "any factors that randomly affect measurement of the variable across the sample" (Jha, 2014, p. 290) and systematic measurement error, that is, "any factors that systematically affect measurement of the variable across the sample" (Jha, 2014, p. 290). In order to reduce measurement error, every tool for data collection has to meet distinct and precise methodological criteria for validity and reliability.

---

[1] Acceptable levels for interrater reliabilities depend on the particular index; see the section "Methods for Calculating Interrater Reliability" in this chapter for more details.

Table 12.3 *Overview of indices for assessing interrater reliability based on level of measurement*

Nominal level	Ordinal and interval level
For two coders:	**Single behaviors/items:**
Cohen's Kappa;	r_{wg} index;
Scott's pi;	Krippendorff's Alpha
Krippendorff's Alpha	
More than two coders:	**For scales:**
Fleiss' Kappa;	ICC;
Scott's pi;	Krippendorff's Alpha
Krippendorff's Alpha	

Interrater Similarity: Agreement and Reliability

A coding scheme for studying interactions should ideally lead to similar results about the category of interest, regardless of who uses it. To assess this interrater similarity, two concepts exist: interrater agreement (IRA) and interrater reliability (IRR). Both assess interrater similarity but they differ in their definition of similarity. IRA refers to the absolute consensus between different coders and focuses on the interchangeability of the coders, whereas the IRR points to the relative consistency between different coders (LeBreton & Senter, 2008; Tinsley & Weiss, 1975). These two concepts are typically used and widely accepted to assess interrater similarity. Therefore, the terms reliability, interrater agreement, and interrater reliability are used synonymously throughout this chapter.

Different methods exist for assessing interrater reliability, with some of them being described below. Depending on the number of coders and the measurement level, some will be more appropriate than others. In general, it is essential to use an index that takes agreement by chance into account for ensuring good interrater reliability.

It is worth calculating and presenting multiple indices for comparison (e.g., Cohen's Kappa and ICC; Howitt & Cramer, 2011; Weingart, 1997) or the observed proportions of positive and negative agreement in addition to Cohen's Kappa values (Cicchetti & Feinstein, 1990; Kolbe et al., 2013). Presenting multiple indices allows for evaluating the categories in a coding scheme critically and for comparing the results with those of other studies.

Table 12.3 provides an overview of how to choose the "right" index for the study and type of data.

Percent agreement, however, is not included in this table because "the convenience of calculating %-agreement, which is often cited as its advantage, cannot compensate for its meaninglessness" (Krippendorff, 2004b, p. 412). It refers to the "percentage of judgments on which coders agree, out of the total number of judgments" (Scott, 1955, p. 322) and is easily calculated. However, it is not chance-corrected and may therefore result in a possible overestimation of the true agreement between two observers (Hallgren, 2012; McHugh, 2012). Moreover, 100 percent of agreement indicates perfect agreement, whereas zero percent indicates no agreement at all. According to Krippendorff (2004b), zero percent agreement has no informative reliability interpretation and it is also rather unrealistic because it means that coders disagree on every category they observe. Percent agreement can only be used for calculating interrater reliabilities for nominal scales and it is limited to only two coders (Krippendorff, 2004b).

Methods for Calculating Interrater Reliability

In the following section, different indices for assessing interrater reliability such as the r_{wg} index, the Intraclass Correlation Coefficient (ICC), Cohen's and Fleiss' Kappa, Scott's pi, as well as Krippendorff's Alpha are described. Depending on the number of coders and the measurement level, some will be more appropriate than others.

Within-Group Interrater Reliability Index (r_{wg} Index). One of the most reported indices for interrater agreement is the r_{wg} index. This index compares the observed variance in ratings and the variance expected in consideration of a null distribution (James, Demaree, & Wolf, 1984). It is generally used to assess agreement when several raters judge a single person on a single variable (LeBreton & Senter, 2008).

The r_{wg} index is estimated by

$$r_{wg} = 1 - (S^2_x / \sigma^{2E})$$

with S^2_x being the observed variance on a variable X over K different observers and with σ^2_E being the variance expected in case of lack of agreement between observers (LeBreton & Senter, 2008). For more details regarding the calculation of r_{wg} index see LeBreton and Senter (2008). The r_{wg} index ranges between 0 and 1, with 1 representing perfect agreement and 0 lack of agreement (LeBreton & Senter, 2008). Brown and Hauenstein (2005) suggest considering values from 0 to .59 as unacceptable levels of agreement, from .60 to .69 as acceptable, and .80 and above as strong levels of agreement.

Intraclass Correlation Coefficient (ICC). Another commonly used measure to assess interrater reliability is the *Intraclass Correlation Coefficient* (ICC), which is based on an one-way random effects analysis of variance (LeBreton & Senter, 2008; Shrout & Fleiss, 1979). It refers to the proportion of observed variance in ratings compared to the total variance in ratings (LeBreton & Senter, 2008). It therefore considers "whether observers were able to agree about summary, or global, behavior measures (frequencies and durations) per observation unit" (Klonek, Quera, & Kauffeld, 2015, p. 285). ICC values are high when the variance between the ratings given by different raters is little. ICC values lower than .40 are seen as poor, values between .40 and .59 as fair, values between .60 and .74 are considered as good, and values above .75 are seen as excellent (Cicchetti, 1994). The ICC is usually calculated when more than two observers are involved (Shrout & Fleiss, 1979). It is also used for assessing interrater reliabilities for ordinal, interval, and ratio scales (Hallgren, 2012).

According to Shrout and Fleiss (1979), the ICC is estimated by

$$\text{ICC} = \frac{\text{BMS} - \text{EMS}}{\text{BMS} + (\text{k} - 1)\text{EMS}}$$

where BMS refers to the mean squares between targets, EMS to the residual sum of squares, and k to the number of coders. For more details regarding the calculation of the ICC see Shrout and Fleiss (1979).

Yoder and Symons (2010) recommend including at least five coding sessions in the ICC calculation or at least ten sessions for more solid results (Bakeman & Quera, 2011). However, these authors do not provide any further details about the duration of these sessions.

Cohens Kappa and Fleiss' Kappa. For nominal scales, *Cohen's Kappa* is suitable to assess interrater reliabilities for two observers, whereas *Fleiss' Kappa* is appropriate for more than two observers (Cohen, 1960; Fleiss, 1971). Both Cohen's Kappa and Fleiss' Kappa refer to the proportion of common agreement with regard to a predefined category or scale that is coded or not. They take chance agreement into account and range from −1 to +1 (Cohen, 1960; Fleiss, 1971). Cohen's Kappa is considered a rather precise index for interrater reliability because it corrects for agreement by chance and is sensitive to the frequency with which categories are chosen: Categories that are chosen less frequently obtain lower estimates of interrater reliability because higher agreement by chance is attributed to the categories chosen more frequently than is required (Howitt & Cramer, 2011; Weingart, 1997). However, Kappa values can be affected by prevalence in the way that a substantial imbalance in the table's marginal totals may lead to low Kappa values despite high agreement between two observers, whereas an asymmetrical imbalance in marginal totals may result in high Kappa values (Feinstein & Cicchetti, 1990).

Cohen's Kappa is estimated by

$$\kappa = \frac{P_0 - P_e}{1 - P_e}$$

with P_0 representing the obtained proportion of agreement between two coders and P_e the proportion coders would be expected to agree by chance (Cohen, 1960). For more details regarding the calculation of Cohen's Kappa see Cohen (1960).

Fleiss' Kappa is estimated by

$$\kappa = \frac{\overline{P}_0 - \overline{P}_e}{1 - \overline{P}_e}$$

with $1 - \overline{P}_e$ being the degree of agreement that is achievable over chance and $\overline{P} - \overline{P}_e$ presenting the degree of agreement that was actually obtained above chance

(Fleiss, 1971). For more details regarding the calculation of Fleiss' Kappa see Fleiss (1971).

Kappa values can be interpreted as follows: Values ≤ 0 indicate no reliability or agreement by chance (Cohen, 1960), values lower than .41 are seen as fair, values between .60 and .80 as substantial, and values above .81 as very good (Landis & Koch, 1977). For robust results, Bakeman, Deckner, and Quera (2005) suggest that 15 to 20 percent of the material should be independently coded by different raters for calculating Kappa. Similarly, Klonek et al. (2015) propose to independently code only a part of the entire observation period in order to be more efficient and economic.

Scott's pi. Another index for calculating interrater reliabilities for nominal scales is *Scott's pi* (Scott, 1955). Cohen's Kappa and Scott's pi have the same formula and both correct for the proportion of agreement that would be expected by chance. However, in contrast to Cohen's Kappa, the expected agreement between different coders is calculated differently for Scott's pi (Craig, 1981): Scott's pi "computes the expected agreement from the proportions of each category in the entire sample of content units" (Craig, 1981, p. 261) and assumes that the proportions in the categories are equal between the observers (Craig, 1981). Scott's pi can be assessed for more than two coders and when different coders have coded subsets of units (Craig, 1981).

Scott's pi is estimated by

$$\pi = \frac{P_0 - P_e}{1 - P_e}$$

with P_0 representing the obtained proportion of agreement between different coders and P_e being the proportion of agreement that is expected by chance (Craig, 1981; Scott, 1955). For more details regarding the calculation of Scott's pi see Scott (1955).

Scott's pi ranges from -1 to $+1$ and according to Craig (1981), the standards for interpreting Kappa values given by Landis and Koch (1977) can also be applied to Scott's pi with values lower than .41 indicating fair reliability, values between .60 and .80 representing substantial reliability, and values above .81 indicating very good reliability.

Krippendorff's Alpha. Another measure for interrater reliability is *Krippendorff's Alpha*, which was originally developed in content analysis and counts pairs of categories that any number of coders have assigned to a single unit of analysis (Hayes & Krippendorff, 2007; Krippendorff, 2004a). It is applicable to samples with missing data and to any scale of measurement, and it takes sample size into account. Krippendorff's Alpha is ranging between 0 and 1, with .67 being the minimum acceptable value and values above .80 indicating substantial reliability (Hayes & Krippendorff, 2007; Krippendorff, 2004a). Alpha cannot be computed with common statistical programs but there is a free macro for SPSS (IBM, 2013) available that allows calculating this reliability coefficient (Hayes & Krippendorff, 2007).

However, interrater reliabilities are seldom perfect (Howitt & Cramer, 2011). If interrater reliabilities remain low after the training procedure, the coding manual should be reviewed in order to answer the following questions: Are there implicit cultural differences in the coding scheme or is a coding scheme not sufficiently culturally sensitive? If the coding scheme is older, is it possible that societal change does not allow for adequate observation based on the coding scheme (e.g., if a coding scheme addresses behavior that is based on stereotypes that have changed since the coding scheme was developed)? Are the categories and codes well defined? Are they too broad or even overlapping and are the definitions unambiguous to understand? The categories of a coding scheme should be very specific because it reduces the coders' cognitive load, which in turn makes coding easier and results in higher interrater reliabilities. These more specific categories can be summarized into larger categories for later analyses without great effort. For instance, Bales' (1950) Interaction Process Analysis (IPA) allows coding main categories at the first step, which can be allocated to more fine-grained subcategories in a second step (see Poole, this volume, Chapter 18).

In addition, the duration of the observation may play an important role for reliability. If the observation time is long, coders may tire, which affects the quality of coding and thus reliability. It is therefore recommended to assess reliability for different time period particularly in case of long observations (Seelandt et al., 2014).

It is important to assess quality of coding continually; I recommend calculating reliabilities regularly after the training procedures, e.g., during every fifth observation or every two weeks, and to provide detailed feedback to coders. This approach avoids subtle and systematic deviations of the coding scheme and ensures that different coders achieve similar results throughout the coding process.

Assessing Validity

In addition to being reliable, a coding scheme should also be valid, which refers to the extent to which a coding scheme measures what it is intended to measure (Dooley, 2001). I will describe face validity, content validity, construct validity, convergent and discriminant validity, as well as predictive or criterion-related validity and provide suggestions on how to increase these different types of validity for behavioral observations.

Face Validity

A coding scheme has *face validity* if its codes simply look as if they are measuring the concepts of interest (Kline, 2015). For instance, observational systems using behavioral marker methodology usually have a high degree of face validity because they consist of predefined behavioral classes with examples of good and poor behavior (Yule et al., 2009). Face validity is not really a measure since it is substantially based on subjective judgments. Subjectivity accompanies the whole research process and influences the selection of codes. However, different raters may have different opinions about the face validity of a coding scheme (Howitt & Cramer, 2011). Using standardized procedures in research serves to overcome subjectivity and assess behavior in ways that can be replicated beyond an individual researcher's subjectivity. Therefore, to assess the validity of a coding scheme more adequately, other types of validity need to be addressed.

Content Validity

Content validity refers to the degree to which a measure reflects all dimensions of the concept of interest (Newman & Newman, 1994). Good content validity is based on an appropriate sample of items or codes representing the construct being measured. Content validity is increased when the items or codes stem from a broad field (Howitt & Cramer, 2011) by combining the following kinds of information:

(1) results from a literature review about the current state of research in the domain of interest,
(2) data obtained by structured or semistructured expert interviews about their specific perceptions on the concepts of interest,
(3) field notes from observations in the corresponding setting to find out what kind of behavior seems to be normal or unusual,
(4) expert reviews about the appropriateness of the items or codes,
(5) a review of existing measures and coding schemes to possibly apply codes or scales or items of existing systems in a measure (Howitt & Cramer, 2011; Weingart, 1997).

In contrast to face validity, experts have to evaluate how well the chosen items or codes cover the concept of interest (Howitt & Cramer, 2011). One possibility to do so is by a group of experts rating items by relevance using the Delphi technique (Clayton, 1997). After the experts have completed their ratings, the results are summarized by calculating, for instance, means, and sent again to the experts to rerate the items again considering the group's measure. If an expert's reevaluation lies outside the group's measure, the expert is asked to explain why the reevaluation deviates from the group's measure (Clayton, 1997). After reevaluation, the results are summarized again. Involving subject matter experts as early as possible in the development and use of coding schemes can be highly valuable.

Construct Validity

Construct validity is the degree to which items or codes measure only or mainly the concept of interest (Cook & Beckman, 2006). Similar to content validity, construct validity is increased by combining the results of expert ratings, observational data, and literature reviews about the concept of interest. However, for some coding schemes, it is more critical to assess content and construct validity than for others. For instance, if a coding scheme simply uses codes such as Question and Statement, there is fairly little doubt that the code is actually measuring questions or statements (see Stiles, this volume, Chapter 44).

Two subtypes of construct validity exist: *convergent* and *discriminant validity*. Convergent validity refers to the degree to which measures that are supposed to assess the same construct are actually related or correlate with each other considerably (Cunningham, Preacher, & Banaji, 2001). Conversely, discriminant validity is the degree to which measures that are measuring different but similar constructs are actually not related to each other or do not correlate, respectively (Howitt & Cramer, 2011). For instance, to test for convergent validity of a coding scheme for assessing teamwork in healthcare teams, one possibility is to use different measures such as Likert-type rating scales, behaviorally anchored scales, or behavioral coding for the same construct and to compare the results afterwards. Seelandt et al. (2014) include an overview of different observational methods for assessing teamwork, communication, and distractors in the operating room that can be used for choosing different measures when assessing convergent validity. Assessing convergent validity is time consuming and requires personal resources because well-trained raters are needed: Using different measures at the same time to assess validity is possible for video-based coding but it is difficult for live, on-site observations because multiple raters need to be involved. During live observations, several raters might be perceived as disturbing for the observed teams and – depending on the setting – space for raters might be limited (e.g., imagine several raters in the operating room together with the surgical team consisting of at least seven people). For this purpose, archival material could be used or similar situations as the context of interest. If a construct is new and nobody has tried to measure it before, it is not possible to assess convergent validity. In that case, however, it is still possible to assess discriminant validity because measures that assess related but distinct constructs can be used. For instance, situation awareness and shared mental models are similar yet distinct constructs. When using measurements for each construct, the results should actually differ, or – in other words – the measure assessing situation awareness should not highly correlate with the measure assessing shared mental models.

Predictive or Criterion-Related Validity

Predictive validity describes how well the measure predicts behavior in the future and can be assessed by correlation (Howitt & Cramer, 2011). Several studies have shown that differences in teamwork measured by certain coding schemes were associated with differences in team performance (see the systematic literature review of Schmutz and Manser, 2013). For example, a behavioral observation study on teamwork and communication within surgical teams has shown that more patient- and case-relevant communication during surgeries is related to better patient outcomes, whereas more patient- and case-irrelevant communication during wound closure is related to worse patient outcomes, namely more postoperative infections (Tschan et al., 2015). Likewise, another study performed lag sequential analyses based on behavioral observations and showed that higher-performing teams have a different interaction pattern compared to lower-performing teams (Kolbe et al., 2014). However, these studies assess or report predictive validity of its measure only implicitly.

For the future and especially for studying team dynamics, it would be extremely important to assess and report predictive validity explicitly. Very often, coding and observational methods are discredited because people claim that it is a waste of time and that they do not predict anything, or at least not better than conventional measures used in teams. Therefore, it would be imperative for progress in team research in general and observational methods in particular to show that this method compared to other methods actually predicts future events better than those conventional methods. This request does not seem to be easily satisfiable because it seems challenging and difficult to show predictive validity, especially in dynamic, fluid teams. In healthcare teams, for instance, it should be taken into account that team composition is frequently changing since healthcare services have to be guaranteed 24/7 and teaching hospitals have rather high turnover rates, which makes it difficult to predict future team behavior.

Conclusion

The purpose of this chapter was to provide information about the content and typical procedure of training coders, the use of coding manuals, as well as introduce the concepts of reliability and validity as they apply specifically to observations and interaction coding. Different approaches and methods for assessing different aspects of each were presented and discussed with regard to studying team interactions.

Controlling and ensuring quality while meeting methodological requirements is time consuming and resource intensive when developing a new instrument or applying an existing instrument for behavioral observations. It is imperative to perform quality control at various stages of the data collection phase, particularly when studying team interactions. Since team interactions are characterized as being dynamic, fluid, and may change over time (Zijlstra, Waller, & Phillips, 2012), the corresponding quality control should consider these attributes. Quality control regarding reliability therefore should be performed (1) at different phases of team interaction (e.g., during routine and nonroutine phases; during the pre-, intra-, and postoperative phases when observing health care teams or after the occurrence of specific events) as well as (2) constantly after a certain number of observations and with different coders during the whole phase of data collection. Extensive training at early stages of the research process is recommended to facilitate and support coders in learning and applying the measure properly. Moreover, (3) validity should be assessed right after the development of the method, and (4) the relationship of reliability and validity should be considered because if a measure is valid that does not mean that it is reliable, and vice versa: a measure can be both reliable and valid, reliable and not valid, and neither reliable nor valid, but never valid and not reliable (Golafshani, 2003; Howitt & Cramer, 2011).

Taken together, it is worth investing time in quality control because it will pay off in the long run, resulting in better interrater reliability, improved validity, and higher data quality.

References

Atkinson, P., Coffey, A., Delamont, S., Lofland, J., & Lofland, L. (2001). *Handbook of Ethnography*. London, UK: Sage.

Bakeman, R., Deckner, D. F., & Quera, V. (2005). Analysis of behavioral streams. In D. M. Teti (Ed.), *Handbook of research methods in developmental science* (pp. 394–420). Oxford, UK: Blackwell Publishers.

Bakeman, R., & Quera, V. (2011). *Sequential analysis and observational methods for the behavioral sciences*. Cambridge, UK: Cambridge University Press.

Bales, R. F. (1950). *Interaction process analysis: A method for the study of small groups*. Oxford, UK: Addison-Wesley.

Bornstein, R. F. (1993). Mere exposure effects with outgroup stimuli. In D. Mackie & D. Hamilton (Eds.), *Affect, cognition, and stereotyping: Interactive processes in group perception* (pp. 195–211). San Diego, CA: Academic Press.

Brown, R. D., & Hauenstein, N. M. (2005). Interrater agreement reconsidered: An alternative to the rwg indices. *Organizational Research Methods*, *8*(2), 165–184. doi:10.1177/1094428105275376

Carthey, J., de Leval, M. R., Wright, D. J., Farewell, V. T., & Reason, J. T. (2003). Behavioural markers of surgical excellence. *Safety Science*, *41*(5), 409–425. doi:10.1016/S0925-7535(01)00076-5

Cicchetti, D. V. (1994). Guidelines, criteria, and rules of thumb for evaluating normed and standardized assessment instruments in psychology. *Psychological Assessment*, *6*(4), 284–290. doi:10.1037/1040-3590.6.4.284

Cicchetti, D. V., & Feinstein, A. R. (1990). High agreement but low kappa: II. Resolving the paradoxes. *Journal of Clinical Epidemiology*, *43*(6), 551–558. doi:10.1016/0895-4356(90)90159-M

Clayton, M. J. (1997). Delphi: A technique to harness expert opinion for critical decision-making tasks in education. *Educational Psychology*, *17*(4), 373–386. doi:10.1080/0144341970170401

Cohen, J. (1960). A coefficient of agreement for nominal scales. *Educational and Psychosocial Measurement*, *20*, 37–46. doi:10.1177/001316446002000104

Cook, D. A., & Beckman, T. J. (2006). Current concepts in validity and reliability for psychometric instruments: theory and application. *The American Journal of Medicine*, *119*(2), 166.e7–166.e16. doi:10.1016/j.amjmed.2005.10.036

Craig, R. T. (1981). Generalization of Scott's index of intercoder agreement. *Public Opinion Quarterly*, *45*(2), 260–264. doi:10.1086/268657

Crossley, J., Marriott, J., Purdie, H., & Beard, J. (2011). Prospective observational study to evaluate NOTSS (Non-Technical Skills for Surgeons) for assessing trainees' non-technical performance in the operating theatre. *British Journal of Surgery*, *98*(7), 1010–1020. doi:10.1002/bjs.7478

Cunningham, W. A., Preacher, K. J., & Banaji, M. R. (2001). Implicit attitude measures: Consistency, stability, and convergent validity. *Psychological Science*, *12*(2), 163–170. doi:10.1111/1467-9280.00328

Dooley, K. (2001). *Social research methods* (4th ed.). Upper Saddle River, NJ: Prentice Hall.

Emerson, R. M., Fretz, R. I., & Shaw, L. L. (2011). *Writing ethnographic fieldnotes* (2nd edn.). Chicago, IL: University of Chicago Press.

Feinstein, A. R., & Cicchetti, D. V. (1990). High agreement but low kappa: I. The problems of two paradoxes. *Journal of Clinical Epidemiology*, *43*(6), 543–549. doi:10.1016/0895-4356(90)90158-L

Fleiss, J. L. (1971). Measuring nominal scale agreement among many raters. *Psychological Bulletin*, *76*(5), 378–382. doi:10.1037/h0031619

Golafshani, N. (2003). Understanding reliability and validity in qualitative research. *The Qualitative Report*, *8*(4), 597–606.

Hallgren, K. A. (2012). Computing inter-rater reliability for observational data: An overview and tutorial. *Tutorials in Quantitative Methods for Psychology*, *8*(1), 23–34. doi:10.20982/tqmp.08.1.p023

Hammersley, M., & Atkinson, P. (2007). *Ethnography: Principles in practice* (3rd edn.). London, UK: Routledge.

Hayes, A. F., & Krippendorff, K. (2007). Answering the call for a standard reliability measure for coding data. *Communication Methods and Measures*, *1*(1), 77–89. doi:10.1080/19312450709336664

Howitt, D., & Cramer, D. (2011). *Introduction to research methods in psychology* (3rd edn.). Harlow, UK: Pearson Education.

Hull, L., Arora, S., Kassab, E., Kneebone, R., & Sevdalis, N. (2011). Observational teamwork assessment for surgery: content validation and tool refinement. *Journal of the American College of Surgeons*, *212*(2), 234–243. doi:10.1016/j.jamcollsurg.2010.11.001

Hull, L., Arora, S., Symons, N. R., Jalil, R., Darzi, A., Vincent, C., & Sevdalis, N. (2013). Training faculty in nontechnical skill assessment: National guidelines on program requirements. *Annals of Surgery*, *258*(2), 370–375. doi:10.1097/SLA.0b013e318279560b

IBM. (2013). IBM SPSS Statistics for Windows, Version 22.0. Armonk, NY: IBM Corporation.

James, L. R., Demaree, R. G., & Wolf, G. (1984). Estimating within-group interrater reliability with and without response bias. *Journal of Applied Psychology*, *69*(1), 85–98. doi:10.1037/0021-9010.69.1.85

Jha, A. S. (2014). *Social research methods*. New Delhi, India: McGraw Hill Education.

Kline, P. (2015). *A handbook of test construction: Introduction to psychometric design*. London, UK: Routledge.

Klonek, F. E., Quera, V., & Kauffeld, S. (2015). Coding interactions in motivational interviewing with computer-software: What are the advantages for process researchers? *Computers in Human Behavior*, *44*, 284–292. doi:10.1016/j.chb.2014.10.034

Kolbe, M., Burtscher, M. J., & Manser, T. (2013). Co-ACT – a framework for observing coordination behaviour in acute care teams. *BMJ Quality and Safety in Health Care*, *22*, 596–605. doi:10.1136/bmjqs-2012-001319

Kolbe, M., Grote, G., Waller, M. J., Wacker, J., Grande, B., Burtscher, M. J., & Spahn, D. R. (2014). Monitoring and talking to the room: Autochthonous coordination patterns in team interaction and performance. *Journal of Applied Psychology*, *99*(6), 1254–1267. doi:10.1037/a0037877

Krippendorff, K. (2004a). *Content analysis: An introduction to its methodology.* (2nd edn.). Thousand Oaks, CA: Sage.

Krippendorff, K. (2004b). Reliability in content analysis: Some common misconceptions and recommendations. *Human Communication Research*, *30*(3), 411–433. doi:10.1111/j.1468-2958.2004.tb00738.x

Landis, J. R., & Koch, G. G. (1977). The measurement of observer agreement for categorical data. *Biometrics*, *33*, 159–174. doi:10.2307/2529310

LeBreton, J. M., & Senter, J. L. (2008). Answers to 20 questions about interrater reliability and interrater agreement. *Organizational Research Methods*, *11*, 815–852. doi:10.1177/1094428106296642

Lehmann-Willenbrock, N., Meinecke, A. L., Rowold, J., & Kauffeld, S. (2015). How transformational leadership works during team interactions: A behavioral process analysis. *The Leadership Quarterly*, *26*(6), 1017–1033. doi:10.1016/j.leaqua.2015.07.003

Mangold. (2014). INTERACT Benutzerhandbuch. Mangold International GmbH (Hrsg.). Retrieved February 16, 2018, from www.mangold-international.com/de/

Martin, P., & Bateson, P. (2007). *Measuring behavior, an introductory guide*. Cambridge, UK: Cambridge University Press.

McGrath, J. E., & Altermatt, T. W. (1999). Observation and analysis of group interaction over time: Some methodological and strategic choices. In M. Hogg & R. Tindale (Eds.), *Blackwell handbook of social psychology: Group processes* (pp. 525–556). London, UK: Blackwell Publishing.

McHugh, M. L. (2012). Interrater reliability: The kappa statistic. *Biochemia Medica*, *22*(3), 276–282. doi:10.11613/BM.2012.031

Newman, I., & Newman, C. (1994). *Conceptual statistics for beginners*. Lanham, MA: University Press of America.

Researchware. (2002). *HyperRESEARCH*. Randolph, MA: ResearchWare, Inc.

Rosenthal, R., & Jacobson, L. (1968). Pygmalion in the classroom. *The Urban Review*, *3*(1), 16–20. doi:10.1007/BF02322211

Schmutz, J., & Manser, T. (2013). Do team processes really have an effect on clinical performance? A systematic literature review. *British Journal of Anaesthesia*, *110*, 529–544. doi:10.1093/bja/aes513

Scott, W. A. (1955). Reliability of content analysis: The case of nominal scale coding. *Public Opinion Quarterly*, *19*(3), 321–325. doi:10.1086/266577

Seelandt, J. C., Tschan, F., Keller, S., Beldi, G., Jenni, N., Kurmann, A., & Semmer, N. K. (2014). Assessing distractors and teamwork during surgery: Developing an event-based method for direct observation. *BMJ Quality & Safety in Healthcare*, *23*, 918–929. doi:10.1136/bmjqs-2014-002860

Shrout, P. E., & Fleiss, J. L. (1979). Intraclass correlations: Uses in assessing rater reliability. *Psychological Bulletin*, *86*(2), 420–428. doi:10.1037/0033-2909.86.2.420

Tinsley, H. E., & Weiss, D. J. (1975). Interrater reliability and agreement of subjective judgments. *Journal of Counseling Psychology*, *22*(4), 358–376. doi:10.1037/h0076640

Tschan, F., Seelandt, J., Keller, S., Semmer, N., Kurmann, A., Candinas, D., & Beldi, G. (2015). Impact of case-relevant and case-irrelevant communication within the surgical team on surgical-site infection. *British Journal of Surgery*, *102*(13), 1718–1725. doi:10.1002/bjs.9927

Weingart, L. R. (1997). How did they do that? *Research in Organizational Behavior*, *19*, 189–239.

Weingart, L. R., Olekalns, M., & Smith, P. L. (2004). Quantitative coding of negotiation behavior. *International Negotiation*, *9*(3), 441–456. doi:10.1163/1571806053498805

Yoder, P., & Symons, F. (2010). *Observational measurement of behavior*. New York, NY: Springer.

Yule, S., Flin, R., Maran, N., Rowley, D., Youngson, G., Duncan, J., & Paterson-Brown, S. (2009). Development and evaluation of the NOTTS behavior rating system for intraoperative surgery. In R. Flin & L. Mitchell (Eds.), *Safer surgery. Analysing behaviour in the operating theatre* (pp. 7–26). London, UK: Ashgate.

Yule, S., Flin, R., Paterson-Brown, S., Maran, N., & Rowley, D. (2006). Development of a rating system for surgeons' non-technical skills. *Medical Education*, *40*(11), 1098–1104. doi:10.1111/j.1365-2929.2006.02610.x

Zijlstra, F. R., Waller, M. J., & Phillips, S. I. (2012). Setting the tone: Early interaction patterns in swift-starting teams as a predictor of effectiveness. *European Journal of Work and Organizational Psychology*, *21*(5), 749–777. doi:10.1080/1359432X.2012.690399

13 Software for Coding and Analyzing Interaction Processes

Michael Glüer

The purpose of software for interaction coding is to support the process of data coding and data analysis. *Data coding* refers to the process of choosing a particular event or time segment and assigning a code to it. For example, a scene in a video where two people argue could be an event for applying a specific code such as "arguing" (referred to as event sampling, Table 13.2). Also, a specific time segment could be considered as a coding-unit (e.g., a video of 60 minutes is divided into ten time segments of six minutes each; referred to as time sampling, Table 13.2). Interaction coding constitutes the first step in the process of doing interaction analysis by assigning specific codes to a selected event or time segment.

The second step of this process is data analysis. *Data analysis* involves the process of assessing and describing events, time segments, and specific interaction patterns. For example, to find out if a teacher's praise is associated with positive reactions by a specific pupil, you need to search for interaction patterns of the events "teacher's praising" and "pupil's reaction." In some software products, such as INTERACT (Mangold International, 2016) or Observer XT (Noldus Information Technology, 2016) the time frame (of the pupil's reaction after a teacher's praise) can even be specified (i.e., in a time frame of two seconds after a teacher's praising). Such analysis techniques are called "contingency or latency analyses." The two coded events can also be used to generate a new event such as "praising and reaction." Creating new codes or events from existing codes, events, or time segments is another part of the analyzing process, which is referred to as *data compilation* (creating new codes). The available software of interaction coding offers either features for both coding and analyzing interactions or only features for coding interactions.

Software programs for interaction coding and analyzing are mostly developed for a specific data type such as video, audio, pictures, or text data, although most products support several data types (Table 13.1).

Software for Video Data Coding and Analysis

There are two leading commercial software products for video data coding: INTERACT (Mangold International, 2016) and Observer XT (Noldus

The author has no affiliation with any mentioned company in this chapter nor any financial or nonfinancial interest in the subject matter or software discussed in this manuscript.

Table 13.1 *Categories of software for interaction coding*

Data categories	Description	Programs
Video	Interaction coding and analysis based on video data	Annotation Tools: ANVIL, ELAN*, EXMARaLDA f4/f5* Catmovie, Transana, Generalized Sequential Querier Etholog INTERACT* Observer XT* Transcriber AG Videograph* QDAS: Aquada7, ATLAS.ti*, DEDOOSE, HyperRESEARCH, MAXQDA*, NVivo*, QDAMiner,
Audio	Interaction coding and analysis based on audio data	Annotation Tools: ANVIL, ELAN*, EXMARaLDA, Transana, f4/f5* INTERACT* Observer XT* Transcriber AG QDAS: Aquada7, ATLAS.ti*, DEDOOSE HyperRESEARCH, MAXQDA*, NVivo*, QDAMiner
Text and picture	Interaction coding and analysis based on text or picture data (e.g., documents, transcribed interviews, tweets; webpages etc.)	QDAS: Aquada7, ATLAS.ti*, DEDOOSE HyperRESEARCH, MAXQDA*, NVivo*, QDAMiner

Note. *= Software that will be introduced; QDAS: Qualitative Data Analysis Software.

Information Technology, 2016). Although both software products offer similar functions, they differ in the program interface and the operation of the software. The most significant difference is the research context for which they have been developed. INTERACT was designed mainly for the field of psychology, whereas Observer XT was designed in the context of biology. Apart from INTERACT and Observer XT, there are many other software tools for specific research purposes or scientific domains. The software Videograph is such a tool; it was originally developed in a German research project to code student-teacher interactions (Rimmele, 2013).

Video data can also be coded and analyzed with annotation, transcription, and qualitative data analysis software (QDAS). Annotation tools are developed in the scientific context of linguistics (Glüer, 2015a). They are tools to code and analyze all kind of language (i.e., spoken language, sign language). The term "annotation" refers to the possibility to comment on language and behavior. To "annotate" is therefore just a synonym for coding. Some of these annotation tools support audio and video data coding such as the Eudico Linguistic Annotator (ELAN; Max Planck Institute for Psycholinguistics, n.d.), ANVIL (Kipp, n. d.) or Transana (Transana, n.d.). Other tools are just made for coding audio data. Another option to code video data is to use transcription tools such as f4/f5, which offer some basic coding options. F4/f5 supports audio as well as video data. Its primary purpose is to transcribe data, but it is also suitable for some basic coding.

Another category of software to code and analyze interactions is qualitative data analysis software (QDAS). QDAS is a category of software developed to code and analyze primarily qualitative data (e.g., applying qualitative methods such as grounded theory or discourse analysis). Recently, some QDAS also support a combination of qualitative and quantitative coding and analyzing (coding by assigning numerical rather than alphabetic codes; e.g., MAXQDA). QDAS support text data (e.g., transcripts of interviews, tweets), pictures, but also video or audio data. Although QDAS offer the possibility to code audio and video files, they offer less usability compared to those products specially designed for video or audio data coding and analysis. This applies especially to the quantification of observational data. For example, most QDAS offer no specific features for sampling methods.

Criteria for Selecting Software

There are several criteria that can help the researcher find the appropriate software (Table 13.2; Glüer, 2010):

(1) *Usability* refers to the easiness and user friendliness of a software product.
(2) *Coding options* refer to the different possibilities to record a code in the software. For example, advanced video data coding software offers the option to assign a specific code to a key of the keyboard.
(3) *Supported sampling methods* refer to the (quantitative) coding of video and audio files. Video and audio data are mainly coded by the help of three different sampling methods: (a) event sampling, (b) time sampling, and (c) sequence sampling (Faßnacht, 2007). In event sampling, every interaction is coded as it occurs. The duration of the interaction is specified by the event itself. In time sampling the video file is fragmented in evenly divided time segments. Sequence sampling is a mix of event sampling and time sampling (Altmann, 1974). The video file is fragmented in individual time segments. The time segment is defined by specific events and the events can have different durations (Faßnacht, 2007; for an example see Glüer, 2013).
(4) *Processing several data files* includes the possibility to work on several data files at the same time. Depending on the data type, this criterion can have a different meaning. For video data, it refers to coding two or more videos from

Table 13.2 *Criteria for selecting software for interaction coding and analyzing (adapted from Glüer, 2010)*

Name of Criterion	Description	Indicators
Usability	Usability refers to the easiness and user friendliness of software.	How easy to use is the software? How stable does the software run? How is the timeline of a video or audio file presented (vertically or horizontally)?
Coding options	Which possibilities has the user to record codes?	How easily can codes be entered? Are there any keyboard shortcuts to assign codes? Can a time frame of a code be used to generate multiple codes? Is it possible to apply multiple coding systems? Can the codes or coding system be saved and transferred to other data projects or software tools?
Supported sampling methods (video or audio data)	Which sampling methods can be realized? And how good is the usability of those methods?	Event sampling (an event is recorded every time it happens. The duration of the event depends on the event itself). Time sampling (data file is fragmented in time segments. For each time segment a single code is given. The duration of the event depends on the specified time segment). Sequence sampling (data file is fragmented in time segments. The duration of a time segment depends on a specific event).
Processing several data files	Is it possible to work with several text, audio, or video files?	How many video files can be played at the same time? How easily can video files be synchronized? Is it possible to switch between the sound source of different video files (e. g., choosing the sound of video 1 or 2)?
Software extensibility (plugins; add-ons)	Can the software be extended by additional components?	Can the software be extended by specific components to analyze, for example, physical data such as heart rate? Can the software be extended by self-written plugins or add-ons?
Data compilation	Is it possible to generate new codes from existing codes?	Can new codes be generated? Generating codes from overlapping events? Generating codes from coding gaps?
Data analysis	Can codes be visualized and analyzed?	Can the interrater reliability be calculated (intraclass coefficient; Cohen's kappa) Can descriptive statistics of the data files be analyzed (e.g., video time, code frequency)? Can codes be visualized?

Table 13.2 (*cont.*)

Name of Criterion	Description	Indicators
Data export	How easily can data be transferred in other software, printed, or exported in different data file formats?	Video and audio files: Can recorded codes be exported? Text files: Can the transcript be customized for export? Are there multifunctional print features (e.g., printing transcript in different ways)? Can data easily be exported in software such as SPSS or MPLUS? Are there any data import functions?
Technical support	Where can you find help if something goes wrong?	Do the developers offer technical support? Are there other support forms (e.g., forums)?
Operation system	Which operation systems are supported?	Does the software support your OS? Does the software support multiple OS such as Linux, MacOS, or Windows?
Time frame precision	How precise and accurate is time information of video and audio files?	Does the software capture milliseconds from audio and video files or picture frames from video files? Can you adjust the data set to the time frame of the video file?
Commercial vs. non-commercial	Commercial, academic, or open source.	Is the software commercial or free (see support and costs)? Was it developed for a specific research area (e.g., linguistic)?
Costs	How expensive is the software?	Cost for software Costs for service Costs for hardware Additional costs

the same scene simultaneously (i.e., cam-1 for teacher and cam-2 for students). For audio or text data it refers to the possibility to open or combine files into a single project.

(5) *Software extensibility* implies the possibility to incorporate external data sources. Some software offers specific add-ons to include physiological data (e.g., heart rate). Other products have the possibility to implement self-written plugins to extend the software capabilities.

(6) *Data compilation* stands for the possibility to generate new codes from existing codes (i.e., from overlaps or time gaps).

(7) *Data analysis* involves visualization, describing, and analyzing the finalized coding (i.e., frequency or mean frequency of codes).

(8) *Data export* enables the user to export data (transcripts, codes) in other software tools, e.g., R-Statistics.

(9) *Technical support* refers to the different ways developers offer support for technical issues. Interaction analysis based on video data is often confronted with difficulties to play back the digital video. Some software developers offer a special service for such issues.

(10) *Supported operation systems* point to the ability to run the software on different operation systems (OS) such as Windows, MacOS, or Linux-based OSs.

(11) *Time frame precision* refers to the accuracy of capturing time values. Depending on the research aim, a researcher may need different time information (e.g., minutes, seconds, or milliseconds). Nevertheless, time should be captured at least in milliseconds and at best in picture frames.

(12) *Commercial vs. noncommercial software* refer to the software origin: Commercial products, developed by companies, are associated with costs (see next point), but offer technical support and innovative features. Noncommercial refers to free or open-source[1] software. They may offer less support and can be error prone sometimes.

(13) *Cost* is probably, for some readers, the most convincing criterion of the product. There are some free products (mostly for coding). Professional software is most times associated with costs.

The following section will introduce eight different software solutions suitable for video coding. Table 13.3 contains an in-depth comparison of the software solution based on these 13 criteria.

INTERACT

INTERACT was developed by Pascal Mangold in Germany (Mangold International, 2017). The initial purpose of the software was to code and analyze video data in the context of developmental psychology, but eventually it became a tool for working with all kinds of video data from any research field. INTERACT offers regular updates with new features. The software is commercial and the Mangold company provides technical support and customer service.

In INTERACT multiple videos can be opened. There is no actual limitation regarding the number of videos that can run at the same time (Mangold International, 2016). The program's interface is one of the easiest for video data coding and analysis. The software comes with a USB flash drive, which also serves as a hardware license key. It supports currently only Windows. A software license (USB flash drive) can only be used by one person/computer at a time. Equipping several computers can be therefore quite cost intensive.

---

[1] The term "free" in free software refers to freedom of using, adapting, and sharing the software (Free Software Foundation, 2016). open-source refers to software where the source code is accessible.

Table 13.3 *A comparison of selected software for interaction coding and analyzing*

Name	INTERACT	Observer XT	Videograph	Eudico Linguistic Annotator	f4/f5	ATLAS.ti	MAXQDA	NVivo
Web page	www.mangold-international.com/en/	www.noldus.com	www.dervideograph.de/enhtmStart.html	https://tla.mpi.nl/tools/tla-tools/elan/	www.audiotranskription.de/english	www.atlasti.com	www.maxqda.com	www.qsrinternational.com
Supported data	Video and audio	Video and audio	Video and audio	Video and audio	Video and audio	Text, pictures, video, audio	Text, pictures, video, audio	Text, pictures, video, audio
Usability	High	Moderate	Moderate	Low	High	High	Moderate	Moderate
Coding options	Many coding options: – Direct coding by mouse or keyboard[a] – Programmable keyboard shortcuts – Simultaneous coding[b] – Comprehensive coding management	Many coding options: – Direct coding by mouse or keyboard[a] – Programmable keyboard shortcuts – Simultaneous coding[b] – Comprehensive coding management	Some coding options: – Direct coding by mouse or keyboard[a] – Ten programmable keyboard shortcuts (no letters) – Simultaneously coding[b] – Basic coding management	Some coding options: – No direct coding by mouse or keyboard[a] – Programmable keyboard shortcuts (no single key coding) – No simultaneous coding[b] – Basic coding management	Few coding options: – Eleven programmable keyboard shortcuts (predefined text elements; no single key coding) – Additional software for coding transcripts (text files) f4analyze	Many coding options: – No direct coding by mouse or keyboard[a] – No simultaneous coding[b] – Comprehensive coding management	Many coding options: – No direct coding by mouse or keyboard[a] – Nine programmable keyboard shortcuts (no single key coding) – No simultaneous coding[b] – Comprehensive coding management	Many coding options: – Direct coding by mouse (not keyboard[a]) – No programmable keyboard shortcuts – No simultaneous coding[b] – Comprehensive coding management

Table 13.3 (cont.)

Name	INTERACT	Observer XT	Videograph	Eudico Linguistic Annotator	f4/f5	ATLAS.ti	MAXQDA	NVivo
Supported sampling methods	All sampling methods: – Sampling setup is very easy	All sampling methods	All sampling methods: – Usability highest with time sampling	No sampling methods: – No feature for sampling methods – Sampling methods can be applied by a workaround – Option for creating regular time segments (time sampling)	No sampling methods: – No feature for sampling methods – Sampling methods can be applied by a workaround – No option for creating regular time segments (time sampling)	No sampling methods: – No feature for sampling methods – Sampling methods can be applied by a workaround – No option for creating regular time segments (time sampling)	No sampling methods: – No feature for sampling methods – Sampling methods can be applied by a workaround – No option for creating regular time segments (time sampling)	No sampling methods: – No feature for sampling methods – Sampling methods can be applied by a workaround – No option for creating regular time segments (time sampling)
Processing several data files	Supports video and audio data: – Plays many videos simultaneously – Videos can be synchronized – Import of external data (e. g., physiological data)	Supports video and audio data: – Plays only two videos simultaneously in the standard version – Videos can be synchronized – Import of external data (e.g., physiological data)	Supports video and audio data: – Plays many videos simultaneously – Videos can be synchronized	Supports video and audio data: – Plays many videos simultaneously – Videos can be synchronized	Supports video and audio data: – Plays many videos simultaneously – Videos can be synchronized	Supports video and audio, text and picture data: – Plays only one video at a time	Supports video and audio, text and picture data: – Plays only one video at a time	Supports video and audio, text and picture data: – Plays only one video at a time

Observer XT

Observer XT was developed by Lucas Noldus (Noldus Information Technology Company, 2016). Observer XT was initially developed for the scientific domain of biology but is currently being used in various scientific areas. It is as powerful as INTERACT, and its primary strength lies within visualization and analysis of all kind of data (e.g., physiological data or data form eye tracking combined with video data). The software is designed for Windows and comes with a USB flash drive, which serves as a hardware license key.

Observer XT offers many features like a facial recognizer for emotions (additional module). The first versions of the Observer XT interface seemed to be somehow complicated. Since then, the company has made significant improvements regarding the user-friendliness of the program. For example, the software offers a three-step interface to set up a project: (1) Setting up the parameters, e.g., sampling method, (2) creating a coding scheme, and (3) defining independent variables. Additionally, Observer XT offers a graphical preview of how the coded data would look in the timeline viewer if the user used a particular setup (e.g., codes with or without duration; Noldus Information Technology, 2015). Introduction videos support the user to initiate the first project. Coding is defined by an aligned key of the keyboard. The time code is shown in hours, minutes, seconds, and frames per second (00h:00min:00sec:00 frames per second). Events are recorded in a vertical timeline (Figure 13.2). Each event can also be visualized in a colored bar on a horizontal timeline. Observer XT also supports coding of several videos at the same time. But there is a limitation of two videos in the standard version with the "media module" and up to four if the user purchases the "multiple media module."

Additionally, there are many options to compile data, for instance, generating a new code from existing codes (merging) or gaps. The analyzing options are numerous, and there are all kinds of descriptive statistics, visualization options, and analyzing techniques. For example, Observer XT supports analysis of specific time segments and subjects, and can analyze coding patterns through, for instance, latency analysis. Moreover, different forms of inter- and intrarater reliability analysis are provided (e.g., Cohen's Kappa).

Observer XT also offers an interface to extend the software and combine it with other software products, e.g., the smart eye tracker. Data can be exported as text files or XLSX files (Microsoft Excel). The company also offers professional support for their software. In sum, Observer XT is a great tool to work with all kinds of observational data. It shows its strength when in-depth analyses are necessary and observational data are combined with data from other sources. Although Noldus profoundly improved the usability, the main disadvantage is still the complexity of the product. Usability is also the biggest difference between INTERACT and Observer XT.

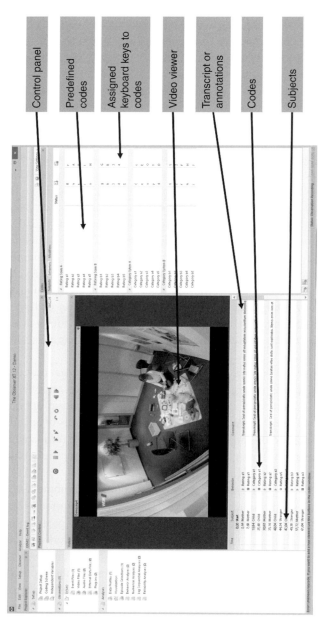

Figure 13.2 Observer XT (version 15.5.927 for Windows). Company: Noldus Information Technology. Demo data file. (Date of screenshot: February 24, 2016, Windows 8.1).

Videograph

Whereas INTERACT and Observer XT are commercial software products, Videograph was developed in a research project at the University of Kiel (Germany). The aim was to develop software to code student-teacher interactions. The software only works on Windows and is not free.

Videograph consists of one central window that includes several secondary windows for video data coding: a video viewer, timeline viewer (data file), and coding and transcription viewer (Figure 13.3). The timeline viewer is horizontal. A recorded code is displayed in the timeline viewer only by a colored bar. The names of the codes themselves are not presented. On the left side of the timeline viewer, an indicator shows the name of the observation instrument or subject of a transcript. The time value of codes cannot be directly viewed in the timeline viewer. For defining codes or transcript videos, there is a coding and transcription viewer. Videograph supports up to 40 subcategories or scales of an observation instrument. A name of an observation category or rating scale can include up to eight signs, and the description can involve 255 signs (Rimmele, 2013). Videograph supports all sampling methods.

Codes can be recorded by clicking the left mouse button on the code in the coding and transcription window (start time) and clicking again for the end time of the code. While one code is recorded (e.g., raising the hand), other codes can be recorded simultaneously (e.g., smiling). Another option is to press a number key on the keyboard (0 to 9). But there is no option to assign a letter key, which restricts the use of a complex coding system by keyboard. However, coding by keyboard only works when the coding and transcription viewer is activated and the right observation instrument (e.g., observation category or rating scale) is marked. In Videograph, a user must switch between different viewers (e.g., video viewer to play the video or the coding and transcription viewer to code or transcribe). As a result, the wrong viewer or observation instrument for coding can often be activated, and the code will not be recorded.

Videograph supports assigning a numerical value to codes, which can be exported to SPSS. The time code shows hours, minutes, and seconds. Therefore, Videograph is not able to record exact time frames of an event (e.g., ms, or by picture frame). Additionally, Videograph supports coding of more than two videos at the same time. According to the Videograph manual, the limit of videos playing simultaneously depends on the resources of the computer (Rimmele, 2013). Videos can also be synchronized within the software, but there are no options for further data compilation or analyses.

In sum, with Videograph basic coding tasks can be completed. However, Videograph is less user-friendly than INTERACT or Observer XT. The biggest issue is the limited time frame precision. For visualizing and analysis, additional software tools are needed. In the last few years, only minor updates were added without including any new features.

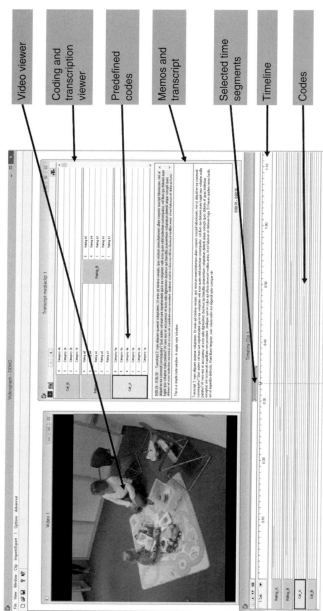

Figure 13.3 *Videograph (version 4.2.1.1X3 for Windows). Developer: Rolf Rimmele. Demo data file (Date of screenshot: February 24, 2016, Windows 8.1). Current version: 4.2.1.26X3, last software updated: January 2015.*

Eudico Linguistic Annotator

The Eudico Linguistic Annotator (ELAN) is an annotation tool that was developed in the Netherlands at the Max Planck Institute for Psycholinguistics, Nijmegen (Max Planck Institute for Psycholinguistics, n.d.). As mentioned before, to "annotate" simply means to code. The software is free of charge and runs under the General Public License. It is supported on different OS such as Windows, MacOS (Apple), and Linux-based systems.

The primary purpose of the software is to code verbal interactions such as verbal language, sign language, and gestures, but it can also be used with every other video project in different scientific areas. It is coding software that does not support any analyzing methods. But it contains some innovative features such as the audio recognizer. With the audio recognizer, an annotation can be automatically generated from the given audio information (Max Planck Institute for Psycholinguistics, 2017).

In ELAN technical terminology is used to refer to the research area of linguistics, which makes it difficult to use in other research areas (Glüer, 2015b). For example, ELAN supports time sampling, but there is no such feature named or described in the software or even in the manual of ELAN. Time sampling, for example, can be created by choosing "create regular annotations" (Glüer, 2012). The software also compromises different annotation modes for (a) fast transcription, (b) generation of events, or (c) synchronizing several videos. ELAN always opens in the annotation mode, which includes several different areas: the video viewer, the audio wave viewer (graphical view of the audio information), the timeline viewer, and the multiple data viewer (Figure 13.4). As in Videograph, the timeline of the data file is horizontal.

The time code of ELAN records in hours, minutes, seconds, and milliseconds (00h:00min:000ms). The timeline is set to one-second steps; it can be adjusted by zooming in and out between ten-second steps and up to ms-steps. The horizontal presentation of annotations (or codes) and the options to zoom in the timeline make ELAN a very useful tool to code on a microanalytic basis.

Codes can be recorded by selecting a time segment with the left mouse button (segment is highlighted blue). By double clicking on the blue mark, an input field appears to enter an annotation or a code. When using an observation instrument, ELAN supports predefined category systems, index systems, or rating scales. Setting up an observation instrument is again complicated. But once it is set up, a code can be recorded by activating a time segment (annotation) and then choosing the favored code from a drop-down menu. Keys on the keyboard can be assigned to a particular code, but the key only works when the selected time segment is activated. Setting up sampling methods is less intuitive compared to INTERACT, Observer XT, and Videograph.

Moreover, it is also possible to code several videos simultaneously. There are also some basic options to compile data (e.g., generating new codes from time gaps

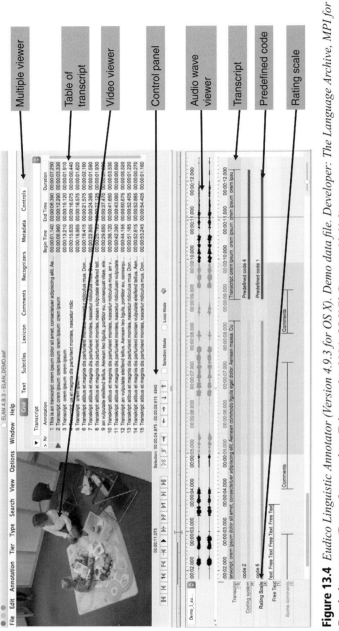

Figure 13.4 *Eudico Linguistic Annotator (Version 4.9.3 for OS X). Demo data file. Developer: The Language Archive, MPI for Psycholinguistics (Date of screenshot: February 24, 2016, OS X El Capitan, 10.11.3).*

between codes) and for descriptive statistics (e.g., frequency or mean). There are numerous options to export data (e.g., text, HTML).

In sum, ELAN is a quite demanding software package for beginners. It is less user friendly compared to INTERACT, Observer XT, and Videograph. There is no option to code an event by just typing a key, and there are no analyzing options. Concerning advantages, the software is free, offers the possibility to apply different sampling methods, and is regularly updated. Due to the horizontal representation of the codes, and the options to zoom in the timeline, it is especially suitable for scale development and microanalysis.

f4 and f5

f4 and f5 are basic tools that allow the user to transcribe video files (f4 = Windows or Linux; f5 = MacOS; Audiotranskription.de, 2012). The commercial software was developed by the German company dr. dresing & pehl GmbH. It captures each annotation by a time stamp (the start or end time of an event). It is also possible to capture time segments by selecting a period in the audio wave viewer (graphical view of the audio information). However, it is not feasible to generate automated time sampling. Also, handling events with time frames is not as comfortable as with INTERACT, Observer XT, ELAN, and Videograph. It is therefore more suitable for users who want to work with the transcript but not with precise time information.

Still, the usability of the software is high concerning transcripts. After a few minutes of using it, the user can handle the software. Coding is done by typing a code directly into the document window or by using a predefined text element that can be entered by keyboard short cuts (Figure 13.5). f4/f5 supports up to ten predefined text elements that can be used as codes, but it is not possible to set up several independent coding systems. f4/f5 only supports one data file at a time. The software cannot be extended with add-ons nor is the software able to compile (i.e., create new codes from gaps) or analyze the data. There are some basic features, such as automatically inserting the name of a person by each time a time stamp is recorded (i.e., Person 1). It is also able to code while playing an audio or video file. For advanced coding, the company distributes another software package that allows comprehensive coding of the transcript of video data: f4analyze (Windows, MacOS, Linux). With f4analyze, memos can be added to each sentence, and additionally different codes can be assigned to the data file. Codes and subcodes can be freely generated and assigned to the sentences in the transcript without a predefined coding system. Double clicking on one code shows all transcripts with the assigned codes (Audiotranskription.de, 2014). Codes can be exported by text file to other software such as MAXQDA (see. next section). The software supports Windows, MacOS, and Linux. f4/f5 is commercial software, but there is an educational discount for universities.

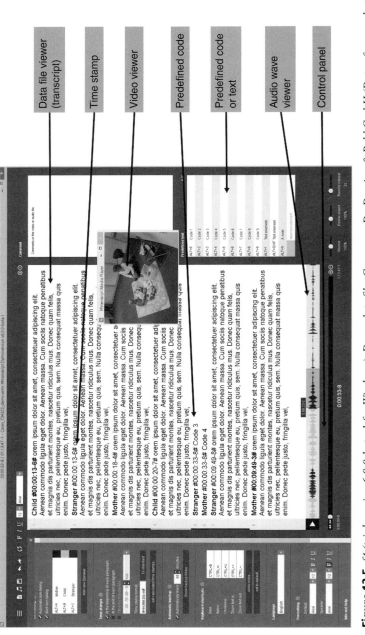

Data file viewer (transcript)

Time stamp

Video viewer

Predefined code

Predefined code or text

Audio wave viewer

Control panel

Figure 13.5 *f4 (trial version 6.0-beta.1 for Windows). Demo data file. Company: Dr. Dresing & Pehl GmbH (Date of screenshot: February 24, 2016, Windows 8.1).*

In sum, f4/f5 is excellent software to transcribe video data. It is easy to use and therefore also suitable for first coding processes. The main disadvantages of this software are that it offers only limited features for the actual coding process and no features for analyzing codes. f4analyze supplements f4/f5 by providing some basic coding features that are mainly suitable for qualitative research questions. The software is also regularly updated.

MAXQDA

The QDAS MAXQDA was first developed in 1989 (VERBIE Software, 2016a). Since then the software has been continually improved. It is a commercial software product, but offers a free time-limited version and an educational discount.

With Version 10, MAXQDA allows for coding video data (VERBIE Software, 2016b). Since 2014, there has also been a version for Windows and MacOS (VERBIE Software, 2016b). MAXQDA offers good usability and various ways to adjust the program to specific research needs. When using the software for the first time, some reading is required to discover all its features. There are several manuals, quick start guides, and video tutorials. Coding of documents (i.e., transcripts) or pictures is done by simply choosing a code by mouse. Coding can alternatively occur by the key of the keyboard, but only for up to nine codes. For text documents, this is not a major issue because no immediate reaction is needed with a static file. MAXQDA additionally offers 300 different symbols (e.g., emojis) to mark and code files.

For video coding, MAXQDA provides basic functions (VERBIE Software, 2016a). Video files are presented in a horizontal timeline as in ELAN or Videograph (Figure 13.6). The coding viewer includes a video viewer, a preview viewer (picture preview of the video segments), an audio wave viewer (graphical view of the audio information), a timeline viewer, and the data file viewer for the codes. Codes are presented by colored bars with the name of the codes. Coding is realized by choosing a time segment in the wave viewer (by mouse) and dragging the mark on predefined codes. The user can also generate a "parent" time segment and "child" time segment for dependent codes (e.g., for time sampling). But there is no specific feature for time sampling such as in INTERACT, Observer XT, or Videograph. In general, MAXQDA is especially helpful to code video data in combination with text files (e.g., interviews). It is less practical for micro-analytic video coding, quantitative coding by categories, or rating scales.

Once data files are coded, there are many ways to visualize data, for instance, codes per document, code relations, comparing codes of different documents, coding sequences of a particular paragraph, or even visual codes in a map. MAXQDA also offers different filter settings to analyze codes by specific variables (i.e., person 1 in an interview transcript). There are also different options to find and show codes, such as searching for overlapping codes (i.e., at least overlapping with

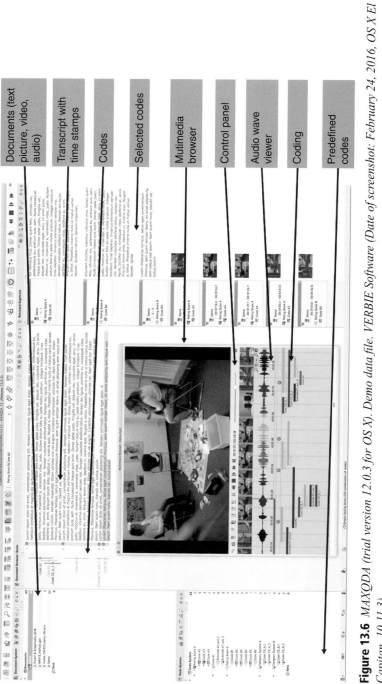

Documents (text picture, video, audio)

Transcript with time stamps

Codes

Selected codes

Mutimedia browser

Control panel

Audio wave viewer

Coding

Predefined codes

Figure 13.6 *MAXQDA (trial version 12.0.3 for OS X). Demo data file. VERBIE Software (Date of screenshot: February 24, 2016, OS X El Capitan, 10.11.3).*

two other codes) or latency analysis (searching for a specific code followed by a specific other code). Codes can be summarized in frequency tables or cross-tables. MAXQDA additionally supports many ways of exporting data. Files can be exported, for example, in Rich Text Format (RTF) or HTML. An outstanding feature of MAQXDA, in comparison to the other QDAS products, is the extra modules for some basic quantitative (e.g., ANOVA) and mixed data analysis. It is also possible to visualize qualitative and quantitative data combined.

ATLAS.ti

Similarly to MAXQDA, the QDAS ATLAS.ti offers the possibility to work with different data files (video, audio, pictures, text) at the same time. ATLAS.ti can be used on Windows and MacOS. It is a commercial software, developed by the ATLAS.ti GmbH.

For beginners, there are handbooks, quick start guides, and video tutorials. Users can start coding immediately after opening video, audio, text, or picture files in the software. There are different options for coding. Users can mark a paragraph, or can just write a note. They can assign a new code or they can use predefined codes. It is also possible to just mark the paragraph for later coding ("in-vivo coding"). Additionally, it is feasible to use a word of a document as a code by itself. When coding different files (i.e., several interviews and videos), users can quickly switch between the files to code one file after the other. Coding of several files can be summarized in one single output.

Any semantic connection between codes can be visualized. Even the way some codes are connected can be highlighted and visualized in a map (Scientific Software Development, 2015).

The video coding window consists of a video player, an audio wave viewer (graphical view of the audio information), and a preview viewer for the video and for the current time segment of a video (Figure 13.7). The time code is displayed in hours, minutes, and milliseconds (00h:00min:00sec:000ms). Codes can be recorded by selecting a time segment within the audio wave viewer with the mouse and then choosing a predefined code or assigning a new one. A marked section can be replayed, and the length of the segment can always be changed. The time code shows the beginning, the end, and the duration of the marked segment. It is also possible to collect snapshots from specific scenes as pictures. As in most QDAS products, video coding is less suitable for specific sampling techniques.

ATLAS.ti analysis features are mostly based on making sense of (semantic) connections between annotations and codes. It offers the possibility to find overlapping codes or a specific combination of codes in documents (Boolean operator). Moreover, there are some quantitative analysis techniques such as cross-tables for frequency. A syntax for exporting data in SPSS is provided as well.

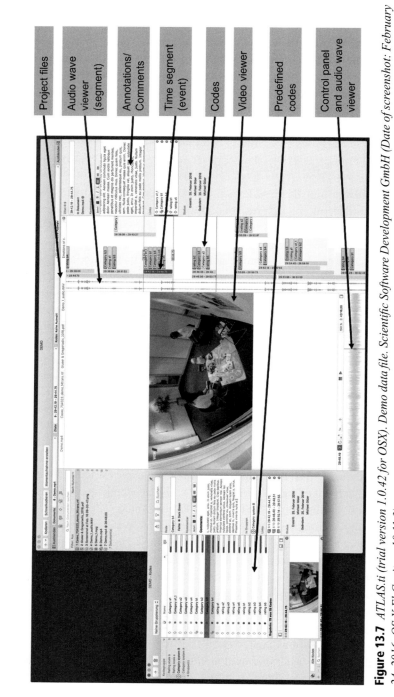

Project files

Audio wave viewer (segment)

Annotations/ Comments

Time segment (event)

Codes

Video viewer

Predefined codes

Control panel and audio wave viewer

Figure 13.7 *ATLAS.ti (trial version 1.0.42 for OSX). Demo data file. Scientific Software Development GmbH (Date of screenshot: February 24, 2016, OS X El Capitan, 10.11.3).*

NVivo

NVivo[3] is another QDAS. It is commercial software with special rates for students and educational institutions. Like the other QDAS, all kinds of qualitative data in documents (i.e., pdf), pictures, video, or audio files can be coded, visualized, and analyzed with NVivo. It also supports direct import from different software tools such as Endnote (QSR International, 2015). It runs on Windows as well as MacOS. Nvivo supports the same coding options already mentioned for MAXQDA and ATLAS.ti. The interface resembles Microsoft Office products because it uses ribbons for navigation (Figure 13.8). Therefore, all needed features can be found easily. Video as well as audio data are displayed by an audio wave (graphical view of the audio information) and video viewer. The horizontal audio wave viewer shows recorded codes by colored bars. It is also possible to show coding by different users. The actual transcript of a video is shown with the time of the segment. It is displayed vertically for each marked time segment. The time code is displayed in hours, minutes, seconds, and milliseconds (00h:00min:0ms). Coding is implemented by choosing a time segment of the video by mouse. The marked segment is pulled on a code in a predefined list of codes on the left side of the video. There is also a selection mode to select a time segment by playing and stopping the video. Codes can be further categorized in subcodes. There is no particular option for sampling methods.

NVivo supports different forms of visualization and data analysis. For example, the user can create word clouds, clusters such as mind-maps of the data, or word-tree maps. It is even possible to draw your own models of the codes and their relationship. Users can search for specific words in transcripts and find related words. As in all the other introduced software, it is possible to consider specific variables to cluster data (i.e., socio-demographic data). These variables can be imported from spreadsheets. NVivo supports creating cross-tables of specific codes and visualizing these data within the software.

Conclusion: How to Decide Which Software to Use?

The selection of the software depends mainly on the data type (video, audio, text, pictures), the specific research needs (code, or analyze data), and the research method being used (qualitative or quantitative). Some software may also support the workflow in a more efficient way than other. This is primarily a question of working preferences. Additionally, depending on the research project, a user may have more or fewer financial resources, which limits the variety of choices dramatically. Sometimes it is recommended to combine different software even of the same software category. For example, ELAN is a great tool for working

[3] There are three different Versions of NVivo: NVivo Starter (only text documents, no video, audio, or pictures), NVivo Pro (i.e., additional data sources), NVivo Plus (i.e., social network analysis).

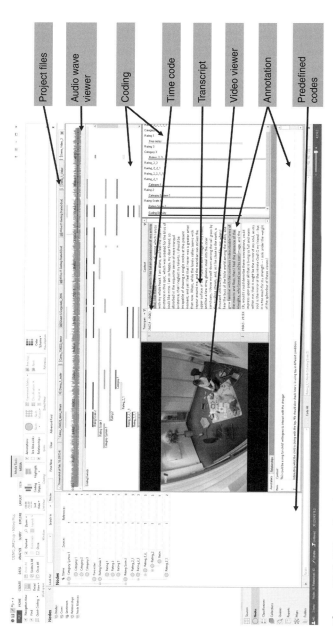

Project files

Audio wave viewer

Coding

Time code

Transcript

Video viewer

Annotation

Predefined codes

Figure 13.8 NVivo Pro (version 11.1.0.411 for Windows). Demo data file. QSR International Software (Date of screenshot: February 24, 2016, Windows 8.1).

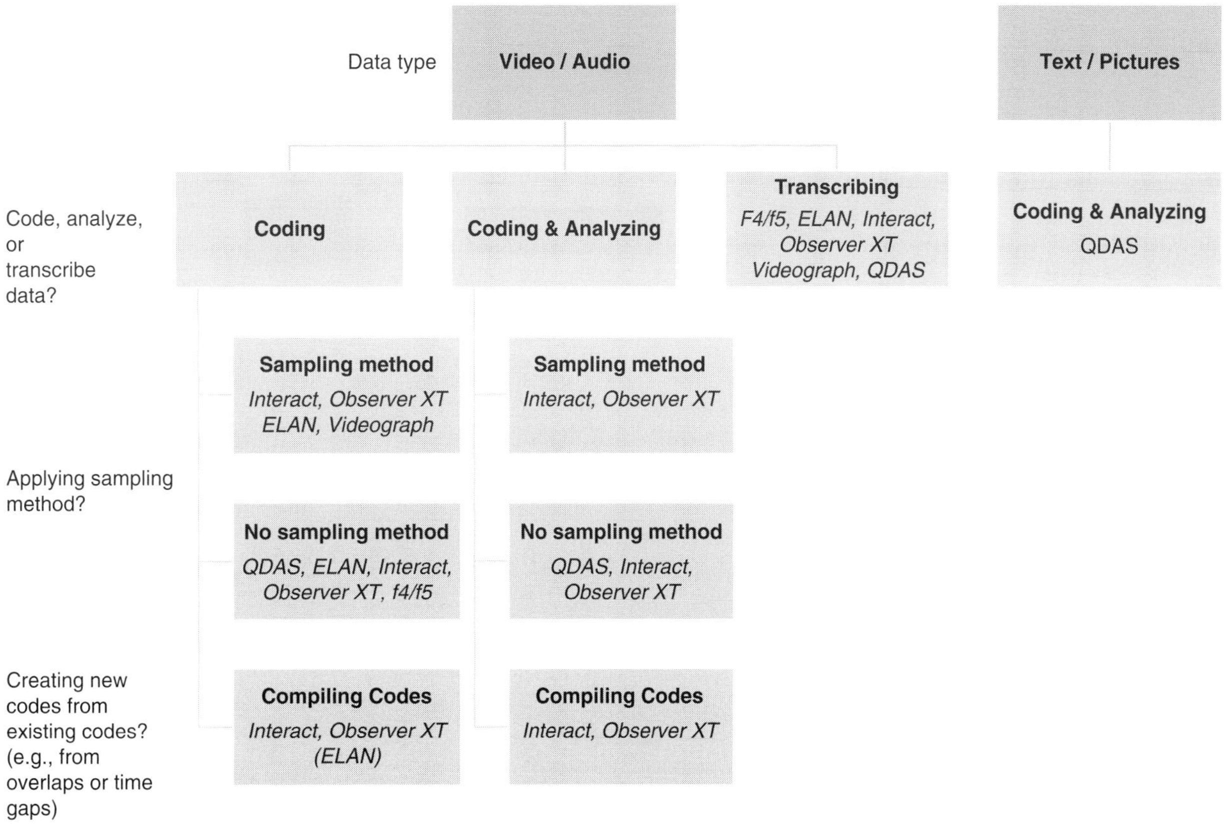

Figure 13.9 *Decision tree for choosing software for interaction coding and analyzing. The order of the software in the boxes is selected by the best fit. QDAS = Qualitative Data Analysis Software (Atlas.ti, MAXQDA; InViVo).*

on a micro-analytic basis and for the development of observation scales, but when it comes to coding, it may slow down the workflow. In INTERACT and Observer XT, the user can code much faster by just pressing a key to start and to end a code. Therefore, using ELAN for developing an observation instrument and using one of the other introduced video software packages for coding and/or analyzing may be a good combination. Of course, one could also use one of the proposed QDAS for coding. But if quantitative codes need to be assigned, based on a sampling method, INTERACT, Observer XT, or Videograph provide many more options to code.

If a user has different data files, such as interviews and video data, QDAS may be the better solution. Selecting between the QDAS is somewhat more challenging. It is again a matter of working preferences and the exact features one is looking for. In this case, it is best to try out different software. Most companies offer a time-limited version that gives real insight into features of interest. Figure 13.9 contains a decision tree on how to choose a software product. First the researcher must decide on the data: video, audio, text, pictures, or a combination. Second, they must decide if the interactions will be coded, analyzed, or just have to be transcribed. Depending on the research question, a specific sampling method or qualitative method may be applied. And finally, there may be the need to create new codes from existing codes (compiling data).

References

Altmann, J. (1974). Observational study of behavior: Sampling methods. *Behavior*, *49*, 715–729. doi:10.1163/156853974X00534

Audiotranskription.de (2014). f4analyse. Software for qualitative text analysis. User manual. Retrieved February 22, 2016, from www.audiotranskription.de/audot/downloadfile.php?k=1&d=29&l=de&c=883a9f6591

Audiotranskription.de (2012). User manual f4. A compact guide on how to use f4. Retrieved February 22, 2016, from www.audiotranskription.de/audot/downloadfile.php?k=1&d=24&l=de&c=e8fa5c88fc

Faßnacht, G. (2007). *Systematische Verhaltensbeobachtung* [Systematic observation of behavior]. Stuttgart, Germany: Reinhardt Verlag.

Free Software Foundation (2016). What is free software? The free software definition. Retrieved January 13, 2017, from www.gnu.org/philosophy/free-sw.en.html

Glüer, M. (2010, September). *Software zur Quantifizierung und Analyse von Videodaten: Ein Überblick über Softwarelösungen* [Software for video data analysis: A review of software products]. Paper presented at the 47. Kongress der deutschen Gesellschaft für Psychologie, Bremen.

Glüer, M. (2012, September). *Durchführung eines Time-Samplings mit ELAN. Workshop zur softwaregestützten Videodatenanalyse – Workshop Unterlagen* [Time sampling with ELAN – Workshop materials]. 48. Kongress der deutschen Gesellschaft für Psychologie, Bielefeld.

Glüer, M. (2013). *Geschenkfreude im Kleinkindalter. Eine empirische Studie zur emotionalen Sozialisation von Kleinkindern in einer Geschenksituation* [Toddlers' joy when receiving a gift. An empirical study of toddlers' emotional socialization in a gift situation]. Hamburg, Germany: Diplomica.

Glüer, M. (2015a). Annotatoren in der Videodatenanalyse: Ein Überblick [Annotation tools for video data analysis. A review; Webpage]. Retrieved January 13, 2017, from www.videodatenanalyse.de/software/annotatoren

Glüer, M. (2015b). Eudico Linguistic Annotator (ELAN): Ein vielseitiger Annotator zur Videodatenanalyse [Eudico Linguistic Annotator (ELAN): A multifunctional annotator for video data analysis; Webpage]. Retrieved January 13, 2017, from www.videodatenanalyse.de/software/annotatoren/elan

Kipp, M. (n.d.). ANVIL: The video annotation research tool [Webpage]. Retrieved January 13, 2017, from www.anvil-software.org/

Mangold International (2017). Mangold: Software and system solutions for research [Webpage]. Retrieved January 13, 2017, from www.mangold-international.com/en/

Mangold International (2016). *INTERACT. User guide. INTERACT version 15.0.* Mangold International GmbH.

Max Planck Institute for Psycholinguistics (n.d.). ELAN [Webpage]. Retrieved January 13, 2017, from http://tla.mpi.nl/tools/tla-tools/elan/

Max Planck Institute for Psycholinguistics (2017). *ELAN – Eudico Linguistic Annotator manual (Version 5.0.0-alpha).* Nijmegen, The Netherlands. Retrieved February 13, 2017, from www.mpi.nl/corpus/manuals/manual-elan.pdf

Noldus Information Technology (2015). *Reference manual. The Observer XT.*

Noldus Information Technology (2016). Noldus: Innovative solutions for behavioral research [Webpage]. Retrieved January 13, 2017, from www.noldus.com

QSR International (2015). *NVivo 11 Plus for Windows. Getting started guide.* Retrieved February 22, 2016, from http://redirect.qsrinternational.com/PlusGSG-nv11-en.htm

Rimmele, R. (2013). *What is Videograph?* [Videograph manual]. Retrieved February 22, 2016, from www.dervideograph.de/videograph_en.pdf

Scientific Software Development (2015). *ATLAS.ti 7. User guide and reference.* Retrieved February 22, 2016, from http://downloads.atlasti.com/docs/manual/atlasti_v7_manual_en.pdf?_ga=1.31324732.2076018714.1389556889

Transana – Qualitative analysis software for text, still image, audio, and video data [Webpage]. (n.d.). Retrieved January 13, 2017, from www.transana.com/

VERBIE Software (2016a). *MAXQDA: The art of data analysis. MAXQDA 12 reference manual.* Retrieved February 22, 2016, from www.maxqda.com/download/manuals/MAX12_manual_eng.pdf

VERBIE Software (2016b). MAXQDA: Qualitative data analysis software [Webpage]. Retrieved February 22, 2016, from www.maxqda.com/

PART IV

Data Analysis and Data Presentation

14 Coding and Counting

Frequency Analysis for Group Interaction Research

Oliver Rack, Carmen Zahn, and Magdalena Mateescu

Frequency Analysis as a Starting Point for Mixed Method Research

Many research designs that investigate group interactions in the field generate data that are discrete or categorical in nature. For instance, occurrences of behaviors such as specific words or statements in group discussions are analyzed and presented as frequency tables. Although frequency analysis is common practice in different areas of nonpsychological research (e.g., astrophysics, Lomb, 1976; literary analysis, Peng & Hengartner, 2002), it is rarely described as a method for group interaction research. This is remarkable because in other areas of scientific psychological research, frequency analysis has repeatedly been described as a systematic procedure (e.g., configurational frequency analysis, CFA, in clinical psychology, Lienert, 1971). Additionally, many authors such as Goodman (1971), Bishop, Fienberg, and Holland (1975), or Haberman (1978) discuss the importance of using frequency data in combination with contingency tables. But despite specialized articles in some experimental psychology journals (e.g., Olzak & Wickens, 1983; Wickens, 1993), the description of frequency analysis as a specific method for group interaction research is rare. Why?

Vokey (2003) notes different reasons. One may be the general form of presentation of frequency analysis in the statistical literature such as handbooks, with emphases and concerns on a very theoretical or methodological level far removed from the practical aspects of the typical experimental psychologist's or group researcher's handling of data. Another reason may be that most books on statistical methods for group researchers do not mention the specific usage of frequency analysis. The relevant aspects and the computational techniques for frequency data are appropriate for contingency tables that are analyzed with the goodness-of-fit approach (tests of independence) developed early in the history of statistics (Pearson, 1916). Furthermore, most data presentations routinely are concerned with correlational rather than experimental and population-based designs (i.e., random sampling) and thus less attention has been devoted to frequency analysis in the area of group interaction research. Therefore, we pose the question here: What is frequency analysis in the area of group interaction research? In the following chapter, we will provide answers to this question and show how interaction researchers can apply this method to learn more about their data.

Frequency Analysis in Group Interaction Research: Empirical Examples

In the different areas of group interaction research, coding systems are a potential starting point for frequency analysis. For example, the Co-ACT coding system (Kolbe, Burtscher, & Manser, 2013, see Part V of this volume) for observing coordination behavior in acute care teams in high-risk, dynamic medical disciplines such as emergency medicine, surgery, and anesthesia can be used to code specific teamwork behaviors. By doing so, the team behaviors are structured in the four quadrants "explicit action coordination," "implicit action coordination," "explicit information coordination," and "implicit information coordination" (for further information, see Kolbe et al., 2013). After the coding procedure, frequency analysis may be used to analyze the occurrence and timing of coordination behavior, thus providing the basis for a detailed understanding of team interaction and performance.

Transferring this empirical example to a more general level, frequency analysis can be described as a process that breaks down complex behaviors into smaller units, assigns them to categories, and then counts their occurrence. Complex behaviors include communication in teams when team members perform a collaborative task, often within a complex socio-technical system (e.g., pilots in a cockpit who prepare the landing of an aircraft, Hutchins, 1995; architects working on a joint construction project, Kvan, 2000; or learners building knowledge in a learning group, Zahn, Pea, Hesse, & Rosen, 2010). By counting the occurrences of qualitatively defined behaviors in a specific context or dataset (e.g., utterances in a group discussion), frequency analysis tries to predict future occurrences. By doing so, qualitative (e.g., behavior coding) and quantitative research procedures (e.g., counting occurrences of pre-defined behaviors) are combined. Hence, we consider frequency analysis as an essential building block to bridge the gap between qualitative and quantitative methods in mixed method research.

Frequency Analysis in Group Interaction Research: Methodological Aspects

As described above, coding systems provide the basis for frequency analysis on an empirical level. From a methodological point of view, frequency analysis is used as a starting point for mixed methods research. Several definitions of mixed methods have emerged over the last years and decades that incorporate different elements of methods, research perspectives, philosophies, and research designs (e.g., Johnson, Onwuegbuzie, & Turner, 2007). In this vein, Cresswell and Plano Clark (2011, p. 5) rely on a definition of mixed methods research that highlights the key components of designing and conducting an empirical mixed methods study:

> In mixed methods, the researcher a) collects and analyzes persuasively and rigorously both qualitative and quantitative data (based on research questions), b) mixes (or integrates or links) the two forms of data concurrently by combining them (or merging them), sequentially by having one build on the other, or

embedding one within the other, c) gives priority to one or to both forms of data (in terms of what the research emphasizes), d) uses the procedures in a single study or in multiple phases of a program of study, e) frames these procedures within philosophical worldviews and theoretical lenses, and f) combines the procedures into specific research designs that direct the plan for conducting the study.

Overall, these key components determine how researchers can integrate quantitative and qualitative methods in empirical studies. Regarding frequency analysis, these core characteristics not only affect how an empirical study is designed and conducted, they also affect how frequency analyses are used in research: (1) either as a standalone procedure or (2) as data or indicators for further analysis. To illustrate the basic idea of using frequency analysis in the nature of mixed methods research, we differentiate research designs. According to Creswell, Plano Clark, and Garrett (2008), different research designs could be developed to conduct mixed methods research. The most prominent differentiation is to distinguish between a triangulation design and a concurrent embedded design. The triangulation design is a design in which quantitative and/or qualitative data are collected and analyzed separately and then merged together to compare or interpret results. In contrast, researchers use the concurrent embedded design when they want to enhance a study based on one method (e.g., quantitative) by including a secondary dataset from another method (e.g., qualitative) (Creswell et al., 2008). In this case, datasets are collected concurrently. What does this mean for frequency analysis? In triangulation designs the results of a frequency analysis are interpreted separately or as standalone results. In embedded designs, the results of the frequency analysis can be used as a basis for further quantitative analysis. In this case, issues of data integration and different sequential mixed method designs such as an explanatory or an exploratory design are relevant to combine qualitative and quantitative data.

Regarding data integration, Bryman (2008) states that it can be challenging to integrate two sets of different forms of data and their results in a meaningful way. Erzberger and Kelle (2003) offer guidelines on integrating two strands of data: (1) designing and implementing comparable topics or questions for both arms (e.g., quantitative and qualitative strands of the study address the same questions or concepts), (2) converting the data so that they can be compared more easily, and (3) using matrices to organize both sets of data into one table. Transferred to frequency analysis, it is often more intuitive for researchers to quantify qualitative data by transformation than to translate quantitative into qualitative data. For example, Witcher and colleagues (2001) transformed their qualitative data into quantitative results by counting themes and calculating frequencies. Thus, the authors determined which themes or topics were mentioned more frequently in their study. Based on a similar strategy, Crone and Teddlie (1995) carry this procedure a step further by quantifying qualitative themes and then conducting statistical analyses on these datasets. These researchers gathered data from teachers and administrators and then computed Chi square tests in order to compare results from schools of varying levels of effectiveness (see also Creswell et al., 2008, p. 73). This can be very useful in experiments, for example, when differences in outcomes of experimental conditions are investigated in relation to group interaction process data.

Besides data integration, researchers need to consider the consequences of having independent samples when merging the results of a frequency analysis based on qualitative codings with quantitative subsamples of a larger dataset (Creswell et al., 2008). This is important because qualitative and quantitative data are usually collected for different purposes, use different quality standards, and require samples of different sizes. On the one hand, it could be a strategy to use the same study participants for both kinds of analyses to compare results. On the other hand, it could be useful to use different participants and different sample sizes. For example, for analyzing group interaction data in a learning group it could be adequate to analyze selected groups (case analyses) with qualitative coding schemes "in depth" for comparisons of more successful learning groups versus less successful groups (e.g., Barron, 2003; Zahn et al., 2010). In this case, small sample sizes would be the consequence. However, it could be interesting to collect subsequently large quantitative datasets to generalize the results from case studies. Hence, it could be an appropriate strategy to have unequal subsamples in qualitative and quantitative strands for the purpose of providing a comprehensive understanding of the situation (for an example of unequal sample sizes, see Hendrix et al., 2001).

Procedures of Frequency Analysis in Group Interaction Research

In this chapter, we present options for calculating and reporting results of frequency analysis. We will explain that depicting simple descriptive frequencies is not the only option to report the results of frequency analysis. After defining the behavior of interest and after developing the coding system (see Figure 14.1), researchers should take into account that the ways in which the data have been collected will affect which statistics may be used and how the results will be reported. Statistical tests of significance can be categorized based on the number of analyzed variables (e.g., bivariate: one independent and one dependent variable; multivariate: more than two variables). Applied to frequency analysis, the researcher needs to decide how the counted behavior frequencies will be handled. Hence, the researcher can decide how the results of a frequency analysis will be used: as standalone results or as a basis for indices and variables for further analysis.

Reporting Frequencies as Standalone Results: Numeric Frequencies, Pie Charts, and Bar Graphs

Frequencies can be reported in different visual forms. In the view of Neuendorf (2002, p. 172ff.), the most important are (1) absolute or relative *numeric*

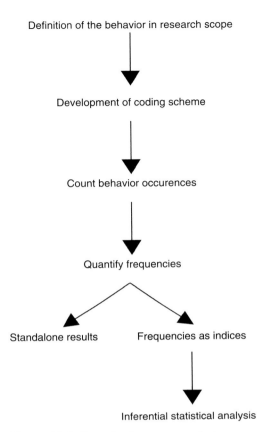

Definition of the behavior in research scope

Development of coding scheme

Count behavior occurences

Quantify frequencies

Standalone results   Frequencies as indices

Inferential statistical analysis

Figure 14.1 *Steps for frequency analysis.*

frequencies, (2) *pie charts* and *bar graphs. Frequencies* show the occurrence of specific data (e.g., the number of questions asked or solutions offered during a group discussion). By doing so, these findings can answer simple research questions such as "What are the frequencies of sexual behaviors and their consequences for viewers as depicted on daytime soap operas?" (Neuendorf, 2002, p. 172). In such cases, frequencies are used as standalone results, no hypotheses are being tested, and no tests of statistical significance are conducted.

To take it a step further, one-sample z-tests can be used to test if the frequency of a code (e.g., a specific behavior) significantly deviates from expected values. Bivariate tests could be used to analyze the relationship between different behaviors. In this regard, contingency tables are types of tables in a matrix format that display the frequency distribution of codes or variables. These tables allow for conclusions about the proportions of different variables in a sample (e.g., the difference of offered solutions during a group discussion between men and women). The difference between the two proportions or between empirical and expected values can be analyzed with various statistical tests, including Pearson's Chi-squared test, G-Test, Fisher's exact test, and Barnard's test. If the proportions of frequencies in the different columns vary significantly between rows, a contingency between the two variables is identified. In other words, the variables or frequencies are not independent but co-vary systematically. We illustrate this use of numeric frequencies by presenting an empirical example from our research project on computer-supported team collaboration (Mateescu, Zahn, Klinkhammer, Rack, & Reiter, 2016). We investigated groups collaborating by using large multitouch tabletop interfaces while brainstorming and working on design tasks. Within the larger project, several studies investigated the influences of task type (brainstorming vs. design) and of workspace structuring (e.g., providing personal workspaces for team members vs. not providing personal workspaces) on collaborative processes and team performance. One experiment is described in more detail below that investigated groups' "territorial" behaviors during task performance.

Table 14.2 shows the interrelations between the type of task and workspace structuring with respect to the amount of observed territorial behavior in a contingency table. By counting the occurrence of the territorial behaviors for the brainstorming task it becomes evident that almost all groups who had no fixed personal workspaces created personal territories on the tabletops whereas most groups in the personal spaces conditions solved the brainstorming task without creating extra personal territories on the tabletop.

Further options to report frequencies as standalone results are *frequency pie charts* and *bar graphs*. Figures 14.3 (pie chart) and 14.4 (bar graph) contain the

Table 14.1 *Description of Empirical Example 1. Data from this experiment were used to exemplify the report of frequencies (see Table 14.2 and Figures 14.3 and 14.4) and spatial mapping of data (see Figures 14.6 and 14.8)*

Empirical Example 1: In this study (Mateescu, Zahn, Klinkhammer, Rack, & Reiter, 2016), we investigated the influences of task type (brainstorming vs. design) and of workspace structuring (e.g., fixed, dynamic, and mobile workspaces vs. no individual workspaces) on the participants' territorial behavior. For workspace structuring, each participant received individual tablets as their "personal workspace," in addition to the large multitouch tabletop for the groups. Participants collaborated in dyads at a large interactive tabletop (see Figure 14.2), where they could use digital tools for writing and moving notes, adding furniture to a room. Dyadic interactions and behaviors were videotaped and coded (e.g., "territorial behavior"). For instance, we coded a dyad to exhibit "territorial behavior" when at least one participant placed their virtual notes on the tabletop in the area in front of them. Interactions with the interface were recorded in logfiles. Logfiles were synchronized with video recordings and were afterwards used to code (e.g., which person completed each interaction).

Table 14.2 *Two-by-four contingency table displaying proportion of groups showing territorial behavior as absolute frequencies (percentage of cell)*

Type of task	No personal workspaces	Workspace structure			
		Fixed	Dynamic	Mobile	TOTAL
Brainstorming	9 of 10 groups (90%)	6 of 11 groups (54%)	4 of 10 groups (40%)	3 of 9 groups (33%)	22 of 40 groups (55%)
Design	2 of 10 groups (20%)	1 of 10 groups (10%)	0 of 10 groups (0%)	1 of 10 groups (10%)	4 of 40 groups (10%)
TOTAL	11 of 20 groups (55%)	7 of 20 groups (33%)	4 of 20 groups (20%)	4 of 19 groups (21%)	

Note: Two independent variables, the type of task (brainstorming vs. design) and workspace structure (fixed, dynamic, mobile vs. no-personal workspaces) were investigated in their effect on participants' territorial behavior. A dyad displayed territorial behavior when at least one member used the area in front of them to staple and organize their own notes while at the same time removing all notes created by the other participant that appeared in that area.

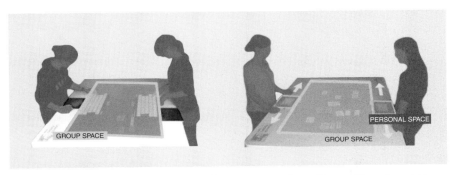

Figure 14.2 *Participants working at interactive tabletop (Experiment 1).*

same information as Table 14.2 as relative and respective absolute frequencies. It is important to note that while pie charts are still largely used, they also tend to be criticized for not being as easy to interpret and understand as bar charts (see Robbins, 2005). In general, pie charts and bar graphs only allow descriptive comparisons but do not provide information about statistical differences.

Overall, the visual presentation of data as pie or bar charts can help to visualize and report the results of frequency analyses. But besides these typical options for presenting frequencies, some more specific options such as log files and density plots offer more possibilities to meaningfully report frequencies in group interaction research.

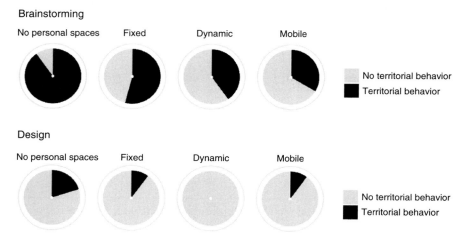

Figure 14.3 *Frequency pie chart. Note: This figure was created with R package ggplot2 (Wickham, 2006).*

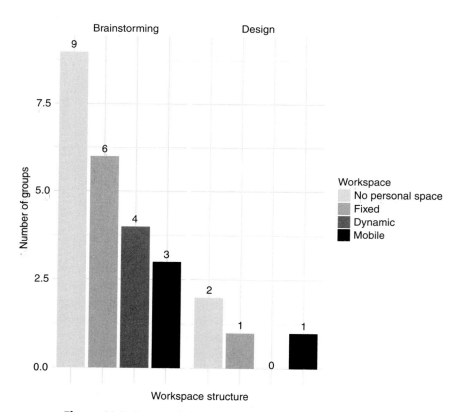

Figure 14.4 *Bar graph displaying absolute frequencies. Note: This figure was created with R package ggplot2 (Wickham, 2006).*

Reporting Frequencies in Group Interaction Research: From Logfiles to Density Plots

Choosing a type of visualization should always be guided by the relationships among variables in the data that the researcher wants to explore and display. In the following, two empirical examples are described to present the results of frequency analysis in group research. Besides summarizing graphs, group interaction data can be temporally mapped (i.e., visualized in relation to a point in time *when* a certain behavior occurs – see Figure 14.5) or mapped to the space in which the behavior takes place (e.g., visualized in relation to a location *where* a certain behavior occurs – see Figures 14.6 to 14.8). Examples 1 and 2 show temporal and spatial mapping of data.

Figure 14.5 shows the results from Empirical Example 2 by mapping groups' behavior to the timeline of the experiment. Such analysis by visualization reveals not only how often a behavior occurs but also the time of occurrence and the co-occurrence of behaviors. For example, all groups in this study had disjunct episodes of zoning and furnishing except for Group 1 in the control condition. This group started by zoning, moved to furnishing, and then made significant changes in the last minutes of the experiment both to the zones and to the furnishing arrangements. A graph such as in Figure 14.5 makes not only the co-occurrence of behaviors salient but also a potential lack of such co-occurrences. For example, in the experimental condition, Group 8 used epistemic actions most of the time whereas Group 21 only used epistemic actions during the zoning phase. Such graphs allow for in-depth analysis of co-occurrences of behavior at group level as well as provide

Table 14.3 *Description of Empirical Example 2. Data from this experiment were used to exemplify the temporal mapping of behavior (see Figure 14.5).*

Empirical Example 2. In Mateescu, Klinkhammer, Reiterer, and Zahn (2015), we were interested in the interaction between the participants working at an interactive tabletop on a design task. Their task was to design a flexible office by partitioning a floor plan in different areas (also called zones, e.g., "silent zones" for concentrated individual office work or "social zones" for informal meetings and mutual social exchange among colleagues) and by furnishing these areas accordingly. Two conditions were compared: The participants in the experimental condition were provided with full interactive functions (such as functions for drawing, dragging, and placing furniture pieces on the floor plan) whereas the control condition was equipped with reduced functionality. The participants' interactions were videotaped and all videos were subsequently analyzed by coding for different types of group behaviors, e.g., type of action with the interface (zoning the office or furnishing) or occurrence of epistemic actions (cf. Kirsh & Maglio, 1994). All videos were segmented into ten-second-intervals, and behaviors were coded for each interval. To ensure reliability, a second independent coder coded 10 percent of the videos.

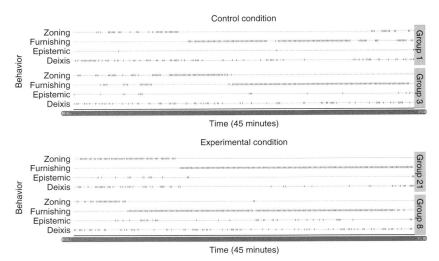

Figure 14.5 *Visualization of observed behaviors (here: according to the design task) on time axes; see description of Empirical Example 2. Note: This visualization was created with R package ggplot2 (Wickham, 2006).*

visualizations of the intensity of the interaction; they help interpret results or form hypotheses with regard to which type of group behavior is more efficient. Figure 14.5 shows the amount of interaction by the density of lines (number of lines per unit of time).

Figures 14.6 to 14.8 show examples for *spatial mapping* of group behaviors from Empirical Example 1. The figures differ in the ways they represent the behaviors (here, interactions with the tabletop interface), with regard to spatial mapping. Figure 14.6 shows *where* the behavior occurred (spatial mapping) as well as *how often* the behavior occurred (the amount of squares and triangles) and *who* performed the behavior (the entity mapping). In Figure 14.7, a heatmap[1] was added to the visualization to make evident *where* most interactions with the interface were performed. The heatmap shows the most used areas as black and areas that were not used at all as white.

In Figure 14.6, participants' interaction with the interface was mapped on the tabletop surface. Two horizontal lines partition the graphical representation of tabletop surface into three equal zones. The visualization makes apparent that the participants in one condition (mobile condition) used the tabletop in a balanced way – the triangles and square cover uniformly most of the surface. This shows that regardless of their positioning at the tabletop, the participants performed interactions on most of the surface of the interactive tabletop. This can be interpreted as a "democratic" way of dyadic interaction with the interface. In contrast, in the

---

[1] A heatmap is a graphical representation used to display information about users' interaction with web pages showing the amount of clicks within a certain area.

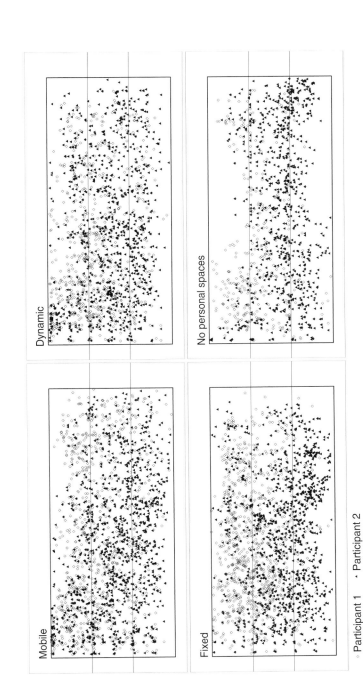

◇ Participant 1 ◂ Participant 2

Figure 14.6 *Density plot of participants' interaction at the interactive tabletop during the brainstorming task. This figure is based on data from Experiment 1. In each dyad one participant's interaction with the interface is coded with a triangle and the other ones with a square.*
Note: Graphic created with R package ggplot2 (Wickham, 2006).

nonpersonal spaces condition the participants created "territories" in front of them and acted more in the nearest one-third of the tabletop around them.

The mosaic graph represented in Figure 14.8 shows the *sum* of participants' interaction with the interface. Here the mapping to the tabletop surface is done in a rather crude approximation in this visualization: The tabletop was partitioned for analysis of the visualization into three equally sized areas A, B, and C, similar to Figure 14.7. Differences in the amount of interaction of the participants with the interface in the four conditions are shown by the relative size of each area. In two experimental conditions (mobile and dynamic), the participants used most of the tabletop interface; however, they used the third of the table farthest away from them slightly less (the amounts of interaction in the area nearest to them and in the middle are almost equal).

Beyond Descriptive Metrics: Frequencies as Indices for Further Analysis

As stated above, the researcher decides on the basis of her research questions and goals how the results of a frequency analysis are used: as standalone results or as a basis for further indices and variables and quantitative analyses. Why is this important?

The visualizations and reports of descriptive metrics such as frequencies are necessary but – in most cases – not sufficient to fully understand complex aspects of group interaction or relationships on a general level (e.g., groups and network perspective; Contractor & Su, 2011). For instance, reporting descriptive frequencies can provide insights in the occurrence of specific behaviors in group discussions, but it does not provide insights into the specific outputs of the group interaction (e.g., group performance). Hence, the use of frequency analysis as a standalone procedure or result could not be defined as a statistically defensible measure to find out whether the observed behaviors have different effects on outcomes of group work. For this reason, frequencies are often used as a basis for inferential statistics by calculating indices for further analysis or further studies. This aspect is specifically relevant for group research because many studies postulate theoretical and empirical relationships (e.g., empirical input-process-output models; Rack, Ellwart, Hertel, & Konradt, 2011) between inputs (e.g., group size, individual motivation of group members), processes (e.g., information sharing), and outcomes (e.g., group performance). Frequency analysis provides a solid basis for more complex data analysis with inferential statistics such as regression analysis or – especially relevant for group research – multilevel modeling (e.g., Kashy & Hagiwara, 2011; Walter & Rack, 2010).

The following procedure exemplifies how frequencies can be turned into indicators (here, collaboration index) and how they can then be related to outcome (here, learning). Empirical Example 3 is drawn from a series of experiments investigating learning with digital video tools from a cognitive-constructivist perspective (Zahn, 2017).

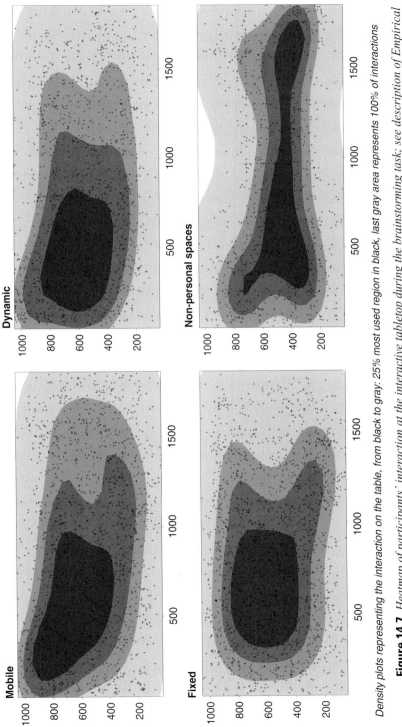

Figure 14.7 *Heatmap of participants' interaction at the interactive tabletop during the brainstorming task; see description of Empirical Example 1. Note: Graphic created with package hdrcde (Hyndman, Einbeck, & Wand, 2009).*

Density plots representing the interaction on the table, from black to gray: 25% most used region in black, last gray area represents 100% of interactions

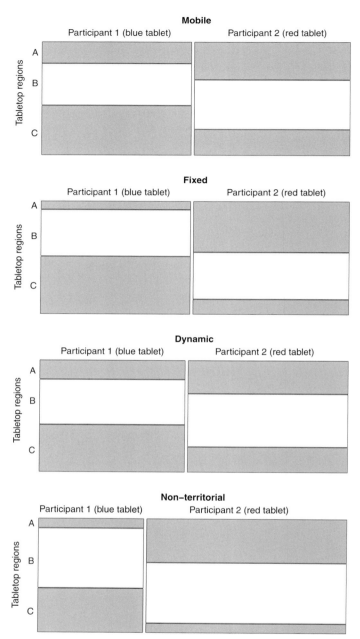

Figure 14.8 *Visualization of the amount of interaction on the tabletop during the brainstorming task – see Experiment 1. The tabletop was partitioned into the three equal sized areas (A, B, and C). The interaction of the two participants is shown in two columns. Note: Graphic created with graphics (R Core Team, 2015).*

Table 14.4 *Description of Empirical Example 3*

Empirical Example 3: In an experimental study (Zahn, Krauskopf, Hesse, & Pea, 2009) on group learning in digital learning environments in history lessons, two types of learning using a web-based video collaboration tool (WebDiver, see http://diver .stanford.edu/) for distinct learning activities were compared: learning by design versus learning by discussion (e.g., Zahn et al., 2009). Dyadic interaction data from a sample of 69 students were collected. The data consisted of written communications between participants in a chat tool and comments written into a video collaboration tool. From these raw data, the quality of the dyadic interactions was analyzed by coding (a) frequencies of content aspects that related directly to the learning contents and goals and (b) aspects of collaboration quality (assessment of the contents of learners' written comments and the overall quality of interactions within dyads from chats). In addition, video recordings were analyzed to determine which comment was written by whom, thereby counting the frequencies of comments created by both participants of the dyads *together* in contrast to frequencies of comments created by one of the partners *alone*. Chat communications within dyads were divided into two subcategories: (1) frequencies of double reference (where participants mutually referred to previous comments) as an indicator of high collaboration quality in general; (2) frequencies of proposals for work structuring as an indicator of coordination activities. The coding results were then integrated to form a collaboration index. This collaboration index was used for further analyses on influences of group collaboration quality on learning outcome and knowledge acquisition. The advantage of frequency analysis in this case is that written comments and chat communications were counted to form a collaboration index that indicates collaboration quality. Thus, a quantitative measure was created relating collaboration quality to the quality of learning (and outcome measures, such as knowledge tests), *bridging the gap between qualitative and quantitative data*. One finding from this analysis, for example, shows that high collaboration quality (index) was correlated with deeper learning (outcome) and transfer (Zahn, 2017).

Limitations and Conclusion

In this chapter, we provided an introduction to frequency analyses for group interaction research. We offered descriptions of important options to use frequency analysis in a typical group interaction research process as a bridge to close the gap between qualitative and quantitative methods. Furthermore, we provided empirical examples to illustrate the prerequisites, requirements, and consequences of using frequency analysis in the field of group research. The most important limitation of frequency analysis is that the quality of frequency analysis depends on the quality of the used coding scheme. For example, if the coding scheme aims at observing unspecific behavioral aspects (e.g., vague differences between the used codes), frequency analysis will provide unclear results. Additionally, coding may vary based on subjective interpretations of the codes by observers, therefore more than one rater is needed (at least for a subsample of the data) and the raters have to be trained (see Seelandt, this volume, Chapter 12). In case of disagreements, additional discussions of codings may be necessary. Hence, coding is often resource intensive. Furthermore, the disadvantage of coding and counting is that it is partly a top-down approach – with coding schemes determining a priori what counts in this case as an indicator for collaboration quality (and what does not count), leaving little room for emergent findings. Finally, the technique of the result visualization should be considered: For example, it is difficult to compare different sections of a given pie chart or to compare data across different pie charts.

Nevertheless, we believe that frequency analysis is a reasonable and meaningful way to investigate group interactions. Although this method could be used as a standalone procedure, it is a notable option to generate behavior-related variables and indices for multivariate statistics to analyze specific relationships in small group research.

References

Barron, B. (2003). When smart groups fail. *The Journal of the Learning Sciences 12* (3), 307–359. doi:10.1207/S15327809JLS1203_1

Bishop, Y. M. M., Fienberg, S. E., & Holland, P. W. (1975). *Discrete multivariate analysis.* Cambridge, MA: MIT Press.

Bryman, A. (2008). Why do researchers integrate/combine/mesh/blend/mix/merge/fuse quantitative and qualitative research? In M. Bergman (Ed.), *Advances in mixed methods research.* Thousand Oaks, CA: Sage.

Contractor, N., & Su, C. (2011). Understanding groups from a network perspective. In A. Hollingshead & M. S. Poole (Eds.), *Research methods for studying groups and teams: A guide to approaches, tools, and technologies* (pp. 284–310). New York, NY: Routledge.

Creswell, J. W., & Plano Clark, V. L. (2011). *Designing and conducting mixed methods research.* Thousand Oaks, CA: Sage.

Creswell, J. W., Plano Clark, V. L., & Garrett, A. L. (2008). Methodological issues in conducting mixed methods research designs. In M. M. Bergman (Ed.), *Advances in mixed methods research* (pp. 66–83). London: Sage.

Crone, L., & Teddlie, C. (1995). Further examination of teacher behavior in differentially effective schools: Selection and socialization processes. *Journal of Classroom Interaction, 30*(1), 1–9.

Erzberger, C., & Kelle, U. (2003). Making inferences in mixed methods: The rules of integration. In A. Tashakkori & C. Teddlie (Eds.), *Handbook of mixed methods in social behavioral research* (pp. 457–490). Thousand Oaks, CA: Sage.

Fairhurst, G. T., Rogers, L. E., & Sarr, R. A. (1987). Manager-subordinate control patterns and judgements about the relationship. In M. L. McLaughlin (Ed.), *Communication yearbook 10* (pp. 395–415). Newbury Park, CA: Sage.

Goodman, L. A. (1971). The analysis of multidimensional contingency tables: Stepwise procedures and direct estimation methods for building models for multiple classifications. *Technometrics, 13*, 33–61.

Haberman, S. J. (1972). Algorithm AS 51: Log-linear fit for contingency tables. *Applied Statistics*, *21*, 218–225.

Hair, J. F., Anderson, R. E., Tatham, R. L., & Black, W. C. (1998). *Multivariate data analysis*. Upper Saddle River, NJ: Prentice Hall.

Hendrix, C. C., Fournier, D. G., & Briggs, K. (2001). Impact of co-therapy teams on client outcomes and therapist training in marriage and family therapy. *Contemporary Family Therapy*, 23(1), 63–82.

Hutchins, E. (1995). How a cockpit remembers its speeds. *Cognitive Science*, *19*, 265–288.

Hyndman, R. J., Einbeck, J., & Wand, M. (2009). The hdrcde package (highest density regions and conditional density estimation). *R package version, 3.1.*

Johnson, R., Onwuegbuzie, A., & Turner, L. (2007). Toward a definition of mixed methods research. *Journal of Mixed Methods Research*, 1(2), pp. 112–133.

Kashy, D. A., & Hagiwara, N. (2012). Analyzing group data. In A. Hollingshead & S. Poole, (Eds.), *Research methods for studying groups: A guide to approaches, tools, and technologies* (pp. 311–328). New York, NY: Routledge.

Kirsh, D., & Maglio, P. (1994). On distinguishing epistemic from pragmatic action. *Cognitive Science*, 18(4), 513–549.

Kolbe, M., Burtscher, M. J., & Manser, T. (2013). Co-ACT – A framework for observing coordination behavior in acute care teams, *BMJ Quality & Safety*, *22*, 596–605.

Kvan, T. (2000). Collaborative design: What is it? *Automation in Construction 9*, 409–415.

Lienert, G. A. (1971). Die Konfigurationsfrequenzanalyse. I. Ein neuer Weg zu Typen und Syndromen. *Zeitschrift für Klinische Psychologie und Psychotherapie*, *19*, 99–115.

Lomb, N. R. (1976). Least-squares frequency analysis of unequally spaced data. *Astrophysics and Space Science*, *39*, 447–462.

Mateescu, M., Klinkhammer, D., Reiterer, H., & Zahn, C. (2015). Influence of Interactive Multi-User Tabletop Technology on Shared Mental Models and Performance: An Experimental Study. Talk at the 17. European Congress of Work and Organizational Psychology, *Symposium "Dynamics of team cognition and team adaptation I – Focus on team cognition."*

Mateescu, M., Zahn, C., Klinkhammer, D., Rack, O., & Reiterer, H. (2016). *Potenziale kollaborativer Medien: Eine empirische Untersuchung am Beispiel interaktiven Tischen*. [Potential collaborative media: An empirical study using the example of interactive tables.] Forschungsbeitrag zum 50. Kongress der Deutschen Gesellschaft für Psychologie [Presentation at the 50th Congress of the German Society for Psychology], Leipzig Deutschland (18–22. 9. 2016).

Neuendorf, K. A. (2002). *The content analysis guidebook*. Thousand Oaks, CA: Sage.

Olson, B. (1994). Sex and the soaps: A comparative content analysis of health issues. *Journalism Quarterly*, *71*, 840–850.

Olzak, L. A., & Wickens, T. D. (1983). The interpretation of detection data through direct multivariate frequency analysis. *Psychological Bulletin*, *93*, 574–585.

Pearson, K. (1916). On a brief proof of the fundamental formula for testing the goodness of fit of frequency distributions and of the probable error of "p". *Philosophical Magazine*, *31*, 369–378.

Peng, R., & Hengartner, H. (2002). Quantitative analysis of literary styles. *The American Statistician*, 56(3), 15–38.

R Core Team (2015). R: A language and environment for statistical computing. R Foundation for Statistical Computing, Vienna, Austria. Retrieved February 15, 2018, from www.R-project.org/.

Rack, O., Ellwart, T., Hertel, G., & Konradt, U. (2011). Team-based rewards in computer-mediated groups. *Journal of Managerial Psychology, 26* (5), 419–438. doi:10.1108/02683941111139029

Robbins, N. B. (2005). *Creating more effective graphs*, Hoboken: Wiley-Interscience.

Stahl, G., Koschmann, T., & Suthers, D. D. (2006). Computer-supported Collaborative Learning. In R. K. Sawyer, (Ed.), *The Cambridge handbook of the learning sciences* (pp. 409–474). Cambridge, UK: Cambridge University Press.

Vokey, J. R. (2003). Multiway frequency analysis for experimental psychologists. *Canadian Journal of Experimental Psychology = Revue Canadienne De Psychologie Experimentale, 57,* 257–264.

Walter, S. G., & Rack, O. (2010). Eine anwendungsbezogene Einführung in die Hierarchisch Lineare Modellierung (HLM). In S. Albers, D. Klapper, U. Konradt, A. Walter, & J. Wolf (Eds.). *Methoden der empirischen Forschung*, S. 293–310. Wiesbaden: Gabler.

Wickens, T. D. (1993). Analysis of contingency tables with between-subjects variability. *Psychological Bulletin, 113,* 191–204.

Wickham, H. (2006). ggplot: An implementation of the grammar of graphics. R package version 2.0.0.

Witcher, A. E., Onwuegbuzie, A. J., & Minor, L. C. (2001). Characteristics of effective teachers: Perceptions of preservice teachers. *Research in the Schools, 8*(2), 45–57.

Zahn, C. (2017). Digital design and learning. Cognitive-constructivist perspectives. In S. Schwan & U. Cress (Eds.), *The psychology of digital learning: Constructing, exchanging, and acquiring knowledge with digital media* (pp. 147–170). Springer International Publishing AG.

Zahn, C., Krauskopf, K., Hesse, F. W., & Pea, R. (2009). Participation in knowledge building "revisited": Reflective discussion and information design with advanced digital video technology. In C. O'Malley, D. Suthers, P. Reimann, & A. Dimitracopoulou (Eds.), *Computer supported collaborative learning practices: CSCL2009 Conference Proceedings.* (pp. 596–600). New Brunswick, NJ: International Society of the Learning Sciences (ISLS).

Zahn, C., Pea, R., Hesse, F. W., & Rosen, J. (2010). Comparing simple and advanced video tools as supports for complex collaborative design processes. *The Journal of the Learning Sciences, 19*(3), 403–440. doi:10.1080/10508401003708399

15 Analysis of Interaction Sequences

Vicenç Quera

Interaction processes unfold in time. In a typical dyadic interaction, the behavior of an individual affects subsequent behaviors of another individual, which in turn affect subsequent behaviors of the former, and so on. Studying the temporal dynamics of an interaction requires knowledge about the order in which individuals participate and behave, the degree to which their behaviors follow each other or overlap, and whether future behaviors can be reliably predicted from past ones during an interaction session. In sum, the aim of such a study is to uncover temporal patterns in the observed sequences.

Systematic observation by trained observers (Bakeman, 2000, 2010; Bakeman & Gottman, 1986, 1997; Bakeman & Quera, 2011, 2012; Martin & Bateson, 2007; Quera & Bakeman, 2000; Yoder & Symons, 2010) is the appropriate method for obtaining precise information about interaction processes. First, a coding scheme must be defined with a research problem in mind. The codes are binary variables (i.e., specific behavior occurs/does not occur) characterizing relevant behaviors of the participants; for example, in research about couple interaction, codes like *Approves, Negates, Complains*, among others, could be applied to each verbal utterance.

Second, a specific technique for observing the interaction and recording it must be used, either continuous act-by-act recording or time sampling. As a result, sequences of code occurrences will be obtained. Depending on the interests of the researchers, codes can be defined either as temporally exclusive (for example, when turn taking is coded in a verbal interaction) or as possibly concurrent (for example, when studying mother-infant face-to-face interaction). In the first case, information about the order in which codes occur will be obtained, whereas in the second case both their order and synchrony will be recorded (for example, when examining whether the mother tends to look at her infant's face in synchrony with the infant babbling). In both cases, code durations may be of interest. If so, observers can take advantage of computer systems to assist coding and provide accurate time recording (see also Glüer, this volume, Chapter 13).

I am greatly indebted to Roger Bakeman, with whom I co-authored the books *Analyzing interaction: Sequential analysis with SDIS and GSEQ*, and *Sequential analysis and observational methods for the behavioral sciences*, and co-developed the GSEQ software for the analysis of interaction sequences. This chapter presents an overview of the fundamental ideas and methods we have been working with during the last quarter of a century.

Third, observer reliability is assessed by comparing recordings from independent and identically trained observers; a high level of observer agreement would indicate that they are interchangeable and that the behavior sequences they obtain can be trusted (Bakeman, Quera, & Gnisci, 2009; Bakeman, Quera, McArthur, & Robinson, 1997; Quera, Bakeman, & Gnisci, 2007; see also Seelandt, this volume, Chapter 12).

And fourth, sequences are analyzed in order to find patterns in them that can address specific research questions (Bakeman, 1978, 2004; Bakeman, Deckner, & Quera, 2005; Bakeman & Quera, 2011; Gottman & Roy, 1990). For example, is cross-complaining more frequent in distressed, or clinical, couples than in nondistressed, or control ones? Does the infant tend to stop crying during an interval of ten seconds after her mother starts holding her? During a project meeting, do positive procedural communications (e.g., "pointing out the main topic") tend to inhibit subsequent negative action statements (e.g., "this never works") and, if so, is the inhibitory effect stronger as time progresses? (Klonek, Quera, Burba, & Kauffeld, 2016). In order to answer these questions, global or summary measures such as rates, percentages, or average durations are in general not useful. Instead, analyses based on transition rates and co-occurrence frequencies among codes, co-occurrence frequencies between time windows anchored to codes, and statistics derived from them can adequately address questions about the temporal dynamics of interaction.

Unlike time-series analysis, which is devised to analyze how continuous variables change across time, the analysis of behavior sequences consists in quantifying temporal relationships among binary behavioral codes that occur in sequence and, in some cases, concurrently as well. Whereas traditional approaches to behavior may assume that results from different units (dyads or groups) can be safely aggregated because differences, if they exist, are negligible, when studying interaction it is always preferable to start analyzing single units separately, not taking for granted that results for different units will be similar. In fact, sequential analyses "from pooled data may differ from the same statistics computed as the mean of individual cases" (i.e., meetings, Bakeman & Quera, 2011, p. 125). Once sequential data for each unit have been analyzed, and patterns have been uncovered, it makes sense to check whether patterns are the same for all units or if differences between them exist. For example, if in a study of group interaction in project meetings it was found that, for every meeting analyzed, positive procedural communications tended to inhibit subsequent negative action statements, then it would make sense to conclude that such inhibitory pattern is likely to be a general phenomenon. Conversely, if positive procedural communications tended to inhibit subsequent negative action statements in some meetings but activate them in some other meetings, then no such conclusion would be warranted, and the researchers would be interested in discerning possible causes for that inter-meeting difference. In the latter case, it is obvious that pooling data across meetings would probably yield misleading results.

Examples

Couples' Verbal Interaction

When couple interaction is observed systematically and only verbal utterances (or "thought units") are of interest, a simple coding scheme can be defined consisting of mutually exclusive and exhaustive codes, separately for wife and husband. For example, WApp (wife approves), WCom (wife complains), WEmo (wife emotes), WEmp (wife empathizes), WNeg (wife negates), and WOth (other wife utterances); and HApp (husband approves), HCom (husband complains), HEmo (husband emotes), HEmp (husband empathizes), HNeg (husband negates), and HOth (other husband utterances). Then, the sequence of utterances coded during an observation session could be as shown in Figure 15.1. As no time information is recorded, only research questions about the order in which utterances occur, or about their relative frequencies, can be addressed. For example, do wife and husband reciprocate verbally, that is, does a code like WCom tend to be followed by HCom (and vice versa) more often than expected by chance? Does WApp tend

```
Event

($Wife    = WCom WEmo WApp WEmp WNeg WOth)

($Husband = HCom HEmo HApp HEmp HNeg HOth)

* Age (Young Adult) Type (Clinic Control);


(Adult, Clinic)

HApp WEmp WEmo HEmp WEmp WNeg WNeg HApp WEmo HEmo WEmp HEmp WCom HCom

HCom WCom HOth WEmo HEmo WEmo HEmo WEmp HEmo WEmo HApp WEmp WEmo HApp

HApp WApp HEmo WEmp HEmp HEmo WEmo WEmo HApp HCom WNeg WNeg WCom HEmo

WEmo HEmp WEmp HEmp WEmo HEmo WEmo WEmo HEmp HNeg HOth HCom WOth WEmo

WApp HApp WEmp WEmo HApp WEmp HCom WCom HEmo WEmo WCom HEmo WEmp HEmp

WEmp HEmp WEmp HApp WCom HCom WNeg HCom WEmp HEmp WEmp HEmp HEmo WEmo

WEmp /
```

Figure 15.1 *An SDIS file containing a sequence of coded utterances during a couple's verbal interaction. The data type (Event), the codes for wife and husband, and two independent variables, with two levels each, are defined at the outset. Only one sequence for a couple is shown here. The first letter in each code denotes speaker (W for wife, H for husband); see text for explanation of the codes. The sequence is read row-wise, from left to right, i.e., first the husband approves (HApp), then the wife empathizes (WEmp); it ends with two wife utterances (WEmo, then WEmp). A wife's utterance can be followed either by a husband's or a wife's utterance, and vice versa. (e.g., WEmp WEmo, or WEmo HEmp). It is assumed that utterances do not overlap in time. No time information was recorded for the codes.*

to be followed by HApp (and vice versa) more often than expected by chance? In research aiming to explore differences in interaction styles between distressed and nondistressed couples a possible research question could be, do distressed wives tend to reciprocate their husbands more than nondistressed wives, specifically, are cross-complaints significantly more frequent in the former than in the latter? (E.g., husband: "I happen to go to work. What have you got to do all day?"; wife: "I'm trying to get along on the money you don't make, that's what"; from Gottman, Notarius, Gonso, & Markman, 1976, p. 8.)

In order to answer such questions, a body of data comprising a sample of couples observed during several sessions would be necessary. Code frequencies should be substantially large in order to apply statistical decision methods about the hypotheses. However, an initial inspection of the sequences may reveal the possible existence of sequential patterns, which can be further analyzed. In the preceding example, subsequences like HEmp WCom HCom, HApp WCom HCom, HCom WCom HOth, and HCom WCom HEmo may be a hint of possible pattern that can be expressed as "the husband tends to complain in response to his wife complaining when his previous utterance was *positive* (approve, empathize), but does not tend to complain in response to his wife complaining when it was *negative* (complain, negate)." That is, the husband possibly responds to his wife in a way that not only depends on her previous behavior, but on his immediately preceding behavior as well. In that example, the specific way in which the husband is responding (not complaining after his wife complained if his previous utterance was negative) could indicate that he is intending to deescalate and avoid conflict.

Mother-Grandmother-Infant Interaction

In the previous example, interaction was represented as a simple sequence in which both the codes' onset and offset times and their possible overlapping were ignored. This simplification can be sufficient for the kind of research questions mentioned. However, certain questions require that interactive behavior be represented in a more complex way. When studying mother-infant interaction at the micro-level, recording precise timings, durations, and synchrony of behavior is often of capital importance. For example, in a study of joint attention to objects in both mother- and grandmother-infant interaction, the following codes are defined (based on Rowland, 1995; see also Bakeman, 2000): A (infant is actively engaged with an object: facial expressions, vocalizations, and motor responses directed to a toy or to an adult handling a toy), P (infant is passively engaged with an object, simply looking to a toy or to an adult handling a toy), N (infant is not engaged), MM (mother maintains infant's attention with verbal comments and facial expressions), MR (mother redirects infant's attention by introducing a new toy or activity), MS (mother supports infant's attention by looking at infant but not physically interacting), MN (mother is not interacting with infant), GM (grandmother maintains infant's attention), GR (grandmother redirects infant's attention), GS (grandmother supports infant's attention), and GN (grandmother is not interacting with infant).While the codes are mutually exclusive and exhaustive for each individual, codes for different individuals can overlap in time. During a session in which a triad of adolescent mother, grandmother, and six-months-old infant were observed, and the codes' onset times were recorded, three parallel sequences, or streams, could be obtained, as shown in Figure 15.2. A time plot of those data is shown in Figure 15.3.

Questions about code frequencies, durations, sequences, and co-occurrences can be answered with those data. For example, does the infant tend to be actively engaged while her mother maintains the infant's attention? Do the grandmother's interactions with the infant tend to last more on average than the mother's? Is the grandmother more successful maintaining the infant's attention than the adolescent mother? Does a positive procedural statement inhibit or facilitate further positive statements in group meetings?

Representing Sequential Data

Interaction sequences can be represented in a variety of ways. When the purpose of the analysis is to obtain statistics for testing hypotheses about sequential or synchronic patterns and for computing association indices among codes, then an appropriate way is to represent them according to the Sequential Data Interchange Standard (SDIS). Details about the features and syntax of SDIS are given in Bakeman and Quera (1992, 1995a, 2011). SDIS is a language for describing sequential data as obtained through direct observation of individuals, interacting dyads, or groups. It permits representing sequential data with or without time information, and with or without co-occurrence among behavioral codes. SDIS data are text files that include: (a) a definition of the data type, a list of the behavioral codes used by the observers, and a list of independent variables (e.g., age, sex, status); and (b) series of codes (plus their occurrence times or their durations, if needed) in the order in which they occurred, organized according to units (i.e., individuals, dyads, groups) and assigned to levels of the independent variables (examples of SDIS files are shown in Figures 15.1 and 15.2).

SDIS defines five types of data: (a) ESD, or Event Sequential Data (or Simple-Code Event), when the stream of behavior is segmented into events and then a single code, without time information, is assigned to each event. (b) MSD, or Multi-Event Sequential Data (or Multi-Code Event), when the stream of behavior is segmented into events and then multiple codes, without time information, are assigned to each event. (c) TDS, or Timed-Event Sequential Data, when the stream of behavior is segmented into events and then codes and their onset, and perhaps also offset, times are assigned to them; the codes may or may not be temporally exclusive and exhaustive. (d) SSD, or State Sequential Data, a particular case of

```
State
($Infant = A P N)
($Grandmother = GM GR GS GN)
($Mother = MM MR MS MN)
* Mother_Skill (Low High);

(Low)
,0:30
% Infant stream:
P,0:30 A,0:36 N,0:39 P,0:42 N,0:47 P,1:00 N,1:06 P,1:23 N,1:27 A,1:44
N,2:00 P,2:37 N,2:40 P,3:06 N,3:10 P,3:19 N,3:24 P,4:52 N,4:57 P,5:02
A,5:10 N,5:17 A,5:42 N,5:45 P,5:54 A,6:01 N,6:08 A,6:12 N,6:15 P,6:24
&
% Grandmother stream:
GN,0:30 GM,0:43 GN,0:56 GR,1:07 GN,1:22 GS,1:30 GM,1:55 GS,1:58
GR,2:00 GS,2:11 GR,2:26 GN,2:34 GR,3:01 GS,3:07 GR,3:11 GM,3:19
GR,3:26 GM,3:38 GS,3:47 GR,3:56 GS,4:06 GR,4:12 GM,4:31 GM,4:39
GS,4:49 GM,5:04 GS,5:12 GR,5:18 GS,5:21 GM,5:27 GR,5:31 GS,5:35
GN,5:41 GR,5:54 GM,5:57 GM,6:07 GN,6:13 GR,6:27
&
% Mother stream:
MM,0:30 MN,0:40 MM,0:56 MN,1:07 MR,1:22 MM,1:25 MS,1:28 MR,1:41
MM,1:44 MM,1:52 MM,1:58 MR,2:13 MS,2:21 MR,2:24 MS,2:28 MM,2:36
MS,2:40 MM,2:44 MR,2:48 MN,2:56 MM,3:01 MS,3:11 MR,4:03 MS,4:10
MR,4:52 MS,4:57 MR,5:02 MS,5:09 MR,5:41 MN,5:45 MR,5:57 MN,6:02
MM,6:10 MN,6:13
,6:30 /
```

Figure 15.2 *An SDIS file containing three parallel sequences of mother-grandmother-infant interaction. The data type (State), the codes for infant, grandmother, and mother, and an independent variable, with two levels, are defined at the outset. Only one sequence for a triad is shown here. See text for explanation of the codes. Codes within each sequence are mutually exclusive and exhaustive, and their onset times are recorded, expressed in minutes and seconds; the offset time for a code equals the onset time for the next code. The first (0.30) and last (6:30) items indicate the session onset and offset times. The sequences are read row-wise, from left to right: the infant was passively engaged (P) from 0:30 to 0:36 (that is, 6 seconds), then actively engaged (A) from 0:36 to 0:39 (3 seconds), and so on; finally, the infant was passively engaged from 6:24 until the session end time, 6:30 (6 seconds). Ampersands separate individual sequences that occur in parallel.*

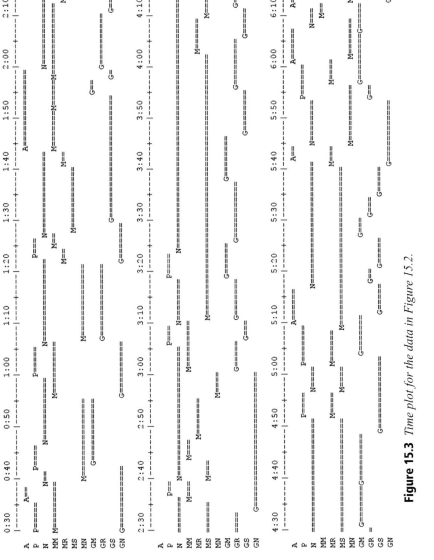

Figure 15.3 *Time plot for the data in Figure 15.2.*

Subject ID _____ Observer _____				
Start time _____ Stop time _____ Date _____				
event	alert	fussy	cry	REM	sleep
1		X			
2	X				
3			X		
4					X
5				X	

Event;
<Infant 32> fussy alert cry sleep REM /

Figure 15.4 *A recording form containing a sequence of mutually exclusive and exhaustive codes, without time information, assigned to an infant's alert states, and its corresponding SDIS representation as Event Sequential Data (ESD).*

TSD in which codes belong to mutually exclusive and exhaustive sets. And (e) ISD, Interval Sequential Data, when time is segmented into equally spaced intervals and one or more codes are assigned to them. Note that the first four data types result from continuous recording, while the latter usually results from a time sampling recording procedure (Bakeman & Quera, 2011; Martin & Bateson, 2007; Yoder & Symons, 2010). Figures 15.4 to 15.8 show different examples of recording forms and their time plots and SDIS representations. For simplicity, only ESD and TSD examples of analysis are dealt with in more detail in this chapter.

Models

In Event Sequential Data, what defines the sequence is the order in which the codes occur in the coding protocol; if they are sorted randomly, it is unlikely that the empirical original sequence is obtained. A sequence of randomly sorted elements has no order, namely, no association exists between one element and the elements occurring before and after it. A random sequence is thus the base model, the null hypothesis against which to compare an observed sequence in order to find out whether sequential associations exist among the codes.

Most behavior sequences are not random; neither are they deterministic, that is, code occurrences cannot usually be predicted with complete certainty from knowledge of previous ones. Generally speaking, behavior sequences are stochastic: Given that a certain code occurs, there is a distribution of transition probabilities for the other (target) codes to occur after it. If the probabilities that the target codes occur vary as a function of the immediately previous given codes only, and if the

Dyad ID _____ Observer _____
Start time _____ Stop time _____ Date _____

event	Infant					Mother	
	alert	fussy	cry	REM	sleep	attentive	inattentive
1		X				X	
2		X					X
3	X					X	
4			X			X	
5					X		X
6					X	X	
7					X		X
8				X			X

Multi;
<Dyad 32> fussy at. fussy in. alert at. cry at. sleep in. sleep at.
sleep in. REM in /

Figure 15.5 *A recording form containing a sequence of two sets of mutually exclusive and exhaustive codes, without time information, assigned to an infant's alert states and her mother's simultaneous behavior, and its corresponding SDIS representation as Multi-Event Sequential Data (MSD).*

Subject ID_____
Observer_____
Date _____

event	onset	offset
fussy	1	3
voc	2	5
alert	3	4
cry	4	8
touch	5	9
voc	7	10
sleep	8	10
REM	10	11

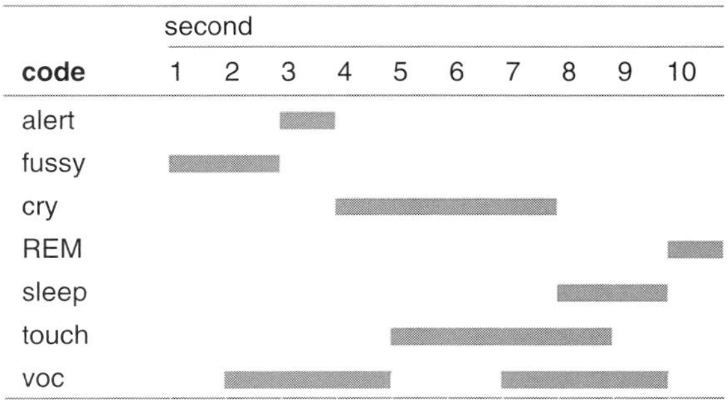

Timed (alert fussy cry REM sleep) touch voc;
<Infant 32>
fussy,1– alert,3– cry,4– sleep, 8– REM,10– &
voc,2–5 touch,5–9 voc,7–10 ,11/

Figure 15.6 *A recording form containing a sequence of exhaustive, but not mutually exclusive, codes with their onset and offset times, assigned to an infant's alert states, its time plot, and the corresponding SDIS representation as Timed-Event Sequential Data (TSD).*

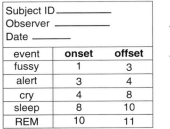

event	onset	offset
fussy	1	3
alert	3	4
cry	4	8
sleep	8	10
REM	10	11

Subject ID _____
Observer _____
Date _____

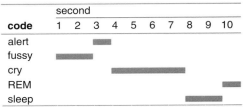

State;
<Infant 32> fussy,1 alert,3 cry,4 sleep,8 REM,10 ,11 /

or:

State;
<Infant 32> fussy=2 alert=1 cry=4 sleep=2 REM=1 /

Figure 15.7 *A recording form containing a sequence of mutually exclusive and exhaustive codes with their onset and offset times, assigned to an infant's alert states, its time plot, and the corresponding SDIS representation as State Sequential Data (SSD).*

Subject ID _____ Observer ____ _____ Date _____

interval	Infant code					Mother code	
	alert	fussy	cry	REM	sleep	touch	voc
1		X					
2		X					X
3	X						X
4			X				X
5			X			X	
6			X			X	
7			X			X	X
8					X	X	X
9					X		X
10				X			
...							

Interval; <Infant 32> fussy, fussy voc, alert voc, cry voc, cry touch *2, cry touch voc, sleep touch voc, sleep voc, REM /

Figure 15.8 *A recording form containing a sequence of time intervals to which two sets of mutually exclusive and exhaustive codes are assigned, and its corresponding SDIS representation as Interval Sequential Data (ISD). The codes define an infant's alert states and her mother's simultaneous behavior.*

distribution of probabilities is the same at any position in the sequence (i.e., if transition probabilities are stationary), then the sequence is described as a discrete time Markov chain (e.g., Stewart, 1994).

A Markov chain is characterized by the distribution of unconditional code probabilities (i.e., for each code, the probability that, if a position in the sequence is selected at random, the code occurs at that position), and by the distributions of conditional, or transition or lag 1, probabilities among the given and target codes. For example, if an event sequence of couple verbal interaction is modeled as a Markov chain, then the matrices shown in Table 15.1 could define it. If the sequence lacked sequential order, then each row of conditional probabilities would be identical to the unconditional ones. However, in that example, while HCom's unconditional probability equals .08, its lag 1 probability after WCom equals .53 (these codes are described in Section 2, Examples). That is, wife complaining tends to be followed by husband complaining, because .53 is greater than .08. On the other hand, HEmo's unconditional probability equals .13, but its lag 1 probability after WCom equals .07. That is, wife complaining does not tend to be followed by husband emoting, because .07 is less than .13. By inspecting the lag 1 probabilities along one column of the matrix we can see how the probability of the target code varies when the given codes vary, and to what extent they differ from the target code's unconditional probability. In sum, variability in probabilities along one column would indicate that the occurrence of the target code for that column is affected (increased or decreased) by the previous, given codes, which would mean that sequential patterns exist in the data.

It must be noted that such implications would be valid only if the probabilities actually were theoretical values. However, as these values are calculated from empirical data, they are in fact estimates of probabilities, which contain a sampling error. Consequently, in order to conclude that some conditional probability is (significantly) greater or less than some unconditional one, a statistical test is needed, as explained in Section 5, Data Analysis. If a substantial amount of conditional probabilities in the matrix differ significantly from their corresponding unconditional ones, then it can be inferred that a Markov chain can be an appropriate model for the sequence.

However, when a sequence is modeled as a Markov chain, it is assumed that the probability of a code occurring at a certain position in the sequence depends on the immediately previous code only; regarding interaction, it means that a behavior can be predicted by taking the previous behavior into account only. Although the Markov chain model can be a reasonable simplification in some cases, usually time dependency among behaviors encompasses lags greater than 1; for example, a husband's utterance may depend not only on the wife's previous utterance (lag 1) but also on a husband utterance previous to it (lag 2). Higher order Markov models can be used to model those more complex cases; they require analyzing multi-dimensional matrices and sample sizes (i.e., sequence lengths) usually bigger than those required by simple Markov chains. For details about Markov models, see Stewart (1994) and Wickens (1982).

Table 15.1 *Unconditional and conditional or lag 1 probabilities for an Event Sequence of couple verbal interaction*

Unconditional probabilities:

WCom	WEmo	WApp	WEmp	WNeg	WOth	HCom	HEmo	HApp	HEmp	HNeg	HOth
.07	.15	.09	.15	.03	.01	.08	.13	.09	.14	.05	.01

Conditional or lag 1 probabilities:

| | | | | | | Target | | | | | | |
Given	WCom	WEmo	WApp	WEmp	WNeg	WOth	HCom	HEmo	HApp	HEmp	HNeg	HOth
WCom	.04	.01	.00	.01	.01	.00	.53	.07	.06	.21	.06	.01
WEmo	.06	.05	.04	.01	.00	.01	.02	.44	.16	.15	.04	.01
WApp	.00	.07	.14	.10	.01	.01	.03	.14	.28	.18	.02	.01
WEmp	.01	.09	.03	.04	.02	.01	.05	.19	.08	.45	.04	.00
WNeg	.06	.05	.06	.03	.11	.00	.23	.06	.14	.12	.14	.02
WOth	.00	.20	.05	.15	.05	.00	.20	.15	.20	.00	.00	.00
HCom	.33	.07	.10	.07	.04	.02	.04	.08	.08	.06	.10	.00
HEmo	.01	.51	.15	.14	.02	.00	.05	.01	.01	.04	.04	.02
HApp	.08	.16	.26	.29	.03	.02	.03	.01	.08	.03	.01	.00
HEmp	.08	.13	.06	.54	.02	.02	.02	.05	.02	.03	.03	.00
HNeg	.17	.19	.14	.08	.17	.00	.09	.05	.04	.00	.06	.02
HOth	.07	.07	.07	.07	.07	.00	.33	.13	.07	.13	.00	.00

Note. Row sums in the matrices equal 1. See text for explanation of the codes.

When interaction is represented as Timed-Event or State Sequential Data, lags are measured in time units (e.g., seconds). For example, in the sequence shown in Figure 15.7, code "fussy" lasts two time units (seconds) and is followed by code "alert," which lasts one time unit; thus, the onset time of "alert" occurs at lag 2 (i.e., is lagged two time units) from the onset time of "fussy." In these cases, it is better to analyze lagged associations by defining time windows anchored to existing codes, and to estimate the lag 0 probability that other codes occur within those windows (Bakeman & Quera, 2011; Chorney, Garcia, Berlin, Bakeman, & Kain, 2010; Hall & Oliver, 1997). A special case is the analysis of synchrony between behaviors, in which each code occurrence is defined as a time window itself. Table 15.2 shows an example of lag 0 conditional probabilities among mother and infant behaviors during

Table 15.2 *Unconditional and conditional or lag 0 conditional probabilities among mother and infant behaviors during episodes of joint attention to objects*

(a) Unconditional probabilities:

IQuiet	IActive	IFuss
.126	.294	.276

Conditional or lag 0 probabilities:

Given	IQuiet	Target IActive	IFuss
MPassive	.376	.330	.295
MActive	.157	.402	.441
MRedirect	.154	.415	.431

(b) Unconditional probabilities:

MPassive	MActive	MRedirect
.133	.318	.305

Conditional or lag 0 probabilities:

Given	MPassive	Target MActive	MRedirect
IQuiet	.269	.387	.344
IActive	.110	.460	.430
IFuss	.093	.482	.425

Note. (a) Conditional probabilities of the infant's codes given the mother's codes. (b) Conditional probabilities of the mother's codes given the infant's codes.

episodes of joint attention to objects, plus unconditional probabilities of each behavior. In this case, the unconditional probability of a code is the probability that, if a time unit is selected at random, the code is occurring in that unit. The lag 0 conditional probability for a pair of given and target codes is the probability that the latter occurs in a time unit given that the former is occurring in the same unit. In the example, while the unconditional probability of the infant being quiet is .126, the probability of being quiet given that her mother is passive is .376. On the other hand, while the unconditional probability of the mother being passive is .133, the probability of being passive given that her infant is quiet is .269. Therefore, the infant tends to be quiet while her mother is passive, and vice versa. By inspecting the conditional probabilities along one column of the matrix, we can see that some values vary according to the given codes (e.g., for MPassive as target, .269, .110, .093), compare them with the corresponding unconditional value (.133), and conclude that the target code is more or less likely to occur depending on the given code (the mother is more likely to be passive while her infant is quiet, and less likely when her infant is either active or fussing). If a new code were defined as a time window of, say, 20 seconds, anchored to the offset of every occurrence of IQuiet, we could estimate the lag 0 conditional probability of MPassive as target, given the time window, and see whether the mother tends to be passive more while her infant is quiet than immediately after her infant ceased to be quiet.

Data Analysis

Conditional and unconditional probabilities are theoretical values. As explained before, they must be estimated from the data, and the estimates are, of course, affected by sampling errors. Therefore, we cannot draw conclusions by simply comparing conditional and unconditional probabilities and deciding on whether they are different or not. Sequential data analysis is based on comparing observed lag frequencies between pairs of codes and global or summary frequencies for individual codes. A common approach is to limit the analysis to lag 1. In this chapter an overview of lag 1 analysis (for Event Sequential Data) and lag 0 analysis (for Timed-Event Sequential Data) is presented. In order to analyze higher orders of sequential association, lags greater than 1 must be explored (Sackett, 1979); log-linear analysis applied to multiple lags is an appropriate approach, which may require long sequences (Bakeman, Adamson, & Strisik, 1995; Bakeman & Quera, 2011). For example, for data like those in Figure 15.1, a log-linear analysis applied to a three-dimensional table with husband codes as givens (lag 0), and subsequent wife (lag 1) and husband (lag 2) codes as targets could reveal: (a) whether lag 1 associations between husband and wife, and between wife and husband codes exist; (b) whether lag 2 associations between husband and subsequent husband codes exist, irrespective of intermediate wife codes; and (c) whether lag 2 associations are independent or not from lag 1 ones. In the latter case, if lag 2 associations did depend on lag 1 ones, then it could be concluded that the way the husband responds to his wife depends on his previous verbal behavior.

Observed Lag Frequencies

Results from a lag 1 analysis of a couple's verbal interaction are shown in Table 15.3; data were Event Sequential and, for that particular analysis, only transitions from husband (given) to wife (target) behaviors were considered, that is, the analysis provided information about how wife responded to husband. Lag 1 frequencies are shown in Table 15.3a. Row and column totals are the global or summary frequencies for these codes; in total, 961 transitions from husband to wife utterances were observed.

Table 15.3 *Lag 1 analysis of a couple's verbal interaction (Event Sequential data)*

(a)

Given	WCom	WEmo	Target WApp	WEmp	WNeg	WOth	Totals
HCom	31	18	28	9	8	4	98
HEmo	4	166	39	42	5	0	256
HApp	14	39	83	70	12	2	220
HEmp	24	39	21	178	8	8	278
HNeg	13	23	24	11	24	1	96
HOth	3	5	1	2	2	0	13
Totals	89	290	196	312	59	15	961

(b)

Given	WCom	WEmo	Target WApp	WEmp	WNeg	WOth	Totals
HCom	9.08	29.57	19.99	31.82	6.02	1.53	98
HEmo	23.71	77.25	52.21	83.11	15.72	4.00	256
HApp	20.37	66.39	44.87	71.43	13.51	3.43	220
HEmp	25.75	83.89	56.70	90.26	17.07	4.34	278
HNeg	8.89	28.97	19.58	31.17	5.89	1.50	96
HOth	1.20	3.92	2.65	4.22	0.80	0.20	13
Totals	89	290	196	312	59	15	961

(c)

Given	WCom	WEmo	Target WApp	WEmp	WNeg	WOth
HCom	8.06	−2.69	2.12	−5.19	0.88	2.12
HEmo	−4.96	14.11	−2.39	−6.41	−3.26	−2.35
HApp	−1.69	−4.58	7.27	−0.23	−0.48	−0.89
HEmp	−0.43	−6.96	−6.30	13.33	−2.69	2.10
HNeg	1.53	−1.40	1.18	−4.63	8.11	−0.43
HOth	1.73	0.66	−1.14	−1.32	1.40	−0.46

Table 15.3 *(cont.)*

(d) Given	WCom	WEmo	**Target** WApp	WEmp	WNeg	WOth
HCom	<.001	.007	.034	<.001	.378	.034
HEmo	<.001	<.001	.017	<.001	.001	.019
HApp	.091	<.001	<.001	.815	.630	.374
HEmp	.668	<.001	<.001	<.001	.007	.036
HNeg	.127	.162	.238	<.001	<.001	.665
HOth	.084	.512	.252	.185	.162	.648

Note. Only transitions from husband (given) to wife (target) behaviors were considered. (a) Observed frequencies. (b) Expected frequencies. (c) Adjusted residuals; significant residuals ($\alpha = .05$) are highlighted: values greater than $+1.96$ are shown in bold, values less than -1.96 are shown in italics. (d) p-values for the adjusted residuals.

Expected Lag Frequencies

If the null hypothesis of no sequential association were true, then the observed lag frequencies would be proportional to their row totals to the same extent as their corresponding column totals are proportional to the total number of transitions. For example, if no sequential association existed between HCom and WCom, then we can estimate that the frequency for that cell would be approximately equal to $98 \times 89 / 961 = 9.08$. That is, under the hypothesis of no association, the expected lag frequency for the cell at row r and column c is computed as:

$$e_{rc} = \frac{f_r \times f_c}{f}$$

where f_r and f_c are the totals for row r and column c, respectively, and f is the total number of transitions. Expected frequencies are shown in Table 15.3b; note that their row and column totals are identical to the observed ones. In some cases, depending on how the behaviors are coded, specific transitions can be impossible; for example, if coding is restricted so that a code cannot follow itself (e.g., if several utterances coded as HCom that occur successively are considered a single instance of HCom) and the code is specified both as given and target, then its auto-transition is not possible, and the table cell contains a structural zero. Lag tables containing structural zeros require that expected frequencies be calculated via an iterative algorithm (for details, see Bakeman & Quera, 1995a, 1995b, 2011).

Chi-square Test

In order to know whether the wife's utterances are sequentially associated to previous husband's utterances, we calculate the Pearson's chi-square statistic for the table:

$$X^2 = \sum_{r=1}^{r=R} \sum_{c=1}^{c=C} \frac{\left(f_{rc} - e_{rc}\right)^2}{e_{rc}}$$

where f_{rc} is the observed lag frequency for the cell at row r and column c, R and C are the number of rows and columns, respectively, and the sums are for all the table cells for which e_{rc} For the data in Table 15.3, $X^2 = 501.49$. If many expected frequencies in the table are not too small (say, not less than 3), then we can assume that, under the null hypothesis, the statistic is distributed as chi-square with degrees of freedom equal to $(R - 1) \times (C - 1)$. In the example, six expected frequencies (16% of the table cells) are less than 3. The 99.9 percentile of the chi-square distribution for $(6 - 1) \times (6 - 1) = 25$ degrees of freedom is 52.6; therefore, as $X^2 = 501.49 > 52.6$, we can reject the null hypothesis with $p < .001$. Consequently, we conclude that wife's utterances are sequentially associated with the previous husband's utterances.

Adjusted Residuals

Once we know that given and target codes are associated, it makes sense to look for possible patterns, that is, transitions that occur significantly more, or less often than expected by chance. In the example, which wife's utterances tend, or do not tend, to occur after which husband's utterances? To this end, Haberman's adjusted residuals (Allison & Liker, 1982; Bakeman & Quera, 1995b, 2011) are computed for all $e_{rc} > 0$:

$$Z_{rc} = \frac{f_{rc} - e_{rc}}{\sqrt{e_{rc} \left[1 - \frac{f_r}{f}\right] \left[1 - \frac{f_c}{f}\right]}}$$

Note that, when the observed lag frequency is greater than the expected one for that cell, the adjusted residual is positive; when the observed is less than the expected, the adjusted residual is negative. The difference is standardized by dividing it by its standard error. Adjusted residuals can be interpreted as z-scores when the row total is not small (say, not less than 30) and the proportion e_{rc}/f_r is not extreme (i.e., it is greater than .10 and less than .90). Therefore, adjusted residuals greater than or equal to $+1.96$ or less than or equal to -1.96 indicate that the observed frequency differs significantly from the expected one, with $\alpha = .05$.

   Table 15.3c shows the adjusted residuals for the example. Most diagonal cells in the table contain positive and significant values, which indicate reciprocity of utterances (HCom-WEmo; HEmo-WEmo; HApp-WApp; HEmp-WEmp; HNeg-WNeg); p-values for the adjusted residuals in those cells are in fact less than .001, as Table 15.3d shows. By reading the table of adjusted residuals along one row, we know how the wife was more likely to respond after a specific husband utterance. For example, the wife tended to complain (8.06, $p < .001$) or approve (2.12, $p = .034$), but did not tend to empathize (-2.69, $p = .007$), after her husband complained. On the other hand, by reading the table along one column, we know which husband's utterances were more likely to occur before a specific wife's utterance. For example, the husband tended to complain (8.06, $p < .001$), but not to empathize (-4.96, $p < .001$), before his wife complained. As both the row total for code HOth (given) and the ratios of the expected frequencies to row totals for code WOth (target) are small, we cannot draw conclusions involving transitions starting at HOth or ending at WOth.

However, when multiple statistical tests (M tests) are performed with a certain alpha level α (in our case, as many tests as cells in the table, i.e., $M = R \times C$), the expected number of false significant results is $\alpha \times M$. In order to keep the global alpha level to α, the Bonferroni correction (Miller, 1966) can be applied by using $\alpha' = \alpha / M$. Then, significant adjusted residuals are those that are greater than or equal to the positive z-score for that α', or less than or equal to the negative z-score for that α'. For the data in Table 15.3, for a global $\alpha = .05$, $\alpha' = .05 / 36 = .001$, $z = \pm 3.29$. For example, with $\alpha' = .001$, the transition HCom-WApp (2.12) would not be considered significant (2.12 < 3.29).

An alternative to applying the Bonferroni correction is using a winnowing technique in order to identify those adjusted residuals that most influence other residuals in the table. As the residuals in the table are dependent on one another (if a cell contains a large and positive residual, then large and negative residuals are found in other cells in its same row and column), probably only some of them are really important, the significance of some others being dependent on them. That redundancy can be filtered out by means of a stepwise analytical procedure: first, the cell with the most significant residual is ignored, or removed (i.e., as if the transition had never been observed), and the residuals for the other cells are calculated; then, the most significant residual obtained at this step is removed, and the residuals recalculated. The process is repeated until no significant residuals are found, and the ones that were removed indicate the transitions that really matter. For details about the winnowing technique, see Bakeman and Quera (1995b, 2011).

When sequences are too short, adjusted residuals cannot be confidently interpreted as z-scores; in that case, an appropriate alternative for obtaining p-values for the transitions among codes is the use of permutation tests. They provide estimations of exact p-values for the transitions without assuming a normal distribution. In essence, the observed sequence is permuted many times (say, 10,000) and a lag table is obtained for each permuted sequence. Then, a distribution of lag frequencies is calculated for each cell in the table by cumulating the transition frequencies for that cell from all the permuted sequences. Those are the expected distributions under the null hypothesis of no sequential association. The p-value for a transition is obtained by calculating the percentile of its observed frequency in the expected distribution for its cell. For details about the use of permutation tests, see Bakeman, Robinson, and Quera (1996) and Bakeman and Quera (2011).

Indices of Association

While adjusted residuals are useful for detecting sequential patterns within a sequence, when the aim is to compare patterns between sequences, alternative statistics are needed. Adjusted residuals and chi-squares depend on sample size. Given that there is a sequential association, the greater the table total the more significant the chi-square can be; also, the greater the row total the more significant the adjusted residuals in that row can be. Therefore, in order to compare sequences from different individuals, dyads, or groups, a statistic that indicates the degree of association not dependent on sample size (i.e., sequence length) is appropriate. Several kinds of such statistics are available; for example, Yule's Q, odds ratios, log odds, and Pearson's phi coefficients (Bakeman, McArthur, & Quera, 1996). They can be calculated for 2 (rows) × 2 (columns) lag tables, and express the degree of association between two binary variables. In the analysis of sequences, the values of the row variable are *given code on/given code off*, and the values of the column variable are *target code on/target code off*. In particular, a Yule's Q calculated for such a table can yield values bounded between +1 (complete positive association) and −1 (complete negative association), with 0 indicating no association. In a lag 0 analysis, complete positive association means that, while the given code is on the target code is always on, and while the given code is off the target code is always off; complete negative association implies given on–target off and given off–target on.

Results from a lag 0 analysis of mother- and grandmother-infant interactions from a study of joint attention to objects are shown in Table 15.4a (based on Rowland, 1995); data were Timed-Event Sequential, and the codes were as defined before. A small sample size of four triads of mother, grandmother, and infant were observed. Infants were: one 6-month-old male, one 6-month-old female, one 12-month-old male, and one 12-month-old female. For each combination of infant age, infant gender, and interacting adult, one 2 × 2, lag 0 table for codes MM/GM (mother or grandmother maintains infant's attention) as given and A (infant is actively engaged) as target were obtained. Tallies in those tables are seconds (720 in total). For example, for the 6-month-old male infant, the MM/Not MM (given)–A/Not A (target) table indicates that in 265 out of 720 seconds the mother was maintaining the infant's attention, and that in 70 out of these 265 seconds the infant was actively engaged. For a 2 × 2 table such as that, Yule's Q is computed as (e.g., Reynolds, 1977):

$$Q = \frac{f_{11} \cdot f_{22} - f_{12} \cdot f_{21}}{f_{11} \cdot f_{22} + f_{12} \cdot f_{21}}$$

Table 15.4 *Lag 0 analysis of mother- and grandmother-infant interactions (Timed-Event Sequential data)*

(a) 6 mo		Mother A	Not A	Totals		Grandmother A	Not A	Totals
Male	MM	70	195	265	GM	25	143	168
	Not MM	25	430	455	Not GM	70	482	552
	Totals	95	625	720	Totals	95	625	720
		A	Not A	Totals		A	Not A	Totals
Female	MM	83	183	266	GM	16	32	48
	Not MM	64	390	454	Not GM	131	541	672
	Totals	147	573	720	Totals	147	573	720
12 mo		A	Not A	Totals		A	Not A	Totals
Male	MM	53	149	202	GM	49	69	118
	Not MM	79	439	518	Not GM	83	519	602
	Totals	132	588	720	Totals	132	588	720
		A	Not A	Totals		A	Not A	Totals
Female	MM	22	180	202	GM	32	46	78
	Not MM	115	403	518	Not GM	105	537	642
	Totals	137	583	720	Totals	137	583	720

(b) 6 mo	Mother	Grandmother
Male	.72 (.06)	.09 (.12)
Female	.47 (.07)	.35 (.14)
12 mo		
Male	.33 (.09)	.63 (.07)
Female	−.40 (.10)	.56 (.09)

Note. (a) Co-occurrence frequencies between infant and mother, and infant and grandmother codes. (b) Yules'*Q*s and *SE*s for the 2 × 2 tables.

and its standard error is:

$$SE_Q = \frac{1 - Q^2}{2} \sqrt{\frac{1}{f_{11}} + \frac{1}{f_{12}} + \frac{1}{f_{21}} + \frac{1}{f_{22}}}$$

For the MM/Not MM (given) – A/Not A (target) table,

$$Q = \frac{70 \cdot 430 - 195 \cdot 25}{70 \cdot 430 + 195 \cdot 25} = .72$$

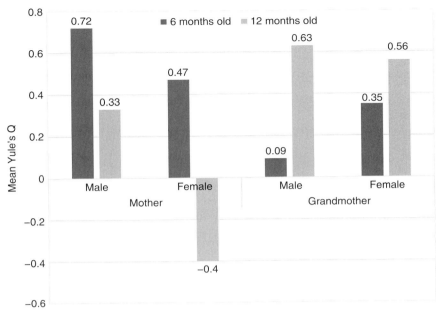

Figure 15.9 *Lag 0 associations (expressed as Yule's Qs) between code A (infant is actively engaged) and codes MM (mother maintains infant's attention) and GM (grandmother maintains infant's attention) in four infants (6-month-old male, 6-month-old female, 12-month-old male, and 12-month-old female).*

which indicates a positive and high lag 0 association, or synchrony, between MM and A; its standard error equals .06 and thus the standardized value is $z = .72 / .06 = 12$, which means that Q is significantly different from zero.

Table 15.4b summarizes the Yules's Qs and their SEs for the eight conditions (see also Figure 15.9). For this small sample we can conclude that: (a) Grandmothers were more effective in maintaining infant's attention with 12-month-olds (Qs = .63 and .56) than with 6-months-olds (Qs = .09 and .35); in fact, ineffective with the 6-month-old male infant ($z = .09 / .12 = .75$, NS). (b) Mothers were more effective with 6-month-olds (Qs = .72 and .47) than with 12-month-olds (Qs = .33 and −.40); in fact, countereffective with the 12-month-old female. (c) Mothers were more effective with male infants than with female infants.

The preceding analysis was an exploration of how synchronic were mother-infant and grandmother-infant interactions, and a very basic sample was observed. In order to test whether infant age and gender have effects on the interactions, a sufficiently big sample of mother-grandmother-infant triads should be observed for each combination of age and gender. Then, one Yule's Q per triad for the MM/Not MM – A/Not A table should be computed (likewise for the GM/Not GM – A/Not A table), and an analysis of variance, and possible t-tests as well, should be carried out to test for the effects of infant age and gender on the

Qs. An alternative statistic to measure degree of association in 2×2 tables is the log odds ratio:

$$Q = ln\, \frac{f_{11}/f_{12}}{f_{21}/f_{22}} = ln\, \frac{f_{11} \cdot f_{12}}{f_{12} \cdot f_{21}}$$

where ln is the natural logarithm. The log odds ratio cannot be computed if any of the four cells has a zero frequency; for that reason, it is customary to arbitrarily add .5 to each cell count. Log odds ratios are bounded between $+\infty$ (complete positive association) and $-\infty$ (complete negative association), with 0 indicating no association. For example, the log odds ratio for the MM/Not MM – A/Not A table at the upper left in Table 15.4a is $r = ln[70 \cdot 430/(195 \cdot 25)] = 1.82$, a positive association.

When researchers are interested in knowing whether sequential associations are dependent on some variables or factors (e.g., in the preceding example, whether the association between MM and A varies between triads) or on a factorial combination of them (e.g., whether that association depends on both the age of the mother and the age of the infant), then the indices of association for 2×2 tables can be used as values of a dependent variable, and an analysis of variance be performed on them. To that end, log odds ratios may be a better choice than Yule's Q when an unbounded measure is needed for performing parametric statistical analyses such as analysis of variance.

Computer Programs

Sequences consisting of codes representing behaviors, either with or without time information, are usually obtained via direct and systematic observation. When the purpose is to represent interactions by means of simple event sequences, usually recording code occurrences with paper and pencil can suffice. However, representing interactions as timed-event sequences can require the use of video recordings; coding them is usually a time intensive task, which can be eased using specialized software like Mangold's INTERACT (www.mangold.de; Mangold, 2006) and Noldus' The Observer (www.noldus.com; Noldus Information Technology, 2003; see also Glüer, this volume, Chapter 13). These programs are useful for recording and representing the data as time plots, for calculating behavioral measures like code frequencies and durations, and for performing basic sequential analyses. In order to run more sophisticated sequential analyses, it is advisable to use program GSEQ, or Generalized Sequential Querier (www.ub.edu/gcai/gseq and www2.gsu.edu/~psyrab/gseq/; Bakeman & Quera, 1995a, 2011, 2012, 2017).

GSEQ computes a variety of simple and sequential contingency table statistics. Simple statistics include frequencies, rates, total durations, proportions, average, minimum, and maximum values of code durations, gaps between consecutive code occurrences, and latencies. Table statistics include lag frequencies, adjusted residuals, chi-squares, expected frequencies and, for 2×2 tables, Yule's Qs, odds

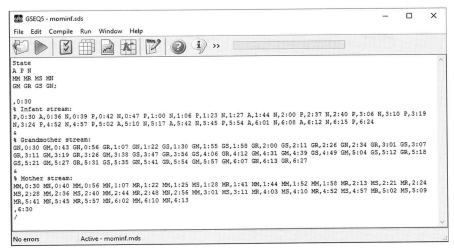

Figure 15.10 *Program GSEQ 5.1. Main window, showing data represented in SDIS format.*

ratios, log odds ratios, and Pearson's phi coefficients. Sequential statistics can be computed for various lags, and separately for each observation session included in a data file or pooled over sessions, levels of an independent variable or factor, or both. Figures 15.10, 15.11, and 15.12 show the data, dialog, and results windows of GSEQ 5.1.

GSEQ can read data files written in the SDIS format. The program includes a compiler for SDIS-formatted data files that checks them for syntactic correctness and converts them into internal files, which are then analyzed with the various analytic procedures included in GSEQ. Data can be entered manually into SDIS files, or converted from other data formats such as those used in Mangold's INTERACT and Noldus' The Observer video-analysis software using the standalone utilities ActSds, OdfSds, and ObsTxtSds (Bakeman & Quera, 2008), which can be downloaded from the GSEQ websites mentioned above. GSEQ's data modification capabilities expand analytic possibilities, which are not available in INTERACT and The Observer. New codes can be created from existing ones using standard logical operations (e.g., and, or, not) or by recoding, lumping, and chaining. A specialized window command permits defining new codes (time windows) that are tied to onsets and/or offsets of existing codes and, in particular, performing time-window sequential analyses.

A use of GSEQ is to produce statistics for export that are then analyzed by standard statistical packages such as R or SPSS, or by standard spreadsheet programs such as Excel. More generally, GSEQ's output consists of simple tab-delimited text files that can be read into and manipulated by any spreadsheet program. GSEQ also includes helpful data plotting routines and procedures for

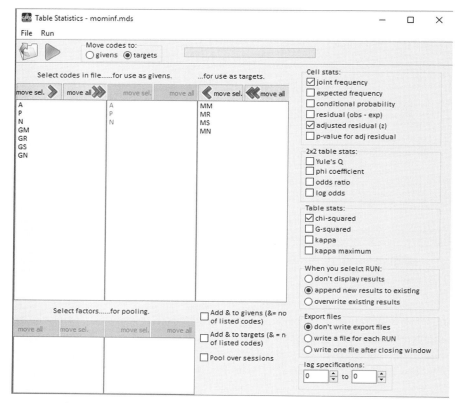

Figure 15.11 *Program GSEQ 5.1. Dialog window for requesting sequential analyses.*

assessing time-based, or point-by-point, interobserver agreement by means of the classic Cohen's kappa and event-based agreement between untimed sequences by means of a coefficient called alignment kappa (Bakeman, Quera, & Gnisci, 2009; Quera, Bakeman, & Gnisci, 2007; Bakeman & Quera, 2011).

Conclusion

In this chapter, an introduction to the methods for the analysis of interaction sequences was presented. When trained systematic observers use predefined categorical variables to record the stream of behaviors that occur when two or more people interact, the process of group interaction is represented as sequences of codes, with or without their onset and offset times; usually, several parallel, or concurrent, sequences must be defined, one per individual. Such sequential data can then be analyzed by means of the GSEQ software, which provides statistical results that indicate which patterns are most likely to occur in the sequences.

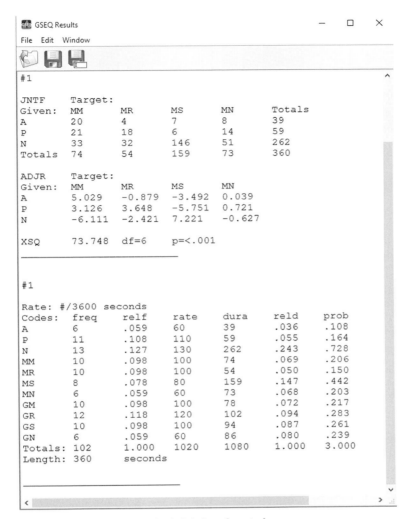

Figure 15.12 *Program GSEQ 5.1. Results window.*

The procedures described above can be termed "classical sequential analysis," and they rely on the use of asymptotic statistics, i.e., the decisions about which patterns are significant in the data are made assuming that certain theoretical probability distributions (for example, the normal distribution) hold. However, that assumption can be sometimes untenable, or impossible to check, as when sequences are short; in those cases, alternative, distribution-free procedures like permutation tests are advisable.

An alternative to the classical sequential analysis, in which associations between behavioral codes are examined in a piecewise manner, is recurrence analysis, which consists in representing graphically in a plot the similarities between parts of a sequence (or between parts of different, perhaps concurrent sequences). This way, sequences can be explored visually as a whole and recurrent patterns can be discovered; also, when two parallel sequences for two interacting individuals are explored using recurrence analysis, possible synchronicities can be revealed. Recurrence analysis of behavioral sequences is a promising and relatively new method (e.g., Buder, Warlaumont, Oller, & Chorna, 2010; Dale, Warlaumont, & Richardson, 2011). Details about this method are found in Bakeman and Quera (2011) and Quera (2008).

References

Allison, P. D., & Liker, J. K. (1982). Analyzing sequential categorical data on dyadic interaction: A comment on Gottman. *Psychological Bulletin*, *91*, 393–403. doi:10.1037/0033-2909.91.2.393

Bakeman, R. (1978). Untangling streams of behavior: Sequential analyses of observation data. In G. P. Sackett (Ed.), *Observing behavior* (Vol. 2, *Data collection and analysis methods*, pp. 63–78). Baltimore, MD: University Park Press.

Bakeman, R. (2000). Behavioral observations and coding. In H. T. Reis & C. K. Judd (Eds.), *Handbook of research methods in social psychology* (pp. 138–159). New York, NY: Cambridge University Press.

Bakeman, R. (2004). Sequential analysis. In M. Lewis-Beck, A. E. Bryman, & T. F. Liao (Eds.), *The SAGE encyclopedia of social science research methods* (Vol. 3, pp. 1024–1026). Thousand Oaks, CA: SAGE Publications.

Bakeman, R. (2010). Reflections on measuring behavior: Time and the grid. In G. Walford, M. Viswanathan, & E. Tucker (Eds.), *The SAGE handbook of measurement* (pp. 221–237). Thousand Oaks, CA: SAGE Publications.

Bakeman, R., Adamson, L. B., & Strisik, P. (1995). Lags and logs: Statistical approaches to interaction (SPPS version). In J. M. Gottman (Ed.), *The analysis of change* (pp. 279–308). Mahwah, NJ: Lawrence Erlbaum.

Bakeman, R., Deckner, D. F., & Quera, V. (2005). Analysis of behavioral streams. In D. M. Teti (Ed.), *Handbook of research methods in developmental science* (pp. 394–420). Oxford, UK: Blackwell Publishers.

Bakeman, R., & Gottman, J. M. (1986). *Observing interaction: An introduction to sequential analysis*. New York, NY: Cambridge University Press.

Bakeman, R., & Gottman, J. M. (1997). *Observing interaction: An introduction to sequential analysis* (2nd edn.). New York, NY: Cambridge University Press.

Bakeman, R., McArthur, D., & Quera, V. (1996). Detecting group differences in sequential association using sampled permutations: Log odds, kappa, and phi compared. *Behavior Research Methods, Instruments, and Computers*, *28*, 446–457. doi:10.3758/BF03200524

Bakeman, R., & Quera, V. (1992). SDIS: A sequential data interchange standard. *Behavior Research Methods, Instruments, and Computers*, *24*, 554–559. doi:10.3758/BF03203604

Bakeman, R., & Quera, V. (1995a). *Analyzing interaction: Sequential analysis with SDIS and GSEQ*. New York, NY: Cambridge University Press.

Towards a T-Pattern Definition

The T-pattern model and detection algorithms, among others, aim at answering questions such as: When behavior A happens, does this make some behavior B, C, D, or E etc. significantly more likely to occur sooner or within a different approximate time interval? Also, when A occurring at t_A predicts a statistically significant increase in the probability of B occurring within some following interval $[t_A + d_1, t_A + d_2]$ (where $0 <= d_1 <= d_2$), is it a causal relation or are A and B non-causally related parts of the same repeated pattern? Is this context-dependent? That is, does the relation only exist when, for example, some event occurred before A or between A and B or when B is a part of another such pattern, for example, with C? Furthermore, when A and B recur as such a pattern, here noted (A $[t_A + d_1, t_A + d_2]$ B) or short (A B), what then tends to happen? No elementary event, C, may be predicted after (A B), but another pattern (C $[t_C + d_1, t_C + d_2]$ D) may be predicted within another interval following (A B), thus forming a more complex pattern: ((A $[t_A + d_1, t_A + d_2]$ B) $[t_{AB} + d_1, t_{AB} + d_2]$ (C $[t_C + d_1, t_C + d_2]$ D)) or short ((A B) (CD)). Note that the values of $d_1 <= d_2$ in each of these intervals may be very different.

The Critical Interval Definition

How to calculate the statistical significance of such relations? The above intervals $[t_A + d_1, t_A + d_2]$ relating a preceding or concurrent behavior A and a following (or concurrent) behavior B are called *critical intervals*. Per definition, here, there is a critical interval relation between two point series t_i; $i = 1..N_A$ and t_j; $j = 1..N_B$, if significantly more than expected by chance of the intervals $[t_i + d_1, t_i + d_2]$ ($i = 1..N_A$) contain at least one occurrence of B, where $0 \leq d_1 \leq d_2$ and $[d_1, d_2]$ is the shortest significant interval with the most such cases. Assume as a *null hypothesis* (fiction) that the two series are independent and B has a constant probability per unit time within the observation period $[1, T]$ given by N_B / T. Here the two series represent the N_A and N_B occurrences of point events, that is, of event-types A and B or of the endings (A) and beginnings (B) of detected T-pattern occurrences.

Per definition, when occurring with that critical distance, instances of A and B form occurrences of the T-pattern (A B), which thus has its own occurrences series. Note that here A and/or B may represent T-patterns of any complexity. A special kind of critical interval called *fast* has a fixed value of $d_1 = 0$. Initially the only kind of critical interval, it now serves as the definition and detection of the T-burst.

The T-Pattern

A T-pattern is a kind of binary tree, for example, ((A B) (C D)) or (A (B C)) or ((A C) D), etc. of critical interval relations between event-types and/or detected T-Patterns. By dropping the binary tree a *T-pattern* can be noted: $X_1 [d_1, d_2]_1 X_2 [d_1, d_2]_2.. X_i [d_1, d_2]_i X_{i+1}.. X_{m-1} [d_1, d_2]_{m-1} X_m$

Where [d_1, d_2] is some critical interval and X is a behavioral event type A or B or C, etc. or a T-pattern, and where the general term X_i [d_1, d_2]$_i$ X_{i+1} means that within occurrences of the pattern, after X_i occurring (ending) at t, X_{i+1} occurs (begins) within a critical interval [t + d_1, t + d_2]. The pattern is said to be of *length* m. Other formal definitions can be found elsewhere (Magnusson, 2000, 2004, 2005, 2006, 2016b, 2017a, and 2017b).

Every T-pattern is thus characterized among others by significant translation symmetry measured by the critical interval relation at all levels and across all its occurrences. With the same critical interval relation at all its nonterminal nodes at all levels a T-pattern is self-similar.

T-Pattern Detection

T-patterns are detected by comparing the occurrences series of all pairs of the coded event-types and the gradually detected T-patterns searching for possible critical intervals between them, and when found, forming the corresponding T-patterns and adding them with their occurrences series to the data.

Creativity

Note that this kind of pattern detection is different from pattern recognition for the detection of a fixed set of known patterns such as printed alphabetical characters. Instead, assuming that behavior is creative, it searches for a more abstract pattern type, thus allowing the detection of entirely new patterns in behavior and other phenomena.

The T-System

The T-pattern model has been extended with other structural types and relations that can be detected with Theme. All have been described to some extent elsewhere (Magnusson, 2000, 2005, 2006, 2016, 2017a, 2017b), but some have not yet been applied in published work. Here T-bursts and T-packets will be described and illustrated.

The T-Burst

The *T-burst* is a univariate T-pattern composed of a single type of component (A, an event-type or T-pattern) recurring at a significantly increased frequency, that is, as bouts or bursts and thus with a fast critical interval relating some of its occurrences. A well-known example is "go" versus a rapid sequence "go go go go," indicating urgency and often evoking a different response. A T-burst may thus strongly predict behavior not predicted by its component occurring alone.

Note that a T-pattern may occur in such bouts and that such T-bursts may occur as parts of T-patterns. As all other T-system terms the occurrence of T-bursts could be symptomatic for certain conditions, cultures, or individuals. See Figure 16.14 and a recent open access online publication (Magnusson, 2017a) and elsewhere (Magnusson, 2006, 2017b).

Syntax and Prediction

Features in Theme deal with the important issue of prediction forwards and backwards (retrodiction) through analysis of relations between *T-components* (event-types or sub-patterns, terminals, or branches) in detected T-patterns. This helps to answer questions such as: When component A occurs, is a T-pattern, Q, containing it likely to be in progress? If so, above a given probability, for example, 80 percent, A is called an 80 percent *T-marker* of Q. A is then called a *T-predictor* of following parts in Q and a *T-retrodictor* of preceding components. Theme usually detects many T-patterns in each project, sometimes hundreds or thousands, containing information of this kind, but its extraction is a daunting task best left to computer algorithms. Easily accessible color-coded examples of T-patterns with T-markers, T-predictors, and T-retrodictors illustrated with diagrams are available online (Magnusson, 2017a, 2017b).

T-Associates and T-Packets

Many kinds of behavior do not occur as parts of a T-pattern, but are significantly related to it. Thus, for example, "talking business" is not a component of dinners generally, but is associated with special cases, that is, "business dinners" and may occur significantly close before, during, and/or after such dinners. The behavior "talking business" is thus called a *positive T-associate* of a business dinner. The relation may also be negative as, for example, "impolite expressions" are avoided during or around "solemn meetings" and are thus called *negative* T-associates. A *T-packet* is defined as some behavior, called the *packet base* (an event-type or a T-pattern), having significant positive and/or negative T-associates, that is, more of its occurrences than expected by chance occur with at least one occurrence (or nonoccurrence) of the associate within or near it.

A packet base may be any recurrent type of event (a point event or a state/interval) such as, for example, a T-pattern or an event-type or any state such as sitting, running, or talking. The intervals or *zones* before and/or after a packet base where the probability of a T-associate is in this sense significantly higher or lower than expectation are called, respectively, its *attraction* and *repulsion zones* (or its +/– *gravity zones*). A T-packet may have any number of associates, positive and/or negative (see Figure 16.17).

Method

Data Collection

Most TPA of interactions with Theme, including the empirical examples below, concerns video recordings. The video files were coded using precursors to the current BehaviorCoder (see below), a free PC-Windows program that can be downloaded from hbl.hi.is and patternvision.com.

Event-Types and the Variable-Value Table (VVT). The coded data are lists of *time-stamped* occurrences of *event-types* (*ETs*) within a continuous observation interval. Each event-type is a behavioral description in terms of a vector of items (elements, values) from predefined but easily modifiable *classes* (nominal variables) that are entered into Theme in a simple text file with the reserved name "vvt. vvt" (variable value table) where, one class or item name per line, a class name begins in the *first column*, and its values follow each starting in *column ≥ 2*:

```
Actor
   sue
   jack
   bill
   b_e
    b
    e
facial
   smile
   blink
location
   corner1
   corner2
locomotion
   run
```

As in this tiny example, the *first class* in a vvt.vvt usually identifies actors (agents, individuals, groups, etc.) and the *second class*, with the reserved name "*b_e*," has the special values "*b*" and "*e*," in that order, for *begin* and *end* (see manual for further specifications).

The values from the vvt.vvt variables are combined to define *event-types*. Each event-type, for example, "sue,b,smile" or "bill,e,run", typically involves an *actor* (agent, individual, group, etc.) and the *beginning* (b) or *end* (e) of behavior having some duration (for example, sitting, walking, talking, etc.). An event-type occurrence (instance) is thus a point event, which occurs (or not) within a discrete time scale unit of any size. The data, T-patterns, and all other T-system terms are thus independent of scale. Units from a few millionths of a second (Nicol, Segonds-

Pichon, & Magnusson, 2015) to days (Hirschenhauser, Frigerio, Grammer, & Magnusson, 2002) have been used in Theme analysis.

The syntax used in defining event-types can be described in terms of nominal vectors of vvt.vvt variables, here, [actor, b_e, face, locomotion, location] where any cell of the vector may be left empty. The values present in each vector thus describe an event, and the data become a list of time stamped event-types. For example:

010 sue,b,run (in time unit 10 sue begins running)
177 bill,e,smile,jack (in time unit 77 bill ends smiling {to/with/at} jack)
394 receiver,b,listen,corner2 (in time unit 394 receiver begins listening in corner2);

where the integer time value represents the smallest discrete time unit used in data, for example, seconds, or tenths or hundredths of seconds, and is referred to as *temporal resolution*.

Theme Raw Data File. The Theme data file is a tab delimited text (.txt) file with only two columns: time and event-type. Time is an integer representing the discrete time unit where the event-type occurred, for example:

5	:
10	sue,b,run
177	bill,e,smile,jack
394	bill,b,listen,corner2
1046	sue,e,run
1236	&

Where ":" and "&" indicate, respectively, start and stop of the continuous observation interval [5, 1236], beginning at time (unit) 5 and ending at time (unit) 1236.

Data Collection Tools

The BehaviorCoder. The time-consuming task of coding behavior, which in most cases cannot yet be automated, is facilitated by multimedia tools such as *BehaviorCoder* (see hbl.hi.is and patternvision.com). Developed especially for Theme analysis, it uses the simple Theme tab delimited text file (.txt) format for immediate entry and analysis with Theme.

LINCE. LINCE is another free coder available on the Internet that can produce data in the Theme format ready for Theme analysis: http://lom.observesport.com/, available in English, Spanish, and Catalan (Gabin, Camerino, Anguera, & Castañer, 2012; for an application in human interaction research, Castañer, Camerino, Anguera, & Jonsson, 2016).

Figure 16.2 *The BehaviorCoder: This figure shows a screenshot of the free multimedia coder BehaviorCoder used to code digital video files and to collect some of the data presented in this chapter. The coder can easily play normally and in slow motion and move the video forward and backward frame-by-frame using the mouse buttons and/or the arrow keys. The vvt.vvt, except for the actor and begin/end classes, are shown at the bottom while the actors appear in the top left (here, x, y, and sys) where they can be selected with the mouse. Switching between begin/end (b/e) values is done by clicking on the B (E) button to the left above the vvt table. The event-types are entered by clicking the values in the vvt.vvt table and are added to the behavior record on the right by simply clicking them. On the left, just above the B/E button, a list of the most recently used codes is built up for one click entry.*

Elan. Elan is an advanced coder that in its current beta version offers output in the Theme data file format. See https://en.wikipedia.org/wiki/ELAN_software and Glüer (this volume, Chapter 13).

The ThemeWatch. A new and different data collection tool is the *ThemeWatch*, developed exclusively for use with smartwatches. By light tapping of the smartwatch screen it allows real-time (time-stamped) coding of an easily modifiable list of events in everyday life (Magnusson, 2017a, 2017b). A simple push on the smartwatch allows sending the Theme data files produced to any previously specified email address (the free app can be downloaded from http://patternvision.com/products/theme-watch/). This tool is not for fast second-by-second coding of behavior, but may help in collecting contextual or background information on a slower scale. It is available also on Apple's App Store and the Android Play Store.

TPA with Theme

The method used is T-pattern detection and analysis (TPA) using Theme searching for T-patterns and related T-system structures. For this a few search parameters need to be set as some of the default values may have to be changed.

Validation. After the detection of T-patterns, questions of validity need to be addressed. Two types of answers are common when using Theme. One answer is statistical, using features built into the software since its beginning. The other relates to more complex issues about the relevance or interest of the detected patterns, depending also on the behavioral coding scheme.

Global Statistical Validation. As some patterns can be found even in random data by pure chance, given the use of large numbers of statistical tests, the question immediately comes up whether the number and complexity of detected patterns exceed random expectation. Theme therefore provides the possibility of repeatedly randomizing and analyzing the data with the same search parameters. In practically all cases, the deviation from random expectation has been far more significant than normally required. Theme produces diagrams that show the difference between findings in original and the average over analyses of randomized data (see Figures 16.8, 16.9, and 16.10).

Single Pattern Validation. This kind of statistical validation is also available for single patterns. The event-type occurrences for the currently selected pattern can be saved to a file and imported for T-pattern detection followed by statistical validation as if only its event-types had been coded.

Figure 16.3 *Search parameter setting. This figure shows the panel used for setting values for the search parameters. See Table 16.1 and text.*

External Validation. A different validation is based on prior knowledge about the behavior analyzed allowing evaluation of the correspondence between the behavior coded and the patterns detected. For this validation no computational answer is provided, but it relies on the researcher's knowledge of both the behavior and T-patterns, as all interpretation of the detected patterns relies on both. In the two illustrative examples presented here, children's *dyadic object exchange* and children's *puzzle solving*, the findings corresponded strongly to prior knowledge while adding new insights.

Setting Theme Search Parameters. The principal search parameters are divided into a few parts. See Figure 16.3 and Theme online manual (Magnusson, 2017b).

The T-Packet Detection Parameters. *Packet Base Type*; here the T-Packet base type is selected, that is, event-types and/or T-patterns. *Packet Significance Level*; sets the significance level to use for T-Associate search. *Minimum*

Table 16.1 *Critical interval (CI) parameters*

Search parameter	Default	Function
Minimum Occurrence	3	minimum occurrences of a pattern
Significance Level	0.005	maximum p value for all CIs
Burst Detection	unchecked	include T-burst detection
Burst Significance	0.005	burst significance level
Max Search Levels	unchecked	max level for bottom-up search
Minimum% of Samples	0 (no limit)	only for multi-sample data
Exclude Frequent ET's	999 (= x)	excludes ETs of mean freq. + x*std

Note: See Figure 16.3 and text.

occurrence; sets the minimum number of occurrences required. *Maximum occurrence;* is also specified as the detection algorithm uses a multinomial statistical test so >15 occurrences of the base may lead to very long (impossible) calculations.

Random Simulation Testing. The type of Monte Carlo testing is selected and the number of repetitions set. *Types of randomizations* – the choices are T-*Shuffling*, T-*Rotation*, or both (see, for example, Magnusson, 2017a, 2017b). Under T-shuffling each series in the raw data is replaced by the same number of random numbers within the observation period. Under T-rotation the observation period [1, T] is considered circular and each series is independently rotated or shifted by a random amount around the origin. *Number of runs per type* – sets the number of randomizations of each type followed by detection. Normally the difference is very big between findings in the raw data versus its randomized versions and usually, for example, 20 runs show vast differences that remain similar for a higher number, but this may depend on the data and the search parameters used. A sufficient value for the intended use may be found by trying out a few numbers and, for practical reasons, using the smallest number needed for the particular project.

Setting, Adapting, Saving, and Retrieving Parameters. The following buttons are: *Set for All* – sets the currently shown parameters values for all the files in the project. *Save search parameters to file* – optionally saves them to a file. *Set parameters from file* – retrieval and setting of parameters stored in a file. *Adapt minimum occurrences to data sets* – provides some help adapting the setting of minimum occurrences in project files of varying durations and/or amounts of data (see Magnusson, 2017b; Theme online manual).

Select Files for Analysis Here the choices are to analyze: *Current data set* – only the current file. *From current data set* – the current file and all files following it in the list at the left of the screen. *All data sets* – all the files in that list (the project).

T-Pattern Selection. When patterns have been detected and validated many options are available. Selections named *quantitative, content*, and *structural* can be made using Theme features as shown in Figures 16.4, 16.5, and 16.6 below. One or more patterns of special interest based on their behavioral content, frequency, and/or structural aspects can thus be selected for analysis including *visualization*.

Structural Selection. When search parameters have been set to search for T-bursts and T-packets, T-patterns that are T-bursts (occur in bouts), or include components that do, can be selected. Similarly, if T-packets are detected, T-patterns including positive and/or negative T-associates can be selected for visualization or other analysis (see Figure 16.6).

Table Generation. Various kinds of tables describing all detected (and selected) patterns can be output as tab-delimited text files for easy entry and analysis with other software (see Theme online manual; Magnusson, 2017b).

Results

This section mostly presents illustrative examples of kinds of structure that can be discovered using Theme and have not been fully illustrated elsewhere.

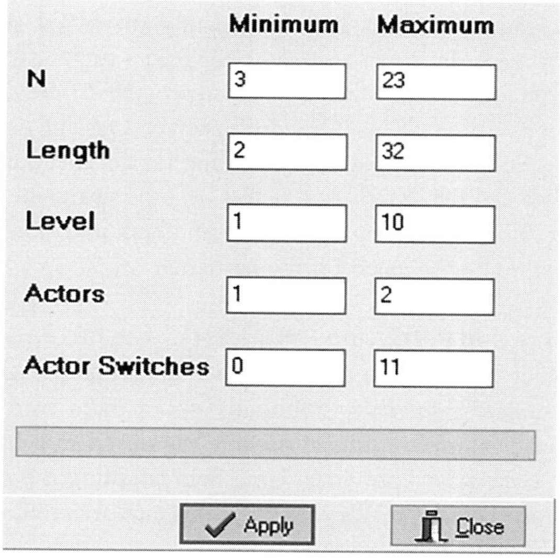

	Minimum	Maximum
N	3	23
Length	2	32
Level	1	10
Actors	1	2
Actor Switches	0	11

✓ Apply   🔟 Close

Figure 16.4 *Quantitative selection. This figures shows how patterns can be selected by narrowing the current value ranges of number of occurrences (N), length (Length), maximum hierarchical level (Level), number of actors involved in the pattern (Actors), and how often there is a switch from one actor to another within the pattern (Actor Switches).*

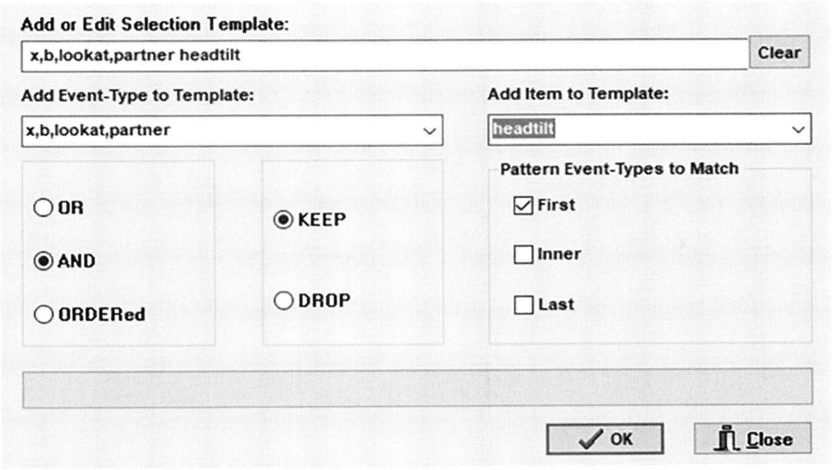

Figure 16.5 *Qualitative selection. This figure shows the panel for selecting patterns according to their behavioral content and, optionally, taking into account its order of appearance. A selection filter is specified as a list of (optionally partial) event-types (Add Event-Type to Template) and/or vvt items (Add Item to Template). Depending on the choice of OR, AND, ORDERed only one, all, or all in the specified order match a pattern. Choice of KEEP or DROP decides whether the matched patterns will be selected or dropped (unselected).*

The first example gives insight into a single dyadic interaction between toddlers playing with and exchanging a picture-viewer under a transparent (acryl) wall that is separating them (Figure 16.7). Here some Theme-features for such *single-sample* analysis are introduced. The second example concerns 16 dyads (samples) where children solve a puzzle together and introduces *multi-sample* files and their analysis.

Single Sample Analysis

The T-pattern search in the toddlers' 13.5 min dyad yielded nearly a thousand T-patterns of various content and complexity (lengths) as can be seen in the Figures 16.8 and 16.9 showing the frequency distribution of their lengths.

Validation of Results. The four figures, 16.8, 16.9, 16.10, and 16.11, show different aspects of the results of Monte Carlo (random simulation) analysis of the data. The results of T-pattern detection in the original data and in randomized versions of the same data are practically always many orders of magnitude beyond the levels of significance normally required. The rare exceptions concern data using very low temporal resolution and/or are collected under difficult (impossible) conditions. The deviations from random expectations also depend on the coding scheme and its relevance for a T-pattern view of the behavior. Monte Carlo results

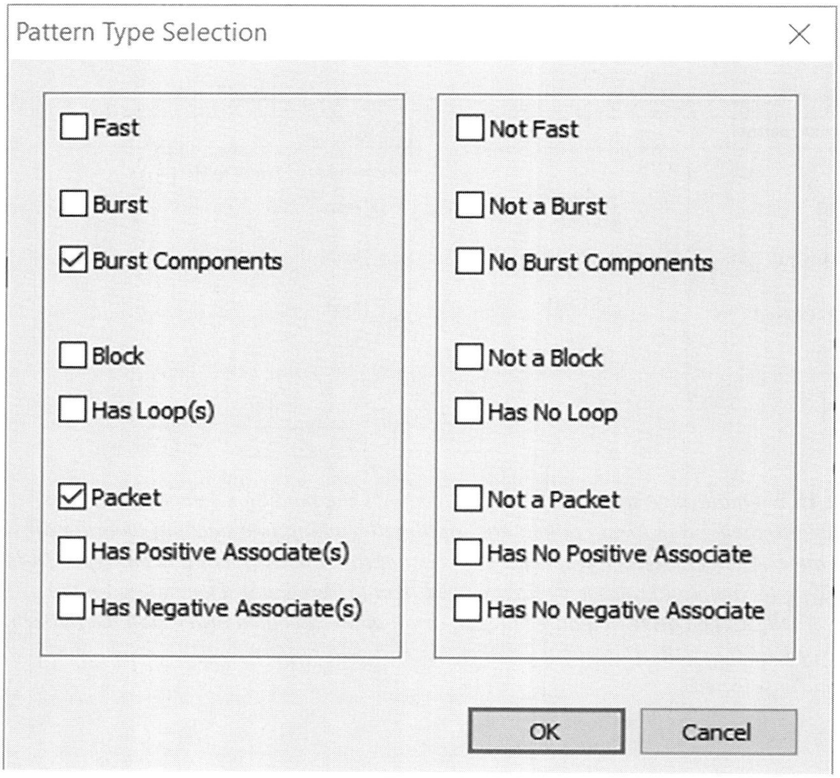

Figure 16.6 *Structural selection. This figure shows the panel for the selection of patterns that (on the left) occur as T-bursts (Burst), have T-bursts components (Burst Components), have +/- T-Associates (Has Positive/Negative Associates), is a packet, that is, has one or more T-associates, has a loop, that is, some pattern components, that is, event-type(s) and/or T-pattern recur within each pattern occurrence.*

are shown here only for the single-sample case, but for multisample data (see below) they are calculated in the same manner and produce the same kinds of Theme diagrams.

Structural Positions of Event-Types. The randomizations also provide an insight into the relative roles and positions of event-types in the detected patterns. See Figure 16.11.

Higher-Level Connections between Event-Types. Theme also provides tables showing higher-level connections between the coded event-types, but some of these only connect at high levels and some not at all. As indicated above, behavioral *connections are often between patterns of simpler units rather than directly between them* (see Figure 16.12).

Figure 16.7 *Two toddlers playing with a picture viewer and exchanging it freely under a transparent acrylic wall separating them.*

T-Patterns Detected in the Toddlers Dyad. Specially developed T-pattern and T-system diagrams facilitate the interpretation of information obtained through TPA with Theme, here illustrated with patterns detected in an object exchange between the two toddlers (Figure 16.7). Figure 16.13 is an example of a Theme diagram showing a simple T-pattern detected in a dyad where the toddlers are called x and y.

Figure 16.14 shows a more complex T-pattern, including a T-burst (411) of a T-pattern (119). It also shows how a T-burst as a part of a complex T-pattern can contribute strongly to prediction. Illustrating an important aspect of Theme diagrams, it also shows the relation between the single *static detection tree* (left) and its (here) four flexible *dynamic occurrence trees;* four *separate entities*, which in spite of the similarity of the trees clearly distinguishes T-pattern detection and Analysis (TPA) from standard cluster analysis.

Multi-Sample Analysis

Theme may analyze separately a single interaction, possibly very short and involving little activity, as well as many interactions, often of varied lengths and activity, concatenated into a single file. Figures 16.15 and 16.16 show data from two of four experimental groups – each with eight dyads – from a study of children's dyadic puzzle solving (Magnusson & Beaudichon, 1997). Given the corpus of all detected T-patterns across the 16 (8+8) samples, it is possible to search for T-patterns that, at any set significance level, occur more in one of the groups, a feature not yet implemented in Theme at the time of the study. The first eight dyads concern a (simple and asymmetric) puzzle-solving situation where the puzzle is simple and one of the two children already knows the solution and is helping the other solve it.

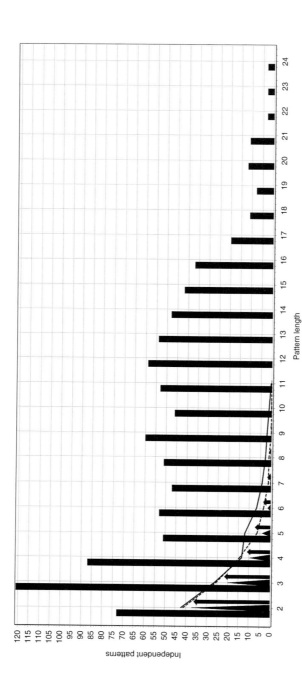

Figure 16.8 *Monte Carlo results 1. This screen capture of Theme shows the number of occurrences of T-patterns of each length, from 2 to 24, and the average number of occurrences of T-patterns of each length detected over 100 repetitions of randomizing and reanalyzing the data. The pyramid is for T-shuffling and the upwards arrow for T-rotation. With 100 randomizations no patterns of length >11 were found under either kind of randomization. In this view other charts concerning the differences between the real data and the randomized can be chosen as can be seen in the following figures.*

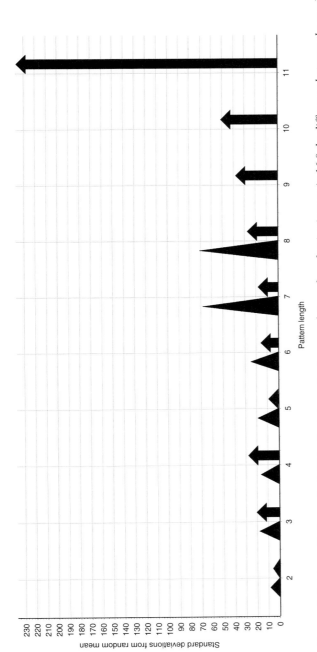

Figure 16.9 *Monte Carlo results 2. This chart shows for the same data and randomizations as in 16.8 the difference between the numbers of occurrences of detected T-patterns in the original data versus the two types of randomized data; pyramids for T-shuffled and upwards arrows for T-rotation.*

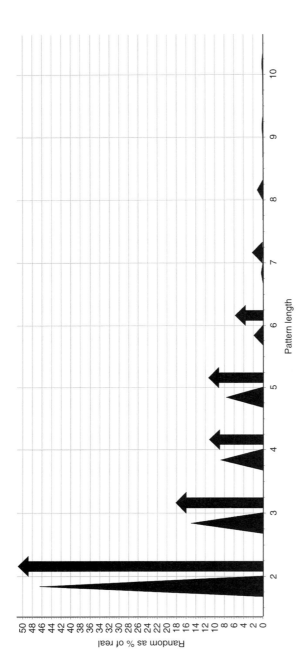

Figure 16.10 *Again for the same data and randomizations, this Theme chart shows the percentage of patterns found under the two randomizations (pyramids=shuffled, upwards arrow=rotated) relative to the detections in the real data and it can be seen that after length 11 no more patterns are found in the 100 times randomized and searched data. In the real data the longest pattern detected is of length 24.*

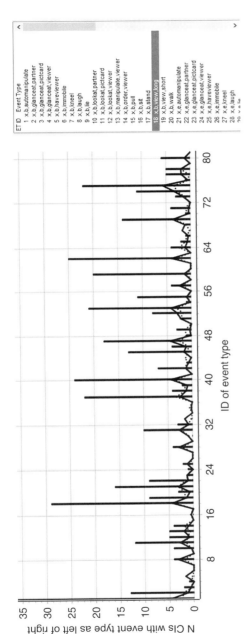

ET ID	Event Type
1	x.b,automanipulate
2	x.b,glanceat,partner
3	x.b,glanceat,pictcard
4	x.b,glanceat,viewer
5	x.b,haveviewer
6	x.b,immobile
7	x.b,kneel
8	x.b,laugh
9	x.b,lie
10	x.b,lookat,partner
11	x.b,lookat,pictcard
12	x.b,lookat,viewer
13	x.b,manipulate,viewer
14	x.b,order,viewer
15	x.b,pull
16	x.b,sit
17	x.b,stand
18	x.b,view,long
19	x.b,view,short
20	x.b,walk
21	x.e,automanipulate
22	x.e,glanceat,partner
23	x.e,glanceat,pictcard
24	x.e,glanceat,viewer
25	x.e,haveviewer
26	x.e,immobile
27	x.e,kneel
28	x.e,laugh
29	x.e,lie

Figure 16.11 *Monte Carlo and event-types. This chart indicates for each event-type the number of other event-types with which it has a direct critical interval relation (level one). The inserted arrows here point to the event-type with the highest number of such relations. Clicking on any column highlights the corresponding event-type in the scrollable list to the right. The lines show the corresponding average numbers in the randomized data, dashed for T-shuffling and full for T-rotation.*

ID	Event Type	e30	e31	e32	e33	e34	e35	e36	e37	e38	e39	e40	e41	e42	e43	e44	e45	e46	e47	e48	e49	e50	e51	e52	e53	e54	e55	e56	e57	e58	e59	e60	e61	e62	e63	e6
28	x,e,laugh																																			
29	x,e,lie																																			
30	x,e,lookat,partner																																			
31	x,e,lookat,pictcard			5					2			5				5		4					5	3		5								4	1	
32	x,e,lookat,viewer								2			3					1																	2	1	
33	x,e,manipulate,viewer																1																			
34	x,e,pull																																			
35	x,e,sit																																			
36	x,e,stand																																			
37	x,e,view,long	3	4	4						2		3					4	4				4	4	3		4			3		3			2		
38	x,e,view,short								2										1																	
39	x,e,walk																																			
40	y,b,automanipulate	4	2	3					2	3		2				3	2	3			3	1	3	1	1	3			1		6			1	1	
41	y,b,crawl																								2									1	1	
42	y,b,glanceat,partner																																			
43	y,b,glanceat,pictcard																																			
44	y,b,glanceat,viewer																																			
45	y,b,haveviewer			7					3			6										7	7	3	3	1					1			5		
46	y,b,headtilt																																	2		
47	y,b,immobile	4							2	1		2																	1							
48	y,b,kneel																												1							
49	y,b,laugh																																			
50	y,b,lie																																			
51	y,b,lookat,partner			4					2			3				4	2						3	5		4								3		
52	y,b,lookat,pictcard			3								1				3					3			1	1	3								2		
53	y,b,lookat,viewer		4	6					2			1	2			6	5	1			2	3	6			6				5				2	1	
54	y,b,manipulate,nose		4														1	1																		
55	y,b,manipulate,viewer								3			6					5	5				7	7	3							1			5		

Figure 16.12 *Higher-level connections. This n * n table shows for each of 28 event-types the hierarchical level (here 1 to 6) where they first connected into the same T-pattern (one or more). It can be seen (inserted circle) that event-type with ID = 11 first co-occurs in a T-pattern with event-type e25 (ID = 25) at level 5.*

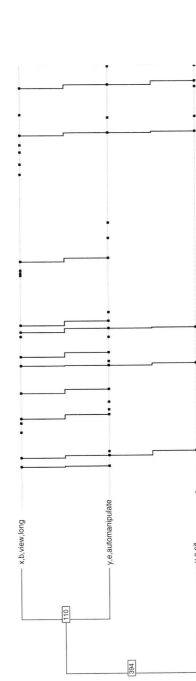

1.000 2.000 3.000 4.000 5.000 6.000 7.000 8.000 9.000 10.000 11.000 12.000

Figure 16.13 *This figure shows on the left a simple T-pattern detection tree with only two critical intervals. At the first level between event-type "x,b,view,long" and "y,e,automanipulate" is a simple T-pattern that at the next level connects with "y,e,sit." All the occurrence points of all three event-types are shown and where they are connected. "X,b,view,long" means child x begins viewing a picture card for more than 3 seconds. "Y,e,automanipulate" means child y ends fiddling with something without watching it. "Y,e,sit" ends sitting. Y was sitting on the floor and may have stood up or started crawling, etc.*

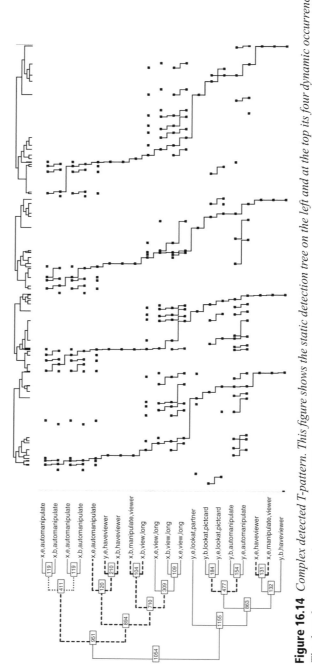

Figure 16.14 *Complex detected T-pattern. This figure shows the static detection tree on the left and at the top its four dynamic occurrences. The dotted connection between pattern 119 and itself forming T-burst 411 means that 119 occurs in such bouts. While occurrences of 119 do not, its bursts, 411, predict every occurrence of the rest of the pattern.*

The following eight dyads are of the opposite complex and symmetric kind where the puzzle is complex and neither child knows the solution and they must discover it together. The simple application of this feature immediately showed, in good agreement with expectations, numerous patterns involving "(giving an) order" in the first group, but practically absent in the latter.

T-Packet with T-Associates and T-Catchment Zones

The T-packet shown below (Figure 16.17) is one of 30 detected in the above toddler's dyad (Figure 16.7). Its base is a T-pattern and it has many positive and negative T-associates. It has a T-catchment (attraction and repulsion zones) for T-associates during, before, and after it. In this case the T-pattern (not shown) that is the T-packet base is a T-burst of a particular behavior in one of the two children. The packet diagram thus shows some of the behavioral context of these bursts in terms of behaviors that tend to associate or disassociate with its occurrence.

Discussion

The T-pattern pattern model with its extensions, the T-system, provide a set of tools for the description and analysis of behavior and interactions. T-pattern detection and analysis (TPA) has a special strength regarding small data and short interactions and the intensive use of the data may reduce the number of subjects and trials needed and thus be valuable for practical and sometimes ethical reasons. Some features of Theme have yet to be applied in empirical research so their value remains to be shown.

Rare events have often been considered a problem in quantitative behavioral analysis and are therefore sometimes excluded by simply not coding them. In TPA, which deals effectively with rare events, they may instead rightly be highly valuable just as the most important events in life and behavior tend to be rare.

In this chapter only dyadic interactions and only among children have been treated directly, but TPA with Theme has been applied in studies of three or more interacting adults (for example, Burgoon, Wilson, Hass, & Schuetzler, 2016; Hardway & Duncan, 2005; Borrie, Jonsson, & Magnusson, 2002).

Conclusion

T-pattern detection and analysis, TPA, developed for the analysis of human behavior and interactions, has proved useful in many kinds of empirical research on behavior and interactions in neurons, animals, and humans at temporal resolutions from microseconds to days. The multimedia coder BehaviorCoder is for precise data collection from video recordings. The new

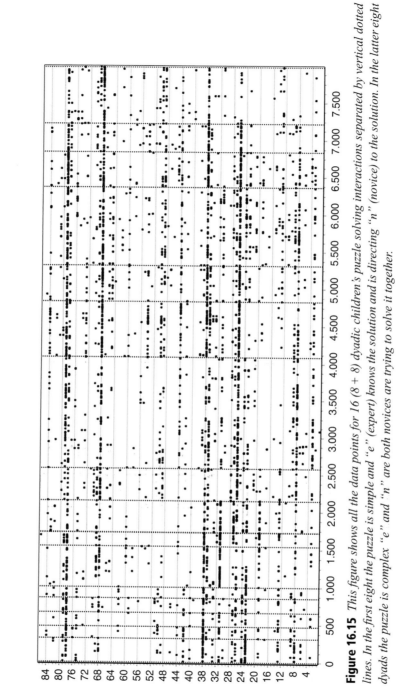

Figure 16.15 *This figure shows all the data points for 16 (8 + 8) dyadic children's puzzle solving interactions separated by vertical dotted lines. In the first eight the puzzle is simple and "e" (expert) knows the solution and is directing "n" (novice) to the solution. In the latter eight dyads the puzzle is complex "e" and "n" are both novices are trying to solve it together.*

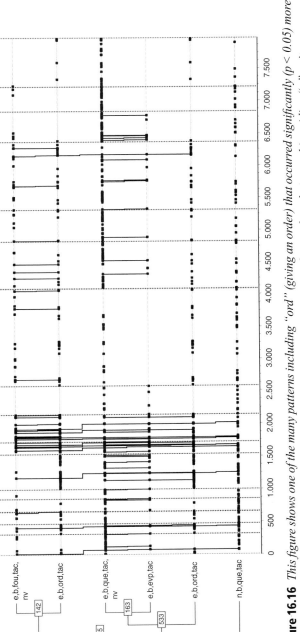

Figure 16.16 *This figure shows one of the many patterns including "ord" (giving an order) that occurred significantly (p < 0.05) more often (and here exclusively) in the first eight dyads with a simple task and where "e" knows the solution and is guiding "n" to it.*

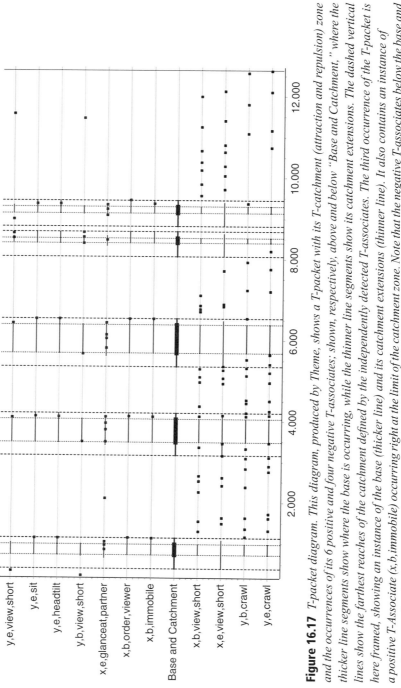

Figure 16.17 T-packet diagram. This diagram, produced by Theme, shows a T-packet with its T-catchment (attraction and repulsion) zone and the occurrences of its 6 positive and four negative T-associates; shown, respectively, above and below "Base and Catchment," where the thicker line segments show where the base is occurring, while the thinner line segments show its catchment extensions. The dashed vertical lines show the farthest reaches of the catchment defined by the independently detected T-associates. The third occurrence of the T-packet is here framed, showing an instance of the base (thicker line) and its catchment extensions (thinner line). It also contains an instance of a positive T-Associate (x,b,immobile) occurring right at the limit of the catchment zone. Note that the negative T-associates below the base and catchment tend to lie outside the catchment. Theme T-packet diagrams normally profit from color coding as can be seen in the Theme online manual (Magnusson, 2017b).

Apple and Android smartwatch application ThemeWatch facilitates more slowly paced real-time coding of events in own behavior and everyday life providing, among other things, contextual information for interactions. Both free and easily acquired from the Internet, the BehaviorCoder and the ThemeWatch were developed to work seamlessly with Theme. The free educational version of the Theme software sufficient for most student and academic projects can now also be easily acquired from the Internet.[1] The future of this approach now lies with those who apply and develop it.

References

Anolli, L., Duncan, S. J., Magnusson, M. S., & Riva, G. (2005). *The hidden structure of interaction: From neurons to culture patterns*. Amsterdam, The Netherlands: IOS Press.

Borrie, A., Jonsson, G. K., & Magnusson, M. S. (2002). Temporal pattern analysis and its applicability in sport: An explanation and exemplar data. *Journal of Sports Sciences*, *20*(10), 845–852.

Burgoon, J. K., Wilson, D., Hass, M., & Schuetzler, R. (2016). Interactive deception in group decision-making: New insights from communication pattern analysis. In M. S. Magnusson, J. K. Burgoon, & M. Casarrubea (Eds.), *Discovering hidden temporal patterns in behavior and interaction: T-pattern detection and analysis with THEME™* (pp. 37–62). Totowa, NJ, US: Humana Press. doi:10.1007/978-1-4939-3249-8_2.

Casarrubea, M., Jonsson, G. K., Faulisi, F., Sorbera, F., Di Giovanni, G., Benigno, A., . . . Magnusson, M. S. (2015). T-pattern analysis for the study of temporal structure of animal and human behavior: A comprehensive review. *Journal of Neuroscience Methods*, *23*, 934–946. doi:10.1016/j.jneumeth.2014.09.024.

Castañer, M., Camerino, O., Anguera, M. T., & Jonsson, G. K. (2016). Paraverbal communicative teaching T-patterns using SOCIN and SOPROX observational systems. In M. S. Magnusson, J. K. Burgoon, & M. Casarrubea (Eds.), *Discovering hidden temporal patterns in behavior and interaction: T-pattern detection and analysis with THEME™* (pp. 83–100). Totowa, NJ: Humana Press. doi:10.1007/978-1-4939-3249-8_4.

Chomsky, N. (1957). *Syntactic structures*. The Hague, The Netherlands: Mouton.

Devlin, K. (2003). *Mathematics: The science of patterns: The search for order in life, mind, and the universe*. New York, NY: Henry Holt.

Duncan Jr., S. D., & Fiske, D. W. (1977). *Face-to-face interaction: Research, methods and theory*. Hillsdale, NJ: Lawrence Erlbaum Associates.

Gabin, B., Camerino, O., Anguera, M. T., & Castañer, M. (2012). Lince: Multiplatform sport analysis software. *Procedia-Social and Behavioral Sciences*, *46*, 4692–4694.

Hardway, C. L. & Duncan, S. D., Jr. (2005). Me first! Structure and dynamics of a four-way family conflict. In L. Anolli, S. D. Duncan, Jr., & M. Magnusson (Eds.),

---

[1] See from hbl.hi.is or patternvision.com.

The hidden structure of social interaction: From neurons to culture patterns.
Amsterdam, The Netherlands: IOS Press.

Hirschenhauser, K., Frigerio, D., Grammer, K., & Magnusson, M. S. (2002). Monthly patterns of testosterone and behavior in prospective fathers. *Hormones And Behavior, 42*(2), 172–181. Retrieved February 14, 2018, from https://doi.org/10.1006/hbeh.2002.1815.

Magnusson, M. S. (1981). Temporal configuration analysis: Detection of a meaningful underlying structure through artificial categorization of a real-time behavioral stream. *Workshop on Artificial Intelligence Uppsala University.* (Part of a 1983 Doctoral Thesis at the Psychological laboratory), University of Copenhagen. Download from http://hbl.hi.is, www.dropbox.com/s/g0iag0fhv4ubmlm/Magnusson%20Uppsala%201981%20paper.pdf.

Magnusson, M. S. (1983). Theme and syndrome: Two programs for behavior research. In D. Edwards & A. Hoeskuldsson (Eds.), *Symposium in applied statistics* (pp. 17–42). Copenhagen: NEUCC, RECKU & RECAU.

Magnusson, M. S. (1996). Hidden real-time patterns in intra- and inter-individual behavior: Description and detection. *European Journal of Psychological Assessment, 12*(2), 112–123. doi:10.1027/1015-5759.12.2.112

Magnusson, M. S. (2000). Discovering hidden time patterns in behavior: T-patterns and their detection. *Behavior Research Methods, Instruments & Computers, 32*(1), 93–110. doi:10.3758/BF03200792

Magnusson, M. S. (2004). Repeated patterns in behavior and other biological phenomena. In U. Griebel & D. K. Oller (Eds.) (2004). *Evolution of communication systems: A comparative approach* (pp. 111–128). Cambridge, MA: A Bradford Book.

Magnusson, M. S. (2005). Understanding social interaction: Discovering hidden structure with model and algorithms. In L. Anolli, S. D. Duncan Jr., & M. S. Magnusson (Eds.), *The hidden structure of social interaction: From neurons to culture patterns* (pp. 3–22). Amsterdam, The Netherlands: IOS Press.

Magnusson, M. S. (2006). Structure and communication in interaction. In G. Riva, M. T. Anguera, B. K. Wiederhold, & F. Mantovani (Eds.), *From communication to presence: Cognition, emotions and culture towards the ultimate communicative experience. Festschrift in honor of Luigi Anolli* (pp. 127–46). Amsterdam, The Netherlands: IOS Press.

Magnusson, M. S. (2016). Time and self-similar structure in behavior and interactions: From sequences to symmetry and fractals. In M. S. Magnusson, J. K. Burgoon, & M. Casarrubea (Eds.), *Discovering hidden temporal patterns in behavior and interaction: T-pattern detection and analysis with THEME™* (pp. 3–35). Totowa, NJ: Humana Press. doi:10.1007/978-1-4939-3249-8_1

Magnusson, M. S. (2017a). Why search for hidden repeated temporal behavior patterns: T-pattern analysis with Theme. *International Journal of Clinical Pharmacology & Pharmacotherapy, 2*, 128. https://doi.org/10.15344/2017/2456-3501/128.

Magnusson, M. S. (2017b). *Theme user manual.* Download from http://patternvision.com/wp-content/uploads/2017/06/Theme-Manual-7-June-2017.pdf.

Magnusson, M. S., & Beaudichon, J. (1997). Détection de "marqueurs" dans la communication référentielle entre enfants [Detection of "markers" in referential communication among children]. In J. Bernicot, J. Caron-Pargue, & A. Trognon, (Eds.), *Conversation, interaction et fonctionnement cogniti [Conversation, interaction and cognitive functioning]* (pp. 315–335). Nancy, France: Presse Universitaire de Nancy.

Magnusson, M. S., Burgoon, J. K., & Casarrubea, M. (2016). *Discovering hidden temporal patterns in behavior and interaction: T-pattern detection and analysis with THEME™*. Totowa, NJ: Humana Press. doi:10.1007/978-1-4939-3249-8

Montagner, H. (1971). Les communications interindividuelles dans les sociétés de guêpes [Interindividual communication in societies of wasps]. *Journal de Psychologie Normale et Pathologique: Intercommunications Chez les Animaux, 3–4*, 281–296.

Montagner, H. (2012). *L'enfant et la communication: Comment gestes, attitudes, vocalisations deviennent des messages* [Child and communication: How gestures, postures, vocalizations become messages]. Collection: Enfances [Collections: Childhood]. Paris, France: Dunod.

Nicol, A. U., Segonds-Pichon, A., & Magnusson, M. S. (2015). Complex spike patterns in olfactory bulb neuronal networks. *Journal of Neuroscience Methods, 239*, 11–17. doi:10.1016/j.jneumeth.2014.09.016

Physiology or Medicine (1973). Press Release. *Nobelprize.org*. Nobel Media AB 2014. Retrieved February 14, 2018, from www.nobelprize.org/nobel_prizes/medicine/laureates/1973/press.html.

Skinner, B. F. (1957). *Verbal behavior* (1st edn.). New York, NY: Appleton-Century-Crofts.

Teerikorpi, P., & Baryshev, Y. (2002). *Discovery of cosmic fractals*. United States of America: World Scientific.

Tinbergen, N. (1963). On aims and methods of ethology. *Zeitschrift für Tierpsychologie, 20*, 410–433. doi:10.1111/j.1439-0310.1963.tb01161.x

17 Interdependence in Small Group Discussion

Joseph A. Bonito and Sarah M. Staggs

The term *interdependence*, as applied to small discussion groups, first appeared in Thibaut and Kelley's (1959) seminal work on the social psychology of groups. At its core, interdependence refers to mutually influential behavior (Van Lange & Balliet, 2015). Influence has several relevant senses as applied to small groups. The most obvious sense of influence is related to preference change, such that a given member's preferred solution at the beginning of a discussion (assuming one has developed a preference prior to or at the onset of deliberation) is different at the end (Pavitt, 2014). Preference change, however, is often the product of other, related types of influence that occur during discussion, including the distribution and management of speaking turns (Bonito & Hollingshead, 1997), making and rebutting arguments (Seibold & Meyers, 2007), keeping the group on task (Gouran & Hirokawa, 1996), managing conflict (De Dreu & Weingart, 2002), and the development and maintenance of relationships (Keyton, 1999). On this account, small group interaction *by definition is interdependent at some level* (Bonito & Sanders, 2011; Poole, 1998).

Our presentation is informed by a view of interdependent behavior as emergent, though constrained by the group's charge, and as contributing to a group's understanding of the situation and context. This position is in contrast to approaches to interdependence that are generally based (either implicitly or explicitly) on some version of the input-throughput-output (IPO) model (Ilgen, Hollenbeck, Johnson, & Jundt, 2005; Pavitt, 2014; Van Lange & Balliet, 2015). A generalized version of the IPO assumes that situational and contextual features, for example task characteristics (Hirokawa, 1990), influence group member cognitions (e.g., Kameda, Ohtsubo, & Takezawa, 1997), which manifest themselves as behavioral patterns that eventually lead to or produce group outcomes. Behavior, then, within the context of the IPO, is conceptualized as a mediator between inputs and outcomes, and the characteristics of group behavior are made more or less likely (if not predetermined) by factors exogenous to discussion. Although we do not doubt that such factors play a role in interaction, the implication of IPO models is that interaction contributes little, if anything, to the process and outcomes that cannot be explained by finding the "right" set of inputs (Bonito & Sanders, 2009). IPO-based approaches, we contend, do little to explain how interaction develops and what it accomplishes because it emphasizes factors exogenous to discussion (e.g., composition, task features). Consequently, we do not address any situational, contextual, or cognitive factors related to interdependence in this chapter.

Interdependent behavior by definition is behavior that is associated within groups – the statistical term for correlated observations is *nonindependence* (Kenny, Kashy, & Cook, 2006). Nonindependence occurs when knowing the value of one person's score or measurement on a variable predicts, in some degree, another person's score or measure on that variable (Kenny & Judd, 1986). For example, participation tends to be highly correlated within groups, such that persons A, B, and C in a given group are frequent participators and persons D, E, and F in another group all participate infrequently (Bonito, 2002). Another example is sequential behavior in the sense that some act types are more or less likely to follow other types (e.g., Lehmann-Willenbrock, Allen, & Kauffeld, 2013). Interdependence and nonindependence are two sides of the same coin. Interdependence is the conceptual veneer that describes and explains observed correlations or sequences of behaviors within groups: "interdependence is nonindependence explained" (Wickham & Knee, 2012, p. 384).

In what follows, we first discuss interdependence in terms of the conceptual features that explain behavior within groups. Following that, we identify several features of interdependent behavior and the reasons why those features produce, or at least provide the basis for, mutual influence during discussion. Finally, we describe several statistical techniques for analyzing interdependent behavior in small decision-making groups. We note that although our discussion is limited to behavior (and primarily verbal behavior at that), the same principles apply to other relevant characteristics of discussion, for example satisfaction (Keyton, 1991) and cohesion (Carron & Brawley, 2000).

Interdependence as Coherence

If interdependence manifests itself as patterns of interaction (in terms of sequences, frequencies, or other types of measures), the issue then concerns what bonds elements of interaction without reference, or at least not giving priority focus, to factors exogenous to interaction. Given, as noted, we assume that interaction is emergent to some degree, we argue that *coherence* is that bond. As Pavitt and Johnson (1999) noted, based on Craig and Tracy (1983), coherence is the principle that participants make contributions to discussion that are "connected to each other in orderly and meaningful ways" (Craig & Tracy, 1983, p. 14). Grice (1975), of course, made coherence the centerpiece of his cooperative principle, arguing that interaction non sequiturs and other seemingly incoherent or irrelevant linguistic forms make sense at deeper levels of meaning by design. For example, one might exclaim "Brilliant!" following another member's admonition that the group stay on task – the exclamation seems overly complimentary given the situation, which lays the groundwork for other meanings to emerge. At the very least, positioning interdependence as coherence provides the basis for focusing our discussion on features of interaction and not on inputs.

One useful way to think about interdependence as coherence is in terms of extremes. At one end, behavior is completely independent – any person's behavior within a group is unrelated to or uninfluenced by what other members say and do. Hewes (1996, 2009) refers to this type of behavior as *egocentrism* and argues that it reflects cases in which persons pursue individual agendas based on internal standards of relevance. At the other extreme of the continuum is *group-centrism*, which implies that coherence and relevance are completely transparent (i.e., made salient during discussion) and shared, such that the only influence on one's behavior is what others said previously and might say subsequently (Bonito & Sanders, 2011).

Neither extreme is plausible, nor did Hewes suggest as much (though he did argue that egocentrism is the baseline against which models of interdependence ought to be judged). For example, egocentrism still requires some semblance of orderly and relevant turn-taking management during discussion (short of chaos), and participants' contributions need not, and often are not, based on or related to what was said previously by others (Corman & Kuhn, 2005). Jones and Gerard (1967) offer a similar take by referring to such behavior as having the appearance of contingency when in fact individuals are acting without considering the behavior of others. Coherence, then, has several properties that influence the connectedness of contributions to group discussion. The first property is the extent to which behavior in groups exhibits or is conceptualized to have turn-by-turn influence. The second property is the depth, in terms of level of abstraction, of the interdependent behaviors in question. We address each property below.

An important question is whether interdependence requires evidence of turn-by-turn influence. Pavitt and Johnson (1999) and Bonito (2007) approached the problem in slightly different but related ways. *Local* coherence occurs when each contribution to discussion is related in some fashion to those that precede and follow it. In fact, Hewes (2009) argued that the best evidence for group-centric speech is *cognitive* change on a turn-by-turn basis – what one *considered* saying at $t + 1$ was fundamentally altered by what another person said at $t + 0$. Bonito and Meyers (2011) acknowledged the importance of interaction sequences but noted that not all aspects of coherence require adjacency, citing, among other pieces of evidence, Corman and Kuhn's (2005) finding that participants who correctly distinguished transcripts of actual discussion from randomly generated sequences focused not on turn-by-turn features but on topics and issues. Thus, *global* coherence is the notion that turn-by-turn influence is not necessary for interdependence; rather, interdependence is evident when contributions are oriented toward some larger issue that transcends turns, for example topics, issues, phases, or matters of process (e.g., if the group decides to vote rather than look for unanimity). Levinson

Table 17.1 *Examples of floor transitions*

Context	Example	Defining characteristic
Floor	ABA-B	B follows A in fourth turn, continuing the pattern in the first three turns
Broken floor	ABA-C	C, not B, follows A in fourth turn, breaking the pattern in the first three turns
New floor	ABAC-A	A follows C in fifth turn, creating floor ACA in turns 3 through 5
Regain	ABAC-B	B follows C in fifth turn, reestablishing the ABA floor started in turns 1 through 3
Nonfloor	ABAC-D	D follows C in fifth turn; no consistent pattern after turns 1–3

Note: Each example begins with speakers A and B holding the floor in turns 1 through 3.

(1983) made a similar point in comparing pragmatic and conversation analytic perspectives on interaction.

The second property of coherence is depth, or the level of abstraction of the behavior of interest. We offer an admittedly coarse but hopefully useful set of abstraction levels related to interdependence. The first is the speaker level, in which participants are distinguished from one another, usually in very generic terms (e.g., Person A, Person B, and so on). One might model turn-by-turn progressions of speakers, with the assumption that some progressions are more relevant than others – it is a local approach to modeling speaking turns. For example, Parker (1988), Stasser and Taylor (1991), and Stasser and Vaughan (1996) were concerned with the *floor*. Parker conceptualized group discussion as fundamentally dyadic in nature (assuming minimum group size of three), such that a pair of speakers directs their comments to one another rather than to the group as a whole. The examples in Table 17.1 are based on Parker's models. The floor was operationalized as a three-sequence progression of speakers in which the same speaker contributed the first and third turns. Consider a four-person group with members identified by a different capital letter and progressions of speakers are represented as a sequence of the identifying letters. Moreover, the model is turn based, which precludes speakers following themselves. A floor exists, for example, when ABA occurs; the sequence ABC is not a floor. Given this definition, there are different trajectories of floor maintenance and transferal, all of which are potentially important for decision making.

Speakers and speaking turns might also be modeled from a global approach. As an example, Fisek and Ofshe (1970) and Shelly and Troyer (2001) examined the development of speaking hierarchies over the course of discussion, finding among other things that persons who speak frequently early in discussion tend to speak frequently throughout. Other prominent models of speaker-based interdependence include work in expectation states (Balkwell, 1994; Skvoretz, 1988; Smith-Lovin, Skvoretz, & Hudson, 1986), in which differential status influences the proportion of speaking turns allocated to and taken by members. Although not specifically identified as a problem of inter-dependence, it is assumed that individuals recognize status differences and that low-status members will decline the floor in favor of their higher-status colleagues.

Content, the next level of vertical interdependence, refers to the words used during discussion and how the words, or groups of words, provided by one-one member influence those provided by others. For example, research based on the hidden profile paradigm (Stasser & Titus, 2003; Wittenbaum, Hollingshead, & Botero, 2004) evaluates discussion content for discrete bits of information distributed to participants prior to discussion. Some information is shared to all members, while some content is given to just one or some of the members. Coders look for that information in the discussion transcripts and identify it as shared or unique. Most studies of the interdependence of infor-mation sharing take a global approach. For example, Bonito and Ruppel (2011) analyzed information sharing during discussion and found that shared informa-tion was largely correlated at the individual level whereas some unique infor-mation was shared at the group level (i.e., if one person provided unique information then another person might do the same). Larson (1997) approached the problem from a different perspective by examining changes in the like-lihood of contributing information as discussion proceeds and found that unique information was integrated into later stages of the process. Local approaches to modeling information sharing are rare. Soller (2004; Soller & Lesgold, 2003) identified a series of sequences that were associated with effective information exchange during online group collaboration. Specifically, effective sequences were those in which new information was followed by explanation and instruction; less successful sequences were those in which new information was poorly explained or doubted by the receiver.

Content assessment lends itself to computer-assisted coding (see Bonito & Keyton, this volume, Chapter 19), which provides opportunities for examining interdependence within and across speaking turns. For example, Nguyen, Boyd-Graber, Resnik, Cai, Midberry, and Wang (2014) used topic model techniques to evaluate a series of discussions from the International Computer Science Institute (ICSI) meeting corpus. The meetings addressed issues related to the development of recording, transcribing, and analytical techniques (e.g., artificial intelligence, coding). Nguyen et al. examined the ICSI data for (a) topic boundaries and shifts, and (b) influence, based on which participants initiated topic changes. Other scholars (e.g., Bonito, 2001) have examined discussion content in terms of statistical similarity, for example, the number of speaking turns that contain the same or similar content, and how similarity influences contributions made by others and assessments of influence and leadership.

The deepest level of interdependence concerns the functional characteristics of discussion (Wittenbaum et al., 2004). Whereas content is expressly about the words used during discussion, functional approaches to group interaction map content onto theoretically relevant mechanisms thought to underlie group processes. Bales (1950) was among the first to identify a set of important group functions and develop a coding system related to them (see this volume, Part V). His interaction process analysis (IPA) is a 12-category system that identifies two broad classes of group functioning, one related to the task itself (e.g., provide information) and the other to relational development and maintenance (e.g., provide support). There have been variations on the theme since (e.g., Hirokawa, 1982), and Bales himself (Bales, Cohen, & Williamson, 1979) updated the IPA into the more comprehensive System for the Multiple Level Observation of Groups (SYMLOG).

The original IPA has two categories, "agrees" and "disagrees," that assume interdependence – presumably one would have to agree or disagree with something said previously by someone else. Other coding schemes assume interdependence or build it in, for example, those that classify conversational argument (Meyers & Brashers, 2010) and conflict and negotiation (Weingart, Brett, Olekalns, & Smith, 2007). Analyses based on functional coding schemes often take a local approach by examining the sequential structure of the categories. For example, Putnam and Jones (1982) noted several different sequential strategies during bargaining negotiations and Lehmann-Willenbrock, Allen, and Kauffeld (2013) identified a range of sequences related to procedural communication during facilitated meetings. Finally, Weingart, Prietula, Hyder, and Genovese (1999) revealed several different trajectories during conflict negotiations, and Pavitt and Johnson (1999, 2002) showed how groups put together proposal sequences. Functional approaches also support global assessments of interdependence. For example, Bonito and Meyers (2011) evaluated data from several different studies and revealed that some types of functional communication are associated, though not necessarily sequentially, at the group level of analysis. Other studies have demonstrated that functional interaction patterns are related to the routineness of situations (Lei, Waller, Hagen, & Kaplan, 2016), the effectiveness of early or emergency response teams (Zijlstra, Waller, & Phillips, 2012), and the performance of anesthesia teams (Kolbe et al., 2014).

Notice that levels of abstraction can be combined or analyzed separately. Research on participation often focuses on the speakers and not what was said (Bonito & Hollingshead, 1997), and other research addresses functional characteristics of interaction without reference to the speakers that produced them (Folger, Hewes, & Poole, 1984; Hirokawa, 1988; Poole, 1998). One might combine levels by addressing the relationship between participant characteristics and the comments produced, for example if experts use different types of influence tactics (Littlepage, Schmidt, Whisler, & Frost, 1995).

Analyzing Interdependence

Statistical analysis of interdependence is a function of theoretical problems and study design, which include choices regarding the features of interdependence of interest (e.g., level of abstraction), and such choices influence the type of group and task used in the study, transcription method (Edwards, 1993), unitization (Guetzkow, 1950), and coding (Folger et al., 1984). In what follows, we offer a brief description of several analytical options based on whether researchers are interested in global or local models of interdependence.

Analysis of Global Interdependence

Global interdependence, as noted, describes a loose connection among comments made during group problem-solving discussions. The term "loose" implies that the connections need not be on a turn-by-turn basis; rather, the connections are made at a more macro level, including phases, topics, and other bracketed features of interaction. We assume that the data have been collected from individuals nested within groups and that the data have not been aggregated at the group level (see Bonito, Ruppel, & Keyton, 2012, for more on this issue). For example, one might code each interaction unit in terms of its function and then count the frequency of each functional type by individuals within groups. A simple approach is to evaluate interdependence in terms of the intraclass correlation (ICC; Hox, 2010; Kenny et al., 2006), which is the ratio of variance between groups (i.e., the extent to which group means vary from the grand mean) to the total variance. In principle, the ICC varies from 0 to 1, though several exceptions to the rule exist, some of which are artifacts related to maximum likelihood estimation and others design based.

Another way to think of the ICC and the global analysis of interdependence is in terms of homogeneity/heterogeneity. An ICC of zero indicates that observations within groups are completely heterogeneous, and an ICC of one means that scores within groups are completely homogeneous. Participation, for example, is homogeneous if each member participated with the same frequency (i.e., no variation within the group), and is heterogeneous when maximally variable (see Coulter, 1989). Another way to think about the problem is in terms of exchangeability and representativeness vis-à-vis the group (see Stapleton, Yang, & Hancock, 2016). In the case of complete homogeneity, each member is a perfect representation of the group score on the variable – if each member participates with the same frequency then the mean participation score is equal to each individual's participation score. In the case of heterogeneity, members' scores are not only variable but few, if any, accurately represent the group. In the case of complete (or nearly complete) homogeneity, as evidenced by ICCs near 1, the researcher might consider aggregating scores at the group level, and in cases of complete (or nearly complete) heterogeneity, one might ignore nesting, although there is some debate on doing so (Kenny et al., 2006; Stapleton et al., 2016).

The ICC is a univariate procedure; the latent group model (LGM; Bonito, Ervin, & Staggs, 2016; Gonzalez & Griffin, 2002) extends the logic of the ICC to assess global interdependence across a range of variables. Consider, for simplicity, the two-variable case, with group discussion coded, for example, for unique and shared information (Bonito & Ruppel, 2011). The group is treated as a latent factor and participants within groups are the "indicators" for the latent factor. Each variable has an ICC estimate, which, as noted, ranges from 0 to 1. Significant ICC estimates indicate a degree of homogeneity such that there is sufficient evidence for group-level influence on the frequency with which members contribute shared and unique information. That amount of variance not accounted for by group is attributable to individual proclivities to contribute information. The LGM also estimates the covariance of the variables at both the group and individual levels of analysis. If the ICCs for the two information variables are significant, then the covariance for the two variables indicates whether groups that contribute shared information also contribute unique information. Like any correlation, the direction can be positive or negative and the value indicates the magnitude. If either or both of the ICCs are not significant then the group-level correlation is meaningless, as one assumes there is no group-level influence on information sharing. Individual level covariances indicate the extent to which an individual who contributes shared information also contributes unique data, beyond group-level influences.

Using this approach, Ervin, Bonito, and Keyton (2017) evaluated functionally based communication within and across four meetings in which participants were asked to design and develop a new kind of remote control. The data were segmented as thought-units (i.e., phrases that contain or imply both a subject and predicate; see Auld Jr. & White, 1956) and the analysis consisted of frequency counts for each unit type for each person (within groups) for each of the four meetings. They found that individual-level correlations for the functional communication types were, with just a few exceptions, evident during the first meeting and persisted throughout all four meetings. Group-level influences on discussion, however, took some time to develop. By the fourth meeting, the ICCs for all four discussion types were significant and substantial, and there were several significant and positive group-level correlations. For example, groups that exchanged information also provided action statements and comments on previous actions. Positive comments were not associated with any of the other functional categories at the group level during any of the meetings.

Many other statistical models are available to evaluate global interdependence for coded behavioral data, including within-and-between analysis (WABA; Dansereau, 2006), the actor-partner interdependence model (Kashy & Kenny, 2000; Kenny & Garcia, 2012), and social relations models (Back & Kenny, 2010; Kenny, 1994). For longitudinal data, one might consider multilevel structural equation models (Heck & Thomas, 2015; Rabe-Hesketh, Skrondal, & Pickles, 2004) and multilevel mixture models (Asparouhov & Muthen, 2008). Both allow specification of latent constructs at the group level, which exist only if there is interdependence within groups on the variable of interest, and mixture models allow the classification of individuals based on trajectories of the interaction variable of interest. We are unaware of mixture modeling applications to small groups, but examples from studies of drug and alcohol abuse have used mixture models to identify classes of trajectories (e.g., latent onset) and predictors of those trajectories (Li, Duncan, & Hops, 2001). Most of these models require large amounts of data, which makes their application to small group research somewhat problematic but not impossible.

Analysis of Local Interdependence

Local interdependence presumes adjacency of speakers, contribution types, or both. Here we focus on discrete sequential models, though other types of sequential analyses exist (e.g., time-series analysis). Sackett (1979) was among the first to address sequential analysis, and many have since broadened our understanding of how to model sequences (Bakeman & Gottman, 1997; Bakeman & Quera, 2011; Cornwell, 2015; Gottman & Roy, 1990; see also Quera, this volume, Chapter 15 and Magnusson, this volume, Chapter 16). The upshot is that the data are arrayed as a sequence of events, which in this case could be speakers, interaction codes, or both. The goal is "to discover the order and the common sequences that characterize the data" (Gottman & Roy, 1990, p. 19); order and sequence, of course, are related to the coding system used and other design features.

Consider the relatively simple example of data from a hidden profile study (Bonito & Ruppel, 2011). The data are coded at the level of the thought-unit as containing either shared (S) or unique (U) information, and the remaining units are coded as other (O). A ten-unit sequence might appear as SSUSSOUUSS. Among other things, it is easy to see that S follows S three times. Less obvious is that U and S display a lag2 relationship, although the intervening event varies; notice the SSU and SOU sequences in the example. Thus, "the history of the system is useful in predicting the future of the system" (Gottman & Roy, 1990, p. 19).

Group scholars often gather interaction data from many groups, which creates a set of issues that require attention. For example, one might choose to analyze each interaction from each group separately or, more likely, evaluate sequential patterns across all interactions. Common practice is to evaluate stationarity and homogeneity before assessing data from all interactions in all groups. Stationarity addresses the consistency of patterns within an interaction, for example (continuing with the hidden profile example above) if the likelihood of S (i.e., shared information) following another S at the beginning of a meeting is the same as that at the end of meeting. Homogeneity evaluates consistency of sequential structure across groups or meetings – is the probability of S following S for Group A the same as that for Group B? Beyond that, there are cases in which theory suggests which patterns to evaluate (Tschan, 1995; Weingart et al., 1999), and in others one uses inductive approaches to identify sequences of interest.

The logic of homogeneity extends to local models of interdependence. If, for example, single-issue offers were always followed by substantiations (e.g., arguments for one's position; see Weingart et al., 1999) or were never followed by them, then the sequence would be true for any two members of the group (assuming speaking turns, in which case a speaker cannot follow himself or herself). On the other hand, if there were no reliable pattern then some members on some occasions might follow an offer with a substantiation but such occasions do not represent what occurs at the group level.

The details for conducting local analyses of interdependence are well beyond the scope of this chapter, but the reader is encouraged to consult Gottman and Roy (1990) for general issues related to sequential analysis; Poole, Van de Ven, Dooley, and Holmes (2000, especially chapter 6) regarding application to group and organizational processes specifically; as well as two chapters in this volume (Quera, Chapter 15; Magnusson, Chapter 16). The statistical tests for evaluating sequences are generally well known to researchers; chi-square and z-tests form the basis for evaluating observed sequences of interest against those assumed under conditions of the null hypothesis (i.e., no association). Gottman and Roy (1990), among others, showed how to use log-linear models to test for both sequence and person effects. More recent advances promise analyzing sequences within latent variable models. For example, dynamic structural equation modeling (Asparouhov, Hamaker, & Muthén, 2017) combines aspects of SEM and Markov models, and scholars have adapted social network analysis to the study of sequences (Cornwell, 2015).

Conclusion

In this chapter, we argued that small group discussion and decision making is interdependent by definition, and we identified several ways in which members influence each other above and beyond preference change. We suggested that coherence is the bond that keeps discussions connected, and we presented two general types of coherence: local and global. We then provided examples of how each type of coherence might be analyzed. Finally, we characterized interdependence in terms of homogeneity/heterogeneity of behavior. Ideally, interdependence during small group discussion lies somewhere near the middle of the homogeneity/ heterogeneity continuum. Individuals often, either intentionally or for other reasons (e.g., intense focus on one's thoughts), make contributions to discussion that seem completely unconnected to the issues and topics that were raised previously or might be relevant to raise subsequently. But to do so throughout the entirety of discussion, while possible, seems socially maladroit and runs counter to the purpose of having groups discuss problems. Of course, in a Gricean (1975) sense, one might behave this way to make a point about the group, its purpose, or its process. On the other hand, to be completely focused on what others say to the exclusion of internally available thoughts and information runs the risk of creating a process that seems uncomfortably close to groupthink (Janis, 1971). Thus, the problem for small group participants is to participate relevantly and coherently while simultaneously addressing issues and problems that are based on insights and logic that are driven by individual cognitive processes.

References

Asparouhov, T., Hamaker, E., & Muthén, B. (2017). Dynamic structural equation models. *Structural Equation Modeling: A Multidisciplinary Journal, 25*, 359–388. https://doi.org/10.1080/10705511.2017.1406803

Asparouhov, T., & Muthen, B. (2008). Multilevel mixture models. In G. R. Hancock & K. M. Samuelsen (Eds.), *Advances in latent variable mixture models* (pp. 27–51). Charlotte, NC: Information Age Publishing.

Auld Jr., F., & White, A. M. (1956). Rules for dividing interviews into sentences. *Journal of Psychology: Interdisciplinary & Applied, 42*, 273–281. https://doi.org/10.1080/00223980.1956.9713040

Back, M. D., & Kenny, D. A. (2010). The social relations model: How to understand dyadic processes. *Social and Personality Psychology Compass, 4*(10), 855–870. https://doi.org/10.1111/j.1751-9004.2010.00303.x

Bakeman, R., & Gottman, J. M. (1997). *Observing interaction: An introduction to sequential analysis* (Vol. 2nd). New York, NY: Cambridge University Press.

Bakeman, R., & Quera, V. (2011). *Sequential analysis and observational methods for the behavioral sciences*. Cambridge, UK: Cambridge University Press.

Bales, R. F. (1950). *Interaction process analysis: A method for the study of small groups*. Cambridge, MA: Addison-Wesley.

Bales, R. F., Cohen, S. P., & Williamson, S. A. (1979). *SYMLOG: A system for the multiple level observation of groups*. New York: Free Press.

Balkwell, J. W. (1994). Status. In M. Foschi & E. J. Lawler (Eds.), *Group processes: Sociological analyses* (pp. 119–148). Chicago: Nelson-Hall.

Bonito, J. A. (2001). An information-processing approach to participation in small groups. *Communication Research, 28*(3), 275–303. https://doi.org/10.1177/009365001028003002

Bonito, J. A. (2002). The analysis of participation in small groups: Methodological and conceptual issues related to interdependence. *Small Group Research, 33*(4), 412–438. https://doi.org/10.1177/104649640203300402

Bonito, J. A. (2007). A local model of information sharing in small groups. *Communication Theory, 17*(3), 252–280. https://doi.org/10.1111/j.1468-2885.2007.00295.x

Bonito, J. A., Ervin, J. N., & Staggs, S. M. (2016). Estimation and application of the latent group model. *Group Dynamics: Theory, Research, and Practice, 20*(3), 126–143. https://doi.org/10.1037/gdn0000044

Bonito, J. A., & Hollingshead, A. B. (1997). Participation in small groups. In B. R. Burleson (Ed.), *Communication yearbook 20* (Vol. 20, pp. 227–261). Newbury Park, CA: Sage.

Bonito, J. A., & Meyers, R. A. (2011). Examining functional communication as egocentric or group-centric: Application of a latent group model. *Communication Monographs, 78*(4), 463–485. https://doi.org/10.1080/03637751.2011.618138

Bonito, J. A., & Ruppel, E. K. (2011). An application of the socioegocentric model to information-sharing discussions: In search of group-level communication influences. *Communication Research, 38*(3), 356–375. https://doi.org/10.1177/0093650210377195

Bonito, J. A., Ruppel, E. K., & Keyton, J. (2012). Reliability estimates for multilevel designs in group research. *Small Group Research, 43*(4), 443–467. https://doi.org/10.1177/1046496412437614

3

Bonito, J. A., & Sanders, R. E. (2009). A different approach to answering a good question: A response to Hewes's models of communication effects on small group outcomes. *Human Communication Research*, *35*(2), 296–303. https://doi.org/10.1111/j.1468-2958.2009.01351.x

Bonito, J. A., & Sanders, R. E. (2011). The existential center of small groups: Member's conduct and interaction. *Small Group Research*, *42*(3), 343–358. https://doi.org/10.1177/1046496410385472

Carron, A. V., & Brawley, L. R. (2000). Cohesion: Conceptual and measurement issues. *Small Group Research*, *31*(1), 89–106. https://doi.org/10.1177/104649640003100105

Corman, S. R., & Kuhn, T. (2005). The detectability of socio-egocentric group speech: A quasi-Turing test. *Communication Monographs*, *72*(2), 117–143. https://doi.org/10.1080/03637750500111849

Cornwell, B. (2015). *Social sequence analysis: Methods and applications*. New York, NY: Cambridge University Press.

Coulter, P. (1989). *Measuring inequality: A methodological handbook*. Boulder: Westview Press.

Craig, R. T., & Tracy, K. (1983). Introduction. In R. T. Craig & K. Tracy (Eds.), *Conversational coherence: Form, structure, and strategy* (pp. 10–22). Beverly Hills, CA: Sage.

Dansereau, F. (2006). Avoiding the "fallacy of the wrong level": A within and between analysis (WABA) approach. *Group & Organization Management*, *31*(5), 536–577. https://doi.org/10.1177/1059601106291131

De Dreu, C. K. W., & Weingart, L. R. (2002). Task versus relationship conflict: A meta-analysis. *Academy of Management Proceedings*, 2002(1), B1–B6. https://doi.org/10.5465/APBPP.2002.7516590

Edwards, J. A. (1993). Principles and contrasting systems of discourse transcription. In J. A. Edwards & M. D. Lampert (Eds.), *Talking data: Transcription and coding in discourse research* (pp. 3–31). Hillsdale, NJ: Erlbaum.

Ervin, J. N., Bonito, J. A., & Keyton, J. (2017). Convergence of intrapersonal and interpersonal processes across group meetings. *Communication Monographs*, *84*(2), 200–220. https://doi.org/10.1080/03637751.2016.1185136

Fisek, M. H., & Ofshe, R. (1970). The process of status evolution. *Sociometry*, *33*(3), 327–346. https://doi.org/10.2307/2786161

Folger, J. P., Hewes, D. E., & Poole, M. S. (1984). Coding social interaction. In B. Dervin & M. J. Voight (Eds.), *Progress in communication sciences* (pp. 115–161). Norwood, NJ: Ablex.

Gonzalez, R., & Griffin, D. (2002). Modeling the personality of dyads and groups. *Journal of Personality*, 70(6), 901–924. https://doi.org/10.1111/1467-6494.05027

Gottman, J. M., & Roy, A. K. (1990). *Sequential analysis: A guide for behavioral researchers*. Cambridge, UK: Cambridge University Press.

Gouran, D. S., & Hirokawa, R. Y. (1996). Functional theory and communication in decision-making and problem-solving groups: An expanded view. In R. Y. Hirokawa & M. S. Poole (Eds.), *Communication and group decision making* (pp. 55–80). Thousand Oaks, CA: Sage.

Grice, H. P. (1975). Logic and conversation. In P. C. Morgan (Ed.) pp. (41–58). New York, NY: Academic Press.

Guetzkow, H. (1950). Unitizing and categorizing problems in coding qualitative data. *Journal of Clinical Psychology*, 6, 47–58. https://doi.org/http://dx.doi.org/10.1002/1097-4679(195001)6:1%3C47::AID-JCLP2270060111%3E3.0.CO;2-I

Heck, R. H., & Thomas, S. L. (2015). *An introduction to multilevel modeling techniques: MLM and SEM approaches using Mplus* (3rd edn.). New York, NY: Routledge.

Hewes, D. E. (1996). Small group communication may not influence decision making: An amplification of socio-egocentric theory. In R. Y. Hirokawa & M. S. Poole (Eds.), *Communication and group decision making* (2nd edn., pp. 179–212). Thousand Oaks, CA: Sage.

Hewes, D. E. (2009). The influence of communication processes on group outcomes: Antithesis and thesis. *Human Communication Research*, 35(2), 249–271. https://doi.org/10.1111/j.1468-2958.2009.01347.x

Hirokawa, R. Y. (1982). Group communication and problem-solving effectiveness I: A critical review of inconsistent findings. *Communication Quarterly*, 30(2), 134–141. https://doi.org/10.1080/01463378209369440

Hirokawa, R. Y. (1988). Group communication and decision-making performance: A continued test of the functional perspective. *Human Communication Research*, 14(4), 487–515. https://doi.org/10.1111/j.1468-2958.1988.tb00165.x

Hirokawa, R. Y. (1990). The role of communication in group decision-making efficacy: A task-contingency perspective. *Small Group Research*, 21(2), 190–204. https://doi.org/10.1177/1046496490212003

Hox, J. J. (2010). *Multilevel analysis: Techniques and applications* (2nd edn). New York, NY: Routledge.

Ilgen, D. R., Hollenbeck, J. R., Johnson, M., & Jundt, D. (2005). Teams in organizations: From input-process-output models to IMOI models. *Annual Review of Psychology*, 56, 517–543. https://doi.org/10.1146/annurev.psych.56.091103.070250

Janis, I. L. (1971). Groupthink. *Psychology Today*, 5, 43–46.

Jones, E. E., & Gerard, H. (1967). *Foundations of social psychology*. Oxford, UK: John Wiley & Sons Inc.

Kameda, T., Ohtsubo, Y., & Takezawa, M. (1997). Centrality in sociocognitive networks and social influence: An illustration in a group decision-making context. *Journal of Personality & Social Psychology*, 73(2), 296–309. https://doi.org/10.1037/0022-3514.73.2.296

Kashy, D. A., & Kenny, D. A. (2000). The analysis of data from dyads and groups. In H. T. Reis & C. M. Judd (Eds.), *Handbook of research methods in social psychology* (pp. 451–477). New York, NY: Cambridge University Press.

Kenny, D. A. (1994). *Interpersonal perception: A social relations analysis*. New York, NY: Guilford Press.

Kenny, D. A., & Garcia, R. L. (2012). Using the actor–partner interdependence model to study the effects of group composition. *Small Group Research*, 43(4), 468–496. https://doi.org/10.1177/1046496412441626

Kenny, D. A., & Judd, C. M. (1986). Consequences of violating the independence assumption in analysis of variance. *Psychological Bulletin*, 99(3), 422–431. https://doi.org/10.1037/0033-2909.99.3.422

Kenny, D. A., Kashy, D. A., & Cook, W. L. (2006). *Dyadic data analysis*. New York, NY: Guilford Press.

Keyton, J. (1991). Evaluating individual group member satisfaction as a situational variable. *Small Group Research*, *22*(2), 200–219. https://doi.org/10.1177/1046496491222004

Keyton, J. (1999). Relational communication in groups. In L. R. Frey, D. S. Gouran, & M. S. Poole (Eds.), *The handbook of group communication theory and research* (pp. 192–224). Thousand Oaks, CA: Sage.

Kolbe, M., Grote, G., Waller, M. J., Wacker, J., Grande, B., Burtscher, M. J., & Spahn, D. R. (2014). Monitoring and talking to the room: Autochthonous coordination patterns in team interaction and performance. *Journal of Applied Psychology*, *99*(6), 1254–1267. https://doi.org/10.1037/a0037877

Larson, J. R. (1997). Modeling the entry of shared and unshared information into group discussion: A review and BASIC language computer program. *Small Group Research*, *28*(3), 454–479. https://doi.org/10.1177/1046496497283007

Lehmann-Willenbrock, N., Allen, J. A., & Kauffeld, S. (2013). A sequential analysis of procedural meeting communication: How teams facilitate their meetings. *Journal of Applied Communication Research*, *41*(4), 365–388. https://doi.org/10.1080/00909882.2013.844847

Lei, Z., Waller, M. J., Hagen, J., & Kaplan, S. (2016). Team adaptiveness in dynamic contexts: Contextualizing the roles of interaction patterns and in-process planning. *Group & Organization Management*, *41*(4), 491–525. https://doi.org/10.1177/1059601115615246

Levinson, S. C. (1983). *Pragmatics*. Cambridge, UK: Cambridge University Press.

Li, F., Duncan, T. E., & Hops, H. (2001). Examining developmental trajectories in adolescent alcohol use using piecewise growth mixture modeling analysis. *Journal of Studies on Alcohol*, *62*(2), 199–210. https://doi.org/10.15288/jsa.2001.62.199

Littlepage, G. E., Schmidt, G. W., Whisler, E. W., & Frost, A. G. (1995). An input-process-output analysis of influence and performance in problem-solving groups. *Journal of Personality & Social Psychology*, *69*(5), 877–889. https://doi.org/10.1037/0022-3514.69.5.877

Meyers, R. A., & Brashers, D. E. (2010). Extending the conversational argument coding scheme: Argument categories, units, and coding procedures. *Communication Methods and Measures*, *4*(1), 27. https://doi.org/10.1080/19312451003680467

Nguyen, V.-A., Boyd-Graber, J., Resnik, P., Cai, D. A., Midberry, J. E., & Wang, Y. (2014). Modeling topic control to detect influence in conversations using nonparametric topic models. *Machine Learning*, *95*(3), 381–421. https://doi.org/10.1007/s10994-013-5417-9

Parker, K. C. (1988). Speaking turns in small group interaction: A context-sensitive event sequence model. *Journal of Personality and Social Psychology*, *54*(6), 965–971. https://doi.org/10.1037/0022-3514.54.6.965

Pavitt, C. (2014). An interactive input–process–output model of social influence in decision-making groups. *Small Group Research*, *45*(6), 704–730. https://doi.org/10.1177/1046496414548353.

Pavitt, C., & Johnson, K. K. (1999). An examination of the coherence of group discussions. *Communication Research*, *26*(3), 303–321. https://doi.org/10.1177/009365099026003002

Pavitt, C., & Johnson, K. K. (2002). Scheidel and Crowell revisited: A descriptive study of group proposal sequencing. *Communication Monographs*, *69*(1), 19–32. https://doi.org/10.1080/03637750216535

Poole, M. S. (1998). The small group should be the fundamental unit of communication research. In J. S. Trent (Ed.), *Communication: Views from the helm for the 21st century* (pp. 94–97). Boston, MA: Allyn & Bacon.

Poole, M. S., Van de Ven, A. H., Dooley, K., & Holmes, M. E. (2000). *Organizational change and innovation processes: Theory and methods for research*. Oxford, UK, and New York, NY: Oxford University Press.

Putnam, L. L., & Jones, T. S. (1982). The role of communication in bargaining. *Human Communication Research*, *8*(3), 262–280. http://dx.doi.org/10.1111/j.1468-2958.1982.tb00668.x

Rabe-Hesketh, S., Skrondal, A., & Pickles, A. (2004). Generalized multilevel structural equation modeling. *Psychometrika*, *69*(2), 167–190. https://doi.org/10.1007/BF02295939

Sackett, G. P. (1979). The lag sequential analysis of contingency and cyclicity in behavioral interaction research. In J. D. Osofsky (Ed.), *Handbook of infant development* (Vol. 1, pp. 623–649). New York, NY: Wiley.

Seibold, D. R., & Meyers, R. A. (2007). Group argument: A structuration perspective and research program. *Small Group Research*, *38*(3), 312–336. https://doi.org/10.1177/1046496407301966

Shelly, R. K., & Troyer, L. (2001). Emergence and completion of structure in initially undefined and partially defined groups. *Social Psychology Quarterly*, *64*(4), 318–332. https://doi.org/10.2307/3090157

Skvoretz, J. (1988). Models of participation in status-differentiated groups. *Social Psychology Quarterly*, *51*(1), 43–57. https://doi.org/10.2307/2786983.

Smith-Lovin, L., Skvoretz, J., & Hudson, C. G. (1986). Status and participation in six-person groups: A test of Skvoretz's comparative status model. *Social Forces*, *64*(4), 992–1005. https://doi.org/10.1093/sf/64.4.992

Soller, A. (2004). Understanding knowledge-sharing breakdowns: A meeting of the quantitative and qualitative minds. *Journal of Computer Assisted Learning*, *20*(3), 212–223. https://doi.org/10.1111/j.1365-2729.2004.00081.x

Soller, A., & Lesgold, A. (2003). A computational approach to analyzing online knowledge sharing interaction. In U. Hoppe, F. Verdejo, & J. Kay (Eds.), *Artificial intelligence in education: Shaping the future of learning through intelligent technologies* (pp. 253–260). Amsterdam, NL: IOS Press.

Stapleton, L. M., Yang, J. S., & Hancock, G. R. (2016). Construct meaning in multilevel settings. *Journal of Educational and Behavioral Statistics*, *41*(5), 481–520. https://doi.org/10.3102/1076998616646200

Stasser, G., & Taylor, L. A. (1991). Speaking turns in face-to-face discussions. *Journal of Personality and Social Psychology*, *60*(5), 675–684. https://doi.org/10.1037/0022-3514.60.5.675

Stasser, G., & Titus, W. (2003). Hidden profiles: A brief history. *Psychological Inquiry*, *14*(3), 304–313. https://doi.org/10.1207/S15327965PLI1403&4_21

Stasser, G., & Vaughan, S. I. (1996). Models of participation during face-to-face unstructured discussion. In E. H. Witte & J. H. Davis (Eds.), *Understanding group behavior* (Vol. 2, pp. 165–192). Mahwah, NJ: Erlbaum.

Thibaut, J. W., & Kelley, H. H. (1959). *The social psychology of groups*. New York, NY: John Wiley.

Tschan, F. (1995). Communication enhances small group performance if it conforms to task requirements: The concept of ideal communication cycles. *Basic and Applied Social Psychology, 17*(3), 371–393. https://doi.org/10.1207/s15324834basp1703_6

Van Lange, P. A. M., & Balliet, D. (2015). Interdependence theory. In M. Mikulincer, P. R. Shaver, J. A. Simpson, & J. F. Dovidio (Eds.), *APA handbook of personality and social psychology, Volume 3: Interpersonal relations* (pp. 65–92). Washington, DC: American Psychological Association. https://doi.org/10.1037/14344-003

Weingart, L. R., Brett, J. M., Olekalns, M., & Smith, P. L. (2007). Conflicting social motives in negotiating groups. *Journal of Personality and Social Psychology, 93*(6), 994–1010. https://doi.org/10.1037/0022-3514.93.6.994

Weingart, L. R., Prietula, M. J., Hyder, E. B., & Genovese, C. R. (1999). Knowledge and the sequential processes of negotiation: A Markov chain analysis of response-in-kind. *Journal of Experimental Social Psychology, 35*(4), 366–393. http://dx.doi.org/10.1006/jesp.1999.1378

Wickham, R. E., & Knee, C. R. (2012). Interdependence theory and the actor–partner interdependence model: Where theory and method converge. *Personality and Social Psychology Review, 16*(4), 375–393. https://doi.org/10.1177/1088868312447897

Wittenbaum, G. M., Hollingshead, A. B., & Botero, I. C. (2004). From cooperative to motivated information sharing in groups: Moving beyond the hidden profile paradigm. *Communication Monographs, 71*(3), 286–310. https://doi.org/10.1080/0363452042000299894

Wittenbaum, G. M., Hollingshead, A. B., Paulus, P. B., Hirokawa, R. Y., Ancona, D. G., Peterson, R. S., . . . Yoon, K. (2004). The functional perspective as a lens for understanding groups. *Small Group Research, 35*(1), 17–43. https://doi.org/10.1177/1046496403259459

Zijlstra, F. R. H., Waller, M. J., & Phillips, S. I. (2012). Setting the tone: Early interaction patterns in swift-starting teams as a predictor of effectiveness. *European Journal of Work and Organizational Psychology, 21*(5), 749–777. https://doi.org/10.1080/1359432X.2012.690399

18 Coding and Analyzing Multiple Levels

Marshall Scott Poole

The social world encompasses multiple levels of meaning and activity. Words, gestures, and behavior form utterances and actions, which link together in interacts, pairs of related acts that link dyads. Interacts, in turn, make up complex interactions performed by groups, which are components of larger organizations, both formal and informal, which in turn constitute societies. Adding to the complexity, in each of the levels just noted we can discern multiple dimensions of meaning, such as task and socioemotional functions of the same utterance. Teasing out the nature of these levels and the dimensions of meaning within them and mapping the connections across levels and dimensions is an important task for interaction analysis.

This chapter will discuss approaches to systematically defining multilevel coding systems and methods for the analysis of multilevel interaction data. Its focus is on coded interaction and directly observed actions or behaviors, not on participants' ratings of interaction or of each other. An extensive and informative discussion of the latter can be found in Kashy and Kenny (2000).

Multilevel coding and analysis has several benefits. First, combining two or more types of meaning introduces valuable nuance into our measurement of interaction. A decision proposal made during an episode of conflict in a group is likely to be quite different in character from one made during a period of group harmony, and combining information about decision function with information about conflict level enables us to operationalize this higher-order meaning (see Poole & Roth, 1989, for an example). As subsequent examples show, adding more than two layers of meaning allows even greater insight. Second, starting with basic units such as speech acts or affect type and combining them in a systematic way to identify more complex, higher-level units increases the reliability of measurement. Generally, small, well-defined units are easier to code reliably, and this base provides a stronger foundation for derivation of more complex higher-order constructs in subsequent stages of the coding and analysis process. Third, multilevel coding and analysis can allow us to identify emergent properties or processes of dyads or groups, such as characteristics of an intimate relationship or teamwork.

This chapter will be organized as follows: First we will introduce some terminology and discuss two cases in which multilevel interaction analysis can be used. Following this, we distinguish two general approaches to linking codings across levels, rule-based and operation-based approaches. The two approaches are explicated through analysis of some exemplary coding systems. We will then discuss methods that can be used to implement rules-based and operation-based multilevel interaction analysis systems.

Terminology: Levels, Dimensions, and Tracks

There are so many possible types of meaning in group interaction that a complete delineation is beyond the scope of this chapter. Instead, we will introduce a few general distinctions that attempt to encompass most of the operations involved in the design of complex coding systems that span multiple levels and dimensions of meaning.

Level of abstraction refers to the breakdown of larger units of meaning, language, or action into smaller units. The smaller units make up the larger units and are subsumed under them. One common set of levels is:

- Word
- Thought unit (independent clause made up of two or more words)
- Speaking turn (multiple clauses by a single communicator)
- Interact (a speaking turn and its response by two different communicators)
- Episode (multiple related interactions by two or more communicators)
- Phase (multiple episodes serving the same general function for the discussion)

In this case the higher levels are defined by the generality of constructs, the number of communicators involved, and the length of the unit. A common strategy in multilevel coding is to work from the smaller unit up, identifying higher-level units based on combinations of lower-level units. To take a simple (and not very interesting) example, we might code the task functions of thought units based on interpretation of the words within them. Then these task functions might be used to characterize a speaking turn as "task focused" or "non-task focused." Once this has been done, pairs of turns can be classified as "task relevant," "non-task relevant," or "mixed" interacts. In turn, analysis of series of interacts would enable classifications of episodes according to their task relevance, and ultimately to the identification of phases based on task focus. Moving up levels enables the coding process to occur in a systematic fashion. Another set of levels common in group and team research is:

- Individual behavior
- Dyadic interaction
- Group/team interaction

These levels are implicitly represented in the earlier set, as word, thought unit, and speaker turn operate at the individual level, interacts at the dyadic level, and episode and phase at the group level. This set of levels is useful because it taps into different realms of constructs commonly of interest to group scholars as the source of different types of effects in group interaction.

To this point, we have assumed that there is one construct per level, arranged in a hierarchical fashion in which lower levels are nested within higher ones. However, it is also possible for there to be more than one *dimension* of meaning in a single level of analysis. For example, a common distinction within levels in group research is between task and socioemotional utterances or acts. Considered together, task and socioemotional functions can define a higher-level construct that represents the combination of the two, such as Bion's (1961) "basic assumptions" (dependency, fight-flight, and pairing).

Coding and analysis across levels and dimensions occur in similar ways, and when this is the case, the term *track* will be used to refer to them generically. A track is a coding of a series of utterances or acts that assigns them to meaningful categories along a single dimension in a single level.

Cases for Multilevel Interaction Coding and Analysis

Two distinct but related cases for multilevel interaction coding and analysis can be identified. The first involves deriving higher-level meanings from two or more lower-level dimensions of meaning. Verbal and nonverbal behaviors and task and socioemotional functions are examples of different dimensions of meaning that can be identified for each of the same sequence of acts. While each dimension provides useful information on its own, by combining them we can generate higher-level constructs. For instance, we could assess the degree of consistency between verbal and nonverbal cues in a speaking turn and categorize turns in terms of their equivocality: clear-cut (if consistent), ambiguous (if inconsistent), or ironic (if contradictory). This more complex construct gives us insight into different aspects of the interaction than do its component dimensions: Bavelas, Black, Chovil, and Mullett (1990), for example, explore a number of ways in which equivocality has significant implications for interpersonal relationships.

The second case involves identification of dyadic or group-level interaction constructs from individual-level actions. For instance, we might code positive and negative affect expressed by each member during a dyadic interaction and then combine this information by looking at interchanges between members to identify the affective tenor of the dyad. If more than two actors are involved, we might want to identify the group's emotional climate based on combinations of affective expressions. In both examples of this second case we are moving from data gathered at the individual level to relation-level or collective constructs.

General Approaches to Defining Inter-Level Relationships

A prerequisite for multilevel coding and analysis is a system that clearly defines the units at each level and specifies the relationships between levels.

There are two different ways in which two levels can be related: They can be related through rules or they can be related through operations. When relationships among levels are delineated by *rules*, there are specific instructions for how to map lower-level codes into higher-level codes. These rule sets also implicitly give the higher-level codes at least part of their meaning. For example, there might be a rule indicating that lower-level acts a and c correspond to higher-level unit A. Part of the meaning of A depends on the meaning of a and c. When relationships between levels are defined by *operations*, algorithms or statistical procedures for aggregating or compiling lower-level units to yield higher-level units are specified. The algorithms or procedures are used in cases in which rules cannot be clearly and comprehensively defined.

We will illustrate the variety of rules- and operations-based approaches with a range of typical examples. As of the writing of this chapter, there is no systematic framework to specify the complete range of choices for inter-level linkage so ostensive definition is the best we can achieve at this point.

Interlevel Linkage via Rules

Well-Specified Rule Systems. The first illustration of a rules-based approach is the Relational Control Communication Coding System (RCCCS), a system designed for research on how partners in interpersonal relationships define themselves and construct their relationships in interaction (Rogers & Farace, 1975; Rogers & Cummings, 2017; described in more detail in Chapter 43 by Friedlander, Escudero, & Heatherington in Part V of this volume). This elegantly specified system first classifies each communicative act based on its format (assertion, question, talkover, noncomplete) and according to how it responds to the previous utterance from the other partner (e.g., support, disconfirmation, extension, topic change). These two codes are then considered together to assign one of three control codes – one-up (dominant), one-down (submissive), or one-across (egalitarian) – which indicates the stance that the act represents toward the partner. For example, an assertion which also responds with support is classified as one-down, while a question that expresses nonsupport is classified as one-up. Then the system moves to the dyadic level and takes pairs of utterances by partners to define five control transaction types at the dyadic level (for example, a pair of successive one-up acts is "competitive symmetry," while a one-up act followed by a one-down act is "complementarity"). Rules explicitly guide the process of moving from the functional and speech act level to control codes and then up to the dyadic transaction level. The system is based on a theoretical rationale that underpins explicit rules for classification of pairs of acts and moves from lower-level units to higher-level units as shown in Figure 18.1.

Bales's (1951) well-known Interaction Process Analysis (IPA) System, described by Keyton in Chapter 23 of Part V, is another example of a well-specified rules-based approach. According to Bales, the task categories in the IPA correspond to the three problems that face all social systems: defining the

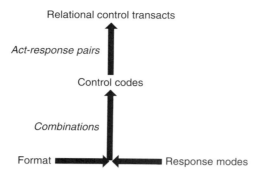

Figure 18.1 *Movement between levels in the RCCCS.*

situation, understanding the situation and available options for addressing it, and selecting and planning implementation of a solution. There are six socioemotional categories corresponding to positive and negative poles: agreement/disagreement, tension expression/release, and solidarity expression/rejection. These categories map onto more general levels: task/socioemotional and positive/negative. As with the RCCCS, the IPA is based on theoretical distinctions, which define the movement from lower to higher levels. For example, the category tension release is identified based on thought units that function as joking or expression of emotions; tension release, in turn, is nested within and partly constitutes the higher-level category of positive socioemotional expression.

Semi-Structured Rule Systems. In the well-specified systems just summarized, all levels are clearly and explicitly linked. Some rule systems do not fully specify all linkages from one level to another, but instead are semi-structured in that they provide clear definitions but leave some room for adaptation to the specifics of the situation when moving from lower- to higher-level constructs. The Conversational Argument Coding Scheme (CASC; Seibold & Weger, 2017) is theoretically grounded in the theory of minimally rational argument and the structuration argument theory. The lowest level of coding classifies acts into argument functions (e.g., assertions, elaborations, challenges, frames). Coding proceeds in a series of passes: (1) separate argument from nonargument; (2) identify issues/topics arguments pertain to; (3) distinguish lines of argument; (4) iterate through classes of functions; and (5) analyze dyadic and group interchanges (Meyers & Brashers, 2010).

In this fifth pass, higher-level constructs are identified in terms of patterns of argument codes. Sequences are chains of consecutive codes such as developing sequences (which advance and elaborate an argument) and diverging sequences (which reflect disagreement). Argument structures represent longer periods of interaction, sometimes involving nonconsecutive acts. Examples include embedded structures that have two or more lines of argument mixed together and tag-team arguments in which two or more members build an argument together. Argument structures are variable in length and so specific rules for identification from lower-order codes cannot be written; instead the authors describe the basic pattern and coders use their pattern recognition faculties to identify them. For this reason, the CACS can be described as semi-structured.

Interlevel Linkage via Operations

Whereas rule-based systems specify connections between levels formally and explicitly, operation-based systems define connections by using statistics or algorithms to identify higher-level constructs. Two ways of doing this are: (1) aggregating lower-level units to yield higher-level constructs or (2) finding patterns of lower-level units that represent higher-level constructs.

Aggregation-Based Operations. The classic study of stages in group problem solving by Bales and Strodtbeck (1951) gives an example of aggregation from a lower level to define higher-level constructs. Bales and Strodtbeck tested a theory of group problem solving that hypothesized that groups would pass through three phases as they solved a problem: an orientation phase, followed by an evaluation phase, and, finally, a control phase. They coded a set of groups using the IPA, divided the coded sessions into thirds, and computed the total number of orientation acts, evaluation acts, and control acts for each third. They then assessed whether profiles of these acts in each third of the discussion reflected the hypothesized phases: If their model was accurate, frequencies of orientation acts would be high in the first phase and decrease over time, evaluation acts should be highest in the middle phase and lower in the first and third, and the frequency of control acts should increase over time. Phases, i.e., higher-order structures of problem-solving interaction, were thus identified through aggregation of lower-level codes.

Pattern-Based Operations. Murase, Asencio, DeChurch, Contractor, Mathieu, and Poole (2015) provide our first example of the use of an algorithm to identify sequential relationships among lower-level codes to define higher-level constructs. Murase et al. conducted a study of entrainment of coordination activities in a multiteam system to test the hypothesis that degree of synchronization in multiteam systems was positively related to team performance. Their analysis distinguished four levels of categorization, as shown in Figure 18.2.

The lowest-level data were log data from a simulation of a multiteam system that had two two-person teams working together to protect a convoy of supplies crossing enemy territory. Each log entry was an action taken by some participant in the game, such as moving from point A to point B or opening a communication channel. The result was a stream of thousands of data points logged consecutively. They employed the sequence analysis application *TraMineR* to identify common short sequences in the data, such as "player 2 moves from A to D::kills enemy:: sends message to player 3." The application identified thousands of short sequences

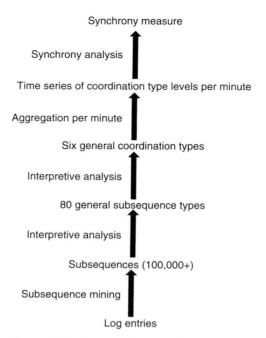

Figure 18.2 *Movement between levels in Murase et al.'s (2015) analysis.*

which were then sorted into eighty more general classes that represented broader functions such as "attacks the enemy." These eighty sub-sequence classes were then sorted into a third level of six categories that indicated within-team and between-team coordination. Data for the game were then divided into one-minute units and the total amount of within- and between-team coordination behaviors each member engaged in was calculated for each minute. This produced a time series of magnitudes of within-team and between-team coordination behaviors for each of the four participants. These time series were then analyzed for degree of synchronization of within- and between-team activities among members, yielding a fourth level of analysis, coefficients indicating four types of synchronization among members of each team for the entire session.

Caveats. One limitation of operation-based definition of higher-level constructs is that different operations may yield different sets of constructs. Defining higher-order constructs by means of aggregation yields different types of meanings than looking for patterns such as sequences in lower-level units (Klein & Kozlowski, 2000).

Connections Between Rule-Based and Operation-Based Approaches

Rule-based and operation-based approaches are not mutually exclusive: As the example of Bales and Strodtbeck (1951) shows, they may be used in concert with each other to define different levels; the IPA employs a rules-based approach to classify utterances into 12 base-level codes that are then mapped into higher-level constructs – orientation, evaluation, control, positive socioemotional, and negative socioemotional acts. These higher-level constructs are then aggregated to provide indicators of the three phases of problem solving.

Operation-based approaches are useful when higher-level units are long compared to the time scale of lower-level units. The leap from a construct such as orientation, which applies to individual acts, to phases that extend over one-third of a discussion and may include tens or even hundreds of acts is a long one. Since phases are typically made up of numerous lower-level codes, aggregation of rules-based categories and identification of patterns made up of these categories offer a systematic means of phase identification. The same is true of other higher-level units, such as a Markovian transition matrix or phase state plot (both of which will be discussed briefly in the following section), which are both derived algorithmically.

Over time, cross-level linkage systems tend to evolve to rule-based formats. In the early stages of the development of any coding system, single or multiple level, the codes are generally derived through a process similar to grounded theory construction (in this case the theory is the theory of the categorical system and linkages across levels). Investigators start with an initial set of functional or grammatical categories, and expand the list as they encounter acts that are not accounted for and as they try to work out specific rules for formerly intuitive and vague category definitions. Rule sets are elaborated and finer, better-delineated definitions evolve, and the final systems often appear to have been designed deductively. Accounts of the historical background of coding systems, however, bear out the trial-and-error, hit-or-miss nature of the process (VanLear & Canary, 2017) (for coding scheme development, see also Tschan, Zimmermann, & Semmer, this volume, Chapter 10).

Methods

A number of methods are available to derive higher-level constructs from lower-level codes. In this section we will address methodologies for aggregation, several approaches for detecting sub-sequence patterns, phasic analysis, state space grid analysis, and visualization techniques.

Methods for Aggregation

As described in the previous section, one way to derive higher-order constructs is by aggregating lower-level codes. The key in this case is defining the unit of aggregation, which is often a time unit, such as a minute, hour, day, or week, but may also be a specific number of lower-level codes, such as ten acts. The choice of unit is dependent in part on the amount of data available. If acts are recorded every hundredth of a second, then a second or minute are probably workable units; longer units such as a week are likely to result in such high totals of acts that they are uninterpretable. If lower-level codes only occur a few times a day, then a week or month may be a more tractable unit.

Ideally, there should be a theoretical rationale for unit of aggregation. In some cases a rationale can be found in general social and behavioral science that provides foundational knowledge. For instance, findings on the limits of human cognitive capacities suggest that if the goal is to map actors' responses to others' acts in immediate interaction, the unit of aggregation should be a few minutes at most. Any unit larger than this would involve more pieces of information than an actor could handle. If each act carries one bit of information, the "magic rule" (Miller, 1956) of "7 plus or minus 2" suggests that around seven prior acts would be a good aggregation unit. In some cases, the immediate theory that informs the research provides a rationale for unit selection. If, for example, the goal was to test Karl Weick's (1979) theory of sensemaking from the *Social Psychology of Organizing*, then the double-interact (a three-act sequence representing act:: response::actor's response to the response) would be the appropriate unit for aggregation.

The result of aggregation is often a simple continuous measure for each unit of analysis, such as total number of positive acts. More complex aggregates are possible, such as the ratio of positive to negative acts. Bales and Strodtbeck (1951) employed a profile measure of the relative levels of orientation, evaluation, control, positive reactions, and negative reactions to define their phases.

Methods for Pattern Recognition and Analysis

Sub-sequence Identification. In some cases short sequences of lower-level codes – two, three, sometimes four units – can be used to identify higher-level constructs. Three approaches for sub-sequences identification can be distinguished: theoretically driven approaches, sequence mining, and stochastic modeling.

Theoretically driven approaches. Meaningful sub-sequence can be defined a priori. In Tschan's (1995) research on communication cycles in teams, cycles were defined as sub-sequence of utterances in which the team is focused on the same part of a task (Tschan, 1995, p. 374). Tschan hypothesized that "ideal communication cycles" – those beginning with orientation or planning and ending with evaluation – would lead to higher levels of team performance than other types of cycles. Tschan used this concept of an ideal cycle as a reference point and coded observed cycles in terms of quality (the degree to which it matched the ideal cycle), and complexity.

Sequence mining. Murase et al. (2015), described above, offers an example of sequence mining. They mapped process by identifying sub-sequences of task-related actions within the larger performance episode on the assumption that sequences of actions were more meaningful indicators of process than individual acts. They first derived a list of all possible sub-sequences between two and four events long based on the stipulation that each step in the sequence must consist of a change in activity (i.e., the steps could not be repetitions of previous activity). This resulted in identification of 148,000 distinct sub-sequences, which were aggregated and reduced to about 80 unique and meaningful short-cycle sequence types. These were further grouped into six activity classes that represented different types of coordination and action within and between teams (a third level recoding of short cycles into classes). The resulting classes were derived by interpreting the derived sub-sequence through the filter of teamwork theory and research.

Like exploratory factor analysis, sequence mining is an inductive method that identifies the large number of sub-sequences of specific lengths in a given whole sequence and relies on the researcher to sort out what the results mean. Sequence-mining algorithms are available in several applications, including the R-package *TraMineR* (Gabadinho, Ritschard, Müller, & Studer, 2011) and STATA (e.g., Brzinsky-Fay, Kohler, & Luniak, 2006).

It is common to think of sequences and sub-sequences in terms of temporally consecutive events, but they may also be composed of nonconsecutive events. In Tschan's plan-act-evaluate sub-sequence, for example, it is not necessarily important that the events be consecutive, but rather that a *plan* code precedes the *act* code and that an *evaluate* code comes after *act*; there may be unrelated events between the three. These other events are treated either as parts of other sub-sequence or as "error." TraMineR and STATA can identify sub-sequences from nonconsecutive events as well as consecutive events.

Another approach to sequence mining is to search for "hidden patterns" of events that occur together within given intervals of time (or sets of acts) at a greater frequency than would be expected by chance. Magnusson's THEME approach (described in Chapter 16 in this handbook) is one way of doing this.

Poole, Lambert, Murase, Asencio, and McDonald (2017) present an extended discussion of sequence approaches. They ground these in process theorizing for groups and organizations.

Stochastic modeling. This approach identifies short sequences based on an underlying model that predicts the probabilities that various short sequences of events will occur in sequences of codes. The basic model is the homogeneous *Markov chain*, which predicts the probability distribution of a set of events (in this case occurrence of event types) at time t + k based on the probability distribution of the same set of event types at time t (see Poole et al., 2000, for a more in-depth description of Markov chain analysis). The structure of this model, as represented by a transition matrix that models the probabilities of transition from one interaction code to another over time, depicts temporal dependencies among interaction types. See Quera (this volume, Chapter 15) for a description.

Another stochastic approach is *relational event modeling* (REM) (Butts, 2008). Relational event modeling allows us to assess whether specific sub-sequences of events occur more often or less often than would be expected by chance in a sequence based on hazard models. Unlike Markov modeling, REM requires the researcher to specify the sequences of interest (e.g., Tschan's [1995], ideal communication cycle) beforehand and build terms into a probabilistic model that is then fit to the sequence data. Hence, it is more dependent on theory of sequence ordering than sequence mining or Markov modeling. Software for conducting REM is available in the Statnet application for R and procedures for conducting REM with interaction data are described in Pilny, Schecter, Poole, and Contractor (2016). Another method for identifying common short sequences, lag sequential analysis, is described by Quera in Chapter 13 of this handbook.

Methods for stochastic modeling of sequences work best when the number of lower level categories is relatively small. As the number of categories increases, more data points are needed to fit the models adequately.

Summary. The three classes of methods discussed in this section rely on the role of sequential structure to give meaning to interaction. Acts or utterances, sequenced in particular ways, give rise to higher-order units of meaning. The sub-sequences identified with these methods can be redefined as higher-level units, which may themselves achieve higher orders of meaning through their sequencing. Alternatively they provide basic units for other types of analysis.

Phasic Analysis. A phase is a period of coherent activity that serves some function in interaction. The best known phasic models are unitary sequence (life cycle) models that posit a set sequence of phases that is uniform across cases, such as Bales and Strodtbeck's (1951) problem-solving model. There are also multiple sequence models, which propose that interaction can follow several different paths, represented by different sequences of phases. Poole and Roth (1989) found, for example, that decision-making groups can follow several different paths as they make decisions: a simple unitary sequence, a sequence in which discussion of solutions predominates, and more complex sequences of problem-solution cycles.

In the case of unitary sequence models, aggregation of lower-level codes can be used to define and ascertain phases if the data correspond to the model. In the case of multiple sequences, it is not possible to divide the interaction into as many intervals as there are phases, since there may be multiple occurrences of the same phases over the course of the interaction. Methods for mapping phases with different lengths and frequency of occurrence are required. TraMineR and STATA both enable this type of analysis, and Holmes and Poole (1991) developed a different method for flexible phase mapping. If a set of interactions is to be analyzed, they can each be mapped and then types of phase progressions can be identified using methods for sequence comparison discussed in the next section.

A significant issue in phasic analysis is whether the lower-level codes are regarded as constituents or indicators of the phases. If the assumption is that the phases are constituted by the acts within them, then the aggregation or pattern of acts corresponds directly to the phase. If the phase is assumed to be an independent higher-order construct (such as a conflict or debate over a proposal) that is indicated by the lower-level codes, then it is necessary to take into account that there may be "error" in the lower-level "observed" codes. When "out-of-phase" codes occur during the phase, they may be a function of error, for example, when a participant tries to introduce a new function but the bid is not accepted by other participants. In this case, it is necessary to "smooth" the sequence by not counting the phasic functions of the error codes, as Holmes and Poole (1991) do in their algorithm for flexible phase mapping.

Sequence Comparison Techniques. When we have multiple instances of the same process – such as multiple cases of groups making a decision – we may ask how similar various instances are in terms of sequential development. Addressing this question can enable identification of higher-level constructs in the form of types of sequences or sub-sequences.

The most straightforward way to derive typologies is to do so via qualitative methods that involve preparation of standard narrative, visual or numerical representations and grouping them according to similarity of appearance. I will discuss this in the section on visualization.

Sequences can also be compared formally using algorithmic methods. Optimal matching (OM) is the most commonly used sequence comparison technique in social scientific research (Brzinsky-Fay & Kohler, 2010). It generates measures of "distance" between pairs of sequences in a set: Similar sequences have low distance values and the more dissimilar a pair of sequences is, the greater the distance. These distances are based on the number of transformation operations – substitution, insertion, and deletion – required to turn one sequence into another (Kruskal, 1983; Cornwell, 2015). Poole et al. (2017) go into more depth on the details of calculating similarities via optimal matching.

To derive typologies of sequences systematically we can analyze the matrix of distances between sequences with cluster analysis and/or multidimensional scaling. The resulting clusters can be used to define different sequence types. Poole and Holmes (1995) present one example of the application of this approach.

Methods for Identifying Relationships among Tracks. Another approach for identifying higher-level constructs from lower-level codings is to identify relationships among two or more tracks. For example, Poole and Roth (1989) coded task function and group climate tracks for decision-making discussions and used the two tracks to define higher-order constructs (e.g., cooperative problem analysis versus conflicted problem analysis). In this case, Poole and Roth used specific definitions to combine the two tracks. For example, when one of the group climate codes, *opposition*, occurred at the same time as the task function code *solution development*, the act was classified as *solution conflict*, a higher-level construct.

Time series synchronization. It is also possible to identify track relationships inductively. One approach for identifying relationships among tracks is analysis of synchrony between time series representing the tracks. In general terms, synchrony refers to stable patterns among two or more sequences. Most time series analysis packages have measures of synchrony; the R package Synchrony (Gouhier & Guichard, 2014), for example, includes measures for directly assessing time series synchrony, but also for the off-set of events to provide indices of how two or more series that are not precisely coordinated still develop in synchronous fashion (harmonic entrainment).

The first step is to segment the sequence into units that allow aggregation of acts on the track into a continuous measure reflecting the amount of each code that occurs during the unit. This yields a time series of continuous values that can be subjected to synchrony analysis. Then this time series can be used to determine cross track synchrony in terms of how multiple tracks reflect similar frequencies of events across a time series. For example, Murase et al. (2015) calculated community-wide synchrony using two event sequences in each of their teams (coordination between teams and coordination within teams). Another measure is "phase lock," an index indicating the stability of the relationship between two tracks over time. Phase lock can be used to identify synchronization and alternation patterns across tracks, which signal different types of inter-track relationships.

State Space Analysis. It is often argued that interaction is a complex dynamic system (e.g., Arrow, McGrath, & Berdahl, 2000). Identification of properties of dynamic complex systems, such as movement in a state space, attractors and repellors, and phase transitions in which the system reconfigures itself, is fundamental to establishing the nature of complex interaction systems. State space models are used to study temporal dynamics in a variety of fields, including engineering, statistics, and economics.

Lewis, Lamey, and Douglas (1999) developed State Space Grid Analysis to facilitate complex dynamic systems analysis for coded data (in their case, socioemotional development in infant-mother interaction). In its simplest format, the state space represents two different dimensions, coded at the same level and temporal granularity. There must be codes on both dimensions for every temporal unit or act. Lewis et al. used values for intensity of the infant's distress and the angle of the infant's gaze at her/his mother, but we could also use task and socioemotional dimensions of interaction. The values of the codes are then mapped onto a two-dimensional grid and the values of the two dimensions plotted over time, as in Figure 18.3.

Movement through this state space can then be tracked and points on the grid that are attractors and repellors are identified. Attractors are combinations of codes that are particularly common and repellors are combinations that rarely occur. Phase transitions are indicated by periods in which movement on the grid becomes more variable and spreads over more cells, followed by "resettling" into a pattern in which there is a new set of attractors and repellors and a new structure of

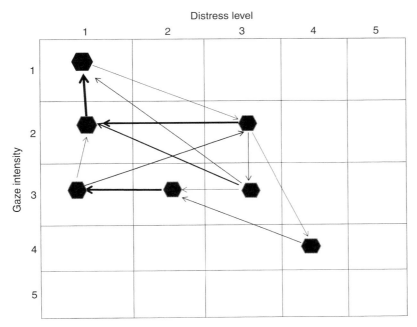

Figure 18.3 *State Space Grid.*

movement. Hollenstein (2007) illustrates graphical and statistical tests for phase transitions.

Visualization. A final approach to identification of patterns across tracks and levels uses graphical techniques to show relations among tracks and across levels. Phase maps and State Space Grids, of course, use visualization for this purpose. Visualizations are most useful when analyzing a large sample of sequences or episodes, because they facilitate comparison of sequences and identification of types through interpretation rather than numerical approaches such as optimal matching. The discerning eye of a knowledgeable researcher is often much better for pattern recognition than computational approaches. *TraMineR* and *STATA*, for example, provide visualizations for the comparison of phase sequences. See also Koch, Ritz, Kleindienst, and Brüngger, this volume, Chapter 20.

Conclusion

Meaning and the social world are multifaceted, layered phenomena, and they best yield their secrets when we can unpack and specify their levels and dimensions of the relationships among them. As this chapter shows, a great deal of effort has been devoted to working out relationships among tracks and levels of meaning and there has been progress in the development of analytical approaches and methods.

The two general approaches to specifying cross-level relationships, by rule and by operation, are complementary. The overall trend is to push to define specific rules linking levels and the combination of tracks within levels, and in some cases this may be possible, whereas in others the best we may be able to do is to develop semi-structured rule sets.

A number of methods are available for defining higher-level constructs from lower-level codings and for the analysis of cross-track and cross-level relationships. While some of them are quite sophisticated statistically, deriving higher-order constructs almost always involves human interpretive analysis to recognize meaningful patterns and to define constructs at higher levels from the many possibilities that these methods tend to yield.

At this point, there are no standardized, canonical methods for coding and analysis across tracks. An important direction for further development is development of standard, replicable methodological schemes for multilevel coding and analysis. It is still the "Wild West" out there in that much methodological improvisation is required and few reliable guides or guidelines exist. But the "West" (or at least the version of it we see in movies) is interesting and a bit fun. There is much room for innovation and building anew.

References

Aisenbrey, S., & Fasang, A. E. (2010). New life for old ideas: The "second wave" of sequence analysis: Bringing the "course" back into the life course. *Sociological Methods and Research, 38,* 420–462. doi:10.1177/0049124109357532

Arrow, H., McGrath, J. E., & Berdahl, J. L. (2000). *Small groups as complex systems: Formation, coordination, development, and adaptation.* Thousand Oaks, CA: Sage.

Bakeman, R., & Gottman, J. M. (1997). *Observing interaction: An introduction to sequential analysis.* Cambridge, UK: Cambridge University Press.

Bales, R. F. (1950). *Interaction process analysis: A method for the study of small groups.* Cambridge, MA: Addison-Wesley.

Bales, R. F., & Strodtbeck, F. L. (1951). Phases in group problem-solving. *Journal of Abnormal and Social Psychology, 46,* 485–495.

Bavelas, J., Black, A., Chovil, N., & Mullett, J. (1990). *Equivocal communication.* Newbury Park, CA: Sage.

Bion, W. R. (1961). *Experiences in groups,* London, UK: Tavistock.

Brzinsky-Fay, C., & Kohler, U. (2010). New developments in sequence analysis. *Sociological Methods and Research, 38,* 359–364. https://doi.org/10.1177/0049124110363371

Brzinsky-Fay, C., Kohler, U., & Luniak, M. (2006). Sequence analysis with Stata. *Stata Journal, 6,* 435–460.

Butts, C. T. (2008). A relational event framework for social action. *Sociological Methodology, 38*, 155–200.

Cornwell, B. (2015). *Social sequence analysis: Methods and applications*. Cambridge, UK: Cambridge University Press.

Gabadinho, A., Ritschard, G., Müller, N. S., & Studer, M. (2011). Analyzing and visualizing state sequences in R with TraMineR. *Journal of Statistical Software, 40*, 1–37.

Gottman, J. M. (1979). *Marital interaction: Experimental investigations*. New York, NY: Academic Press.

Gouhier, T. C., & Guichard, F. (2014). Synchrony: Quantifying variability in space and time. *Methods in Ecology and Evolution, 5*, 524–533.

Hollenstein, T. (2007). State space grids: Analyzing dynamics across development. *International Journal of Behavioral Development, 31*, 384–396. doi:10.1177/0165025407077765

Holmes, M., & Poole, M. S. (1991). The longitudinal analysis of interaction. In B. Montgomery & S. Duck (Eds.), *Studying interpersonal interaction* (pp. 286–302). New York, NY: Guilford.

Kashy, D. A., & Kenny, D. A. (2000). The analysis of data from dyads and groups. In H. T. Reis & C. M. Judd (Eds.), *Handbook of research methods for social psychology*. Cambridge, UK: Cambridge University Press.

Klein, K. J., & Kozlowski, S. W. J. (Eds.) (2000). *Multilevel theory, research, and methods in organizations: Foundations, extensions, and new directions*. San Francisco, CA: Jossey-Bass.

Kruskal, J. B. (1983). Sequence comparison. In D. Sankoff & J. B. Kruskal (Eds.), *Time warps, string edits, and macromolecules: The theory and practice of sequence comparison* (pp. 1–21). Reading, MA: Addison-Wesley.

Lewis, M. D., Lamey, A. V., & Douglas, L. (1999). A new dynamic systems method for the analysis of early socioemotional development. *Developmental Science, 2*, 457–475.

Meyers, R. A., & Brashers, D. E. (2010). Extending the conversational argument coding scheme: Argument categories, units, and coding procedures. *Communication Methods and Measures, 4*, 27–45.

Miller, G. A. (1956). The magical number seven, plus or minus two: Some limits on our capacity for processing information. *Psychological Review, 63*(2), 81–97.

Murase, T., Asencio, R., DeChurch, L. A., Contractor, N., Mathieu, J. E., & Poole, M. S. (2015, November). *The effect of synchronization of group processes on multiteam system effectiveness*. Group Communication Division, National Communication Association Conference, Las Vegas, NV.

Pilny, A., Schecter, A., Poole, M. S., & Contractor, N. (2016). An illustration of the relational event model to analyze group interaction processes. *Group Dynamics: Theory, Research, and Practice, 20*, 181–195. http://dx.doi.org/10.1037/gdn0000042.

Poole, M. S., & Holmes, M. E. (1995). Decision development in computer-assisted group decision making. *Human Communication Research, 22*, 90–127.

Poole, M. S., Lambert, N., Murase, T., Asencio, R., & McDonald, J. (2017). Sequential analysis of processes. In A. Langley & H. Tsoukas (Eds.), *Sage handbook of process organization studies* (pp. 254–270). Beverly Hills, CA: Sage.

Poole, M. S., & Roth, J. (1989). Decision development in small groups IV: A typology of decision paths. *Human Communication Research, 15*, 323–356.

Poole, M. S., Van de Ven, A. H., Dooley, K., & Holmes, M. E. (2000). *Organizational change and innovation processes: Theory and methods for research*. New York, NY: Oxford University Press.

Rogers, L. E., & Cummings, J. A. (2017). Relational communication control. In C. A. VanLear & D. J. Canary (Eds.) *Researching interactive communication behavior* (pp. 93–106). Thousand Oaks, CA: Sage.

Seibold, D. R., & Weger, H. W. (2017). The conversational argument coding scheme. In VanLear, C. A., & Canary, D. J. (Eds.), *Researching interactive communication behavior: A sourcebook of methods and measures* (pp. 159–174). Los Angeles, CA: Sage.

Tschan, F. (1995). Communication enhances small group performance if it conforms to task requirements: The concept of ideal communication cycles. *Basic and Applied Social Psychology, 17*, 371–393.

VanLear, C. A., & Canary, D. J. (2017). *Researching interactive communication behavior: A sourcebook of methods and measures*. Los Angeles, CA: Sage.

Weick, K. E. (1979). *The social psychology of organizing*. Reading, UK: Addison-Wesley.

19 Introduction to Machine Learning

Teaching Computers to Code Group Interaction Data

Joseph A. Bonito and Joann Keyton

This chapter offers an overview of supervised machine learning (SML) and its application to coding transcribed data of group interaction. SML is a type of computer-based text processing that uses human-coded data to train the software to identify relationships between the text and the codes. Examples include sentiment analysis (Taboada, Brooke, Tofiloski, Voll, & Stede, 2011), the purpose of which is to measure opinions about a particular topic from a variety of text sources (e.g., blogs), and identifying political orientation from Twitter feeds (Colleoni, Rozza, & Arvidsson, 2014). Applied to group interaction, machines are trained to classify discussion from a set of human-coded exemplars. Ideally, a well-trained machine and its underlying mathematical representation of the data can be used to classify new, unlabeled, or uncoded data. Thus, one might train a machine on transcribed data that were human-coded, for example, with Bales' (1950) interaction process analysis (IPA) and in turn use the machine to code data from other groups without having to use human coders.[1]

SML follows a deductive or top-down approach to coding, in which both text and human-generated codes are the input that allows the machine to learn which content goes with which codes (Burscher, Odijk, Vliegenthart, Rijke, & Vreese, 2014; Burscher, van Spanje, & de Vreese, 2015). The coding system itself is developed by researchers and derived from theory, for example functional communication (Gouran, Hirokawa, Julian, & Leatham, 1993; Wittenbaum et al., 2004), or from general features of group interaction, such as argument (Meyers & Brashers, 2010). In contrast, *unsupervised machine learning* is an inductive or bottom-up process – the machine identifies a series of text clusters from which the researcher chooses the most interpretable set (Lambert, 2001). The difference between supervised and unsupervised approaches is clear – the former requires the development and assessment of a coding system *in advance* of its computer application whereas the latter *depends* on computer algorithms to identify latent structures in the data.

As most group researchers are (painfully) aware, much time and effort are required to collect and process group interaction data. Details for recording and

---

[1] The ability of a trained machine to code new data depends crucially on the match between the discussion contexts from which the training and new datasets were collected. IPA seems applicable across many discussion tasks but might not work as well with some types of meetings, for example brainstorming (Scheerhorn, Geist, & Teboul, 1994).

transcribing data are certainly important, and choices made at these stages influence analytic options that follow (Edwards, 1993). Here, and for supervised machine learning, we assume that the data have been transcribed and unitized reliably by humans (Guetzkow, 1950). Unitization choice, of course, depends on both theoretical and practical concerns – in some cases, it makes sense to segment at the speaking-turn level, for example, when speaker exchange is of interest, and in other cases smaller units are warranted or desired (Auld Jr. & White, 1956; see also Reed, Metzger, Kolbe, Zobel, & Boos, this volume, Chapter 11).

Large datasets are generally useful because machine classification improves as the size of the training set increases – the more coded exemplars provided, the better the machine's *understanding* of the relationship between content and labels. Data from group interactions illustrate this problem, because such data can generate corpora of many thousand units. For example, Beck and Keyton (2009; Keyton & Beck, 2009) studied three different *bona fide* groups (see Putnam & Stohl, 1990) and recorded 16 different meetings on a variety of issues and topics. The interactions were transcribed and segmented at the thought-unit level, producing in excess of 15,000 units across the 16 meetings. For studying group interaction, most laboratory studies and some field studies likely provide enough data for developing successful machine learning algorithms.

Although SML offers promise, we caution readers not to get overly excited by – or overly concerned with – computer-assisted coding of group interaction. Reliable application of most coding schemes requires some degree of intuition and experience, and the development of the *training set* (the human-coded interaction units that are used to train the machine) is only as good as the rationale that underlies the coding system in question. But there is evidence that computer software can be trained to code interaction just about as well as humans, at least under some circumstances (e.g., Colleoni et al., 2014). The obvious advantage to using SML to code group interaction is the ability to process many thousands of message units quickly and reliably and that the system can be reliably applied to new, uncoded data. The problems of recording, transcribing, and unitizing discussion data still exist, though work on those fronts suggests some degree of help is on the way (Jarnow, 2016; Maas et al., 2017), and somewhat ironically advancement in interaction transcription is itself a complex machine learning problem.

The Mechanics of Supervised Machine Learning

Here we discuss the mechanics of machine learning using the AMI dataset. We first describe the dataset then discuss how the data are prepared for analysis. Following that, we demonstrate the process of machine learning using R's *tm* (Feinerer & Hornik, 2017; Meyer, Hornik, & Feinerer, 2008) and *RTextTools packages* (Jurka, Collingwood, Boydstun, Grossman, & van Atteveldt, 2014), though other packages are available, for example those based on the Python programming language (Ivezić, Connolly, VanderPlas, & Gray, 2014). Following that, we discuss our results and the application of SML to group discussion data.

The AMI Dataset

The AMI Meeting Corpus, released in 2006, is a multimodal dataset consisting of 100 hours of meeting recordings. Thus, it is an obvious choice for supervised machine learning, as the dataset consists of enough transcribed meetings to allow for the *training* as well as the coding of the units of interactions. A 15-member European-funded multidisciplinary consortium created this corpus. One of the consortium goals was to develop meeting technology that improves work-group effectiveness by giving better access to the group's history. The data have been used for the purpose of testing technological developments in meeting management and recording and transcribing technologies. The design of the dataset, however, was broadly conceived as natural, uncontrolled conversations, such that scholars in linguistics, organizational and social psychology, speech and language engineering, video processing, and multimodal systems would find value in the dataset. About two-thirds of the data were generated using a scenario in which the participants assume different roles in a design team (i.e., project manager, marketing expert, user interface designer, industrial designer), taking a design project from kick-off to completion over the course of a day. These are the data used for this chapter. Many journal articles and conference presentations have been made with these data, especially in the field of Computer Science; the data continue to be used and were the most widely used source of data at the 2013 Interspeech Conference (International Speech Communication Association, comprised primarily of speech science and technology engineers). Details of the dataset can be found at http://groups .inf.ed.ac.uk/ami/corpus/.

A set of guidelines were produced by the consortium to standardize manual transcription completed with the Transcriber tool developed at University of California, Berkeley. All transcriptions were verified through a two- or three-pass system. The first pass was the transcription from multichannel audio to text, the second pass was for verification, and the third pass (when needed) identified spelling or format problems. Transcripts are time-synchronized with the digitized audio recordings and feature microphone channel IDs for distinguishing speakers. Carletta (2007) provides an evaluative review of the corpus; Hain et al. (2007) provide a review of the technical specifications of the transcribing system and techniques used to evaluate the transcript data.

The AMI Corpus and the research studies based on it are different than the meeting transcripts typically used in the Communication discipline. Rather, the AMI Corpus was developed to explore engineering problems (e.g., detecting speaker overlap, identifying formal and informal roles based on prosody or eye gaze) for which solutions can be developed and applied to human-machine interfaces. Typically, these engineering problems are not content reliant, nor are they centrally interested in human-human interactions. However, since the corpus became available, researchers are beginning to explore its potential for identifying and understanding verbal and nonverbal characteristics of interactive talk (Bonito, Keyton, & Ervin, 2017; Ervin, Bonito, & Keyton, 2017; Gorisch, Wells, & Brown, 2012).

Consistent with previous research (e.g., Bonito, 2003; Bonito & Meyers, 2011; Meyers, 1989), participants' speech was coded at the thought-unit level (Auld Jr. & White, 1956). Thought units correspond to an independent clause, though shorter units that imply a complete thought (e.g., backchannels) were also included. The consequence of using the thought unit instead of speaking turns is that a given turn often contains several complete thoughts, though there is evidence that speaking turns and thought units are highly correlated (Tsai, 1977).

Each of the AMI groups analyzed here participated in four different discussions in the same order, resulting in four transcripts per group. The task itself was to design a new type of remote control. The discussions, in order, were the project kick-off, functional design, conceptual design, and detailed design. Time between discussions was used for individual work on the project. The kick-off consisted of participants becoming acquainted with the task and each other. The functional design task established user requirements, working design, and technical functionality, whereas the conceptual design discussions focused on the components, properties, and materials to be used in the remote control. Finally, the participants finalized the look and feel of the remote during the detailed design discussions.

An excerpt from the AMI dataset is presented in Table 19.1. It is from group ES2002 at the beginning of the second discussion in which participants were instructed to develop the functional design of the remote control. The data were

Table 19.1 *Excerpt from the AMI Corpus*

Unit	Speaker	Text	Code
1	B	Um, so so far, just to recap you've got volume and channel control and	Inform
2	C	There's um on and off, um volume and channel, and skip to certain channels with the numbers	Inform
3	B	Right okay	Assess
4	D	Well, one one way I would look at this um would be that we a approach the different controls in terms of um like control types	Suggest
5	D	so that for the user it's very clear what they want to do where they go	Inform
6	B	Mm-hmm yeah	Backchannel

segmented at the thought-unit level. Although speaker designation is generally not useful for classification, we include it here for readability. The *text* and *code* columns contained the transcribed discussion and human-assigned codes, respectively. In what follows, we use the excerpt to illustrate several of the data processing steps.

Preprocessing the AMI Data

It is often important to reduce *noise* in the data, which is defined as text characteristics that impede or hinder classification (Taboada et al., 2011). Several preprocessing options to reduce noise are available for the terms or words in a dataset (Grimmer & Stewart, 2013), the most important of which is stemming. For example, consider the words *group, groups, groupings*, and *grouped*. One could choose to treat each as a separate term but it is often preferable to convert the last three to *group*. There are linguistic reasons for stemming, but the practical effect is to reduce the number of terms in the term-document matrix. Consider two documents (i.e., discussion units), the first of which contains "group" and the second "groups." Assuming the two units/documents have no other words in common, stemming would identify each document has having the word stem "group" in common; without stemming, the two texts/documents would have no common words. Word commonality across documents is the basis for classification, so it is clear that stemming plays a vital role in the process.

Other preprocessing options that affect the dimensionality of the term-document matrix include (a) removing capitalization (e.g., so that "Group" and "group" are treated as the same term), (b) converting numbers to their text equivalents (i.e., "9" becomes "nine") or removing numbers entirely if the research application warrants it, and (c) identifying stop words, a vector of terms that is excluded from the analysis. Some programs have prepackaged stop-word lists, which usually include grammatical functions words (e.g., "the", "a", "an") that are usually, but not always, unhelpful for classification.[2] Most programs allow the user to include custom stop words, usually words that occur so frequently across the document vector space as to be relatively useless for classification. For example, Bonito (2001) asked groups to develop a psychological profile of a fictitious person named Jim, and because participants mentioned the word "Jim" often, it was included in the list of stop words.

Representing the AMI Data as Numbers

The AMI data are unitized at the level of the thought unit. Thus, each thought unit is considered a *document* – a separate entity in the corpus that contributes to how the machine learns the relationship among the words in the data that allows for

---

[2] Although our explication is based on the English language, machine learning is obviously not restricted to any language.

Table 19.2 *Term-document matrix for the AMI data extract*

Term	Document					
	1	2	3	4	5	6
approach	0	0	0	1	0	0
certain	0	1	0	0	0	0
channel	1	2	0	0	0	0
clear	0	0	0	0	1	0
control	1	0	0	2	0	0
differ	0	0	0	1	0	0
far	1	0	0	0	0	0
got	1	0	0	0	0	0
just	1	0	0	0	0	0
like	0	0	0	1	0	0

classification. The words in each document provide the basis for analysis and classification. The *term-document matrix* consists of an array containing the unique words in the dataset in the rows and each document as a column, whereas the *document-term matrix* has the documents in the rows and terms in the columns. (Although our example uses the term-document matrix some packages work with document-term version.) The cells are frequency counts of the number of times a given word appears in a particular document. Ignoring the coding for a moment, applying the preprocessing described above (and adding "um" to the software's list of standard stop words) the data in the example contain 27 unique words. For example, the first unit in the excerpt reduces to "far just recap youv got volum channel control." The most frequently occurring words are "channel" and "control," each of which occurs three times in the excerpt. The resulting term-document matrix for this excerpt is 27 terms (the rows) × 6 documents (the columns), with each cell containing each term's frequency in each document. The first 10 rows are presented in Table 19.2.

One can see that the word "channel" occurs in documents 1 and 2, though of course that is evident from simply inspecting the text. Obviously, the term-document matrix grows quite rapidly as the number of documents is added to the corpus but the logic is the same; words co-occur in some documents but not others. And co-occurrence is exactly the point, or in this case the starting point, for machine learning. Returning to the excerpt in Table 19.1 and now considering the human-generated codes, units (i.e., documents) 1 and 2 were both coded as *inform* and both contain the words "channel" and "volume." In fact, in this excerpt, those two words do not occur in the other four units. It appears then that those two words are linked with the category *inform*. Notice, however, that the fifth unit was also coded as *inform* but does not contain either "channel" or "volume." Moreover, the term "control" appears twice in unit 4, which is coded as *suggest* and once in the first unit, which, as noted, is coded as *inform*.

Obviously, the same category can include different terms and the same term can appear in several different categories. This is an important issue and it is helpful at this point to revisit coding of interaction data to address it. More often than not, coding rules depend on several interaction features, only one of which is content. As an example, perhaps the simplest coding scheme is identifying shared and unique information from hidden profile designs (Stasser & Titus, 2003), as in most cases the distribution of information is known to the researcher prior to the study. Thus, if a researcher-provided piece of information is given to all participants prior to interaction, when mentioned during discussion it is coded as *shared*. The same process applies to unique information. But other coding schemes require intuition in addition to, or sometimes in opposition to, the content.

For example, Bales' (1950) IPA contains 12 codes, one of which is *gives suggestion*. Most native speakers of English know what a suggestion sounds or looks like in an English transcript, and the words "one way" in unit 4 from the extract above gives the impression that a suggestion is being made. There are many variations on the theme but other tokens of *give suggestion* include "maybe," "what if," "why don't we," and so on. In that sense, *gives suggestion* is seemingly independent of the task, a type of interaction unit that occurs across contexts. For example, one presumably gives suggestions when discussing budgets, or making hiring decisions, or deliberating a criminal case. Another category in the IPA is *gives information*, which contains terms that are specific to the task or charge. Thus, giving information during a budget meeting, for example, might consist of revenue and expenditure estimates; in a jury deliberation giving information is focused on evidence and testimony.

In addition to the content-category relationship, coding schemes often depend, sometimes implicitly, on unit sequencing. For example, a unit coded as *asks for suggestions* is likely to be followed by suggestions, and *asks for information* generally compels members to provide information. Most machine-learning software treats units as independent (cf. Nguyen et al., 2013), which excludes sequential relationships from the learning algorithm. To further complicate matters, machine-learning algorithms generally treat words *within units* as independent, so that "remote control" does not refer to the device but rather to two distinct terms. Software can be tweaked to investigate higher-order n-grams (i.e., the term-document matrix consists of word pairs or triplets rather than single words) though there is conflicting evidence as to the utility of doing so (Grimmer & Stewart, 2013).

The preceding identifies problems familiar to researchers who have grappled with processing group interaction data. Yet the point is clear – machine-learning accuracy is only as good as the reliability and validity of the coding system in question. High reliability implies that many of the issues described above (e.g., nonindependent content) have been resolved so that independent coders consistently and reliably assign units to categories. Machine-learning models are simply mathematical representations of the relationship between content and classification, and therefore lack anything resembling representational validity (Poole & Folger, 1981). The use of "automated methods ... implies that the models should be evaluated based on their ability to perform some useful social scientific task" (Grimmer & Stewart, 2013, p. 270). For group researchers in particular the processing and classification of group interaction data seems a useful task indeed.

Machine Learning in Practice

Despite the caveats and cautions provided above, there is great potential in applying machine-learning algorithms to group-interaction data. We turn to an illustration of supervised machine learning using the full AMI dataset (Carletta, 2007; Carletta et al., 2006). We used the *gold standard* transcripts provided on the AMI website. Our own estimate (Bonito et al., 2017) of unitization reliability based on the segmented and coded transcripts is $U = .019$, and the best reported estimate for intercoder reliability is *kappa* = .67 (Reidsma, Heylen, & Op Den Akker, 2009). In what follows, we use the R packages *tm* (Feinerer & Hornik, 2017; Meyer et al., 2008) and *RTextTools* (Jurka et al., 2014) to process the data from the AMI study. In addition to preprocessing the text, the researcher is faced with a range of choices regarding the conversion of text to numbers. For the most part, we skip the statistical details related to machine learning and instead describe the primary choices and their consequences. We encourage the interested reader to consult James, Witten, Hastie, and Tibshirani (2013) for general principles and modeling issues and Grimmer and Stewart (2013) for issues particular to text classification and applications in the social sciences.

The AMI data consist of 110,795 coded thought units. We chose to remove from the data units coded as *stall, fragment, be negative, be positive, elicit offers or suggestions, elicit comment about understanding, comment about understanding, backchannel,* and *other* because they either occurred infrequently or we judged the category-to-text relationship too vague to be reliable. The remaining data consisted of 72,308 thought units. From this we chose a random sample of 10,000 units for this example, as doing so provides an unbiased set for machine learning (Hand, 2006).[3]

We preprocessed the data as described above except we decided not to use the built-in list of English stop words because many of the words contained in it were deemed useful for classification. For example, the word "right" signifies agreement

---

[3] Some reasons for taking a random sample of units include, for example, that coders might develop a better handle on the coding as they coded more examples, that units appear more frequently early or later in the interaction, that coders might get bored the more units coded, and so on.

and "seem" indicates a qualification.[4] Rather, we limited word length to a minimum of three characters (the default in the R *tm* package); shorter words (and single letters, e.g., "a") were automatically excluded from the analysis. Thus, the preprocessing produced a dataset with 2,833 unique words (that were three characters and longer as well as *stemmed*). An important choice at this stage is term weighting, which is the process by which some words are given more classification importance than others. There are several options, only two of which are described here. The first weighs terms by frequency, with the most frequently occurring terms having the most weight in the classification process. Thus, the terms "yeah" ($N = 1517$) and "think" ($N = 694$), which ranked first and second, respectively, would have the most weight. The second option is to use the *inverse document frequency* (IDF) function, which gives the most weight to terms that appear most frequently in the fewest documents or units. In essence, the IDF identifies words with the greatest discriminatory power; words that occur quite frequently across many documents or occur only once in the dataset have little classificatory weight. For this example, we chose the IDF.

The Process of How the Machine Learns

At this point we are ready to employ SML to code the AMI data. The 10,000 units that we sampled from the entire corpus were further divided into the *training* ($N = 9,000$) and *testing* ($N = 1,000$) sets. The former, as the name implies, is used to train the machine in terms of the relationship between text and categories, and is not used in the data analysis; the second set is coded for data analysis by the machine using the developed classification probabilities. The testing set then contains the codes assigned by humans and those assigned by the machine. The testing set allows the comparison of human- and computer-generated codes using a variety of metrics, which we explain below.

Another choice facing the researcher in the process is the specification of the clustering functions that link the terms to the codes (James et al., 2013). The functions in effect train the software to associate content with categories. Many functions are available – short descriptions of and reference for those offered in *RTextTools* are provided in Jurka et al. (2014). Rather than choose one, however, researchers typically use several in what is termed an *ensemble approach*. For this example we used maximum entropy (ME), support vector machine (SVM), and glmnet (GLM), as they require the least amount of computer-processing resources. As we shall see, some functions perform better than others.

Tables 19.3 and 19.4 produce familiar-looking *confusion* matrices (also called an *error matrix*) that allow the researcher to visualize the performance of an algorithm in a supervised environment. The rows are the human-generated codes and the columns are those produced by the machine. The matrix in Table 19.3 is based on the SVM function and the one in Table 19.4 on the ME function. The diagonals

---

[4] The standard English stop word list appears at https://github.com/arc12/Text-Mining-Weak-Signals /wiki/Standard-set-of-english-stopwords.

Table 19.3 *Support vector machine (SVM) and human coding confusion matrix*

Human	Machine					
	1	2	3	4	5	6
1. Assess	191	0	1	84	1	1
2. Elicit assessment	6	4	0	22	0	1
3. Elicit information	2	0	4	41	0	2
4. Inform	45	1	3	423	0	14
5. Offer	2	0	0	15	2	1
6. Suggest	13	0	0	89	0	32

Table 19.4 *Maximum entropy (ME) and human coding confusion matrix*

Human	Machine					
	1	2	3	4	5	6
1. Assess	195	4	4	63	1	11
2. Elicit assessment	7	6	3	14	0	3
3. Elicit information	4	0	9	25	4	7
4. Inform	74	7	40	298	7	60
5. Offer	4	0	0	7	6	3
6. Suggest	25	3	5	59	3	39

indicate the agreement and the off-diagonals identify the type of disagreement. Perhaps the simplest and most familiar place for the researcher to start to evaluate machine performance is to calculate the proportion of exact agreement, which is the sum of the agreements (diagonals) to the matrix total. The estimates are .55, .66, and .65 for ME, SVM, and GLM, respectively. Thus, SVM and GLM demonstrate approximately 65 percent agreement with human coding, and the ME function seems to perform somewhat worse than the other two.

Other performance assessments include *precision* and *recall*. Precision is the ratio of correctly coded units (i.e., agreement between machine and human) for a given category by the machine to all of the units coded in that category by the machine.[5] Thus, precision for *assessments* for SVM (see Table 19.3) is 191/259 = .74; the machine guessed correctly on 74 percent of the units it coded as *assessments*. Precision for the other categories is calculated in similar fashion. Recall is the ratio of correctly coded units for a given category to all units

---

[5] This calculation ignores potential unreliability among human coders. In many applications, the first step in data processing is for coders to independently categorize a subset of the data, after which any disagreements are resolved. Once the process results in acceptable intercoder reliability, the final step is to divide the corpus into smaller, more manageable parts for coders to evaluate independently. Errors at this stage are likely, which clearly has some bearing on how well the machine does its job.

Table 19.5 *Averaged validation metrics for machine-learning algorithms*

	Precision	Recall	f-score
SVM	.661	.340	.385
GLMNET	.502	.307	.320
Maximum Entropy	.388	.377	.375

Table 19.6 *Ensemble validation for machine-learning algorithms*

Ensemble size	Coverage	Percent ensemble recall
n > = 1	1.00	.66
n > = 2	.98	.67
n > = 3	.51	.71

coded in that category by the human. For *assessments* in Table 19.3, recall is 191/278 = .69. What does this mean? Examining Table 19.3, we see that human coders identified 19 more assessments than did the machine (278 vs. 259) but when the machine did classify a unit as an *assessment*, it matched the human coders 69 percent of the time. The estimates by category for SVM are interesting for several reasons. Notice, for example, that recall for *inform* is quite high (87 percent) but that precision is lower (63 percent) primarily because the machine was more likely to code a unit as *inform* than were human coders. Finally, one may average the precision and recall scores for each function, though clearly doing so would give infrequently classified categories the same weight. The package *RTextTools* provides an *f*-score, which is the weighted average of precision and recall. Table 19.5 contains aggregated performance estimates for each function.

Two other validation strategies help evaluate performance. The first is *ensemble agreement*, which assesses agreement among the classification functions used in the analysis. Here we used SVM, ME, and GLM and results are presented in Table 19.6. The first column is called *coverage* and identifies the proportion of units on which the three functions agreed. The second column, *recall*, is the agreement between the functions and the human-generated codes. Thus, two of the functions agreed on 98 percent of the units and those codes agreed with human codes 67 percent of the time. All three functions agreed on 51 percent of the cases, and for those cases there was 71 percent agreement with the human coders. Thus, it appears for these data that agreement among the classification functions does not guarantee agreement with human coders. Using more functions might increase both ensemble agreement (or the aggregation of different estimation methods), as well as agreement between the ensemble and human coders.

The second form of validation is called *cross-validation*, which is a three-step process of training, model selection, and model testing (Grimmer & Stewart, 2013). In practice, cross-validation is often used by sampling subsets from the trained data and assessing each subset's performance on another training subset. One then computes the average accuracy of each pass or *fold*. This allows the examination of performance beyond that estimated from the testing set. The researcher may select any number of folds, though the size of the training set has some bearing on the number of folds that might be used (Fushiki, 2011). For this example, cross-validation using four folds produced average accuracy (i.e., agreement scores between machine and human) estimates of 80 percent for ME and 64 percent for SVM.

Assessing Disagreement

At this point it is helpful to compare human- and machine-coding disagreements in order to get a sense of the feature/classification mismatches. We present a small subset of the disagreements in Table 19.7. It is important to restate that the units are randomly drawn from the corpus and therefore are not in sequence (units within the table have no interaction-based relationship). In addition, the issues and problems here are particular to the classification scheme used to code the AMI data. Different tasks and/or coding schemes will likely display other types of problems.

The first column in Table 19.7 is the text for each unit. The remaining columns, labeled *Human, ME, SVM,* and *GLM,* contain human-generated codes and the three computer-generated classifications. Thus, the document in row 1 "Yeah, whatever" was coded as an *inform* by the human coder, and as an *assessment* by all three computer algorithms. Before proceeding, it is helpful to consider the AMI coding manual (Guidelines for Dialogue Act and Addressee Annotation Version 1.0, 2005). The instruction for *inform* is quite simple and perhaps overly vague: "the inform act is used by speaker to give information" (p. 12). Instructions for *suggest* are similarly straightforward:

> The speaker expresses an intention relating to the actions of another individual, the group as a whole, or a group in the wider environment. Sometimes, SUGGEST can take the form of a question, especially when the speaker is not sure that the group will accept the idea or suggestion. (Guidelines, 2005, p. 15)

Identifying *assessments*, however, is much more involved and unlike *suggest* and *inform*, the instructions reference previous discussion such that it is an evaluation of what someone or the group as a whole said. According to the instructions, *assessments*

> include, among other things, accepting an offer, expressing agreement/ disagreement or any opinion about some information that's been given, expressing uncertainty as to whether a suggestion is a good idea or not, evaluating actions by members of the group, such as drawings. (Guidelines, 2005, p. 17)

Table 19.7 *A sample of human/machine disagreements*

Text	Human	ME	SVM	GLM
Yeah, whatever	Inform	Assess	Assess	Assess
Yeah well, I was just gonna throw out there the thought about um personalising the remote control	Suggest	Assess	EI	EI
The looks remain the same	Inform	Assess	EI	EI
We can pretty much just do whatever we want	EI	Assess	EI	EI
Is that okay?	EA	Assess	Assess	Assess
why shouldn't we take a basic battery?	EA	Suggest	Offer	Offer
So we could say that was our target.	Suggest	Inform	EI	EI
So we could get it down to what?	EI	Suggest	Offer	Offer
It's just to indicate something's on	Inform	Suggest	EI	EI
Well we'll consider both	Offer	Suggest	EI	EI

Note: EA = Elicit Assessment; EI = Elicit Information; coding units displayed here are not in sequence.

Assessments, on this account and within this coding scheme, have a built-in sense of interdependence; as noted, the algorithms used here clearly treat each document/unit independently and thus cannot use preceding interactions to identify or classify the current unit.

Disagreements between machine and human coding may also hinge on a number of other factors. For example, perusal of the data reveals that nouns of objects appear frequently in the *inform* category. Of course, nouns also appear in other categories, but they are more abstract and not as directly related to the remote control being produced. For example, in Table 19.6, "the looks remain the same" is coded by a human coder as *inform* as "the looks" is a synonym for "the design." But, all three versions of machine coding coded this segment as *assess* or *elicit information*. A second consideration quite important to some group-interaction scholars is that machine learning does not take into account *how* a message is delivered. Nonverbals (e.g., facial expressions, raising/lower voice while speaking, saying something in an ironic tone) can be central to a coder's decision in assigning thought units to categories. Third, the way in which the AMI data were segmented is not equivalent to more traditional social science views on unitizing. For this corpus, segmentation is described as broken up "into whatever chunks the transcribers thought were handy" or "not important" (Guidelines, 2005, p. 5).

Conclusion

In this chapter, we provided an introduction of interaction coding completed by supervised machine learning. Analyses we conducted demonstrate that "yes," supervised machine learning can be a useful tool for researchers who code by hand. By examining agreements, as well as disagreements, between human and machine coding, we illuminate some of the difficulties of relying on machine coding when researchers are interested in messages and meanings. However, machine learning is an important technological accomplishment, and our expectation is that it will continue to improve. We finish the chapter with some of our thoughts in an attempt to answer questions you may have after reading this chapter.

If machine coding can be improved, it may come through technological advancement, more discrete coding schemes, or development of clustering algorithms specific to interaction data. Humans are likely to be better at coding interaction in settings in which messages are comprised of more abstract words requiring the coder to rely upon the context to be understood. Perhaps information about the context can be drawn from information about the data-collection context (as well as the transcripts) and provided as *contextual coding rules* in addition to the coding rules for category assignment. As scholars continue to improve machine coding, then the ability to train on data from one context and apply it to another context becomes possible.

Another way to evaluate machine coding is to reconsider the level of satisfactory agreement. We believe that one reason a relatively high level of agreement was achieved between the machine algorithms and human coders is because a majority of codes were categorized as *inform*. For the most part, message units labeled in this way do not depend on sequential structure, at least not like some of the other codes (and coding schemes). Working with machine coding might also result in scholars revisiting what is considered a satisfactory level of agreement for publication. One aspect of the moderate agreement achieved with machine coding reported here is that sequences of talk were not considered in the analyses (cf. Nguyen et al., 2013). Creative experiments with textual datasets (and many coding schemes) may help to establish new guidelines for expectations of unitizing and coder reliability for future research. While group interaction scholars are most interested in sequences of group member talk, other interesting analyses could be developed by eliminating a pure sequence requirement.

Another disadvantage of machine coding is the exclusion of short units of talk (e.g., "yeah") that communication researchers, in particular, believe are important for understanding how a conversation unfolds, as well as identifying power dynamics within a group. The worst-case scenario is that machine learning will be deemed as not suitable for interaction analysis because it focuses only on message unit and not on the sequences of message units. The best-case scenario is that machine learning would encourage group scholars to identify and test more macro properties and principles of human speech.

Essentially, *groupies* (those that study group interaction) and *geeks* (those that create social signal processing technologies) are beginning to talk across disciplinary boundaries (e.g., the workshop on Interdisciplinary Insights into Group and Team Dynamics, held in 2016[6] or the special issue of *Small Group Research*, Issue

---

[6] See www.4tu.nl/ht/en/news/!/112600/workshop-group-dynamics/.

5, Vol. 48, 2017). It is these types of interdisciplinary collaborations that will ultimately create tools that improve the current state of machine-learning coding. These collaborations will require patience and time as scholars relearn to identify, process, code, and analyze transcribed interaction data in different ways.

References

Auld Jr., F., & White, A. M. (1956). Rules for dividing interviews into sentences. *Journal of Psychology: Interdisciplinary & Applied, 42*, 273–281. https://doi.org/10.1080/00223980.1956.9713040

Bales, R. F. (1950). *Interaction process analysis: A method for the study of small groups.* Cambridge, MA: Addison-Wesley.

Beck, S. J., & Keyton, J. (2009). Perceiving strategic meeting interaction. *Small Group Research, 40*, 223–246. https://doi.org/10.1177/1046496408330084

Bonito, J. A. (2001). An information-processing approach to participation in small groups. *Communication Research, 28*, 275–303. https://doi.org/10.1177/009365001028003002

Bonito, J. A. (2003). A social relations analysis of participation in small groups. *Communication Monographs, 70*, 83–97. https://doi.org/10.1080/0363775032000133755

Bonito, J. A., Keyton, J., & Ervin, J. N. (2017). Role-related participation in product design teams: Individual- and group-level trends. *Communication Research, 44*(2), 263–286. https://doi.org/10.1177/0093650215618759

Bonito, J. A., & Meyers, R. A. (2011). Examining functional communication as egocentric or group-centric: Application of a latent group model. *Communication Monographs, 78*, 463–485. https://doi.org/10.1080/03637751.2011.618138

Burscher, B., Odijk, D., Vliegenthart, R., Rijke, M. de, & de Vreese, C. H. (2014). Teaching the computer to code frames in news: Comparing two supervised machine learning approaches to frame analysis. *Communication Methods and Measures, 8*, 190–206. https://doi.org/10.1080/19312458.2014.937527

Burscher, B., van Spanje, J., & de Vreese, C. H. (2015). Owning the issues of crime and immigration: The relation between immigration and crime news and anti-immigrant voting in 11 countries. *Electoral Studies, 38*, 59–69. https://doi.org/10.1016/j.electstud.2015.03.001

Carletta, J. (2007). Unleashing the killer corpus: Experiences in creating the multi-everything AMI Meeting Corpus. *Language Resources and Evaluation, 41*, 181–190. https://doi.org/10.1007/s10579-007-9040-x

Carletta, J., Ashby, S., Bourban, S., Flynn, M., Guillemot, M., Hain, T., ... Wellner, P. (2006). The AMI meeting corpus: A pre-announcement. In S. Renals & S. Bengio (Eds.), *Machine learning for multimodal interaction* (Vol. 3869, pp. 28–39). Springer Berlin Heidelberg. Retrieved from http://link.springer.com/chapter/10.1007/11677482_3

Colleoni, E., Rozza, A., & Arvidsson, A. (2014). Echo chamber or public sphere? Predicting political orientation and measuring political homophily in twitter using big data. *Journal of Communication, 64*, 317–332. https://doi.org/10.1111/jcom.12084

Edwards, J. A. (1993). Principles and contrasting systems of discourse transcription. In J. A. Edwards & M. D. Lampert (Eds.), *Talking data: Transcription and coding in discourse research* (pp. 3–31). Hillsdale, NJ: Erlbaum.

Ervin, J. N., Bonito, J. A., & Keyton, J. (2017). Convergence of intrapersonal and interpersonal processes across group meetings. *Communication Monographs, 84*, 200–220. https://doi.org/10.1080/03637751.2016.1185136

Feinerer, I., & Hornik, K. (2017). tm: Text Mining Package (Version R package version 0.7–1). Retrieved from https://CRAN.R-project.org/package=tm

Fushiki, T. (2011). Estimation of prediction error by using K-fold cross-validation. *Statistics and Computing, 21*, 137–146. https://doi.org/10.1007/s11222-009-9153-8

Gorisch, J., Wells, B., & Brown, G. J. (2012). Pitch contour matching and interactional alignment across turns: An acoustic investigation. *Language and Speech, 55*, 57–76. https://doi.org/10.1177/0023830911428874

Gouran, D. S., Hirokawa, R. Y., Julian, K. M., & Leatham, G. B. (1993). The evolution and current status of the functional perspective on communication in decision-making and problem-solving groups. In J. Anderson (Ed.), *Communication yearbook 16* (pp. 573–600). Newbury Park, CA: Sage.

Grimmer, J., & Stewart, B. M. (2013). Text as data: The promise and pitfalls of automatic content analysis methods for political texts. *Political Analysis, 21*, 267–297. https://doi.org/http://dx.doi.org/10.1093/pan/mps028

Guetzkow, H. (1950). Unitizing and categorizing problems in coding qualitative data. *Journal of Clinical Psychology, 6*, 47–58. https://doi.org/http://dx.doi.org/10.1002/1097-4679(195001)6:1%3C47::AID-JCLP2270060111%3E3.0.CO;2-I

Guidelines for Dialogue Act and Addressee Annotation Version 1.0. (2005). Retrieved February 14, 2018, from http://groups.inf.ed.ac.uk/ami/corpus/Guidelines/dialogue_acts_manual_1.0.pdf

Hain, T., Wan, V., Burget, L., Karafiat, M., Dines, J., Vepa, J., & Lincoln, M. (2007). The AMI system for the transcription of speech in meetings. In *IEEE International Conference on Acoustics, Speech and Signal Processing, 2007. ICASSP 2007* (Vol. 4, p. IV-357–IV-360). https://doi.org/10.1109/ICASSP.2007.366923

Hand, D. J. (2006). Classifier technology and the illusion of progress. *Statistical Science, 21*, 1–14. https://doi.org/10.1214/088342306000000060

Interdisciplinary Insights into Group and Team Dynamics. (2017). Special Issue: *Small Group Research, 48*, 519–630.

Ivezić, Ž., Connolly, A. J., VanderPlas, J. T., & Gray, A. (2014). *Statistics, data mining, and machine learning in astronomy: A practical Python guide for the analysis of survey data*. Princeton, NJ: Princeton University Press.

James, G., Witten, D., Hastie, T., & Tibshirani, R. (2013). *An introduction to statistical learning: with applications in R* (1st edn. 2013, Corr. 6th printing 2016 edition). New York, NY: Springer.

Jarnow, J. (2016). Why our crazy-smart AI still sucks at transcribing speech. Retrieved March 16, 2017, from www.wired.com/2016/04/long-form-voice-transcription/

Jurka, T. P., Collingwood, L., Boydstun, A. E., Grossman, E., & van Atteveldt, W. (2014). RTextTools: Automatic text classification via supervised learning (Version

R package version 1.4.2). Retrieved from https://CRAN.R-project.org/package=RTextTools

Keyton, J., & Beck, S. J. (2009). The influential role of relational messages in group interaction. *Group Dynamics: Theory, Research, and Practice*, *13*, 14–30. https://doi.org/10.1037/a0013495

Lambert, B. L. (2001). Automatic content analysis of pharmacist-patient interactions using the Theme Machine document clustering system. In M. West (Ed.), *Progress in communication sciences, Volume 17: Applications of computer content analysis* (pp. 103–122). Westport, CT: Ablex.

Maas, A. L., Qi, P., Xie, Z., Hannun, A. Y., Lengerich, C. T., Jurafsky, D., & Ng, A. Y. (2017). Building DNN acoustic models for large vocabulary speech recognition. *Computer Speech & Language*, *41*, 195–213. https://doi.org/10.1016/j.csl.2016.06.007

Meyer, D., Hornik, K., & Feinerer, I. (2008). Text mining infrastructure in R. *Journal of Statistical Software*, *25*, 1–54. https://doi.org/10.18637/jss.v025.i05

Meyers, R. A. (1989). Testing persuasive argument theory's predictor model: Alternative interactional accounts of group argument and influence. *Communication Monographs*, *56*, 112–132. https://doi.org/10.1080/03637758909390254

Meyers, R. A., & Brashers, D. E. (2010). Extending the conversational argument coding scheme: Argument categories, units, and coding procedures. *Communication Methods and Measures*, *4*, 27–45. https://doi.org/10.1080/19312451003680467

Nguyen, V., Boyd-Graber, J., Resnik, P., Cai, D. A., Midberry, J. E., & Wang, Y. (2014). Modeling topic control to detect influence in conversations using nonparametric topic models. *Machine Learning*, *95*, 381–421. doi:10.1007/s10994-013-5417-9

Poole, M. S., & Folger, J. P. (1981). A method for establishing the representational validity of interaction coding systems: Do we see what they see? *Human Communication Research*, *8*, 26–42. https://doi.org/http://dx.doi.org/10.1111/j.1468-2958.1981.tb00654.x

Putnam, L. L., & Stohl, C. (1990). Bona fide groups: A reconceptualization of groups in context. *Communication Studies*, *41*, 248–265. https://doi.org/10.1080/10510979009368307

Reidsma, D., Heylen, D., & Op Den Akker, R. (2009). On the contextual analysis of agreement scores. In M. Kipp, J. Martin, P. Paggio, & D. Heylen (Eds.), *Multimodal corpora: From models of natural interaction to systems and applications* (pp. 122–137). Berlin, Germany: Springer-Verlag. Retrieved from http://dl.acm.org/citation.cfm?id=1809277.1809288

Scheerhorn, D., Geist, P., & Teboul, J. B. (1994). Beyond decision making in decision-making groups: Implications for the study of group communication. In L. R. Frey (Ed.), *Group communication in context: Studies of natural groups.* (pp. 247–262). Hillsdale, NJ: Lawrence Erlbaum.

Stasser, G., & Titus, W. (2003). Hidden profiles: A brief history. *Psychological Inquiry*, *14*, 304–313. https://doi.org/10.1207/S15327965PLI1403&4_21

Taboada, M., Brooke, J., Tofiloski, M., Voll, K., & Stede, M. (2011). Lexicon-based methods for sentiment analysis. *Computational Linguistics*, *37*, 267–307. https://doi.org/10.1162/COLI_a_00049

Tsai, Y. (1977). Hierarchical structure of participation in natural groups. *Behavioral Science*, *22*(1), 38–40. https://doi.org/10.1002/bs.3830220106

Wittenbaum, G. M., Hollingshead, A. B., Paulus, P. B., Hirokawa, R. Y., Ancona, D. G., Peterson, R. S., & Yoon, K. (2004). The functional perspective as a lens for understanding groups. *Small Group Research*, *35*, 17–43. https://doi.org/10.1177/1046496403259459

20 TINT

A Technique for Visualizing Team Processes

Julia Koch, Frank Ritz, Cornelia Kleindienst, and Jonas Brüngger

The present chapter focuses on the description of TINT (Team INTeraction), a technique that allows capturing and visualizing team processes throughout their development in time by taking collective, complex, dynamic, and naturalistic aspects into account. TINT supports researchers in exploring and understanding how teams organize their interactions within a naturalistic work setting, and to assess effective team behavior for a successful task fulfillment. Teams have to collectively adapt their team members' activities to the dynamic situational demands of the sociotechnical system to monitor and control its functioning and outcomes. In order to do so, the team members need to pursue shared goals, coordinate their activities, and be responsive to each other. They coordinate their intentions and actions based on cognitive representations of not only themselves but also the other team members. Such collective action can be described as "joint cooperative activities" (Bratman, 1992; Tomasello, Carpenter, Call, Behne, & Moll, 2005). TINT focuses on joint activities teams carry out to integrate individual knowledge and to elaborate and execute collective plans that help them to meet their common goals under the given situational requirements. For operationalization purposes, we draw on the concept of macrocognition (Cacciabue & Hollnagel, 1994; Klein, Ross, Moon, Klein, Hoffman, & Hollnagel, 2003). Macrocognitions describe specific types of joint team activities, e.g., detecting an unexpected situation, generating hypotheses about the situation, creating a strategy for achieving a desired state of their work system, and collectively executing action plans (Patterson, Miller, Roth, & Woods, 2010). This takes place in a realistic working context, which is typically characterized by complexity, ambiguity, high risks, time pressure, and conflicts of goals (Klein, Ross, Moon, Klein, Hoffman, & Hollnagel, 2003).

TINT allows focusing on the team as the examination unit and visualizing its joint team processes in a holistic and comprehensive manner. The resulting visualization can be used not only for in-depth assessment among researchers but also as a basis to stimulate discussion and reflection among the assessed teams. The possibility to include the teams' perspectives in the analysis process is what makes TINT an innovative and useful complement to quantitative analyses focusing on aggregated individual behavior data regarding frequencies and patterns (e.g., Stachowski, Kaplan, & Waller, 2009; Waller, 1999; Waller, Gupta, & Giambatista, 2004; Zala-Mezö, Wacker, Künzle, Brüesch, & Grote, 2009). TINT complements existing research methods with a more interpretative and naturalistic approach that respects that team processes are reciprocally embedded in specific work contexts and influenced by dynamic task demands. It is suitable not only for the enrichment of field and simulator-based studies to deepen scientific knowledge but also for an initialization of organizational learning processes about effective team processes in practice.

TINT: General Overview

TINT comprises a procedural framework of three steps to capture, visualize, and analyze the temporal development of joint team activities. It serves as a holistic analysis, complemented by a closer qualitative examination. In this chapter, we give a concrete example of how to apply TINT by describing how we used it for our case study of teams in a nuclear power plant adapting to an unexpected and novel event. TINT is meant to be adapted and transferred to various contexts and kinds of teamwork to assess the development of team processes over a certain period of time. It can be used to describe single cases of teamwork or to compare multiple cases (e.g., high- vs. low-performing teams), as we did in our study.

Context of the Development of TINT

We developed TINT against the background of a project in a nuclear power plant (as a part of the project "TeamSafe," see Ritz, Kleindienst, Brüngger, & Koch, 2015). Analogous to other types of high-risk organizations (Perrow, 1999), nuclear power plants employ teams that are responsible for permanently monitoring the system in a control room. They act in the event of incidents to ensure a safe functioning of the system. High-risk organizations are highly complex sociotechnical systems, in which developments can never fully be anticipated, and safety-critical events are not completely preventable (Grote, Weichbrodt, Günter, Zala-Mezö, & Künzle, 2009; Ritz, 2012). This has significant consequences for control room teams: While standardized procedures guide their course of action and coordinate their collaboration during their daily routine, manuals and guidelines may become obsolete in the face of an unexpected and up to that point novel event. In order to adapt and reestablish a safe system state, the teams need to develop a new action plan on the spot. This requires a fundamental change from a rule-driven towards a flexible work mode of collective problem solving (Vidal, Carvalho, Santos, & dos Santos, 2009). Burke, Stagl, Salas, Pierce, and Kendall (2006, p. 1190) describe team adaptation as "a change in team performance, in response to a salient cue or cue stream, that leads to a functional outcome for the entire team." According to the authors' concept, team adaptation encompasses a series of macrocognitions (situation assessment, plan formulation, plan execution, and team learning), which occur simultaneously, dynamically, and recursively at a team level.

Data Collection

We designed TINT as a technique for the analysis of scenario-based teamwork in a simulator or in the field. In either case, data should be collected in the form of video recordings, as they ensure the required flexibility for data coding and re-examining of key phases. For our study, control room teams of a nuclear power plant worked on a safety-critical scenario in a high-fidelity simulator. This approach was chosen because such safety-critical work situations in nuclear power plants are extremely rare to observe under real-world conditions. The scenario was designed in collaboration with instructors of the plant's training unit. It simulated a previously unknown situation that could not be handled by following standardized procedures and that would become safety-critical if not adequately managed. An initial leakage in the feed water pipe led to an increase of pressure and temperature within the containment. The team in the control room was given several notifications and alerts that call for immediate actions specified in the manual. Usually, the leakage would be identifiable due to an altered flow rate and could be repaired by simply following the manual. Due to an unfortunate combination with a second leakage in another part of the system, the situation in our scenario was not clearly interpretable. Therefore, the teams could not follow the entire standard procedure to identify the leaking pipe. They were required to notice the two leakages, to localize them, and to develop an appropriate action plan to solve the problem to prevent it from affecting the safety of the system. The training instructors of the power plant stopped the scenario as soon as the team decided on a definitive action plan and was about to execute it. Time pressure was moderate, which allowed for sufficient discussion within the team. With their consent, teams were recorded on video. The training instructors of the power plant rated the teams' technical performance, which we used as a basis to select specific cases for analysis.

How to Apply TINT

In the following, we will describe how to structure, visualize, and analyze the collected data with TINT. We illustrate the description of the technique with the example of a group comparison we conducted in our study. Based on the ratings of the training instructors (see previous paragraph), we selected the highest (team A) and the lowest (team B) performing teams for comparison. The description of our group comparison will give the readers a concrete idea of how TINT can be applied.

Figure 20.1 depicts the three steps researchers have to proceed through to apply TINT. In step 1, the recorded scenario is structured into segments for analysis. In step 2, macrocognitions throughout the scenario are coded and visualized for an analysis and team comparison regarding the frequency, duration, and temporal arrangement of several types of macrocognitions. Moreover, TINT includes a complementary qualitative analysis of specific scenario intervals (step 3). Said analysis deepens the understanding of how and why observed teams organize certain interaction sequences.

Step 1: Scenario Structuring

Initially, the storyline of the scenario is subdivided into different intervals to facilitate the analysis and allow comparison between different teams. The interval definitions are the same for all assessed cases (e.g., high- and low-performing teams). Each interval is characterized by a scenario-specific change in the situational demand, such as the need to assess the situation or to take immediate action to prevent further escalation. As an example, Table 20.1 depicts the interval definitions we set for our scenario.

Based on the interval definitions, the recorded scenario is coded separately for each team. The coding can then be visualized as presented in Figure 20.2: The timeline depicts the duration of the entire scenario of a team in minutes, and black brackets indicate the coded intervals 1 to 5 (according to the numbers in Table 20.1). The goal of this first step is to create orientation markers that facilitate the comparison across teams. As the intervals indicate different situational demands, it can be useful to compare the teams for each separate interval. The first interval marks the actual start of the scenario, which in our case is when the first system alarm went off and the team initiated problem-detection and situation assessment. The time can thus be counted from this point on, resulting in a total scenario time of 45 minutes for team A and 30 minutes for team B.

Table 20.1 *Example of interval definitions*

Intervals	Situational demands
1	Problem detection and situation assessment, triggered by a system-generated alarm
2	Immediate manual-based action to prevent further escalation
3	Reassessment of the situation, triggered by system parameters that are not clearly interpretable by means of the operator manual
4	Completing the current section for the immediate actions in the operator manual
5	Develop a further action plan

Figure 20.1 *The three steps of TINT.*

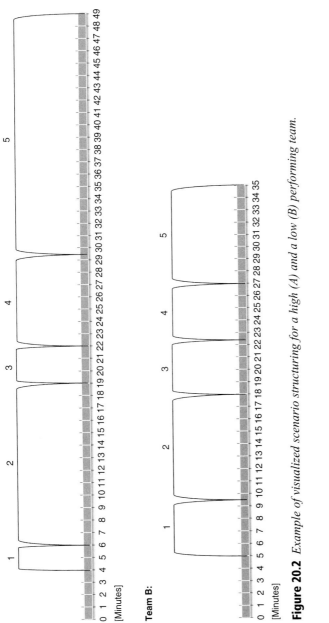

Figure 20.2 *Example of visualized scenario structuring for a high (A) and a low (B) performing team.*

Step 2: Visualization

In step 2, the joint activities of the team are captured and visualized. For the operationalization of joint team activities, TINT draws on the concept of macro-cognition (e.g., Fiore et al., 2010; Klein, Ross, Moon, Klein, Hoffman, & Hollnagel, 2003). Macrocognitions are "the internalized and externalized high-level mental processes employed by teams to create new knowledge during complex, one-of-a-kind, collaborative problem solving" (Letsky, Warner, Fiore, Rosen, & Salas, 2007, p. 7). High-level processes, in turn, include "combining, visualizing, and aggregating information to resolve ambiguity in support of the discovery of new knowledge and relationships" (Letsky, Warner, Fiore, Rosen, & Salas, 2007, p. 7). These processes occur in dynamical, iterative, recursive, and nonlinear phases of collaborative problem solving (Fiore et al., 2010). Numerous specific examples of macrocognition activities are described in literature (e.g., Klein et al., 2003; Patterson et al., 2010; Rosen, Fiore, Salas, Letsky, & Warner, 2008), such as detecting, sense making, planning, deciding, executing, or coordinating. In our study, we chose to focus on detecting, sense making and planning, updating, and executing. For each of these macrocognitions, we agreed on a definition that suited our context. According to Letsky et al. (2007), macrocognitions encompass externalized processes associated with observable actions carried out by the team and internalized processes that can only be measured indirectly. We are aware of the difficulties and limitations associated with measuring internalized team processes (e.g., building of shared mental models or team situation awareness; see e.g., Cooke, Gorman, Myers, & Duran, 2013; Cooke, Salas, Kiekel, & Bell, 2004). For this reason, we advise to focus on the externalized mental processes that are observable and describable. For each macrocognition type to assess, we defined specific behavioral markers indicating starting and ending points for coding. Table 20.2 exemplarily shows the definition and behavioral markers we used for "detecting."

Table 20.2 *Example of definition and behavioral markers for coding of the macrocognition type "detecting"*

Definition of macrocognition		Behavioral markers for coding
Detecting	"Noticing that events may be taking an unexpected (positive or negative) direction that require explanation and may signal a need or opportunity to reframe how a situation is conceptualized (sensemaking) and/or revise ongoing plans (planning) in progress (executing)." (Patterson et al., 2010, p. xxvi).	At least two team members . . . circulate in the control room to check different displays, exchange descriptive information about system parameters, and discuss the need to assess the situation.

Based on the behavioral markers, two researchers independently code the macrocognitions for each team. This allows for comparison and discussion of the codings among the researchers. The goal is to reach consensus for all differences in coding, resulting in one final coding version for each team. After that, the codings are visualized on the timeline in the form of circles. Figure 20.3 depicts an example of the resulting visualization. The timeline shows the duration of the scenario, and the circles indicate the starting and ending points of each coded macrocognition phase. The bigger the circle, the longer the duration of the macrocognition phase it represents. The diverse types of macrocognition are distinguished by different tints of grey of the circles (see the legend in Figure 20.3) Overlapping sections indicate an episode during which the team worked in different subgroups (each subgroup must include at least two persons so that there can be coded any macrocognitions, see Table 20.2). The visualization is not tied to specific software. It can be drawn on the computer (e.g., in Word, PowerPoint, or any graphics software) or by hand on a large paper, according to the preference of the researchers and their plan of how to discuss the results with the teams later on. In order to highlight the different types of macrocognition in the visualization, we recommend using tints of colors instead of grey.

The visualization provides a basis for analyzing and comparing the team adaptation processes (1) in terms of frequencies and durations of all types of macrocognition, and (2) in terms of sequences of various macrocognition phases. In the following, we will provide examples of potential ways for analysis.

Frequencies and Durations. Summing up the frequency and duration of all macrocognition phases (i.e., all circles of the same type) gives a quantitative overview of how often a team engaged in a new type of macrocognition and how much time it invested in each. This can be compared in relation to the other types of macrocognition per team and in relation to other teams. As Table 20.3 showcases for our study, both teams invested most of their scenario time in executing activities, around half of it in sense-making and planning activities, and the smallest percentage in detecting problems and updating. Team A invested a slightly lower proportion of the total scenario time in detecting problems, sense making and planning, and executing activities than was the case for team B, but a higher proportion in updating. On average, however, the high-performing team A spent more time on each phase of sense making and planning, updating, and executing than the low-performing team B, and changed to a new phase less frequently. The frequencies and proportions can also be calculated separately for certain scenario intervals. As explained before, the overlapping circles in Figure 20.3 indicate the periods where the teams worked in parallel subgroups (joint activities of at least two team members). This is the reason why the added duration of all macrocognition phases per team in Table 20.3 is more than the total scenario time. The total time of work in subteams (i.e., all overlapping areas) in relation to the total time of work among all team members gives an impression of how a team coordinates its collaboration during the scenario. In our example, team

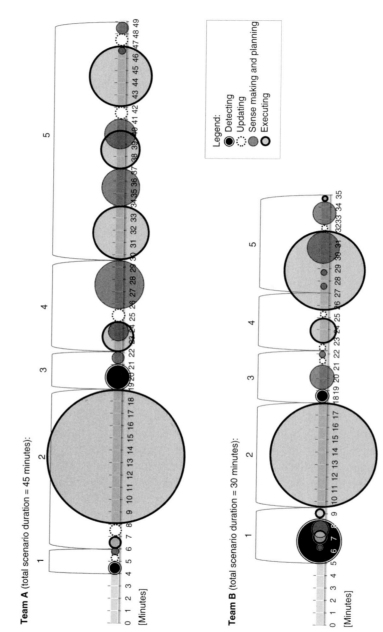

Figure 20.3 *Example of visualization of macrocognition phases for a high (A) and a low (B) performing team.*

Table 20.3 *Example of frequency rates and durations of macrocognition activities for a high (A) and a low (B) performing team*

		Detecting problems	Sense making and planning	Updating	Executing
Team A[1]	Total frequency	2	8	5	6
	Average frequency per 10 minutes	0.4	1.8	1.1	1.3
	Total duration	3.0 min	14.0 min	4.5 min	27.0 min
	Average duration	1.5 min	1.8 min	0.9 min	4.5 min
	Proportion in relation to scenario time	6.7%	31.1%	10.0%	60.0%
Team B[2]	Total frequency	2	8	4	5
	Average frequency per 10 minutes	0.7	2.7	1.3	1.7
	Total duration	4.5 min	10.0 min	2.0 min	20.0 min
	Average duration	2.3 min	1.3 min	0.5 min	4.0 min
	Proportion in relation to scenario time	15.0%	33.3%	6.7%	66.7%

Note. [1] total scenario time = 45 min. [2] total scenario time = 30 min.

A spent 92 percent of the scenario time in macrocognition among all team members, and 8 percent on the level of subgroups. In team B, the amount of time spent in subgroups was higher, at 22 percent.

Sequences The visualization (Figure 20.3) allows for explorative detection of sequences of various macrocognition phases that differ between the teams in terms of their chronological arrangement. In our example, we extracted and described three sequences that differed between team A and team B. These sequences are presented as examples in Table 20.4.

Step 3: Closer Examination

Step 3 of TINT serves a closer qualitative analysis of specific macrocognition phases, scenario intervals, or sequences that seem particularly relevant after the observation and analysis during the first two steps. The purpose of step 3 is to intensify the analysis qualitatively by asking a series of analytical questions (observation scheme, Table 20.5). This can be conducted together with the assessed teams. For this purpose, we recommend presenting selected excerpts of the video to the teams and discuss them along the lines of the analytical questions of the observation scheme. Alternatively, the teams can be involved after step 3 by putting the findings of steps 2 and 3 and possible elaborated hypotheses up for discussion.

Table 20.4 *Examples of different macrocognition sequences for a high (A) and a low (B) performing team*

No.	Team A		Team B	
	Sequence	Description	Sequence	Description
1		Joint first assessment at the beginning of the scenario carried out by all team members jointly.		First assessment at the beginning of the scenario carried out in subgroups.
2		Continuous re-assessment of the current course of action through an alternation of phases of executing and sense making/planning.		No alternating pattern of executing and sense making/planning identifiable for the re-assessment.
3		Alignment of understanding of all team members through updating after every episode of work in subgroups.		Episode of work in subgroups is not completed by an updating phase.

Table 20.5 *Observation scheme for closer analysis*

	Aspects	Analytical questions
Why	Function for team adaptation process	• How is the phase positioned in the chronology of the scenario? • How does the course of action change due to the phase? • What function does the phase have for the overall team adaptation process?
How	Coordination behaviors	• How is the phase initiated? • How does the shift supervisor coordinate information exchange among the team members? • How does the phase end?
	Communication behaviors	• Who is speaking? • What is being discussed (e.g., cause analysis)? • How does the shift supervisor deal with a sense of unease? • Which team members bring in additional information, ideas, doubts, or questions? • How does the shift supervisor actively encourage team members to bring in additional information, ideas, doubts, or questions? • What are the reactions to a team member speaking up?

Yin (2009) emphasizes that the important objective of a case study is to examine some relevant "how" and "why" questions about the relationship of events over time, and not merely to observe time trends alone. The questions on the "why" dimension are supposed to deepen the understanding of the function-specific macrocognition phases have for the overall scenario, i.e., how they contribute to the team's effective task fulfillment. As an example, sequence number 3 in Table 20.4 fulfills the function to align the team members' collective understanding after having worked in parallel. The questions on the "how" dimension explore how interaction is organized within certain phases, intervals, or sequences in terms of the team's coordination and communication behavior. The questions entail relevant topics found in literature about team adaptation, such as the sense of unease (Fruhen, Flin, & McLeod, 2014; Ritz & Koch, 2015), speaking up, coaching, and psychological safety (Edmondson, 2003). The scheme can be complemented or altered according to the context and the research objective. The questions are supposed to be answered for every macro-cognition phase, sequence, or scenario interval of interest separately. To sum up the findings, the observations are subsequently aggregated and compared across teams.

Discussion

TINT is a technique to examine from a new angle how teams organize their interaction through joint cooperative activities. It complements common quantitative approaches of analysis with a more interpretative approach that allows for description and comparison of specific cases at a team level and considers their dynamic and naturalistic characteristic. The benefit of TINT lies in in the holistic and tangible nature of its outcome, which displays team processes in their temporal development during a scenario. The resulting visualization intends to allow for in-depth analysis by researchers as well as for providing a valuable basis to enter into a substantial dialogue with practitioners (e.g., team members of the assessed teams or training instructors of the organization). It can be used to stimulate and moderate collective reflections and discussions about effective organization of collective interaction within the assessed teams. Involving the teams in the research process adds several benefits: From a scientific point of view, their participation enriches the analysis, as they can provide additional information that gives indications about the internalized processes behind the observable macrocognition behaviors and allows for communicative validation. From a practical point of view, it provides the teams an opportunity to develop a shared understanding and a common language, which in turn form crucial elements for organizational learning (Nonaka, 1994). TINT visualizations can be used to stimulate collective reflection during which tacit knowledge is made explicit and an organizational learning process is initialized about the competences and resources empowering teams for effective cooperation.

TINT also has limitations. We are aware that the explorative and interpretative approach of the technique can be criticized for its subjectivity and its low empirical validity for research purposes. Although step 2 encompasses quantitative measures, these must be treated as explorative indicators. In our case study, for example, it cannot be conclusively assessed if higher or lower proportions of work in subgroups are effective for or are hampering team adaptation (Table 20.3). The frequency rates and durations must be interpreted along with the qualitative findings by taking the scenario and its context into account, resulting in a "kaleidoscopic picture" of the case (Boos, 1992, p. 42), and by drawing comparisons to findings of other studies about team interaction. Clearly, the technique is designed for in-depth case study analysis and the formulation of new hypotheses but it is not useful for the analysis of a large number of cases. Yet it is possible to apply TINT to several comparable cases (e.g., high-performing teams in different scenarios) to compare the outcomes and find similarities, which indicate effective patterns of team processes at a more generalizable level and provide a basis for theory development (Boos, 1992).

The technique's rough procedural framework leaves a high degree of freedom for its application. It can be transferred to any other context of teamwork to learn more about how teams organize their interaction. This can encompass environments with a low degree of standardization but also highly standardized settings to examine variations in the application of manuals among teams (Savioja, Norros, Salo, & Aaltonen, 2014). TINT can basically be adapted to the assessment of any form of processes that occur at a team level and that can be observed through externalized, observable team members' actions. This can be any types of macrocognition similar to the ones we have used, or other joint cooperative activities within teams, such as deciding (Patterson et al., 2010), coordination or communication processes, uncertainty management, activities of attention (Klein et al., 2003), or (shared) leadership behavior (Künzle et al., 2010). The technique can be suited to various requirements of experimental and quasi-experimental settings for both simulator-based and field study setups, on the condition that the sequence of interest can be recorded on video. We hope to inspire other researchers to use TINT as a foundation to be refined and adapted to their specific context and purpose.

References

Boos, M. (1992). A typology of case studies. In M. Ó. Súilleabháin, E. A. Stuhler, & D. J. de Tombe (Eds.), *Research on cases and theories*, Vol. 1 (pp. 5–16). Mering: Hampp.

Bratman, M. E. (1992). Shared cooperative activity. *The Philosophical Review, 101*(2), 327–341. doi:10.2307/2185537

Burke, C. S., Stagl, K. C., Salas, E., Pierce, L., & Kendall, D. (2006). Understanding team adaption: A conceptual analysis and model. *Journal of Applied Psychology, 91*, 1189–1297. doi:10.1037/0021-9010.91.6.1189

Cacciabue, P. C., & Hollnagel, E. (1994). Simulation of cognition: Applications. In J.-M. Hoc, P. C. Cacciabue, & E. Hollnagel (Eds.), *Expertise and technology. Cognition & human-computer cooperation* (pp. 55–74). Mahwah, NJ: Lawrence Erlbaum.

Cooke, N. J., Gorman, J. C., Myers, C. W., & Duran, J. L. (2013). Interactive team cognition. *Cognitive Science, 37*, 255–285. doi:255-285.10.1111/cogs.12009

Cooke, N. J., Salas, E., Kiekel, P. A., & Bell, B. (2004). Advances in measuring team cognition. In E. Salas & S. M. Fiore (Eds.), *Team cognition: Understanding the factors that drive process and performance* (pp. 83–106). Washington, DC: American Psychological Association. doi:10.1037/10690-005

Edmondson, A. C. (2003). Speaking up in the operating room: How team leaders promote learning in interdisciplinary action teams. *Journal of Management Studies, 40*(6), 1419–1452. doi:10.1111/1467-6486.00386

Fiore, S., Rosen, M., Smith-Jentsch, K. A., Salas, E., Letsky, M., & Warner, N. (2010). Toward an understanding of macrocognition in teams: Predicting processes in complex collaborative contexts. *Human Factors, 52*(2), 203–224. doi:10.1177/0018720810369807

Fruhen, L. S., Flin, R., & McLeod, R. (2014). Chronic unease for safety in managers: A conceptualisation. *Journal of Risk Research, 17*(8), 869–979. doi:10.1080/13669877.2013.822924

Grote, G., Weichbrodt, J.C., Günter, H., Zala-Mezö, E., & Künzle, B. (2009). Coordination in high-risk organizations: The need for flexible routines. *Cognition, Technology & Work, 11*, 17–27. doi:10.1007/s10111-008-0119-y

Klein, G., Ross, K. G., Moon, B. M., Klein, D. E., Hoffman, R. R., & Hollnagel, E. (2003). Macrocognition. *IEEE Intelligent Systems, 18*(3), 81–85. doi:10.1109/MIS.2003.1200735

Künzle, B., Zala-Mezö, E., Wacker, J., Kolbe, M., Spahn, D. R., & Grote, G. (2010). Leadership in anaesthesia teams: The most effective leadership is shared. *Quality & Safety in Healthcare, 19*, 1–6. doi:10.1136/qshc.2008.030262

Letsky, M., Warner, N., Fiore, S. M., Rosen, M. A., & Salas, E. (2007). Macrocognition in complex team problem solving. *Proceedings of the 12th International Command and Control Research and Technology Symposium (12th ICCRTS)*, Newport, RI, June 2007. Washington, DC: US Department of Defense Command and Control Research Program.

Nonaka, I. (1994). A dynamic theory of organizational knowledge creation. *Organization Science, 5*, 14–37. doi:10.1287/orsc.5.1.14

Patterson, E. S., Miller, J. E., Roth, E. M., & Woods, D. D. (2010). Macrocognition: Where do we stand? In E. S. Patterson & J. E. Miller (Eds.), *Macrocognition metrics and scenarios: Design and evaluation for real-world teams* (pp. xxiii–xxxi). Hampshire, UK: Ashgate Publishing.

Perrow, C. (1999). *Normal accidents. Living with high-risk technologies*. Princeton, NJ: Princeton University Press.

Ritz, F. (2012). Organizational trust and trust in automated systems as predictors for safety related team performance: Results from a cross-cultural study. In G. Salvendy & W. Karwowski (Eds.), *Advances in human factors and ergonomics 2012, 14 Volume Set: Proceedings of the 4th AHFE Conference* 21–25 July 2012 (pp. 7249–7258). Boca Raton, FL: CRC Press.

Ritz, F., Kleindienst, C., Brüngger, J., & Koch, J. (2015). Coping with unexpected safety-critical situations through adaptation: A concept for resilient (simulator) team training. *6th International Conference on Applied Human Factors and Ergonomics, AHFE 2015, Procedia Manufacturing*, *3*, 1865–1871.

Ritz, F., & Koch, J. (2015). Die Entwicklung sicherheitsgerichteten Führungsverhaltens zur Bewältigung von kritischen Systemzuständen durch Leitwarten-Teams in der Kerntechnik [The development of safety-oriented leadership behavior to handle critical system conditions by control room teams in nuclear power engineering]. In M. Grandt & S. Schmerwitz (Eds.), *Kooperation und kooperative Systeme in der Fahrzeug- und Prozessführung [Cooperation and cooperative systems in vehicle and process management]* (pp. 171–186). Bonn, DE: Deutsche Gesellschaft für Luft- und Raumfahrt.

Rosen, M. A., Fiore, S. M., Salas, E., Letsky, M., & Warner, N. (2008). Tightly coupling cognition: Understanding how communication and awareness drive coordination in teams. *The International C2 Journal*, *2*(1), 1–29.

Savioja, P., Norros, L., Salo, L., & Aaltonen, I. (2014). Identifying resilience in proceduralised accident management activity of NPP operating crews. *Safety Science*, *68*, 258–274. doi: 10.1016/j.ssci.2014.04.008

Stachowski, A., Kaplan, S. A., & Waller, M. J. (2009). The benefits of flexible team interaction during crises. *Journal of Applied Psychology*, 94, 1536–1543. doi:10.1037/a0016903

Tomasello, M., Carpenter, M., Call, J., Behne, T., & Moll, H. (2005). Understanding and sharing intentions: The origins of cultural cognition. *Behavioral and Brain Sciences*, *28*, 675–735. doi:10.1017/S0140525X05000129

Vidal, M. C. R., Carvalho, P. V. R., Santos, M. S., & dos Santos, I. J. L. (2009). Collective work and resilience of complex systems. *Journal of Loss Prevention in the Process Industries*, *22*, 516–527. doi:10.1016/j.jlp.2009.04.005

Waller, M. J. (1999). The timing of adaptive group responses to nonroutine events. *Academy of Management Journal*, *42*(2), 127–137. doi:10.2307/257088

Waller, M. J., Gupta, N., & Giambatista, R. C. (2004). Effects of adaptive behaviors and shared mental models on control crew performance. *Management Science*, *50*(11), 1534–1544. doi:10.1287/mnsc.1040.0210

Yin, R. K. (2009). *Case study research: Design and methods* (4th edn.). Los Angeles, CA: Sage.

Zala-Mezö, E., Wacker, J., Künzle, B., Brüesch, M., & Grote, G. (2009). The influence of standardisation and task load on team coordination patterns during anaesthesia inductions. *Quality and Safety in Health Care*, *18*(2), 127–130. doi:10.1136/qshc.2007.025973

PART V

Coding Schemes for Interaction Research

Overview of Part V

The coding schemes presented in detail in this section constitute a small selection from a large body of work developed by many researchers over the years since the beginning of systematic behavioral observation (see the Appendix for an additional selection of published coding schemes). We have sorted the coding schemes into six areas based on the constructs that they address.

- General group process systems
- Argument, conflict, and negotiations
- Coordination and coherence
- Cognition and meta-cognition
- Personality and team behavior
- Roles and relationships

Although this categorization is not perfect, it does provide some structure to researchers who are looking for a specific area or construct. Within each area, chapters are sorted alphabetically based on the name of the coding scheme. All coding schemes follow a template that allows for a quick comparison of coding schemes and a quick review of all relevant information. Table V.1 presents the template with the information covered in each section and an explanation of what to expect in this section.

Table V.1 *Overview of coding scheme template*

Section	Explanation
Name of the coding scheme	Short title of the coding scheme as well as common abbreviation
Keywords	Central keywords indicating constructs being measured
Summary	Overview and short description of the purpose of the coding scheme
Description of the coding scheme	Introduction to theoretical background and development; description of the coding scheme including codes used, their definition, and examples for each code
Comparable instruments	Differences and similarities with other comparable instruments
Goals of the instrument	Types of research questions that can be addressed
Available versions	For instance, languages, online/electronic, paper, etc.
Applicability	Laboratory, field, real-time coding, etc.
Practical application	Prospective coding time per minute • Time required for coder training • Technical requirements (computer, recording devices, coding keyboards, etc.) • Description of unitizing independent of coding; what is considered a coding unit, how is it defined? • Is a training manual available? How can it be obtained? • Light version: possibilities to shorten the coding scheme for economy reasons and to improve applicability in the field
Quality assessment	Reliability testing Validity testing
Data aggregation and analysis	Aggregation of data and recommendations for further analysis of the data that goes beyond standard techniques and methods
Previous studies	Previous studies that used the instrument as well as a short description of their results
Original publication	Original publication of the coding scheme; if applicable: later versions or improvements, or previous versions, if available: contact address of authors where more information could be obtained
References	All references cited in the text

General Group Process Systems

21 The Advanced Interaction Analysis for Teams (act4teams) Coding Scheme

Simone Kauffeld, Nale Lehmann-Willenbrock, and Annika L. Meinecke

General Information

Name of Coding Scheme

Advanced Interaction Analysis for Teams (act4teams)

Keywords

Work groups, team meetings, meeting interactions, group processes, functional communication, dysfunctional communication, social dynamics

Summary

The Advanced Interaction Analysis for Teams (act4teams) coding scheme is a theory-based, validated tool for measuring the fine-grained problem-solving dynamics that occur in groups and teams. It has been applied across a wide range of group interaction settings, cultural contexts, and research questions. The unit of analysis is a thought unit situated within the temporal group communication flow. The act4teams coding scheme distinguishes four broad facets of verbal group communication: problem-focused statements, procedural statements, socio-emotional statements, and action-oriented statements. These four facets amount to a total of 43 mutually exclusive and exhaustive behavioral categories. Act4teams is typically applied to videotaped group interactions leading to event data including time stamps.

Description of the Coding Scheme

The act4teams coding scheme is based on an extensive review of past research on team competences, problem-solving, decision-making, and relational

The three authors are in alphabetical order and contributed equally to this chapter.

processes in groups (for a detailed theoretical underpinning of the coding scheme, see Kauffeld, 2006a, and Kauffeld & Lehmann-Willenbrock, 2012). The act4teams coding scheme distinguishes problem-focused statements, procedural statements, socio-emotional statements, and action-oriented statements.

An overview of the act4teams coding scheme is presented in Table 21.1. Each verbal statement within a given group interaction fits one and only one of the categories (i.e., exhaustive and mutually exclusive coding) within the four broader facets of group communication.

First, *problem-focused statements* are aimed at understanding and analyzing the problem at hand, discussing ideas, and developing ideas and solutions. Moreover, asking for and sharing information is also classified as problem-focused communication. Overall, the problem-focused facet of the coding scheme comprises 11 fine-grained behavioral categories, such as "describing a problem" or "arguing for a solution."

Second, *procedural statements* are aimed at structuring the group process, and both positive and negative procedural statements are distinguished. Positive procedural statements help to facilitate goal accomplishment and guide the group

Table 21.1 *Act4teams coding scheme for coding group interactions*

Problem-focused statements	Procedural statements	Socio-emotional statements	Action-oriented statements
Problem	**Positive**:	**Positive**:	**Positive, proactive**:
Describing a problem	Goal orientation	Encouraging	Expressing positivity
Connections	Clarifying	participation	Taking responsibility
with problems	Procedural suggestion	Providing support	Action planning
Defining the objective	Procedural question	Active listening	**Negative,**
Solution	Prioritizing	Reasoned	**counterproductive**:
Describing a solution	Time management	disagreement	No interest in change
Problem with a	Task distribution	Giving feedback	Complaining
solution	Visualization	Humor	Seeking someone to blame
Arguing for a solution	Summarizing	Separating opinions	Denying responsibility
Organizational	**Negative**:	from facts	Empty talk
knowledge	Losing the train of	Expressing feelings	Ending the discussion early
Knowing who	thought	Offering praise	
Question	(running off	**Negative**:	
	topic)	Criticizing/backbiting	
		Interrupting	
		Side conversations	
		Self-promotion	

Additional codes:

Pause; laughter; incomprehensible; incomplete sentence (cut off by an interruption); other (not fitting any of the above codes)

discussion. Nine positive procedural behavioral categories are distinguished, for instance, "clarifying" and "summarizing." Negative procedural statements, in contrast, lead to a loss of structure in the group discussion process. Verbal behaviors such as running off topic or contributing numerous irrelevant examples are coded as "losing the train of thought."

Third, *socio-emotional statements* capture the relational interaction among group members and, again, are both positive and negative in nature. Positive socio-emotional statements can be coded into nine distinct behavioral categories including "providing support," "humor," and "offering praise." Negative socio-emotional statements are further differentiated into four behavioral categories, for instance "interrupting" and "criticizing/backbiting."

Fourth, *action-oriented statements* describe group members' willingness to take responsibility and action to improve their work. Again, positive and negative statements are distinguished. Positive, action-oriented (or proactive) statements include three behavioral categories: "expressing positivity," "taking responsibility," and "action planning." Negative, action-oriented (or counteractive) statements, in contrast, comprise six distinct categories that denote a lack of initiative and interest, such as "complaining," "seeking someone to blame," or "denying responsibility."

In addition to these 43 distinct behavioral categories, five additional behavioral categories are available (see Table 21.1). These additional categories are assigned when none of the group members talk for 20 seconds or longer ("pause"), when group members laugh ("laughter"), when a statement is not comprehensible due to sound issues or mumbling ("incomprehensible"), when a speaker is interrupted midsentence ("interrupted sentence"), or when a statement does not fit into any of the other behavioral categories ("other"), which rarely occurs.

Comparable Instruments

The act4teams coding schemes shares some common ground with prior classification systems for intra-group interactions, such as IPA (Bales, 1950), SYMLOG (Bales & Cohen, 1979), and KONFKOD (Fisch, 1994). However, act4teams extends these previous coding schemes by including both positive and negative communication behaviors, as well as action-oriented communication, an important facet when studying teams in the workplace that share a history and a future (Kauffeld, 2006a).

Goals of the Instrument

The act4teams coding scheme is suitable for group settings in which group members discuss problems, debate different ideas, find solutions, and make decisions. As act4teams captures the entire flow of conversational events that are exchanged among group members, it provides insights into the fine-grained temporal dynamics in group interactions. For example, previous research using the act4teams coding scheme has identified emergent patterns in group interactions such as complaining and solution cycles (Kauffeld, 2007; Kauffeld & Meyers, 2009; Lehmann-Willenbrock & Kauffeld, 2010), humor patterns (Lehmann-Willenbrock & Allen, 2014), and positivity patterns (Lehmann-Willenbrock, Chiu, Lei, & Kauffeld, 2017). Moreover, previous research has used the act4teams coding scheme to study intercultural differences in group interactions (Lehmann-Willenbrock, Allen, & Meinecke, 2014) and emergent discussion roles (Lehmann-Willenbrock, Beck, & Kauffeld, 2016). As such, the act4teams coding scheme is especially suitable for studying fine-grained temporal processes in groups focusing on the moment-to-moment dynamics of verbal conduct at the conversational event level.

Available Versions

The act4teams coding scheme was originally designed for German-speaking work groups and was first published in 2000 under its original German name "Kasseler Kompetenz Raster" (Cassel competency grid; Kauffeld, Grote, & Frieling, 2000; see also Kauffeld, 2006b; Kauffeld, 2010). The original version included two additional behavioral categories – "economical thinking" and "changing the topic" – which were later excluded due to their infrequent occurrence.

The coding scheme is available in German and English and has been successfully applied to German, Dutch, US, and Swiss group interaction data.

Applicability

The act4teams coding scheme is applicable across a wide range of group interaction settings, including team meetings, group problem-solving conversations, and group creativity interactions. However, it is less suitable for situations where group members simply share information but do not discuss information and ideas.

The act4teams coding scheme is typically applied to field data and video-taped interactions among actual team members (Kauffeld, 2006a). However, it has also been applied in laboratory studies in the past (e.g., Lehmann-Willenbrock & Allen, 2017; Lehmann-Willenbrock et al., 2014). Due to its high level of granularity, we do not recommend using the entire act4teams coding scheme for real-time (ad hoc) coding. However, simplified versions of the act4teams coding scheme have been applied successfully in live coding settings in the past. Further information and paper-pencil templates for real-time coding are available upon request from Simone Kauffeld.

Practical Application

Coding Time

Using a software solution (see details below), one minute of videotaped group interaction amounts to a coding effort of 8–15 minutes. However, this coding effort depends on a number of factors such as group size, sound quality, language/dialect, the complexity of the topic that is being discussed, and coders' experience.

Coder Training

Training coders requires approximately 200 hours, including studying and discussing the coding handbook, coding sample transcripts, coding group discussions that were specifically designed for training purposes, and coding at least one group discussion from a field setting for reliability check purposes.

Technical Requirements

Coding with act4teams does not necessarily have to be software assisted. However, we strongly advise to do so to minimize the coding effort and facilitate data processing and analysis. INTERACT software (Mangold, 2014) has typically been used with act4teams. An external coding keyboard can further help in sequencing and annotating the video data.

Unitizing

The unit of analysis is a thought unit, which constitutes the smallest meaningful segment of behavior that can be coded into one of the 43 behavioral categories in act4teams. This is usually a simple sentence containing a subject and predicate. However, it can also be a single word such as "okay." A new unit is parsed when one of the following occurs:

- The speaker changes (turn-taking).
- Within a conversational turn, the speaker voices several statements where each expresses a complete thought (e.g., first describing a problem and then asking a question).
- A speaker stays within the same category but the main argument changes. For example, the speaker lists three different solutions in a row (coded as three separate "solution" statements). Thus, the same categories may be repeated.
- A speaker talks for longer than 20 seconds. This rule helps to reconstruct the interaction process temporally (i.e., a speaker who stated three acts in a row could not have spoken longer than one minute).

Training Manual

We developed a self-learning tool, including the coding handbook (German and English), standardized transcripts, standardized training videos, and corresponding standard solutions, to facilitate the training process and to provide coders with extensive materials so that they can learn at their own pace. The training tool is available upon request from Simone Kauffeld.

Simplified Version

Depending on the application context, the specific categories can be summarized to form larger aspects of group interaction (e.g., Klonek, Quera, Burba, & Kauffeld, 2016). Moreover, the coding scheme can be adapted such that only a smaller number of categories are applied. For example, the coding scheme can be used to focus only on positive procedural communication (van der Haar, Koeslag-Kreunen, Euwe, & Segers, 2017). The decision to focus on a narrower set of behavioral categories in the act4teams scheme should be driven by the specific research question and/or practical application context at hand.

Quality Assessment

Reliability

Act4teams has shown excellent overall interrater reliability in previous studies, with Cohen's Kappa (in the case of two coders) or Fleiss' Kappa (among larger pools of coders) ranging from .81 to.90 (e.g., Kauffeld & Lehmann-Willenbrock, 2012; Lehmann-Willenbrock & Allen, 2014; Lehmann-Willenbrock, Meinecke, Rowold, & Kauffeld, 2015).

Moreover, for the seven larger aspects in the act4teams coding scheme (i.e., problem-solving statements, positive procedural statements, negative procedural statements, positive socio-emotional statements, negative socio-emotional statements, positive action-oriented statements, and negative action-oriented statements), the code-specific Cohen's Kappa yielded a mean value of .72 (SD = .16; Klonek et al., 2016). Moreover, the average intraclass correlation coefficient (ICC; two-way random, absolute agreement) was .85 (SD = .22; Klonek et al., 2016), which indicates high agreement upon summary measures among observers.

Validity

Concerning content validity, findings show that the 43 behavioral categories within the act4teams coding scheme successfully cover a wide range of group communication behaviors, and only an extremely small fraction of behavioral units cannot be classified using the act4teams coding scheme (Kauffeld, 2006a). Moreover, the act4teams categories have been related to numerous outcome criteria. In particular, a large study based on 92 videotaped organizational team meetings showed distinct relationships between the act4teams categories and team meeting satisfaction, team productivity, and organizational functioning more broadly (Kauffeld & Lehmann-Willenbrock, 2012). There are three key takeaways from this study. First, dysfunctional communication categories, such as criticizing others or complaining, were more strongly related to outcome measures than their functional counterparts (e.g., providing praise or expressing positivity), such that "bad is stronger than good" in terms of dysfunctional and functional team behaviors. Second, the frequency of sharing problems was unrelated to the outcome criteria, whereas naming solutions and analyzing problems and solutions (e.g., discussing causes and consequences of problems and solutions) showed positive relationships to team and organizational outcomes. Thus, teams need to dig deeper into the problem-solving process in order to be successful. Finally, results showed that action-planning statements – albeit infrequent – were particularly important for meeting satisfaction and team productivity. Thus, teams need to agree on tangible actions to make sure that solutions and decisions that are discussed during the meeting are also implemented after the meeting is over.

In sum, these findings provide support for the criterion-related validity of the act4teams coding scheme, and show that the coding scheme can be used to discriminate between more or less successful groups, which points to the construct validity of the coding scheme. Likewise, the act4teams coding scheme has been used to discriminate between self-managing teams and traditional work groups (Kauffeld, 2006b). For example, findings revealed that self-managing teams use more procedural communication and less often lose the train of thought in details and examples than traditional work groups.

In terms of convergent and discriminant validity, several studies showed distinct correlational patterns between the act4teams categories and similar or dissimilar constructs. For example, solution-focused leader behaviors coded with act4teams have been successfully related to ratings of transformational leadership style (Lehmann-Willenbrock et al., 2015). The categories "cross-linking problems" (i.e., naming causes and consequences of problems) and "procedural statements" have been shown to be related to group members' perceptions of innovation. Positive action-oriented statements have been shown to be positively related to organizational citizenship behavior (see Kauffeld, 2006a, for more detailed information).

Data Aggregation and Analysis

Typically, an analysis with act4teams leads to a stream of sequentially coded group behaviors. Each unit of analysis includes the specific onset and offset times (in hours, minutes, seconds, and frames per second), the speaker, and the specific behavioral category. This stream of data can be analyzed to detect emergent interaction patterns or to derive summary measures. Potential summary measures include raw frequencies, relative frequencies (as a percentage), and behavior rates (standardized to a specific time period). Previous studies using act4teams usually reported behavior rates standardized to a 60-minute time period, to account for differing meeting lengths.

Previous Studies

Researchers using the act4teams coding scheme must be willing to spend a considerable amount of time training coders and analyzing the data. While this process is demanding – especially in comparison to survey methods – the subsequent possibilities to analyze the data are manifold. Previous studies showed that coding one hour of videotaped group interactions led to 800–1200 coded units. Thus, act4teams can provide fine-grained insights into social dynamics in groups and teams.

References

Original Publications

Kauffeld, S. (2006a). *Kompetenzen messen, bewerten, entwickeln [Measuring, evaluating, and developing competencies]*. Stuttgart, Germany: Schäffer-Poeschel.

Kauffeld, S., Grote, S., & Frieling, E. (2000). Die Diagnose beruflicher Handlungskompetenz: Das Kasseler-Kompetenz-Raster [Diagnosis of professional competence: The Cassel competency grid]. In K. A. Geißler & W. Loos (Eds.), *Handbuch Personalentwicklung* (pp. 1–22). Cologne, Germany: Deutscher Wirtschaftsdienst.

Meinecke, A. L., & Lehmann-Willenbrock, N. (2015). Social dynamics at work: Meetings as a gateway. In J. A. Allen, N. Lehmann-Willenbrock, & S. G. Rogelberg (Eds.), *The Cambridge handbook of meeting science* (pp. 325–356). New York: Cambridge University Press.

Other References

Bales, R. F. (1950). *Interaction process analysis: A method for the study of small groups*. Cambridge, MA: Addison-Wesley.

Bales, R. F., & Cohen, S. P. (1979). *SYMLOG: A system for the multiple level observation of groups*. New York, NY: Free Press.

Fisch, F. (1994). Eine Methode zur Analyse von Interaktionsprozessen beim Problemlösen in Gruppen [A method for the analysis of interaction processes during group problem solving]. *Gruppendynamik*, 25, 149–168.

Kauffeld, S. (2006b). Self-directed work groups and team competence. *Journal of Occupational and Organizational Psychology*, 79, 1–21. doi:10.1348/096317905X53237

Kauffeld, S. (2007). Jammern oder Lösungsexploration: Eine sequenzanalytische Betrachtung des Interaktionsprozesses in betrieblichen Gruppen bei der Bewältigung von Optimierungsaufgaben [Complaining or exploration of solutions: A sequential examination of interaction processes in work groups when completing optimization tasks]. *German Journal of Work and Organizational Psychology, 51*, 55–67. doi:10.1026/0932-4089.51.2.55

Kauffeld, S. (2010). Das Kasseler-Kompetenz-Raster [The Cassel competency grid]. In W. Sarges, H. Wottawa, & C. Roos (Eds.), *Handbuch wirtschaftspsychologischer Testverfahren, Band II: Organisationspsychologische Instrumente* (2nd edn., pp. 165–173). Lengerich, Germany: Pabst.

Kauffeld, S., Grote, S., & Frieling, E. (2000). Die Diagnose beruflicher Handlungskompetenz: Das Kasseler-Kompetenz-Raster [Diagnosis of professional competence: The Cassel competency grid]. In K. A. Geißler & W. Loos (Eds.), *Handbuch Personalentwicklung* (pp. 1–22). Cologne, Germany: Deutscher Wirtschaftsdienst.

Kauffeld, S., & Lehmann-Willenbrock, N. (2012). Meetings matter: Effects of team meeting communication on team and organizational success. *Small Group Research, 43*, 128–156. doi:10.1177/1046496411429599

Kauffeld, S., & Meyers, R. (2009). Complaint and solution-oriented circles: Interaction patterns in work group discussions. *European Journal of Work and Organizational Psychology, 18*, 267–294. doi:10.1080/13594320701693209

Klonek, F. E., Quera, V., Burba, M., & Kauffeld, S. (2016). Group interactions and time: Using sequential analysis to study group dynamics in project meetings. *Group Dynamics: Theory, Research, and Practice, 20*, 209–222. doi:10.1037/gdn0000052

Lehmann-Willenbrock, N., & Allen, J. A. (2014). How fun are your meetings? Investigating the relationship between humor patterns in team interactions and team performance. *Journal of Applied Psychology, 99*, 1278–1287. doi:10.1037/a0038083

Lehmann-Willenbrock, N., & Allen, J. A. (2017). Well, now what do we do? Wait … : A group process analysis of meeting lateness. *International Journal of Business Communication. Advance online publication.* doi:10.1177/2329488417696725

Lehmann-Willenbrock, N., Allen, J. A., & Meinecke, A. L. (2014). Observing culture: Differences in U.S.-American and German team meeting behaviors. *Group Processes & Intergroup Relations, 17*, 252–271. doi:10.1177/1368430213497066

Lehmann-Willenbrock, N., Beck, S. J., & Kauffeld, S. (2016). Emergent team roles in organizational meetings: Identifying communication patterns via cluster analysis. *Communication Studies, 67*, 37–57. doi:10.1080/10510974.2015.1074087

Lehmann-Willenbrock, N., Chiu, M. M., Lei, Z., & Kauffeld, S. (2017). Understanding positivity within dynamic team interactions: A statistical discourse analysis. *Group & Organization Management, 42*, 39–78. doi:10.1177/1059601116628720

Lehmann-Willenbrock, N., & Kauffeld, S. (2010). The downside of communication: Complaining cycles in group discussions. In S. Schuman (Ed.), *The handbook for working with difficult groups: How they are difficult, why they are difficult, what you can do* (pp. 33–54). San Francisco, CA: Jossey-Bass/Wiley.

Lehmann-Willenbrock, N., Meinecke, A. L., Rowold, J., & Kauffeld, S. (2015). How transformational leadership works during team interactions: A behavioral process analysis. *The Leadership Quarterly*, *26*, 1017–1033. doi:10.1016/j.leaqua.2015.07.003

Mangold. (2014). INTERACT user manual. Retrieved from www.mangold-international .com

van der Haar, S., Koeslag-Kreunen, M., Euwe, E., & Segers, M. (2017). Team leader structuring for team effectiveness and team learning in command-and-control teams. *Small Group Research*, *48*, 215–248. doi:10.1177/1046496417689897

22 The Discussion Coding System (DCS)

Carsten C. Schermuly

General Information

Name of Coding Scheme

The Discussion Coding System (DCS)

Keywords

Nonverbal behavior, dominance, affiliation, decision making

Summary

The Discussion Coding System (DCS) is a coding scheme to code verbal and nonverbal communication processes in groups. Nonverbal behavior (facial expression, body posture, gesture, and paralanguage) is coded on two basic dimensions: affiliation and dominance. This coding makes it possible to identify the interpersonal character of an act, in addition to its function. The DCS is easy to use and has the ability to code different-sized groups engaged in a variety of task types. Coding software was developed that contributes to the efficiency of the coding process.

Description of the Coding Scheme

According to Boos (1995), communication processes have a sequential, reciprocal, and simultaneous nature, and different information overlaps at the same time. The simultaneous character of communication is taken into account in the DCS by coding each speech act according to its functional and interpersonal meaning (Schermuly & Scholl, 2012).

In the functional domain, speech is coded according to what kind of function the act had for the interaction process. Three different main categories are captured here: content acts, socioemotional acts, and regulation acts. Content acts refer to task-related information such as arguments, data, and facts, but also beliefs and

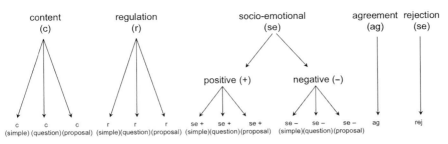

Figure 22.1 *Hierarchical structure of the functional categories (Schermuly & Scholl, 2012, p. 16).*

attitudes concerning content issues (e.g., "This organization has 300 employees"). Socioemotional acts are separated into positive (e.g., "I like your work") and negative ones (e.g., "Your behavior in this group is unacceptable"). The differentiation between content and the socioemotional categories is influenced by the Interaction Process Analysis (IPA, Bales, 1950). Regulation acts (e.g., "Now, we discuss the next item of the agenda") were introduced in a coding scheme by Fisch (1994) and serve to structure and to ease the interaction processes (Sjøvold, 2007). They are critical for the efficiency and the success of groups (Kolbe, 2007). Besides these main categories, two further subcategories are coded: proposals and questions. Proposals are important for the productivity of a group (Scharpf & Fisch, 1989) and questions help, for example, to develop a transactive memory system (Brauner, 2006). Proposals and questions can occur in all three main categories and therefore indicate a subtype of each. Finally, the reactions that an act provokes are coded. This is done according to two basic reactions, rejection and agreement, which are also part of the IPA. The hierarchical structure of the categories in the functional domain is displayed in Figure 22.1.

Additionally, every act is rated regarding the interpersonal meaning that the speaker communicates to the addressee of the message. For Luxen (2005, p. 332), "affiliation and dominance are the ink with which human action is written" and they are universal dimensions of social cognition (Fiske, Cuddy, & Glick, 2006). Each act, independent of the functional category in which it was coded, is rated regarding the extent to which the speaker nonverbally communicated affiliation or dominance. For example, a proposal can be made with nonverbal signals of affiliation or dominance and it might be important for the success if it is accompanied by more dominant or submissive signals. The dominant and affiliative character of an act is evaluated on two five-point rating scales (see Figure 22.2): very submissive (1) to very dominant (5), and very hostile (1) to very friendly (5).

To increase the reliability of the coding, both bipolar dimensions are operationalized in a double way. The behavioral operationalization focuses on nonverbal behavior (see for example Table 22.1, first column). The behaviors belong to different nonverbal channels such as facial expression and glance, body posture, gesture, and paralanguage. Because nonverbal behavior can be interpreted ambiguously (e.g., was it

Table 22.1 *Examples for the behavior- and adjective-oriented operationalization*

Pole	Nonverbal behaviors	Adjectives
Dominance	relaxation stimuli (e.g., asymmetrical arms and legs position, sideways lean of the torso, hand relaxation, neck relaxation, reclining angle); postural expansion; to speak in a clear, firm voice	assertive, self-assured, proud
Submissiveness	to look up from below; to heighten the voice; to make the body small	shy, hesitant, subservient
Hostility	to raise the voice; to raise the chin; to turn away from someone	ruthless, vicious, merciless
Friendliness	to smile and laugh with other(s); to speak tenderly; small interpersonal distance	empathetic, considerate, generous

Note. See for the complete operationalization Schermuly and Scholl (2012, p. 38–40)

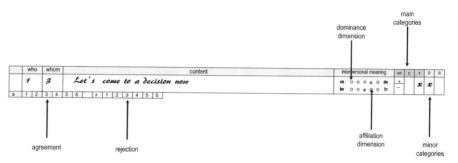

Figure 22.2 *DCS coding sheet when the paper-pencil version is used; su = submissive; do = dominance; ho = hostile; fr = friendly; se = socio-emotional; c = content; r = regulation; p = proposal; q = question; a = agreement; r = rejection.*

a friendly or hostile smile?), the adjective-based operationalization (see for example Table 22.2, second column) is a check in addition to the behaviors to rate the interpersonal meaning of an act correctly. First, an observer identifies a behavior that usually stands for a specific expression (e.g., smile = friendly). Then, the observer relates the impression to the adjective-based operationalization and checks whether the smile was actually communicated, for example, empathetically or viciously. The adjectives stem from the Interpersonal Adjective List (IAL, Jacobs & Scholl, 2005), which measures the general interpersonal style of people. Example behaviors and adjectives are shown in Table 22.1 (all adjectives and behaviors are listed in Schermuly & Scholl, 2011, 2012). Figure 22.2 displays the coding sheet for the paper-pencil version.

Table 22.2 *Selection of studies using DCS*

Study	Study Aims
Ianiro et al. (2013) Ianiro & Kauffeld (2014) Ianiro, Lehmann-Willenbrock, & Kauffeld (2015)	Testing the consequences of dominant and affiliative nonverbal behavior in coaching processes for the relationship quality and goal attainment
Schermuly (2011)	The consequences of different leadership styles on team outcomes such as task satisfaction and performance in a hidden profile task were tested. The communication variables measured with DCS (for example, dominance and affiliation behavior, content and regulation acts) served as mediators.
Schröder, Netzel, Schermuly, & Scholl, (2013)	The DCS was expanded concerning a third interpersonal dimension (activation) and then, for the first time, Affect-Control-Theory (Heise, 2007) was tested with nonverbal behaviors.
Meyer et al. (2016)	Micro-level leadership behavior, leader evaluations, and team decision quality were analyzed. Above all, leader question behavior measured with DCS was associated with team decision quality.
Kämmer, Gaissmaier, Reimer, & Schermuly (2014)	The functional categories of DCS were used to test the recognition heuristic in a team context.
Meyer & Schermuly (2012)	The consequences of diversity fault lines on team decisions were tested. The elaboration of task-relevant information, which was measured with DCS, served as a mediator.

Comparable Instruments

Regarding the functional codes in particular, the DCS has its roots in well-established coding instruments. These functional elements of the DCS coding system build on the IPA (Bales, 1950) and the KONFKOD (Fisch, 1994). Bales assumes that during group processes, task and socioemotional demands have to be fulfilled, and so both meta categories of the IPA were integrated into the DCS. Fisch (1994) states that to capture group interactions adequately a third category for regulation acts is necessary, and so this category is also integrated into the DCS.

However, there are also differences concerning the IPA and the KONFKOD. Agreements and rejections are discrete categories that do not automatically belong to the socioemotional domain. Suggestions and questions can be coded in all three functional categories (e.g., "don't be so resentful"). But neither instrument considers that every statement, regardless of its primary function in the interaction process, can be accompanied by an interpersonal emotional meaning. As well, a content act or a regulation act (e.g., "Let's come to the next point") can be displayed with more or less dominance and affiliation, which can be crucial for the outcome of this act.

Goals of the Instrument

DCS was developed to answer research questions in different group situations. This makes it possible to compare results and to gain more general findings about group processes (see Table 22.2 for an overview of the application of DCS in different group settings). Another goal was to code not only verbal but also nonverbal behavior on two basic interpersonal dimensions. This makes it possible, for example, to identify general interaction and leadership styles in the interpersonal circumplex spanned by the dimensions of dominance and affiliation. Schermuly and Scholl (2012) coded, for example, the movie *12 Angry Men* with the DCS. They showed that the jurors displayed different interaction styles concerning both the interpersonal dimensions, and that some jurors changed their interaction styles during the group discussion. The juror who convinced all other jurors behaved moderately dominantly, but was neutral on the affiliation dimension. Furthermore, it is possible with DCS to code the functional but also the interpersonal character of communication acts. In this way it is possible to analyze if specific communication acts are more successful or evoke different reactions if they are displayed with a specific nonverbal character. For example, do regulation acts receive more agreements if they are communicated in a dominant-friendly way or is a dominant-neutral style more successful? Do clients show more self-disclosure if the counselor shows complementary or similar behaviors on the two interpersonal dimensions? Because the DCS considers the generally accepted dimensions of dominance and affiliation, several theories such as Interpersonal Theory or Affect Control Theory can be tested.

Available Versions

The instrument is available in German (Schermuly & Scholl, 2011) and in English (Schermuly & Scholl, 2012). The coding software exists only in German (Schermuly & Scholl, 2011). The coding software is available at Hogrefe for €346.[1] It runs on the Windows software system (starting with Windows 2000).

Applicability

The DCS can be, and has been, used in the laboratory and in the field. It is especially useful in coding decision making processes in groups. The coding of

---

[1] See www.testzentrale.de.

nonverbal behavior allows identifying, for example, nonverbal circles (e.g., domi-nant-friendly acts are answered with submissive-friendly acts that lead to more dominant-friendly acts) in teams or dyads that are not obvious to interaction partners. For example, Ianiro, Lehmann-Willenbrock, and Kauffeld (2015) showed that patterns of reciprocal friendliness were predictable for the later experienced working alliance between coach and client. But the development of groups and their knowledge exchange can also be captured. Finally, real-time coding is possible, but compared to video-supported coding the reliability clearly decreases (see Schermuly & Scholl, 2011; 2012).

Practical Application

The basis of the coding process is sense units. The interaction process is divided into sense units with the help of seven standardized rules. An example of these rules is the speaker rule (new act if the speaker changes). A new act is also coded if the addressee of an act changes or the main function changes (e.g., speaker starts with a regulation act and then states a socioemotional act) (see all rules in Schermuly & Scholl, 2012).

The coding time of the DCS was measured in several studies (see Schermuly, 2011). In the video-supported application, coding takes four times the discussion time on average. Depending on the research question and the analyzing strategy, only specific parts of the DCS can be chosen and coded. For example, it is an option to code only who speaks to whom and the interpersonal dimensions. This decreases the coding time significantly. A detailed manual is available (Schermuly & Scholl, 2011), as is a two-day standardized training course that has proven effective (see for a description Schermuly & Scholl, 2011). The DCS can be used in a paper-pencil version, but can also be supported using the DCS coding software. When the coding software is used the data can be exported into Excel, SPSS, or other software to conduct specific statistical analyses. The software automatically pro-duces a report about the most important group variables and can visualize the discussion processes in detail.

Quality Assessment

Reliability

DCS was tested in several studies (see for an overview Schermuly & Scholl, 2012). The reliability results show that all kappa values for the functional categories lie higher than .61. More than 50 percent of the kappa values lie even higher than .81, which approaches a perfect agreement according to Sachs (1999). For the interper-sonal dimensions of the DCS, unadjusted intraclass correlations (ICC) were calcu-lated. The mean ICC for affiliation is .83 and for dominance it is .73. Both values are satisfactory, but the coding of the affiliation dimension proves more reliable. The reliabilities for live coding are considerably lower (Schermuly & Scholl, 2012).

Validity

The validity of the DCS was tested in several studies. For example, there exist significant positive correlations between trait dominance measured with IAL and dominance behavior measured with DCS ($r = .27$; $p < .01$) as well as between trait affiliation (also measured with IAL) and DCS affiliation ($r = .18$; $p < .05$), thus showing support for convergent validity. Extraversion is also associated with dominance ($r = .26$; $p < .01$) and agreeableness with affiliation ($r = .25$; $p < .01$) (Schermuly et al., 2010). Assessing construct validity, participants who were primed with a scrambled sentences test on dominant behavior style were coded as significantly more dominant with DCS than participants who were primed with a more submissive behavior style ($M_{do} = 2.79$ ($SD = .45$); $M_{su} = 2.62$ ($SD = .47$), $F(1,58) = 3.45, p < .07$, $\eta^2 = .06$). Concurrent validity testing of the DCS and KONFKOD shows high agreement between the three main categories (see Schermuly & Scholl, 2012).

For criterion-related validity, for example, high negative relationships were found between dominant-hostile behavior from a supervisor, and satisfaction with supervisor and task ($\rho = -.73$, $p < .01$ and $\rho = -.32$, $p < .01$). Positive correlations were found between friendly supervisor behavior and leader satisfaction ($r = .43$, $p < .01$) as well as task satisfaction ($r = .21$, $p < .10$) (Schermuly, 2011). Furthermore, different functional categories and team performance were associated (Meyer et al., in press; Meyer & Schermuly, 2012). Ianiro et al. (2013) found that mimicry behavior in coaching is associated with higher relationship quality. The more similarity the coach and the client show between their dominance and affiliation behavior in the first coaching session, the higher the client perceives the relationship quality at the end of the coaching ($r = .57$; $p < .01$).

Data Aggregation and Analysis

Data can be analyzed on the level of sense units. This makes it possible to conduct sequential analyses. In addition, an aggregation of the data is an option. This can be done at the person-oriented level (e.g., how successful was a group member with a specific nonverbal style or how many proposals were stated by a person?), or at the group level (e.g., how friendly was the interpersonal exchange in the group?). Future research should use the DCS in important field settings more often to measure and analyze nonverbal interaction processes that are not directly noticeable by the team and observers. This is important because, as shown above, dominance and affiliation are associated, for example, with satisfaction and relationship variables. New contexts for the use of the DCS include, for example, communication processes in group therapies, job interviews and assessment centers, operating rooms, or management boards.

Previous Studies

Studies using DCS are summarized in Table 22.2.

References

Original Publications

Schermuly, C. C., & Scholl, W. (2011). *Instrument zur Kodierung von Diskussionen (IKD) [Discussion Coding System (DCS)]*. Göttingen, Germany: Hogrefe.

Schermuly, C. C., & Scholl, W. (2012). The Discussion Coding System (DCS). A new instrument for analyzing communication processes. *Communication Methods and Measures*, *6*, 12–40.

Other References

Bales, R. F. (1950). *Interaction process analysis. A method for the study of small groups*. Cambridge, MA: Addison-Wesley.

Boos, M. (1995). Die sequentielle Strukturierung sozialer Interaktion [The sequential structure of social interaction]. In W. Langenthaler & G. Schiepek (Hrsg.), *Selbstorganisation und Dynamik in Gruppen* (pp. 209–221). Münster: Lit.

Brauner, E. (2006). Kodierung transaktiver Wissensprozesse (TRAWIS). Ein Verfahren zur Erfassung von Wissenstransfers in Interaktionen [Transactive Knowledge Coding System (TRAWIS): A schema for the assessment of knowledge transfer in interactions]. *Zeitschrift für Sozialpsychologie*, *37*, 99–112. doi:10.1024/0044-3514.37.2.99

Fisch, R. (1994). Eine Methode zur Analyse von Interaktionsprozessen beim Problemlösen in Gruppen [A method for the analysis of interaction processes during group problem solving]. *Gruppendynamik*, *25*, 149–168.

Fiske, S. T., Cuddy, A. J. C., & Glick, P. (2006). Universal dimensions of social cognition: Warmth and competence. *Trends in Cognitive Sciences*, *11*, 77–83. http://dx.doi.org/10.1016/j.tics.2006.11.005

Heise, D. R. (2007). *Expressive order. Confirming sentiments in social action*. New York, NY: Springer.

Ianiro, P. M., & Kauffeld, S. (2014). Take care what you bring with you: How coaches' mood and interpersonal behavior affect coaching success. *Consulting Psychology Journal: Practice and Research*, *66*, 231–257. http://dx.doi.org/10.1037/cpb0000012

Ianiro, P. M., Lehmann-Willenbrock, N., & Kauffeld, S. (2015). Coaches and clients in action: A sequential analysis of interpersonal coach and client behavior. *Journal of Business and Psychology*, *30*, 435–456. http://dx.doi.org/10.1007/s10869-014-9374-5

Ianiro, P. M., Schermuly, C. C., & Kauffeld, S. (2013). Why interpersonal affiliation and dominance matter: An interaction analysis of the coach-client relationship. *Coaching: An International Journal of Theory, Research & Practice*, *6*, 25–46. http://dx.doi.org/10.1080/17521882.2012.740489

Jacobs, I., & Scholl, W. (2005). Interpersonale Adjektivliste (IAL): Die empirische Umsetzung theoretischer Circumplex-Eigenschaften für die Messung interpersonaler Stile [Interpersonal Adjective List (IAL): The empirical implementation of theoretical circumplex characteristics for the measurement of interpersonal styles]. *Diagnostica, 51*, 145–155. http://dx.doi.org/10.1026/0012-1924.51.3.145

Kämmer, J. E., Gaissmaier, W., Reimer, T., & Schermuly, C. C. (2014). The adaptive use of recognition in group decision making. *Cognitive Science, 38*, 911–942. http://dx.doi.org/10.1111/cogs.12110

Kolbe, M. (2007). *Koordination von Entscheidungsprozessen in Gruppen. Die Bedeutung expliziter Koordinationsmechanismen.* [Process coordination in decision making groups. The meaning of explicit coordination mechanisms]. Saarbrücken, Germany: VDM Verlag Dr. Müller.

Luxen, M. F. (2005). Gender differences in dominance and affiliation during a demanding interaction. *The Journal of Psychology, 139*, 331–347. http://dx.doi.org/10.3200/JRLP.139.4.331-347

Meyer, B., Burtscher, M. J., Jonas, K., Feese, S., Arnrich, B., Tröster, G., & Schermuly, C. C. (2016). What good leaders actually do: Micro-level leadership behavior, leader evaluations, and team decision quality. *European Journal of Work and Organizational Psychology, 25*(6), 773–789. http://dx.doi.org/10.1080/1359432X.2016.1189903

Meyer, B., & Schermuly, C. C. (2012). When beliefs are not enough: Examining the interaction of diversity faultlines, task motivation, and diversity beliefs on team performance. *European Journal of Work and Organizational Psychology, 21*, 456–487. http://dx.doi.org/10.1080/1359432X.2011.560383

Sachs, L. (1999). *Angewandte Statistik. Anwendung statistischer Methoden (Applied statistics. Application of statistical methods).* Berlin, Germany: Springer.

Scharpf, U., & Fisch, R. (1989). Das Schicksal von Vorschlägen in Beratungs- und Entscheidungssitzungen. Ein Beitrag zur Analyse inhaltlicher Aspekte der Interaktion bei der Entscheidungsfindung in Gruppen [The fate of proposals in consultation and decision situations. A contribution to the analysis of content aspects of interaction in group decision-making]. *Gruppendynamik, 20*, 283–296.

Schermuly, C. C., Schröder, T., Nachtwei, J. & Scholl, W. (2010). Das Instrument zur Kodierung von Diskussionen (IKD): Ein Verfahren zur zeitökonomischen und validen Kodierung von Interaktionen in Organisationen [The Discussion Coding System (DCS): An instrument for valid and time-efficient coding of interactions in organizations]. *Zeitschrift für Arbeits- und Organisationspsychologie, 54*, 149–170. http://dx.doi.org/10.1026/0932-4089/a000026

Schröder, T., Netzel, J., Schermuly, C. C., & Scholl, W. (2013). Culture-constrained affective consistency of interpersonal behavior. A test of affect control theory with nonverbal expressions. *Social Psychology, 44*, 47–58.

Sjøvold, E. (2007). Systematizing person-group relations (SPGR). A field theory of social interaction. *Small Group Research, 38*, 615–635.

23 Interaction Process Analysis (IPA)

Joann Keyton

General Information

Name of Coding Scheme

Interaction Process Analysis (IPA)

Original Publication

Bales, R. F. (1950). *Interaction process analysis: A method for the study of small groups*. Cambridge, MA: Addison-Wesley.

Keywords

Interaction analysis, IPA, conversation, task-oriented, relational, socioemotional, small groups

Summary

Bales' (1950a, 1950b) Interaction Process Analysis (IPA) was one of the earliest coding schemes that prescribed both the process of unitizing and analyzing acts within and between speakers in naturally occurring conversation. IPA was developed to distinguish between and clarify the functions of task-oriented and relational components comprising group interaction. The focus of this coding scheme is the function of the *act* (i.e., complete thought), which is derived from interpreting the reaction of a communicator to another communicator's act. IPA was developed on the foundation that group members both act and react to others in group conversations. Its 12 categories for coding acts are organized into four macro categories of socioemotional/positive reactions, socioemotional/negative reactions, task/attempted answers, and task/questions. The coding scheme focuses on process and is agnostic to the content of the interaction.

Description of the Coding Scheme

During the period 1947 to 1950, the American social psychologist Robert Freed Bales (1916–2004) developed Interaction Process Analysis (IPA). Based initially in his research of self-help meetings of Alcoholics Anonymous, the broadest presentation of IPA appears in his seminal book, *Interaction Process Analysis: A Method for the Study of Small Groups* (1950b). Influenced by the contributions by Kurt Lewin's (1939) field theory, Bales' contributions are noted for bringing attention to the group as a social system.

Bales' Interaction Process Analysis (1950b) theory has been described as both well developed and unified in the theoretical premise that people act and react in groups. These actions are observable verbal (i.e., any type of utterance) or nonverbal (e.g., facial expressions, gestures, bodily attitudes, emotional signs that are directed to others in a group) behaviors (i.e., acts) that can be identified by other group members and coded by observers. The IPA coding scheme distinguishes between acts that are task related and those that are relationally focused. Working from a transcript, observers code each group members' acts into a 12-category coding scheme. The first three categories (represented by the code of 1 through 3) are positive socioemotional reactions (i.e., shows solidarity/seems friendly; shows tension release/dramatizes; agrees); the last three categories (represented by the codes of 10 through 12) are negative socioemotional reactions (i.e., disagrees; shows tension; shows antagonism/seems unfriendly). The six middle categories are task-related behaviors separated into answers (i.e., gives suggestions; gives opinions; gives orientation/information) and questions (i.e., asks for orientation/information; asks for opinions; asks for suggestions). The codes for the answer categories are 4 through 6; the codes for the question categories are 7 through 9.

Bales' Interaction Process Analysis requires that coders identify every act of every group member as a socioemotional act or a task-related act. Within those two broad categories, a coder must make a further distinction of which six socioemotional codes or which six task-related codes best represent the act. Theoretically, the two dimensions function at the same time as group members interact; however, each act contributes to either the socioemotional reality or the task of the group. Theoretically, the two dimensions are interdependent and inseparable.

Bales argued that group members must try to achieve a balance, or equilibrium, between these two dimensions. As he explained, every group has some degree of difficulty in adapting to the task. To overcome this difficulty, every group develops social mechanisms that help members differentiate themselves from one another; as group members do so, the social dimension of the group may suffer. That is, task-oriented interaction can cause deterioration in the group's social structure. Conversely, as group members try to strengthen their interpersonal bonds through socioemotional interaction, the task can suffer. These ideas were formalized in Bales and Strodtbeck (1951) as an explanation of the common problems of perception and communication that occur in groups that meet over time.

Interestingly, Bales did not have the expectation that a group's interaction would be evenly balanced with regard to (a) distribution of acts across the 12 categories, or (b) group member interaction, which would normally be interwoven, for example, with socioemotional talk immediately following task-oriented talk. Bales did hypothesize that task-oriented group interaction would be punctuated with short bursts of socioemotional talk. Research has generally found that task-oriented acts outnumber socioemotional acts (e.g., Beck & Keyton, 2014). Depending on the climate of the group, negative socioemotional acts could outnumber positive socioemotional acts (see Beck, Paskewitz, Anderson, Bourdeaux, & Currie-Mueller, 2017; Dennis, Kunkel, & Keyton, 2008; Keyton & Beck, 2009; Lofstrand & Zackrisson, 2014).

Comparable Instruments

One of the unique aspects of IPA is that all acts comprising an interaction are coded. Transcripts are segregated into speaking turns; speaking turns are unitized into thought units. IPA was not designed to isolate certain types of acts for coding (e.g., coding only acts that represent leadership or conflict).

Bales' (1950b) Interaction Process Analysis was the springboard for Bales and Cohen's (1979) SYMLOG, or the SYstem for the Multiple Level Observation of Groups. SYMLOG extends Bales' IPA two-dimensional coding scheme into three dimensions representing (1) dominance versus submissiveness, (2) friendliness versus unfriendliness, and (3) instrumentally controlled versus emotionally expressive behaviors. Whereas IPA is used for coding interaction after it happens by researchers, SYMLOG captures the subjective experience of group members as they rate themselves and all other group members on 26 adjective phrases immediately after participating in group interaction. SYMLOG ratings can be done on a paper form or through software. Initially, trained coders coded self-help groups in real time. This practice, however, has declined. More suitable is a coding version of SYMLOG developed by Beck and Fisch (2000).

Goals of the Instrument

IPA was developed for assessing face-to-face naturally occurring interaction. Bales (1950b) declared that an act "is the smallest discriminable segment of verbal or nonverbal behavior" that can be coded (p. 37). IPA is suited for answering questions about the balance of task and socioemotional utterances across a group's interaction period. This question is not applied to individual group members, but to the group as an interacting whole. This task/socioemotional balance can be explored in one group meeting, as well as across a group's multiple meetings. Initially intended for answering questions about the social relationships of group members in social or relational groups (e.g., self-help groups), IPA has been used by researchers as a basis for evaluating group performance relative to other constructs in task-oriented groups (see Hackman, 1975). More recently, IPA has been the basis for theorizing about message interdependence among group members (see Beck & Keyton, 2012).

Research-oriented goals are the focus of IPA, as researchers must record the group interaction, and transcribe, unitize, and finally code the interaction. IPA can also be used to provide feedback to groups that meet regularly over time, as the interval between meetings would allow a facilitator to conduct the coding and develop the analyses as feedback to group members.

Available Versions

Bales' original version of the theory and methodology is available in Bales (1950b). Others (Keyton, 1997, 2003) have provided condensed versions of the theory and necessary steps for coding.

Applicability

Originally, Bales developed IPA for use with task-oriented self-analytical groups but believed that IPA could be used with any type of group, especially work groups. More commonly, IPA is a research tool, as the results from IPA coding can be used to analyze how group members communicate with one another and achieve their common tasks. Communication scholars, in particular, have applied IPA theory and method to analyze the group talk of ad hoc task groups in experimental designs (Hiltz, Johnson, & Turoff, 1986), weekly meetings of a breast cancer support group (Beck & Keyton, 2014; Dennis, Kunkel, & Keyton, 2008), weekly meetings of a nonprofit business (Beck & Keyton, 2009), online support group posts (Maloney-Krichmar & Preece, 2000), online group discussions (Fahy, 2005), microblogging (Guo & Goh, 2014), and the interaction of players in online multiplayer video games (Pena & Hancock, 2006). In some of these instances, researchers have reported giving feedback to groups based on the research results.

Practical Application

In using IPA for research, the most practical considerations include: (a) how the group interaction will be audio recorded and transcribed, (b) who will verify the transcription to the audio, (c) who will unitize and code the transcript, and (d) who will analyze the results. It is not possible for one person to complete these tasks, as unitizing and coding reliability must be established with another coder. Student research assistants are often employed (with training and supervision) to complete the tasks.

The unitizing and coding of a transcript is functionally dependent upon the quality of the recording of the group interaction and the accuracy of the transcription. Consumer-quality digital voice recording equipment produces sufficient quality for transcription; however, the use of a consumer-grade, low-profile, omnidirectional table microphone significantly improves the recording, and is the least obtrusive. Speakers can also wear individual lapel mics and be recorded on professional-grade recording device with multiple inputs; these recordings can be unified by using Audacity®, free, open source, cross-platform audio software for multi-track recording and editing. Researchers report transcribing the recording themselves, or using professional or student transcribers. In either case, the transcript must be (a) verified to the audio recording, and (b) prepared such that every turn at talk is attributable to a group member. Unfortunately, to date, digital transcription software is not satisfactory for automatically transcribing multi-voice recordings.

Unitizing and coding transcripts is time and labor intensive. Training for all who participate in unitizing and/or coding is required. As Jordan and Henderson (1995) describe, "group work is also essential for incorporating novices because interaction analysis is difficult to describe and is best learned by doing . . . [as] apprentices, newcomers are gradually socialized into an ongoing community of practice in which they increasingly participate" (pp. 43–44). Training is best done with all coders together.

After describing the interaction context, training typically is comprised of these steps: (a) creating conceptual clarity about *complete* thoughts or *thought units*, (b) reviewing and discussing unitized interaction from another project, (c) practicing unitizing as a group on data from the current project, and (d) reviewing the unitizing practice as a group. Novice researchers must be reminded that a turn at talk may be a complete thought unit or may be coded as several thought units. If the researcher is satisfied with unitizing performance, and while the group of coders is still together, individual coders are given transcripts to unitize independently. These unitizing attempts are then reviewed by the group, with the researcher adding or correcting as necessary. At this point, the researcher can give individual unitizing assignments to coders; and the following coder meeting is devoted to a second person independently unitizing the material. When sufficient unitizing reliability (i.e., .9 or above) is achieved among all coder dyads, coders may work independently on unitizing. Unitizing is generally straightforward when the transcript is of lab groups or online communication. However, unitizing is more difficult when interactants (a) take long turns at speaking, (b) talk over one another, or (c) are dealing with complex issues.

Once all material is unitized, training for the coding scheme begins repeating the steps above. Coding is more difficult than unitizing and takes considerably more time, as coders must choose and apply one of the 12 codes. Some scholars reduce coding anxiety by having coders first make the binary decision of *is this unit task related or socioemotionally related?* Once that decision is made, coders then select from one of six subordinate task or socioemotional codes. Intercoder reliability of .80 is acceptable; .90 is preferable (Neuendorf, 2002).

For both unitizing and coding, coders can only work individually once satisfactory intercoder reliability is achieved. Throughout the unitizing and coding process, all coders should have access to the audio recording. Researchers should also check for coder drift as coding proceeds across many transcripts.

Because researchers work on interaction from different contexts and of different modes, standard times for training, coding, or unitizing have not been established. Nor does a coding manual, outside of Bales' articles, exist.

Quality Assessment

Reliability

Few studies have assessed the validity or reliability of Bales' Interaction Process Analysis. A central issue of reliability is establishing interrater coding reliability. Training of coders is required, but researchers have not reported difficulty in developing reliability among coders. Nor have researchers reported difficulty with maintaining coding reliability across a group's interactions, or among different group interactions. The one exception occurs in the unitizing and/or coding of complex interactions as described above.

Reliability is reported twice – first for unitizing reliability and then coding reliability – when using IPA. Unitizing reliability is generally considered satisfactory at .9 or above. When this level of unitizing is achieved among all unitizing dyads, coders may work independently on unitizing.

Coding reliability has a slightly lower threshold and is considered suitable when all coding dyads achieve intercoder reliability of .85 to .90. Coders can only code independently once satisfactory intercoder reliability is achieved. Coder drift should be assessed for large datasets. Information about training, how unitizing and coding reliability was established, and degrees of unitizing and coder reliability should be reported in the manuscript. Some researchers have reported that categorizing validity can be practically evidenced by coding consistency (Rourke & Anderson, 2004). Krippendorff (2004) explains that lack of reliability "limits the chance of validity" (p. 212) and cautions researchers that "reliability does not guarantee validity" (p. 213).

Validity

Poole and Folger (1981) examined the representational validity of IPA and found that it performed better than other coding systems (Fisher's [1970] Decision Proposal Coding System, and Mabry's [1975] Pattern Variable Coding System) for conflict over opinions, assertions of opinions, information exchange, and summarization of others' views and opinions. Given the differences of types of groups in which IPA has been deployed, the validity of the theory and coding scheme is high. The functional nature of the theory and coding scheme is applicable to face-to-face and online groups regardless of the content of their interactions. Shortly after, Allen, Comerford, and Ruhe (1989) reported a validity study of IPA. Factor analysis was used on the data of two individuals who coded while the interaction took place. No mention is made of a unitizing step. Their results did not confirm the structures of IPA codes as four broad categories (i.e., questions, attempted answers, positive socioemotional, negative socioemotional); the 12 categories that comprise IPA; the pairwise structure (e.g., gives orientation, asks for orientation); or socioemotional as distinct from task.

Data Aggregation and Analysis

Because IPA focuses on the function, rather than the content, of talk, it is possible to aggregate data from IPA studies for secondary analyses. Researchers have begun to investigate with sequential analysis (a) the degree to which stationarity, or the consistency in the transition among functional contribution types across the entirety of a group discussion, is present; as well as (b) the degree to which homogeneity, or transition among functional contribution types across groups or meetings, is present (see Ervin, Bonito, & Keyton, 2017).

Previous Studies

Keyton and Beck (2009) coded sequences of talk in breast cancer support group interaction and discovered that task-socioemotional-task message sequences help group members accomplish different relational and task goals. Results confirm earlier claims that relational influence stems from both task and relational messages. Using IPA coding and focusing on the interaction of the group leader, Beck and Keyton (2014) found that broad categories of task-oriented facilitation techniques (changing the focus, clarification) and one category of socioemotional facilitation techniques (showing support) dominated the support groups' conversation. The results suggest that support group facilitators need the ability to facilitate both task and relational aspects of social support.

Research using IPA to study communication in health settings continues; see Beck, Paskewitz, Anderson, Bourdeaux, and Currie-Mueller (2017). Research exploring communication through digital behavior has also utilized Bales' IPA; see Li, Rau, Li, and Maedche (2017); and Choi, Im, and Hofstede (2016).

References

Original Publication

Bales, R. F. (1950b). *Interaction process analysis: A method for the study of small groups.* Cambridge, MA: Addison-Wesley.

Other References

Allen, W. R., Comerford, R. A., & Ruhe, J. A. (1989). Factor analytic study of Bales' Interaction Process Analysis. *Educational and Psychological Measurement, 49,* 701–707. doi:10.1177/001316448904900325

Bales, R. F. (1950a). A set of categories for the analysis of small group interaction. *American Sociological Review, 15,* 257–263.

Bales, R. F., & Cohen, S. P. (1979). *SYMLOG: A system for the multiple level observation of groups.* New York, NY: Free Press.

Bales, R. F., & Strodtbeck, F. L. (1951). Phases in group problem-solving. *Journal of Abnormal and Social Psychology, 44,* 485–495.

Beck, D., & Fisch, R. (2000). Argumentation and emotional processes in group decision-making: Illustration of a multilevel interaction process analysis approach. *Group Processes & Intergroup Relations, 3,* 183–201. doi:10.1177/1368430200003002005

Beck, S. J., & Keyton, J. (2009). Perceiving strategic meeting interaction. *Small Group Research, 40,* 223–246. doi:10.1177/1046496408330084

Beck, S. J., & Keyton, J. (2012). Team cognition, communication, and message interdependence. In E. Salas, S. F. Fiore, & M. Letsky (Eds.), *Theories of team cognition: Cross-disciplinary perspectives* (pp. 471–494). New York, NY: Routledge.

Beck, S. J., & Keyton, J. (2014). Facilitating social support: Member-leader communication in a breast cancer support group. *Cancer Nursing, 37,* E36–43. doi:10.1097/NCC.0b013e3182813829

Beck, S. J., Paskewitz, E. A., Anderson, W. A., Bourdeaux, & Currie-Mueller, J. (2017). The task and relational dimensions of online social support. *Health Communication, 32,* 347–355. doi:10.1080/10410236.2016.1138383

Choi, K. S., Im, I., & Hofstede, G. J. (2016). A cross-cultural comparative analysis of small group collaboration using mobile twitter. *Computers in Human Behavior, 65,* 308–318. doi:10.1016/j.chb.2016.08.043

Dennis, M. R., Kunkel, A., & Keyton, J. (2008). Problematic integration theory, appraisal theory, and the Bosom Buddies Breast Cancer Support Group. *Journal of Applied Communication Research, 36,* 415–436. doi:10.1080/00909880802094315

Ervin, J., Bonito, J., & Keyton, J. (2017). Convergence of intrapersonal and interpersonal processes across group meetings. *Communication Monographs, 84,* 200–220. doi:10.1080/03637751.2016.1185136

Fahy, P. (2005). Online and face-to-face group interaction processes compared using Bales' Interaction Process Analysis (IPA). Retrieved February 14, 2018, from www.eurodl.org/materials/contrib/2006/Patrick_J_Fahy.htm

Fisher, B. A. (1970). Decision emergence: Phases in group decision-making. *Speech Monographs, 7*, 53–66. doi:10.1080/03637757009375649.

Guo, H., & Goh, D.H-L. (2014). "I Have AIDS": *Content analysis of postings in HIV/AIDS support group on a Chinese microblog, 34*, 219–226. Retrieved February 14, 2018, from www.eurodl.org/materials/contrib/2006/Patrick_J_Fahyhtm.

Hackman, J. R. (1975). Group tasks, group interaction process, and group performance effectiveness: A review and proposed integration. *Advances in Experimental Social Psychology, 8*, 45–99. doi:10.1016/S0065-2601(08)60248-8

Hiltz, S. R., Johnson, K., & Turoff, M. (1986). Experiments in group decision making communication process and outcome in face-to-face versus computerized conferences. *Human Communication Research, 13*, 225–252 doi:10.1111/j.1468-2958.1986.tb00104.x

Jordan, B., & Henderson A. (1995). Interaction analysis: Foundations and practice. *The Journal of the Learning Sciences, 4*, 39–103.

Keyton, J. (1997). Coding communication in decision-making groups: Assessing effective and ineffective process. In L. R. Frey & J. K. Barge (Eds.), *Managing group life: Communication in decision-making groups* (pp. 236–269). Boston, MA: Houghton Mifflin.

Keyton, J. (2003). Observing group interaction. In R. Y. Hirokawa, R. S. Cathcart, L. A. Samovar, & L. D. Henman, *Small group communication: Theory and practice* (8th edn., pp. 256–266). Los Angeles, CA: Roxbury.

Keyton, J., & Beck, S. J. (2009). The influential role of relational messages in group interaction. *Group Dynamics, 13*, 14–30. doi:10.1037/a0013495

Krippendorff, K. (2004). *Content analysis: An introduction to its methodology* (2nd edn.). Thousand Oaks, CA: Sage.

Lewin, K. (1939). Field theory and experiment in social psychology. *American Journal of Sociology, 44*, 868–896. doi:10.1086/218177

Li, Y., Rau, P-L. P., Li, H., & Maedche, A. (2017). Effects of a dyad's cultural intelligence on global virtual collaboration. *IEEE Transactions on Professional Communication, 60*, 56–75. doi:10.1109/TPC.2016.2632842.

Lofstrand, P., & Zakrisson, I. (2014). Competitive versus non-competitive goals in group decision-making. *Small Group Research, 45*, 451–464. doi:10.1177/1046496414532954

Mabry, E. A. (1975). An instrument for assessing content themes in group interaction. *Speech Monographs, 42*, 191–297. doi:10.1080/03637757509375904

Maloney-Krichmar, D., & Preece, J. (2002). *The meaning of an online health community in the lives of its members: Roles, relationships and group dynamics*. Published in the proceedings of the IEEE 2002 International Symposium on Technology and Society: Social Implications of Information and Communication Technology. doi:10.1109/ISTAS.2002.1013791

Maloney-Krichmar, D., & Preece, J. (2005). Multilevel analysis of sociability, usability, and community dynamics in an online health community. *ACM Transactions on Computer-Human Interaction, 12*, 201–232. doi:10.1145/1067860.1067864

Neuendorf, K. A. (2002). *The content analysis guidebook*. Thousand Oaks, CA: Sage.

Pena, J., & Hancock, J. T. (2006). An analysis of socioemotional and task communication in online multiplayer video games. *Communication Research, 33*, 92–109. doi:10.1177/0093650205283103

Poole, M. S., & Folger, J. P. (1981). A method for establishing the representational validity of interaction coding systems: Do we see what they see? *Human Communication Research, 8,* 26–42. doi:10.1111/j.1468-2958.1981.tb00654.x

Rourke, L., & Anderson, T. (2004). Validity in quantitative content analysis. *Educational Technology Research and Development, 52*(1), 5–18.

24 TEMPO

A Time-Based System for Analysis of Group Interaction Process

Janice R. Kelly, Maayan Dvir, and Danielle M. Parsons

General Information

Name of Coding Scheme

Time-by-Event-by-Member Pattern Observation (TEMPO)

Keywords

Time-based, temporal patterning, task production, group process, member support, group well-being, group interaction

Summary

The Time-by-Event-by-Member Pattern Observation (TEMPO) system is a 22-category hierarchically organized system for coding primarily verbal behavior in group interactions. The system distinguishes between contributions to task content versus process and proposals versus evaluations of those contributions. The system also has categories that tap nontask activities, particularly those relevant to member support and group well-being. Importantly, these activities are referenced with respect to which member made the contribution and the time and duration of each contribution. Thus, this system is particularly applicable to questions of temporal patterns of activities in group interaction.

Description of the Coding Scheme

TEMPO was developed to be a comprehensive and time-sensitive coding system that is applicable to a wide variety of groups and tasks. TEMPO stands for Time-by-Event-by-Member Pattern Observation system – thus it codes *who* (Member) says *what* (Event) and *when* (Time). The system is based on McGrath's (1991) Time, Interaction, and Performance (TIP) theory of group performance and interaction. TIP theory emphasizes temporal processes in group interaction and

Table 24.1 *The TEMPO coding system*[a]

Production function categories Propose	
Content	Process
1. New – task content	1. Goals – quality/quantity production standards
2. Prior – prior content revisited	2. Strategies – how to do the task
3. Dictate – repeat content as in dictate to writer or to others who didn't hear	3. Acts – keep task moving, process tasks not 1 or 2

Evaluate	
Content	Process
1. Agree with/accept – proposed content	1. Agree with/accept – proposed process
2. Clarify/modify – proposed content	2. Clarify/modify – proposed process
3. Disagree – with content that is otherwise accepted	3. Disagree – with a process that is otherwise adopted
4. Reject – content that is proposed	4. Reject – process that is proposed

Nonproduction categories
T. Task digression – talking about content or process that has already been accepted. The discussion or comment does not move the task forward
P. Personal comments – comments about oneself that do not move the task forward
I. Interpersonal comments – responses to other's personal comments that do not move the task forward
R. React to experiment – look up at recording booth, react to the time limit, comment about being recorded, etc.
D. Digressions – comments about the specifics of the situation that don't fit anywhere else
U. Uninterpretable – you can tell who spoke but not what they said, or you can't tell who spoke
S. Silence – periods of no overt activities (no one is speaking or writing)
W. Writing – for periods of silence because the scribe is writing

Note. [a]Based on Futoran, Kelly, and McGrath (1989).

group functions that are relevant to task production, as well as to other aspects of group interactions such as group well-being and member support.

Who? TEMPO is designed to identify behaviors of individual members and their individual contribution to the group product. Thus, in addition to data regarding the task contributions and process of the group as a whole, the pattern of contributions of each member can be identified.

What? The TEMPO coding system contains 22 categories that capture statements that are relevant and constructive to task production across a wide range of tasks, as well as statements that serve nontask production functions (see Table 24.1). Production functions include proposals of content or process, as well as evaluations of content or process. A proposal of content (PC) is a contribution that is directly related to the goal of the group's activity, for example providing a possible solution to a problem. Proposals of content include (1) offering a new content proposal that was not previously suggested, (2) revisiting a topic that was previously discussed, and (3) repeating content to scribes or to others who didn't hear. Note that proposals of content (PC) can be further coded after the interaction for the quality of that contribution, such that it can be tied directly to the final group outcome (e.g., were high-quality proposals of content incorporated into the final group outcome). A proposal of process (PP) addresses comments and recommendations regarding the way in which the group should approach the task, for example suggesting to allocate roles to the different members or to start by reviewing all the relevant materials. Proposals of process include (1) declaring goals or standards the group should consider, (2) suggesting strategies the group should apply, or (3) performing other acts that contribute to the flow and continuation of the work on the task. Group members may also evaluate both content (EC) and process (EP) proposals made by fellow group members: (1) Agree with or accept a proposal, (2) clarify, ask for clarifications, or suggest modifications to a proposal, (3) express disagreement with a proposal although it is still considered and may be adopted by the group, or (4) reject a proposal completely, as it is off the table.

One of the unique characteristics of TEMPO is that it recognizes that group members may engage in behavior that is not productive to the task, and thus eight categories are designated for nonproduction functions. These include (T) discussing the task in a way that does not contribute to the efforts to move forward, such as discussing a proposal that has already been accepted, (R) reacting to the experimental environment, and (D) discussing matters that are off-topic. Matters that may not concern the group goal but may affect the well-being of the group members include (P) personal and (I) interpersonal comments. TEMPO also accounts for times of (W) writing and of (S) silence, in which no one speaks or writes for a time period of two seconds or more. Lastly, when someone speaks but the coder cannot interpret the words or recognize which member speaks it is coded as (U) uninterpretable.

When? As group interaction occurs and develops over time, the TEMPO system emphasizes the temporal patterning of the interaction and its process. Coders code for the time at which an event occurs, as well as the duration of the event. Coders can also code for cycles of activity—a period of time when interaction is devoted to a particular theme.

Comparable Instruments

The TEMPO system shares some features in common with other coding systems. For example, the act4teams coding system (Kauffeld & Lehmann-Willenbrock, 2012) contains process-focused categories (problem-focused statements and procedural statements), as well as content statements (action-oriented statements). The Micro-Co coding system (Kolbe, Strack, Stein, & Boos, 2011) also has categories that tap into process (instructions and structurings) as well as content (declaring and questions) and is also hierarchically structured. In addition, the system shares some features in common with the Bales (1950) Interaction Process Analysis system. For example, both systems allow for the coding of task contributions (Active and Passive Task Contributions in the Bales system and Propose and Evaluate Content in the TEMPO system). However, the TEMPO system is explicitly time-based and preserves the temporal ordering of contributions. In addition, the system allows for individual task contributions to be later coded for quality so that these individual contributions can be tied directly to the quality of the final outcome or task product of the group. The system also allows for the coding of longer cycles of group activity.

Goals of the Instrument

TEMPO was developed to code for group member activities during group interaction (Event) in a way that is sensitive to who makes the contribution (Member) and when the contribution (Time) was made. Additional goals of the system are:

- To provide a flexible set of categories that could be applied to a wide range of tasks and conceptual issues.
- To permit the investigator to tie the quality of task contributions directly to task performance.
- To allow the investigator to look for activity patterns in group interaction across time.

TEMPO can be used to address questions such as:

- How do group and task features affect the temporal flow of interaction within the group?
- How does that flow of interaction affect the temporal flow of influence among group members?
- How do those temporal patterns of interaction and influence affect the rate and quality of group task performance?

Available Versions

Currently, TEMPO is only available in English. It has been used in the past primarily with paper and pencil coding of videotaped group interaction. However, it could be adapted for other languages and online use.

Applicability

TEMPO is applicable to both field and laboratory research. Videotaping of the group interaction is recommended in order to capture the temporal spacing of member interaction at a fine-grained level. However, it is possible to use the system to code in real time if one is merely interested in the sequencing of acts. Collapsing the system to its five hierarchical categories would also improve one's ability to use the system in real time.

Practical Application

Coding Time

It takes coders approximately two hours to code 10 minutes of a three-person interaction using all 22 TEMPO categories. Coding time may vary by group size, number of coders, and the hierarchical level at which the system is used.

Coder Training

Time required for training coders is approximately two to four hours per coder. Interrater reliability for the first hierarchical level (task vs. nontask) is generally high, whereas the second (propose vs. evaluate content vs. process plus nontask) and third hierarchical levels (full 22 categories) often produce more moderate inter-rater reliabilities.

Technical Requirements

We advise using computer-based records for coding TEMPO (see Glüer, Chapter 13, this volume). Software possibilities include any software that allows a researcher to define their own categories and code event strings. Recording devices (either audio or video) are generally required for application of TEMPO given that real-time coding is difficult without extensive training.

Unitizing

Units of analysis are based on events that consist of three facets: the group member who originated the act, the type of act (by coding category), and the time at which the act began (reported in seconds). Each unit is coded by assigning one of 22 coding categories. An example coding unit for an event where an individual agreed with previously proposed content would be labeled EC1 (Evaluate Content 1: Agree). At a more macro level, the researcher can code for cycles of activity that involve the contribution, evaluation, and modification of a content theme. Content proposals can also be evaluated for quality and can then be tied to task performance.

Training Manual

A training manual as well as a full description of the coding scheme are available from the first author.

Simplified Version

The coding process can be simplified, depending on the researcher's hypotheses, to five basic categories of Level 2 (Process Content, Evaluation Content, Propose Process, Evaluate Process, and Nontask Activity). From there, the researcher can choose to expand parts of the coding scheme, for instance by differentiating between agreements and disagreements within content evaluations. Furthermore, analysis can be simplified by collapsing data across time into "time blocks."

Quality Assessment

Reliability

In Karau and Kelly (1992), five coders, all blind to the conditions of the study, coded in common 10-minutes segments of one-sixth of the videotapes of the group interactions. The mean percentage agreement among all possible pairs of raters at the 22-category component level of the system was 73 percent. The mean percentage agreement among all possible pairs of raters at a hierarchically collapsed level (direct task activity, nontask activity, content evaluations, and process activity) was 93 percent. Straus (1997) assessed component-level interrater reliability using Cohen's Kappa. Three raters coded in common approximately 10 percent of group interaction transcripts. Cohen's Kappa exceeded .80 for the vast majority of rater-pairs on component categories.

Validity

No validity studies have been conducted for this system. Discriminant validity could be established by coding a set of groups using both TEMPO and another system to determine how TEMPO provides contributions that are independent from the other system.

Data Aggregation and Analysis

Each act recorded references (1) the group member who contributed the act, (2) the type of act (system coding category), and (3) the temporal location of the act. Aggregation generally involves collapsing this three-dimensional matrix on its temporal axis, its coding category axis, and/or its member axis. For example, if temporal and member axes are collapsed, the frequency of acts within each coding category can be examined. If the member axis is preserved, the frequency of acts within each coding category by member can be examined. Preserving some aspects of the temporal dimension (for example, dividing the interaction into four equal segments) allows an examination of the frequency of acts within each coding category across time or per member across time. The 22 coding categories are arranged hierarchically, and thus can be collapsed into higher order groupings (e.g., proposing new, prior, and dictating task content can be collapsed into propose content). Karau and Kelly (1992) took this latter approach and used ANOVA to analyze the proportion, rate, and total frequency of direct task activity, nontask activity, content evaluations, and process activity across the conditions of their study.

Previous Studies

Studies applying TEMPO have addressed face-to-face versus computer mediated group processes (Straus, 1997), the development of improved online learning programs (Liu & Burn, 2007), group process variations by task type (Straus, 1999), and virtual reality communication (Nordbäck, & Sivunen, 2013). One example of TEMPO is provided by Karau and Kelly (1992), who were interested in examining the effects of time abundance and time scarcity on both group interaction process and the quality of the written group solutions. Group interactions were videotaped and coded by five judges using a hierarchically collapsed version of TEMPO. Researchers found that time scarcity resulted in higher task focus, but the highest-quality end product was produced by groups working at optimal time conditions. Interestingly, the quality of proposed solutions (PC1s) did not differ across time limit conditions.

References

Original Publication

Futoran, G. C., Kelly, J. R., & McGrath, J. E. (1989). TEMPO: A time-based system for analysis of group interaction process. *Basic and Applied Social Psychology, 10,* 211–232. doi:10.1207/2s15324834basp1003.2

Other References

Bales, R. F. (1950). *Interaction process analysis: A method for the study of small groups.* Cambridge, MA: Addison-Wesley.
Karau, S. J., & Kelly, J. R. (1992). The effects of time scarcity and time abundance on group performance quality and interaction process. *Journal of Experimental Social Psychology, 28,* 542–571. doi:10.1016/0022-1031(92)90045-L

Kauffeld, S., & Lehmann-Willenbrock, N. (2012). Meetings matter: Effects of team meetings on team and organizational success. *Small Group Research*, *43*, 130–158. doi:10 1177/1046496411429599

Kolbe, M., Strack, M., Stein, A., & Boos, M. (2011). Effective coordination in human group decision making: MICRO_CO: A micro-analytical taxonomy for analyzing explicit coordination mechanisms in decision-making groups. In M. Boos et al. (Eds.), *Coordination in Human and Primate Groups* (pp. 199–219). Berlin, Germany: Springer-Verlag. doi:10.1007/978-3-642-15355-6_11

Liu, Y. C., & Burn, J. M. (2007). Improving the performance of online learning teams – A discourse analysis. *Journal of Information Systems Education*, *18*, 369–379.

McGrath, J. E. (1991). Time, interaction, and performance (TIP): A theory of groups. *Small Group Research*, *22*, 147–174. doi:10.1177/1046496491222001

Nordback, E., & Sivunen, A. (2013). Leadership behaviors in virtual team meetings taking place in a 3D virtual world. 46th Hawaii International Conference on System Sciences. doi:10.1109/HICSS.2013.380

Straus, S. G. (1997). Technology, group process, and group outcomes: Testing the connections in computer-mediated and face-to-face groups. *Human-Computer Interaction*, *12*, 227–266. doi:10.1207/s15327051hci1203_1

Straus, S. G. (1999). Testing a typology of tasks: An empirical validation of McGrath's (1984) Group Task Circumplex. *Small Group Research*, *30*, 166–187. doi:10.1177/104649649903000202

Argument, Conflict, and Negotiations

25 ARGUMENT

A Category System for Analyzing Argumentation in Group Discussions

Margarete Boos and Christina Sommer

General Information

Name of Coding Scheme

ARGUMENT

Keywords

Argumentation, debate, decision-making, functioning morality, social representations

Summary

The goal of ARGUMENT is to analyze the structure of argumentation in a debate or general group discussion. The system's analysis of argumentation structure follows the concept of argument developed by Toulmin (1958). In his model of argument, Toulmin differentiates six elements of argumentation: grounds, qualifiers, claim, warrants, backing, and rebuttal. Using this model, verbal contributions to a group discussion can be segmented and coded according to these elements to identify structural characteristics of argumentation, e.g., deductive versus inductive ways of reasoning in a discussion.

Description of the Coding Scheme

ARGUMENT originates from a research project where moral decision making in medical settings was investigated, based on the concept of "functioning morality" articulated by Bergmann and Luckmann (1999). They describe the moral decision-making processes in everyday life, pointing out that moral judgments are interpersonally negotiated. From this perspective, moral decisions are put to practice through the actions and interactions of persons in social relationships or group settings. Morality can therefore be understood as a prime example of social representations (Moscovici, 1981, 1984).

Social representations form a set of concepts, statements, and social explanations originating in daily life that regulate interindividual communications. A crucial point of social representations theory is that "the purpose of all representations is to make something unfamiliar, or unfamiliarity itself, familiar" (Moscovici, 1984, p. 24). To achieve this function, social representations theory supposes two specific processes representing the dynamic of social representations: *anchoring* and *objectification* (Moscovici, 1984).

Through the *anchoring* mechanism, an alien event or concept that must be understood is integrated by molding it within the context of existing concepts. A basic example of an anchoring mechanism is our everyday use of personal experiences or culturally shared input gleaned from literature, theatre, radio, Internet, etc., in order to socially navigate our way around an unknown cultural setting or foreign country, especially when facing a personally unknown experience such as, say, attending the opera for the first time. Such (pre-)existing concepts, no matter how unknown on an individual basis, can be understood as socially shared. Consequently, anchoring is not simply an individual process of assimilation, but rather a process of drawing on social or group knowledge. In the second formation process of social representations – *objectification* – these abstract schemes formed during the anchoring process are transformed or "objectified" into concrete mental content.

Moscovici (1984) has argued that "representations are the outcome of an unceasing babble and a permanent dialogue between individuals" (p. 951). In other words, social representations do not remain unchangeable content once they have been established as a social norm, but instead are subjected to an enduring dialogue where different positions are debated and contested (Moscovici, 1984).

This leaves us with the question as to how we may analyze the structure (anchoring and objectification) of arguments in a way that gives consideration to their richness, while still taking into account that they should be seen as a group process to reflect the social representations aspect. The brief example in Figure 25.1 using medical moral dilemmas, which has been structured according to Toulmin (1958), may be useful to clarify our analytical structure underlying argumentation.

This example highlights how the sequence of debate in itself is an important datum. If we assume a principle-based reasoning to be deductive in nature, the *claim* to discontinue force-feeding, which is concluded as a decision, marks the start of the argument and arguably one would expect it to be *warrant*ed early on: "Discontinuing force-feeding exercises the patient's immutable right of self-determination, if a patient has chosen to die." But starting the argument on the following *grounds* and leading to the *conclusion* using the sequence of debate illustrated in Figure 25.1 is more inductive: "The patient wanted to die, but he is currently incapacitated, so we cannot really know whether or not that decision holds; ergo, we should not discontinue force-feeding." In a nutshell, this framework allows to rate the different aspects of an argument by their respective function relative to the individual case. This framework is also suitable to structure group-based arguments.

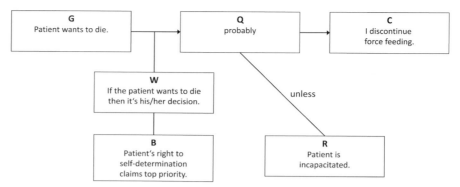

Figure 25.1 *Toulmin's (1958) model of argumentation. Note. G = grounds: reasons or supporting evidence that bolster claim; Q = qualifier: specification of limits to claim, warrant, and backing; C = claim: the position being argued for; W = warrant: principle, provision, or chain of reasoning that connects grounds to claim; B = backing: support, justification, reasons to back warrant; R = rebuttal: counterexamples and counter-arguments.*

In his model of argument, Toulmin (1958) discriminates six elements of argumentation: grounds, qualifiers, claim, warrants, backing, and rebuttal (see Figure 25.1). A claim (C) represents the goal or discovery of the argument. The grounds (G) support the claim. They are the underlying foundations that substantiate the truth of the claim. Figuratively, the grounds are like the ingredients of a cake (C) – they comprise factual data. At the very least, an argument is composed of a claim and of a ground. Warrants (W) define the way of argumentation. Warrants back up the reliability of progression from grounds to claim, as is process progression described in the recipe of a cake. Examples of warrants are rules of thumb and legal principles. The backing (B) provides a supportive statement for the warrant. Backing is additional information that is presupposed by the warrant, such as scientific laws or statistics. The backing facilitates the decision whether the warrant has merit. The rebuttal contains the exceptional case that overrides the validity of the warrant. The argumentation element of qualifier indicates the possible weaknesses or strengths of G, W, and B to point toward C. Qualifiers (e.g., probably, certainly, presumably) mark the relationship of C to G, W, and B. X-(G) implies that a previously established claim, warrant, or rebuttal is used as grounds for a subsequent claim (Voss, Tyler, & Yengo, 1983).

Comparable Instruments

There exist comparable coding schemes for analyzing argumentation, conflict, and negotiations in dyadic or group discussions (see for instance this volume, Chapters 26–29). The specificity of ARGUMENT is its focus on the logical structure of an argument, which means that the codes only represent the six basic elements of an argument.

Goals of the Instrument

ARGUMENT's purpose is to disassemble the process of argumentation into basic logical elements. It is applicable not only to the discussion of moral dilemmas, but to a wide range of interaction contexts where there is controversy and arguments/counterarguments are exchanged. For example, one could investigate whether argumentation training changes patterns in debate and how novices' and experts' structure of argumentation differs.

In a study investigating the interaction of two moral modes – justice and care – (Gilligan, 1982), it was shown that according to the moral mode (care or justice) and the moral dilemma at hand, participants in group discussions on a medical/ethical dilemma draw on structurally linked as well as substantially distinct patterns of argumentation (Sommer et al., 2011). The structure of justice arguments tended to be more deductive, as warrants (principle, provision, or chain of reasoning that connects grounds to claim) were used earlier in the argument; whereas the formal structure of care arguments seemed to be more flexible, that is, inductive as well as deductive.

Available Versions

Currently, ARGUMENT is available in English and German. There is no problem in applying the simple basic idea to any other language.

Applicability

ARGUMENT is applicable both in the laboratory and in field settings. In both settings, it is recommended to audio- and video-record the verbal interactions that are to be studied, allowing for more precise analysis. Its application ranges from group discussions on moral dilemmas, to the study of mock juries while deliberating a legal case, and to more basic debates such as the analysis of argumentation in couples' or family conflict.

Practical Application

Coding Time

Coding time required is approximately four to six minutes of coding per one minute of interaction time. However, this strongly depends on the density and complexity of the argumentation tackled in the conversation.

Coder Training

Time required for training coders depends on their previous experience with (a) other coding schemes, (b) the respective coding software, and (c) the respective field (e.g., everyday talk versus interaction between experts).

Technical Requirements

Potential coding software that can be applied includes all software that allows users to define their own categories and – if necessary for the research question – to log time and duration of each code.

Unitizing

In applying this system, group discussions should be videotaped and transcribed. Afterwards, the transcripts are divided into arguments, whereby an argument consists of at least two elements: a ground and a claim (Toulmin, 1958; Voss et al., 1983). The ground(s) (G) support the claim. Grounds are the underlying foundations that substantiate the perceived truth of the claim. Together, they comprise the basic data of any debate, as an argument is minimally composed of a claim and of a ground.

Training Manual

A basic coding manual in German is available from the first author.

Simplified Version

As the structure of arguments must be analyzed exhaustively, there is no light version. Nevertheless, it is up to the researcher to focus the coding on the arguments concerning preselected topics or fields of debate, e.g., only task-oriented arguments and no relationship-oriented arguments.

Quality Assessment

Reliability

Interrater reliability was assessed by two independent coders applying the six elements of ARGUMENT to group discussions of medical students on a medical dilemma. The group discussions were transcribed. Then, the records were divided into arguments following the concept of argument by Toulmin (1958) and Voss et al. (1983). A total of 779 arguments were chosen randomly for the analysis of inter-rater agreement (30 percent of 2570 arguments). The reliability for delimiting the arguments amounted to kappa = .76. This inter-rater agreement is considered high (Fleiss, 1981).

The coding manual can be found at http://hdl.handle.net/2142/35315 (last retrieved on February 18, 2018).

Other References

Bales, R. F. (1950). *Interaction process analysis*. Reading, MA: Addison-Wesley.

Fisher, B. A. (1970). Decision emergence: Phases in group decision making. *Communication Monographs, 37*, 53–66.

Markman, H. J., Renick, M. J., Floyd, F. J., Stanley, S. M., & Clements, M. (1993). Preventing marital distress through communication and conflict management training: A 4- and 5-year follow-up. *Journal of Consulting and Clinical Psychology, 61*(1), 70–77.

Poole, M. S., & Dobosh, M. (2010). Exploring conflict management processes in jury deliberations through interaction analysis. *Small Group Research, 41*, 408–426.

Poole, M. S., & Roth, J. (1989b). Decision development in small groups V: Test of a contingency model. *Human Communication Research, 15*, 549–589.

Poole, M. S., Holmes, M., & DeSanctis, G. (1991). Conflict management in a computer-supported meeting environment. *Management Science, 37*, 926–953.

Sambamurthy, V., & Poole, M. S. (1992). The effects of variations in capabilities of GDSS designs on management of cognitive conflict in groups. *Information Systems Research, 3*, 224–251.

Sillars, A. L., Coletti, S. F., Parry, D., & Rogers, M. A. (1982). Coding verbal conflict tactics: Nonverbal and perceptual correlates of the "avoidance-distributive-integrative" distinction. *Human Communication Research, 9*, 83–95.

27 Micro-Conflict Coding Scheme

Susannah B. F. Paletz and Christian D. Schunn

Name of Coding Scheme

Micro-Conflict Coding Scheme

Keywords

Conflict, disagreement, micro-conflict, communication, micro-processes, interpersonal, teams

Summary

This scheme guides independent coders to assess the presence or absence of micro-conflicts (brief disagreements) at the turn, utterance, or text-based micro levels (e.g., YouTube comments). This scheme has been used with transcribed and audio-videotaped corpora of interpersonal communication, but could also be extended to social media and online communication. In addition to identifying disagreement, this scheme offers guidance for contingent dimensions of the micro-conflicts, such as affect and type (e.g., relationship or task). Past studies have used this coding scheme to examine science and engineering design teams of varying sizes and expertise levels (e.g., Paletz, Schunn, & Kim, 2013; Paletz, Chan, & Schunn, 2016, 2017).

Description of the Coding Scheme

Intrateam conflict is often defined as perceived discrepancies between parties (Jehn & Bendersky, 2003), containing cognitive, behavioral, and affective features (Barki & Hartwick, 2004). It is typically divided up into different types: task conflict (conflicts about the work at hand); process conflict (conflicts about how the work might be accomplished, such as scheduling); and relationship conflict (about personal values, personality, and liking/disliking of others, Jehn,

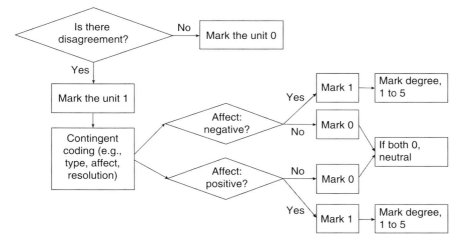

Figure 27.1 *Conflict coding and an example of a contingent code (Affect).*

1997). Another dimension is the degree to which the conflict is characterized by negative affect (Amason, 1996) or positive affect (Jehn & Bendersky, 2003). While relationship conflict is more likely than task conflict to have negative affect (Paletz et al., 2011), suggesting overlap, these two dimensions – the type and affectivity of the conflict – are considered to be different elements of conflict (Jehn & Bendersky, 2003).

We focus on the *expression* of disagreement as it occurs between at least two people (Bendersky, Bear, Behfar, Weingart, Todorova, & Jehn, 2014), at a relatively low level of granularity such as the turn or utterance, rather than larger units, such as five-minute intervals (Paletz et al., 2011). The coding scheme uses the following steps:

- This scheme starts with a set of heuristics to assist the coder with assessing the presence or absence of disagreement in the course of a conversation. Conflicts can be assessed at micro-levels of entire turns or utterances (clauses, or thought statements; Chi, 1997), but individual words would be too fine-grained (e.g., it would be difficult to identify the conflict by word in the utterance, "Well, I like cheese more"). Audio-video data should be attended to, not just transcripts alone. The initial code is whether the unit contains disagreement (1) or not (0; see Figure 27.1); the coder draws on the text content and context of the conversation to make this judgment, in combination with the tone, facial expression, and body language of the speaker, if those data are available.[1]

- A direct contradiction is considered a micro-conflict, but a standalone addition or a clarification is not. For example, if Person A says, "you need to go to the store

---

[1] We have tried coding transcripts without the audio-video cues of tone and body language, and reliability is lower (and coding more difficult) than with those other cues.

today to get milk" and Person B says, "We don't need milk" or "Yeah, but I can't do it today," those are disagreements; if Person B says, "Yeah, but I also need to get coffee," it is not a conflict. The simple existence of "but" or "no" does not constitute a conflict in and of itself (e.g., the response "No" to "We can't go there, can we?" is an agreement).

- A contradiction that is clearly a joke (and not meant seriously) is not a disagreement, but a jokingly said true disagreement is.
- Continuous or semicontinuous disagreement utterances on the same precise topic can be combined to be different micro-conflict events (see Table 27.1). Thus, the topic of disagreement needs to be understandable and documented by the coder (e.g., about whether an engineering team can use a specific kind of material), versus only being an unexplained and brief "but" without any further content. Documenting the topic of the conflict enables coding other aspects of the conflict. The coders therefore need to learn about the domain under discussion. Sometimes the topic is strongly implied rather than explicitly stated, however, including a general displeasure with another person's values. Relationship conflict, for example, can include generally disdainful comments (e.g., "you're stupid"), which imply a disagreement with the other person's image or sense of worth.
- There is no micro-conflict if a person simply makes an assertion or suggestion, unless that assertion directly contradicts something someone else said before.
- If a person begins a disagreement, the continuing turns and/or utterances that are explanations and justifications of the disagreement should also be coded as disagreement (marked as 1). However, if everyone else present is clearly agreeing with the person who was initially stating a disagreement, these later explanations no longer count as a conflict, because no one is in disagreement. This situation is rare, as usually it is ambiguous by silence whether listeners are in agreement or not. However, take this hypothetical example between two people: "We should use a smaller screw size, like three mm;" "I think that'll slip through the holes as bored, we need at least six mm;" "Oh, yeah, you're right;" and "Otherwise, we are going to lose our screws." The last turn is not a disagreement any more, though if it had occurred before the agreement, it would be counted as a disagreement.
- Disagreements that later turn out to be misunderstandings should still be coded as conflict.

Because of the subjectivity of identifying micro-conflicts, it is important that at least two independent coders assess *all* of the materials/corpus (100% double coding) and resolve all discrepancies via consensus, which includes listening, watching, and reading for each code (presence/absence of conflict and any contingent codes, see below). The coders should regularly meet to run reliability statistics, and review their assessments; all disagreements should be resolved by consensus.

The coding instructions for this scheme were further refined (Paletz, Chan, & Schunn, 2017; Paletz, Sumer, & Miron-Spektor, 2017). In the context of

Table 27.1 *Example of a micro-conflict event*

Speaker number	Transcript[2]	Micro-conflict	Task conflict	Process conflict	Relationship conflict	Conflict notes
1	Yeah	0				
1	it's huge	0				
1	\<missing words\> compromise it	0				
2	If we can't get that to work	0				
2	then we're in trouble	0				
1	No,	1	1	0	0	Conflict Event 110107_1F-C2: S1 disagrees with S2's assessment that they'll be in trouble if they can't get specific feature to work; they'll win because they already achieved enough to complete the project (lines 113–116). Focus is on the tool so mainly task conflict.
1	no	1	1	0	0	Conflict Event 110107_1F-C2
1	we're not	1	1	0	0	Conflict Event 110107_1F-C2
1	Then we've won	1	1	0	0	Conflict Event 110107_1F-C2
1	This worked	1	1	1	0	Conflict Event 110107_1F-C2; utterance refers to both the tool and past process success.
1	That's it	1	1	0	0	Conflict Event 110107_1F-C2; Person 1 is firmly finishing their disagreement (next row is another speaker)

professional design, discussants often raise constraints against, or limitations regarding, an idea. For instance, in designing an electric car, constraints might

[2] For this particular transcript, no gestures were noted, except in the third row, "multiple people talking," which was why there were missing words.

include specific limits on the size, cost, weight, and driving distance (minimum and maximum). Judging whether voicing a constraint (e.g., "we have to make sure it can get 200 miles, at least") is also a disagreement can be difficult. Signs that a constraint may be a disagreement include: (1) if the constraint undermines or negates the initial idea, versus implying a slight modification to the idea; (2) tone (e.g., contemptuous versus neutral); and (3) whether the constraint blossoms into an explicit, full-scale disagreement. In this last case, if it is clear that the initial constraint statement is a tentative way to start to voice the disagreement, it is counted as a disagreement.

After conflict is identified, the scheme includes contingent coding and can include more aspects of conflict by those using the scheme. Because the three dimensions of task, process, and relationship conflict can co-occur at the utterance level, these are coded separately as three different, nonexclusive codes (e.g., "we need to buy another wrench" is both process and task). Other dimensions include affect using two separate scales (presence/absence and then intensity of negative versus positive affect, see Figure 27.1) and whether the conflict was resolved within 25 utterances (or one minute; Paletz et al., 2011), a time unit that has been found to be meaningful for micro-process and/or cognitive temporal dynamics (e.g., Chan, Paletz, & Schunn, 2012; Christiansen & Schunn, 2009; Paletz, Chan, & Schunn, 2017). During coder consensus meetings, the coders should pay attention to the topic of conflict events, as well as the parties involved in the conflict. Coding mismatches may arise not from the nature of the conflict, but from differing views of the topic of discussion or where the conflict starts/ends.

Comparable Instruments

Conflict is commonly measured via self-report (Bendersky et al., 2014; Jehn & Mannix, 2001). However, self-report surveys may measure lay assumptions of behavior rather than actual behavior (Staw, 1975), and brief conflicts may be difficult for individuals in the conversation to notice and remember (Gottman & Notarius, 2000). Jehn (1997) developed her typology of task, process, and relationship conflict through assessing interviews and behavior. Conflict has been identified in archival data (e.g., Bearman, Paletz, Orasanu, & Thomas, 2010), and in a coarser-grained way in observed interactions (e.g., family disagreements, Vuchinich, 1987), but these have not resulted in consistent, published coding schemes. Many behavioral coding schemes include conflict (e.g., Bales, 1951; Kuhn & Poole, 2000), and/or different aspects of disagreement (e.g., criticizing in act4teams, Kauffeld, 2006; Kauffeld & Lehmann-Willenbrock, 2012). However, these schemes assess conflict as mutually exclusive of other behaviors. Coan and Gottman (2007) created the Specific Affect Coding System (SPAFF) to assess specific affective states that occur during experimentally manipulated marital conflict, rather than identifying conflict itself. SPAFF identifies differences between, for instance, contempt, anger, and domineering patterns of behavior, and could be used after conflict has been already identified using the micro-conflict scheme (Neff et al., 2012).

Goals of the Instrument

This coding scheme can be used to assess the prevalence and dynamic patterns of disagreements in conversations, including cycles of escalations and de-escalations (Srikanth, Harvey, & Peterson, 2016; Weingart, Behfar, Bendersky, Todorova, & Jehn, 2015). It can also be used for examining the relationship (co-occurrence or temporal relationship) between micro-conflicts and any other variable that is also identified. For example, one can detect a relationship between micro-conflicts and immediate, subsequent uncertainty in spoken conversations, as well as whether the micro-conflicts co-occur simultaneously with uncertainty (Paletz, Chan, & Schunn, 2016, 2017). When conceptualized at such a micro-level, it becomes possible to test theories about the impact of the directness and oppositional intensity of how conflict is expressed (Weingart, et al., 2015) and its potential for encompassing positive affect (Todorova, Bear, & Weingart, 2014).

Available Versions

A version of the coding scheme, in English, was published in Paletz et al. (2011), although a more refined version is available from the authors.

Applicability

The main constraints of the scheme are that the behavior in question must be recorded, as conversations need to be read and re-read (and listened to, and watched) multiple times in order to judge conflict. That noted, the scheme can be used on any conversation, although data that lack tone, visuals, and context will be harder to code. Still, this scheme should be applicable to social media or text-only data (e.g., text messages), even though it has yet to be applied to those settings.

Practical Application

Coding is time consuming, ranging from two to twenty minutes per minute of video for initial coding, not including consensus. Faster coding occurs when few turns have conflict, whereas slower coding occurs in conflict-rich and/or expert domains. Turns are faster to code than utterances. In addition, consensus can take at least six minutes for each minute of video. Coder training may take more than 40 hours, depending on the difficulty of learning the domain being discussed. A manual and initial training materials can be made available, but most training should also occur on materials specific to the new task. We use Excel versions of transcripts with each unit (e.g., turn) on a different row; if available, a column for gestures and other transcriber observations in the next column;[3] and a column just for micro-conflict assessments (see Table 27.1). In this manner, additional codes (e.g., uncertainty, analogy, affect, type of conflict) can be added to the Excel spreadsheet as subsequent columns. Given that Excel is compatible with or can export to most statistical software packages, this format enables easy data transfer and analysis.

We have used utterances (clauses, or thought statements; Chi, 1997; Paletz et al., 2013) and turns (Paletz, Sumer, & Miron-Spektor, 2017) as the unit of coding. Units should be created independent of coding as part of the transcription process by trained transcribers. Other potential units for this coding scheme include parcels of speech with inter-pausal silences of a particular number of milliseconds (e.g., 200 ms), tweets, sentences, and comments on online news stories. Grain sizes larger than a turn and smaller than a thought statement are not recommended.

Quality Assessment

Reliability

Coding units are determined by trained transcribers. The reliability of this coding scheme for the identification of conflict is modest, ranging from kappa = .44 to .74 for two coders.[4] This low kappa reliability reflects the low base rate of conflict in general (Bakeman, Quera, McArthur, & Robinson, 1997): Indeed, the raw agreement between two coders for the lowest reliabilities was still over 90 percent (Paletz, Sumer, & Miron-Spektor, 2017). To ensure high quality, we require exhaustive double coding (or triple coding, if the resources are available) and resolving all discrepancies through discussion and re-watching/listening to the source material. That method reduces noise and increases confidence in the validity of the coding (Smith, 2000). Additional coders may also increase reliability. The contingent code dimensions typically had higher reliability, with the presence of positive and negative affect and whether a conflict was resolved ranging from kappas of .69 to .72, and the intensity of negative and positive affect had ICCs from .79 to .81 (Paletz et al., 2011).

---

[3] Although we collect this information in our Excel transcripts, if the coders are also watching and listening, the written gesture data may not be necessary for the coding.

[4] For subjective coding, Landis and Koch (1977) suggested that kappas from .40 to .59 are moderate, .60 to .79 are substantial, and .80 and above are outstanding.

Validity

To validate the coding scheme (Paletz, Sumer, & Miron-Spektor, 2017), we compared the presence of micro-conflicts in five-turn aggregates with relevant word sets distilled by the Linguistic Inquiry Word Count (LIWC) software (Pennebaker, Boyd, Jordan, & Blackburn, 2015). The LIWC automatically counts words in previously validated word lists. In English conversations of a multi-national design team, we coded 321 minutes (3,108 turns), which were aggregated into 475 segments of speech, including 52 micro-conflict events. Controlling for significant covariates, negation words were 84 percent more likely during micro-conflict events compared to baseline speech (baseline segments were at least ten turns separated from micro-conflict events, Paletz, Sumer, & Miron-Spektor, 2017). More subtly, differentiation words (e.g., hasn't, but, else) were 38 percent more common during and 24 percent more common just after a micro-conflict compared to baseline, statistically controlling for team size. Assent (e.g., OK, yes) words were 59 percent less frequent during conflict events and 28 percent less frequent during delayed post-conflict compared to baseline, controlling for significant team covariates (Paletz, Sumer, & Miron-Spektor, 2017). These findings suggest that the conflicts had a different lexical pattern than utterances without conflict, indicating convergent and discriminant validity.

Data Aggregation and Analysis

The typical output of the coding scheme is a series of 0s and 1s assigned to each different unit (see Table 27.1, includes conflict type and consensus documentation). Disagreements of contiguous or quasi-contiguous units are aggregated into micro-conflict *events* on the same topic. In our studies, we have aggregated nonconflict units into five turns, ten utterances, and 25 utterances, depending on how the dataset had been unitized and the hypothesized speed of the other (nonconflict) phenomena being studied, such as temporal relationships with cognitive processes. This data structure enables the analysis of time-lagged or time-phase data of the effects of a micro-conflict event on subsequent processes in the next minute or half-minute.

Previous Studies

We have used this coding scheme with professional scientists, student engineers, and professional designers. Process micro-conflicts were more common early in the lifecycle of teams and in meetings of a group with more challenges versus a group with fewer challenges (Paletz et al., 2011). Overall conflict was more common in meetings of Scandinavians compared to more diverse meetings (Paletz, Sumer, & Miron-Spektor, 2017). Process and negative micro-conflicts significantly preceded within-discipline analogies, which represent a moderate distance between the target issue and the domain from which problems, solutions, and comparisons were drawn (Paletz, Schunn, & Kim, 2013). We have also used this method to examine the temporal relationship between disagreement and uncertainty (Paletz et al., 2016; Paletz, Chan, & Schunn, 2017). LIWC insight words (e.g., think, know, consider) were more common during expressed micro-conflicts than baseline (Paletz, Sumer, & Miron-Spektor, 2017).

References

Original Publications

The first version is explained and published in:

Paletz, S. B. F., Schunn, C. D., & Kim, K. H. (2011). Conflict under the microscope: Micro-conflicts in naturalistic team discussions. *Negotiation and Conflict Management Research, 4*, 314–351. doi:10.1111/j.1750-4716.2011.00085.x

However, an updated and improved version was used in the following two works:

Paletz, S. B. F., Chan, J., & Schunn, C. D. (2017). The dynamics of micro-conflicts and uncertainty in successful and unsuccessful design teams. *Design Studies, 50*, 39–69. doi:10.1016/j.destud.2017.02.002

Paletz, S. B. F., Sumer, A., & Miron-Spektor, E. (2017). Psychological factors surrounding disagreement in multicultural design team meetings. *CoDesign*. https://doi.org/10.1080/15710882.2017.1378685

Other References

Amason, A. (1996). Distinguishing the effects of functional and dysfunctional conflict on strategic decision making: Resolving a paradox for top management teams. *Academy of Management Journal, 39*, 123–143. doi:10.2307/256633

Bakeman, R., Quera, V., McArthur, D., & Robinson, B. F. (1997). Detecting sequential patterns and determining their reliability with fallible observers. *Psychological Methods, 2*, 357–370. doi:10.1037/1082-989X.2.4.357

Bales, R. F. (1951). *Interaction process analysis: A method for the study of small groups.* Cambridge, MA: Addison-Wesley Press.

Barki, H., & Hartwick, J. (2004). Conceptualizing the construct of interpersonal conflict. *International Journal of Conflict Management, 15*, 216–244. doi:10.1108/eb022913

Bearman, C. R., Paletz, S. B. F., Orasanu, J., & Thomas, M. J. W. (2010). The breakdown of coordinated decision making in distributed systems. *Human Factors, 52*, 173–188. doi:10.1177/0018720810372104

Bendersky, C., Bear, J., Behfar, K. J., Weingart, L. R., Todorova, G., & Jehn, K. A. (2014). Identifying gaps between the conceptualization of conflict and its measurement. In N. Ashkanasy, O. Ayoko, & K. A. Jehn (Eds.), *Handbook of research in conflict management* (pp. 79–89). Cheltenham, UK: Edward Elgar. doi:10.4337/9781781006948

Chan, J., Paletz, S. B. F., & Schunn, C. D. (2012). Analogy as a strategy for supporting complex problem solving under uncertainty. *Memory and Cognition, 40*, 1352–1365. doi:10.3758/s13421-012-0227-z

Chi, M. T. H. (1997). Quantifying qualitative analysis of verbal data: *A practical guide. Journal of Learning Sciences*, 6, 271–315. doi:10.1207/s15327809jls0603_1

Christensen, B. T., & Schunn, C. D. (2009). The role and impact of mental simulation in design. *Applied Cognitive Psychology, 23*, 327–344. doi:10.1002/acp.1464

Coan, J. A., & Gottman, J. M. (2007). The Specific Affect (SPAFF) coding system. In J. A. Coan & J. J. B. Allen (Eds.) *Handbook of emotion elicitation and assessment* (pp. 106–123), New York, NY: Oxford University Press.

Gottman, J. M., & Notarius, C. I. (2000). Decade review: Observing marital interaction. *Journal of Marriage and the Family, 62*, 927–947. doi:10.1111/j.1741-3737.2000.00927.x

Jehn, K. A. (1997). A qualitative analysis of conflict types and dimensions in organizational groups. *Administrative Science Quarterly, 42*, 530–557. doi:10.2307/2393737

Jehn, K. A., & Bendersky, C. (2003). Intragroup conflict in organizations: A contingency perspective on the conflict-outcome relationship. *Research in Organizational Behavior, 25*, 187–242. doi:10.1016/s0191-3085(03)25005-x

Jehn, K. A., & Mannix, E. A. (2001). The dynamic nature of conflict: A longitudinal study of intragroup conflict and group performance. *Academy of Management Journal, 44*, 238–251. doi:10.2307/3069453

Kauffeld, S. (2006). Self-directed work groups and team competence. *Journal of Occupational and Organizational Psychology, 79*, 1–21. doi:10.1348/096317905X53237.

Kauffeld, S., & Lehmann-Willenbrock, N. (2012). Meetings matter: Effects of team meetings on team and organizational success. *Small Group Research, 43*, 130–158. doi:10.1177/1046496411429599

Kuhn, T., & Poole, M. S. (2000). Do conflict management styles affect group decision making? Evidence from a longitudinal field study. *Human Communication Research, 26*, 558–590. doi:10.1111/j.1468-2958.2000.tb00769.x

Landis, J. R., & Koch, G. G. (1977). The measurement of observer agreement for categorical data. *Biometrics, 33*, 159–174. doi:10.2307/2529310

Neff, R., Jankovic, S., Wolf, M., Tacey, P., Paletz, S. B. F., & Schunn, C. D. (2012). Affect and conflict in student engineering teams. Poster presented at the International Society for the Psychology of Science and Technology Conference, Pittsburgh, PA.

Paletz, S. B. F., Chan, J., & Schunn, C. D. (2016). Uncovering uncertainty through disagreement. *Applied Cognitive Psychology, 30*, 387–400. doi:10.1002/acp.3213

Paletz, S. B. F., Schunn, C. D., & Kim, K. H. (2013). The interplay of conflict and analogy in multidisciplinary teams. *Cognition, 126*, 1–19. doi:10.1016/j.cognition.2012.07.020

Pennebaker, J. W., Boyd, R. L., Jordan, K., & Blackburn, K. (2015). *The development and psychometric properties of LIWC2015*. Austin, TX: University of Texas at Austin. Retrieved February 14, 2018, from http://liwc.wpengine.com/wp-content/uploads/2015/11/LIWC2015_LanguageManual.pdf. doi:10.15781/T29G6Z.

Smith, C. P. (2000). Content analysis and narrative analysis. In H. T. Reis & C. M. Judd (Eds.), *Handbook of research methods in social and personality psychology* (pp. 313–335). Cambridge, UK: Cambridge University Press.

Srikanth, K., Harvey, S., & Peterson, R. (2016). A dynamic perspective on diverse teams: Moving from the dual-process model to a dynamic coordination-based model of diverse team performance. *Academy of Management Annals, 10*, 453–493. doi:10.1080/19416520.2016.1120973

Staw, B. M. (1975). Attribution of the "causes" of performance: A general alternative interpretation of cross-sectional research on organizations. *Organizational Behavior and Human Decision Processes, 13*, 414–432. doi:10.1016/0030-5073(75)90060-4

Todorova, G., Bear, J. B., & Weingart, L. R. (2014). Can conflict be energizing? A study of task conflict, positive emotions, and job satisfaction. *Journal of Applied Psychology, 99*, 451–467. doi:10.1037/a0035134

Vuchinich, S. (1987). Starting and stopping spontaneous family conflicts. *Journal of Marriage and the Family, 49*, 591–601. doi:10.2307/352204

Weingart, L. R., Behfar, K. J., Bendersky, C., Todorova, G., & Jehn, K. A. (2015). The directness and oppositional intensity of conflict expression. *Academy of Management Review, 40*, 235–262. doi:10.5465/amr.2013-0124

28 OFFER

Behaviorally Coding Indirect and Direct Information Exchange in Negotiations

Jeanne Brett, Jingjing Yao, and Zhi-Xue Zhang

General Information

Name of Coding Scheme

OFFER Coding Scheme

Keywords

Negotiation, strategy, offer, multi-issue offers, questions and answers, substantiation, behavioral coding, direct information exchange, indirect information exchange

Summary

Negotiators exchange information about their interests and priorities indirectly via offers and substantiation (attempts to influence the counterpart to make concessions) as well as directly via a reciprocal exchange of questions and answers (Pruitt, 1981). We developed OFFER to code indirect as well as direct information exchange. Interests are the underlying reasons for the positions that negotiators are taking – why they want what they want. Priorities are the relative importance of issues and issue options to negotiators. Negotiators use insight about each other's interests and priorities to make offers that trade-off one party's low-priority issue for the other party's high-priority issue. Trade-off agreements are called value creating because each negotiator gets more of what is most important to that negotiator. Value-creating agreements are generally operationalized by the negotiators' joint gains (the sum of each negotiator's gains).

Description of the Coding Scheme

OFFER is grounded in Pruitt's (1981) theorizing that there is indirect information about interests and priorities embedded in negotiators' offers. Although offers reflect negotiators' positions – direct information about what negotiators want – Pruitt (1981) reasoned that across a series of offers nego-tiators would concede on low-priority issues and hold firm on high-priority issues. He recognized that most negotiators were unlikely to engage in the second-order information processing that is required to infer interests and priorities indirectly from offers and patterns of offers. Consider this example of a negotiation between a chef and an entrepreneur. They have four issues to negotiate: how much capital each will contribute (seven options), location (five options), vehicle (five options), and quality of kitchen equipment (five options). Not surprisingly, each wants the other to put in the major portion of the capital. The first offer from the entrepreneur is likely to require that the chef put in 80 percent of the capital; they purchase a new panel truck, because it can be used for advertising; and used kitchen equipment can be rented. The chef's counteroffer comes back requiring the entrepreneur to put in 80 percent of the capital, approves of the new panel truck, but demands new top-quality kitchen equipment. Looking for the interests underlying these two offers, we can infer that each negotiator has an interest in the other's contributing the majority of the capital, but that the entrepreneur is also interested in the panel truck, while the chef is primarily interested in the quality of the kitchen equipment.

The OFFER coding scheme uses speaking turns – all one negotiator says until the next negotiator begins to speak – as its unit of analysis. The OFFER coding scheme uses five codes: information about interests or priorities (Q&A); substan-tiation about positions (S) – that is, justifying and arguing for positions; making an offer on a single issue (SIO); making a multi-issue offer (MIO); and miscellaneous (M). See Table 28.1 for the OFFER coding scheme.

Table 28.1 *OFFER coding scheme*

Code	Definition	Example
SIO	Single-issue offer	I'll agree to pay 50 percent of the capital investment.
MIO	Multi-issue offer	I'll agree to pay 50 percent of the capital investment, if I can have new top-quality kitchen equipment.
Q&A	Reciprocal questions and answers concerning negotiators' interests and priorities	Quality kitchen equipment is my priority.
S	Substantiation – all types of influences attempts including argument, comparisons, threats	The kitchen equipment I propose is the standard for chefs trained like me at the Culinary Institute.
M	Miscellaneous – assign when no theoretical code is applicable	We should talk about kitchen equipment.

Comparable Instruments

OFFER is based on Pruitt's (1981) distinction between indirect and direct information sharing. This is a somewhat different theory from those underlying other negotiation-strategy coding schemes. For example, De Dreu, Evers, Beersma, Klewer, & Nauta's (2001) coding scheme is based on the dual concern model (Pruitt & Rubin, 1986). Liu (2009), Olekalns and Smith (2000), and Weingart, Thompson, Bazerman, and Carroll's (1990) coding scheme is based on the behavioral theory of negotiation (Walton & McKersie, 1965).

We built OFFER because other methods of coding negotiation strategy ignore offers (De Dreu et al., 2001), aggregate offers with other integrative strategy codes (Olekalns, Brett, & Weingart, 2004), or leave offers as a standalone category (Liu, 2009). Some distinguish single and multi-issue offers (Weingart et al., 1990) and others just measure offers (Adair & Brett, 2005).

OFFER is more parsimonious – it has five codes – than other negotiation strategy coding schemes that code at a much more molecular level of analysis and then aggregate. For example, Olekalns and colleagues (2004) used 32 codes aggregated into six clusters using correspondence analysis.

Goal of the Instrument

We built OFFER because of an anomaly in the empirical data showing relationships between use of negotiation strategy, as measured by other instruments, and outcomes. In Western culture, negotiators generally use a direct series of questions and answers about interests and priorities to generate insight into each other's interests and priorities, and use that information to make trade-off agreements that create value. When Western culture negotiators engage in a series of offers and substantiation (justification for the offer), they fail to generate insight and create value (Kong, Dirks, & Ferrin, 2014). Eastern culture negotiators are less likely than Western culture negotiators to engage in a direct series of questions and answers about interests and priorities. However, research shows that they still generate insight and create value (Adair, Okumura, & Brett, 2001; Adair & Brett, 2005; Liu, 2009). They may be doing so indirectly, by drawing inferences from offers and substantiation, as proposed by Pruitt (1981).

We built OFFER to test the hypothesis that negotiators, particularly those from Eastern cultures, can draw inferences about each other's priorities and interests from offers and patterns of offers and use that indirect information to make trade-offs that generate value-creating agreements. Evidence that they are doing so would be if (a) Eastern culture negotiators are using questions and answers about interests and priorities less than Western culture negotiators, (b) Eastern culture negotiators' insight into each other's interests and priorities is equivalent to that of

Western culture negotiators, (c) Eastern culture negotiators' joint gains are equivalent to those of Western culture negotiators, and (d) Eastern culture negotiators' use of offers predicts their insight and joint gains.

OFFER coding operationalizes the process of negotiation by measuring indirect information sharing via single and multi-issue offers and direct information sharing via questions and answers about negotiators' interests and priorities and substantiation. Negotiation strategy data coded using OFFER can be used as mediating variables or mechanisms for explaining the effects of independent variables or manipulations on negotiation outcomes. Some examples of the types of research questions that could use OFFER are:

(1) How do independent variables and their interactions, e.g., negotiators' cultures, power, status, trust, or manipulated factors affect use of negotiation strategies?
(2) What is the pattern of response to different types of strategy, e.g., mimic and reciprocate, complement, remain steadfast, within a negotiation, and why?
(4) What is the pattern of strategic transition across trajectories of the negotiation?
(5) How does the negotiation process affect economic and subjective negotiation outcomes?

Available Versions

The OFFER codebook is available in English and Chinese.

Applicability

OFFER is applicable regardless of whether the negotiations occur in the laboratory, online, or in the field. However, OFFER coding based on transcripts is preferable, because it is easy to double check, but coding directly based on video or audio recordings is also feasible.

Practical Application

Coding Time

The coding speed depends on how complicated the negotiation is, e.g., how many issues, whether issues are quantified, and what the research question is. Indirect information exchange (i.e., SIO and MIO) are relatively easy to identify, e.g., "I'll agree to paying 50 percent of the capital investment, if I can have new, top-quality kitchen equipment" (MIO). Coding direct information sharing requires coders to understand Q&A and S. For example, "quality kitchen equipment is my priority" (Q&A) versus "we should talk about kitchen equipment" (M); "The kitchen equipment I want is the standard for chefs trained like me at the Culinary Institute" (S) versus "I've had 5 years of culinary experience" (M).

Coder Training

Coder training can take five–six hours. It involves (a) becoming familiar with the negotiation exercise, (b) becoming familiar with the code, (c) practicing coding with the trainer, (d) coding individually and comparing with the trainer and other coder, and (e) recalibrating where the coder is showing discrepancies. If coding numerous transcripts over a period of weeks, coders will need to recheck their reliability. We recommend coding a common transcript or a common section of the same transcript every five–ten transcripts.

Technical Requirements

Any recording device or software is appropriate, so long as each voice is recorded with equal quality. Coding software for qualitative analysis, for example, atlasti.com or nvivo (www.qsrinternational.com/nvivo-product), can be useful, especially for training coders and checking reliability, but it is not necessary. As long as speaking turns are uniquely identified, coding can be done in a spreadsheet.

Unitizing

The unit of OFFER coding is the speaking turn – one party's speech until the beginning of the other party's speech, regardless of its length. Very brief interruptions, e.g., mmh, yes, signaling "I am listening," may be coded as separate speaking turns or ignored depending on the research question. Native language transcribers can usually identify speaking turns highly reliably from audio recordings when there are only two voices. In multiparty negotiations, video recordings may be necessary to ensure reliability of unitizing, especially if the research question requires separating what role said what, for example, if analyzing data using an actor partner interaction model (APIM) (Kenny, Kashy, & Cook, 2006), or fitting a sequential model.

Training Manual

Training manual in English or Chinese versions is available upon request from the authors.

Quality Assessment

We conducted an empirical study applying OFFER to data from 50 Chinese executive MBA dyads negotiating the *Cartoon* exercise in Mandarin. Negotiations were recorded and recordings were transcribed. We recruited and trained two Chinese coders who were blind to our hypotheses. Training followed the pattern outlined above until coders' ICC(2) were greater than or equal to .70. Coders then coded five transcripts independently and one commonly, so ICC(2) could be checked, until coding had been completed.

Reliability

Coders coded multi-issue offers, associating each offer with negotiators' role, buyer or seller. For the two coders agreement was ICC(1) = .66 and ICC(2) = .79. Speaking turns that were not coded as offers were then coded as direct information sharing about interests and priorities (Q&A), substantiation (S), or miscellaneous (M). Cohen's kappa for this coding was $\kappa = .65$, indicating substantial agreement between coders (Landis & Koch, 1977).

Validity

We used two criteria, insight and joint gains, to evaluate the validity of the coding. Both were measured at the end of the negotiation. Insight is the extent to which negotiators accurately detected the relative importance of the two integrative issues (i.e., runs and financing terms). To measure insight, negotiators rate how important each issue is to the counterparty and to themselves. Joint gains are the sum of the two negotiators' individual gains.

Direct information sharing, Q&A and S, were not significantly related to insight. Multi-issue offers, which were operationalized as the proportion of MIO to total offers (SIO plus MIO), were significantly related to insight. Using the APIM model (Kenny et al., 2006) to control for interdependence between negotiators, the actor and partner effects were significant and positive. These results show that negotiators' use of multi-issue offers positively predicted their own insight as well as their counterparts' insight.

To test whether insight mediated the relationship between negotiators' use of multi-issue offers and their joint gains, we aggregated the actor and partner measures of multi-issue offers and insight to the dyad level (joint gains refer to the dyad's outcome). The highly interdependent nature of negotiation theoretically permits this aggregation, and statistical results supported it: for multi-issue offers ICC(1) = .59, r_{wg} = .95, and for insight ICC(1) = .38, r_{wg} = .84. Results based on 1,000 bootstrap samples (Hayes, 2012) showed that dyads' multi-issue offers positively predicted dyads' insight, and dyads' insight positively predicted their joint gains. The direct effect of dyads' multi-issue offers was not significant, while the indirect effect of multi-issue offers via insight on joint gains was significant. This suggested that dyads' insight mediated the relationship between negotiators' use of multi-issue offers and joint gains. This mediated relationship is evidence that these Chinese negotiators were using multi-issue offers as an indirect source of information about their counterpart's interests and priorities and then using that insight to negotiate high joint gains.

Data Aggregation and Analysis

Speaking turn-level data can be aggregated across time or across members of a negotiation dyad or group, assuming ICC(1) and ICC(2) statistics justify doing so, or these data can be analyzed in a disaggregated manner. For example, Adair and Brett (2005) analyzed data by quartiles and Curhan and Pentland (2007) used thin slices. However, we caution that information may be lost in aggregation and recommend instead using APIM or other multi-level models that take interdependence into account.

Previous Studies

Yao, Zhang, and Brett (2017). The studies in this paper provide empirical evidence that both actors' and partners' trust propensity as well as their negotiation behaviors affect the development of trust in negotiation. Yao, Brett, and Zhang (2017). Negotiation data from Chinese executives and two independent datasets of American executives show that there is a low-trust path to joint gains based on multi-issue offer strategy, which is motivated by a high holistic mindset.

References

Original Publications

Yao, J., Brett, J., & Zhang, Z. X. n.d. *Multi-issue offers: A low-trust path to joint gains in negotiations*. Paper presented at the International Association for Conflict Management conference, Berlin, Germany, July 2017.

Yao, J., Zhang, Z. X., & Brett, J. (2017). Understanding trust development in negotiations: An interdependent approach. *Journal of Organizational Behavior*, *38*(5), 712–729.

Other References

Adair, W. L., & Brett, J. M. (2005). The negotiation dance: Time, culture, and behavioral sequences in negotiation. *Organization Science*, *16*(1), 33–51. doi:10.1287/orsc.1040.0102

Adair, W. L., Okumura, T., & Brett, J. M. (2001). Negotiation behavior when cultures collide: The United States and Japan. *Journal of Applied Psychology, 86*(3), 371–385. doi:10.1037/0021-9010.86.3.371

Curhan, J., & Pentland, A., (2007). Thin slices of negotiation: Predicting outcomes from conversational dynamics within the first 5 minutes. *Journal of Applied Psychology, 92*(3), 802–811. doi:10.1037/0021-9010.92.3.802

De Dreu, C., Evers, A. Beersma, B., Klewer, E., Nauta, A. (2001). A theory based measure of conflict management in the workplace. *Journal of Organizational Behavior, 22* (6), 645–668. doi:10.1002/job.107

Hayes, A. F. 2012. PROCESS: A versatile computational tool for observed variable mediation, moderation, and conditional process modeling. (White paper). Retrieved February 16, 2018, from www.afhayes.com/public/process2012.pdf

Kenny, D. A., Kashy, D., & Cook, W. L. 2006. *Dyadic data analysis*. New York, NY: Guilford Press.

Kong, D. T., Dirks, K., & Ferrin, D. (2014). Interpersonal trust within negotiations: Meta-analytic evidence, critical contingencies, and direction for future research. *Academy of Management Journal, 57*(5), 1235–1255. doi:10.5465/amj.2012.0461

Landis, J. R., & Koch, G. G. 1977. The measurement of observer agreement for categorical data. *Biometrics, 33*(1), 159–174. doi:10.2307/2529310

Liu, M. (2009). The intrapersonal and interpersonal effects of anger on negotiation strategies: A cross-cultural investigation. *Human Communication Research, 35*(1), 148–169. doi:10.1111/j.1468-2958.2008.01342.x

Olekalns, M. Brett, J. M., & Weingart, L. R. 2004. Phases, transitions and interruptions: The processes that shape agreement in multi-party negotiations. *International Journal of Conflict Management: Special Issue on Processes in Negotiation, 14* (3), 191–211. doi:10.1108/eb022898

Olekalns, M., & Smith, P. L. (2000). Understanding optimal outcomes: The role of strategy sequences in competitive negotiations. *Human Communication Research, 26*(4), 527–57. doi:10.1111/j.1468-2958.2000.tb00768.x

Pruitt, D. G. 1981. *Negotiation Behavior*. New York, NY: Academic Press.

Pruitt, D., & Rubin, J. (1986). *Social conflict: Escalation, stalemate, and settlement*. New York, NY: Random House.

Walton, R. E., & McKersie, R. B. (1965). *A behavioral theory of labor negotiations: An analysis of a social interaction system*. Ithaca, NY: Cornell University Press.

Weingart, L. R., Thompson, L. L., Bazerman, M. H., & Carroll, J. S. (1990). Tactical behavior and negotiation outcomes. *International Journal of Conflict Management, 1*(1), 7–31. doi:10.1108/eb022839

29 VTCS

Verbal Tactics Coding Scheme

Alan L. Sillars

General Information

Name of Coding Scheme

<u>V</u>erbal <u>T</u>actics <u>C</u>oding <u>S</u>cheme (VTCS)

Keywords

Conflict tactics, conflict strategies, couple conflict, couple communication, observed communication

Summary

The VTCS identifies communication tactics in observed conflict or problem-solving discussions. Most research has involved couple conflict, but it has also been used to study several other contexts (e.g., computer-assisted negotiation, conflict on television, conflicts of college roommates). The VTCS classifies each statement in a discussion based on the function it serves in managing, escalating, or minimizing conflict issues. The initial coding scheme (Pike & Sillars, 1985; Sillars, 1980) collapsed specific tactics into three general strategies for managing conflict – *integrative, distributive*, and *avoidance*. The revised coding scheme (Sillars, 1986) replaced the three-strategy distinction with seven, more descriptive macrocategories, as research suggested that the avoidance and integrative categories were not homogeneous (Sillars et al., 1983). The revised system can still be adapted to collapse tactics into a smaller set of macro-categories when this serves research goals. In the revised system, *denial and equivocation, topic management, noncommittal*, and *irreverent* codes minimize direct discussion of conflict, with the first two representing the clearest examples of avoidance tactics. *Analytic* and *conciliatory* tactics may both contribute to integrative/cooperative conflict management but in different ways – analytic codes promote information sharing, whereas conciliatory codes protect the other's face and promote relationship repair. Confrontative codes are competitive, face-threatening tactics equivalent to the distributive category in the original coding scheme.

Description of the Coding Scheme

The VTCS identifies 25 conflict tactics nested under seven main distinctions: (1) *denial and equivocation*, (2) *topic management*, (3) *noncommittal remarks*, (4) *irreverent remarks*, (5) *analytic remarks*, (6) *confrontative remarks*, and (7) *conciliatory remarks*. Table 29.1 summarizes the categories, definitions, and examples from marital conflict discussions. *Denial and equivocation* refers to statements that deny or obscure the presence of conflict between participants. *Topic management* refers to statements that shift the discussion away from conflict issues.

Table 29.1 *Summary of VTCS codes and examples from marital discussions*

Conflict codes	Illustrations
A. Denial and equivocation	
Direct denial. Statements that deny that a conflict is present.	"That's not a problem."
Implicit denial. Statements that imply denial by providing a rationale for a denial statement, although denial is not explicit.	"We've never had enough money to disagree over" (when discussing disagreements over money).
Evasive remarks. Failure to acknowledge or deny the presence of a conflict following a statement or inquiry about the conflict by the partner.	"That could be something that a person might resent but I don't know."
B. Topic management	
Topic shifts. Statements that terminate discussion of a conflict issue before each person has fully expressed an opinion or before the discussion has reached a sense of completion.	"Okay, the next issue is . . . " (statement occurs before each person has disclosed their opinion on the topic).
Topic avoidance. Statements that explicitly terminate discussion of a conflict issue before it has been fully discussed.	"I don't want to talk about that."
C. Noncommittal remarks	
Noncommittal statements. Statements that neither affirm nor deny the presence of conflict and that are not evasive replies or topic shifts.	"The kids are growing up so fast I can't believe it."
Noncommittal questions. Unfocused and conflict-irrelevant questions.	"What do you think?"
Abstract remarks. Abstract principles, generalizations, or hypothetical statements.	"All people are irritable sometimes."
Procedural remarks. Procedural statements that supplant discussion of conflict.	"You aren't speaking loudly enough."

Table 29.1 (*cont.*)

D. Irreverent remarks	
Friendly joking. Friendly joking or laughter.	"We need to either clean the house or torch it" (with friendly intonation).

E. Analytic remarks	
Descriptive statements. Nonevaluative statements about observable events related to conflict.	"I criticized you yesterday for getting angry with the kids."
Disclosive statements. Nonevaluative statements about events related to conflict that the partner cannot observe, such as thoughts, feelings, intentions, motivations, and past history.	"I swear I never had such a bad week as that week."
Qualifying statements. Statements that explicitly qualify the nature and extent of conflict.	"Communication is mainly a problem when we're tired."
Soliciting disclosure. Nonhostile questions about events related to conflict that cannot be observed (thoughts, feelings, intentions, motives, or past history).	"What were you thinking when you said . . . "
Soliciting criticism. Nonhostile questions soliciting criticism of oneself.	"Does it bother you when I stay up late?"

F. Confrontative remarks	
Personal criticism. Remarks that directly criticize the personal characteristics or behaviors of the partner.	"Sometimes you leave and you don't say goodbye or anything. You just walk right out."
Rejection. Statements in response to the partner's previous statements that imply personal antagonism toward the partner in addition to disagreement.	"Oh come on." "You're exaggerating."
Hostile imperatives. Requests, demands, arguments, threats, or other prescriptive statements that implicitly blame the partner and seek change in the partner's behavior.	"If you're not willing to look for a new job then don't complain to me about it."
Hostile jokes. Joking, teasing, or sarcasm that is at the expense of the partner and is accompanied by hostile intonation.	"Every time you send me flowers, two days later I get the bill."
Hostile questions. Directive or leading questions that fault the partner.	"Who does most of the cleaning around here?"
Presumptive remarks. Statements that attribute thoughts, feelings, motivations, or behaviors to the partner that the partner does not acknowledge.	"You're purposely making yourself miserable."
Denial of responsibility. Statements that minimize or deny personal responsibility for conflict.	"That's not my fault."

Table 29.1 (*cont.*)

G. Conciliatory remarks	
Supportive remarks. Statements that refer to understanding, support, acceptance, positive regard for the partner, shared interests and goals, compatibilities, or strengths of the relationship.	"I can see why you would be upset."
Concessions. Statements that express a willingness to change, show flexibility, make concessions, or consider mutually acceptable solutions to conflicts.	"I think I could work on that more."
Acceptance of responsibility. Statements that attribute responsibility for conflict to self or to both parties.	"I think we've both contributed to the problem."

Noncommittal remarks are statements that neither acknowledge nor deny conflict. Noncommittal remarks represent a neutral style of communication reminiscent of casual conversation. *Irreverent remarks* make light of conflict in a friendly way. *Analytic remarks* provide or seek information about a conflict issue in a nonconfrontational manner. *Confrontative remarks* are verbally competitive statements, such as insults, criticism, and hostile jokes. *Conciliatory remarks* express supportiveness or desire for reconciliation (see Sillars & Wilmot, 1994, for general discussion of codes, early findings, and conceptual links).

The codes focus primarily on verbal (vs. nonverbal) communication and interpret statements based on conventional meanings accessible to observers who are members of the same culture (e.g., what would normally count as personal criticism vs. neutral description of conflict). Members of Eastern and Western cultures draw analogous distinctions between avoidant, competitive, and integrative conflict tactics (Oetzel et al., 2001), although cultural insiders might interpret the function of specific statements differently. Aside from presuming general cultural knowledge, VTCS codes are relatively objective and require only modest inference about participants' subjective intent. However, a few categories require inference about whether a remark is hostile or friendly (e.g., *hostile questions* vs. *seeking disclosure*), based on intonation and other contextual information.

VTCS codes assume that discussions focus on conflict issues salient to participants. For example, the denial and equivocation codes apply when individuals downplay an area of perceived conflict and not, for example, to positive relationship talk of a general nature. To ensure relevance to conflict, researchers either provide individuals with instruction to discuss and resolve an acknowledged problem (e.g., Cohen & Bradbury, 1997), limit coding to discussion topics privately reported to be areas of conflict (e.g., Sillars, Pike, Jones, & Murphy, 1984), or screen interactions for conflict episodes using independent criteria and limit VTCS coding to these episodes (e.g., Poole et al., 1991).

Comparable Instruments

Similar coding schemes for couple conflict include the Marital Interaction Coding System (MICS, Heyman, Weiss, & Eddy, 1995), the Couples Interaction Scoring System (CISS, Gottman, 1979), and the Kategoriensystem für Partnerschaftliche Interaktion (KPI, Hahlweg, 2004). Sillars and Overall (2017) compare these and other conflict coding systems. Several categories in the VTCS overlap with the MICS, CISS, and KPI. For example, each has categories for description or disclosure and most have codes for criticism and mind reading (i.e., *presumptive attribution* in the VTCS). However, the VTCS distinguishes avoidance and nonengagement tactics (*denial and equivocation, topic management, noncommittal remarks, irreverent remarks*) to a greater extent than most similar coding methods. The VTCS can also distinguish direct versus indirect forms of confrontation (McNulty & Russell, 2010).

Goals of the Instrument

The coding scheme is designed to yield detailed analysis of conflict patterns in observed interactions based on verbal tactics. It can address a variety of research questions, such as:

• How pre-interaction expectations, attributions, and beliefs relate to enacted conflict patterns;
• How biological sex, gender, and personality relate to conflict patterns;
• How individuals influence one another during conflict through reciprocal and compensatory sequential patterns of interaction;
• How conflict patterns relate to outcomes, such as conflict management, satisfaction, relationship change, and effective decision making;
• Whether conflict patterns mediate adaptation to external stress over time;
• How the directness of communication about conflict relates to mutual understanding about conflict issues;
• How conflict over digital communication media compares with face-to-face conflict.

Available Versions

Currently, there are no special versions or translations of the VTCS.

Applicability

The VTCS is best suited for coding structured conflict discussions, recorded either in a lab or the field (e.g., couple conversations recorded at home). The full version of the VTCS requires recordings and/or written transcripts. Real time coding and analysis of unstructured conflict interactions are potentially feasible with adaptations that simplify coding (described below).

Practical Application

Coding Time

Time required for coding varies, but trained and efficient coders require five minutes or more per minute of recorded interaction, when working with written transcripts (with units of analysis previously marked) and audio or video recordings. Transcription and unitizing require additional time.

Coder Training

Researchers can expect to spend 15 hours on coder training (Gill, Christensen, & Fincham, 1999) and additional time for regular meetings to discuss coder disagreements and guard against drift and decay during the coding process.

Technical Requirements

Coders should hear audio or watch video recordings while coding. Coding is more efficient when assisted by written transcripts.

Unitizing

Speaking turns or thought units serve as the unit of analysis (except for ratings across an entire discussion, described under "light version").

Training Manual

A detailed training manual (Sillars, 1986) can be downloaded from www .researchgate.net/profile/Alan_Sillars/contributions.

Simplified Version

The VTCS can be simplified by coding only summary conflict codes and not subcategories (e.g., Bradbury, Campbell, & Fincham, 1995; Comstock & Strzyzewski, 1990), or rating general strategies across a discussion, rather than coding individual statements (Sillars et al., 2014). Canary, Cunningham, and Cody (1988) created a self-report questionnaire based on VTCS codes and other items. Others used VTCS codes to identify general strategies from open-ended descriptions of conflict (Cloven & Roloff, 1991; Shearman, Dumlao, & Kagawa, 2011).

Quality Assessment

Reliability

Intercoder reliability ranged from .78–.87 (Scott's pi) across four studies of marital conflict (Sillars et al., 1984; Sillars, Weisberg, Burggraf, & Zietlow, 1990; Zietlow & Sillars, 1988).

Validity

In a validation study, verbal tactics correlated in the expected manner with observer perceptions of interactions and with nonverbal behaviors (e.g., gestures, eye gaze, speech hesitation; Sillars, Coletti, Parry, & Rogers, 1982). Multiple studies show that VTCS codes relate to relationship satisfaction, attributions, conflict severity, and other perceptions of relationship partners.

Data Aggregation and Analysis

VTCS codes can be aggregated in multiple ways to reflect research goals, including three general strategies (i.e., *avoidance, integrative, negative*, Cohen & Bradbury, 1997; *avoidance, integrative, distributive*; Pike & Sillars, 1985), four categories (*avoidance, confrontative, analytic, conciliatory*; Burggraf & Sillars, 1987; *avoidance, direct negative, indirect negative, constructive*; McNulty & Karney, 2004), or seven categories (Zietlow & Sillars, 1988). Codes are used to examine base rates and sequential structure of verbal tactics, with studies consistently showing strong overall reciprocity of verbal tactics (e.g., Pike & Sillars, 1985).

Previous Studies

Research has considered how conflict tactics identified by the VTCS relate to attributions and expectancies for conflict (Bradbury & Fincham, 1992; McNulty & Karney, 2002, 2004; Sillars, 1980, 1981, 1985), communication goals (Keck & Samp, 2007), values and beliefs about marital (Sillars et al., 1983) and family communication (Sillars et al., 2014), relationship power (Overall, Hammond, McNulty, & Finkel, 2016), psychological gender (Bradbury et al., 1995), depression and neuroticism (Cohen & Bradbury, 1997; Hellmuth & McNulty, 2008; McNulty, 2008), intersubjective understanding and cognitive recall of interactions

(Sillars et al., 1984; Sillars, Weisberg, Burggraf, & Zietlow, 1990), sex differences (Burggraf & Sillars, 1987), life stages of couples (Zietlow & Sillars, 1988), and relationship satisfaction, both concurrently and over time (Bradbury et al., 1995; McNulty & Karney, 2004; McNulty & Russell, 2010; Neff & Karney, 2007; Sillars et al., 1983). Other studies examine verbal tactics during negotiations conducted over computers versus face to face (Poole et al., 1991; Rhee, Pirkul, Jacob, & Barhki, 1995) and family conflicts depicted on television (Comstock & Strzyzewski, 1990).

References

Original Publications

Sillars, A. L. (1980). The sequential and distributional structure of conflict as a function of attributions concerning the locus of causality and stability of conflicts. In D. Nimmo (Ed.), *Communication Yearbook 4* (pp. 217–235). New Brunswick, NJ: Transaction Press. [VTCS applied to discussions of college roommates]

Sillars, A. L., Pike, G. R., Jones, T. S., & Redmon, K. (1983). Communication and conflict in marriage. In R. Bostrom (Ed.), *Communication yearbook 7* (pp. 414–429). Beverly Hills, CA: Sage. [First application to marital conflict]

Revised Coding System

Zietlow, P. H., & Sillars, A. L. (1988). Life stage differences in communication during marital conflicts. *Journal of Social and Personal Relationships*, 5, 223–245. doi:10.1177/026540758800500206

Other References

Bradbury, T. N., Campbell, S. M., & Fincham, F. D. (1995). *Journal of Personality and Social Psychology*, 68, 328–341. doi:10.1037/0022-3514.68.2.328

Bradbury, T. N., & Fincham, F. D. (1992). Attributions and behavior in marital interaction. *Journal of Personality and Social Psychology*, 63, 613–628. doi:10.1037/0022-3514.63.4.613

Burggraf, C. S., & Sillars, A. L. (1987). A critical examination of sex differences in marital communication. *Communication Monographs*, 54, 276–294. doi:10.1080/03637758709390233

Canary, D. J., Cunningham, E. M., & Cody, M. J. (1988). Goal types, gender, and locus of control in managing interpersonal conflict. *Communication Research*, 15, 426–446. doi:10.1177/009365088015004005

Cloven, D. H., & Roloff, M. E. (1991). Sense-making activities and interpersonal conflict: Communicative cures for the mulling blues. *Western Journal of Speech Communication*, 55, 134–158. doi:10.1080/10570319109374376

Cohan, C. L., & Bradbury, T. N. (1997). Negative life events, marital interaction, and the longitudinal course of newlywed marriage. *Journal of Personality and Social Psychology, 73*, 114–128. doi:10.1037/0022-3514.73.1.114

Comstock, J., & Strzyzewski, K. (1990). Interpersonal interaction on television: Family conflict and jealousy on primetime. *Journal of Broadcasting and Electronic Media, 34*, 263–282. doi:10.1080/08838159009386742

Gill, D. S., Christensen, A., & Fincham, F. D. (1999). Predicting marital satisfaction from behavior: Do all roads really lead to Rome? *Personal Relationships, 6*, 369–387. doi:10.1111/j.1475-6811.1999.tb00198.x

Gottman, J. M. (1979). *Marital interactions: Experimental investigations*. New York, NY: Academic Press.

Hahlweg, K. (2004). Kategoriensystem für Partnerschaftliche Interaktion (KPI): Interactional coding system (ICS). In P. K. Kerig & D. H. Baucom (Eds.), *Couple observational coding systems* (pp. 122–142). Mahwah, NJ: Lawrence Erlbaum.

Hellmuth, J. C., & McNulty, J. K. (2008). Neuroticism, marital violence, and the moderating role of stress and behavioral skills. *Journal of Personality and Social Psychology, 95*, 166–180. doi:10.1037/0022-3514.95.1.166

Heyman, R. E., Weiss, R. L., & Eddy, J. M. (1995). Marital Interaction Coding System: Revision and empirical evaluation. *Behaviour Research and Therapy, 33*, 737–746. doi:10.1016/0005-7967(95)00003-G

Keck, K. L., & Samp, J. A. (2007). The dynamic nature of goals and message production as revealed in a sequential analysis of conflict interaction. *Human Communication Research, 33*, 27–47. doi:10.1111/j.1468-2958.2007.00287.x

McNulty, J. D., & Russell, V. M. (2010). When "negative" behaviors are positive: A contextual analysis of the long-term effects of problem-solving behaviors on changes in relationship satisfaction. *Journal of Personality and Social Psychology, 98*, 587–604. doi:10.1037/a0017479

McNulty, J. K. (2008). Neuroticism and interpersonal negativity: The independent contributions of perceptions and behaviors. *Personality and Social Psychology Bulletin, 34*, 1439–1450. doi:10.1177/0146167208322558

McNulty, J. K., & Karney, B. R. (2002). Expectancy confirmation in appraisals of marital interactions. *Personality and Social Psychology Bulletin, 28*, 764–775. doi:10.1177/0146167202289006

McNulty, J. K., & Karney, B. R. (2004). Positive expectations in the early years of marriage: Should couples expect the best or brace for the worst? *Journal of Personality and Social Psychology, 86*, 729–743. doi:10.1037/0022-3514.86.5.729

Neff, L. A., & Karney, B. R. (2007). Stress crossover in newlywed marriage: A longitudinal and dyadic perspective. *Journal of Marriage and Family, 69*, 594–607. doi:10.1111/j.1741-3737.2007.00394.x

Oetzel, J. G., Ting-Toomey, S., Yokochi, Y., Masumoto, T., Yokochi, Y., Pan, X., Takai, J., & Wilcox, R. (2001). Face and facework in conflict: A cross-cultural comparison of China, Germany, Japan, and the United States. *Communication Monographs, 68*, 235–258. doi:10.1080/03637750128061

Overall, N. C., Hammond, M. D., McNulty, J. K., & Finkel, E. J. (2016). Power in context: Relationship and situational power interact to predict men's aggression. *Journal of Personality and Social Psychology, 111*, 195–217. doi:10.1037/pspi0000059

Pike, G. R., & Sillars, A. L. (1985). Reciprocity of marital communication. *Journal of Social and Personal Relationships*, *2*, 303–324. doi:10.1177/0265407585023005

Poole, M. S., Holmes, M., & Desanctis, G. (1991). Conflict management in a computer-supported meeting environment. *Management Science*, *37*, 926–953. doi:10.1287/mnsc.37.8.926

Rhee, H-S., Pirkul, H., Jacob, V., & Barhki, R. (1995). *Effects of computer-mediated communication on group negotiation: An empirical study.* Proceedings of the 28th Annual Hawaii International Conference on System Sciences. Wailea, HI.

Shearman, S. M., Dumlao, R., & Kagawa, N. (2011). Cultural variations in accounts by American and Japanese young adults: Recalling a major conflict with parents. *Journal of Family Communication*, *11*, 105–125. doi:10.1080/15267431.2011.554499

Sillars, A. L. (1981). Attributions and interpersonal conflict resolution. In J. H. Harvey, W. J. Ickes & R. F. Kidd (Eds.), *New directions in attribution research, Volume 3* (pp. 279–305). Hillsdale, NJ: Erlbaum.

Sillars, A. L. (1985). Interpersonal perception in relationships. In W. J. Ickes (Ed.), *Compatible and incompatible relationships* (pp. 277–305). New York, NY: Springer-Verlag.

Sillars, A. L. (1986). *Procedures for coding interpersonal conflict: The Verbal Tactics Coding Scheme (VTCS).* Unpublished manuscript, University of Montana.

Sillars, A. L., Coletti, S. F., Parry, D., & Rogers, M. A. (1982). Coding verbal conflict tactics: Nonverbal and perceptual correlates of the "avoidance-distributive-integrative" distinction. *Human Communication Research*, *9*, 83–95. doi:10.1111/j.1468-2958.1982.tb00685.x

Sillars, A., Holman, A., Richards, A., Jacobs, K., Koerner, A., & Reynolds-Dyk, A. (2014). Conversation and conformity orientations as predictors of observed conflict tactics in parent-adolescent discussions. *Journal of Family Communication. 14*, 16–31. doi:10.1080/15267431.2013.857327.

Sillars, A., & Overall, N. C. (2017). Coding observed interaction (pp. 199–216). In C. A. VanLear & D. J. Canary (Eds.), *Researching communication interaction behavior: A sourcebook of methods and measures.* Thousand Oaks, CA: Sage.

Sillars, A. L., Pike, G. R., Jones, T. S., & Murphy, M. A. (1984). Communication and understanding in marriage. *Human Communication Research*, *3*, 317–350. doi:10.1111/j.1468-2958.1984.tb00022.x

Sillars, A. L., Weisberg, J., Burggraf, C. S., & Zietlow, P. H. (1990). Communication and understanding revisited: Married couples' understanding and recall of conversations. *Communication Research*, *17*, 500–502. doi:10.1177/009365090017004006

Sillars, A. L., & Wilmot, W. W. (1994). Communication strategies in conflict and mediation. In J. Wiemann & J. A. Daly (Eds.), *Strategic interpersonal communication* (pp. 163–190). Hillsdale, NJ: Erlbaum.

Coordination and Coherence

30 CoCo

A Category System for Coding Coherence in Conversations

Margarete Boos

General Information

Name of Coding Scheme

Coherence in Conversations (CoCo)

Keywords

Conversational coherence, topic management, topic coordination, topic development

Summary

The goal of the Coding Conversational Coherence (CoCo) category system is to measure conversational coherence, i.e., the degree to which communication partners develop topics collaboratively by (a) referring to each other's verbal contributions and (b) framing and bridging those contributions within a joint task and interpersonal context. Conversational coherence is assumed to serve two elementary functions of conversation management: the coordination of conversation flow and the management of interpersonal relations (Cornelius & Boos, 2003). Noncoherent conversation leads to disrupted, disjointed topical flow and is associated with low interpersonal interest, politeness, and sympathy toward other group members and their topics (Cappella, 1994; Ng & Bradac, 1993). The CoCo category system consists of seven categories and is organized along a continuum from noncoherent to coherent mechanisms. This allows for calculating a coherence coefficient to measure coherence quantitatively and for comparing coherence quality of group discussions.

Description of the Coding Scheme

Topics structure everyday conversations and form the agenda of group meetings. Topics do not appear automatically; they are the product of collaborative activities of conversation partners (Crow, 1983). Topics fulfill at least five psycho-logical functions in communication (Boos & Cornelius, 2001). First, topics serve as a structure where speakers can co-orient with their utterances (Newcomb, 1959). Second, a topic focuses the attention of communication partners towards a joint issue (Grosz, 1977). We all know the metaphor of the "common thread" running through a conversation that is easy to follow, versus "going off at a tangent," which describes conversation that loses focus and containment, such as in small talk. Third, topics span a temporal-spatial context. They exhibit relative duration com-prising multiple utterances, which means that topics conflate multiple contributions to one single context of meaning. Besides this temporal connotation, there is also a spatial one – the "context space" containing interconnected topical sequences (Reichman, 1978). Fourth, topics solve a system problem in social interaction. By concentrating the interaction system on topics, a native system complexity can be built and confined to the system environment (Luhmann, 1972). Thus, topics constitute simple social systems (Willke, 1978) by providing a transient commu-nication structure, for example the brief encounter of mutually unfamiliar people at a bus station. This structure serves as a focus of joint perception and helps to establish a social meaning structure. Hence, depending on the strength of the social meaning structure, more stable and longer-lasting social entities like social rela-tionships and groups can develop. Fifth, topics not only function as a generating mechanism of a social system, but also enable memory. In recapitulating a conversation or trying to tell others about a conversation where they had not been present, we stick to the topics that were discussed. Topics are the condensation or macro structure of a discourse's global meaning (van Dijk, 1977), i.e., a hierarchically structured semantic representation of the conversation. That means that topics serve as cognitive schemata to plan, perform, understand, store, and reproduce discourse. Reichman (1978) calls topics mental models of a conversation.

Hewes (1996) found that 84 percent of speech in decision-making groups was linked to turn-taking rules rather than topics. In his view of socioegocentric communication in small groups, Hewes argues that participants often only think aloud about the task, which means talking in monologues. Thus, a collective monologue rather than dialogue emerges where contributions are only lined up but not knotted substantially. Many studies in small group research come to the result that there is no systematic relation between their interaction and communication process with their outcome, i.e., decision or problem solu-tion. Pavitt and Johnson (1999) therefore postulate to first test whether there is communication in the strict sense of the word, which means whether a discussion is coherent enough before it is investigated whether the communication process affects the outcome.

Conversational coherence can be conceptualized as a communicative compe-tence consisting of the ability and motivation to establish an orderly and mean-ingful discourse and smooth topic development (Craig & Tracy, 1983; Tracy, 1985). If communication partners refer to each other's verbal contributions, develop topics jointly, and maintain them until they are explicitly concluded, this is also interpreted as motivation to show interest, politeness, and friendliness (Ng & Bradac, 1993) by the partners and by bystanders.

Even though coherence is defined as an identifiable language behavior, we have a methodical problem in measuring coherence, as we cannot quantify language meaning. But we can quantify the degree to which meaning changes: We can code coherence as a relational concept of topic development from utterance to utterance during the conversation. As Crow (1983) puts it: "The topic of a conversational act is coded not for a specific content but for the coherence of its content in relation to prior and subsequent acts."

CoCo is based on the categories of topic management defined by Crow (1983). The category system distinguishes between coherent and noncoherent topic management devices and a category "no clear others" for speech acts that are not understandable or cannot be clearly categorized. Coherent topic management mechanisms include "maintaining current topic," "topic shading," "renewal of group topic," and "renewal of topic given by a communication partner." Noncoherent mechanisms include "inserts," "initiation of new topic," and "renewal of own topic" (see descriptions in Table 30.1).

A coefficient of coherence can be calculated by dividing the difference between the sum of messages coded in the coherent topic management categories plus the sum of messages coded in the noncoherent topic management categories by the sum of messages in the coherent and the noncoherent categories. The coefficient – ranging between −1 and +1 –permits comparisons between groups that work for unequal periods of time, or have unequal rates of interaction.

Table 30.1 *Topic management mechanisms*

Mechanism	Description
Maintaining	Current topic is maintained.
Topic shading	A topic is shifted by developing subtopics.
Renewal of group topic	A topic that already has been established in the group discussion is renewed.
Renewal of topic given by a communication partner	A topic introduced by one of the discussion partners is renewed.
Renewal of own topic	A topic that was introduced by the speaker her/himself is renewed.
Insert	A newly introduced topic is not developed further (e.g., introjection, parenthesis).
Initiation of new topic	A new topic is introduced, either as an abrupt topic shift or at clearly defined places during a conversation (e.g., at the beginning, after a break)
No clear others	The content of an utterance is not understandable.

Comparable Instruments

Crow (1983) developed a category system to measure topic management in interpersonal conversations. Our coding scheme builds on Crow's approach and differentiates the category "renewal" into three separate categories in order to distinguish coherent and noncoherent ways of taking up topics that had been introduced and/or further elaborated during a discussion.

Goals of the Instrument

CoCo's purpose is to measure conversational coherence in conversations and group discussions. An index of coherence allows quantitative assessment and comparisons between group discussions in different conditions. In a study comparing face-to-face and synchronous computer-mediated discussions (Boos & Cornelius, 2001), conversational coherence predicted mutual understanding and task orientation in both conditions. In synchronous text-based computer-mediated communication like chats, all participants can receive and send messages simultaneously, which impedes clarity about the topic and topical reference of messages. When members of computer-mediated groups were trained in strategies for creating coherence and developing topics collaboratively during their chat processes such as explicitly referencing to already established topics, they could actively adapt their communication behavior to the media restrictions, establish coherence of their conversation, and reach higher levels of satisfaction with the group decision process.

CoCo is applicable to a wide range of interaction contexts. For example, one could investigate whether the degree of coherence of an individual group member is systematically associated with his or her hierarchical position. Also, one could investigate to what extent conversational coherence is perceived by others as a communicative competence and how it relates to positive social perception.

Available Versions

Currently, CoCo is available in German and English. There is no problem to apply the simple basic idea to any other language.

Applicability

CoCo is applicable both in the laboratory and in field settings. In both settings, it is recommended to audio- and video-record the verbal interactions that are to be studied, allowing for more precise analysis. Application examples include the investigation of couples' everyday conversations (Crow, 1983), the study of decision-making sessions in groups (Cornelius, 1996), and the analysis of text-based synchronous group discussions via computer networks on dilemmas (Cornelius, 2001).

Although it is assumed that the one-dimensional structure of CoCo in combination with the suggested coherent and noncoherent categories should facilitate its use in live coding, e.g., of meetings, this remains to be empirically tested. Likewise, CoCo has thus far only been used for coding audio- or video-taped and transcribed conversations.

Practical Application

Coding Time

Coding time required is approximately five to six minutes of coding per one minute of interaction time. However, this depends on the complexity and multitude of topics tackled in the conversation. If the coding is reduced to the simple distinction between coherent and noncoherent devices, live coding should be possible.

Coder Training

Time required for training coders depends on their previous experience with (a) other coding schemes, (b) the respective coding software, and (c) the respective field (e.g., small talk versus interaction between experts).

Technical Requirements

Potential coding software that can be applied includes all software that allows a user to define their own categories and – if necessary for the research question – to log the time and duration of each code. Given the current advancements in coding applications for smartphones and similar devices, they represent an easy-to-use and literally lighter alternative to using notebooks for real-time coding (e.g., during assemblies, meetings, interviews).

Unitizing

The length of coding units can vary from a whole speaking turn to single propositions according to the SynSeg syntax-based segmentation method (Reed, Metzger, Kolbe, Zobel, & Boos, this volume, Chapter 11).

Training Manual

A comprehensive coding manual in German is available from the author.

Simplified Version

Depending on the research question, it might suffice to reduce the coding system to only the two main categories, coherent versus noncoherent topic management devices. For example, if a researcher wants to investigate if coherent behavior in an interpersonal encounter leads to the perception of being a communicative competent person, it seems possible to apply only CoCo's main distinction between coherent and incoherent mechanisms.

Quality Assessment

Reliability

Interrater reliability was assessed by two independent coders applying the eight suggested CoCo categories on coding a randomly chosen face-to-face decision-making session of a four-person group consisting of n = 347 units (Cornelius & Boos, 2003). Analysis of Cohen's κ showed a mean value of κ = 0.84, representing very good agreement (Fleiss, 1981).

Validity

CoCo was developed on a theoretical and empirical base, thus we assume that it has sufficient content validity. Predictive validity was tested using data of face-to-face and computer-mediated group discussions. Conversational coherence correlated significantly with mutual understanding and satisfaction with team process (Cornelius & Boos, 2003). Cross-validity was measured applying CoCo together with two other relevant category systems: The method for violations of local and neutral coherence developed by Piontkowski, Oehlschlegel-Haubrock and Hoelker (1997) as well as the system to code communication cycles in group behavior from Tschan (1995) to 39 face-to-face group discussions with three participants each and a mean duration of 10 minutes (Boos & Cornelius, 2001). There were high positive correlations between the coherence coefficient and "local coherence" (Pearson correlation .59), "cycle quality" (.54), and "communication flow" (.28). These results confirm CoCo as a valid instrument to comprehend the degree of conversational coherence in group discussions.

Data Aggregation and Analysis

We recommend applying CoCo to group-level coding. Coherence is a collective concept as it refers to the collaborative development and management of topics in an interpersonal conversation or a group discussion. Coding cannot be executed for each member separately like in many other coding systems. To decide whether an utterance is coherently linked to the utterance before, the coder has to take into consideration the sequential flow of conversation as it appears and cannot segment the conversation into person- or role-based parts. This group-based coding nevertheless allows for applying data analysis strategies on the individual level such as role-specific degrees of coherence or use of specific topic management behavior.

Previous Studies

CoCo has been applied to the study of group decision making in face-to-face and computer-mediated groups (Cornelius, 1996; Cornelius & Boos, 1999, 2003).

References

Original Publications

Boos, M., & Cornelius, C. (2001). Bedeutung und Erfassung konversationaler Kohärenz in direkter und computervermittelter Kommunikation [Meaning and Measurement of Conversational Coherence in Direct and Computer-mediated Communication]. In F.W. Hesse & H.F. Friedrich (Eds.). *Partizipation und Interaktion im virtuellen Seminar* (pp. 55–80). Muenster, Germany: Waxmann.

Cornelius, C., & Boos, M. (2003). Enhancing mutual understanding in synchronous computer-mediated communication by training: Trade-offs in judgmental tasks. *Communication Research, 30,* 147–177. doi.org/10.1177/0093650202250874

Other References

Boos, M., Riethmüller, M., & Cornelius, C. (2013). Sozialer Einfluss in Chat-Gruppen: Geschlechtsspezifische Auswirkungen auf konversationale Partizipation und Kohärenz [Social influence in chat groups: Gender-specific effects on conversational participation and coherence]. *Gruppendynamik & Organisationsberatung, 44,* 445-460. doi.org/10.1007/s11612-013-0226-y

Cappella, J. N. (1994). The management of conversational interaction in adults and infants. In M. L. Knapp & G. R. Miller (Eds.), *Handbook of Interpersonal Communication* (pp. 380–418). Thousand Oaks, CA: Sage.

Cornelius, C. (1996). *Themenentwicklung in Gruppendiskussionen [Topic development in group discussions].* University of Konstanz: Unpublished Diploma Thesis.

Cornelius, C. (2001). *Gegenseitiges Verständnis in Computerkonferenzen. Voraussetzungen und Folgen konversationaler Kohärenz in Entscheidungsfindungsgruppen im Medienvergleich [Mutual understanding in computer conferences: Conditions and effects of conversational coherence in decision-making groups].* Muenster, Germany: Waxmann.

Cornelius, C., & Boos, M. (1999). Es lohnt sich, kohärent zu sein! [It is worthwile to be coherent!] In U.-D. Reips (Ed.), *Aktuelle Online Forschung – Trends, Techniken, Ergebnisse [Current internet science – trends, techniques, results]*. Zürich, Switzerland: Online Press. Retrieved February 12, 2018, from http://iscience .deusto.es/archive/reips/books/tband99/pdfs/a_h/cornelius.pdf

Craig, R. T., & Tracy, K. (Eds.), *Conversational coherence: Form, structure, and strategy*. Beverly Hills, CA: Sage.

Crow, B. K. (1983). Topic shifts in couples' conversations. In R. T. Craig & K. Tracy (Eds.), *Conversational coherence: Form, structure, and strategy* (pp. 136–156). Beverly Hills, CA: Sage.

Fleiss, J. L. (1981). *Statistical methods for rates and proportions* (2nd edn.). New York, NY: Wiley.

Grosz, B. J. (1977). *The representation and use of focus in a system for understanding dialogs*. Proceedings of the Fifth International Joint Conference on Artificial Intelligence (pp. 67–76). Cambridge, Massachusetts. Retrieved February 12, 2018, from www.ijcai.org/Proceedings/77-1/Papers/009.pdf

Hewes, D. E. (1996). Small group communication may not influence decision making. An amplification of socio-egocentric theory. In R. Hirokawa & M. S. Poole (Eds.), *Communication and group decision making* (pp. 179–211). Beverly Hills, CA: Sage.

Luhmann, N. (1972). Einfache Sozialsysteme [Simple social systems]. *Zeitschrift für Soziologie, 1*, 51–65. doi.org/10.1515/zfsoz-1972-0105.

Newcomb, T. M. (1959). Individual systems of orientation. In S. Koch (Ed.), *Psychology: A study of a science, Vol. 3* (pp. 384–422). New York, NY: McGraw-Hill.

Ng, S. H., & Bradac, J. J. (1993). *Power in language: Verbal communication and social influence*. Beverly Hills, CA: Sage.

Pavitt, C., & Johnson, K. K. (1999). An examination of the coherence of group discussions. *Communication Research, 26*, 303–321. doi.org/10.1177/009365099026003002

Piontkowski, U., Oehlschlegel-Haubrock, S., & Hoelker, P. (1997). Annaeherung oder Abgrenzung? [Approximation or avoidance?] *Zeitschrift für Soziologie, 26*, 128–138. doi.org/10.1515/zfsoz-1997-0204

Reichman, R. (1978). Conversational coherency. *Cognitive Science, 2*, 283–327. doi.org/10 .1207/s15516709cog0204_1

Tracy, K. (1985). Conversational coherence: A cognitively grounded rules approach. In R. L. Street & J. N. Cappella (Eds.), *Sequence and pattern in communicative behaviour* (pp. 30–49). London: Edward Arnold.

Tschan, F. (1995). Communication enhances small group performance if it conforms to task requirements: The concept of ideal communication cycles. *Basic and Applied Social Psychology, 17*, 371–393. doi.org/10.1207/s15324834basp1703_6

Van Dijk, T. A. (1977). *Text and context. Explorations in the semantics and pragmatics of discourse*. New York, NY: Longmann.

Willke, H. (1978). Elemente einer Systemtheorie der Gruppe: Umweltbezug und Prozesssteuerung [Elements of a systems theory of groups: Environment relationship and process steering]. *Soziale Welt, 29*, 343–357. Retrieved February 12, 2018, from www.jstor.org/stable/40877230

31 Co-ACT

A Framework for Observing Coordination Behavior in Acute Care Teams

Michaela Kolbe

General Information

Name of Coding Scheme

Observing Coordination Behavior in Acute Care Teams (Co-ACT)

Keywords

Acute care teams, explicit coordination, implicit coordination, framework

Summary

The goal of Co-ACT is to facilitate future acute care team (ACT) research by presenting a framework that provides a shared language of teamwork behaviors, allows for comparing previous and future ACT research, and offers a measurement tool for ACT observation. The Co-ACT (Observing Coordination Behavior in Acute Care Teams) framework consists of four quadrants organized along two dimensions (explicit vs. implicit coordination; action vs. information coordination). Co-ACT provides not only a framework for organizing behavior codes but also offers respective categories for succinctly measuring teamwork in ACTs. It aims at guiding and comparing ACT study results.

Description of the Coding Scheme

Teamwork represents a major factor contributing to medical errors, in surgery second only to lack of competence (Gawande, Zinner, Studdert, & Brennan, 2003). This raises the question as to which best practices of teamwork allow health care teams to work effectively, prevent errors, and improve patient safety. Research investigating this question looks at ACTs, i.e., health care teams in high-risk, dynamic disciplines such as emergency medicine, surgery, and anesthesia. These teams represent action teams; that is, teams of highly skilled specialists who work together for brief performance events that require flexibility and improvisation in an unpredictable context, often under high time pressure and with unstable team membership (Sundstrom, de Meuse, & Futrell, 1990). Teamwork in action teams rarely focuses on long-term goal achievement or on team building. Instead, it serves the purpose of coordination during brief performance sequences, for example during the induction of general anesthesia. Using the genuine advantages of behavior observation, patient safety research has investigated teamwork behaviors that are particularly effective for promoting team performance. Especially in the last decade, teamwork behaviors such as leadership, coordination, and communication have been studied in a variety of high-risk health care contexts using behavior observation. As one side effect, the number, scope, and variety of behavior taxonomies used for this research are growing. Even for observing acute care teams, almost a dozen taxonomies exist (Fletcher et al., 2004; Grote, Kolbe, Zala-Mezö, Bienefeld-Seall, & Künzle, 2010; Kolbe, Künzle, Zala-Mezö, Wacker, & Grote, 2009; Manser, Howard, & Gaba, 2008; Mazzocco et al., 2009; Parker, Yule, Flin, & McKinley, 2011; Thomas, Sexton, & Helmreich, 2004; Tschan et al., 2011; Undre, Sevdalis, & Vincent, 2009; Williams, Lasky, Dannemiller, Andrei, & Thomas, 2010; Yule, Flin, Paterson-Brown, & Maran, 2006). This divergence of observation measures reflects the current divergence of the field but complicates the comparison and convergence of research findings. Co-ACT is intended to serve as meta-taxonomy that facilitates comparison, integration, and convergence of findings from different observational studies. The model of team coordination in health care action teams (Kolbe, Burtscher, Manser, Künzle, & Grote, 2011) and the results of previous observation studies provided the theoretical basis and empirical evidence, respectively, for the Co-ACT framework. Co-ACT consists of four quadrants (explicit action coordination, implicit action coordination, explicit information coordination, implicit information coordination). For each quadrant, three categories are suggested (Figure 31.1). Further codes (e.g., acknowledgment) can be added as amendments.

Goals of the Instrument

Co-ACT's purpose is to provide direction for future observational research on ACTs by pointing out which behaviors to observe. Co-ACT captures those behaviors that are specifically relevant for ACT performance (e.g., team member monitoring) while disregarding behaviors that are relevant in longer-lived teams (e.g., team building and development). This ACT-specificity of Co-ACT aims for generalizability across tasks occurring within ACTs as well as for comparative studies with respect to different ACT disciplines. For example, one could investigate whether the effectiveness of specific behaviors such as "talking to the

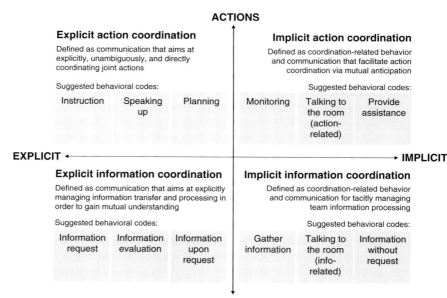

Figure 31.1 *Co-ACT. Framework for observing coordination behavior in acute care teams. (Adapted from Kolbe, Burtscher, & Manser, 2013).*

room" varies between surgery and anesthesia. Also, one could investigate to what extent the relationship between ACT behavior and ACT performance depends on temporal and situational factors and how ACTs coordinate adaptively using Co-ACT. For example, implicit information coordination may be appropriate during routine situations but not during a complex crisis with ambiguous information (Tschan, Semmer, Hunziker, & Marsch, 2011).

Co-ACT allows for assessing the occurrence and timing of coordination behavior, thus providing the basis for a detailed understanding of team interaction. Addressing the rating versus describing behavior challenge of observation-based ACT research (Kolbe et al., 2013), this represents a significant advantage compared to existing static taxonomies of health care teamwork, in which the assumed quality of behaviors is rated or self-assessed as an overall score for a given episode. Co-ACT can be used to study the dynamics of the coordination process, revealing insights into the immediate functions of specific behaviors for the ongoing team interaction and performance.

Available Versions

Currently, Co-ACT is available in German and English. Given the dense dynamics of interactions in ATCs, software-supported coding is recommended.

Applicability

Co-ACT is applicable in both the simulated and the clinical settings. In both settings, it is recommended to audio- and video-record the interactions that are to be studied, allowing for more precise analysis. The 12 Co-ACT categories should be considered as suggestions, which can serve relatively well for measuring coordination behavior in most clinical and simulated situations of ACTs. Based on the specific research question, modifying some of the suggested categories would be appropriate. For instance, some studies (Weiss et al., 2014; Weiss, Kolbe, Grote, Spahn, & Grande, 2017b) focused on the quality and impact of "speaking-up" behavior, therefore Co-ACTs *speaking-up* category was refined with respect to speaking-up content (e.g., suggestion vs. opinion vs. problem, Morrison, 2011). The refined *speaking-up* category retains its position within the Co-ACT framework, that is, it still represents explicit action coordination behavior.

Although we assume that the simple two-dimensional structure of Co-ACT in combination with the limited number of suggested categories should facilitate its use, this remains to be explicitly tested. Likewise, Co-ACT has so far been used only for coding video-taped data but not for live coding. As other taxonomies used for live observation include more codes than Co-ACT, we assume that Co-ACT has the potential to provide the observer with a manageable set of codes for live behavior observation.

Practical Application

Coding Time

Coding time required is approximately 12 minutes of coding per one minute of interaction time for the full version. However, this strongly depends on action density.

Coder Training

Time required for training coders depends on their previous experience with (a) other coding schemes, (b) the respective coding software, and (c) the respective field (e.g., surgery).

Technical Requirements

Potential coding software that can be applied includes all software that allows a user to define their own categories and to log time and duration of each code. Given the current advancements in coding applications for smart phones and similar devices, they represent an easy-to-use and literally lighter alternative to using notebooks for real-time coding (e.g., during long surgical procedures).

Unitizing

Duration of coding units can vary from few frames (e.g., quick team member monitoring) to even a minute (e.g., information evaluation). A coding unit begins as soon as one of the codes can be identified on the basis of the behavioral markers of the coding manual, and it ends when the actor stops showing the respective behavioral markers. If a user wants to code the behavioral stream exhaustively, we recommend adding a "dummy-code" for noncodable utterances.

Training Manual

A comprehensive coding manual is available from the first author of the original publication.

Simplified Version

As noted above, the 12 Co-ACT categories should be considered a suggestion; based on the specific research question, specifying some of the suggested categories while not coding others could be appropriate. For example, if a researcher wants to investigate if certain forms of explicit coordination were related to team performance during nonroutine situations, it seems possible to apply only Co-ACT's explicit codes and specify them by distinguishing different types of instructions such as specific (e.g., "Jack, start chest compressions now, please") vs. unspecific instructions (e.g., "Could someone start chest compressions, please").

Quality Assessment

Reliability

Interrater reliability was assessed by two independent coders applying the 12 suggested Co-ACT categories for coding two videotapes of complete inductions of general anesthesia at a large teaching hospital. Overall, they coded 266 events. Analysis of Cohen's κ showed a mean value of $\kappa = .77$, representing substantial strength of agreement (Landis & Koch, 1977). The category *information request* achieved the highest ($\kappa = 1.00$) and the category *planning* the lowest ($\kappa = .33$) reliability. Since those categories with low κ values tended to occur only rarely (e.g., n = 3 for *planning*) and κ values are affected by prevalence (Feinstein & Cicchetti, 1990), the observed proportions of positive and negative agreement were analyzed (Cicchetti & Feinstein, 1990). Results show that codes with lower κ values had low observed proportions of positive agreement but very high proportions of negative agreement (Kolbe et al., 2013).

Validity

Co-ACT was developed on a theoretical and empirical base, thus it is assumed that it has sufficient content validity. Predictive validity was tested using data of simulated inductions of general anesthesia, selected Co-ACT codes correlated significantly with team performance (Kolbe, Burtscher, & Manser, 2011). More validity tests are required.

Data Aggregation and Analysis

Applying Co-ACT to individual-level coding is recommended for two reasons. First, interaction in ACTs is very dense and each team member is continuously engaged in coordination and/or task work – making team-level coding almost impossible. Second, individual-level coding allows for applying certain data analysis strategies on the team level such as role-specific lag sequential analysis, pattern analysis, network analysis, and multilevel analysis, all of which transfer individual-level data to richer and more elaborate team-level data of team coordination than any team-level coding would allow for.

Previous Studies

Co-ACT has been applied to the study of team interaction in anesthesia in simulated (Kolbe et al., 2012; Weiss et al., 2014; Weiss et al., 2017a, 2017b) as well as clinical settings (Kolbe et al., 2014).

References

Original Publication

Kolbe, M., Burtscher, M. J., & Manser, T. (2013). Co-ACT: A framework for observing coordination behaviour in acute care teams. *BMJ Quality & Safety*, *22*, 596–605. doi:10.1136/bmjqs-2012-001319.

Other References

Cicchetti, D. V., & Feinstein, A. R. (1990). High agreement but low kappa: II. Resolving the paradoxes. *Journal of Clinical Epidemiology*, *43*, 551–558. doi:org/10.1016/0895-4356(90)90159-M

Feinstein, A. R., & Cicchetti, D. V. (1990). High agreement but low kappa: I. The problems of two paradoxes. *Journal of Clinical Epidemiology*, *43*, 543–549. doi:org/10.1016/0895-4356(90)90158-L

Fletcher, G., Flin, R., McGeorge, P., Glavin, R., Maran, N., & Patey, R. (2004). Rating non-technical skills: Developing a behavioral marker system for use in anaesthesia. *Cognition, Technology and Work*, 165–171.

Gawande, A. A., Zinner, M. J., Studdert, D. M., & Brennan, T. A. (2003). Analysis of errors reported by surgeons at three teaching hospitals. *Surgery*, *133*, 614–621. doi:10:1067/msy.2003.169

Grote, G., Kolbe, M., Zala-Mezö, E., Bienefeld-Seall, N., & Künzle, B. (2010). Adaptive coordination and heedfulness make better cockpit crews. *Ergonomics*, *52*, 211–228. doi:10.1080/00140130903248819

Kolbe, M., Burtscher, M. J., & Manser, T. (2011). Analyzing communication to understand how healthcare action teams coordinate. Paper presented at the *5th International Workshop on Behavioral Science Applied to Acute Care Teams*, Zurich, Switzerland.

Kolbe, M., Burtscher, M. J., Wacker, J., Grande, B., Nohynkova, R., Manser, T., ... Grote, G. (2012). Speaking-up is related to better team performance in simulated anesthesia inductions: An observational study. *Anesthesia & Analgesia*, *115*, 1099–1108. doi:10.1213/ANE.0b013e318269cd32

Kolbe, M., Grote, G., Waller, M. J., Wacker, J., Grande, B., Burtscher, M., & Spahn, D. (2014). Monitoring and talking to the room: Autochthonous coordination patterns in team interaction and performance. *Journal of Applied Psychology*, *99*, 1254–1267. doi:org/10.1037/a0037877

Kolbe, M., Künzle, B., Zala-Mezö, E., Wacker, J., & Grote, G. (2009). Measuring coordination behaviour in anaesthesia teams during induction of general anaesthetics. In R. Flin & L. Mitchell (Eds.), *Safer surgery. Analysing behaviour in the operating theatre* (pp. 203–221). Aldershot, UK: Ashgate.

Landis, J. R., & Koch, G. G. (1977). The measurement of observers agreement for categorical data. *Biometrics*, *33*, 159–174. doi:10.2307/2529310

Manser, T., Howard, S. K., & Gaba, D. M. (2008). Adaptive coordination in cardiac anaesthesia: A study of situational changes in coordination patterns using a new observation system. *Ergonomics*, *51*, 1153–1178. doi:10.1080/00140130801961919

Mazzocco, K., Petitti, D. B., Fong, K. T., Bonacum, D., Brookey, J., Graham, S., ... Thomas, E. J. (2009). Surgical team behaviors and patient outcomes. *Am J Surg*, *197*(5), 678–685.

Morrison, E. W. (2011). Employee voice behavior: Integration and directions for future research. *The Academy of Management Annals*, *5*(1), 373–412. doi:10.1080/19416520.2011.574506

Parker, S. H., Yule, S., Flin, R., & McKinley, A. (2011). Towards a model of surgeons' leadership in the operating room. *BMJ Quality & Safety*, *20*, 570–579. doi:10.1136/bmjqs.2010.040295

Sundstrom, E., de Meuse, K. P., & Futrell, D. (1990). Work teams. Applications and effectiveness. *American Psychologist*, *45*, 120–133. doi:10.1037/0003-066X.45.2.120

Thomas, E. J., Sexton, J. B., & Helmreich, R. L. (2004). Translating teamwork behaviours from aviation to healthcare: Development of behavioural markers for neonatal resuscitation. *Qual Saf Health Care*, *13*(suppl 1), i57–i64. doi:10.1136/qshc.2004.009811

Tschan, F., Semmer, N. K., Vetterli, M., Gurtner, A., Hunziker, S., & Marsch, S. U. (2011). Developing observational categories for group process research based on task and coordination-requirement analysis: Examples from research on medical emergency-driven teams. In M. Boos, M. Kolbe, P. Kappeler, & T. Ellwart (Eds.), *Coordination in human and primate groups* (pp. 93–118). Heidelberg, Germany: Springer.

Undre, S., Sevdalis, N., & Vincent, C. (2009). Observing and assessing surgical teams: The Observational Teamwork Assessment for Surgery (OTAS). In R. Flin & L. Mitchell (Edsr.), *Safer surgery. Analysing behaviour in the operating theatre* (pp. 83–101). Aldershot, UK: Ashgate.

Weiss, M., Kolbe, M., Grote, G., Dambach, M., Marty, A., Spahn, D. R., & Grande, B. (2014). Agency and communion predict speaking up in acute care teams. *Small Group Research*, *45*, 290–313. doi:10.1177/1046496414531495

Weiss, M., Kolbe, M., Grote, G., Spahn, D. R., & Grande, B. (2017a). We can do it! Inclusive leader language promotes voice behavior in multi-professional teams. The Leadership Quarterly. Advance online publication. https://doi.org/10.1016/j.leaqua.2017.09.002

Weiss, M., Kolbe, M., Grote, G., Spahn, D. R., & Grande, B. (2017b). Why didn't you say something? Using after-event reviews to affect voice behavior and hierarchy beliefs in multi-professional action teams. *European Journal of Work and Organization Psychology*, *26*(1), 66–80. doi:org/10.1080/1359432X.2016.1208652

Williams, A. L., Lasky, R. E., Dannemiller, J. L., Andrei, A. M., & Thomas, E. J. (2010). Teamwork behaviours and errors during neonatal resuscitation. *Quality and Safety in Health Care*, *19*(1), 60–64.

Yule, S., Flin, R., Paterson-Brown, S., & Maran, N. (2006). Non-technical skills for surgeons in the operating room: A review of the literature. *Surgery*, *139*, 140–149.

32 SO-DIC-OR

Simultaneous Observation of Distractions and Communication in the Operating Room

Sandra Keller and Franziska Tschan

General Information

Name of Coding Scheme

Simultaneous Observation of Distractions and Communication in the Operating Room (SO-DIC-OR)

Keywords

Communication coding in surgery, distraction coding in surgery, timed event coding, coding application

Summary

The goal of this timed event-coding scheme is to observe the occurrences of distractors, communication, and aspects of context in a specific work setting, the operating room (OR). The coding scheme is centered on the perspective of the surgeons performing the surgery. Possible applications include timed assessment of distractors and communication in the OR; it can be used for direct observation when video-recording is not possible. A special feature is the easy combination with collecting qualitative data (comment function; see below).

Description of the Coding Scheme

The coding scheme was developed to directly and simultaneously observe two important influences on teamwork in surgery – distractions and communication, and to assess context factors of surgeries.

Surgeries are carried out by interdisciplinary teams composed of surgeons who perform the surgery; scrub nurses who work within the sterile field directly with the surgeons and pass instruments to the surgeon; circulating nurses who work outside of the sterile field and are responsible for tasks around the surgery, among others taking phone calls or bringing new instruments into the room; anesthetists; and often technicians who perform specialized tasks. Team sizes of surgical teams vary between five and 10 or more professionals (Zheng, Fung, Fu, Panton, & Swanstrom, 2015). Although the whole surgical team collaborates closely, the members of the different disciplines perform many tasks in parallel. For example, while the surgeons are operating, the circulating nurses may bring and unwrap new material; anesthetists may give medication or insert a tube; a technician may adjust a technical device, and so forth.

Because of the high number of team members present and the numerous technical devices used, surgeries are often noisy (Hodge & Thompson, 1990; Katz, 2015), and there are many potential distractions (Sevdalis, Undre, McDermott, Giddie, Diner, & Smith, 2014). Noise and distractions impair not only impair individual (surgical) performance (Feuerbacher, Funk, Spight, Diggs, & Hunter, 2012), but also can interfere with communication and collaboration (Keller, Tschan, Beldi, Kurmann, Candinas, & Semmer, 2016; Way, Long, Weihing, Ritchie, Jones, Bush, & Shinn, 2013) and may thus have a negative impact on team performance, including patient outcomes (Kurmann, Peter, Tschan, Muhlemann, Candinas, & Beldi, 2011). Communication is a key factor of good collaboration and teamwork. On the one hand, the exchange of task-related communication enhances team performance (Bedwell, Ramsay, & Salas, 2012); this has also been found in surgeries (Mazzocco, Petitti, Fong, Bonacum, Brookey, Graham, Lasky, Sexton, & Thomas, 2009; Tschan, Seelandt, Keller, Semmer, Kurmann, Candinas, & Beldi, 2015). On the other hand, socio-emotional communication or communication that is not directly relevant to the task influences the social climate of a team (Barsade & Knight, 2015), but can also lower attention to the task and hurt team performance (Tschan et al., 2015). To assess these important influences on the surgical process, the coding scheme includes codes to assess typical distractors during surgeries as well as task-related, task-irrelevant, and socioemotional communication.

Influences of distractions and communication on the team process and performance are dependent on many context factors. An example is different surgical phases that have different concentration requirements (Wadhera, Parker, Burkhart, Greason, Neal, Levenick, Wiegmann, & Sundt, 2010). The coding scheme therefore includes codes to measure contextual aspects.

The coding scheme was developed for in-vivo observation – the observers are present in the OR and observe and code while the surgical team works. It has mutually exclusive codes (this means that one and only one code can be chosen at any given moment). It is set up on software that allows to timestamp events – this means that the exact real time of choosing a code is noted. For the originally published version (Seelandt et al., 2014), we used a spreadsheet solution with a macro that included a timestamp (Microsoft Excel). The actual coding scheme is set up on an iPad app (Tschan et al., 2016) that, again, timestamps each coding. Duration of events cannot be assessed with either software solution. Doing real-time coding while a complex interaction such as a surgery is done is a heavy burden for the coder's attention. The number of codes therefore is limited and the codes are defined rather specifically to allow the observer to rapidly make the decision about which code to use. Table 32.1 presents the codes and provides examples.

Aspects of the *context* are also coded and include time of incision and time of wound closure; change of personnel (for example, a new surgeon joins the group during the procedure); incidents (a specific incident occurs, for example an unplanned x-ray to locate a missing sponge).

Comment function: The iPad application that is used is set up to automatically open a comment function (open text) after a code has been confirmed; this allows the observer to add a free text with further details or comments related to the code. These comments allow for later fine-grained coding and additional qualitative analyses.

Comparable Instruments

To our knowledge, there is no instrument that assesses both distractors and communication in the surgical context within the same coding scheme. However, the distraction codes of the scheme were inspired by existing instruments (Healey, Sevdalis, & Vincent, 2006; Sevdalis, Healey, & Vincent, 2007). In comparison to SO-DIC-OR, these instruments not only assess distractors, but also include information about their immediate effects. If distractors are the main interest, these instruments are more complete and detailed than SO-DIC-OR. For communication during surgeries, existing instruments assess the quality of communication for specific professions in the OR (surgeons, anesthetists, scrub nurses) using behavioral rating scales for the whole or part of a procedure. This method yields a summary score across the whole procedure as compared to timed codes when a behavior or event occurs (Flin, 2013; Sevdalis, Davis, Koutantji, Undre, Darzi, & Vincent, 2008; Undre, Sevdalis, & Vincent, 2009; Yule, Flin, Maran, Rowley, Youngson, & Paterson-Brown, 2008). Behavioral rating scale assessments are of limited use for the analyses of specific aspects of the team process. Coding schemes for communication developed in fields other than surgery contain similar codes to the ones included in SO-DIC-OR (Bales, 1950; Futoran, Kelly, & McGrath, 1989; Kolbe, Künzle, Zala-Mezo, Wacker, & Grote, 2009).

Goals of the Instrument

A wide variety of research questions can be addressed using the instrument. *Descriptive* questions include the distribution of codes over time or in

Table 32.1 *Examples of SO-DIC-OR codes of distractions and communication in surgical teams (for the original version see Seelandt et al., 2014)*

Code	Qualifiers[1]	Description	Example
distractors			
Side conversations	Intensity (low, medium, highly distracting) who (nurses, anesthesia, visitors etc.)	Conversations among team members not working directly at the operating table (e.g., circulating nurses, anesthetists)	Anesthetists organize coffee breaks; circulating nurses discuss new instruments
Noise distractors	Intensity	Noise events (except side conversations)	Loud noises while unpacking new instruments
Technical distractors (alarms, beepers, incoming phone calls)	Intensity What, where	Patient or technical alarm sounds, incoming phone calls	A perfusor alarm goes off
Door openings	Door denomination	Door opens and closes	
Communication with/in the sterile team			
Case-relevant communication	Intensity (low, medium, high volume) who to whom	Task-related communication: Communication related to patient or procedure	First and second surgeons plan the next steps; surgeon informs anesthetist that they have to prepare a stomach tube
Teaching	Who to whom	Communication related to teaching	Surgeon explains to resident a specific anatomical structure
Problem solving	Who	Interruption of surgery to engage in a discussion about a specific problem related to the surgery	Surgeons discuss whether they have to re-sect a specific part of the pancreas
Case-irrelevant communication	Who to whom	Communication that is not related to the current case	The surgical team talks about sports; talks about another patient
Release tension	Who	Joking or laughter	The resident tells surgical jokes
Tension	Who to whom intensity	Tense conversations or conflicts	The surgeon yells at the resident because he/she does not hold the camera steady

Note: [1]Qualifiers are not part of the original system (Seelandt et al., 2014).

different phases of a surgery. It is possible to *compare* distractors and communication across different surgeries or the same surgeries performed by different teams or in different contexts, and to study the effects of interventions or training on team processes. *Relationships* between observations and other process variables can be assessed (for example, between noise and communication, see Keller et al., 2016), as well as relationships between processes and outcomes (for example, team communication and patient outcomes; see Tschan et al., 2015). Because the observations are timestamped, *process analyses* are also possible.

The coding scheme can easily be adapted to different contexts and more specific research questions. For example, for one specific analysis we added an additional specification (brings material) to the code "door opening" to assess how often a door opening included someone to get material and was thus clearly related to the task.

We believe that the coding scheme can be adapted to other contexts than surgery, for example for teams working in potentially distracting environments such as construction crews. It is easily possible to omit or add codes, and thus to adapt the coding scheme to the need of the researcher.

Available Versions

A detailed coding manual is available in German and French, and a general description in English (Seelandt et al., 2014). Initially, the application was set up on Excel, but the newest version is set up on Adjustable Field Notes, a payable, generic iPad app suitable for this or similar coding schemes (Tschan, Holzer, Semmer, Keller, Zimmermann, Huber, Beldi, & Stolz, 2016).

Applicability

The coding scheme is designed for in-vivo, real-time coding. The codes can be used for video-coding, but for this we do not suggest using the app, because the timestamp function records real time when coding, which may not be practical if coding from videos is done. The coding scheme can easily be adapted to different research questions and can certainly be adapted to other teams than surgical teams or other circumstances, and it can be set up on other platforms.

Practical Application

Coding Time

SO-DIC-OR is done in vivo, and the time used to code is the time of observation. On average, coders apply two codes per minute, this includes using the commenting function. After the observation, the files have to be manually "cleaned" before being analyzed. The cleaning includes a first quality check and correction of typos in comments. The required time for cleaning is about 15 minutes per one hour of observation.

Coder Training

Time required for coder training is at least 35 hours, most often more. Coders need to familiarize themselves with the specific context of operating rooms (OR), including how to dress and behave in an OR. Training sessions include context training, theoretical training, hands-on training under supervision, comparing novice and expert coding, and reliability testing after each training session. Regular re-training is necessary; every fifth surgical procedure is observed by two coders to constantly assess reliability; regular meetings also are held among the coders to discuss coding issues. Coders observe real surgeries and are sometimes confronted with difficult patient situations and with difficult team situations; this can be emotionally straining for the coders. This is addressed during the training. In addition, after each observation, coders write a short debriefing, where he or she reflects on the situation and emotional involvement. We also make sure that a senior member of the team is accessible per phone in case a more thorough debriefing is necessary. The necessity of extended debriefings is about one in 70 observed surgeries.

Technical Requirements

SO-DIC-OR can be used with many platforms. The initial version was set up as a spreadsheet, but the current version is set up on an iPad application (Tschan et al., 2016). Data are available as csv files, with one timed coding unit per line. There is no included option of data summary; researchers will have to work based on the raw data.

Unitizing

Event-sampling. Events are defined as units in time. Communication events are defined as uninterrupted communication related to the same topic.

Training Manual

A training manual is available in German and French from the authors.

Simplified Version

Categories can be dropped or added at the researcher's discretion.

Quality Assessment

Reliability

Reliability has been tested using Cohen's kappa and intraclass correlation coefficients for each code in four different conditions: across the entire surgery, in the first hour of a surgery, after three hours into surgeries to assess interobserver quality over time (two observers who coded throughout the surgery), and as comparison between observers who coded the first three hours and a new observer that joined after three hours into the surgery to assess fatigue effects (Seelandt et al., 2014). With very few exceptions, interobserver agreement was high to very high.

Validity

Validity related to other instruments has not been assessed.

Data Aggregation and Analysis

The app that we are using records data in a spreadsheet format with one line per timed event (including qualifiers and comments). The observational codes are string variables that can be recoded into numbers for statistical analysis. Data can be aggregated (for example, using functions of known statistics programs) for the whole procedure or according to context or time variables (for example, for every five minutes, or for phases of the surgery), or they can used for sequential analysis.

Previous Studies

A description of the coding system is published (Seelandt et al., 2014). An analysis investigating the association between distractions, respectively communication and the most frequent complication, surgical site infections based on 167 surgeries, showed that measured distractors were not predictive of surgical site infections, whereas more case-relevant information exchange and less case-irrelevant communication were related to a lower probability of surgical site infection, in other words, to better patient outcome (Tschan et al., 2015). Another study combined noise level measures with observed distractions and communication and showed that noise peaks impaired task-related communication (Keller et al., 2016).

References

Original Publication

Seelandt, J. C., Tschan, F., Keller, S., Beldi, G., Jenni, N., Kurmann, A., Candinas, D., & Semmer, N. K. (2014). Assessing distractors and teamwork during surgery: Developing an event-based method for direct observation. *BMJ Quality & Safety, 23*, 918–929. doi:10.1136/bmjqs-2014-002860

Other References

Bales, R. F. (1950). *Interaction process analysis; a method for the study of small groups.* Cambridge, MA: Addison-Wesley Press.

Barsade, S. G., & Knight, A. P. (2015). Group affect. *Annual Review of Organizational Psychology and Organizational Behavior, 2*(1), 21–46. doi:10.1146/annurev-orgpsych-032414-111316

Bedwell, W. L., Ramsay, P. S., & Salas, E. (2012). Helping fluid teams work: A research agenda for effective team adaptation in healthcare. *Translational Behavioral Medicine, 2*(4), 504–509. doi:10.1007/s13142-012-0177-9

Feuerbacher, R. L., Funk, K., Spight, D. H., Diggs, B. S., & Hunter, J. G. (2012). Realistic distractions and interruptions that impair simulated surgical performance by novice surgeons. *Archives of Surgery, 147*(11), 1026–1030. doi:doi:10.1001/archsurg.2012.1480

Flin, R. (2013). Non-technical skills for anaesthetists, surgeons and scrub practitioners (ANTS, NOTSS, and SPLINTS). Retrieved February 16, 2018, from http://patient safety.health.org.uk/sites/default/files/resources/non_technical_skills_for_a naesthetists_surgeons_and_scrub_practitioners.pdf

Futoran, G. C., Kelly, J. R., & McGrath, J. E. (1989). TEMPO: A time-based system for analysis of group interaction process. *Basic and Applied Social Psychology, 10*(3), 211–232. doi:10.1207/s15324834basp1003_2

Healey, A. N., Sevdalis, N., & Vincent, C. (2006). Measuring intra-operative interference from distraction and interruption observed in the operating theatre. *Ergonomics, 49*, 589–604. doi:10.1080/00140130600568899

Hodge, B., & Thompson, J. F. (1990). Noise pollution in the operating theatre. *Lancet, 335* (8694), 891–894. doi:10.1016/0140-6736(90)90486-O

Katz, J. D. (2015). Noise in the operating room. *Survey of Anesthesiology, 59*(1), 60. doi:10.1097/ALN.0000000000000319

Keller, S., Tschan, F., Beldi, G., Kurmann, A., Candinas, D., & Semmer, N. K. (2016). Noise peaks influence communication in the operating room. An observational study. *Ergonomics, 59*(12), 1541–1552. doi:10.1080/00140139.2016.1 159736

Kolbe, M., Künzle, B., Zala-Mezo, E., Wacker, J., & Grote, G. (2009). Measuring coordination behavior in anaesthesia teams during induction of general anaesthetics. In R. Flin & L. Mitchell (Eds.), *Safer surgery: Analysing behavior in the operating theatre* (pp. 203–222). London, UK: Ashgate.

Kurmann, A., Peter, M., Tschan, F., Muhlemann, K., Candinas, D., & Beldi, G. (2011). Adverse effect of noise in the operating theatre on surgical-site infection. *British Journal of Surgery*, 98(7), 1021–1025. doi:10.1002/bjs.7496

Mazzocco, K., Petitti, D. B., Fong, K. T., Bonacum, D., Brookey, J., Graham, S., Lasky, R. E., Sexton, J. B., & Thomas, E. J. (2009). Surgical team behaviors and patient outcomes. *American Journal of Surgery*, 197(5), 678–685. doi:S0002-9610(08)00459-5 [pii] 10.1016/j.amjsurg.2008.03.002

Sevdalis, N., Davis, R., Koutantji, M., Undre, S., Darzi, A., & Vincent, C. A. (2008). Reliability of a revised NOTECHS scale for use in surgical teams. *American Journal of Surgery*, 196(2), 184–190. doi:0.1016/j.amjsurg.2007.08.070

Sevdalis, N., Healey, A. N., & Vincent, C. A. (2007). Distracting communications in the operating theatre. *Journal of Evaluation in Clinical Practice*, 13(3), 390–394. doi:10.1111/j.1365-2753.2006.00712.x

Sevdalis, N., Undre, S., McDermott, J., Giddie, J., Diner, L., & Smith, G. (2014). Impact of intraoperative distractions on patient safety: a prospective descriptive study using validated instruments. *World Journal of Surgery*, 38(4), 751–758. doi:10.1007/s00268-013-2315-z

Tschan, F., Holzer, E., Semmer, N. K., Keller, S., Zimmermann, J., Huber, S. A., Beldi, G., & Stolz, M. (2016). *Adjustable Field Notes – A 5$ iPad application to observe team interactions*. Paper presented at the 10th International Meeting for Behavioral Science in Surgery & Acute Care Settings, November 11–12, 2016, Aberdeen.

Tschan, F., Seelandt, J., Keller, S., Semmer, N. K., Kurmann, A., Candinas, D., & Beldi, G. (2015). Impact of case-relevant and case-irrelevant communication within the surgical team on surgical site infection. *British Journal of Surgery*. doi:10.1002/bjs.9927

Undre, S., Sevdalis, N., & Vincent, C. (2009). Observing and assessing surgical teams: The Observational Teamwork Assessment for Surgery (OTASS). In R. Flin & L. Mitchell (Eds.), *Safer surgery. Analysing behaviour in the operating theatre* (pp. 83–102). London, UK: Ashgate.

Wadhera, R. K., Parker, S. H., Burkhart, H. M., Greason, K. L., Neal, J. R., Levenick, K. M., Wiegmann, D. A., & Sundt, T. M., 3rd. (2010). Is the "sterile cockpit" concept applicable to cardiovascular surgery critical intervals or critical events? The impact of protocol-driven communication during cardiopulmonary bypass. *Journal of Thoracic and Cardiovascular Surgery*, 139(2), 312–319. doi:10.1016/j.jtcvs.2009.10.048

Way, T. J., Long, A., Weihing, J., Ritchie, R., Jones, R., Bush, M., & Shinn, J. B. (2013). Effect of noise on auditory processing in the operating room. *Journal of the American College of Surgery*, 216(5), 933–938. doi:10.1016/j.jamcollsurg.2012.12.048.

Yule, S., Flin, R., Maran, N., Rowley, D., Youngson, G., & Paterson-Brown, S. (2008). Surgeons' non-technical skills in the operating room: Reliability testing of the NOTSS behavior rating system. *World Journal of Surgery*, 32(4), 548–556. doi:10.1007/s00268-007-9320-z

Zheng, B., Fung, E., Fu, B., Panton, N. M., & Swanstrom, L. L. (2015). Surgical team composition differs between laparoscopic and open procedures. *Surgical Endoscopy and Other Interventional Techniques*, 29(8), 2260–2265. doi:10.1007/s00464-014-3938-3

Cognition and Metacognition

33 CASoRL

Coding Scheme for the Analysis of Social Regulation of Learning

Cornelia Schoor

General Information

Name of Coding Scheme

Coding Scheme for the Analysis of Social Regulation of Learning (CASoRL).

Keywords

Social regulation of learning; collaborative learning; cooperative learning; socially shared regulation; co-regulation; other-regulation; socially shared metacognition

Summary

Regulation of learning refers to the metalevel of monitoring, evaluating, and controlling of different aspects of the learning process. In collaborative learning, not only one's own learning process has to be regulated, but also those of the other group members and the whole group. Several kinds of regulation in collaborative learning can be differentiated, which are referred to in this chapter as different modes of social regulation of learning.

The goal of the Coding Scheme for the Analysis of Social Regulation of Learning (CASoRL) is to facilitate and inspire future research on different modes of social regulation of learning. CASoRL is based on the theoretical framework of Schoor, Narciss, and Körndle (2015). In a first step, regulatory utterances are identified (auxiliary level). In a second step, these are coded with regard to the social perspective of operations, products, standards, and evaluations (based on the COPES model by Winne & Hadwin, 1998) (principal level). CASoRL allows researchers to distinguish a variety of modes of social regulation of learning.

Description of the Coding Scheme

Collaborative learning refers to "a situation in which two or more people learn or attempt to learn something together" (Dillenbourg, 1999, p. 1). While

Practical Application

Coding Time

Coding time depends heavily on the proportion of regulatory units, with a higher proportion of regulatory units producing longer coding times. With a low proportion of regulatory units, the coding time per minute of computer-based chat data is about one minute for an experienced coder. Data from face-to-face interaction probably produce more utterances per minute, resulting in longer coding times.

Coder Training

Time required for coder training strongly depends on their prior knowledge about regulation in learning and/or about metacognition. For coders familiar with the concept of social regulation of learning, the expected training time is about one hour. More time is needed for coders unfamiliar with social regulation of learning because they need to familiarize themselves with the concepts of regulation and sharedness and learn to identify examples of these in the data.

Technical Requirements

There are no technical requirements. Software used for coding must allow the definition of own categories and multiple coding dimensions for coding the content of the coding units and the perspectives of the four OPES components. It is recommended to use recording devices because the coding of the perspectives in the OPES components is time consuming.

Unitizing

Coding can be applied to sentences, turns, or even episodes depending on the research question. Coding of the different perspectives seems to be easier for smaller units because the perspectives can change within bigger units such as episodes. The decision for the coding unit and the segmentation into units should be done in a first step independent from and prior to the coding.

Training Manual

A coding manual is available from the author.

Simplified Version

There is no light version. On the contrary, the present coding scheme could be expanded, for example, by coding the perspective of the OPES components not only for regulatory coding units but also for planning and task definition.

Quality Assessment

Reliability

Interrater reliability was assessed based on a small pilot study on computer-supported collaborative learning (Schoor & Deiglmayr, in prep.). The data of 14 dyads (527 turns) were coded by two independent raters. The inter-rater reliability over all categories of the auxiliary level of content coding was κ = .78, which is substantial (Landis & Koch, 1977). Fifty-two turns were coded acceptance and seven turns were coded regulation by both raters. The low proportion of regulation is not unexpected as learners often do not engage in regulation spontaneously (e.g., Bannert, 2009; Schoor & Bannert, 2012). For the differentiation of acceptance and regulation versus the rest, the interrater reliability was κ = .68, which is also substantial (Landis & Koch, 1977). The interrater reliability for regulation, however, was only κ = .34 (fair agreement, Landis & Koch, 1977), which was probably due to the very small proportion of regulation in these data. As for the principal level of analyzing the perspective of regulation (*I, you*, or *we perspective* on operations, products, evaluation, and standards), the overall agreement was κ = .84 (almost perfect, Landis & Koch, 1977). In fact, the agreement was perfect for operations, evaluation, and standards, but not for products. A closer look showed a problem in defining individual and collaborative tasks that was not due to the coding scheme; rather, a careful definition of what is considered an individual or a collaborative task within the group work has to be made for every study in which the coding scheme is to be used.

Validity

CASoRL was developed on a theoretical and empirical base, therefore it is assumed that it has sufficient content validity. In our small pilot study (Schoor & Deiglmayr, in prep.), dyads applying regulation showed a descriptively better performance in the group product, which – maybe due to the very small sample size – was not significant. Explicit empirical validity tests are required.

Data Aggregation and Analysis

Data resulting from the coding reflect one kind of regulation per coding unit, e.g., the turn. In the case of the analysis of turns or sentences, it is recommended to analyze and interpret sequences of units. For example, socially shared regulation utterances only seem meaningful (i.e., socially shared) if there is an uptake, i.e., if another group member also applies socially shared regulation. Therefore, further data analysis should not be limited to frequency analysis, but should also include analyses of chronological or temporal sequences.

Previous Studies

Being a new tool, CASoRL has so far been applied only in a not-yet-published small pilot study on the effect of different distributions of learning material across learning partners in computer-supported collaborative learning (Schoor & Deiglmayr, in prep.). The results show no relation of regulation to the distribution of learning material.

References

Bannert, M. (2009). Promoting self-regulated learning through prompts: A discussion. *Zeitschrift für Pädagogische Psychologie*, *22*(2), 139–145.

Boekaerts, M. (1999). Self-regulated learning: Where we are today. *International Journal of Educational Research*, *31*, 445–457.

Brydges, R., Manzone, J., Shanks, D., Hatala, R., Hamstra, S. J., Zendejas, B., & Cook, D. A. (2015). Self-regulated learning in simulation-based training: A systematic review and meta-analysis. *Medical Education*, *49*(4), 368–378. doi:10.1111/medu.12649

Dillenbourg, P. (1999). What do you mean by "collaborative learning"? In P. Dillenbourg (Ed.), *Collaborative Learning* (pp. 1–19). Oxford, UK: Elsevier.

Grau, V., & Whitebread, D. (2012). Self and social regulation of learning during collaborative activities in the classroom: The interplay of individual and group cognition. *Learning and Instruction*, *22*(6), 401–412. doi:10.1016/j.learninstruc.2012.03.003

Hurme, T.-R., Merenluoto, K., & Järvelä, S. (2009). Socially shared metacognition of pre-service primary teachers in a computer-supported mathematics course and their feelings of task difficulty: A case study. *Educational Research and Evaluation*, *15*(5), 503–524. doi:10.1080/13803610903444659

Iiskala, T., Vauras, M., Lehtinen, E., & Salonen, P. (2011). Socially shared metacognition of dyads of pupils in collaborative mathematical problem-solving processes. *Learning and Instruction*, *21*(3), 379–393.

Järvelä, S., & Hadwin, A. F. (2013). New frontiers: Regulating learning in CSCL. *Educational Psychologist*, *48*(1), 25–39. doi:10.1080/00461520.2012.748006

Landis, J. R., & Koch, G. (1977). The measurement of observer agreement for categorical data. *Biometrics*, *33*(1), 159–174.

Rogat, T. K., & Adams-Wiggins, K. R. (2014). Other-regulation in collaborative groups: implications for regulation quality. *Instructional Science*, *42*(6), 879–904. doi:10.1007/s11251-014-9322-9

Schoor, C., & Bannert, M. (2012). Exploring regulatory processes during a computer-supported collaborative learning task using process mining. *Computers in Human Behavior*, *28*(4), 1321–1331. doi:10.1016/j.chb.2012.02.016

Schoor, C., & Deiglmayr, A. (in prep.). *Aufteilung von Informationen auf verschiedene Dokumente beim individuellen und kooperativen computerunterstützten Lernen* [Distribution of information on different documents during computer-supported individual and cooperative learning]. Manuscript in preparation.

Schoor, C., Narciss, S., & Körndle, H. (2015). Regulation during cooperative and colla-borative learning: A theory-based review of terms and concepts. *Educational Psychologist, 50*(2), 97–119. doi:10.1080/00461520.2015.1038540

Winne, P. H., & Hadwin, A. F. (1998). Studying as self-regulated learning. In D. J. Hacker, J. Dunlosky, & A. C. Graesser (Eds.), *Metacognition in educational theory and practice* (pp. 277–304). Mahwah, NJ: Lawrence Erlbaum.

Zimmerman, B. J. (2013). From cognitive modeling to self-regulation: A social cognitive career path. *Educational Psychologist, 48*(3), 135–147. doi:10.1080/00461520.2013.794676

34 Coding Scheme for Group Creativity

Chia-Yu Kou and Sarah Harvey

General Information

Name of Coding Scheme

Coding Scheme for Group Creativity

Keywords

Collective Creativity, Creative Process, Group Interaction, Idea Evaluation, Meetings

Summary

The proposed coding scheme is designed to aid researchers who study collective creative processes. Coding categories follow creativity theory, including idea introduction, idea discussion, and idea decision. The coding scheme was inductively derived by analyzing over 50 hours of group interactions in meetings. We also provide a mapping template for researchers to aggregate the codes by outlining individual codes to a visual synopsis of the creative process, which would be particularly useful to observe patterns in ongoing group discussion.

Description of the Coding Scheme

Meetings are vital for group creativity as the location where creative solutions often develop. Novel ideas and solutions often rely on small, diverse teams to recombine individuals' domain-specific knowledge and skill (Mannix & Neale, 2005; Milliken & Martins, 1996) into new ideas (Nemeth, 1997). Essentially, group creativity occurs when group members stimulate one another's divergent thinking, and their individual ideas are aggregated to creative output (George, 2007; Kurtzberg & Amabile, 2000; Nemeth, 1986; Paulus & Yang, 2000; Sacramento, Dawson, & West, 2008). However, why are some groups more creative than others? How can interactions among group members influence creativity?

Our approach to these questions was rooted in the analysis of the creative process in meetings. Using meetings as a means to tap into how group creativity unfolds has two benefits. First, studying meetings can reveal embedded group dynamics through which the group works. For example, certain ideas may initiate shared moments of connections between individuals that simulate long creative dialogues (Hargadon & Bechky, 2006). Second, meeting conversations enable researchers to observe both idea generation and idea evaluation. Research in creativity has traditionally emphasized the idea generation side of the creative process (Collins & Loftus, 1975; Diehl & Stroebe, 1987; Diehl & Stroebe, 1991; Litchfield, 2008; McGrath, 1984; Osborn, 1953; Paulus & Yang, 2000), but recent studies found that idea evaluation is often ingrained in the creative processes regardless of the stage of the process in which a group is engaged (e.g., Harvey & Kou, 2013; Jackson & Poole, 2003). For instance, groups may not follow Osborn's brainstorming rules. Instead, group members may favor certain ideas, criticize ideas, and provide praise for good ideas throughout the creative process (Hargadon & Bechky, 2006; Jackson & Poole, 2003; Long-Lingo & O'Mahony, 2010), suggesting evaluation as an integral part of creative processes.

Drawing on these theoretical insights, our coding scheme is developed inductively to capture creative processes. There are three coding categories: idea generation, idea evaluation, and idea decision (see Table 34.1). The coding unit begins as soon as coders identify idea-related conversation, and it ends when coders stop seeing the conversation listed in the coding scheme (for a similar approach see Jackson & Poole, 2003). Idea generation statements are divided into two categories: presenting a new idea or developing an idea by groups. A new idea can be a single overarching idea (e.g., a new model), or the subset of an overarching idea (e.g., particular issues with the new models). Idea evaluation statements comprise four categories: exchanging information, agreeing and elaborating on the idea, disagreeing and refining the idea, and integrating multiple ideas. Idea decision registers the end state of the idea, where it can be accepted, rejected, or undecided. Codes may cover multiple speakers (for example please see Table 34.1, accepting and rejecting ideas). The scheme is particularly useful when researchers are interested in comparing the number of ideas formulated across multiple groups, and comparing contributions across each speaker throughout the creativity process.

Comparable Instruments

Our scheme closely relates to Jackson and Poole's (2003) scheme. Their scheme includes "idea generation," "criticizing," and "clarifying," corresponding to "develop and present new ideas," "disagree with the idea," and "elaboration" in

Table 34.1 *Group creativity coding scheme*

Categories	Codes	Example
Idea generation related statement	Present new idea	"I'll speak for the next few minutes about a model."
	Develop new idea	"I would like to suggest that we don't define intangible and don't use the term . . ."
Idea evaluation related statement	Information exchange related to idea	"We did a market analysis . . . 72% of those in that survey said that . . ."
	Agree & elaborate on idea	"I think you're right about this. Maybe it's an agreement among us on . . ."
	Disagree with & refine idea	"The models [that have been discussed] are interesting. I don't think anyone really jumps out at me as being 'the' model [that we should go with]."
	Integrate multiple ideas	"I think we need to look at it obviously not as an either/or type of situation. It could be either done by either ways. We need to make sure what we adopt are both capable of dealing with the different approaches."
Idea decision related statement	Accept idea	Member 1: "We've built out a very robust recommendation here." Member 2: "I agree." Member 3: "I agree also." Member 1: "Let's consider that done."
	Reject idea	Member 1: "I don't think race is needed as part of the minimum dataset . . ." Member 2: "Okay, let's move on."

Note. Adapted from Harvey and Kou (2013, p. 354).

our coding scheme here. Jackson and Poole's scheme focuses solely on the idea generation part of the creative process, and it does not include codes for information sharing, evaluating ideas, and idea decisions.

Because our scheme draws on the assumption that interactions are the key to predicting group outcomes, our scheme is also similar to team process coding schemes such as act4team (Kauffeld & Lehmann-Willenbrock, 2012) and Bales' Interaction Process Coding scheme (Bales, 1950). However, our coding scheme solely focuses on idea-related components, and therefore it can be viewed as a condensed version of team process coding schemes. Our coding scheme is helpful for mapping out patterns of idea evolution over time. This prevents forcing coding of lengthy conversations into a single category when the statement is complex (Fahy, 2006).

Goals of the Instrument

The coding scheme can be applied to laboratory and field settings where teams discuss ideas. The scheme helps researchers to identify creative moments in ongoing interactions and capture idea-related discussion. It is most directly applicable to research questions related to the group creative process. It is also suitable for answering questions about "how" that process works. For instance, one could investigate how team-level factors such as diversity, shared experience, or conflict may affect the nature of the creative process. Researchers may also be able to use the codes to capture different processes and connect those processes to creative outcomes. Codes can further provide an overview of ongoing creative activities. This is useful when researchers study ongoing group interactions over time. For instance, researchers could uncover conditions that trigger the pursuit of creative solution in the first place, and evaluate the influence of immediate group interactions on generating creative ideas.

Available Versions

The instrument is available in English. It can be used with paper-pencil methods and coding software, such as Nvivo or MaxQDA.

Applicability

The coding scheme could be applied to primary data collected in the laboratory and the field, as well as a secondary dataset (such as online discussion forum or meeting transcriptions). Meeting transcriptions are essential. Real-time coding in a field context is not possible because it is extremely difficult to recognize when an idea has been returned to (e.g., built on, integrated), without returning back to the previous discussion. Audio recording is sufficient to produce transcriptions, and video-recording is not essential. Meeting transcriptions are of particular importance in the field setting for two reasons. First, coding itself requires a general understanding of the grand task in the study context and the role of each participant. Second, in a field setting, the discussion may consist of continuous conversations over months. Meeting transcriptions will allow precise tracking of idea generation and evaluation.

Practical Application

Coding Time

Coding time is approximately three codes per minute. Coding every sentence in the transcription is not necessary. In our experience, when meetings are designated to generate creative solutions, there will be texts left uncoded, which often relate to the introduction of individuals, a recap of meeting discussions, and a summary of future actions. These texts can serve as a source to check codes in idea generation and idea decision categories.

Coding time would be longer when (1) a coder lacks detailed technical knowledge and familiarity with idea content in dense discussions, since initial coding requires first reading through the transcripts at least three times before attempting coding; (2) ideas are discussed across meetings, since this increases coding time because coders have to return to previous sections of discussions in order to follow the pattern of discussion and understand how new comments are related to prior discussion.

Coder Training

We suggest three hours' training for coders to familiarize them with the application of the codes in the research context, although the time needed for coder training varies depending on their familiarity with the context and previous coding experience.

Technical Requirements

A recording device is essential when researchers collect their data; otherwise, there are no special technical requirements. If a researcher wishes to use secondary data, coders need to adjust their coding rule to accommodate the local languages. For instance, researchers coding discussion forums on the Internet may include smiley emoji in the coding rules, suggesting participants agree with the idea presented.

Training Manual

A training manual is available upon request from the corresponding author. Before coding, we suggest coders gain a good understanding of the group's background, the nature of the project, agenda and activities in each meeting, and jargon used in the project. This helps coders identify idea-related conversation. Researcher training, therefore, should focus on becoming embedded in the team meeting context.

Simplified Version

The coding scheme provided here should be short enough to apply to the field setting directly.

Quality Assessment

Reliability

Codes were developed in a qualitative tradition, aiming to derive theoretically relevant categories, i.e., abstracting theoretical meaning, rather than necessarily describing precise actions that happened. To ensure the quality of the coding scheme, an interrater reliability check is done between two authors. Codes were counted as in agreement if the two coders assigned the same code to statements. For 70 coded statements randomly selected from meeting transcripts over coding categories, Cohen's kappa between two coders was .77, indicating a high level of reliability (Landis & Koch, 1977). Discrepancies were discussed and resolved afterward and then updated to the coding scheme. Second, authors coded three meeting transcripts and compared the overall discussion patterns that resulted from their coding over time. The authors agreed on all three meetings.

Validity

Our coding scheme was inductively developed. This should assure sufficient content validity. However, construct and predictive validity test should be assessed.

Data Aggregation and Analysis

If researchers are interested in how ideas unfold over time, we propose a two-step method to map out the evolution of ideas over the course of meetings through a visual synopsis (Langley, 1999). The unit of analysis here is the meeting. Researchers can draw visual synopsis after coding is completed, as a data analysis technique. This is useful when researchers want to describe interaction patterns from the same sample over time.

First, by using the template in Table 34.2, researchers write down ideas generated in the meetings in the idea column on the left. In the time columns, when an

Table 34.2 *Visual synopsis template (preliminary format)*

Idea	Time (register speaking sequence or time)													End state (register whether idea is accepted, rejected, or undecided)
1														
2														
etc.														

Table 34.3 *Visual Synopsis Example*

Idea	Time																End state
P1	G													A			Accepted
P2						G	E							A			Accepted
P3								G	E	E	E						Undecided
P4	G	E	E	E	E	E	A										Accepted
P5					G	E								A			Accepted
P6								G	E	E	E		E				Undecided
P7				G	E	E								A			Accepted
P8								G	E			E	E	E	E E E	A	Undecided

Note. A refers to the group made a decision – Idea is accepted; G refers to idea generation; E refers to idea evaluation.

idea is proposed, coders note "G" in the cell. When the discussion on a specific idea occurred, coders note "E" in the cell. When the idea is decided, coders note "A" as idea accepted or "R" as idea rejected in the cell. Time columns can be used to record sequence of speaking (see example in Table 34.3), or record time interval if that suits coders' needs. In the end state column, this indicates the end state of an idea: whether the idea is accepted, rejected, or undecided. After recording all coded segments, looking across the rows shows the discussion pattern for a specific idea; looking across the columns indicates the shift of idea discussion during a particular period.

Table 34.3 is an example of applying one of the coded meetings from our data to the template provided in Table 34.2. It shows the discussion pattern of this particular meeting. For ideas P1, P2, and P5 in Table 34.3, the group mentioned the idea at the beginning, but the idea did not trigger a group decision until later in the meeting. We also identified the nature of a discussion about ideas, such as whether group members were agreeing or disagreeing with the ideas during discussion. Aggregating codes in the visual map template as in Table 34.2 will allow researchers to compare different processes (e.g., Harvey & Kou, 2013).

Previous Studies

The coding scheme has so far been applied to field research on group creativity in the health care policy group setting (Harvey & Kou, 2013). A similar methodology has also been applied to examining boardroom discussions (Harvey, Currall, & Hammer, in press).

References

Original Publication

Harvey, S., & Kou, C. Y. (2013). Collective engagement in creative tasks: The role of evaluation in the creative process in groups. *Administrative Science Quarterly, 58,* 346–386. doi:10.1177/0001839213498591

Other References

Bales, R. F. (1950). A set of categories for the analysis of small group interaction. *American Sociological Review, 15,* 257–263. doi:10.2307/2086790

Bales, R. F., & Cohen, S. P. (1979). *SYMLOG: A system for the multiple level observation of groups.* New York, NY: Free Press.

Collins, A., & Loftus, E. (1975) The spreading-activation theory of semantic processing. *Psychological Review, 82,* 407–428. doi:dx.doi.org/10.1037/0033-295X.82.6.407

Diehl, M., & Stroebe, S. (1987). Productivity loss in brainstorming groups: Toward the solution of a riddle. *Journal of Personality and Social Psychology*, *53*, 497–509. doi:dx.doi.org/10.1037/0022-3514.53.3.497

Diehl, M., & Stroebe, S. (1991). Productivity loss in brainstorming groups: Tracking down the blocking effect. *Journal of Personality and Social Psychology*, *61*, 392–403. doi:dx.doi.org/10.1037/0022-3514.61.3.392

Fahy, P. J. (2006). Online and face-to-face group interaction processes compared using Bales' Interaction Process Analysis (IPA). *European Journal of Open, Distance, and E-learning*, 1. Retrieved July 7, 2016 from www.eurodl.org/materials/contrib/2006/Patrick_J_Fahy.htm

George, J. M. (2007). Creativity in organizations. *Academy of Management Annals*, *1*, 439–477. doi:doi.org/10.1080/078559814

Gersick, C. J. (1988). Time and transition in work teams: Toward a new model of group development. *Academy of Management Journal*, *31*, 9–41. doi:10.2307/256496

Hargadon, A. B., & Bechky, B. A. (2006). When collections of creative become creative collectives: A field study of problem solving at work. *Organization Science*, 17, 484–500. doi:doi.org/10.1287/orsc.1060.0200

Harvey, S., Currall, S. C., & Hammer, T. (in press). Decision diversion in diverse teams: Findings from inside a corporate boardroom. *Academy of Management Discoveries*. doi:10.5465/amd.2015.0129.

Jackson, M. H., & Poole, M. S. (2003). Idea-generation in naturally occurring contexts. *Human Communication Research*, *29*, 560–591. doi:10.1111/j.1468-2958.2003.tb00856.x

Kauffeld, S., & Lehmann-Willenbrock, N. (2012). Meetings matter: Effects of team meetings on organizational success. *Small Group Research*, *43*, 130–158. doi:doi.org/10.1177/1046496411429599

Kurtzberg, T. R. & Amabile, T. M. (2000). From Guilford to creative synergy: Opening the black box of team-level creativity. *Creativity Research Journal*, *13*, 285–294. doi:doi-org.ucd.idm.oclc.org/10.1207/S15326934CRJ1334_06

Landis, J. R., & Koch, G. G. (1977). The measurement of observers agreement for categorical data. *Biometrics*, *33*, 159–174. doi:10.2307/2529310

Langley, A. (1999). Strategies for theorizing from process data. *Academy of Management Review*, *24*, 691–710. doi:10.5465/AMR.1999.2553248

Litchfield, R. (2008). Brainstorming reconsidered: A goal-based view. *Academy of Management Review*, *33*, 649–668. doi:10.5465/AMR.2008.32465708

Long-Lingo, E., & O'Mahony, S. (2010). Nexus work: Brokerage on creative projects. *Administrative Science Quarterly*, *55*, 47–81. doi:doi.org/10.2189/asqu.2010.55.1.47

Mannix, E., & Neale, M. A. 2005. What differences make a difference? The promise and reality of diverse teams in organizations. *Psychological Science in the Public Interest*, *6*, 31–55. doi:10.1111/j.1529-1006.2005.00022.x

McGrath, J. (1984). *Groups: Interaction and performance*. Englewood Cliffs, NJ: Prentice Hall.

Milliken, F. J., & Martins, L. L. 1996. Searching for common threads: Understanding the multiple effects of diversity in organizational groups. *Academy of Management Review*, *21*, 402–433. doi:10.5465/AMR.1996.9605060217

Nemeth, C. J. (1986). Differential contributions of majority and minority influence. *Psychological Review, 93*(1), 23–32. doi:dx.doi.org.ucd.idm.oclc.org/10.1037/0033-295X.93.1.23

Nemeth, C. J. (1997). Managing innovation: When less is more. *California Management Review, 40*, 59–74. doi:doi.org/10.2307/41165922

Osborn, A. (1953). *Applied imagination.* New York, NY: Scribner.

Paulus, P. B., & Yang, H. (2000). Idea generation in groups: A basis for creativity in organizations. *Organizational Behavior and Human Decision Processes, 82*, 76–87. doi:10.1006/obhd.2000.2888

Sacramento, C. A, Dawson, J. F., & West, M. A. (2008). Team creativity: More than the sum of its parts? In M. D. Mumford, S. T. Hunter, & K. E. Bedell-Avers (Eds.), *Research in multi-level issues, vol. 7: Multi-level issues in creativity and innovation* (pp. 269–287). Bingley, UK: Emerald Books.

35 Analyzing Critical Thinking in Group Constellations

From Discourse Analysis to Analyzing Social Modes of Thinking

Maree J. Davies, Katharina Kiemer, and Adam Dalgleish

General Information

Name of Coding Scheme

Critical Discourse Analysis

Keywords

Critical thinking; small group discussion; dialogic teaching

Summary

Multiple research and policy documents highlight the relevance of critical thinking capabilities; for example, for democratic participation in a society (e.g., Bolhuis, 2003), coping with the demands of the twenty-first century (e.g., Paul & Binker, 1990), or contributing to the social and economic welfare of a society (e.g., Bloom & Watt, 2003). "Critical thinking refers to the use of cognitive skills or strategies that increase the probability of a desirable outcome. Critical thinking is purposeful, reasoned, and goal-directed. It is the kind of thinking involved in solving problems, formulating inferences, calculating likelihoods, and making decisions" (Halpern, 1999, p. 70) To assess critical thinking (CT) a variety of methods have been established, mostly focusing on the individual: standardized test measures (Ennis, 1962; Facione, 1990), self-report scales (Galotti, Clinchy, Ainsworth, Lavin, & Mansfield, 1999), or content analysis tools (Newman, Webb, & Cochrane, 1995). What is missing from measurements on critical thinking is a group perspective capturing the benefits of shared thinking for knowledge construction and understanding (Thayer-Bacon, 2000; Wegerif et al., 2017). Also, measurement tools of critical thinking tend to be discipline specific, focusing on argument strength, critical disposition, or bias. So far, these different perspectives have not been merged into a single measurement tool. This coding scheme attempts to address these gaps in existing research.

Description of the Coding Scheme

Critical thinking is mostly described and researched from an individual's point of view – for example, the ability to engage in purposeful, self-regulatory judgement – and based on a view that focuses on hierarchical models of thinking (Bloom et al., 1956) and deconstructing arguments for logic (for example, Zohar, Weinberger, & Tamir, 1994). In addition, psychometric and self-report measurement tools used to assess critical thinking have an inborn focus of critical thinking as an individual process. Yet, in recent years, research, particularly educational research, has focused on social modes of thinking and reasoning (Wegerif et al., 2017). Quintessential for this research is the understanding that talking and engaging in argument is a social mode of thinking that supports knowledge construction and understanding. This new focus on group interactions necessitates new developments in measurement tools that go beyond the individual and capture the interaction in its entirety. To this purpose we devised a coding scheme assessing the level of critical thinking in small-group discussions by dissecting individual contributions of critical thinking (see Table 35.1) to arrive at a group measure.

Critical thinking is also commonly aligned with a market-based approach to education to strengthen innovative and competitive advantages in the knowledge-based global economy (Bloom & Watt, 2003). In this context, critical thinking is related to measurements of dispositions and skills through psychometric testing (Ennis, 1962; Facione, 1990; Sternberg, 1987; Watson & Glaser, 1980). A relatively recent addition to the field of critical thinking has been in the argument of including intuition, emotion, and imagination thinking (Thayer-Bacon, 2000). However, what seems to be missing from this literature is the view of critical thinking as a collective, dialogic exercise drawing on sociopolitical issues. As well as an individual able to think logically, analytically, and with reason is the concern with the individual recognizing the hierarchical structures in society and the consideration of wider perspectives and ethical consequences (Apple, 2010; Freire, 1970; hooks, 1994, 2010; Postman & Weigartner, 1969). These skills have, so far, been largely ignored in the assessment of critical thinking. Therefore, this coding scheme was also devised to specifically combine the *philosophical, educational*, and *sociological* views on critical thinking, which past studies have left unconsidered. Table 35.1 summarizes the codes and provides example excerpts from group discussions. Codes are not mutually exclusive, meaning that each case (individual person) can be coded per unit of analysis (an individual's contribution) on each code in each category.

Table 35.1 *Summary of indicators of critical thinking (CT) in group interactions*

Category	Code	Description	Example
Philosophical view on CT	A – Argument	Speaker provides a group of statements, some of which (the reasons) are intended to support another (the conclusion) Conclusions usually need an indicator such as therefore, thus, consequently, so.	"This painting was done during the time when nuclear testing was controversial and the two heads look like nuclear heads so I think the Salvador Dali picture might be about nuclear testing."
	E – Providing a statement of evidence	Speaker provides clear evidence for a claim by supporting their argument with data or relevant examples (Facione, 1990). Speaker may use words such as because, since, for the reason that, assuming that.	"There was nuclear testing at Bikini Atoll between 1946 and 1958, and Dali was painting then, so then the picture might represent the destruction of humanity from the tests."
	B – Building on to the discussion	Speaker stays on topic and builds on the discussion but the statement does not include evidence.	"It looks like a head full of activity, or smoke to me."
	CE – Critical Engagement	Evidence of a speaker providing a strong or insightful counter example to a particular argument or point. Shows engagement with and critical thought about ideas presented. (Facione, 1990)	"The tree is closer to the explosion than the other head though, so maybe it doesn't represent the destruction of humanity but the destruction of nature?"
	RAB – Recognizing Availability Bias	Speaker recognizes that, just because they see an idea presented often, it does not make it true (Kahneman, 2011)	"I heard on the news that there was a flood of migrants to Germany. I wonder what they mean by a flood of migrants though?"
	RCB – Recognizing Confirmation Bias	Speaker recognizes that, they believe something because the information confirms previously existing belief or biases (Kahneman, 2011)	"I am worried about flying now because of a possible terrorist attack. But I wonder if that is because terrorist attacks are made such a big deal in the media?"
Sociological view on CT	PS – Power Structure	Speaker identifies a relevant societal power structure, showing knowledge of contexts likely to impact arguments. External influences such as media, politics, gender, ethnicity, religion are examples (Apple, 2010; Giroux, 2015; McLaren, 2016).	"Only 200 Micronesians inhabited the islands when the US conducted the nuclear tests, I think they thought they would get away with it because they are such a big and powerful country."
	SASQ – Situated awareness question	Speaker asks who in society would challenge our group's view.	Who would challenge our view?

Table 35.1 (*cont.*)

Category	Code	Description	Example
	SAC – Situated Awareness Challenge	Speaker suggests what other group(s) in society may challenge the group's view on the discussion topic; gender, ethnicity, political, socio-economic, and religious different perceptions may be suggested (Freire, 1970; Ladson-Billings & Tate, 2006) and those with disabilities or learning differences.	"A person who holds liberal views might not agree with our view that health insurance should be compulsory."
	SASG – Situated Awareness – Self and Group	Speaker acknowledges why the group or themselves would hold a particular perspective such as how gender, ethnicity, political, socio-economic, and religious influences might shape perceptions of you or other people in different contexts (hooks, 1994, 2010; Delpit, 1995).	"New Zealand has a strong anti-nuclear history so perhaps that is why we think it is about nuclear testing."
Educational view on CT	DM – Discourse Management	A question or statement that aims to keep the group on task, a sign of positive and honest engagement with ideas (Facione, 1990).	"I think we are getting side tracked." "We haven't heard from Peter, what do you think, Peter?"
	UQ – Uptake Question	Student seeking further information from a student in the group (Nystrand, Wu, Gamoran, Zeiser, & Long, 2003).	"When you said you think your family would think the nuclear testing was necessary why do you think that, Sara?"
	HLQ – High-Level Question	Student seeking further information by asking either a question that elicits a generalization, analysis, or speculative question (Applebee, Langer, Nystrand, & Gamoran, 2003).	Generalization – "Would all artists have been anti-nuclear?" Analysis – "I wonder if Dali had a friend involved in the nuclear testing and that inspired him to paint the picture?" Speculation – "I wonder to what extent would famous artists like Dali impact political opinion with their work?"
	IIE – Imagination/ Intuition/Emotion	Opening up the discussion to new ideas that haven't yet been explored (Thayer-Bacon, 2000).	"Maybe there is another message than the effect of nuclear testing that Dali was trying to say."

Comparable Instruments

Newman and colleagues (1995) presented an extensive set of indicators for critical and uncritical thinking in computer-supported collaborative learning settings based on Henri (1991) and focusing particularly on cognitive reasoning skills and problem-solving. Also, Jeong (2003) presented a content analysis tool to assess the quality of online discussions and their relationship to critical thinking. The present coding scheme is different from these previous attempts in that it uses multiple views of critical thinking to assess the quality of the critical thinking. Furthermore, we hold a strong group perspective; specifically, as well as assessing the quality of individuals' critical thinking during discussion, we also assess the quality of the critical thinking of the group's interaction. Also, in contrast to these previous instruments, the unit of analysis is not a unit of meaning (Henri, 1992; Jeong, 2003) or an entire online post (Garrison et al., 2001), but the contribution of an individual participant to the group discussion. It is also more diverse in its application, as it does not require threaded discussions as input (Jeong, 2003).

Goals of the Instrument

First and foremost, the goal of this coding scheme is to provide a framework and a measurement tool for critical thinking in group situations, namely small-group discussions; that is, it provides a more well-rounded and inclusive scheme than previous attempts by including the traditional philosophical, educational, and sociological perspectives. Consequently, research questions that can be studied using the coding schemes could include, "What percentage of interactions include awareness of who would challenge the group's views?", "What percentage of interactions include arguments with justified reasoning?", and "What percentages of questions appear to encourage depth of discussion?". As such, apart from directing future research into this direction and offering a tool for observational research, it can be used as a blueprint for desired behavior; for example, in professional development (Correnti & Rowan, 2007).

Available Versions

The critical thinking coding scheme is available in English and German from the first author as a digital copy.

Applicability

Thus far, the coding scheme was used in field studies only, although it is also conceivable to apply it to laboratory settings. In the development process, the focus was on small-group discussions occurring during classroom instruction, but the application to other settings in which small groups of people come together to discuss an issue and generate a joint understanding is feasible as well; for example, analysis of study groups, management and council meetings, health care, and so on.

For a precise analysis, video-recording is advisable. Using only audio-recordings runs the risk of not being able to identify who is speaking and thus misjudging participants' engagement in critical thinking during small-group discussions. So far, the coding scheme has been used only for coding recorded footage and not for real-time coding. Given the complexity of analyzing individual statements of participants according to eleven categories, it seems unlikely that in its present form the coding scheme is open to real-time coding.

Practical Application

Coding Time

In the current study the average coding time was two minutes of coding per one minute of transcript. Coding very much depends on participants' engagement in small-group discussions and as such the number of relevant turns, as well as coders' experience with coding in general and this coding scheme in particular, are important.

Coder Training

The time required for training coders depends on their previous experience with (a) other coding schemes, (b) the respective coding software, and (c) coders' knowledge in the field (dialogic teaching, critical thinking, reasoning, and so on). Coders achieved acceptable reliability within approximately 15–20 hours of training.

Technical Requirements

Depending on the format of the data (written transcripts of small-group discussions, video footage), technical requirements differ. Generally the use of supportive software such as MAXQDA, Dedoose for written transcripts, or INTERACT, ELAN, and Nvivo is considered more than helpful (see also Glüer, this volume, Chapter 13). Potential coding software includes all software that allows a user to define categories. Logging and analysis of the duration of each code is optional, but can offer additional interesting insight into small-group discussions.

Unitizing

The coding scheme uses event sampling; each group participant is seen as a separate case and each of their contributions as a separate event which can be analyzed for every code in each category. Of interest for the analyses are the frequencies of the different codes, as well as the sequential analysis of the codes in their chronological order during group interaction.

Training Manual

A comprehensive coding manual is currently in development and can be obtained from the first author.

Quality Assessment

Reliability

One-third of the transcripts were coded by two coders for comparison, and interrater reliability was calculated using Cohen's Kappa. Reliability was strong, with $\kappa = .90$. Where there were disagreements, these were resolved through discussion and consensus.

Validity

At the time of writing this chapter, validity analyses are still being conducted. These will be updated once completed.

Data Aggregation and Analysis

Data are coded on an individual level but analyzed on a group level. Of interest is the frequency of each code as well as the total sum of codes during an episode of group discussion. The critical thinking quality of a group is derived from the relative number of codes applied to an episode of talk, with higher numbers of codes assigned (relative to the total amount of segments) indicating higher critical thinking quality.

Previous Studies

The tool was only developed relatively recently and is still being revised based on preliminary results and practical experiences in its use. In its current form it has been applied in a field-experiment study in upper secondary schools and higher education institutes in New Zealand. In a longitudinal study, students' critical thinking during group discussions was analyzed after their teachers engaged in long-term professional development on dialogic teaching.

References

Apple, M. (Ed.). (2010). *Global crisis, social justice, and education*. New York, NY: Routledge.

Applebee, A. N., Langer, J. A., Nystrand, M., & Gamoran, A. (2003). Discussion-based approaches to developing understanding: Classroom instruction and student performance in middle and high school English. *American Educational Research Journal, 40*(3), 685–730. http://dx.doi.org/10.3102/00028312040003685

Bakhtin, M. (1986). *Speech genres and other late essays*. Austin, TX: University of Texas Press.

Bloom, B. S., Engelhart, M. D., Furst, E. J., Hill, W. H., & Krathwohl, D. R. (1956*). Taxonomy of educational objectives: The classification of educational goals. Handbook I: Cognitive domain*. New York, NY: David McKay Company.

Bloom, M., & Watt, D. (2003). *Solving Canada's innovation conundrum: How public education can help*. Ottawa, ON: Conference Board of Canada.

Bolhuis, S. (2003). Towards process-oriented teaching for self-directed lifelong learning: A multidimensional perspective. *Learning and Instruction, 13*(3), 327–347. http://doi.org/10.1016/S0959-4752(02)00008-7

Correnti, R., & Rowan. B. (2007). Opening up the black box: Literacy instruction in schools participating in three comprehensive school reform programs. *American Educational Research Journal, 44*(2), 298–339, doi:10.3102/0002831207302501

Delpit, L. (1995). *Other people's children: Cultural conflict in the class-room*. New York, NY: Free Press.

Ennis, R. H. (1962). A concept of critical thinking: A proposed basis for research in the teaching and evaluation of critical thinking ability. *Harvard Educational Review, 32*(1), 81–111.

Facione, P. A. (1990). *Critical thinking: A statement of expert consensus for purposes of educational assessment and instruction. Research findings and recommendations*. Newark, DE: American Philosophical Association.

Freire, P. (1970). *Pedagogy of the oppressed*. London: The Continuum Publishing Company.

Galotti, K. M., Clinchy, B. M., Ainsworth, K. H., Lavin, B., & Mansfield, A. F. (1999). A new way of assessing ways of knowing: The Attitudes Toward Thinking and Learning Survey (ATTLS). *Sex Roles, 40*(9), 745–766. doi:10.1023/A:1018860702422

Garrison, D. R., Anderson, T., & Archer, W. (2001). Critical thinking, cognitive presence, and computer conferencing in distance education. *American Journal of Distance Education, 15*(1), 7–23. http://dx.doi.org/10.1080/08923640109527071

Giroux, H. (2015). *Education and the crisis of public values: Challenging the assault on teachers, students, and public education*. New York, NY: Peter Lang Publishing, Inc.

Halpern, D. F. (1999). Teaching for critical thinking: Helping college students develop the skills and dispositions of a critical thinker. *New Directions for Teaching and Learning, 80*, 69–74. doi:10.1002/tl.8005

Henri, F. (1991) Computer conferencing and content analysis. In C. O'Malley (Ed.), *Computer Supported Collaborative Learning* (pp. 117–136). Heidelberg, Germany: Springer-Verlag.

Henri, F. (1992). Computer conferencing and content analysis. In A. R. Kaye (Series Ed.), *NATO ASI Series: Vol. F 90. Collaborative learning through computer conferencing* (pp. 117–136). Berlin, Germany: Springer.

hooks, b. (1994). *Teaching to transgress: Education as the practice of freedom.* New York, NY: Routledge.

hooks, b. (2010). *Teaching critical thinking: Practice wisdom.* New York, NY: Routledge.

Jeong, A. C. (2003). The sequential analysis of group interaction and critical thinking in online. *The American Journal of Distance Education, 17*(1), 25–43. http://dx.doi.org/10.1207/S15389286AJDE1701_3

Kahneman, D. (2011). *Thinking, fast and slow.* New York, NY: Farrar, Straus and Giroux.

Ladson-Billings, G. J., & Tate, W. (2006). *Education research in the public interest: Social justice, action, and policy.* New York, NY: Teachers College Press.

McLaren, P. (2016). *Life in schools: An introduction to critical pedagogy in the foundations of education.* New York, NY: Routledge.

Newman, D. R., Webb, B., & Cochrane, C. (1995). A content analysis method to measure critical thinking in face-to-face and computer supported group learning. *Interpersonal Computing and Technology, 3*(2), 56–77.

Nystrand, M., Wu, L. L., Gamoran, A., Zeiser, S., & Long, D. (2003). Questions in time: Investigating the structure and dynamics of unfolding classroom discourse. *Discourse Processes, 35*(2), 135–198. doi:10.1207/S15326950DP3502_3

Paul, R. W., & Binker, A. J. A. (1990). *Critical thinking: What every person needs to survive in a rapidly changing world.* Center for Critical Thinking and Moral Critique, Sonoma State University, Rohnert Park, CA 94928.

Postman, N., & Weigartner, C. (1969). *Teaching as a subversive activity.* New York, NY: Delacorte Press.

Sternberg, R. J. (1987). Introduction. In B. Baron & R. J. Sternberg (Eds.), *Teaching thinking skills: Theory and practice.* New York, NY: Freeman.

Thayer-Bacon, B. (2000). *Transforming critical thinking: Thinking constructively.* New York, NY: Teachers College Press.

Watson, G., & Glaser, E. M. (1980). *Watson-Glaser critical thinking appraisal.* San Antonio, TX: PsychCor.

Wegerif, R., Fujita, T., Doney, J., Linares, J. P., Richards, A., & Van Rhyn, C. (2017). Developing and trialing a measure of group thinking. *Learning and Instruction, 48*, 40-50.

Zohar, A., Weinberger, Y., & Tamir, P. (1994). The effect of the biology critical thinking project on the development of critical thinking. *Journal of Research in Science Teaching, 31*(2), 183–196. doi:10.1002/tea.3660310208

36 Identifying Teacher and Student Contributions during Assessment Conversations

The Elevate Coding Scheme

Erin Marie Furtak and Katharina Kiemer

General Information

Name of Coding Scheme

The Elevate Coding Scheme

Keywords

Formative assessment, formative assessment conversations, eliciting student ideas, teacher feedback, teacher questions, student-teacher interaction, classroom interaction

Summary

Formative assessment researchers have argued that teachers and students should engage in whole-class conversations in which teachers ask open-ended questions, students share their thinking, and teachers and students provide helpful, informational feedback to advance student thinking and learning (e.g., Shepard, 2000). To help us understand variations in student achievement in a larger study of formative assessment classroom practices, we developed and validated a coding scheme for teacher and student talk turns which involves four sets of codes: teacher questions to elicit student ideas, teacher exposition, student response, and teacher feedback.

Description of the Coding Scheme

Formative assessment, the process of teachers eliciting student ideas and responding to them during the course of instruction, has been a focus of much research in the past 20 years (Penuel & Shepard, 2016). The phrase "formative assessment" has been used to describe both the material tasks (Bennett, 2011) as well as the process by which teachers attend to student ideas in whole-class interactions (Coffey, Hammer, Levin, & Grant, 2011). Duschl and Gitomer (1997, p. 43) described these interactions as "assessment conversations," or whole-class instructional dialogues in which a diversity of student ideas and representations are shared.

The Elevate Coding Scheme was designed to analyze these types of formative assessment conversations and to make distinctions between higher- and lower-quality teacher and student contributions to them. Building on previous literature, we define higher-quality formative assessment conversations as those in which teachers ask open-ended, authentic questions (e.g., those starting with "Why," "How," or "What do you think?") to provide room for students to share their ideas (e.g., Cazden, 2001; Michaels, O'Connor, & Resnick, 2008). Student contributions involve longer, extended expressions of ideas, and even arise spontaneously and in response to other students rather than only in response to teacher questions. Teachers build on student ideas and provide helpful feedback to move students forward in their learning (Shepard, 2000). In doing so, they provide information about the quality of student performance, cueing students for particular types of responses, and asking follow-up questions that push students to improve the clarity and quality of their scientific explanations. These types of feedback have been positively associated with student learning (Hattie & Timperley, 2007; Kluger & DeNisi, 1996), and are central to many definitions of quality formative assessment (Wiliam, 2007). In other cases, teachers providing neutral responses or acknowledging student contributions without immediately evaluating them can encourage students to continue to share their thinking (e.g., "OK"). Rephrasing or revoicing student ideas can serve the function of letting students know their ideas have been heard (O'Connor & Michaels, 1993).

Based on a continuous approach to formative assessment conversations, the Elevate Coding Scheme can also capture lower-quality, more traditional student-teacher interactions in which teachers are in control of classroom discourse (e.g., Jurik, Gröschner, & Seidel, 2013; Kobarg & Seidel, 2007), the teacher is viewed as the ultimate source of knowledge ("primary knower," Bernstein, 2000), and student ideas are only drawn out for the purpose of evaluating them (Mercer, 2010; Reznitskaya, 2012). These exchanges often feature the Initiate-Respond-Evaluate (IRE) sequence of instruction, in which teachers ask simple questions, students give short, constrained, responses, and then teachers provide evaluative feedback (Cazden, 2001; Mehan, 1979). This type of discourse structure scarcely leaves time or space for students to voice their ideas and expand on their thinking (Seidel, Prenzel, Wittwer, & Schwindt, 2007).

We provide an overview of the coding scheme in Table 36.1. Before applying any codes, the verbal classroom interaction is segmented in teacher and student talk turns. Following, each talk turn is assessed on the basis of three categories for teacher statements (teacher question, teacher exposition, teacher feedback), and one for student responses. Within each category codes are ranked in order of

Table 36.1 *Elevate coding scheme*

Code		Description	Example
Teacher question			
0	Not present	Teacher talk turn does not contain a question.	
1	Instructional	Teacher talk turn cued elicitation of students' ideas; teacher asks questions while providing heavy clues for the information being sought.	"What's the answer to number 2?"
2	Eliciting student ideas	Teacher talk turn asks students to share their ideas, conceptions, opinions or interpretations.	"What might happen to these other guys?" "Why are the two species able to coexist?"
Teacher exposition/lecture			
0	Teacher exposition	Teacher talk turn is about content or procedural information about the classroom activity, not in response to a previous student statement or question.	"At the top you have big concepts, today our big concepts are reproductive success and adaptation. Those are kind of like genetic variability in the way you're going to put them on the paper. Your job is to connect all of these ten words, write them down in a way that makes sense with those two big concepts."
1	No teacher exposition	Teacher talk turn refers back to a student utterance.	Student: "It naturally trends towards specific traits." Teacher: "Okay, so it trends toward a specific trait."
Teacher feedback			
0	Not present	Teacher talk turn contains no response to student idea.	
1	Evaluative or limiting	Teacher talk turn is evaluative, or teacher interrupts student and finishes student thought.	"No." "Good Job."
2	Neutral	Teacher talk turn repeats or revoices students' words, other neutral response.	"I see." "OK."
3	Pushing student thinking	Teacher talk turn promotes students' thinking by asking them to elaborate their responses or by asking for more information about the previous question; provides descriptive or helpful feedback about quality of student idea.	"The fact that you said, like, 'pass on those genes' made that a really good answer."

Table 36.1 (*cont.*)

Code	Description	Example
Student responses		
0 Constrained	Student talk turn represents a one-word or short answer, is inauthentic, and does not reveal nature of student's thinking.	"I don't know." "Yes"
1 Extended	Student talk turn is an extended student utterance, which reveals student thinking in some way.	"Somewhere in the genes there was a mutation where the offspring have like longer legs … "
2 Question	Student talk turn is a question of the teacher or another student. All questions count as questions, regardless of topic.	" … so that came from when there were less complex species that had that?"

quality, with 0 representing that the code is not present in a given talk turn, and higher-quality codes assigned with higher numerical values (e.g., a question that elicits student thinking is given a higher rank than asking an instructional question). Consequently, codes within any category are mutually exclusive, but all categories are applied to each talk turn. In the case of the "Teacher Exposition" code, which was originally used as a 0 "not present" versus 1 for "present," we reverse the value in Table 36.1 to indicate that, in the context of formative assessment conversations, we view teachers providing extended mini-lectures or commentary on student ideas (teacher exposition) as being a lower-quality practice as compared to referring back to a student utterance (no teacher exposition).

Goals of the Instrument

The Elevate Coding Scheme is a tool designed to help researchers distinguish between the formative assessment conversations described above and more constrained, traditional forms of classroom discourse. Drawing on previous frameworks for the analysis of formative assessment conversations (Ruiz-Primo & Furtak, 2006, 2007), it aims to provide insights into both the quality and quantity of certain teacher talk moves, both at the level of an individual talk turn and in aggregates within and across lessons. It assigns lower-quality values to teacher and student talk turns associated with the IRE-sequence (Mehan, 1975), and higher-quality values to the open-ended, authentic student-teacher interactions that occur in formative assessment conversations (e.g., Michaels, O'Connor, & Hall, 2013).

Available Versions

The Elevate Coding Scheme is currently available in English only. In its present version, the coding scheme has been used to code directly from video footage in appropriate software. Coding from transcripts is also feasible; however, given the amount of student-teacher interaction sequences during whole class discussions in classrooms, software-supported coding is strongly recommended.

Applicability

Formative assessment conversations are not restricted to high school classrooms, but can be encountered in any learning context (e.g., university, medical training); as such, the Elevate Coding Scheme can be used in all these contexts. Thus far, the Elevate Coding Scheme has been applied to videotapes of high school biology classrooms; however, the four coding categories are content-neutral so could be applied to any setting in which the elicitation of ideas, student contributions, and teacher responses to those contributions are of interest. Compared with prior coding schemes which target teacher-student discourse (e.g., Pehmer, Kiemer, Gröschner, & Seidel, 2014; Seidel & Prenzel, 2006), the present coding scheme not only focuses on quantity (frequencies), but also on quality (by creating aggregate variables). Due to the necessity to rerun talk turns multiple times in order to categorize them adequately, real-time coding does not seem feasible.

Practical Application

Coding Time

Approximately one–two minutes.

Coder Training

Training time for coders varies, depending on their level of expertise with regard to formative assessment conversations and their experience with coding video- or audio-footage in general. Coders achieved acceptable reliability within approximately 15–20 hours of training.

Technical Requirements

Recording devices, preferably in the form of video cameras with high-quality microphones, are needed for the application of the Elevate Coding Scheme, since real-time coding is not an option. Video recording facilitates the process of determining who is speaking in a whole class discussion; however, we envision that audio recordings can be used as data as well. Any coding software needs to allow for defining individual events, which can be coded on multiple categories.

Unitizing

The coding scheme uses event sampling. An event is defined here as a speaker's talk turn. In a first pass, coders segment the recordings according to talk turns (teacher; student). After achieving satisfactory levels of agreement, in a second pass these coding units are then coded for content. Specifically, each unit is coded for each category described above (Table 36.1).

Training Manual

A comprehensive coding manual can be obtained from the first author.

Quality Assessment

Reliability

In a previous study (Furtak et al., 2016), two raters independently coded 20 percent of 89 total videos (stratified across teacher, school, and study year for a total of 2018 talk turns and nearly 17 hours of video) and established acceptable levels of agreement with Cohen's κ as follows: teacher question = .90; teacher exposition = .86; teacher feedback = .86; student response = .85.

Validity

A researcher (Furtak et al., 2016) who was not familiar with the teachers used summary coded data to sort teachers into instructional "profiles," or those with higher frequencies of codes associated with traditional instruction (e.g., asking closed-ended questions and providing evaluative responses), those with enactment more associated with formative assessment (e.g., asking open-ended questions, giving informational feedback), and those whose instruction was typically a mixture of the two. Two researchers who did not code the data, but who worked with teachers in the study, independently sorted the teachers into these three categories based upon their impressions of the teachers' instructional approaches. When the different sorting approaches were compared, both processes led to teachers being placed in the same categories (traditional, formative assessment, mixed), indicating the coding system captured similar patterns observed in more holistic, long-term observations of teachers.

Data Aggregation and Analysis

The data have been aggregated in two ways: first, in terms of frequencies of categories of code, and second, by creating mean quality variables based on the codes. The first analysis involved generating descriptive statistics based on teacher and student talk turns for each code within the different categories. The second involved a numeric value assigned to each teacher coding category reflecting its quality (student codes were not used in this analysis), with increasing values representing higher quality questions and feedback, as indicated in Table 36.1. Hence, each instance of a teacher asking a question was treated as an occasion that could be assigned a particular score (min = 1, max = 2), and each instance of a teacher providing feedback could be treated as an occasion that could be assigned a particular score (min = 1, max = 3). For further analysis, averages across occasions are calculated to generate variables for mean question quality and mean feedback quality across occasions.

Previous Studies

Precursors of this coding scheme were successfully used in studies by Ruiz-Primo and Furtak (2006; 2007), who distinguished among different types of formative assessment cycles of eliciting student ideas, students responding, and then teachers responding and then using student ideas to provide feedback. These studies demonstrated that teachers who completed more informal formative assessment cycles with their students in the course of classroom conversations had students with higher scores on embedded formative assessments.

Codes for teacher question and feedback quality have also been used to track changes in teachers' classroom practices in a longitudinal study (Furtak et al., 2016). Teachers who participated in a three-year professional learning experience intended to support their abilities to identify, interpret, and respond to student thinking showed significant gains in the quality of their questions and feedback.

References

Bennett, R. E. (2011). Formative assessment: A critical review. *Assessment in Education: Principles, Policy & Practice, 18*(1), 5–25. doi:10.1080/0969594X.2010.513678

Bernstein, B. B. (2000). *Pedagogy, symbolic control and identity-theory, research, critique* (2nd edn.). London, UK: Taylor & Francis Publishers, Ltd.

Cazden, C. B. (2001). *Classroom discourse: The language of teaching and learning.* Portsmouth, NH: Heinemann.

Coffey, J. E., Hammer, D., Levin, D. M., & Grant, T. (2011). The missing disciplinary substance of formative assessment. *Journal of Research in Science Teaching, 48* (10), 1109–1136. doi:10.1002/tea.20440

Duschl, R. A., & Gitomer, D. H. (1997). Strategies and challenges to changing the focus of assessment and instruction in science classrooms. *Educational Assessment, 4*(1), 37–73. http://dx.doi.org/10.1207/s15326977ea0401_2

Furtak, E. M., Kiemer, K., Swanson, R., DeLeon, V., Circi, R., Morrison, D., & Heredia, S. (2016). Developing teachers' attention and response to student thinking through long-term professional development: Results of a longitudinal study. *Instructional Science. 44*, 267–291. doi:10.1007/s11251-016-9371-3

Hattie, J., & Timperley, H. (2007). The power of feedback. *Review of Educational Research, 77*(1), 81–112. https://doi.org/10.3102/003465430298487

Jurik, V., Gröschner, A., & Seidel, T. (2013). How student characteristics affect girls' and boys' verbal engagement in physics instruction. *Learning and Instruction, 23*, 33–42. doi:10.1016/j.learninstruc.2012.09.002

Kluger, A. N., & DeNisi, A. (1996). The effects of feedback interventions on performance: A historical review, a meta-analysis, and a preliminary feedback intervention theory. *Psychological Bulletin, 119*, 254–284. doi:0033-2909/96/S3.00

Kobarg, M., & Seidel, T. (2007). Prozessorientierte Lernbegleitung-Videoanalysen im Physikunterricht der Sekundarstufe I. *Unterrichtswissenschaft, 35*(2), 148–168.

Mehan, H. (1979). *Learning lessons*. Cambridge, MA: Harvard University Press.

Mercer, N. (2010). The analysis of classroom talk: Methods and methodologies. *British Journal of Educational Psychology, 80*(1), 1–14. doi:10.1348/000709909X479853

Michaels, S., O'Connor, M. C., & Hall, M. W. (2013). *Accountable Talk sourcebook: For classroom conversation that works*. Institute of Learning. University of Pittsburgh. Retrieved April 20, 2017 from ifl.pitt.edu/index.php/download/index/ats.

Michaels, S., O'Connor, M. C., & Resnick, L. B. (2008). Deliberative discourse idealized and realized: Accountable Talk in the classroom and in civic life. *Studies in Philosophy and Education, 27*(4) 283–297. doi:10.1007/s11217-007-9071-1

O'Connor, M. C., & Michaels, S. (1993). Aligning academic task and participation status through revoicing: Analysis of a classroom discourse strategy. *Anthropology and Education Quarterly, 24*(4), 318–335. http://dx.doi.org/10.1525/aeq.1993.24.4.04x0063k

Pehmer, A.-K., Kiemer, K., & Gröschner, A. (2014). *Produktive Lehrer-Schüler-Kommunikation: ein Kategoriensystem zur Erfassung Produktiver Gesprächsführung im Klassengespräch und in Schülerarbeitsphasen*. Friedl-Schöller Endowed Chair for Teaching and Learning Research. TUM School of Education, Technische Universität München.

Penuel, W. R., & Shepard, L. A. (2016). Assessment and teaching. In D. H. Gitomer & C. Bell (Eds.), *Handbook of Research on Teaching* (5th edn., pp. 787–850). Washington, DC.: American Educational Research Association.

Reznitskaya, A. (2012). Dialogic teaching: Rethinking language use during literature discussions. *The Reading Teacher, 65*(7), 446–456. doi:10.1002/TRTR.01066

Ruiz-Primo, M. A., & Furtak, E. M. (2006). Informal formative assessment and scientific inquiry: Exploring teachers' practices and student learning. *Educational Assessment, 11*(3 & 4), 237–263. http://dx.doi.org/10.1080/10627197.2006.9652991

Ruiz-Primo, M. A., & Furtak, E. M. (2007). Exploring teachers' informal formative assessment practices and students' understanding in the context of scientific inquiry. *Journal of Research in Science Teaching*, 44(1), 57–84. doi:10.1002/tea.20163

Seidel, T., & Prenzel, M. (2006). Stability of teaching patterns in physics instruction: Findings from a video study. *Learning and Instruction*, 16(3), 228–240. doi:0.1016/j.learninstruc.2006.03.002

Seidel, T., Prenzel, M., Wittwer, J., & Schwindt, K. (2007). Unterricht in den Naturwissenschaften. In M. Prenzel, C. Artelt, J. Baumert, W. Blum, M. Hammann, E. Klieme, & R. Pekrun (Eds.), *PISA-Konsortium Deutschland. PISA 2006. Die Ergebnisse der dritten internationalen Vergleichsstudie* (pp. 147–180). Münster, Germany: Waxmann.

Shepard, L. A. (2000). The role of assessment in a learning culture. *Educational Researcher*, 29(7), 4–14. https://doi.org/10.3102/0013189X029007004

Wiliam, D. (2007). Keeping learning on track: Classroom assessment and the regulation of learning. In J. F. K. Lester (Ed.), *Second handbook of mathematics teaching and learning* (pp. 1053–1098). Greenwich, CT: Information Age Publishing.

37 Hidden Profile Discussion Coding

Tracing Synergy in Group Decisions

J. Lukas Thürmer, Frank Wieber, Thomas Schultze, and Stefan Schulz-Hardt

General Information

Name of Coding Scheme

Hidden Profile Discussion Coding

Keywords

Hidden profile paradigm, group decisions, group performance, group interaction, unshared information, synergy

Summary

Group interaction can empower groups to outperform even their best members; unfortunately, such strong *synergy* is rare. The prototypical decision situation where synergy through interaction is possible is called a *hidden profile* (HP). The two main characteristics of these situations are that (1) each group member has new, unshared information that the other group members do not have, and (2) integrating this unshared information implies a different, better decision alternative than each member's information alone. The hidden profile coding scheme is designed to code the initially shared and unshared information that is mentioned during the group discussion. The hidden profile coding scheme therefore aims to directly observe group decision processes that potentially lead to synergy.

Description of the Coding Scheme

The hidden profile paradigm and coding scheme stand in the tradition of highly formalized, structural approaches to groups such as social decision schemes (Davis, 1973) and social interaction sequence (Stasser & Davis, 1981). More recently, hidden profile research has been conducted in a wide range of fields, including organizational management (Brodbeck, Kerschreiter, Mojzisch, & Schulz-Hardt, 2007; Lightle, Kagel, & Arkes, 2009), motivation science (Sassenberg, Landkammer, & Jacoby, 2014; Thürmer, Wieber, & Gollwitzer, 2015), and economics (Maciejovsky & Budescu, 2013). The key question in this research is whether and how groups make better decisions than individuals in hidden profiles (i.e., attain *synergy*).

Groups typically fail to solve hidden profiles (Stasser & Titus, 1985, 2003). Studying group decisions, Schulz-Hardt, Brodbeck, Mojzisch, Kerschreiter, and Frey (2006) distributed attributes of four applicants for a position of an airline pilot so that each group member received information favoring a suboptimal alternative (i.e., advantages of the best applicant and disadvantages of the other candidates were unshared). A group discussion then would have allowed groups to consider all information and identify the best candidate, a task that overall only 35 percent of the groups mastered. In contrast, when full information was available at the onset – a situation where groups cannot achieve synergy – all groups picked the best candidate (100 percent). This finding is representative of the literature: A meta-analysis including 65 studies shows that groups are eight times less likely to make the optimal decision in a hidden profile situation as compared to situations where sufficient information is available to every group member from the onset (Lu, Yuan, & McLeod, 2012). Groups thus typically fail to attain synergy in hidden profiles.

The hidden profile coding scheme (Schulz-Hardt et al., 2006) charts the information flow during group discussions to analyze why groups (do not) attain synergy. The complete information that the group received prior to the discussion (i.e., all group members' information combined) is the basis of the coding scheme (left column, Table 37.1). The researcher also needs to know which information was shared and which information was unshared prior to the discussion. Each coding category (Mentioned, Repeated) is subdivided by group member to indicate who mentioned or repeated an item.

An information item (e.g., "Applicant A is boastful") is coded when two conditions are fulfilled: First, the information item is linked to the respective decision alternative explicitly, by context, or by designation (e.g., "I know something about Person A") and, second, the content of the information item is reproduced

Table 37.1 *Sample coding sheet*

Information item	Mentioned by group member			Repeated by group member		
	X	Y	Z	X	Y	Z
Applicant A:						
Has excellent spatial cognition	0	1	0	0	3	0
Has very good leadership skills	1	0	0	1	1	0
Is sometimes hectic	0	0	0	0	0	0
Is boastful	0	0	1	2	1	0

adequately either by referring to the main terms or synonyms (e.g., "he is more of a boastful type").

When an information item is brought up for the first time, it is coded as "Mentioned." Each information item can thus only be mentioned once by one group member. When an item is brought up again after another information item has been discussed, this is coded as "Repeated." Each information item can be repeated by any group member multiple times. Researchers can either code directly into Table 37.1 or first write lists of which items are mentioned when. The latter approach is useful to analyze the order in which information comes up.

Comparable Instruments

The advantage of the hidden profile paradigm is that the overall information available is determined a-priori by the researchers. As a consequence, the coding scheme is simple, requires minimal coder training, and coding requires little time.

Many different variants of the hidden profile discussion coding scheme exist and we only discuss selective examples. Stasser, Taylor, and Hanna (1989) introduced coding hidden profile discussions and used a coding scheme that only contains the "mentioned" category. Kolb and van Swol (2016) and Larson, Foster-Fishman, and Keys (1994) coded the order and the time when each information item was mentioned, and used INTERACT software or paper-and-pencil-coding, respectively. Without coding actual group discussions, Nevicka, Ten Velden, De Hoogh, and Van Vianen (2011) inferred the discussion content from group members' recall of information after the discussion. Although this method may be highly efficient, it is questionable if it is reliable since group members may not remember all mentioned items after the discussion is over.

A potential limitation of the hidden profile coding scheme is that it ignores all utterances that do not constitute information. Other aspects of group interaction are therefore not captured and researchers may combine hidden profile coding with more elaborate techniques of coding group interaction. Complementary coding schemes could moreover be used to code for the social processes in a group.

Goals of the Instrument

Hidden profile discussion coding allows investigating the information exchange during group discussions (Stasser et al., 1989). For instance, Schulz-Hardt et al. (2006) found that dissent between group members facilitates solving hidden profiles and used the hidden profile discussion coding scheme to test two proposed mechanisms: First, any dissent should increase discussion intensity and decrease bias toward shared information and toward members' suboptimal prediscussion preferences, and thereby increase discussing the best alternative. Second, a proponent of the best alternative should directly increase discussing the best alternative.

In general, coding the mentioned information allows studying at least three types of questions: (1) factors that affect discussion intensity, (2) factors that influence discussion bias, and (3) how increased intensity and decreased bias contribute to improved decisions. Depending on the design of a study and the sample size, it may be possible to test more than one of these questions simultaneously. Recent research further indicates that the biased repetition of information contributes to the failure to solve hidden profiles (Schulz-Hardt, Giersiepen, & Mojzisch, 2016). Researchers may therefore have specific hypotheses regarding those repetitions (e.g., that an intervention that increases repetitions of preference-inconsistent information should increase decision quality; Thürmer et al., 2015).

Available Versions

The hidden profile coding scheme has been used in many countries (e.g., the Netherlands; De Wilde, Ten Velden, & De Dreu, 2017; the United States; Kolb & van Swol, 2016; and Germany; Thürmer et al., 2015), and translating the coding scheme is easy. A greater challenge may be translating the decision cases that include the information on the decision alternatives. Depending on the wording and the cultural background, information items may differ in their valence and even the preferences for decision alternatives may change. Additional pre-testing may therefore be required.

Applicability

A pre-requisite for using this coding scheme is the complete list of all the available information on the decision alternatives. This is easy to ensure in laboratory experiments, where the researcher controls which information is available to each group member from the onset. However, the development of laboratory paradigms is challenging since it requires extensive pretesting of the information items and the decision alternatives.

In field settings, knowledge of the information available to each team member prior to the discussion is also necessary. Although this information is not always available, many team decision situations entail records of this information and can therefore be studied with the hidden profile discussion scheme. For instance, Stasser, Abele, and Parsons (2012) obtained data from a leadership training program, where executives participated in a personnel selection task. Executives first obtained information on different candidates through a computer system and then decided on the best candidate in small-group discussions. Because the computer recorded which information was obtained, Stasser et al. could analyze video-recordings of the group discussions with a variant of the hidden profile discussion coding scheme. Another example is a committee meeting where each committee member shares his or her notes from before the discussion. Researchers could code each member's prediscussion notes and then analyze records of the group discussion with the hidden profile coding scheme. Moreover, health care providers are required to keep detailed records of every patient's information that is available to them. Discussions and decisions by interprofessional medical teams could therefore be analyzed with the hidden profile discussion scheme. Similarly, educators commonly keep individual records about their students and then discuss how to proceed with each student at teachers' conferences. Researchers could use these records to code and analyze decisions in an education context. Few studies have investigated hidden profiles in field settings, and we believe that this is a highly promising area for future research.

Practical Application

Coding Time

The coding scheme is easy to use, requires minimal coder training, and coding is fast. One minute of a group discussion requires little more than one minute coding time, potentially allowing for real-time coding. However, we recommend using video recordings of the group discussions to increase coding accuracy and to allow for assessing intercoder agreement. Usually, coders are proficient after coding interactions of one or two test groups, which usually last 10 to 25 minutes each. The coding can be conducted on standard personal computers with any spreadsheet software (e.g., Microsoft Excel, Microsoft, 2016; or Libre Office Calc, The Document Foundation, 2017).

Coder Training

No extensive training is required; the coding rules are described above.

Unitizing

Each information item (i.e., attribute of a decision alternative) that was provided to participants at the onset (e.g., "Applicant A is boastful," see above for coding rules) is considered a coding unit. As this definition leaves little room for interpretation, it allows for high objectivity in the coding process. Utterances other than information are not coded.

Simplified Version

One could consider only coding the first instances when information is mentioned, ignoring repetitions. However, the coding scheme is very efficient and the need to further shorten the coding scheme should hardly ever occur.

Quality Assessment

Reliability

This coding scheme is highly reliable, usually attaining between 80 percent and 95 percent agreement rates between coders; Schulz-Hardt et al. (2006) report 87 percent agreement. Other studies using variants of the coding scheme report 99 percent (Greitemeyer, Schulz-Hardt, Brodbeck, & Frey, 2006), 87 percent (Stasser & Stewart, 1992), 95 percent (Thürmer et al., 2015), and 95 percent (Winquist & Larson, 1998) agreement (if separate agreements for different types of information are reported, we reproduce agreement for unshared items).

Validity

The content validity of the coding scheme is high, since it contains all the information of the decision cases. In line with this theoretical argument, the measures obtained commonly predict group decision quality; in a meta-analysis, Lu and colleagues (2012) observed an average effect of information exchange on decision quality of $r = .56$ and an average effect of discussion focus on decision quality of $r = .25$. We are not aware of further formal validity testing.

Data Aggregation and Analysis

Most commonly, the coding output is analyzed at the group level (i.e., aggregated across all group members), and with regard to the two main obstacles in solving hidden profiles: Insufficient discussion intensity (groups do not discuss the problem sufficiently), and discussion bias (e.g., groups mainly discuss information that supports suboptimal pre-discussion preferences). Both obstacles prevent groups from talking about the correct alternative. Schulz-Hardt et al. (2006) used the following measures of discussion intensity (with higher values indicating greater intensity):

- duration of the discussion (assessed separately from discussion videos)
- proportion of information items mentioned (i.e., mean of proportion shared and proportion unshared)
- average repetition rate of these information items.

The measures of discussion bias assess how much the discussion focuses on shared information or on information supporting pre-discussion preferences, respectively.[1] Instead of using absolute numbers of items, these measures use proportions of proportions. The reasoning is as follows: The number of overall items available per category may vary. For instance, a suboptimal alternative most likely has fewer positive items than the optimal alternative. Comparing the number of items mentioned would therefore not represent the bias correctly. Proportions (the ratio of items mentioned divided by the overall number of items available) take the overall number of items available into account, and therefore avoid this problem. However, the proportion in one category (e.g., shared information) is not very informative if one does not take into account how this number relates to the overall proportion of information discussed (e.g., shared information and unshared information). Therefore, the bias measures below use proportions of proportions (the ratio of the proportion of items mentioned in the respective category divided by the overall proportion of items mentioned). This approach further has the advantage that the bias measures can be interpreted across decision situations (i.e., when different amounts of information are available): .50 represents an unbiased discussion, values closer to 1 represent a discussion biased toward the initial preference or shared information, respectively, and values closer to 0 represent a discussion biased against the initial preference or for unshared information, respectively. Schulz-Hardt et al. (2006) used the following measures of discussion bias[2] (see also Stasser, Vaughan, & Stewart, 2000):

- The bias toward mentioning shared information (that all members know at the onset of the discussion) instead of unshared information (that is new to all but one member) is calculated by dividing the proportion of shared information mentioned by the overall proportion of information mentioned (shared plus unshared):

$$\frac{Proportion\ of\ Shared\ Information\ Mentioned}{(Proportion\ Shared\ +\ Proportion\ Unshared)}$$

- One may also want to calculate the bias toward mentioning preference-consistent information (i.e., positive aspects of the preferred alternative and negative aspects of the non-preferred alternatives). Since group members may have different pre-discussion preferences, measures of preference consistency need to be calculated for each group member separately and then averaged. This is a problem when analyzing the number of items mentioned: Since each item can only be mentioned once, a preference-consistent mention by one group member makes it impossible for another group member to mention this (potentially preference-inconsistent) item. Schulz-Hardt et al. therefore did not include this measure.

---

[1] Note that shared information supports suboptimal preferences in hidden profile situations.
[2] Calculating requires knowing group members' initial preferences. These are commonly assessed before the group discussion.

- The bias toward repeating shared information instead of unshared information is calculated by dividing the repetition rate of shared information by the overall repetition rate (shared plus unshared):

$$\frac{Repetition\ Rate\ of\ Shared\ Information}{(Repetition\ Rate\ Shared\ +\ Repetition\ Rate\ Unshared)}$$

- Lastly, the repetition bias for information in line with the pre-discussion preference is calculated by dividing the repetition rate of preference consistent information by the overall repetition rate (preference consistent plus preference inconsistent):

$$\frac{Repetition\ Rate\ Preference\ Consistent\ Information}{(Repetition\ Rate\ Consistent\ +\ Repetition\ Rate\ Inconsistent)}$$

Moreover, an overall discussion bias score (i.e., including the focus on shared and preference-consistent information) may be calculated from the repetition of preference-consistent and shared information.

It is also possible to code and calculate these measures separately for each different group member or to code the sequence of information mentioned. These analyses will offer a benefit if differences between group members or across time are of interest. For example, members who prefer the same decision alternative as most other group members (majority) can be compared to members who hold an idiosyncratic preference (minority) with regard to differences in their introduction and repetition of information. Or, building on this, differences between minorities that change the group's final decision and those who do not can be calculated. Lastly, the introduction of information over time allows testing whether unshared information is more likely to be mentioned later on in the discussion (Larson et al., 1994).

Previous Studies

Versions of this coding scheme have been used in dozens of studies, and the literature on hidden profiles is vast. One meta-analysis (Lu et al., 2012) and several review papers (Brodbeck et al., 2007; Schulz-Hardt & Mojzisch, 2012; Sohrab, Waller, & Kaplan, 2015; Stasser & Titus, 2003) provide comprehensive overviews of the literature on hidden profiles and studies that used variants of this coding scheme.

References

Original Publication

Schulz-Hardt, S., Brodbeck, F. C., Mojzisch, A., Kerschreiter, R., & Frey, D. (2006). Group decision making in hidden profile situations: Dissent as a facilitator for decision quality. *Journal of Personality and Social Psychology*, *91*, 1080–1093. doi:10.1037/0022-3514.91.6.1080

Other References

Brodbeck, F. C., Kerschreiter, R., Mojzisch, A., & Schulz-Hardt, S. (2007). Group decision making under conditions of distributed knowledge: The information asymmetries model. *Academy of Management Review*, *32*, 459–479. doi:10.5465/AMR.2007.24351441

Davis, J. H. (1973). Group decision and social interaction: A theory of social decision schemes. *Psychological Review*, *80*, 97–125. doi:10.1037/h0033951

De Wilde, T. R. W., Ten Velden, F. S., & De Dreu, C. K. W. (2017). The neuropeptide oxytocin enhances information sharing and group decision making quality. *Nature: Scientific Reports*, *7*, 40622. doi:10.1038/srep40622

Greitemeyer, T., Schulz-Hardt, S., Brodbeck, F. C., & Frey, D. (2006). Information sampling and group decision making: The effects of an advocacy decision procedure and task experience. *Journal of Experimental Psychology: Applied*, *12*, 31–42. doi:10.1037/1076-898x.12.1.31

Kolb, M. R., & van Swol, L. M. (2016). Manipulating a synchronous or separatist group orientation to improve performance on a hidden profile task. *Group Processes & Intergroup Relations*. doi:10.1177/1368430216647188

Larson Jr., J. R., Foster-Fishman, P. G., & Keys, C. B. (1994). Discussion of shared and unshared information in decision-making groups. *Journal of Personality and Social Psychology*, *67*, 446–461. doi:10.1037/0022-3514.67.3.446

Lightle, J. P., Kagel, J. H., & Arkes, H. R. (2009). Information exchange in group decision making: The hidden profile problem reconsidered. *Management Science*, *55*, 568–581. doi:10.1287/mnsc.1080.0975

Lu, L., Yuan, Y. C., & McLeod, P. L. (2012). Twenty-five years of hidden profiles in group decision making. *Personality and Social Psychology Review*, *16*, 54–75. doi:10.1177/1088868311417243

Maciejovsky, B., & Budescu, D. V. (2013). Markets as a structural solution to knowledge-sharing dilemmas. *Organizational Behavior and Human Decision Processes*, *120*, 154–167. doi:10.1016/j.obhdp.2012.04.005

Microsoft. (2016). Microsoft Office Excel.

Nevicka, B., Ten Velden, F. S., De Hoogh, A. H. B., & Van Vianen, A. E. M. (2011). Reality at odds with perceptions. *Psychological Science*, *22*, 1259–1264. doi:10.1177/0956797611417259

Sassenberg, K., Landkammer, F., & Jacoby, J. (2014). The influence of regulatory focus and group vs. individual goals on the evaluation bias in the context of group decision making. *Journal of Experimental Social Psychology*, *54*, 153–164. doi:10.1016/j.jesp.2014.05.009

Schulz-Hardt, S., Giersiepen, A., & Mojzisch, A. (2016). Preference-consistent information repetitions during discussion: Do they affect subsequent judgments and decisions? *Journal of Experimental Social Psychology*, *64*, 41–49. doi:10.1016/j.jesp.2016.01.009

Schulz-Hardt, S., & Mojzisch, A. (2012). How to achieve synergy in group decision making: Lessons to be learned from the hidden profile paradigm.

European Review of Social Psychology, *23*, 305–343. doi:10.1080/10463283.2012.744440

Sohrab, S. G., Waller, M. J., & Kaplan, S. (2015). Exploring the hidden-profile paradigm: A literature review and analysis. *Small Group Research*, *46*, 489–535. doi:10.1177/1046496415599068

Stasser, G., Abele, S., & Parsons, S. V. (2012). Information flow and influence in collective choice. *Group Processes & Intergroup Relations*, *15*, 619–635. doi:10.1177/1368430212453631

Stasser, G., & Davis, J. H. (1981). Group decision making and social influence: A social interaction sequence model. *Psychological Review*, *88*, 523–551. doi:10.1037/0033-295X.88.6.523

Stasser, G., & Stewart, D. (1992). Discovery of hidden profiles by decision-making groups: Solving a problem versus making a judgment. *Journal of Personality and Social Psychology*, *63*, 426–434. doi:10.1037/0022-3514.63.3.426

Stasser, G., Taylor, L. A., & Hanna, C. (1989). Information sampling in structured and unstructured discussions of three- and six-person groups. *Journal of Personality and Social Psychology*, *57*, 67–78. doi:10.1037/0022-3514.57.1.67

Stasser, G., & Titus, W. (1985). Pooling of unshared information in group decision making: Biased information sampling during discussion. *Journal of Personality and Social Psychology*, *48*, 1467–1478. doi:10.1037/0022-3514.48.6.1467

Stasser, G., & Titus, W. (2003). Hidden profiles: A brief history. *Psychological Inquiry*, *14*, 304–313. doi:10.1080/1047840X.2003.9682897

Stasser, G., Vaughan, S. I., & Stewart, D. D. (2000). Pooling unshared information: The benefits of knowing how access to information is distributed among group members. *Organizational Behavior and Human Decision Processes*, *82*, 102–116. doi:10.1006/obhd.2000.2890

The Document Foundation. (2017). LibreOffice Calc. Retrieved from www.libreoffice.org

Thürmer, J. L., Wieber, F., & Gollwitzer, P. M. (2015). A self-regulation perspective on hidden-profile problems: If–then planning to review information improves group decisions. *Journal of Behavioral Decision Making*, *28*, 101–113. doi:10.1002/bdm.1832

Winquist, J. R., & Larson, J. R., Jr. (1998). Information pooling: When it impacts group decision making. *Journal of Personality and Social Psychology*, *74*, 371–377. doi:10.1037/0022-3514.74.2.371

38 TRAWIS

Coding Transactive Knowledge and Knowledge Exchange

Elisabeth Brauner

General Information

Name of the Coding Scheme

Transactive Knowledge Interaction System (TRAWIS)

Keywords

Transactive memory, knowledge exchange, knowledge transfer, knowledge acquisition, mental models, content coding, knowledge development over time

Summary

The goal of the Transactive Knowledge Interaction System (TRAWIS) is to code knowledge exchange and transfer during group interaction, specifically, transactive memory processes (what people know about other people's knowledge and the interactions between and among people when exchanging knowledge). Utterances are coded based on their reference to two basic dimensions: (1) type of knowledge addressed, that is, whether the person refers to object-level knowledge or to metaknowledge; (2) cognitive focus of the person, that is, reference to personal knowledge or to social knowledge. Possible applications include transactive memory assessment, knowledge management, team development, or information processing in teams. TRAWIS allows operationalizing transactive memory as a process variable and enables both practitioners and basic researchers to study knowledge exchange processes as they occur in group interaction.

Description of the Coding Scheme

TRAWIS was developed for interaction process analysis of transactive memory. Transactive memory is defined as the knowledge that people acquire about knowledge of others as well the knowledge-relevant processes that occur among people (Wegner, 1995). These knowledge-relevant processes represent the way in which transactive memory is constructed, activated, and operated. Most early research on transactive memory focused on investigating who knows what rather than on the interactive processes that lead to knowledge exchange (e.g., Moreland, Argote, & Krishnan, 1996; Wegner, Giuliano, & Hertel, 1985). TRAWIS presents a well-tested instrument to assess processes that lead to the development of transactive memory.

Theoretical basis for the development of TRAWIS are two basic dimensions of knowledge that can be addressed in verbal communication. The first dimension is the type of knowledge addressed in an utterance, which indicates whether a person is referring to object-level knowledge or meta-level knowledge (or metaknowledge). Object-level knowledge comprises the knowing of facts, events, or concepts and is stored in a person's memory. Metaknowledge is knowledge *about* object-level knowledge, which indicates whether object-level knowledge exists or not. For instance, knowing that my paternal grandfather's date of birth was October 18, 1888, is object-level knowledge. Knowing *that* I know my paternal grandfather's birthday is meta-knowledge, which means knowing that this knowledge exists in one's memory. At the same time, knowing that I *don't know* my maternal grandfather's date of birth is metaknowledge as well, in this case metaknowledge about a lack of object-level knowledge (see Brauner, 2002). The response to a question such as "When is your grandfather's birthday?" will be object-level knowledge (actually providing the date), whereas the response to a question such as "Do you know your grandfather's birthday?" would be meta-level knowledge. Responses to meta-level questions can be *yes, no, I am not sure, I think I know, I feel I know but cannot recall right now* (for various kinds of meta-level knowledge, see Brauner, 2002).

The second relevant dimension in TRAWIS is whether personal knowledge or social knowledge is addressed in an utterance. Personal knowledge is knowledge (object-level or meta-level) that a person stores in their own memory. Social knowledge is knowledge that a person assumes, or expects, or believes to be stored in another person's memory. Social knowledge again could be object-level knowledge or meta-level knowledge. Social object-level knowledge is concrete knowledge that Person A believes that Person B holds. If Person A is correct and Person B indeed holds respective knowledge, then this knowledge can be considered shared knowledge between Person A and Person B. Social meta-level knowledge is knowledge that Person A believes B holds albeit without Person A actually holding the same knowledge that A believes B should have. This knowledge is what is usually referred to as "knowing what others know." Interaction addressing personal knowledge can be considered to be monitoring and controlling of individual cognition whereas interaction addressing social knowledge can be considered monitoring and controlling of social information processes (Brauner, 2002, 2006).

These two dimensions form four basic categories: personal metaknowledge, social metaknowledge, personal object-level knowledge, and social object-level knowledge. Each of these four basic categories contains three specific categories that refer to types of knowledge exchanged (see Table 38.1). Furthermore, two additional categories can be assigned to utterances that address group coordination

Table 38.1 *TRAWIS classification of utterances based on their role in knowledge exchange during conversation*

	Focus on personal knowledge	Focus on social knowledge
Object-level knowledge	accepting/taking in information (learning new information)	accepting/rejecting other's inferences (agreeing or disagreeing with statements)
	drawing inferences, developing hypotheses (creating new information)	referring to other's specific knowledge or to shared knowledge; (showing shared expertise)
	using personal object-level knowledge (sharing expertise)	searching for information (when knowing who has it)
Meta-level knowledge	using personal metaknowledge (showing existing expertise)	searching for information (when not knowing who has it)
	rejecting/denying having knowledge or metaknowledge	using metaknowledge about other (showing knowledge about other's expertise)
	accepting/not accepting responsibility for information	assigning/not assigning responsibility (defining expertise areas)
Categories not related to knowledge exchange	group coordination	
	other remarks, remaining utterances that cannot be categorized	

Note. This table is modified based on Brauner (2006, Table 1).

processes or other utterances that do not address knowledge exchange or that cannot be categorized.

Comparable Instruments

The act4teams coding scheme (Kauffeld, Lehmann-Willenbrock, & Meinecke, this volume, Chapter 21) contains several codes that can be considered addressing monitoring and controlling of knowledge within a group (see below section on validity). No specialized coding schemes measuring transactive memory exist that operationalize transactive knowledge processes as embedded in a theoretical framework.

Goals of the Instrument

TRAWIS was developed to analyze the function of utterances for monitoring and controlling individual cognition and social information processing in group discussions. It can be used in the laboratory and in the field. For process analysis in laboratory groups, questions may address knowledge transfer in teams. For groups in the field, questions of knowledge management, knowledge exchange, and effective team knowledge development over time may be studied. Such questions can include:

- Degree of learning achieved by a team
- Development of a shared knowledge base (knowledge integration)
- Development of shared mental models
- Acquisition of knowledge about other team members' expertise (metaknowledge)
- Stages of team development of knowledge acquisition
- Task dependence of transactive knowledge acquisition
- Differences in transactive knowledge acquisition between types of teams
- Differences in knowledge acquisition between types of communication (e.g., face-to-face vs. computer-mediated communication)
- Knowledge management in teams and organizations
- Change of knowledge processes over time

Available Versions

Currently, TRAWIS is available in English and German. It can be used with paper-pencil methods as well as using coding software. Duration of codes does not have to, but can, be recorded. Recording further information, such as exact time of code, who speaks, to whom, etc. can be useful but is not required.

Applicability

TRAWIS is applicable both in the laboratory and in the field. In both environments, it is recommended to audio- and preferably video-record the interactions that are to be studied. Recording will allow for more precise analysis due to the fact that coding of 14 categories requires coders to engage in cognitive processing that is fairly complex and can be time consuming. However, it is possible to reduce coding to the four basic categories, which will allow well-trained coders to code real-time discussions. This is particularly recommendable if there are objections to recording of participants (e.g., consent to analyze but no consent to record).

Practical Application

Coding Time

Coding time required is approximately nine minutes of coding per one minute of interaction time for the full version.

Coder Training

Time required for training coders depends slightly on the experience of coders with other coding schemes. For an experienced coder, two to five hours of training should suffice. For inexperienced coders, between ten and 20 hours should be expected.

Technical Requirements

Technical requirements for using TRAWIS depend on the preference of the researchers (paper-pencil vs. computer-assisted coding). Potential software that can be used includes all software that allows a researcher to define their own categories and code events rather than intervals or states. Coding keyboards can be helpful but are not required. Recording devices are required for application of the full version of TRAWIS because real-time coding is not possible.

Unitizing

Units of analysis are based on events that can be understood as "thought units" (Bakeman & Gottman, 1997) or sense units (Boos, 1996). For the full version of TRAWIS, unitizing should be done in a first step by two independent coders, reliability of coding units should be assessed, and thereafter actual coding conducted. Each unit is coded by assigning one of 14 coding categories (12 codes for knowledge-relevant processes; one code for group coordination; one code for units that are not knowledge-relevant or are not codable).

Training Manual

A training manual, coding flow chart, as well as a full description of the coding scheme are available from the author.

Simplified Version

To abbreviate and simplify the coding process, a shortened version with only the four basic categories (personal meta-level, social meta-level, personal object-level, and social object-level) can be used by trained coders for real-time coding. Furthermore, event-sampling or time-sampling techniques can be used to limit analyses to specific points in time.

Quality Assessment

Reliability

Interrater reliability was assessed using three independent coders at two different points in time: (1) at the end of the coder training, and (2) three months later. Each

Table 38.2 *Coding reliability comparison of three different coders*

	t_1		t_2	
	κ	κ$_{max}$	κ	κ$_{max}$
Coder 1 and 2	.81	.93	.76	.91
Coder 2 and 3	.83	.96	.80	.92
Coder 1 and 3	.82	.92	.74	.87

time, 300 units each of three different group discussions were coded (900 units in total) by each of the three coders. Table 38.2 shows the results.

Given that theoretically Kappa can achieve values between −1 and +1, reliabilities for TRAWIS can be considered very good despite the slight decline towards the end of the three-month coding period. According to Landis and Koch (1977, p. 165) values between .81 and 1.0 can be considered "almost perfect," between .61 and .80 "substantial," and between .41 and .60 "moderate."

Validity

Previous research shows very good validity of TRAWIS. Data presented by Piontkowski, Böing-Messing, Hartmann, and Keil (2003) show that TRAWIS achieves discriminant validity based on comparison with the Interaction Process Analysis system (IPA) by Bales (1950). Both coding systems are independent although they focus on the same types of units. TRAWIS codes knowledge-relevant processes whereas IPA addresses the structural and relationship aspect of interactions. In a different study (Brauner, Kauffeld, Siem, & Buschek, unpublished data), 44 practice groups were coded using TRAWIS and the Cassel Competence Grid (CCG) (e.g., Kauffeld, 2006; now act4teams, Kauffeld et al., this volume, Chapter 21). Results show significant positive correlation between group coordination in TRAWIS and positive utterances addressing structure in CCG. Furthermore, the knowledge-relevant processes concerning *knowledge disclosure* and *retaining of knowledge* correlated positively with *knowledge management* in CCG. *Knowing Who* in CCG moreover shows significant positive correlation with the two TRAWIS categories *Assign/don't Assign Responsibility* and *Use Personal Object-level Knowledge*. Finally, *Knowledge about the Organization* in CCG correlated positively with *Social Object-level Knowledge* in TRAWIS (for more details, see Brauner, 2006).

Data Aggregation and Analysis

Data can be analyzed by aggregating at the level of the basic dimension as well as at the level of individual categories. Analyses can include frequencies of dimensions or categories and contingencies of sequences of dimensions or of categories. Sequential analyses (e.g., Bakeman & Gottman, 1997) or pattern analysis (e.g., Stachowski, Kaplan, & Waller, 2009) are recommended particularly for understanding the development of knowledge exchange over time.

Previous Studies

Studies applying TRAWIS have addressed development of transactive memory over time (Brauner, 2002), development of social metacognition, decision-making processes (Piontkowski et al., 2003), and transactive memory processes and performance in groups (Brauner, 2002).

References

Original Publication

Brauner, E. (2006). Kodierung transaktiver Wissensprozesse (TRAWIS). Ein Verfahren zur Erfassung von Wissenstransfer in Interaktionen [Transactive Knowledge Coding System (TRAWIS): A schema for the assessment of knowledge transfer in interactions]. *Zeitschrift für Sozialpsychologie [Journal of Social Psychology]*, *37*, 99–112. [Available in English from the author] http://dx.doi.org/10.1024/0044-3514.37.2.99

Other References

Bakeman, R., & Gottman, J. M. (1997). *Observing interaction: An introduction to sequential analysis*. Cambridge, UK: Cambridge University Press.

Brauner, E. (2002). *Transactive knowledge systems in groups and organizations*. Habilitationsschrift, Germany: Humboldt-University in Berlin.

Brauner, E., Kauffeld, S., Siem, B. & Buschek, S. (unpublished data). *Competencies in transactive knowledge systems in groups of practitioners. Process analyses with the Cassel Competence Grid and Transactive Knowledge Coding (TRAWIS)*.

Landis, R. D., & Koch, G. G. (1977). The measurement of observer agreement for categorical data. *Biometrics*, *33*, 159–174.

Moreland, R. L., Argote, L., & Krishnan, R. (1996). Socially shared cognition at work: Transactive memory and group performance. In J. L. Nye & A. M. Brower (Eds.), *What's social about social cognition? Research on socially shared cognition in small groups* (pp. 57–84). Thousand Oaks, CA: Sage.

Piontkowski, U., Böing-Messing, E., Hartmann, J., Keil, W., & Laus, F. (2003). Transaktives Gedächtnis, Informationsintegration und Entscheidungsfindung im Medienvergleich [Transactive memory, knowledge integration, and decision making in a comparison of media]. *Zeitschrift für Medienpsychologie*, *15*, 60–68. https://doi.org/10.1026//1617-6383.15.2.60

Stachowski, A. A., Kaplan, S. A., & Waller, M. J. (2009). The benefits of flexible team interaction during crisis. *Journal of Applied Psychology, 94,* 1536–1543. http://dx .doi.org/10.1037/a0016903

Wegner, D. M. (1995). A computer network model of human transactive memory. *Social Cognition, 13,* 319–339. http://dx.doi.org/10.1521/soco.1995.13.3.319

Wegner, D. M., Giuliano, T., & Hertel, P. T. (1985). Cognitive interdependence in close relationships. In W. I. Ickes (Ed.), *Compatible and incompatible relationships* (pp. 253–276). New York, NY: Springer.

Personality and Team Behavior

39 The Behavior Analysis Coding System

An Applied, Real-time Approach for Measuring and Improving
Interactive Skills

Samuel Farley, Rose Evison, Neil Rackham,
Rod Nicolson, & Jeremy Dawson

General Information

Name of Coding Scheme

The Behavior Analysis Coding System

Keywords

Interactive skills, process-analysis, real-time coding, behavior analysis, short-cycle feedback

Summary

The goal of the behavior analysis (BA) approach is to code, in real time, individuals' sequential utterances during team meetings, thereby providing objective data that can be used for immediate post-meeting behavioral feedback. The approach was developed during industrial training courses to improve employee's interactive skills. Although a comprehensive 13-category system has been established, the value of the BA system involves principles for category development and the provision of immediate feedback to help people improve their interactions with others. Accordingly, BA could help teams improve language use (Leshed et al., 2009), dysfunctional team processes (Johnson, Hollenbeck, Scott DeRue, Barnes, & Jundt, 2013), and performance (Gabelica, Van den Bossche, Segers, & Gijselaers, 2012).

Description of the Coding Scheme

High-quality team meetings are needed to support organizational effectiveness. Kauffeld and Lehmann-Willenbrock (2012) published data on this link in 2012, yet before the evidence had been established, the notion prompted Rackham, Honey, and Colbert (1971) to investigate ways of improving employee communication in meetings.

Rackham et al. (1971) started with the assumption that in order to bring about improvements in people's interactive skills, you first need a system for measuring their verbal behavior. Changes in verbal behavior can then be achieved by observing people's interactions and providing feedback on how often they use specific behaviors (Morgan, Rackham, & Hudson, 1974). When feedback is accompanied by suggestions on more effective behaviors and advice on practicing new behaviors, over time people can improve their communicative repertoire. This approach, which Rackham et al. labelled behavior analysis, has roots in psychomotor skill learning and was also influenced by Interaction Process Analysis (IPA, Bales, 1950). The application of these ideas to the work context was novel, and Rackham et al. developed a set of criteria for creating category systems relevant to industry.

Rackham et al. (1971) used the following criteria to establish categories: (1) a coding category must describe a verbal behavior which can change during training, (2) categories must be mutually exclusive, (3) categories must be meaningful to participants and observers, (4) the category system must permit high interrater reliability when used by different observers, and (5) categories should be related to the outcomes of interactions (Morgan et al., 1974). One of the category systems produced via the BA approach is outlined in Table 39.1; however behavior analysis was always viewed as a process rather than a specific set of categories (Rackham & Morgan, 1977).

Over the course of a four-year research project with the British Overseas Airways Corporation (BOAC), Rackham et al. developed and tested five category systems while training supervisory teams in communication skills (Rackham & Morgan, 1977). The behavioral categories developed during this project were reduced using cluster analysis into a set of "meta-categories," which reflected the way the behaviors were used (Morgan et al., 1974). The four meta-categories were Initiating (behaviors related to idea and suggestion creation), Clarifying (behaviors that create a common understanding), Reacting (behaviors that establish agreement and disagreement), and Process Behaviors (behaviors that balance people's contributions).

Rackham and Morgan (1977, p. 31) outlined the definitions of a 13-category instrument (see Table 39.1), which was the fifth and final system produced during a four-year project with BOAC. Although this category system and meta-category framework denote one of the prevalent approaches in practice, several other category systems have been established (Evison & Ronaldson, 1975; Rackham, 1988). Therefore, one of the advantages of the BA process is that researchers and practitioners can develop their own categories to address specific research questions or training goals, as long as they adhere to the BA principles.

Table 39.1 *The 13-category BA coding system (Rackham & Morgan, 1977, p. 31)*

Meta-categories	Behavioral categories
Initiating behaviors	1. *Proposing*: Behavior which puts forward a new concept, suggestion or course of action (and is actionable).
	2. *Building*: Behavior which extends or develops a proposal which has been made by another person (and is actionable).
Clarifying behaviors	3. *Giving information*: Behavior which offers facts, opinions or clarification to other individuals.
	4. *Seeking information*: Behavior which seeks facts, opinions or clarification from another individual or individuals.
	5. *Summarizing*: Behavior which summarizes, or otherwise restates in compact form, the content of the previous discussions or considerations.
	6. *Testing understanding*: Behavior which seeks to establish whether or not an earlier contribution has been understood.
Reacting behaviors	7. *Supporting*: Behavior which involves a conscious and direct declaration of support or agreement with another person or his / her concepts.
	8. *Disagreeing*: Behavior which involves a conscious, direct and reasoned declaration of difference of opinion, or criticism of another person's concepts.
	9. *Blocking/difficulty stating*: Behavior which places a block in the path of a proposal or concept without offering any alternative proposal and without offering a reasoned statement of disagreement.
	10. *Defending/attacking*: Behavior which attacks another person or defensively strengthens an individual's own position. Defending/attacking behaviors usually involve overt value judgements and often contain emotional overtones.
	11. *Open*: Behavior which exposes the individual who makes it to risk of ridicule or loss of status. This behavior may be considered the opposite of defending/attacking, including with this category admissions of mistakes or inadequacies provided that these are made in a non-defensive manner.
Process behaviors	12. *Bringing in*: Behavior which is a direct and positive attempt to involve another group member.
	13. *Shutting out*: Behavior which excludes, or attempts to exclude, another group member (e.g., interrupting, talking over).

Comparable Instruments

When developing the BA coding system, Rackham et al. (1971) examined the work of Bales (1950) and Heyns and Zander (1953). Similar to Bales (1950) IPA, behavior analysis is a method of systematically coding all verbal utterances that occur within a group. However, unlike IPA, BA adopts a natural language format whereby the categories are named using accessible terminology. For example, category names such as *Supporting, Disagreeing*, and *Seeking Information* are intuitive to observers and participants. The BA coding system also shares similarities with the Act4teams coding system (Kauffeld, 2006), in that both were developed to categorize verbal statements in team meetings. Although, Act4teams is a 44-category system, whereas BA category systems adopt fewer categories to facilitate real-time coding and user-friendly feedback.

The BA approach has been applied in various contexts. Rackham (1988) conducted a series of experimental studies examining the *Seeking Information* questions asked by sales people, which uncovered a sequence of questions that led to success in sales. Furthermore, Evison and Ronaldson (1975) used the original 13 categories as a base to develop an instrument that captured the behavioral profiles of counselors practicing different forms of counselling.

Goals of the Instrument

BA seeks to improve interactive skills by providing people with communication feedback immediately after a specific event. This is known as short-cycle feedback and it involves coding verbal behavior in real time and using the coded data to improve interactions. Since BA allows users to define and develop their own categories, it can be used in multiple settings.

One area where BA could be usefully applied is the training of team processes. Team processes are defined as "members' interdependent acts that convert inputs to outcomes through cognitive, verbal, and behavioral activities directed toward organizing task work to achieve collective goals" (Marks, Mathieu, & Zaccaro, 2001, p. 357). In comparison with research examining performance feedback, relatively little research has addressed the outcomes of process feedback (Gabelica et al., 2012). Recent research has shown that team training within medical contexts is beneficial (Hughes et al., 2016), therefore BA could complement existing training exercises.

Available Versions

Behavior analysis can be conducted using pencil and paper on a coding matrix. More recently an iPad app has been developed to facilitate real-time coding followed by instant feedback (contact the authors for further information).

Applicability

Behavior analysis is predominantly a real-time, field-based method that has been used for employee development in such companies as IBM, BP, and

Xerox. Most iterations of the BA coding system involve 11–15 categories, although the number of categories can be reduced depending on the user's motivations. Since BA evolved as an exhaustive system (the observer should be able to assign any statement to a category), one of the drawbacks of coding schemes with fewer categories is that many behaviors will not match category definitions (Rackham & Morgan, 1977). One way to bypass this problem involves including an "other" or "dustbin" category for any verbal behaviors that do not fall neatly into the adopted categories. This method is preferable to not coding the "other" categories at all, because it allows the user to determine the percentages of all categories that were coded within a meeting.

Practical Application

Coding Time

BA is a real-time coding methodology, thus one minute of interaction is equivalent to one minute of coding.

Coder Training

An extensive three-phase training system was developed to train 88 observers for a project that used BA in higher education. Phase 1 involved an online training course designed for use on an iPad app. After logging into the app, observers watched videos that introduced the categories. After watching the videos, the observers coded simulated audio meetings and the app calculated their kappa values (the observer's answers were scored against an experienced coder's scores). Phase 2 of the training involved a full-day face-to-face session whereby observers were reintroduced to the categories via lectures, small group activities, and further coding practice. Phase 3 involved another day of face-to-face training to ensure that the observers could code reliably and give feedback to teams. Overall, the training takes around 20 hours.

Technical Requirements

Technical requirements depend on whether the observer wishes to use the pencil-paper coding matrix or the iPad app. Data obtained using the latter method records time stamps and can be uploaded into software packages (e.g., Excel, SPSS), whereas the pencil-paper method necessitates manual data input. The app is designed for Apple's IOS software and equivalent versions are available for desktop computers.

Unitizing

Codes are applied to distinct speech units and an individual may receive more than one code during the same speaking turn. For example, the statement "Excellent suggestion, Callum, shall we do that after lunch?" would receive two codes: *Supporting* and then *Proposing*. When using the app, the observer taps on a team member's name as they start speaking, the observer then taps on the behavioral category once it becomes obvious which behavior the speaker is using. The length of time that the speaker uses the behavior is recorded by an internal timer within the app.

Training Manual

Details of the comprehensive observers training program are available from the authors.

Simplified Version

A short version has not been developed.

Quality Assessment

Reliability

Historically, the reliability of BA coding was assessed using Spearman's rho, and once observers had met the criterion of .90 and above, they were considered reliable coders. However, Cohen's kappa is now used to evaluate inter-rater reliability. A software program has been developed to compare the codes applied by the trainee observers (to audio test-tapes) with "gold standard" codes applied by experienced coders. After hearing each statement, the trainee observer has a few seconds to apply the right code to a statement before the program plays the next statement. This program was recently used to evaluate the reliability of 88 observers who participated in the training program, and the mean reliability of the observers at the end of training was $\kappa = .71$ ($SD = .10$).

Assessing the interrater reliability of coding conducted in the field necessitates two observers coding the same meeting at the same time. At present, field reliability is calculated using Cohen's Kappa, and the results show that the reliability varies across categories. Since the app records time stamps it may be possible to obtain a criterion for the sequential reliability in the future.

Validity

The predictive validity of certain BA categories was tested in a pilot study, which revealed that the pattern of correlations between categories and outcomes conformed to expectations (Farley, Nicolson, Rackham, Evison, & Dawson, 2016). For instance, the *Supporting Ideas* and *Supporting People* categories were positively correlated with meeting satisfaction, whereas *Defending/Attacking* and *Disagreeing* were negatively correlated with meeting satisfaction. Further research is needed to determine the discriminant validity of the categories and to cross-validate them with similar coding systems, such as act4teams (Kauffeld, 2006) and TEMPO (Futoran, Kelly, & McGrath, 1989) (see also Kauffeld, Lehmann-Willenbrock, & Meinecke, this volume, Chapter 21; Kelly, Dvir, & Parsons, this volume, Chapter 24).

Data Aggregation and Analysis

Data are captured at the individual level as the coder categorizes the verbal statements of each individual team member. However, the data can be aggregated to the team level; for example the team may wish to determine the number of supporting statements compared to the number of disagreements in a one-hour meeting. Therefore, the observer can choose whether to provide team-level feedback, individual-level feedback, or both. In addition, analyses can include category frequencies, time each individual spent talking (in seconds and as a percentage), as well as sequential information. However, speaking time and sequential information can only be obtained when the app program is used.

The observer's method of providing feedback aligns with evidence-based, best-practice recommendations: Feedback should be provided to the whole group immediately after the period of interaction (DeShon, Kozlowski, Schmidt, Milner, & Wiechmann, 2004; Hey, Pietruschka, Bungard, & Joens, 2000), it should be given in a nonthreatening manner by an impartial individual (Gabelica, Van den Bossche, De Maeyer, Segers, & Gijselaers, 2014), it should be clear (London & Sessa, 2006), and after receiving it teams should be encouraged to reflect and evaluate its content (Konradt, Schippers, Garbers, & Steenfatt, 2015).

Previous Studies

Rackham and Morgan (1977) examined leaders who were judged as effective meeting chairs; they found that the chairs commonly used *Testing Understanding, Summarizing*, and *Proposals*, but rarely *Disagreed* or *Supported Others*. Similarly, Rackham and Carlisle (1978a, 1978b) compared skilled negotiators with average negotiators, finding that the former used significantly more *Testing Understanding, Seeking Information*, and *Summarizing* than the latter.

A recent program of research has started to examine how the BA approach can be used as a university teaching tool. The HE context seemed particularly appropriate, as although universities generally seek to develop teamwork ability by assigning students a mandatory team working task (Vik, 2001), often little is done to support teamwork skills through training and feedback (Hansen, 2006).

During this research program, the original categories have been modified, as the *Open* and *Blocking* categories have been discarded and new categories have been developed (the updated category scheme is available from the authors on request).

This approach has been relabeled as "Behavior in Teams" (BiT) analysis and has the goal of providing students with the behavioral skills needed to work in teams.

An experimental study within this research program examined the behaviors used by 771 students who were organized into 139 teams. The data obtained during the study can help answer important questions, such as do teams who receive process feedback perform better than those that do not? What behaviors are commonly used by effective teams? And do demographic variables (e.g., age, gender, and cultural background) alter the extent to which people participate in meetings? The answers to these questions will reveal knowledge that can assist the way team behaviors are taught and applied.

References

Original Publications

Rackham, N., Honey, P., & Colbert, M. (1971). *Developing interactive skills*. Guilsborough, Northants: Wellens Publishing.

Rackham, N., & Morgan, T. (1977). *Behaviour analysis in training*. Maidenhead, Berkshire: McGraw-Hill Book Co Ltd.

Other References

Bales, R. F. (1950). *Interaction process analysis: A method for the study of small groups*. Cambridge, MA: Addison Wesley.

DeShon, R. P., Kozlowski, S. W., Schmidt, A. M., Milner, K. R., & Wiechmann, D. (2004). A multiple-goal, multilevel model of feedback effects on the regulation of individual and team performance. *Journal of Applied Psychology, 89*(6), 1035–1056. http://dx.doi.org/10.1037/0021-9010.89.6.1035

Evison, R., & Ronaldson, J. B. (1975). A behaviour category instrument for analysing counselling interactions. *British Journal of Guidance and Counselling, 3*(1), 82–92. http://dx.doi.org/10.1080/03069887508256301

Farley, S., Nicolson, R., Rackham, N., Evison, R., & Dawson, J. (2016). *The Behaviour in Teams (BIT) approach to providing team process feedback in meetings: A pilot study and research proposal*. The Institute of Work Psychology International Conference, June, 23–21, 2016. Sheffield, United Kingdom.

Futoran, G. C., Kelly, J. R., & McGrath, J. E. (1989). TEMPO: A time-based system for analysis of group interaction process. *Basic and Applied Social Psychology, 10*(3), 211–232. http://dx.doi.org/10.1207/s15324834basp1003_2

Gabelica, C., Van den Bossche, P., De Maeyer, S., Segers, M., & Gijselaers, W. (2014). The effect of team feedback and guided reflexivity on team performance change. *Learning and Instruction, 34*, 86–96. http://dx.doi.org/10.1016/j.learninstruc.2014.09.001

Gabelica, C., Van den Bossche, P., Segers, M., & Gijselaers, W. (2012). Feedback, a powerful lever in teams: A review. *Educational Research Review, 7*(2), 123–144. http://dx.doi.org/10.1016/j.edurev.2011.11.003

Hansen, R. S. (2006). Benefits and problems with student teams: Suggestions for improving team projects. *Journal of Education for Business*, *82*(1), 11–19. http://dx.doi.org /10.3200/JOEB.82.1.11-19

Hey, A. H., Pietruschka, S., Bungard, W., & Joens, I. (2000). Feedback as a supporting system for work groups. In M. Vartiainen, F. Avallone, & N. Anderson (Eds.), *67 Innovative theories, tools, and practices in work and organizational psychology* (pp. 125–140). Seattle, WA: Hogrefe & Huber Publishers.

Heyns, R. W., & Zander, A. F. (1953). Observation of group behavior. In L. Festinger & D. Katz (Eds.), *Research methods in the behavioral sciences* (pp. 381–417). New York, NY: Holt, Rinehart and Winston.

Hughes, A. M., Gregory, M. E., Joseph, D. L., Sonesh, S. C., Marlow, S. L., Lacerenza, C. N., Benishek, L.E., King, H.B., & Salas, E. (2016). Saving lives: A meta-analysis of team training in healthcare. *The Journal of Applied Psychology*, *101*(9), 1266–1304. http://dx.doi.org/10.1037/apl0000120

Johnson, M. D., Hollenbeck, J. R., Scott DeRue, D., Barnes, C. M., & Jundt, D. (2013). Functional versus dysfunctional team change: Problem diagnosis and structural feedback for self-managed teams. *Organizational Behavior and Human Decision Processes*, *122*(1), 1–11. http://dx.doi.org/10.1016/j.obhdp.2013.03 .006

Kauffeld, S. (2006). Self-directed work groups and team competence. *Journal of Occupational and Organizational Psychology*, *79*(1), 1–21. http://dx.doi.org/10 .1348/096317905X53237

Kauffeld, S., & Lehmann-Willenbrock, N. (2012). Meetings matter: Effects of team meetings on team and organizational success. *Small Group Research*, *43*(2), 130–158. http://dx.doi.org/10.1177/1046496411429599

Konradt, U., Schippers, M. C., Garbers, Y., & Steenfatt, C. (2015). Effects of guided reflexivity and team feedback on team performance improvement: The role of team regulatory processes and cognitive emergent states. *European Journal of Work and Organizational Psychology*, *24*(5), 777–795. http://dx.doi.org/10.1080 /1359432X.2015.1005608

Leshed, G., Perez, D., Hancock, J. T., Cosley, D., Birnholtz, J., Lee, S., McLeod, P. L., & Gay, G. (2009). Visualizing real-time language-based feedback on teamwork behavior in computer-mediated groups. In *Proceedings of the SIGCHI Conference on Human Factors in Computing Systems* (pp. 537–546). ACM. http://dx.doi.org/10.1145/1518701.1518784

London, M., & Sessa, V. I. (2006). Group feedback for continuous learning. *Human Resource Development Review*, *5*(3), 303–329. http://dx.doi.org/10.1177 /1534484306290226

Marks, M. A., Mathieu, J. E., & Zaccaro, S. J. (2001). A temporally based framework and taxonomy of team processes. *Academy of Management Review*, *26*(3), 356–376. http://dx.doi.org/10.5465/AMR.2001.4845785

Morgan, T., Rackham, N., & Hudson, H. (1974). DIS: Three years on. *Industrial and Commercial Training*, *6*(6), 248–257. http://dx.doi.org/10.1108/eb003406

Rackham, N. (1988). *SPIN Selling*. New York, NY: McGraw-Hill.

Rackham, N., & Carlisle, J. (1978a). The effective negotiator-Part I: The Behaviour of Successful Negotiators. *Journal of European Industrial Training*, *2*(6), 6–11. http://dx.doi.org/10.1108/eb002297

Rackham, N., & Carlisle, J. (1978b). The effective negotiator-Part 2: Planning for negotiations. *Journal of European Industrial Training*, *2*(7), 2–5. http://dx.doi.org/10.1108/eb002302

Rackham, N., Honey, P., & Colbert, M. (1971). *Developing interactive skills*. Guilsborough, Northants: Wellens Publishing.

Rackham, N., & Morgan, T. (1977). *Behaviour analysis in training*. Maidenhead, Berkshire: McGraw-Hill Book Co Ltd.

Vik, G. N. (2001). Doing more to teach teamwork than telling students to sink or swim. *Business Communication Quarterly*, *64*(4), 112–119. http://dx.doi.org/10.1177/108056990106400413

40 Groupness/Entitativity Observational Coding (GEOC)

A Coding System to Assess Groupness or Entitativity in Groups

José Navarro and Rocío Meneses

General Information

Name of Coding Scheme

Groupness/Entitativity Observational Coding (GEOC)

Original Publication

This observational coding system is based on two previous sources: first, a theoretical framework developed by Meneses, Ortega, Navarro, and Quijano (2008) and, second, a questionnaire published by Navarro, Meneses, Miralles, Moreno, and Loureiro (2015). This coding system has not been published before.

Keywords

Groupness, groupiness, entitativity, groupality, group development, group maturity, social aggregates, emergent process

Summary

The goal of this observational coding system is to provide an assessment of the groupness/entitativity of groups, allowing us to distinguish a real group from a mere social aggregate. Accordingly, not all groups are functioning as developed groups; some groups achieve high degrees of development (real groups), whereas others only remain mere social aggregates. This distinction is useful in contexts in which real groups are required, for example, at work when teamwork is needed, but also in other social contexts (e.g., community psychology, intergroup relationships) in which this emergent process (i.e., groupness, groupiness, or entitativity) is important to consider. It can also be useful in research when it is necessary to guarantee that researchers are working with real groups (not mere aggregates of individuals) in lab experiments or field studies.

Description of the Coding Scheme

Which criteria define a real group? How would it be possible to distinguish groups from mere social aggregates? These classic questions (e.g., Campbell, 1958; Sherif, 1967) continue to be relevant (Meneses, Ortega, Navarro, & Quijano, 2008; Wageman, Hackman, & Lehman, 2005; West & Lyubovnikova, 2012). In a review study, Meneses et al. (2008) found that what specialized literature has called groupness, entitativity, or groupality is an emergent state that defines a group as a "real" group. Groupness is the extent to which a group is perceived more as a group than a mere collection of individuals and to whether certain sets of people constitute a group (McGrath, 1984). Size, interdependence, and interaction patterns reflect the level of groupness of a given group in McGrath's (1984) view. Meanwhile, entitativity refers to a set of properties that allows a collection of people to be perceived as a group according to their interaction level, common goals, common results, similarity between group members, and the importance of the group to its members (e.g., Hamilton & Sherman, 1996; Lickel et al., 2000; Moreland & McMinn, 2004). Groupness and entitativity have represented the two major current research lines about this topic; however, as Meneses et al. (2008) showed, both represent the same theoretical construct: the key characteristics that can define a group as a real group, something more than a simple aggregate of people.

At this point both theoretical approaches have proposed a set of criteria that can be used to identify whether a set of people is a "real" group or not; in particular, these approaches consider interrelationship, identification, coordination, and orientation to group goals as the key criteria to define any group (Meneses et al., 2008). These criteria are relatively similar to those proposed by Wageman et al. (2005) in their team diagnostic survey. We will describe briefly these criteria.

Interrelationship refers to the interactions among members, to the establishment of interpersonal feelings and behaviors among them (e.g., frequent interaction among members) and structural elements (e.g., patterns of interaction that form in the group). Group identification refers to the degree to which members see themselves as a group, enabling them to decide whether someone belongs to the group or not, and the importance the group has for them. Coordination refers to the management of interdependent behaviors, resources, and technologies properly in order to achieve the group's goals. Finally, orientation to group goals refers to the degree to which group members agree on, and commit themselves to the achievement of, a common project (Meneses et al., 2008; Meneses & Navarro, 2015; Navarro et al., 2015).

Understood in this way, groupness and entitativity have been measured using classic questionnaires (e.g., Carpenter & Radhakrishnan, 2002; Lickel et al., 2000; Navarro et al., 2015). The team diagnostic survey developed by Wageman et al. (2005) could be another useful tool for this purpose. However, the previously mentioned criteria that define groupness or entitativity can also be assessed through observational coding.

Table 40.1 *Groupness/entitativity observational coding (GEOC)*

Criterion and its definition	Example of behaviors to observe
Interrelationship Definition: The interactions among members; the establishment of interpersonal feelings and behaviors among members	• Members participate actively in group activities • Eye contact among members • Attention directed toward who intervenes • Members are given feedback about their contributions
Group identification Definition: The degree to which members see themselves as a group and the importance the group has for members	• Use of common language expressions and language codes (e.g., presence of own group expressions, terms, and so on) • Comparisons with other groups occur • Use of the term "we" • A specific group name is used
Coordination Definition: The management of behaviors, resources, and technologies in order to achieve the group goals	• Appearance of mimetic behaviors (e.g., body movements, similar clothing used) • Existence of defined and different roles (e.g., differences among members in responsibilities, task assignments, competences showed, and so on) • Information about how to work together is provided and used • Absence of redundant functions among the different roles played • Appearance of behaviors showing anticipation on members' needs • Helping behaviors among members
Orientation to group goals Definition: The degree to which group members agree on and commit themselves to the achievement of a common project	• Established action plans are followed • Expressing feelings of identification with the group goals • New group goals are made by members • Existence of a language oriented to a common task

Note. Criterion and its definition are based on Arrow et al. (2000); Campbell (1958); Hamilton et al. (1998); Meneses et al. (2008).

In Table 40.1 we present some examples of behaviors of each of the aforementioned criteria that can be used as a rating system by observers to judge the group interaction process as a whole. To apply it, we can use the behavioral examples proposed like a checklist with different degrees of occurrence, for example, rarely–at times–very often, and rate each of the criteria (e.g., if all the behaviors proposed in one criterion are observed very often we can rate it with the maximum score).

Goals of the Instrument

The GEOC is useful to assess the groupness or entitativity of any group in any particular context. It can be used for academic purposes (e.g., lab experiments, field studies) and for managerial issues as well (e.g., diagnosis of teams in an organization). In more detail, the GEOC can be useful:

- to determine whether any group is a real group and not a mere collection of people (this is important in academic research about group or team behavior or in applied fields in which team diagnosis can be important);
- to be included in any research that uses IPO or IMOI models (Ilgen, Hollenbeck, Johnson, & Jundt, 2005), for example, as a moderator or a mediator;
- to be included in any organizational assessment interested in knowing the level of development of their work teams;
- to be used in social and community assessments interested in knowing the development or maturity of the groups involved.

Comparable Instruments

There are different alternatives to assess groupness or entitativity using questionnaires (e.g., Lickel et al., 2000; Carpenter & Radhakrishnan, 2002; Navarro et al., 2015). However, a retrospective review of the psychological literature (i.e., PsycInfo database) covering a period of twenty-two years (from 1994 to 2016) and using different keywords (i.e., "groupness," "entitativity," and "groupality") was carried out and we did not find any observational system useful for this purpose.

Since 1994, the Group Development Observation System (GDOS), based on the unified Wheelan (1994) model, has been used and validated (Wheelan, Davidson, & Tilin, 2003). But this tool is specifically designed to identify the *developmental stage* of a group at the time of observation. The GEOC instrument proposed by us is based on the aforementioned theoretical model (Meneses et al., 2008), and its main interest is to identify the degree of groupness or entitativity (i.e., if a group is a real group rather than a mere aggregation of different people) regardless of the stages of development. Moreover, the GDOS focuses entirely on verbal communication; it requires session filming and transcribing using a codification of thoughts expressed by members of the group as eight categories that define the system, and finally contrast evaluators' codifications (Wheelan, Verdi, & McKeage, 1994; Wheelan et al., 2003). Finally, evaluators are required to be certified by GDQ Associates, Inc. All these features make the use of GDOS expensive and laborious.

In contrast, verbal and nonverbal behaviors are encoded within the GEOC during the group dynamic, according to the four criteria proposed by the theoretical model (Meneses et al., 2008). Moreover, the focus on the groupness/entitativity phenomenon provides an advantage in relation to simply measuring coordination behaviors;

it would be necessary here to remember that coordination is a criterion included among the groupness/entitativity key criteria, but other criteria are equally important (see Table 40.1). The checklist proposed is brief and easy to code by anyone with a solid training in group dynamics observation (e.g., having post-graduate studies). Different coders can contrast their assessments in order to guarantee a more reliable measure. These characteristics make the GEOC economical in time and money.

Available Versions

GEOC is available in English and Spanish. However, as we propose the observation of behaviors (see Table 40.1), translation to other languages would be easy. This observational system can be used by taking notes electronically or using a paper-pencil procedure.

Applicability

GEOC can be applicable both in the laboratory and in the field settings. The best way to apply this observational system is to observe the group when members are interacting. For example, in a team it can be useful to apply GEOC while they are working together. Following common ethical guidelines it would be necessary to get a general consent form from the group (i.e., the members) with regard the observation of their interactions. To have a more reliable assessment of the group, different applications should be done from different samples of how the group interacts. Moreover, due the fact that the topic of interest is an evolving process we can expect changes in it over time.

Practical Issues

Coding Time per Minute

We consider that GEOC allows real-time process analyzing of an actual situation of the group of interest. This means that we need the same time as that taken by the group interaction process.

Time Required for Coder Training

Like others group observational systems, GEOC would require coders trained in group dynamics observation. Specialized training in group dynamics, by postgraduate students for example, is strongly recommended (for example, having received a minimum of 100 hours of training).

Technical Requirements

The GEOC only requires notetaking (e.g., paper-pencil uses, computer notes, etc.). There are no other special technical requirements.

Training Manual

A brief manual with some guidelines is available from the authors. In the manual we have also included some possible interventions to enhance groupness/entitativity considering the different criteria included in the construct.

Quality Issues

Reliability and Validity

Because this is the first time that we are proposing the GEOC system we cannot report published results about its reliability and validity. However, this system is based on previous research using the questionnaire format of this tool (e.g., Navarro et al., 2015; Navarro, Meneses, Nadal, & Landsberger, 2016). In these studies, the survey format has shown good values of reliability (Cronbach's alpha values ranged from .70 to .89). Moreover, with this questionnaire we have been able to develop successive studies of validity (content, convergent, criterion, and incremental) that have shown remarkable results of the tool (e.g., correlations values around .75 with other measures of entitativity, or R^2 values around .40 as a predictor of group performance; see Navarro et al., 2015; Navarro et al., 2016).

Data Aggregation and Analysis

Data should be considered at the group level, because the construct of interest is exclusively situated at the group level. Due to the nature of the groupness/entitativity construct, it would be useful also to obtain a measure of each of the four criteria included: interrelationship, identification, coordination, and orientation to group goals. In this way, the GEOC will provide a general measure of the groupness/entitativity of the group and a measure of each of its four criteria as well (see Table 40.1). Considering the general measure and the different criteria at the same time can be useful for diagnostic purposes and to better orientate posterior interventions (e.g., intervene to increase the amount of interrelationships, or intervene to promote identification with the group).

To obtain a group level measure, the average from the coders assessment can be used jointly with measures of reliability (e.g., ICC[1] and ICC[2]; see Bliese, 2000). Moreover, as we have already said, we strongly recommend the application of the observational system several times per group, considering the evolving nature of the construct of interest. For example, for a project team that will be working for a certain period of time it would be useful to measure groupness/ entitativity at the beginning of the project team, in the middle of its lifetime, and at the end (or just before the end of the project).

Previous Studies Using the Instrument

This observational system is new and has not been previously used, despite being based on previous theoretical and empirical research that has shown the utility of the construct of groupness/entitativity (e.g., Carpenter & Radhakrishnan, 2002; Meneses et al., 2008; Navarro et al., 2015).

References

Original Publications

Meneses, R., Ortega, R., Navarro, J., & de Quijano, S. D. (2008). Criteria for assessing the level of group development (LGD) of work groups: Groupness, entitativity, and groupality as theoretical perspectives. *Small Group Research*, *39*, 492–514. doi:10.1177/1046496408319787

Navarro, J., Meneses, R., Miralles, C., Moreno, D. I., & Loureiro, V. (2015). What distinguish teams from social aggregates? A tool to assess the group development. *Anales de Psicología*, *31*, 921–929. doi:10.6018/analesps.31.3.183831

Other References

Arrow, H., McGrath, J. E., & Berdahl, J. L. (2000). *Small groups as complex systems. Formation, coordination, development, and adaptation*. Thousand Oaks, CA: Sage.

Bliese, P. D. (2000). Within-group agreement, non-independence, and reliability: Implications for data aggregation and analysis. In K. J. Klein & S. W. Kozlowski (Eds.), *Multilevel theory, research, and methods in organizations* (pp. 349–381). San Francisco, CA: Jossey-Bass, Inc.

Campbell, D. T. (1958). Common fate, similarity, and other indices of the status of aggregates of persons as social entities. *Behavioral Science*, *3*, 14–25. doi:10.1002/bs.3830030103

Carpenter, S., & Radhakrishnan, P. (2002). The relation between allocentrism and perceptions of ingroups. *Personality and Social Psychology Bulletin*, *28*, 1528–1537. doi:10.1177/014616702237580

Hamilton, D. L., & Sherman, S. J. (1996). Perceiving persons and groups. *Psychological Review*, *103*, 336–355. doi:10.1037/0033-295X.103.2.336

Hamilton, D. L., Sherman, S. J., & Lickel, B. (1998). Perceiving social groups: The importance of the entitativity continuum. In C. Sedikides & J. Schopler (Eds.), *Intergroup cognition and intergroup behavior* (pp. 47–74). Mahwah, NJ: Erlbaum.

Ilgen, D. R., Hollenbeck, J. R., Johnson, M., & Jundt, D. (2005). Teams in organizations: from input-process-output models to IMOI models. *Annual Review of Psychology, 56,* 517–43. doi:10.1146/annurev.psych.56.091103.070250

Kauffeld, S., & Lehmann-Willenbrock, N. (2008). Teamdiagnose und Teamentwicklung [Team diagnosis and team development]. In I. Jöns (Eds.), *Erfolgreiche Gruppenarbeit. Konzepte, Instrumente, Erfahrungen [Successful group work. Concepts, instruments, experiences]* (pp. 30–41). Wiesbaden: Gabler.

Kozlowsky, S. W. J., & Ilgen, D. R. (2006). Enhancing the effectiveness of work groups and teams. *Psychological Science in the Public Interest, 7,* 77–124. doi:10.1111/j.1529-1006.2006.00030.x

Lickel, D., Hamilton, D., Lewis, A., Sherman, S., Wieczorkowska, G., & Uhles, A. N. (2000). Varieties of groups and the perception of group entitativity. *Journal of Personality and Social Psychology, 78,* 223–246. doi:10.1037/0022-3514.78.2.223

McGrath, J. E. (1984). *Groups: Interaction and performance.* Englewood Cliffs, NJ: Prentice-Hall.

Meneses, R., & Navarro, J. (2015). ¿Cómo mejorar la eficacia de los equipos a través de los procesos grupales? Un ejemplo en la industria automotriz. [How to improve the effectiveness of teams through group processes? An example in the automotive industry]. *Papeles del Psicólogo, 36,* 224–229.

Moreland, R. L., & McMinn, J. G. (2004). Entitativity and social integration: Managing beliefs about the reality of groups. In V. Yzerbyt, C. Judd, & O. Corneille (Eds.), *The psychology of group perception: Perceived variability, entitativity, and essentialism* (pp. 311–325). New York, NY: Psychology Press.

Navarro, J., Meneses, R., Nadal, M., & Landsberger, E. (2016). Desarrollo y desempeño en equipos de proyecto: Validez incremental de la escala de desarrollo grupal [Team development and team performance: Incremental validity of the group development scale]. *Anuario de Psicología, 46,* 8–16. doi:10.1016/j.anpsic.2016.06.002

Sherif, M. (1967). *Social interaction. Process and products. Selected papers by Muzafer Sherif.* Chicago, IL: Aldine Publishing Company.

Wageman, R., Hackman, J. R., & Lehman, E. (2005). Team Diagnostic Survey. Development of an instrument. *The Journal of Applied Behavioral Science, 41,* 373–398. doi:10.1177/0021886305281984

West, M., & Lyubovnikova, J. (2012). Real teams or pseudo teams? The changing landscape needs a better map. *Industrial and Organizational Psychology, 5,* 25–28. doi:10.1111/j.1754-9434.2011.01397.x

Wheelan, S., Davidson, B., & Tilin, F. (2003). Group development across time: Reality or illusion?. *Small Group Research, 34,* 223–245. doi:10.1177/1046496403251608

Wheelan, S., & Hochberger, J. (1996). Validation studies of the group development questionnaire. *Small Group Research, 27,* 143–170. doi:10.1037/1061-4087.55.3.179

Wheelan, S. A. (1994). *Group processes: A development perspective.* Boston: Allyn & Bacon.

Wheelan, S. A., Verdi, A. F., & McKeage, R. (1994). *The group development observation system: Origins and application.* Philadelphia, PA: PEP Press.

41 Assessing Group Interactions in Personality Psychology

The Münster Behavior Coding-System (M-BeCoSy)

Marc Grünberg, Jana Mattern, Katharina Geukes, Albrecht C. P. Küfner, and Mitja D. Back

General Information

Name of Coding Scheme

The Münster Behavior Coding-System (M-BeCoSy)

Keywords

Social behavior, group interactions, interpersonal circumplex, small groups, personality psychology

Summary

The Münster Behavior Coding-System (M-BeCoSy) aims at a comprehensive assessment of essential individual differences in social behavior during group interactions. It allows to code and rate individual behaviors across seven behavioral domains (expressiveness, dominance, arrogance, warmth, aggressiveness, negative affect behavior, intellectual competence behavior), three behavioral channels (verbal, paraverbal, nonverbal), and three levels of abstraction (macro-, meso-, micro-level). Moreover, M-BeCoSy is available in different versions with each capturing behavioral domains and channels in different levels of detail. Its modular composition allows for tailored analyses of individual differences in a variety of group interaction contexts, e.g., small group research in developmental, educational, personality, and social psychology as well as professional contexts such as assessments, leadership coaching, team diagnostics in organizations, counseling, and educational environments.

Description of the Coding Scheme

Group interactions are a major context for the expression of individual differences in behavior, making tools for the assessment of behaviors in groups highly useful for the study of personality. While behavioral observation within groups is well established in other fields of psychology such as organizational psychology and social psychology, the few previous coding schemes in personality psychology (see Bakeman, 2000, and Furr & Funder, 2009, for overviews) focused on individual (Back, Schmukle, & Egloff, 2009; Borkenau, Mauer, Riemann, Spinath, & Angleitner, 2004; Kirschbaum, Pirke, & Hellhammer, 1993) or dyadic settings (Cuperman & Ickes, 2009; Funder, Furr, & Colvin, 2000). Therefore, we developed a novel coding scheme – the Münster Behavior Coding System. It enables the observation of individual differences in social behaviors during group interactions.

M-BeCoSy focuses on key behavioral domains derived from the Interpersonal Circumplex (Wiggins, 1979, 1991): expressiveness, dominance, arrogance, and warmth. This set is extended by adding three behavioral domains that are often investigated in personality research, have relevant social effects, and show substantial variation across individuals: aggressiveness, negative affect behavior, and intellectual competence behavior (e.g., Bettencourt, Talley, Benjamin, & Valentine, 2006; Borkenau et al., 2004; Leising & Bleidorn, 2011).

Within each behavioral domain, we defined specific behavioral indicators, which are behaviors that represent, or indicate, the presence of not directly observable psychological constructs. These indicators were selected based on (a) a top-down approach in which we performed extensive literature research on personality and interpersonal behavior as well as on existing coding schemes within and outside of personality psychology (including well-established schemes for the coding of emotions, e.g., Ekman & Friesen, 1977; and of marital interaction behavior, e.g., Gottman, 1994), and (b) a bottom-up approach, in which we analyzed video-recordings of a large group-interaction study (Geukes, Breil, Hutteman, Nestler, Küfner, & Back, 2017; also see https://osf.io/q5zwp, Geukes, Nestler, Küfner, & Back, 2016) with regard to the observability of specific behavioral indicators and their variability across individuals. To allow for breadth and representativeness in behavioral coverage, selected indicators vary across behavioral channels (paraverbal, nonverbal, and verbal). Also, to combine the advantages of holistically processed behavioral information and the objective perception of specific movements, behavioral indicators are assessed at different levels of abstraction including the macro-level (global ratings of a behavioral domain; e.g., shows expressive behavior), meso-level (circumscribed behavioral expressions; e.g., ratings of cheerful facial expression), and micro-level (specific behavioral acts with or without duration; e.g., counting of number of smiles) (see Cairns & Green, 1979; Furr & Funder, 2009). Almost all behavioral indicators at the micro-level are assessed by codings whereas most indicators at the meso-level and those at the macro-level are assessed by ratings.

The structure of M-BeCoSy is summarized in Figure 41.1. M-BeCoSy has a modular composition, that is, modules of behavioral indicators can be selected based on the question at hand and the intended extensiveness of assessment (e.g., selected behavioral domains, channels, and/or levels of abstraction). Moreover, M-BeCoSy is available in three different versions ranging from

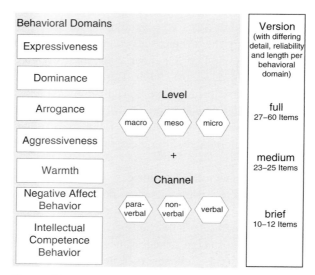

Figure 41.1 *The Münster Behavior Coding System – Overview.*

a small (10–12 indicators per domain), to a medium-sized (23–25 indicators per domain), to a full version (27–60 indicators per domain). Whereas these versions differ with respect to the level of detail and reliability due to the different numbers of items included, every version incorporates all of the behavioral domains (expressiveness, dominance, arrogance, warmth, aggressiveness, negative affect behavior, intellectual competence behavior) and covers meso- and micro-levels as well as all channels (paraverbal, nonverbal, and verbal) of behavioral assessment in group interactions. Table 41.1 summarizes exemplary codings and ratings for each behavioral domain. For research purposes with extremely limited resources, an ultra-brief behavioral screening version that only includes one macro-level rating for each behavioral domain is also available.

Comparable Instruments

The development of M-BeCoSy was informed by a number of existing behavioral coding and rating approaches. Previous instruments focused on other social contexts, on specific levels of abstraction, and on selected behavioral domains or items. One of the most widely used instruments in personality psychology, the Riverside Behavioral Q-sort (RBQ, Funder et al., 2000), assesses a range of single behavioral items on a meso-level in the context of dyadic interactions. Other well-established coding systems, such as The Facial Action Coding System (FACS, Ekman & Friesen, 1977), assess emotional expressions on a micro-level and focus on a set of specific emotions shown for example in facial expressions. In addition,

Table 41.1 *Exemplary codings (micro-level) and ratings (meso-level) of the Münster Behavior Coding System*

Behavioral domain	Type	Channel	Exemplary codings and ratings
Expressiveness	micro	paraverbal	# of cheerful-funny laughter, giggle
	meso	nonverbal	expressive lively facial expressions
Dominance	micro	nonverbal	# of dominant pointing gestures
	meso	paraverbal	vibrant and powerful voice
Arrogance	micro	verbal	# of arrogant-patronizing comments
	meso	nonverbal	arrogant-back-leaning body posture
Aggressiveness	micro	paraverbal	# of aggressively drowning others out
	meso	nonverbal	rejective body posture
Warmth	micro	paraverbal	# of agreeing, responsive sounds while others talk
	meso	verbal	friendly-polite statements
Negative affect behavior	micro	nonverbal	# change of arm/hand position
	meso	paraverbal	nervous-precarious faltering, tense voice
Intellectual competence behavior	micro	verbal	# expressed new ideas, interesting, creative remarks
	meso	paraverbal	fluent, clear way of speaking

Note. M-BeCoSy's codings and ratings comprise all combinations of type and channel for each dimension. The table only contains selected example codings and ratings for each behavioral domain.

there are various approaches that have been developed in the context of specific study designs (Back et al., 2009; Borkenau et al., 2004; Leising & Bleidorn, 2011), most of which measure individual behaviors via behavioral ratings in clearly defined behavioral tasks. M-BeCoSy adds to these existing instruments by providing a generic coding scheme that can be applied to all kinds of group interaction contexts and that consists of a broader array of behavioral domains and levels of abstraction (including codings at a micro-level in addition to macro- and meso-level ratings). This allows both a broad applicability across research contexts and specific research questions as well as capturing each behavioral domain in more detail. At the same time there are several behavioral indicators contained in M-BeCoSy that are similar to or even directly matching items assessed by existing instruments, which allows for close comparisons with published research.

Goals of the Instrument

M-BeCoSy was developed for behavioral analyses of individual differences during group interactions. It allows investigating a wide range of different research topics, such as

- the direct behavioral assessment of circumscribed traits from the interpersonal circumplex such as dominance, expressiveness, warmth, and arrogance, as well as of selected traits of the Big Five, for example by using codings or ratings from the behavioral domains of expressiveness and dominance (extraversion), arrogance, aggressiveness, and warmth (agreeableness), negative affect (neuroticism), and intellectual competence (openness)
- the assessment of predefined, context-specific behaviors that may be evaluated on an objective scale ranging from positive to negative (i.e., interpersonal skills)
- the behavioral mediation of social consequences of personality (e.g., interaction behaviors underlying the effects of personality on popularity, status, social exclusion, leadership)
- behavioral cues explaining the accuracy and biases in interpersonal perceptions (including self-, other-, and meta-perceptions)
- effects of gender composition, situational context, and task characteristics on behavioral dynamics
- intraindividual behavioral dynamics (e.g., behavioral flexibility versus consistency within and across contexts, density distribution parameters, if-then contingencies, behavioral flux and spin)

Available Versions

Currently, M-BeCoSy is openly available in English and German: https://osf.io/x7fc4/. Three versions are available: a small version including 73 indicators (10–12 indicators per domain), a medium-sized version including 167 indicators (23–25 indicators per domain), and a full version including 284 indicators (27–60 indicators per domain). In addition, there is an ultra-small screening version with one global rating for each behavioral domain. Software-supported coding is recommended but not necessary.

Applicability

M-BeCoSy has been originally designed to be applied in laboratory contexts in which group interactions are observed and videotaped. The coding scheme was first tested in an interactive laboratory study (https://osf.io/q5zwp/, Geukes, Nestler, et al., 2016), which showed its applicability to interpersonal situations with groups of four to six participants. Most behavioral indicators of M-BeCoSy, however, also can be assessed in other social contexts including larger groups, dyadic interactions, and even in individual behavioral observations. M-BeCoSy can, thus, be assessed in a wide range of research contexts (e.g., personality, social, developmental, pedagogical, clinical, and I/O psychological research) and applied contexts (e.g., in personnel assessment situations *laboratory and in the field: The PILS and CONNECT study.* Manuscript submitted for publication.

Geukes, K., Hutteman, R., Nestler, S., Küfner, A. C. P., & Back, M. (2016, August 24). *CONNECT.* Retrieved February 16, 2018, from osf.io/2pmcr

Geukes, K., Nestler, S., Hutteman, R., Dufner, M., Küfner, A. C. P., Egloff, B., Denissen, J. J. A., & Back, M. D. (2017). Puffed up but shaky selves: State self-esteem level and variability in narcissists. *Journal of Personality and Social Psychology, 112,* 769–786. doi:10.1037/pspp0000093

Geukes, K., Nestler, S., Hutteman, R., Küfner, A. C. P., & Back, M. D. (2017). Trait personality and state variability: Predicting individual differences in within- and cross-context fluctuations in affect, self-evaluations, and behavior in everyday life. *Journal of Research in Personality, 69,* 124–138. https://doi.org/10.1016/j.jrp.2016.06.003

Geukes, K., Nestler, S., Küfner, A. C. P., & Back, M. (2016, July 1). PILS – Personality Interaction Laboratory Study. Retrieved February 16, 2018, from osf.io/q5zwp

Gottman, J. M. (1994). *What predicts divorce? The relationship between marital processes and marital outcomes.* Hillsdale, NJ: Lawrence Erlbaum Associates.

Kirschbaum, C., Pirke, K. M., & Hellhammer, D. H. (1993). The 'Trier Social Stress Test'— a tool for investigating psychobiological stress responses in a laboratory setting. *Neuropsychobiology, 28,* 76–81. doi:10.1159/000119004

Leckelt, M., Küfner, A. C., Nestler, S., & Back, M. D. (2015). Behavioral processes underlying the decline of narcissists' popularity over time. *Journal of Personality and Social Psychology, 109* (5), 856–871. doi:10.1037/pspp0000057

Leising, D., & Bleidorn, W. (2011). Which are the basic meaning dimensions of observable interpersonal behavior? *Personality and Individual Differences, 51,* 986–990. doi:10.1016/j.paid.2011.08.003

Nestler, S., Grimm, K. J., & Schönbrodt, F. D. (2015). The social consequences and mechanisms of personality: How to analyse longitudinal data from individual, dyadic, round-robin, and network designs. *European Journal of Personality, 29,* 272–295. doi:10.1002/per.1997

Wiggins, J. S. (1979). A psychological taxonomy of trait-descriptive terms: The interpersonal domain. *Journal of Personality and Social Psychology, 37,* 395–412. doi:10.1037/0022-3514.37.3.395

Wiggins, J. S. (1991). Agency and communion as conceptual coordinates for the understanding and measurement of interpersonal behavior. In W. M. Grove & D. Ciccetti (Eds.), *Thinking clearly about psychology: Vol. 2. Personality and psychopathology* (pp. 89–113). Minneapolis, MN: University of Minnesota Press.

Roles and Relationships

42 BRRICS

Brief Romantic Relationship Interaction Coding Scheme

Mikhila N. Wildey and S. Alexandra Burt

General Information

Name of Coding Scheme

Brief Romantic Relationship Interaction Coding Scheme (BRRICS)

Keywords

Romantic relationships, global coding, brief coding, affect coding, macroanalytic coding, couples interaction

Summary

The BRRICS was specifically developed for use with large samples of couples with observational interaction data. The coding scheme uses minimal resources, coders are not required to have advanced training in couple dynamics, and establishing intercoder reliability is relatively quick and easy. It includes eight codes assessing the global dynamics of the relationship, four at the individual level and four at the dyadic level. These codes include assessing positive and negative attributes at the individual and dyadic levels, the demand-withdraw pattern of communication, and an overall global rating of satisfaction of the relationship.

Description of the Coding Scheme

The BRRICS was developed for researchers interested in couple dynamics who may not have the time or resources to devote to more complex video coding. Each code is an interval variable rated on a Likert scale. The full coding scheme including complete descriptions of codes is presented in Table 42.1. Positive affect and negative affect are first rated separately for each partner. These codes were developed in light of research indicating that couples who communicate with more negative affect and less positive affect tend to be more dissatisfied in their relationships (e.g., Caughlin, Huston, & Houts, 2000). These codes are based on similar

Table 42.1 *Full coding scheme with descriptions of codes*

Level	Code	Rating
Individual Codes – Wife (code after 1st pass)	**Positive affect**: Smiling, laughing, humorous statements, and statements that make the partner feel understood and validated. Examples: outright jokes of the "one-liner variety," proposals that are clearly facetious solutions to the problem, statements emphasizing the humorous aspects of a situation or problem, paraphrasing the partner's statements, reflecting feelings, giving positive feedback, and expressing care, concern, or understanding of the person's feelings. Does NOT include nervous laughter or smiling, or humor with a sarcastic or hostile undertone.	None 1–2 instances A few/several instances Moderate amounts – about half the time Substantial amounts – over half the time but not the entire time Constantly throughout the interaction
	Negative affect: Any instance of a harsh tone or facial expression. Includes statements with negative content including criticism, nonverbal responses that communicate hostility, and disagreements said with harsh tone that do not further the discussion.	None 1–2 instances A few/several instances Moderate amounts – about half the time Substantial amounts – over half the time but not the entire time Constantly throughout the interaction
Individual Codes – Husband (code after 1st pass)	**Positive affect**: Same as description under Wife positive affect	None 1–2 instances A few/several instances Moderate amounts – about half the time Substantial amounts – over half the time but not the entire time Constantly throughout the interaction
	Negative affect: Same as description under Wife negative affect	None 1–2 instances A few/several instances Moderate amounts – about half the time Substantial amounts – over half the time but not the entire time Constantly throughout the interaction None

Table 42.1 (*cont.*)

Level	Code	Rating
Dyadic codes (code after 2nd pass)	**Positive reciprocity**: Positive affect at the dyadic level (i.e., back and forth exchanges of positive affect). Overall positivity and warmth in the couple. Code for smiling, laughing, and joking with each other (but do not code for hostile humor).	1–2 instances A few/several instances Moderate amounts – about half the time Substantial amounts – over half the time but not the entire time Constantly throughout the interaction
	Negative reciprocity: Negative affect at the dyadic level (i.e., back and forth exchanges of negative affect). Code for hostility, harsh tone, frowning, and/or criticism towards each other.	None 1–2 instances A few/several instances Moderate amounts – about half the time Substantial amounts – over half the time but not the entire time Constantly throughout the interaction
	Demand/withdraw pattern: This is a characteristic pattern in which one partner "nags" the other partner who then withdraws (or "shuts down") from the interaction. In this pattern, one partner will continue to voice complaints, push the other partner to do something, or criticize the other partner while the other partner withdraws from the conversation and stops responding in an appropriate fashion. Often times, the withdrawal of one partner will make the demanding partner become even more demanding. Circle to what degree this pattern is present. This pattern is often gendered such that women make the demands while men withdraw, but the reverse may also be found.	No Somewhat Yes
	Overall Satisfaction: Rate how much you feel this couple is satisfied and happy in their relationship with one another.	Extremely Low Low Neither Low nor High High Extremely High

codes found in the Rapid Marital Interaction Coding Scheme (RMICS; Heyman, 2004). Positive affect includes behaviors such as smiling, laughing, joking, expressions of empathy, understanding, and validation. Negative affect includes behaviors such as criticism, harsh tones or facial expressions, hostility, and sarcasm. Positive Reciprocity and Negative Reciprocity are both rated for each couple and are essentially dyadic measures of positive and negative affect between the couple. That is, Positive [Negative] Reciprocity is rated when one partner exhibits a positive [negative] behavior towards the other partner and the other partner responds in a positive [negative] manner. These six codes (positive and negative affect for each partner, positive and negative reciprocity at the dyadic level) are rated on a six-point scale (1 = "Never," 2 = "1–2 instances," 3 = "A few/several instances," 4 = "Moderate amounts – about half the time," 5 = "Substantial amounts – over half the time but not the entire time," 6 = "Constantly throughout the interaction"). Raters tally the frequency of these behaviors while also gauging the overall time spent engaging in the behavior during the interaction to determine the rating for the code. Raters are told to attend more closely to the overall time involved in the behavior after a tally of three (i.e., a rating of "3") given that tallying a precise number of behaviors would involve more viewings of the interaction.

Demand-withdraw pattern is also assessed at the dyadic level. This pattern characteristically involves one partner approaching conflict (e.g., "nagging" the other partner) while the other partner avoids conflict (e.g., withdraws or "shuts down"; Christensen & Heavey, 1990), and the pattern has been consistently linked to greater relationship distress (e.g., Christensen, Eldridge, Catta-Preta, Lim, & Santagata, 2006). Raters record "Yes," "Somewhat," or "No" for the presence, slight presence, or absence of the pattern, respectively. Finally, an Overall Satisfaction code asks raters to identify the degree to which they felt the couple in the interaction was satisfied and happy with their relationship on a five-point scale (1 = "Extremely Low," 2 = "Low," 3 = "Neither High nor Low," 4 = "High," 5 = "Extremely High"). This rating is meant to serve as an observer-reported global estimation of satisfaction that can be compared to or used in place of self-report measures of satisfaction, especially given that satisfaction is frequently used as a dependent variable in couples research (see Fincham & Beach, 2006).

Comparable Instruments

The BRRICS is a macroanalytic coding scheme, meaning it is designed to capture global themes in couple dynamics versus microanalytic coding schemes, which typically provide a large amount of specific information on the couple's relationship. Only a couple of existing macroanalytic coding schemes are most comparable to the BRRICS, though both are more intensive in various ways than the BRRICS. The Marital Interaction Coding System-Global (MICS-G; Weiss & Tolman, 1990) assesses six global communication patterns using a Likert-type rating scale. Although it contains only a few codes, it involves greater training time than the BRRICS (i.e., approximately ten hours) and is generally only used by advanced clinicians. The Interaction Dimensions Coding System (ICDS; Julien, Markman, & Lindahl, 1989) consists of nine individual-level codes and five dyadic codes. Although coding time is relatively brief (i.e., two passes of the interaction plus 5–10 minutes to assign ratings after the second pass), training time is also far more extensive (i.e., about 50 hours) than that for the BRRICS. Raters must also attend to 24 coding dimensions during each viewing of the interaction (i.e., nine for each spouse and five overall), thereby making it significantly more complicated for raters than the BRRICS.

Goals of the Instrument

Many research questions can be answered with the BRRICS. Researchers who generally rely on self-reports of romantic relationships may benefit from the addition of observational data rated via the BRRICS to increase confidence in their findings through the use of multiple methods of measurement. The BRRICS ratings can be used as predictors, outcomes, or potential mediators/moderators of relationships between other variables. For example, researchers can test how observed negative affect influences divorce outcomes, how personality influences observed relationship satisfaction, and how the observed demand-withdraw pattern moderates the relationship between psychopathology and relationship satisfaction. The BRRICS ratings can also be used to examine how couple dynamics influence other relationships (e.g., the degree to which couple conflict is related to outcomes in children). Finally, if observational data on couples is available at multiple time points, BRRICS ratings can be used in longitudinal data analyses to measure changes in couple dynamics over time.

Available Versions

Currently, the BRRICS is only available in English. It can be used with paper-pencil methods or can be entered into an online coding system.

Applicability

The BRRICS can be used in both lab and field settings where couple interactions can be audio- and video-recorded to be later coded. Recording is necessary in order to allow raters to code at both the individual level and dyadic level, which requires two passes of viewing the interaction. It may be possible to adapt the BRRICS for use in a real-time discussion between couples, but the coding scheme would likely need to be restricted to only rating at the individual level or the dyadic level.

Practical Application

Coding Time

Prospective coding time involves viewing the coding unit twice (i.e., once attending to individual-level codes and once attending to dyadic codes) and a few minutes to assign ratings after each viewing.

Coder Training

Training is minimal and typically involves two hours of in-person training and rating about ten coding units to establish adequate reliability. Coders need no prior experience in the area of romantic relationship research (e.g., can be undergraduate students) but a researcher more knowledgeable in couple dynamics should initially train coders. During the first hour of training, the researcher will watch a coding unit with coders and discuss possible ratings for each code. Coders should then independently rate five coding units (two passes each) and reliability should be assessed. The researcher should then discuss problems/ questions encountered by coders during a second hour of training and come to a mutual agreement on how the coding units should have been rated. Coders should then independently rate five additional coding units and reliability should be assessed again. Although additional rounds of training may be necessary to establish adequate reliability, prior research has shown that only two hours were needed (Humbad et al., 2011).

Technical Requirements

Audio-visual equipment is necessary to view the interactions.

Unitizing

Most researchers will typically make use of the BRRICS with short interactions (e.g., ten minutes) involving the couple engaging in a discussion where both partners take turns (e.g., discussing a conflict). With shorter interactions, the entire interaction can be a coding unit. However, researchers can select a smaller portion of the interaction as a coding unit, especially if the entire interaction is lengthy (e.g., one hour).

Training Manual

There is no training manual for this coding scheme. The full coding scheme with description of codes in Table 42.1 and the assistance of a trainer knowledgeable in couple dynamics is all that is necessary.

Quality Assessment

Reliability

Interrater reliability was initially assessed in Humbad et al. (2011) using intraclass correlations (ICCs) between four raters for each of the eight codes across
118 ten-minute marital interactions. ICCs greater than .70 are considered acceptable (e.g., Labreton, Burgess, Kaiser, Atchley, & James, 2003). Given the low
endorsement of "Somewhat" and "Yes" for the demand/withdraw item in the
sample (i.e., 11 percent of the interactions), the two ratings were collapsed into
a single category denoting the presence of any degree of the pattern. Cohen's
Kappa was calculated for this item, and values of at least .60 are considered good
(Landis & Koch, 1977). ICCs ranged from .73 to .82 for all items (refer to
Humbad et al., 2011 for a complete table), and Cohen's Kappa for the demand/
withdraw pattern was .60.

Validity

Humbad et al. (2011) compared ratings of the BRRICS codes to other measures of
the marital relationship for validity purposes. Each of the eight codes were
compared to both spouse's self-report of marital adjustment based on the
Dyadic Adjustment Scale (DAS; Spanier, 1976), and they were compared to the
Conflict Severity and Conflict Frequency scales in the Children's Perception of
Interparental Conflict measure (CPIC; Grych, Seid, & Fincham, 1992), which is
a measure where each couple's children reported on their perceptions of their
parents' relationship. The BRRICS codes all correlated in expected directions
with the above measures. Correlations between the BRRICS codes and the DAS
ranged from $r = .30$ to .67, and correlations among the BRRICS codes and the two
scales of the CPIC ranged from $rs = -.25$ to $-.46$, suggesting that the associations
between the BRRICS codes and these measures ranged from small to large in
size. For a detailed table of these associations, please refer to Humbad et al.
(2011).

Data Aggregation and Analysis

Given the BRRICS codes are interval variables assessed using
a Likert rating scale, the ratings can then be used in additional analyses on
the romantic relationship. If there is a small degree of endorsement in the
Demand-Withdraw Pattern code (i.e., few couples were rated as "Somewhat"
or "Yes"), it is recommended researchers consider collapsing these categories
into one category denoting the presence of any level of the Demand-
Withdraw Pattern.

Previous Studies

One study used a twin design and found the etiology of child conduct problems was not moderated by the quality of the parents' relationship (Burt, Wildey, & Klump, 2015). A second study found the effect of individuals' negative [positive] behaviors on relationship satisfaction was reduced [magnified] when partners engaged in fewer negative [greater positive] behaviors and magnified [reduced] when partners engaged in greater negative [fewer positive] behaviors (Chow & Ruhl, 2018). A third study found that externalizing psychopathology was negatively associated with relationship satisfaction, even after controlling for observed positive and negative affect (Wildey, Donnellan, Klump, & Burt, submitted).

References

Original Publication

Humbad, M. N., Donnellan, M. B., Klump, K. L., & Burt, S. A. (2011). Development of the Brief Romantic Relationship Interaction Coding Scheme (BRRICS). *Journal of Family Psychology*, 25, 759–769. http://dx.doi.org/10.1037/a0025216

Other References

Burt, S. A., Wildey, M. N., & Klump, K. L. (2015). The quality of the interparental relationship does not moderate the etiology of child conduct problems. *Psychological Medicine*, 45, 319–332. doi:10.1017/S003329171400138X

Caughlin, J. P., Huston, T. L., & Houts, R. M. (2000). How does personality matter in marriage? An examination of trait anxiety, interpersonal negativity, and marital satisfaction. *Journal of Personality and Social Psychology*, 78, 326–336. doi:10.1037//0022-3514.78.2.326

Chow, C. M., & Ruhl, H. (2018). Congruity of observed social support behaviors and couple relationship quality. *European Journal of Social Psychology*, 48, 62–71. doi:10.1002/ejsp.2302

Christensen, A., Eldridge, K., Catta-Preta, A. B., Lim, V. R., Santagata, R. (2006). Cross-cultural consistency of the demand/withdraw interaction pattern in couples. *Journal of Marriage and Family*, 68, 1029–1044. doi:10.1111/j.1741-3737.2006.00311.x

Christensen, A., & Heavey, C. L. (1990). Gender and social structure in the demand/withdraw pattern of marital conflict. *Journal of Personality and Social Psychology*, 59, 73–81. http://dx.doi.org/10.1037/0022-3514.59.1.73

Fincham, F. D., & Beach, S. R. H. (2006). Relationship satisfaction. In A. L. Vangelisti & D. Perlman (Eds.), *The Cambridge Handbook of Personal Relationships* (pp. 579–594). New York, NY: Cambridge University Press.

Grych, J. H., Seid, M., & Fincham, F. D. (1992). Assessing marital conflict from the child's perspective: The Children's Perception of Interparental Conflict Scale. *Child Development, 63*, 558–572. doi:10.1111/j.1467-8624.1992.tb01646.x.

Heyman, R. E. (2004). Rapid Marital Interaction Coding System (RMICS). In P. K. Kerig & D. H. Baucom (Eds.), *Couple observational coding systems* (pp. 67–93). Mahwah, NJ: Lawrence Erlbaum.

Julien, D., Markman, H. J., & Lindahl, K. M. (1989). A comparison of global and micro-analytic coding systems: Implications for future trends in studying interactions. *Behavioral Assessment, 11*, 81–100. doi:10.1007/BF00962701

Labreton, J. M., Burgess, J. R. D., Kaiser, R. B., Atchley, E. K., & James, L. R. (2003). Variance hypothesis and interrater reliability and agreement: Are ratings from multiple sources really dissimilar? *Organizational Research Methods, 6*, 80–128. doi:10.1177/1094428102239427

Landis, J. R., & Koch, G. G. (1977). The measurement of observer agreement for categorical data. *Biometrics, 33*, 159–174. doi:10.2307/2529310

Spanier, G. B. (1976). Measuring dyadic adjustment: New scales for assessing the quality of marriage and similar dyads. *Journal of Marriage and the Family, 38*, 15–28. doi:10.2307/350547

Weiss, R. L., & Tolman, A. O. (1990). The Marital Interaction Coding System – Global (MICS-G): A global companion to the MICS. *Behavioral Assessment, 12*, 271–294.

Wildey, M. N., Donnellan, M. B., Klump, K. L., & Burt, S. A. (submitted). Using multiple methods to evaluate associations between externalizing psychopathology, personality, and relationship quality: A replication and extension. *Journal of Personality Disorders*.

43 (Family) Relational Communication Control Coding System

Myrna L. Friedlander, Valentín Escudero, and Laurie Heatherington

Myrna L. Friedlander, Valentín Escudero, and Laurie Heatherington

General Information

Name of Coding Scheme

(Family)[1] Relational Communication Control Coding System – (F)RCCCS

Keywords

Interpersonal communication, relational communication, interpersonal control, dominance, submission, symmetry, complementarity

Summary

The RCCCS dyadic coding system and its extension to the family/group context (FRCCCS) were developed to operationalize interpersonal control (dominance, submission) in social relationships through the analysis of verbal communication. The two primary interaction patterns, *symmetry* and *complementarity*, are differentiated by the structural and pragmatic similarity or dissimilarity of contiguous speaking turns. Nonverbal relational behavior can also be coded alongside the verbal messages (Siegel, Friedlander, & Heatherington, 1992).

Description of the Coding Scheme

As explained in Rogers and Escudero (2004b), the RCCCS and its adaptation to the family context (FRCCCS) were derived through multiple lines of theorizing. The RCCCS (Rogers, 1979; Rogers & Farace, 1975; Rogers & Millar, 1979) evolved from Gregory Bateson's (e.g., 1979) writings about *double description* in human communication. From this perspective, one person's verbal

---

[1] This notation signifies that the FRCCCS was modified from the original RCCCS.

message to another person is viewed as having no relational value in itself. Rather, meaningful interactional patterns are formed through the combination of one unit of action with the subsequent unit of action to create two fundamental interaction patterns: *symmetry* and *complementarity*. Symmetry occurs when each member of the dyad behaves toward the other as the other member behaved toward him or her, either in a domineering, submissive, or transitory (neutral) manner. Complementarity occurs when one person's domineering behavior is accepted by the other person, who responds with submissiveness, and vice versa.

A number of steps are involved in coding and then summarizing the relational patterns in a dialogue. First, each message within a speaking turn is coded in terms of its grammatical format (e.g., assertion, question, talkover) and its response mode, or its pragmatic function in relation to the preceding message by the other speaker (e.g., answer, order, topic change). The combination of format and response mode results in a *message code*, such as "talkover/topic change." Second, a *control code* is assigned to each message code using specific definitions. For example, a talkover/topic change is defined as one-up (↑; domineering), an assertion that offers support to the other speaker is defined as one-down (↓; submissive), and an assertion that extends the theme is defined as one-across (→; transitory or neutral).

The next step involves determining the sequential pattern of control codes wherein speaker A's message is the antecedent to speaker B's reply, and B's reply is the antecedent to speaker A's next message in the sequence. The contiguity of control codes forms one of nine possible patterns, the most salient of which are complementarity (↑↓ and ↓↑) and competitive (↑↑) or submissive (↓↓) symmetry. Consider the example below:

A to B: Let's just stop talking about this. I just can't listen to it anymore. . . . (assertion/instruction, ↑)

B to A: Just don't tell me what to do all the time! (talkover/order, ↑)

A to B: Sorry. I wasn't trying to upset you. (assertion/support, ↓)

The sequence A to B/B to A is competitive symmetry (↑↑), whereas the sequence B to A/A to B is complementarity (↑↓).

Finally, the percentages of symmetrical, complementary, and transitory patterns are determined by dividing each type of pattern by the total number of patterns in the dialogue. In the above example, there are only two sequential patterns, 50 percent of which are symmetrical (A to B ↑, followed by B to A ↑) and 50 percent of which are complementary (B to A ↑, followed by A to B ↓).

The FRCCCS (Friedlander & Heatherington, 1989) was expanded from the RCCCS to identify triadic interaction patterns within a group of three or more individuals. For example, a speaker can direct a message to two (or more) people simultaneously by interrupting their ongoing dialogue. Alternately, a speaker's direct message to one person may contain an indirect message to another person, as in:

SON TO THERAPIST [CHANGING THE TOPIC]:	My father doesn't understand me at all.
THERAPIST TO SON:	How do you suppose your relationship with him will improve when he starts treating you more like an adult?
FATHER TO THERAPIST:	I'm trying, but he won't give me a chance.

In this example, Son's direct message to Therapist is ↑ (assertion/topic change), with an indirect ↑ (assertion/nonsupport) message to Father. Therapist's reply is called a *coalitionary move* due to the simultaneous one-down (↓, open question/ extension) message to Son, who is the "direct target" of the message, and one-up ↑ (assertion/instruction) message to Father, the "indirect target" of the message. Father's interruption of the dialogue between Son and Therapist is called an *intercept* (↑) to both targets, Therapist (directly) and Son (indirectly). Moreover, within this three-message sequence, the contiguous dyadic patterns are complementarity (Son-Therapist ↑/Therapist-Son ↓) and competitive symmetry (Therapist-Father ↑/Father-Therapist ↑).

Comparable Instruments

The most similar instrument to the RCCCS is Tracey's (e.g., Tracey, Heck, & Lichtenberg, 1981) operationalization of *topic determination*, or complementarity in dyadic conversations. This measure differs from the RCCCS in that only one aspect of a message is considered, *topic initiation* or *topic following*. Whereas a high degree of topic determination characterizes complementarity, a low degree characterizes symmetry.

The Interpersonal Communication Rating System (e.g., Strong et al., 1988) operationalizes complementarity (and anti-complementarity) in line with interpersonal personality theory (Sullivan, 1953). Complementarity is observed when two speakers' contiguous messages are dissimilar on the dominance-submission axis of the interpersonal circle but similar on the friendly-hostile axis. In contrast to the RCCCS, this measure does not take into account the structure of messages, and the interpersonal codes (e.g., self-effacing, distrustful) require a greater consideration of content.

See Friedlander (1993) for a discussion of the similarities and differences between these measures in the context of psychotherapy research.

Goals of the Instrument

Using the (F)RCCCS, researchers can determine the preponderance of different patterns of interaction to determine which one is most characteristic of a dyad's relationship. In group studies, researchers can study the preponderance of symmetry in relation to speaker characteristics such as gender, role (physician versus patient), or perceived marital satisfaction. Additionally, analyses of the codes can identify the range and average message control intensity, variability of codes, and rigidity of interactional patterns. Reciprocity can be studied to determine, for example, whether one speaker's ↑ messages significantly "activate" the other speaker's ↑ messages, resulting in competitive symmetry (e.g., Muñiz de la Peña, Friedlander, & Escudero, 2012). Episodes of interaction can also be studied to pinpoint, for example, precisely when competitive symmetry changed to complementarity within a defined conflict event (Rogers & Escudero, 2004b).

Available Versions

The FRCCCS coding manual is used for coding dyadic and family communication. This manual, available in both English and Spanish, can be downloaded without charge from http://softa-soatif.com/otros-instrumentos-2.

Applicability

Because of the complexity of the coding process, the instrument requires verbatim transcripts of video-/audio-recorded social interactions rather than coding in real time. Although use of the transcript alone is sufficient, the optimal procedure involves use of both recordings and transcripts. Although no application has been designed specifically for either the RCCCS or FRCCCS, various software programs can provide a configuration of the coding system with the computer's keyboard in order to synchronize the coding with the video on the computer screen.

Practical Application

Coding Time

Two hours are needed to code each hour of interaction for judges (observers) who have received solid training in the instrument. However, the coding time can vary depending on the difficulty of the data (e.g., conflictual dyadic discussions and discussions among three or more individuals).

Coder Training

Solid training of coders requires at least 30 hours. The FRCCCS training manual is comprehensive in describing every step and relevant aspect of the training, including multiple examples of accurate coding as well as procedures and tables to illustrate the computation of interjudge reliabilities. The reliability statistic is

Cohen's *kappa* for categorical data; kappa is computed separately for the three dimensions (identification of speaker and target(s), format, and response mode). *Kappa* is computed for each pair of coders; a mean kappa is calculated if three or more coders are used.

The first phase of training involves developing a basic knowledge of the coding manual with its various coding examples. The second phase involves individual practice (it is recommended that coders be given two hours of videotapes for this initial independent practice) followed by conjoint sessions in which the judges discuss their results and errors are corrected. As the coding material becomes more difficult, the joint meetings involve clarifying the judges' areas of doubt or subtleties in the coding.

During the training process, at least two tests of interjudge reliability should be conducted. When a satisfactory level of reliability is achieved (i.e., mean $k \geq .75$ for each of the three coding dimensions), the judges can proceed to code the research data. In order to create the optimal dataset for the statistical analysis, all coding discrepancies should be negotiated to consensus.

In coding the actual research data, coders should be randomly assigned to the various transcripts. At least one-third of the sample should be coded independently by two or more of the trained coders, allowing interjudge reliabilities to be assessed at the beginning, middle, and end of the coding process.

Technical Requirements

Technology can optimize the coding process. As mentioned above, computer software can be configured for synchronizing the codes with the videos.

Quality Assessment

Reliability

The interjudge reliability of the RCCCS was amply demonstrated in initial studies using percent agreement as the index, in (among others) studies of marital communication (Ericson & Rogers, 1973; Mark, 1971) and subsequent studies using Cohen's *kappa* as the index, in the domains of marital communication (O'Donnell-Trujillo, 1981), counseling (Heatherington & Allen, 1984; Lichtenberg & Barké, 1981; Tracey & Miars, 1986), and school consultation (Erchul, 1978). Several studies demonstrated various dimensions of construct and criterion validity of the original RCCCS (Ayers & Miura, 1981; Folger & Sillars, 1980; Heatherington, 1988; Tracey & Miars, 1986).

Regarding the psychometric properties of the FRCCCS, high interjudge agreement on the unitization of messages, formats, and response codes was found in the development of the measure, with mean $\kappa = .96$, .84, and .66, respectively, after

30–40 hours of training (Friedlander & Heatherington, 1989). Evidence of the construct validity of the triadic-based extension of the FRCCCS to family groups was provided by Gaul, Simon, Friedlander, Heatherington, and Cutler (1990), and the validity of its extension to nonverbal behavior was tested in three studies (Siegel, Friedlander, & Heatherington, 1992).

Validity

The utility of the RCCCS and FRCCCS in research of various kinds (case study, task analysis, hypothesis testing) and modalities (individual and family therapy and supervision processes) demonstrates its value for studying diverse domains of human interaction (see Heatherington & Friedlander, 2004, for a summary).

Data Aggregation and Analysis

The (F)RCCCS was developed to analyze complete social communication episodes, although shorter segments can be analyzed depending on the design of a particular research study. For example, some of the psychotherapy studies that used this instrument aggregated therapy sessions of the same case or from different cases for comparative purposes.

Previous Studies

The (F)RCCCS has been used to describe the interpersonal control patterns in couples' relationships (e.g., Rogers & Escudero, 2004b), in individual and family psychotherapy (Heatherington & Friedlander, 2004, Muñiz de la Peña et al., 2012), in clinical supervision (Friedlander, Siegel, & Brenock, 1989), and in medical (Cecil & von Friederichs-Fitzwater, 2004) and managerial contexts (Fairhurst, 2004) (see Escudero, Friedlander, & Lee, this volume, Chapter 3, for a review).

Original Publication

The Relational Communication Control Coding System (RCCCS; Escudero & Rogers, 2004; Ericson & Rogers, 1973; Rogers & Farace, 1975) and its adaptation, the Family Relational Communication Control Coding System (FRCCCS; Friedlander & Heatherington, 1989), are thoroughly described in the above references.

References

Original Publications

Ericson, P. M., & Rogers, L. E. (1973). New procedures for analyzing relational communication. *Family Process*, *12*, 245–267. doi:10.1111/j.1545-5300.1973.00245.x

Escudero, V., & Rogers, L. E. (2004). Analyzing relational communication. In L. E. Rogers & V. Escudero (Eds.), *Relational communication: An interactional perspective to the study of process and form.* (pp. 3–21). Mahwah, NJ: Lawrence Erlbaum Associates.

Friedlander, M. L., & Heatherington, L. (1989). Analyzing relational control in family therapy interviews. *Journal of Counseling Psychology*, *36*, 139–148. doi:10.1037/0022-0167.36.2.139

Rogers, L. E., & Farace, R. V. (1975). Relational communication analysis: New measurement procedures. *Human Communication Research*, *1*, 222–239. doi:10.1111/j.1468-2958.1975.tb00270.x

Other References

Ayers, J., & Miura, S. Y. (1981). Construct and predictive validity of instruments for coding relational control. *Western Journal of Speech Communication*, *45*, 159–171.

Bateson, G. (1979). *Mind and nature: A necessary unity.* New York, NY: Bantam Books.

Cecil, D. W., & von Friederichs-Fitzwater, M. (2004). Relational control in physician-patient interaction. In L. E. Rogers & V. Escudero (Eds.), *Relational communication: An interactional perspective to the study of process and form* (pp. 179–195). Mahwah, NJ: Lawrence Erlbaum Associates.

Erchul, W. P. (1978). A relational communication analysis of control in school consultation. *Professional School Psychology*, *2*, 113–124.

Fairhurst, G. T. (2004). Organizational relational control research: Problems and possibilities. In L. E. Rogers & V. Escudero (Eds.), *Relational communication: An interactional perspective to the study of process and form* (pp. 197–215). Mahwah, NJ: Lawrence Erlbaum Associates.

Friedlander, M. L. (1993). Does complementarity promote or hinder client change in brief therapy? A review of the evidence from two theoretical perspectives. *The Counseling Psychologist*, *21*, 457–486. doi:10.1177/0011000093213010

Friedlander, M. L., Siegel, S. M., & Brenock, K. (1989). Parallel processes in counseling and supervision: A case study. *Journal of Counseling Psychology*, *36*, 149–157. doi:10.1037/0022-0167.36.2.149

Friedlander, M. L., Wildman, J., & Heatherington, L. (1991). Interpersonal control in structural and Milan systemic family therapy. *Journal of Marital and Family Therapy*, *17*, 395–408. doi:10.1111/j.1752-0606.1991.tb00909.x

Gaul, R., Simon, L., Friedlander, M. L., Heatherington, L., & Cutler, C. (1991). Correspondence of family therapists' perceptions with FRCCCS coding rules for triadic interactions. *Journal of Marital and Family Therapy*, *17*, 379–393. doi:10.1111/j.1752-0606.1991.tb00908.x

Heatherington, L. (1988). Coding relational control in counseling: Criterion validity. *Journal of Counseling Psychology, 35,* 41–46.

Heatherington, L., & Friedlander, M. L. (1987). *Family Relational Communication Control Coding System.* Unpublished manuscript. Williams College, Williamstown, MA.

Heatherington, L., & Friedlander, M. L. (1990). Complementarity and symmetry in family therapy communication. *Journal of Counseling Psychology, 37,* 261–268. doi:10.1037/0022-0167.37.3.261

Heatherington, L., & Friedlander, M. L. (2004). From dyads to triads, and beyond: Relational control in individual and family therapy. In L. E. Rogers & V. Escudero (Eds.), *Relational communication: An interactional perspective to the study of process and form* (pp. 103–129). Mahwah, NJ: Lawrence Erlbaum Associates.

Muñiz de la Peña, C., Friedlander, M. L., Escudero, V., & Heatherington, L. (2012). How do therapists ally with adolescents in family therapy? An examination of relational control communication in early sessions. *Journal of Counseling Psychology, 59,* 339–351. doi:10.1037/a0028063

Rogers, L. E. (1979). *Relational communication control coding manual.* (Available from L. E. Rogers, Department of Communication, University of Utah, Salt Lake City, Utah 84112).

Rogers, L. E., & Escudero, V. (Eds.) (2004a). *Relational communication: An interactional perspective to the study of process and form.* Mahwah, NJ: Lawrence Erlbaum Associates.

Rogers, L. E., & Escudero, V. (2004b). Relational communication patterns in marital interaction. In L. E. Rogers & V. Escudero (Eds.), *Relational communication: An interactional perspective to the study of process and form* (pp. 83–102). Mahwah, NJ: Lawrence Erlbaum Associates.

Rogers, L. E., & Millar, F. (1979). Domineeringness and dominance: A transactional view. *Human Communication Research, 5,* 238–246.

Siegel, S. M., Friedlander, M. L., & Heatherington, L. (1992). Nonverbal relational control in family communication. *Journal of Nonverbal Behavior, 16,* 117–139. doi:10.1007/BF00990326

Strong, S. R., Hills, H. I., Kilmartin, C. T., DeVries, H., Lanier, K., Nelson, B. N., ... Meyer, C. W., III, (1988). The dynamic relations among interpersonal behaviors: A test of complementarity and anticomplementarity. *Journal of Personality and Social Psychology, 54,* 789–810. doi:10.1037/0022-3514.54.5.798

Sullivan, H. S. (1953). *The interpersonal basis of psychiatry.* New York, NY: Norton.

Tracey, T. J., Heck, E. J., & Lichtenberg, J. W. (1981). Role expectations and symmetrical/complementary therapeutic relationships. *Psychotherapy: Theory, Research and Practice, 18,* 338–344. doi:10.1037/h0088384

44 Verbal Response Modes Taxonomy

William B. Stiles

General Information

Name of Coding Scheme

Verbal Response Modes Taxonomy

Keywords

Verbal response modes, speech acts, interpersonal relationships, grammatical form versus pragmatic intent, interpersonal process coding

Summary

The verbal response modes (VRM) taxonomy is a general-purpose classification of speech acts that can be applied by coders to any sort of spoken or written discourse. The grammatical form and interpersonal intent of each utterance are each coded into one of eight modes: Disclosure, Edification, Question, Acknowledgment, Advisement, Confirmation, Interpretation, or Reflection. The modes reflect the *micro-relationship* of speaker to other (the relationship enacted in one utterance) and can be aggregated to describe speaker-to-other relationships in verbal interactions of any length along such dimensions as attentiveness, directiveness, and presumptuousness. The speaker and/or other may be individuals or collectivities.

Description of the Coding Scheme

The VRM taxonomy classifies speech acts; that is, the categories describe what people *do* when they say something (disclose, interpret, advise, etc.) rather than the content of what they say (Stiles, 1981). The taxonomy is based on theoretical principles in a way that ensures the categories are mutually exclusive and exhaustive, in the sense that every comprehensible utterance can be classified into one and only one mode. Each utterance is coded twice, once for its grammatical form and once for its pragmatic intent.

The pragmatic intent of each utterance is coded as reflection (R), acknowledgment (K), interpretation (I), question (Q), confirmation (C), edification (E), advisement (A), or disclosure (D). These VRM codes are assigned according to three *principles of classification*, each of which can take the value of *speaker* or *other* (see Stiles, 1992):

(1) *source of experience*: whether the utterance's topic is information held by the speaker or by the other,

(2) *frame of reference*: whether the utterance is expressed from the speaker's own point of view or from a point of view shared with the other, and

(3) *presumption*: whether the speaker uses knowledge only of his or her own experience and frame of reference (speaker) or instead presumes knowledge of what the other's experience or frame of reference is, was, will be, or should be (other).

As shown in Table 44.1, these three forced choices place every utterance into one of the eight mutually exclusive intent categories. These categories are exhaustive in the sense that every comprehensible utterance can be coded. The designation *uncodable* (U) is used only for utterances that are incomprehensible.

The grammatical form definitions, also shown in Table 44.1, were based on the observation that each mode has an associated set of grammatical features and that utterances can be classified on the basis of these features alone, regardless of the intent classification (see Stiles, 1992). Thus, each utterance is classified twice, once for form and once for intent using the same eight mode names. Utterances in which form and intent coincide are called *pure modes*; utterances in which form and intent differ are called *mixed modes*. For example, "Remove your shoes before you enter" is coded as advisement form (imperative) with advisement intent (guiding the other's behavior), a pure advisement, abbreviated AA. On the other hand, "I would appreciate your removing your shoes before you enter" is coded as disclosure form (first-person singular) with advisement intent (guiding the other's behavior), a mixed mode, abbreviated DA.

Comparable Instruments

Many systems have been used to code response modes or interpersonal speech acts, including those designed to assess psychotherapeutic and conversational techniques (e.g., Bales, 1970; Elliott et al., 1987; Goodman & Dooley, 1976; Orlinsky, Grawe, & Parks, 1994). A distinctive feature of the VRM taxonomy is its basis in the theoretical principles of classification, source of experience, frame of reference, and presumption.

Table 44.1 *Taxonomy of verbal response modes*

Source of experience	Frame of reference	Presumption	
		Speaker (no presumption)	Other (presumption)
Speaker	Speaker	DISCLOSURE (D)	ADVISEMENT (A)
		Form: Declarative; first-person singular ("I") or first-person plural ("we") where other is not a referent.	*Form*: Imperative, or second person with verb of permission, prohibition, or obligation.
		Intent: Reveals thoughts, feelings, wishes, perceptions, or intentions.	*Intent*: Attempts to guide behavior; suggestions, commands, permission, prohibition.
Speaker	Other	EDIFICATION (E)	CONFIRMATION (C)
		Form: Declarative; third person (e.g., "he," "she," "it").	*Form*: First-person plural ("we") where referent includes other.
		Intent: States objective information.	*Intent*: Compares speaker's experience with other's; agreement, disagreement, shared experience or belief.
Other	Speaker	QUESTION (Q)	INTERPRETATION (I)
		Form: Interrogative, with inverted subject-verb order or interrogative words.	*Form*: Second person ("you"); verb implies an attribute or ability of the other; terms of evaluation.
		Intent: Requests information or guidance.	*Intent*: Explains or labels the other; judgments or evaluations of other's experience or behavior.
Other	Other	ACKNOWLEDGMENT (K)	REFLECTION (R)
		Form: Nonlexical or contentless utterances; terms of address or salutation.	*Form*: Second person; verb implies internal experience or volitional action.
		Intent: Conveys receipt of or receptiveness to other's communication; simple acceptance, salutations.	*Intent*: Puts other's experience into words; repetitions, restatements, clarifications.

Goals of the Instrument

The VRM system is particularly appropriate for addressing questions involving social roles and interpersonal relationships as these are manifested verbally. It is sensitive to dimensions of relative status, intimacy, and dominance, and it offers fine-grained descriptions of the great variety of tasks performed in social encounters.

Available Versions

The VRM system has been applied and described in Spanish (Caro, 1993; Caro & Stiles, 1997) and Dutch (Meeuwesen, 1984; Meeuwesen, Schaap, & van der Staak, 1991) as well as in English.

Applicability

VRMs can be coded from written documents, verbatim transcripts, audio or video recordings or live interactions. Coding of complex or rapidly moving interaction from audio or video recordings is more difficult but possible; coders working from recordings may need to replay them several times to catch all utterances.

Practical Application

Coding Time

Experienced coders can code most utterances in clearly articulated speech from good-quality audio recordings in real time. Inexperienced coders or coding of ungrammatical or hard-to-understand speech, poor recordings, unfamiliar types of interactions, or other complexities may take much longer.

Coder Training

Undergraduate volunteers have been able to learn the system well enough to code competently in 30–40 hours (see studies reviewed in Stiles, 1992). Basic training can draw on a computer-assisted training program available at www.users.miamioh.edu/stileswb/archive.htmlx. This can be followed by practice on transcripts of verbal interactions of the same type as are being studied (e.g., medical interviews; group psychotherapy), with regular meetings to discuss verbal constructions characteristic of that type. The manual (Stiles, 1992) includes explanations of how to code many difficult constructions. Coders continue to improve in speed and accuracy for a long time as they gain experience.

Technical Requirements

VRMs can be coded from written documents, verbatim transcripts, audio or video recordings or live interactions.

VRM form codes are based on grammatical features (see Table 44.1), so grammatical, nonelliptical utterances can be coded in isolation. In natural speech, elliptical, incomplete, and ungrammatical utterances require reference to context. VRM intent codes classify the speaker's intended meaning and therefore must be understood in context. In practice, VRM intent can usually be coded in a context of a few preceding utterances, but some utterances may be understandable only in the context of earlier events.

Unitizing

The VRM coding unit is the utterance, which is defined as a simple sentence (single predicate), independent clause, nonrestrictive dependent clause, multiple predicate, or term of acknowledgment, evaluation, or address.

The VRM system allows any size of summarizing unit. Most VRM studies have summarized over an encounter or a segment of an encounter. Utterances have most often been aggregated separately for each speaker; however, it is possible to aggregate by dyad or by larger groups. In some applications, codes of single utterances are reported.

Training Manual

A detailed coding manual is included in Stiles (1992). At the time of writing this chapter, the book is out of print, but it is available in libraries and online. An electronic prepublication version of the book and a digital coder training program are available online at no cost at the following web address. A computer-assisted coder training program is also available there at no cost from www.users .miamioh.edu/stileswb/archive.htmlx.

Simplified Version

It is possible to use only the VRM form codes or only the VRM intent codes (see Table 44.1).

Quality Assessment

Reliability

Reliability depends on coders' ability, training, and experience, the index being used, and the nature and variability of the material being coded. Reliability also varies across the VRM categories; common categories within a particular form of discourse are usually coded more reliably than rare categories. Experienced coders can achieve high reliability on frequently used categories in most sorts of conversations. Because of the complexities, decontexturalized examples of VRM reliabilities are not a good guide. However, for experienced, paid coders working from audiotapes, the intraclass correlation coefficient designated ICC(1,1) by Shrout and Fleiss (1979) was .96 for therapist interpretation form percentages and .84 for interpretation intent percentages in psychotherapy sessions, where interpretation was fairly common (Stiles, Shapiro, & Firth-Cozens, 1988). For volunteer undergraduate coders working from transcripts, Cohen's Kappa was .91 for edification form and .79 for edification intent but only .62 for interpretation form and .45 for interpretation intent in experimental laboratory conversations between students and professors, where edification was common but interpretation was rare (Cansler & Stiles, 1981). For a discussion of practical issues in coding and reliability, see Chapter 11 in Stiles (1992).

Validity

The VRM codes are descriptive categories, and it makes little sense to ask if they are valid (e.g., is the question category a valid measure of being a question?). Some people might define the terms differently, however (e.g., disclosure might be defined differently by different investigators).

Derivative indices, such as the role dimensions (see next section), have demonstrated construct validity (see Stiles, 1992, Chapter 4, for a review). For example, interviewers (e.g., doctors, psychotherapists, courtroom interrogators) are much more *attentive* than interviewees (patients, clients, witnesses). In mixed-status dyads (e.g., teacher-student, senior-freshman, psychotherapist-client, doctor-patient), the higher-status member is consistently more *presumptuous* than the lower-status member (Stiles et al., 1997).

Data Aggregation and Analysis

The VRM system offers a variety of aggregate measures for characterizing an encounter. These include:

(1) The *frequency or percentage of each form or intent*; for example, the frequency of Acknowledgment form aggregated across intents or the percentage of Edification intent aggregated across forms to yield a profile for a particular role or relationship.

(2) Three *role dimensions*, which are labeled as (a) informativeness versus attentiveness, (b) unassumingness versus presumptuousness, and (c) directiveness versus acquiescence, correspond to the proportion of speaker versus other values on source of experience, presumption about experience, and frame of reference, respectively. To put this another way, the VRM coding system considers each utterance as simultaneously representing one or the other pole on all three role dimensions. For example, an edification such as "The accident was on the ninth of September" (EE) is considered as simultaneously informative, acquiescent, and unassuming. A question such as "Was it a pretty bad car

accident?" (QQ) is considered as attentive, directive, and unassuming. An advisement such as "Now turn this way" (AA) is considered as informative, directive, and presumptuous.

(3) The *frequency or percentage of each pure or mixed mode*, for example, the frequency of KK or the percentage of DE can yield a more subtle way to characterize a verbal exchange. For example, although "Could you scoot forward a bit?" (QA) is directive in both form and intent, it is attentive and unassuming in form (question) but informative and presumptuous in intent (advisement). As a result, it is subtly more polite than its pure-mode counterpart, "Scoot forward a bit" (AA).

Previous Studies

The VRM taxonomy has been used extensively to study medical interviews (e.g., Cape & Stiles, 1998; Meeuwesen, Schaap, & van der Staak, 1991; Shaikh, Knobloch, & Stiles, 2001) and psychotherapy (e.g., Anderson, Knobloch-Fedders, Stiles, Ordonez, & Heckman, 2012; Stiles & Shapiro, 1995). It has also been applied to public discourse such as presidential speeches (Miller & Stiles, 1986), labor-management negotiations (Hinkle, Stiles, & Taylor, 1988), and radio call-in programs (Henricks & Stiles, 1989). Studies have found systematic relations between VRM indices and interpersonal relationship variables in a wide variety of ordinary conversations. For example, in initial interactions, both men and women used more disclosure if they or their partner were judged attractive (Stiles, Walz, Schroeder, Williams, & Ickes, 1996). Women tended to be more attentive than men under some conditions, particularly within committed relationships such as married or dating couples (Stiles et al., 1997). High and moderate trait anxious university students (but not the low trait anxious students) used higher percentages of disclosure when speaking about an anxiety-arousing topic than when speaking about a happy topic (Stiles, Shuster, & Harrigan, 1992). VRM coding can also be used to analyze group interaction (see Stiles, 1986, for a worked-through example). VRM indices describe the relationship of the speaker to the other (author to addressee), so it is necessary to keep track of who is speaking and who being spoken to, as a speaker may have very different relationships with different people in a room.

References

Original Publication

Stiles, W. B. (1992). *Describing talk: A taxonomy of verbal response modes*. Newbury Park, CA: Sage.

Other References

Anderson, T., Knobloch-Fedders, L., Stiles, W. B., Ordonez, T., & Heckman, B. D. (2012). The power of subtle interpersonal hostility in psychodynamic psychotherapy: A speech acts analysis. *Psychotherapy Research, 22*, 348–362. doi:10.1080/10503307.2012.658097

Bales, R. F. *Personality and interpersonal behavior.* New York, NY: Holt, Rinehart & Winston, 1970.

Cansler, D. C., & Stiles, W. B. (1981). Relative status and interpersonal presumptuousness. *Journal of Experimental Social Psychology, 17*, 459–471.

Cape, J. D., & Stiles, W. B. (1998). Verbal exchange structure of general practice consultations with patients presenting psychological problems. *Journal of Health Psychology, 3*, 5–21. doi:10.1177/135910539800300101

Caro, I. (1993). Actos de habla de pacientes y terapeutas: Un análisis de la terapia lingüística de evaluación a través de los Modos de Respuesta Verbal [Patients' and therapists' speech acts: The linguistic therapy of evaluation analyzed through the Verbal Response Modes]. In I. Caro (Ed.), *Psicoterapia e investigación de procesos [Psychotherapy and process research].* Valencia, Spain: Promolibro (Colección de Psicología Teorética).

Caro, I., & Stiles, W. B. (1997). *Vamos a traducir los MRV* (let's translate the VRM): Linguistic and cultural inferences drawn from translating a verbal coding system from English into Spanish. *Psychiatry, 60*, 233–247.

Elliott, R., Hill, C. E., Stiles, W. B., Friedlander, M. L., Mahrer, A. R., & Margison, F. R. (1987). Primary therapist response modes: Comparison of six rating systems. *Journal of Consulting and Clinical Psychology, 55*, 218–223.

Goodman, G., & Dooley, D. (1976). A framework for help-intended interpersonal communication. *Psychotherapy: Theory, Research and Practice, 13*, 106–117. doi:10.1037/h0088322

Henricks, W. H., & Stiles, W. B. (1989). Verbal processes on psychological radio call-in programs: Comparison with other help-intended interactions. *Professional Psychology: Research and Practice, 20*, 315–321. doi:10.1037/0735-7028.20.5.315

Hinkle, S., Stiles, W. B., & Taylor, L. A. (1988). Verbal processes in a labour/management negotiation. *Journal of Language and Social Psychology, 7*, 123–136. doi:10.1177/0261927X8800700203

Meeuwesen, L. (Ed. and Trans.) (1984). *Handleiding voor een taxonomie van verbale antwoordwijzen: Een beschrijving en bewerking van Stiles "Verbal Response Modes (V.R.M.)".* Vakgroep Klinische Psychologie, University of Nijmegen, Nijmegen, The Netherlands.

Meeuwesen, L., Schaap, C., & van der Staak, C. (1991). Verbal analysis of physician-patient communication. *Social Science & Medicine, 32*, 1143–1150. doi:10.1016/0277-9536(91)90091-P

Miller, N. L., & Stiles, W. B. (1986). Verbal familiarity in American presidential nomination acceptance speeches and inaugural addresses (1920–1981). *Social Psychology Quarterly, 49*, 72–81. doi:10.2307/2786858

Orlinsky, D. E., Grawe, K., & Parks, B. K. (1994). Process and outcome in psychotherapy – Noch einmal. In A. E. Bergin & S. L. Garfield (Eds.), *Handbook of psychotherapy and behavior change* (4th edn., pp. 270–376). New York, NY: Wiley.

Shaikh, A., Knobloch, L. M., & Stiles, W. B. (2001). The use of a verbal response mode coding system in determining patient and physician roles in medical interviews. *Health Communication, 13*, 49–60. doi:10.1207/S15327027HC1301_05

Shrout, P. E., & Fleiss, J. L. (1979). Intraclass correlations: Uses in assessing rater reliability. *Psychological Bulletin, 86*, 420–428.

Stiles, W. B. (1978a). *Manual for a taxonomy of verbal response modes*. Chapel Hill: Institute for Research in Social Science, University of North Carolina at Chapel Hill.

Stiles, W. B. (1978b). Verbal response modes and dimensions of interpersonal roles: A method of discourse analysis. *Journal of Personality and Social Psychology, 36*, 693–703.

Stiles, W. B. (1981). Classification of intersubjective illocutionary acts. *Language in Society, 10*, 227–249.

Stiles, W. B. (1986). Development of taxonomy of verbal response modes. In L. S. Greenberg & W. M. Pinsof (Eds.), *The psychotherapeutic process: A research handbook* (pp. 161–199). New York, NY: Guilford Press.

Stiles, W. B., Lyall, L. M., Knight, D. P., Ickes, W., Waung, M., Hall, C. L., & Primeau, B. E. (1997). Gender differences in verbal presumptuousness and attentiveness. *Personality and Social Psychology Bulletin, 23*, 759–772. doi:10.1177/0146167297237009

Stiles, W. B., & Shapiro, D. A. (1995). Verbal exchange structure of brief psychodynamic-interpersonal and cognitive-behavioral psychotherapy. *Journal of Consulting and Clinical Psychology, 63*, 15–27. doi:10.1037//0022-006X.63.1.15

Stiles, W. B., Shapiro, D. A., & Firth-Cozens, J. A. (1988). Verbal response mode use in contrasting psychotherapies: A within-subjects comparison. *Journal of Consulting and Clinical Psychology, 56*, 727–733.

Stiles, W. B., Shuster, P. L., & Harrigan, J. A. (1992). Disclosure and anxiety: A test of the fever model. *Journal of Personality and Social Psychology, 63*, 980–988. doi:10.1037/0022-3514.63.6.980

Stiles, W. B., Walz, N. C., Schroeder, M. A. B., Williams, L. L., & Ickes, W. (1996). Attractiveness and disclosure in initial encounters of mixed-sex dyads. *Journal of Social and Personal Relations, 13*, 305–314. doi:10.1177/0265407596132009

Appendix

Table A.1 *Overview of published coding schemes*

Name of coding scheme	Reference	Synopsis
Argument		
AAO – Argumentative Analysis of Options	Horita, M. (2000). Folding arguments: A method for representing conflicting views of a conflict. *Group Decision and Negotiation, 9*(1), 63–83. doi:10.1023/A:1008796822813	Coding system based on modal logic created to develop a strategic map for conflict analysis.
CAS – Conversational Argument Scheme and CACS – Conversational Argument Coding Scheme	Meyers, R. A., & Brashers, D. (2010). Extending the Conversational Argument Coding Scheme: Argument categories, units, and coding procedures. *Communication Methods and Measures, 4*(1/2), 27–45. doi:10.1080/19312451003680467	Looks to analyze argument structures and the interaction that occurs during an argument. Coding scheme allows researchers to track how people develop and share ideas during interaction.
	Canary, D. J., & Seibold, D. R. (2010). Origins and development of the Conversational Argument Coding Scheme. *Communication Methods and Measures, 4*(1/2), 7–26. doi:10.1080/19312451003680459	
Coordination & leadership		
Leadership Coding System (multiteam systems MTS)	Bienefeld, N., & Grote, G. (2014). Shared leadership in multiteam systems: How cockpit and cabin crews lead each other to safety. *Human Factors, 56*(2), 270–286. doi:10.1177/0018720813488137	Coding scheme based on Yukl's (2006) framework of leadership functions, designed for the operationalization of leadership.
MICRO-CO	Kolbe, M., Strack, M., Stein, A., & Boos, M. (2011). Effective coordination in human group decision	Coding scheme developed to measure coordination mechanisms used by group members during decision-

Table A.1 (*cont.*)

Coordination & leadership

	making: MICRO-CO: A micro-analytical taxonomy for analysing explicit coordination mechanisms in decision-making groups. In *Coordination in human and primate groups* (pp. 199–219). Berlin & Heidelberg: Springer.	making discussion. MICRO-CO permits a detailed analysis of the coordinative function of statements made during group discussion.

Exchange of knowledge and information

Social Information Processing Analysis (SIPA)	Fisher, B. A., Drecksel, G. L., & Werbel, W. S. (1979). Social Information Processing Analysis (SIPA): Coding ongoing human communication. *Small Group Behavior, 10*(1), 3–21. doi:10.1177/0090552679101001	Coding Scheme for assessing information processing at the social level, organized within four dimensions: Source of Information; Time Orientation; Information Assembly Rules; Equivocality Reduction

Decision making

Design Meeting Interaction	Olson, G. M., Olson, J. S., Carter, M. R., & Storrøsten, M. (1992). Small group design meetings: An analysis of collaboration. *Human-Computer Interaction, 7*(4), 347–374. doi:10.1207/s15327051hci0704_1	Coding scheme focuses on the problem-solving aspects of design in collaborative group work. Scheme is organized into a set of ten activity categories that capture the general nature of the design.
KONFKOD – Konferenz-kodierung	Fisch, R. (1994). Eine Methode zur Analyse von Interaktionsprozessen beim Problemlösen in Gruppen. *Gruppendynamik, 25*(2), 149–168.	Method for analyzing decision and problem-solving processes in groups.
Measuring Deliberation	Stromer-Galley, J. (2007). Measuring deliberation's content: A coding scheme. *Journal of Public Deliberation, 3*(1), 1–37.	Coding scheme used to describe the process and content of deliberation, organized into four categories: problem, metatalk, process, and social.

Family and relationships

Couples Interaction Scoring System (CISS)	Gottman, J., Markman, H., & Notarius, C. (1977). The	Coding schemes (CISS and RCISS) used to measure the interaction and

Table A.1 (cont.)

Family and relationships

	topography of marital conflict: A sequential analysis of verbal and nonverbal behavior. *Journal of Marriage and Family, 39*(3), 461–477. doi:10.2307/350902	satisfaction in married couples. CISS consists of four categories (husband disagree, wife disagree, husband mind read, and wife mind read). RCISS is based on a rating system and validation shows that they can assess humor, anger, disgust-contempt, sadness, whining, and fear.
Rapid Couple Interaction Scoring System version (RCISS; Gottman, 1996)	Krokoff, L. J., Gottman, J. M., & Hass, S. D. (1989). Validation of a global rapid couples interaction scoring system. *Behavioral Assessment, 11*(1), 65–79.	
SPAFF – Specific Affect Coding System	Coan, J. A., & Gottman, J. M. (2007). The specific affect coding system (SPAFF). In J. A. Coan & J. J. B. Allen (Eds.), *Handbook of emotion elicitation and assessment* (pp. 106–123). New York, NY: Oxford University Press.	Coding scheme used to systematically observe affective behavior in the context of marital conflict. Designed so that the global category of positive and negative affect could be assessed. Consists of five positive aspects and 12 negative aspects.
MICS – Marital Interaction Coding Scheme	Heyman, R. E., Weiss, R. L., & Eddy, J. M. (1995). Marital Interaction Coding System: Revision and empirical evaluation. *Behaviour Research and Therapy, 33*(6), 737–746. doi:10.1016/0005–7967(95)00003-G	Coding scheme composed of eight categories used to analyze interactions within a marriage. Categories include blame, invalidation, validation, facilitation, propose change, irrelevant, description, attention, and inattention.
Relationship Communication coding scheme	Mark, R. A. (1971). Coding communication at the relationship level. *Journal of Communication, 21*(3), 221–232. doi:10.1111/j.1460–2466.1971.tb00920.x	Relationship coding scheme that codes speaker, speech, and metaspeech (response to preceding statement) and defines nine relational codes to assess relationships.
Marriage conflict coding scheme	Rausch, H. L., Barry, W. A., Hertel, R. K., & Swain, M. A. (1974). *Communication conflict and marriage*. Oxford, England: Jossey-Bass.	Coding scheme aimed to assess interaction during conflicts within marriages. Scheme is composed of six interactive categories (cognitive, resolving, reconciling, appealing, rejecting, and coercing)

Table A.1 (*cont.*)

Family and relationships

		aimed at presenting ways to study the interactions of married couples in conflict-laden contexts.
Marital quality and gender differences in parent-child interactions	Kerig, P. K., Cowan, P. A., & Cowan, C. P. (1993). Marital quality and gender differences in parent-child interaction. *Developmental Psychology, 29*(6), 931–939. doi:10.1037/0012–1649.29.6.931	Coding scheme aiming to study marital quality or gender based on parent-child interactions. Coding composed of nine categories (responses, interpersonal focus, positive expressions, negations, disengagement, overriding/low expectations, control, assert, and challenge/cognitively stimulate) grouped into three broader categories (positive response, negative response, and assertions).
Child Development Coding Scheme	Bakeman, R., & Adamson, L. B. (1984). Coordinating attention to people and objects in mother-infant and peer-infant interaction. *Child Development, 55*(4), 1278–1289. doi:10.2307/1129997	Coding scheme for children's coordination of attention in mother-infant and peer-infant interaction. Coding scheme consisting of six categories (unengaged, on-looking, persons, objects, passive joint, and coordinated joint) developed to assess how infants coordinate their attention to people and objects.
DPICS II – Dyadic parent-child interaction coding system II	Eyberg, S. M., Bessmer, J., Newcomb, K., Edwards, D., & Robinson, E. A. (1994). *Dyadic parent–child interaction coding system-II: A manual.* (Social and Behavioral Sciences Documents, No. 2897). San Rafael, CA: Select Press.	Direct observational-based method comprised of 24 categories, used to assess parent-child interactions.
Family Interaction Coding Scheme	Grotevant, H. D., & Carlson, C. I. (1987). Family interaction coding systems: A descriptive review. *Family Process*, 26(1), 49–74.	Article reviews 13 coding systems of interaction within families and discusses them with regard to description of codes, administrative procedures, reliability, validity, and use in basic and applied contexts.

Table A.1 *(cont.)*

Family and relationships

Family observational coding systems	Kerig, P. K., & Lindahl, K. M. (Eds.). (2000). *Family observational coding systems: Resources for systemic research.* Psychology Press.	Collection of coding systems and resources for observing interactions in families.
Couple Observational Coding Systems	Kerig, P. K., & Baucom, D. H. (Eds.) (2004). Couple observational coding system. New York, NY: Routledge Taylor and Francis.	Collection of observational coding methods for couple's research.
SCIFF – System for Coding Interactions and Family Functioning	Lindahl, K. M., & Malik, N. (2000). The System for Coding Interactions and Family Functioning. In Kerig, P. K., & Lindahl, K. M. (Eds.). *Family observational coding systems: Resources for systemic research* (pp. 77–92). Philadelphia, PA.: Brunner/Mazel.	Coding scheme for the behavioral assessment of family functioning focusing on conflict, disagreement, and problem solving. Coding is based on various dimensions, e.g. family level, dyadic/couple's level, parent level, child level.
ABC Mealtime Coding System	Fiese, B. H., Winter, M. A., & Botti, J. C. (2011). The ABCs of family mealtimes: Observational lessons for promoting healthy outcomes for children with persistent asthma. *Child Development, 82*(1), 133–145. doi:10.1111/j.1467–8624.2010.01545.x	A micro-coding system designed to assess five dimensions of mealtime behavior (action-oriented, behavior control, meal-oriented behavior, positive communication, and critical communication) during meal time.
Mother Adolescent Interaction Task (MAIT)	Pineda, A. Q., Cole, D. A., & Bruce, A. E. (2007). Mother–adolescent interactions and adolescent depressive symptoms: A sequential analysis. *Journal of Social and Personal Relationships, 24*(1), 5–19. doi:10.1177/0265407507072564	Behavioral coding system composed of three categories (critical behavior, depressive behavior, and positive behavior) to test mother-adolescent interactions, specifically, the emotion regulation and depressive symptoms of their adolescent offspring.
RELCOM Analyzing Relationship Communication	Fisher, B. A., & Drecksel, G. L. (1983). A cyclical model of developing relationships: A study	Coding scheme looking at communication within relationships based on five categories

Table A.1 (*cont.*)

Family and relationships

	of relational control interaction. *Communications Monographs, 50*(1), 66–78. doi:10.1080/03637758309390154	(domineering, structuring, equivalence, deferring, and submitting) of relational control modes used for interaction analysis, specifically, to discover progressive pattern of relational control of newly acquainted pairs.

Human-machine interaction

SInA – Systemic Interaction Analysis	Lohse, M., Hanheide, M., Rohlfing, K. J., & Sagerer, G. (2009). Systemic interaction analysis (SInA) in HRI. In *Proceedings of the 4th ACM/IEEE international conference on Human robot interaction* (pp. 93–100). ACM.	Coding scheme for assessing the interaction between humans and robots

Negotiation

Negotiation Coding Scheme	Donohue, W. A., Diez, M. E., & Hamilton, M. (1984). Coding naturalistic negotiation interaction. *Human Communication Research, 10*(3), 403–425. doi:10.1111/j.1468-2958.1984.tb00025.x	Codes interactions within the negotiation process. Coding system made up of 20 categories used for analyzing communication strategies in negotiations interaction (attacking, defending, and regressing).
Negotiation Behavior Coding Scheme (second one)	Weingart, L. R., Olekalns, M., & Smith, P. L. (2004). Quantitative coding of negotiation behavior. *International Negotiation, 9*(3), 441–455. doi:10.1163/1571806053498805	Coding scheme to look at interactions taking place during negotiation processes by observing negotiation behaviors coded via six categories/strategies (integrative info, create value, distributive info, chain value, push to closure, and process management).
Integrative and Distributive Negotiation Tactics	Weingart, L. R., Hyder, E. B., & Prietula, M. J. (1996). Knowledge matters: The effect of tactical descriptions on negotiation behavior and outcome. *Journal of Personality and Social Psychology, 70*(6), 1204–1217. doi:10.1037/0022-3514.70.6.1205	Coding scheme focused on the use of integrative and distributive tactics. Identifies general negotiation behaviors including offers, information provision, questions, procedural comments, and reactions. These general behaviors are further divided into 14 subcategories.

Table A.1 (*cont.*)

Nonverbal communication

| Facial Action Coding System | Ekman, P., & Friesen, W. (1978). Facial action coding system: A technique for the measurement of facial movement. *Palo Alto: Consulting Psychologists.*

Ekman, P., & Friesen, W. V. (1976). Measuring facial movement. *Environmental Psychology & Nonverbal Behavior, 1*(1), 56–75. doi:10.1007/BF01115465

Ekman, P., Freisen, W. V., & Ancoli, S. (1980). Facial signs of emotional experience. *Journal of Personality and Social Psychology, 39*(6), 1125–1134. | Coding system designed to measure all visible facial behavior, distinguishing between 44 action units (minimal units that are anatomically separate and visually distinguishable). Generally speaking, the system allows for the examination of a participant's entire record of expressive behavior. |

Physician-patient communication and care communication

HIM – Hill Interaction Matrix	Hill, W. F. (1971). The Hill Interaction Matrix. *Personnel & Guidance Journal, 49*(8), 619–622.	Allows therapist to assess the therapeutic quality of an interaction within a small (therapy) group.
MIPS – Medical Interaction Process System	Ford, S., & Hall, A. (2004). Communication behaviours of skilled and less skilled oncologists: A validation study of the Medical Interaction Process System (MIPS). *Patient Education and Counseling, 54* (3), 275–282. doi:10.1016/j.pec.2003.12.004	Coding scheme for analyzing the interactions between oncologists and individuals with cancer consisting of 15 variables.
RIAS – Roter Interaction Analysis system	Roter, D., & Larson, S. (2002). The Roter interaction analysis system (RIAS): Utility and flexibility for analysis of medical interactions. *Patient Education and Counseling, 46* (4), 243–251.	An interaction analysis system for coding medical dialogue
SABICS	Zhou, Y., Cameron, E., Forbes, G., & Humphris, G. (2012). Development of a novel coding scheme (SABICS) to record nurse-child interactive behaviours in a community dental	Coding scheme for nurse-child interactions in a community for dental preventive intervention.

Table A.1 (*cont.*)

Physician-patient communication and care communication

	preventive intervention. *Patient Education and Counseling, 88*(2), 268–276. doi:10.1016/j. pec.2012.01.001	
SCCAP – Siminoff Communication content & Affect program	Siminoff, L. A., & Step, M. M. (2011). A comprehensive observational coding scheme for analyzing instrumental, affective, and relational communication in health care contexts. *Journal of Health Communication, 16*(2), 178–197. doi:10.1080/10810730.2010.535109	Revised coding scheme to look at medical interactions. Coding scheme grounded in communication theory comprised of three groups (content themes, communication types, & observer ratings) used to measure communication in health care settings.
Verbal Behaviour Coding System (physician-patient relationship)	Street, R. J., Gordon, H. S., Ward, M. M., Krupat, E., & Kravitz, R. L. (2005). Patient participation in medical consultations: Why some patients are more involved than others. *Medical Care, 43*(10), 960–969. doi:10.1097/01. mlr.0000178172.40344.70	A system that codes communication measures from audiotapes in physician-patient relationship and especially the patient participation. Coding system comprised of three types of speech acts (asking questions, assertive responses, and expressions of concern or other negative emotions) to examine the extent to which patient participation in medical interactions is influenced.
4HCS – Four Habits Coding Scheme	Krupat, E., Frankel, R., Stein, T., & Irish, J. (2006). The Four Habits Coding Scheme: Validation of an instrument to assess clinicians' communication behavior. *Patient Education and Counseling, 62*(1), 38–45. doi:10.1016/j.pec.2005.04.015	Coding instrument used to improve clinicians' communication skills. Coding scheme consisting of 23 items used widely to describe clinicians' communication behavior. The tool has the potential to be of utility to researchers and evaluators as well as educators and clinicians.

Rumors

RIAS – Rumor Interaction Analysis System	Bordia, P., & DiFonzo, N. (2004). Problem solving in social interactions on the Internet: Rumor as social cognition. *Social Psychology Quarterly, 67*(1), 33–49. doi:10.1177/ 019027250406700105	Coding scheme that categorizes rumors within a group. Coding scheme comprised of 14 categories to analyze rumors transmitted on various internet discussion groups over the life of each rumor.

Table A.1 (*cont.*)

Software		
LIWC – Linguistic Inquiry and Word Count	Kahn, J. H., Tobin, R. M., Massey, A. E., & Anderson, J. A. (2007). Measuring emotional expression with the Linguistic Inquiry and Word Count. *The American Journal of Psychology, 120*(2), 263–286. doi:10.2307/20445398	A text analysis software program. LIWC calculates the degree to which people use different categories of words across a wide array of texts, including emails, speeches, poems, or transcribed daily speech via four dimensions (summary language variables, linguistic dimensions, other grammar, & psychological processes) with each having numerous subcategories.

Relational communication		
Relational Linking System	VanLear, C. A., Sheehan, M., Withers, L. A., & Walker, R. A. (2005). AA Online: The enactment of supportive computer mediated communication. *Western Journal of Communication, 69*(1), 5–26. doi:10.1080/10570310500033941	Coding scheme consisting of two dimensions: self-presentation (four subcategories) & other-orientation (six subcategories) used to compare behaviors and interaction patterns in online AA groups.

Teacher-student interaction		
Quantifying verbal interactions – four coding schemes	Martens, B. K., Erchul, W. P., & Witt, J. C. (1992). Quantifying verbal interactions in school-based consultation: A comparison of four coding schemes. *School Psychology Review, 21*(1), 109–124.	Focuses on the link between interpersonal communication processes to school-based consultation outcomes in the United States. Description and comparison of four coding schemes; application during consultation interviews. The four coding schemes: Bergan and Tombari's (1975) Consultation Analysis Record (CAR), Rogers and Farace's (1976) relational communication coding system (R-F), Folger and Puck's (1976) request-centered coding system (F-P), and Tracey and Ray's (1984) topic following-topic initiation coding system (T-R).

Table A.1 (*cont.*)

Teacher-student interaction

AET-SSBD ADHD-SOC BOSS COC DOF SECOOS SOS	Volpe, R. J., DiPerna, J. C., Hintze, J. M., & Shapiro, E. S. (2005). Observing students in classroom settings: A review of seven coding schemes. *School Psychology Review, 34*(4), 454–474.	Seven coding schemes reviewed that are used for direct observational assessment of student classroom behavior: Academic Engaged Time Code of the Systematic Screening for Behavior Disorders (AET-SSBD; Walker & Severson, 1990); ADHD School Observation Code (ADHD-SOC; Gadow, Sprafkin, & Nolan, 1996); Behavioral Observation of Students in Schools (BOSS; Shapiro, 2004); Classroom Observation Code (COC; Abikoff & Gittelman, 1985); Direct Observation Form (DOF; Achenbach, 1986); State-Event Classroom Observation System (SECOS; Saudargas, 1997); Student Observation System of the Behavioral Assessment System for Children-2 (SOS; Reynolds & Kamphaus, 2004).
FIAC – Flanders Interaction Analysis Categories	Flanders, N. A. (1970). *Analyzing teacher behavior.* Boston, MA: Addison-Wesley P. C. Flanders, N. A. (1961). Analyzing teacher behavior. *Educational Leadership, 19*(3), 173–200.	Coding scheme for teacher-student interactions comprising seven categories for teacher statements (clarify feeling constructively, praise or encourage, clarify, develop or make use of ideas suggested by students, ask questions, lecture, give directions, & criticize), two categories for students (student talk initiated by the student, and student talk in response to the teacher), and one category used to indicate silence or confusion.

Team efficacy behavior

Action Cycles	Tschan, F. (2002). Ideal cycles of communication (or cognitions) in triads, dyads, and individuals. *Small*	System used to measure the quality of task-related communication related to group productivity. Content, action regulation (orientation, planning,

Table A.1 (cont.)

Team efficacy behavior

	Group Research, 33(6), 615–643. doi:10.1177/1046496402238618	evaluation), communication cycles, and cycle characteristics are coded. Ideal cycles were defined as starting with orientation or planning and ending with evaluation. Quality of each cycle calculated based on proportion of ideal cycles.
Collective Construction of Work Group Moods (observer's instrument)	Bartel, C. A., & Saavedra, R. (2000). The collective construction of work group moods. *Administrative Science Quarterly, 45*(2), 197–231. doi:10.2307/2667070	Coding scheme developed for behavioral indicators comprising of eight categories (high activation, activated pleasant, pleasant, unactivated pleasant, low activation, unactivated unpleasant, unpleasant, and activated unpleasant) called the mood circumplex model, used to measure observation for work group moods.
DE-CODE: A coding scheme for assessing debriefing interactions	Seelandt, J.C., Grande, B., Kriech, S., & Kolbe, M. (2017). DE-CODE: A coding scheme for assessing debriefing interactions. *BMJ Simulation and Technology Enhanced Learning*. Published Online First: 08 November 2017. doi: 10.1136/bmjstel-2017-000233	DE-CODE is designed as micro-level measurement tool for coding debriefing conversations during simulation-based training.
Explicit professional oral communication observation tool	Kemper, P. F., van Noord, I., de Bruijne, M., Knol, D. L., Wagner, C., & van Dyck, C. (2013). Development and reliability of the explicit professional oral communication observation tool to quantify the use of non-technical skills in healthcare. *BMJ Quality and Safety, 22*(7), 586–595. doi:10.1136/bmjqs-2012–001451	Coding system comprising six dimensions (assertiveness, working with others; task-oriented leadership; people-oriented leadership; situational awareness; planning and anticipation) to measure and quantify the use of nontechnical skills by direct observations of explicit professional oral communication in clinical situations. Each dimension is specified into several concrete items reflecting verbal behaviors.

Table A.1 (*cont.*)

Team efficacy behavior

Group Development Observation System	Wheelan, S. A., Verdi, A. F., McKeage, R., Wheelan, S. A., & Verdi, A. F. (1992). Group Development Observation System. *Sex Roles, 27*(1/2), 1–15.	Coding scheme for categorizing verbal behavior in developmental group phases comprised of seven categories (dependency statements, counterdependency statements, fight statements, flight statements, pairing statements, counterpairing statements, and work statements) used to investigate communication patterns in groups.
MUMIN	Allwood, J., Cerrato, L., Jokinen, K., Navarretta, C., & Paggio, P. (2007). The MUMIN coding scheme for the annotation of feedback, turn management and sequencing phenomena. *Language Resources and Evaluation, 41*(3–4), 273–287. doi:10.1007/s10579-007–9061-5	Coding scheme looking at multimodal expressions in interactions, comprised of two main categories: modality specific (three expression type subcategories: facial displays; gestures; and speech) and multimodal communication.
SYMLOG – System for the Multiple Level Observation of Groups	Bales, R. F., Cohen, S. P., & Williamson, S. A. (1979). *SYMLOG: A system for the multiple level observation of groups*. New York, NY: Free Press. Bales, R. F., & Cohen, S. P. (1982). *SYMLOG: Ein System für die mehrstufige Beobachtung von Gruppen*. Stuttgart, Germany: Klett-Cotta. Hare, A. P. (2000). Social interaction systems: Theory and measurement: Book review. *Group Dynamics: Theory, Research, And Practice, 4*(2), 199–208. doi:10.1037/1089–2699.4.2.199	SYMLOG System is a theory of personality and group dynamics, integrated with a set of practical methods for measuring and changing behavior and values in a democratic way. System is designed for small natural groups. Interactions are coded in terms of a three-dimensional space that encompasses the dimensions dominant to submissive; friendly to unfriendly; and instrumentally controlled to emotionally expressive.

Index